DUNGEONS & DRAGONS® · CAMPAIGN SETTING

FORGOTTEN REALMS®

GAME DESIGN: **Ed Greenwood, Sean K Reynolds, Skip Williams, Rob Heinsoo**

ADDITIONAL DESIGN: **James Wyatt**

DEVELOPER: **Richard Baker**

EDITORS: **Michele Carter, Julia Martin, John D. Rateliff**

EDITORIAL ASSISTANCE: **Steven E. Schend**

MANAGING EDITOR: **Kim Mohan**

FORGOTTEN REALMS CREATIVE DIRECTOR: **Richard Baker**

DIRECTOR OF RPG R&D: **Bill Slavicsek**

BRAND MANAGER: **Jim Butler**

CATEGORY MANAGER: **Keith Francis Strohm**

VISUAL CREATIVE DIRECTOR: **Jon Schindehette**

ART DIRECTOR: **Robert Raper**

TYPOGRAPHERS: **Angelika Lokotz, Sonya Percival**

FORGOTTEN REALMS LOGO DESIGN: **Robert Campbell, Sherry Floyd**

COVER DESIGN: **Sherry Floyd, Robert Campbell, Robert Raper**

INTERIOR ARTISTS: **Todd Lockwood, Sam Wood, Matt Wilson, Carlo Arellano, Stephanie Pui-Mun Law**

CARTOGRAPHERS: **Rob Lazzaretti, Todd Gamble, Dennis Kauth**

INTERIOR DESIGN & LAYOUT: **Robert Campbell, Robert Raper**

ADDITIONAL GRAPHIC DESIGN: **Sherry Floyd, Dee Barnett, Cynthia Fliege**

DIGI-TECH SPECIALIST: **Joe Fernandez**

BUSINESS MANAGER: **Anthony Valterra**

PROJECT MANAGER: **Justin Ziran**

PRODUCTION MANAGER: **Chas DeLong**

Based on the original DUNGEONS & DRAGONS® rules created by E. Gary Gygax and Dave Arneson and the new DUNGEONS & DRAGONS game designed by Jonathan Tweet, Monte Cook, Skip Williams, Richard Baker, and Peter Adkison.

Special Thanks: Ed Greenwood, Jeff Grubb, George Krashos, Eric L. Boyd, Bryon Wischstadt, Todd Lockwood, John Gallagher, Larry Weiner

U.S., CANADA, ASIA, PACIFIC, & LATIN AMERICA
Wizards of the Coast, Inc.
P.O. Box 707
Renton WA 98057-0707

(Questions?) 1-800-324-6496

EUROPEAN HEADQUARTERS
Wizards of the Coast, Belgium
P.B. 2031
2600 Berchem
Belgium
+32-70-23-32-77

620-T11836-001

Visit our website at www.wizards.com/forgottenrealms

contents

Within these covers is your guide to the land of Faerûn. Read carefully, and ye will uncover more of its glories, byways, and dangers than ye might learn in a year of perilous travels. More adventurers should be so well informed when they venture into realms wild and strange. If they were, more might live to tell their own tales.

I am Elminster of Shadowdale, called by some the Old Sage, and called far worse things by others. I've walked these realms for over a thousand years. Yet, I am far from the oldest, wisest, or mightiest being to walk the ground of Faerûn with my well-worn boots—and that is truth. But if ye learn the long history of my deeds, ye'll know precisely what I stand for and what I am. And that's a rare and precious thing, knowing yourself. Do ye know exactly what ye stand for?

Think on that while I let my tongue loose for a bit and roll the splendid sights of these lands over ye like the great green waves that crash on the rocks below where Mount Waterdeep rises up out of the cold and mighty Sea of Swords. Let me speak of the wonders bards sing of under the starry night sky all over these fair lands. Let me tell ye of soft blue moonlight and spell stars in the hair of elven women, their bare shoulders all silver, dancing under the trees of the High Forest—just as the ghosts of their fair vanished kin still dance under the moon in ruined, fiend-roamed Myth Drannor.

Let me speak of brawling, bustling Waterdeep, the beautiful towers of Silverymoon, and of a hundred other proud cities with their lanterns and rumbling carts and shadowed alleys and dripping sewers, their intrigues and strivings and riches. Let me whisper of the realms below, the Underdark, a world of sunless caverns where cruel elves with obsidian skin, purple-hued mind flayers, and things far worse battle in the depths beneath your feet, and gems are born in the hottest deeps where rock flows like water.

Heed my tales of old magic in forgotten tombs or marked by standing stones and portals that with a single stride span half of Faerûn. Beware cold claws that reach from the shadows and proudly sneering courtiers in gleaming finery whose honeyed tongues and sly plots are colder and more perilous still than steely talons. Hear tell of wild places where dragons battle each other in the sky and ruins only adventurers—like ye—have seen that are haunted by fearsome beholders, shape-changing horrors, and oozing things made of eyes and tentacles that lurk . . . and hunger.

Hold, and listen well! If ye heed not a word of mine in all your days, remember this: Faerûn needs its heroes.

I'm one such to some, though I am old and battered and have left a heap of bloody, bitter mistakes behind me high enough to bury empires. Your sword must flash beside my faltering spells, for Faerûn faces new, rising dooms that I cannot face alone. Our homelands stand in worse peril now than ever before. Old evils stir, or return unlooked-for, looming like storm clouds over the darkened hills. Strife and change tear asunder nations and cities. Who can see who shall rise over all? Even the monks of far Candlekeep, who guard well the words of the prophet Alaundo who is never wrong, cannot know.

It might just be ye, if your swords and spells are ready and your heart bold. Faerûn needs ye, lest we fall unguarded to the dangers all around.

Adventurer, I am Elminster, and I say to ye that these forgotten realms are yours to discover, reforge, and defend, yours to make anew in winning your own crown. Go forth and take up arms against the perils that beset us!

—Elminster of Shadowdale
Mirtul, Year of Wild Magic

Welcome to the world of Faerûn, a place of great heroes and stark evil, encompassing lands of magic, mystery, and high peril.

Bold knights dare the crypts of dead monarchs, seeking glory and treasure. Insolent rogues prowl the dank alleyways of ancient cities, plotting their next exploit. Devout clerics wield mace and spell, questing against the terrifying powers that threaten the land. Cunning wizards plunder the ruins of fallen empires, delving fearlessly into secrets too dark for the light of day. Dragons, giants, black-hearted villains, demons, savage hordes, and unimaginable abominations lurk in horrible dungeons, endless caverns, ruined cities, and the vast wild places of the world, thirsting for the blood of heroes.

This is the land of Faerûn, a continent of heart-stopping beauty and ages-old evil. It is your land to shape, to guide, to defend, to conquer, or to rule. It is a land trod by noble heroes and unredeemable villains, a great and terrible company to which you and your fellows now belong.

Welcome to the FORGOTTEN REALMS® campaign setting.

The Land of Faerûn

From the bitter, windswept steppes of the Endless Waste to the storm-lashed cliffs of the Sword Coast stretches a wide, wild land of shining kingdoms and primal wilderness. Faerûn is only one continent of the world known as Toril. Other lands lie in distant corners of the world, but Faerûn is the center of it all, the crossroads and crux upon which all else turns. Dozens of nations, hundreds of city-states, and countless tribes, villages, and settlements dot its expanse.

The continent of Faerûn measures more than thirty-five hundred miles from east to west and twenty-five hundred from north to south. It includes sun-blasted deserts, vast forest deeps, forbidding mountains, and gleaming inland seas. Across this vast expanse travel minstrels and peddlers, caravan merchants and guards, soldiers, sailors, and steel-hearted adventurers carrying tales of strange, glorious, faraway places. Good maps and clear trails can take even an inexperienced youth with dreams of glory far across Faerûn. Thousands of restless young would-be heroes from backcountry farmsteads and sleepy villages arrive in Waterdeep and the other great cities every year in search of wealth and renown.

Known roads may be well traveled, but they are not necessarily safe. Fell magic, deadly monsters, and cruel local rulers are all perils that you face when you fare abroad in Faerûn. Away from the main roads and the great cities, the countryside is far wilder than the city folk remember. Even farms and freeholds within a day's walk of Waterdeep itself may fall prey to monsters, and no place in Faerûn is safe from the sudden wrath of a dragon.

The People

Faerûn is home to hundreds of intelligent creatures, ranging from the teeming kingdoms of humankind to the secret fastnesses of terrible creatures whose entire species numbers a score or less. Like humans, these peoples run the gamut from grotesque to beautiful, from murderous to beatific.

The great story of Faerûn is, in many ways, that of the rise of humankind and the fading of the ancient empires of those who came before. Over thousands of years, humans have brought an end to the old ways. Elven cities lie in ruins, abandoned to human encroachment. Hills and dells once the homes and hunting grounds of goblins and giants are now dotted with human fields and pastures.

Human pride and folly have brought untold disaster down on Faerûn more than once, and the ever-growing lands of humans encroach on the territories of older races both benign and fierce. The fundamental questions are clear: Can the old races survive the dominance of humankind? Or will humans overreach themselves, as they have done so many times before, and bring down upon all a dark age of unimaginable horror?

The Civilized Folk

Of the many races of Toril, a dozen or so account for nine-tenths of all folk who live in the world today. Humans are the most numerous. They are a race of kingdom-builders, merchants, wizards, and clerics whose crowded cities lie scattered across the fair face of the continent. Young and vigorous in comparison to the other races, humans hold the future of Faerûn in their hands—for good or for ill.

While humans were still eking out a subsistence in scattered, disorganized bands, two older races—dwarves and elves—raised mighty realms in the mountains and forests. The zenith of both races is now past, but Faerûn is filled with wonders of stone, wood, and magic they wrought at the heights of their power. Grim dwarven citadels filled with the clamor of industry and breathtaking elven cities as graceful as spun glass still stand, even as year by year human dominion grows.

Though they never commanded the power of the dwarves or the elves, halflings and gnomes have adapted better to the rise of humankind. Halflings have prospered, taking advantage of the situations created by the cultural conflicts between the humans and the elder races. Although halflings hold lands exclusively for their people in only a handful of places, their settlements can be found throughout most human lands. Gnomes prefer more reclusive dwellings and do not raise mighty cities, but, like the halflings, their homes and settlements are scattered through a dozen human lands.

Other races are sometimes considered civilized folk, too, despite their smaller numbers. Centaurs and fey roam the great northern forests, good of heart but growing ever more wary of human incursions. Merfolk rule vast underwater domains in the warm seas of the south. Proud wemics roam the endless plains of the Shaar. But their numbers are few compared to even a small human land.

Savage Peoples and Monsters

Against the young human lands and the ancient refuges of the older races stand ranged a great number of enemies. Foremost among these are the savage peoples—goblins, orcs, ogres, and all their kin. Breeding fierce warriors in dark mountain fortresses and noisome cavern dens, they regularly burst forth from their strongholds to pillage and slaughter villages and towns unfortunate enough to lie in their path.

Faerûn is home to creatures far more malevolent, cruel, and calculating than orc chiefs and rampaging ogres. The deeps of the Underdark house sinister and powerful beings such as the drow, the beholders, and the mind flayers. These terrible creatures dream of enslaving the surface lands and feasting on human cattle while they rule as the overlords of all Toril.

Neither the uncounted hordes of goblinkind nor the dark powers that lie beneath the surface world are the most dangerous threat to human cities and realms, however. That honor must be reserved for the most terrible and awesome creatures of Faerûn—the dragons. No one knows just how many dragons soar through the icy spires of the Spine of the World or slither through the depths of the Forest of Wyrms, but even a single dragon can spell doom for a city. From time to time, great numbers of dragons take flight at once and wing across the face of Faerûn in a terrifying rage, burning and devouring at will.

Heroes—and Villains

Faerûn is a land of heroes both light and dark, and you must choose where you will stand in the struggle to come. Regardless of race or station, the most notable creatures to roam Faerûn are its heroes and their enemies. In the courts of kings, the dens of thieves, and the citadels of dark powers, companies of questers, treasure seekers, monster slayers, and freebooters struggle to preserve the things they hold dear and to vanquish the enemies who would destroy them.

The most dangerous creature on Faerûn is, as you might expect, a person with the ruthlessness to do whatever is necessary to achieve her goal. Even a dim-witted ogre can guess what a red dragon might want when it appears on the horizon, but fathoming the purposes and designs of a scheming wizard or unscrupulous merchant lord is far more difficult.

A world of magic

Toril is steeped in magic. It permeates the entire world. Fallen empires thousands of years old left *portals* and wrecked towers scattered across the landscape that are still filled with potent enchantments. Haughty wizards whose spells can lay low entire armies plot against each other as they pursue their studies into ever more powerful—and more dangerous—fields of arcane lore. Deities channel divine energy through their mortal agents to advance the causes that interest them. Adventurers of all types, evil and good, wield mighty spells seemingly at will.

Most Faerûnians never learn to speak a spell, but magic touches their lives in ways they do not always see. Skilled wizards and sorcerers serve the monarchs of the land, plying their spells to defend their realms against attack and to watch their enemies' movements. Clerics intercede with the deities to invoke their blessings as real and tangible benefits to the endeavors of the community. Monstrous aberrations of twisted magic and warped energy are often the deadliest creatures to prey on Faerûn's common folk, and adventurers armed with enchanted steel are the land's first line of defense against such perils.

Ancient wonders

The history of Faerûn is dominated by the cyclic rise and cataclysmic destruction of empires founded on knowledge of the intricacies of magic. The Imaskari wrought magical *portals* to bridge the gap between worlds, only to be destroyed by the god-kings of the slave races they imported to Faerûn. Their lost realm now lies beneath the dust desert of Raurin. The mighty Empire of Netheril dominated the center of the continent, its skies graced by floating cities and its wizards commanding unimagined might. They reached too far and were destroyed in a magical catastrophe of world-shaking proportions, forever changing the workings of magic itself. Realms such as Narfell and Raumathar, Athalantar and Cormanthyr, Illefarn and Hlondath have left their ruins throughout the world.

Magic both old and strong still slumbers in the wreckage of these ancient realms. Every year some new marvel is rediscovered in an old ruin: a spell never before seen or a wondrous item of great power and high purpose. More often, though, blights and perils long forgotten or magical abominations that should never see the light of day emerge to trouble the world anew, unearthed by those ignorant or unscrupulous enough to seek them out.

Mages, priests, and minstrels

Crumbling towers and buried vaults of elder lands hold power and peril beyond compare, but it is the living wielders of magic who shape Faerûn's future. Every land in Faerûn is home to the lonely towers of reclusive wizards and the fortresslike temples of clerical orders.

Practitioners of the Art, the wreaking of arcane magic, include the most powerful mortals to walk the face of Toril. Mysterious enchanters, proud diviners, and depraved necromancers roam Faerûn, engaged in their own secretive business. Some seek deeper knowledge

and greater power, others toil in the service of dark masters, and others still strive to right wrongs wherever they find them. Any person with the wits of a fence post treads cautiously in the presence of sorcerers or wizards, for who can guess at their purposes and designs?

Invokers of divine magic, also known as the Power, include the clerics of Faerûn's multitudinous goddesses and gods. Devoted to the service of their patron deities, they run the gamut from priests of Tempus who march with armies to scholarly clerics who carefully protect knowledge in the hoary halls of the Inner Chamber of Deneir and the Seat of Lore of Oghma in Berdusk. The deities of Faerûn watch over every corner of the world and aspect of life, and only a fool would ignore their mortal agents.

Wizards and clerics are not the only wielders of magic in the world. Druids and rangers serve nature deities and guard the deep forests. Bards wander the land, carrying news and gossip with their magical songs. Faerûn is a land rich with wielders of magic, and their works and deeds topple thrones and shake empires.

The forgotten realms campaign

This book describes in brief a wide and wonderful world. Most readers will see its wonders and survive its perils for themselves through the medium of the DUNGEONS & DRAGONS® game. The information in this work provides you, the Dungeon Master, with a sketch, a snapshot, of a complete, living, breathing fantasy world in which to set your D&D® game. It's a setting for your adventures, a background for your characters and plots, a set of suggestions for how you could play a continuing game, and a source of ideas for how to develop a world of your own.

What you need to play

You'll need a copy of the DUNGEONS & DRAGONS *Player's Handbook, Dungeon Master's Guide,* and *Monster Manual* to best use the material in this book. The *Monster Compendium: Monsters of Faerûn* sourcebook is also extremely useful, providing game descriptions of many creatures mentioned in this book.

If you've never played D&D before, this book may not be for you quite yet. If you've never played a roleplaying game before, start with the *D&D Adventure Game* before tackling the FORGOTTEN REALMS *Campaign Setting.* If you're already familiar with roleplaying games, you may want to start with the D&D *Player's Handbook* and play for a while to familiarize yourself with the game system.

Where do I start?

Players beginning a FORGOTTEN REALMS campaign should start by creating a FORGOTTEN REALMS character. Talk with your DM about the character options he intends to make available in his FORGOTTEN REALMS game. After that, Chapter 1: Characters is the first place to go. Chapter 2: Magic is also useful if you create a spellcasting character, and Chapter 5: Deities is important if you are going to play a cleric, druid, paladin, or ranger character.

If you're a Dungeon Master starting a FORGOTTEN REALMS campaign, you should read most of this book eventually. It's filled with ideas for plots and villains, rules options to give your game a distinctive Faerûnian flavor, and tools to help you to run a comprehensive and cohesive FORGOTTEN REALMS game. For the DM, Chapter 8: Running the Realms is the best place to start.

ELMINSTER

Male human (Chosen of Mystra) Ftr1/Rog2/Clr3/Wiz20/ Acm5/Epic4: CR 39; Medium-size humanoid; HD 1d10+7 plus 2d6+14 plus 3d8+21 plus 14d4+98; hp 219; Init +10; Spd 30 ft.; AC 29 (touch 17, flat-footed 25); Atk +17/+12/+7 melee (1d8+6/19–20, +5 *thundering longsword*) or +15/+10/+5 ranged touch (by spell); SA Sneak attack +1d6, turn undead 6/day; SQ Archmage high arcana, Chosen immunities, Chosen spell-like abilities, detect magic, enhanced Constitution, enhanced Intelligence, epic-level benefits, evasion, silver fire; SR 21; AL CG; SV Fort +17, Ref +13, Will +17; Str 13, Dex 18, Con 24, Int 24, Wis 18, Cha 17. Height 6 ft. 2 in.

Skills and Feats: Alchemy +27, Balance +6, Climb +5, Concentration +34, Decipher Script +9, Diplomacy +6, Handle Animal +7, Heal +8, Hide +8, Intimidate +11, Intuit Direction +6, Jump +5, Knowledge (arcana) +27, Knowledge (geography) +22, Knowledge (history) +17, Knowledge (Dalelands local) +17, Knowledge (nature) +17, Knowledge (nobility) +17, Knowledge (the planes) +22, Knowledge (religion) +8, Listen +13, Move Silently +8, Open Lock +6, Perform (dance) +6, Ride +8, Scry +27, Search +9, Sense Motive +11, Spellcraft +29, Spot +14, Swim +5, Tumble +5; Blooded, Craft Staff, Craft Wondrous Item, Expertise, Forge Ring, Heighten Spell, Improved Initiative, Luck of Heroes, Scribe Scroll, Skill Focus (Spellcraft), Spell Focus (Enchantment), Spell Focus (Evocation), Spell Penetration, Twin Spell.

Special Qualities: Archmage High Arcana: Arcane reach, mastery of counterspelling, mastery of elements, spell power +4 (total). Chosen Immunities: Elminster is completely unaffected by attacks that duplicate these effects: *detect thoughts, disintegrate, Evard's black tentacles, feeblemind, finger of death, fireball, magic missile, sunburst, temporal stasis.* Chosen Spell-like Abilities (all 1/day): *dispel magic, lesser ironguard, see invisibility, shapechange, Simbul's synostodweomer* (converts prepared spells into 2 points of healing per spell level), *spider climb, teleport without error, thunderlance, true seeing.* Detect Magic (Su): Line of sight. Enhanced Constitution: The Chosen of Mystra template adds +10 to Elminster's Constitution. Enhanced Intelligence: Elminster used *wish* spells to increase his Intelligence. His Intelligence score has a +4 inherent bonus included in its value. Epic-Level Benefits: Bonus spell level ×4 (included in the listing below), six effective levels of wizard and five of archmage (included in above total). Silver Fire (Su): See Chapter 2 for details.

Cleric Spells per Day: 4/4/3. Base DC = 14 + spell level, 16 + spell level for evocation and enchantment spells. Domains: Magic (use spell trigger or spell completion devices as a 26th-level wizard), Spell (+2 bonus on Concentration and Spellcraft checks). Caster level 3rd.

Wizard Spells per Day: 4/6/6/6/5/4/5/3/3/3/1/1/1/1. Base DC = 21 + spell level, 23 + spell level for evocation and enchantment spells. Caster level 25th.

Signature Possessions: Ring of protection +3, amulet of natural armor +5, bracers of armor +7, ring of regeneration, mantle of spell resistance, +5 thundering longsword, Elminster's eversmoking pipe. As a very powerful wizard, Elminster has access to incredible resources and can acquire or make almost any nonartifact item he might need, given time.

Like his onetime apprentice Vangerdahast, this ancient wizard is finally starting to seem truly old, prone to long reveries in which he sees again people and places now long vanished. The strongest of Mystra's Chosen rarely moves directly against his foes, preferring to work through younger and more vigorous heroes.

The Sage of Shadowdale for years confounded the Zhentarim, the Red Wizards of Thay, and a hundred rival mages while at the same time training and rearing a long succession of apprentices who all became superb spellcasters in their own right. Before that he foiled renegade Chosen, helped found the Harpers, and raised several of the Seven Sisters. During the Time of Troubles, he saved Toril by holding Mystra's power inside himself, surviving by his wits and the aid of the ranger Sharantyr rather than by his magic. He's also a passable fighter and thief and a superb dancer.

Elminster is a consummate actor and delights in acts of whimsy, helping the needy and lovelorn, and dispensing poetic justice to those who deserve it. He has a heart of gold, a deep need to bring tyrannical, pompous, and cruel persons low, and a crotchety, "Don't push me" manner. After knowing the love of the goddess Mystra, nothing awes him or leaves him much afraid.

Illustration by Sam Wood

Elminster

CHARACTER DESCRIPTION TERMS

The nonplayer character descriptions in this book, whether presented in a section of their own or in a brief parenthetical mention in the text, use a lot of abbreviations. See Chapter 8: Running the Realms for information about characters of higher than 20th level.

Character Abbreviations: *Standard Classes:* Bbn, barbarian; Brd, bard; Clr, cleric; Drd, druid; Ftr, fighter; Mnk, monk; Pal, paladin; Rgr, ranger; Rog, rogue; Sor, sorcerer; Wiz, wizard. *Specialist Wizards:* Abj, abjurer; Cjr, conjurer; Div, diviner; Enc, enchanter; Evo, evoker; Ill, illusionist; Nec, necromancer; Tra, transmuter. *DUNGEON MASTER's Guide Prestige Classes:* Arc, arcane archer; Asn, assassin; Blk, blackguard; Def, dwarven defender; Lor, loremaster; Shd, shadowdancer. *FORGOTTEN REALMS Prestige Classes:* Acm, archmage; Chm, divine champion; Dev, arcane devotee; Dis, divine disciple; Gld, guild thief; Hrp, Harper scout; Hie, hierophant; Hth, hathran; Prp, Purple Dragon knight; Red, Red Wizard; Rnc, runecaster; Sha, shadow adept; Skr, divine seeker. *DUNGEON MASTER's Guide NPC Classes:* Adp, adept; Ari, aristocrat; Com, commoner; Exp, expert; War, warrior.

Other Abbreviations: LG, lawful good; NG, neutral good; CG, chaotic good; LN, lawful neutral; N, neutral; CN, chaotic neutral; LE, lawful evil; NE, neutral evil; CE, chaotic evil; Str, Strength; Dex, Dexterity; Con, Constitution; Int, Intelligence; Wis, Wisdom; Cha, Charisma; HD, Hit Dice; hp, hit points; Init, initiative bonus; Atk, attacks; Spd, speed; AC, Armor Class; SA, special attacks; SQ, special qualities; AL, alignment; SV, saving throw bonuses; Fort, Fortitude; Ref, Reflex; Will, Will.

Characters

additional features to Step 2: Choose Class and Race (choose a region here as well), Step 7: Select a Feat, and Step 8: Review Description we describe in this chapter.

character races

Faerûn is home to hundreds of intelligent races and gives rise to dozens and dozens of potentially heroic paths. In a FORGOTTEN REALMS campaign, a number of new character races are available for players. The standard races described in the *Player's Handbook* are present in Faerûn, although they're often known by names specific to Toril, the planet the continent of Faerûn is located on. For example, the standard dwarf is known as the shield dwarf, although gold dwarves and gray dwarves are commonplace adventurers. Moon elves, rock gnomes, and lightfoot halflings correspond to the *Player's Handbook* elf, gnome, and halfling, respectively. Humans and half-orcs don't have any specific subraces in Faerûn, but your choice of home region (see below) adds a new level of detail to these characters, too.

character classes

Some of the classes described in the *Player's Handbook* have significant new opportunities in the FORGOTTEN REALMS setting. For example, every cleric chooses a patron deity from the expansive Faerûnian pantheon. Many of these deities have access to new domains not described in the *Player's Handbook*. In addition to the prestige classes described in the *DUNGEON MASTER's Guide*, your character can now aspire to join one of a number of new prestige classes specific to Faerûn. While beginning characters won't qualify for the archmage class, the Faerûnian prestige classes are something a character may choose to strive toward right from 1st level.

character region

The *Player's Handbook* only requires you to choose a race and a class, but the FORGOTTEN REALMS campaign setting also gives you the ability to further define your character by choosing a region in which your character grew up (or at least gained most of her early experience). Your native region helps define your character as part of the world of Toril and gives you additional choices for which feats and equipment you can have.

Each race and class description lists a number of suggested regions in which that type of character is particularly common or encouraged by the principal culture. If you choose a region where your character's class is favored, your character gains access to special regional

Guarded wizards of Thay, distrusted by the common folk of the Dalelands, seek deeper knowledge in the elven ruins of Cormanthor. Determined clerics of Tyr wander the cold lands of the Moonsea, battling against the sinister influence of the Zhentarim. Stout-hearted shield dwarves seek to free the plundered citadels of their ancestors from the feral orcs and ogres that occupy them. Almost any kind of fantasy hero or villain may find a home in the FORGOTTEN REALMS® campaign setting. Faerûn is an old continent with hundreds of disparate cultures.

In this world, your fighter is not defined simply by his Strength score of 16 and his mastery of the bastard sword. He is defined by his homeland, his training, and his background. Just as the Dungeon Master (DM) carefully crafts adventures to highlight the magic and perils of the far-scattered lands of Faerûn, each player contributes to the campaign a character whose personality, motivations, and attitudes reflect the heroes—or the villains—of a land shrouded in mystery, myth, and legend.

creating a forgotten realms character

Any character created using the rules in the *Player's Handbook* works as a FORGOTTEN REALMS character, but this chapter explains how to create a character tailored for Faerûn and grounded in all the rich detail of the setting. To create a 1st-level character, turn to the beginning of the *Player's Handbook* and use the steps outlined in the Character Creation Basics section. Follow the *Player's Handbook* steps in character creation but add in the feats and bonus starting equipment. See Table 1–4: Character Regions for a list of the possible regions and the specific benefits, and consult the Regional Feat Regions map to help in selecting a region.

Region-specific skills

A character's region may also affect his or her list of skills. As a general rule, characters with the Knowledge skill often focus on the region in which they grew up, although characters may focus on regions in which they have lived as adults or which they have studied in books.

Regional Focus: A character may choose to add a regional focus to the geography, history, nature, nobility and royalty, or religion areas of the Knowledge skill. The regional focus provides a +2 bonus on Knowledge checks that pertaiun to the region in question. For example, a character may choose Knowledge (Sembian history) instead of Knowledge (history) in order to be particularly adept at Knowledge (history) checks pertaining to Sembia.

Local Knowledge: The Knowledge (local) skill per se does not

Converting Core D&D Characters to Forgotten Realms Characters

If you created a character with the *Player's Handbook* and would like to bring that character into the FORGOTTEN REALMS campaign setting, the biggest point of conversion lies in the differences between the pantheons. Table 1–1: Deity Conversion shows which FORGOTTEN REALMS deities correspond to the *Player's Handbook* deities.

TABLE 1–1: DEITY CONVERSION

Player's Handbook Deity	FORGOTTEN REALMS Deity
Boccob	Azuth, Mystra, Savras, Velsharoon
Corellon Larethian	No change
Ehlonna	Mielikki
Erythnul	Cyric, Garagos, Malar
Fharlanghn	Selûne, Shaundakul
Garl Glittergold	No change
Gruumsh	No change
Heironeous	Torm, Tyr
Hextor	Bane, Loviatar
Kord	Lathander, Tempus, Uthgar
Moradin	No change
Nerull	Cyric, Malar, Talona
Obad-Hai	Silvanus
Olidammara	Oghma, Sune, Tymora
Pelor	Ilmater, Lathander, Torm
St. Cuthbert	Helm, Hoar, Tyr
Vecna	Shar, Velsharoon
Wee Jas	Azuth, Kelemvor
Yondalla	No change

Also, the subraces of Faerûn vary from those presented in the *Player's Handbook* and the *Monster Manual.* For simplicity, choose the FORGOTTEN REALMS subrace that matches the racial ability score modifiers for your character. Standard elves become moon elves, standard dwarves become shield dwarves, standard gnomes become rock gnomes, and standard halflings become lightfoot halflings.

exist in a Forgotten Realms campaign. Instead, a character who chooses Knowledge (local) must specify the region his knowledge applies to. For example, someone familiar with the legends and personalities of Sembia would take the Knowledge (Sembia local) skill.

New feats

This chapter introduces a number of new feats appropriate to various lands and cultures of Faerûn. A shield dwarven cleric might learn to fix her spells to objects through the Inscribe Rune feat, while a Mulhorandi mage could delve into the dangerous lore of the Shadow Weave and learn to tap sources of magical energy that most wizards dare not touch. Of course, all the feats described in the *Player's Handbook* are still available to Faerûnian characters.

Races of Faerûn

Faerûn is inhabited by hundreds of different races. Some races are native and have lived here for uncounted thousands of years. Others arrived over centuries of migration and conquest from other planes and worlds. The races most commonly found as player characters—humans, dwarves, elves, half-elves, half-orcs, halflings, and gnomes—are descended from both Faerûnian natives and immigrants from other worlds. Because of their complex ancestry, members of most of these races and subraces display a wide range of skin and hair colors.

As a further consequence of their mixed heritage, humans, dwarves, elves, and the other major races of Faerûn have much in common with their kin on other worlds. Rather than repeating facts that have been established in the *Player's Handbook*, this section focuses on the ways in which the races and subraces of Faerûn differ from the standard races described in the *Player's Handbook*.

Languages: Automatic and bonus languages for all races appear in the race descriptions, since Faerûn is home to a number of unique tongues. In the case of races for which "home region" appears in the race description—for example, humans or planetouched—the language selection is determined by the character's home region. See Table 1–4: Character Regions for details.

A character's choice of race and region determines her automatic and bonus languages. Table 1–4: Character Regions supersedes the automatic and bonus language information in the *Player's Handbook*. However, the following languages are always available as bonus languages to characters, regardless of race or region: Abyssal (clerics), Aquan (water genasi), Auran (air genasi), Celestial (clerics), Common, Draconic (wizards), Dwarven, Elven, Gnome, Goblin, Giant, Gnoll, Halfling, Ignan (fire genasi), Infernal (clerics), Orc, Sylvan (druids), Terran (earth genasi), and Undercommon. Druids also know Druidic in addition to their other languages.

Regions: Each race description gives the primary regions or strongholds of the race. Characters can choose one of these regions for their home region, they can default to the general racial entry for their region, or they can choose to be from elsewhere in Faerûn. The information given in this section helps you construct a character, but does not directly affect your character's starting feats or equipment. The regions/cultural descriptions that key into the regional feats and equipment on Table 1–4: Character Regions are those listed in the Classes section.

HUMANS

Compared to most of the nonhuman races, who tend to get along with others of their own race reasonably well, the humans of Faerûn are divided into innumerable competing nations, states, sects, religions, bandit kingdoms, and tribes. Humans argue about anything, fight about most things they argue about, and hold dear among their many deities quite a few who actively encourage that type of behavior.

The longer-lived races of elves and dwarves tend to have respect for individual humans who deserve it without necessarily respecting the entire race. The elves have difficulty forgetting that the first human empires of Netheril, Raumathar, Narfell, and other ancient lands were built upon magical secrets borrowed or looted from the elves. The fact that those early human empires invariably corrupted themselves with evil magic does not reassure the elves. The dwarves, particularly the shield dwarves of northern Faerûn, respect humans as fierce warriors, but fear that there would be little room for their race in a world dominated by humankind.

Humans don't see it that way, of course. Their greatest heroes outshine the deities themselves, or become deities in their own right. Unfortunately, the same could be said of humanity's greatest villains, and that is the challenge facing any human adventurer. Power comes at a cost.

Regions: Humans can be found in almost every corner of Faerûn. Decide what character class you wish to play and pick a region listed in the class description, consult Table 1–4: Character Regions or browse through Chapter 4: Geography for a region that seems appropriate to your character.

Racial Abilities: Human characters, regardless of region, have all the human racial traits given in Chapter 2 of the *Player's Handbook* except as follows:

- **Automatic Languages:** Common, home region. Bonus Languages: Any (other than secret languages, such as Druidic).

DWARVES

Dwarves ruled vast kingdoms beneath hill and mountain long before humans wandered into Faerûn. Many sages suspect that the first dwarves came to Faerûn millennia ago in a great migration from another plane. However, it occurred so long ago that evidence of it is almost nonexistent, and meanwhile the dwarves are now as natural a part of Faerûn as the mountains themselves. The two main dwarven subraces are the shield dwarves of northern Faerûn and the gold dwarves of the far south. The gray dwarves, or duergar, are an Underdark race less common than their surface kindred. The gray dwarves are generally evil, although a few exiles defy this rule.

Male dwarves of any type take pride in their beards, the most remarkable of any race. Some female dwarves of Faerûn can grow beards, too, often passing as males among the nondwarves of the surface lands. Dwarven women may choose to shave their beards to match human-style expectations of beauty, while others glory in luxurious plaited beards that match their hair or wear sharply cut goatees.

For many generations the dwarven race declined in numbers from endless wars with orcs and their kin. However, in the Year of Thunder (1306 DR), the great god Moradin bestowed a new blessing upon his people. The dwarves tell different stories about the source of this blessing, which they refer to as the Forge or the Thunder Blessing. Some say that it was the result of a mighty quest by a dwarven heroine. Others say that Moradin had planned to reforge his peoples' souls all along. Whatever the source of the blessing, the birthrate among dwarves has soared until it is now fully half as high as that of a young and vigorous human land.

The new dwarven generation is commonly referred to as the thunder children. Nearly a fifth of dwarven births after the Thunder Blessing have resulted in identical or fraternal twins. The thunder children share little of the fear and distrust of arcane magic possessed by their ancestors. Most dwarves still feel more comfortable wielding an axe instead of a wand, but many thunder children, particularly the twins, study wizardry or the sorcerer's arts.

In the past few years, these thunder children have come of age, and dwarves are once again a common sight in Faerûn. Many young stout folk leave their homes in groups of a hundred or more to found new clans in hills unclaimed by other dwarves. Others have chosen to wander the world, seeking glory and wealth.

folk of faerûn

Ah, humans, now. There're a lot of us, to be sure, flung far across all these lands, and more besides, across the sundering seas. We battle like orcs and dream like elves and work harder than all but the dwarves at their forges—and we cover Faerûn.

There was a time when any fool could have told you where the folk of this land or that came from, but now we sail or ride so far and often that we're all from everywhere. Even the most isolated villages hold folk who hail from they know not where.

Yet you can still tell something of where someone hails from by their hair and build and skin and manner, though any traveler knows not to assume too much from a quick glance. Remember that, and hearken:

If you look upon tall build, pale skin, hair of flame or straw, and eyes of hazel or blue, slow to speak, apt to frown at cities and go wide-eyed in wonder at finery or magic, then you look upon a Northerner of the Sword Coast. If such a one has darker hair, more muscular build and speaks swifter, he may be from the Moonsea North, or easterly in the Cold Lands. Both kindreds roar at war and in drink, and like to sing—long rising and falling chants. They spit and growl and can speak many words with their glares.

If folk are of medium height and all manner of hues about their hair and eyes, you gaze upon Heartlanders. They're more stocky—burly, some say—in the Dales, and apt to be fine-featured and handsome in Cormyr and Tethyr, with more Southern blood (black hair, yellow or orange eyes, and dusky skin) in Waterdeep, Amn, the Dragon Coast, and Sembia. Heartlanders are soft-spoken and careful, knowing well how easy it is to offend, with so many folk brushing blades past each other.

The folk of Turmish are dark brown in the skin and black in the hair. The Vilhon Reach and the Border Kingdoms about the Lake of Steam are crossroads where all folk mix and marry—and look it. Courtesy and fair speech are virtues in these lands, and these folk weave wondrous compliments into every greeting.

Calimshan, now, is a place of dusky skin—nut-brown to ochre—with much black body hair that the sun may bleach almost white. Shorn and shaved and oiled often, such hides turn golden. Thayans are much the same. Dark dun skins can be seen in the Old Empires, alongside red eyes and paler skins, many the hue of new parchment. The slaves there betray many bloodlines from other lands.

Proud they are, all these people, and sharp of brows and looks, with finely chiseled features.

In the lands around the Easting Reach they turn slender and shorter and agile, soft-spoken again like Heartlanders. Beyond, in Rashemen and Narfell, skins go swarthier and manners are hard as a well-made blade. It is said that no Nar can rest until he avenges the smallest slight with blood, and any Rashemi is capable of finding an insult in the most innocuous of remarks.

Why the gods make us all different, only they know.

—Olram Faravaerr, Merchant of Mintarn

Illustration by Matt Wilson

Shield Dwarf · Gold Dwarf · Gray Dwarf · Human · Rock Gnome · Deep Gnome

Gold Dwarves

Unlike the shield dwarves, the gold dwarves maintained their great kingdom in the Great Rift and did not decline in terrible wars against evil humanoids. While they practiced some magic, they never acquired the hubris that caused the downfall of some human nations. Confident and secure in their remote home, the gold dwarves gained a reputation for haughtiness and pride.

Since the Thunder Blessing, many young gold dwarves have left the Great Rift and are exploring the rest of Faerûn. The folk of other lands have learned that while some gold dwarves are aloof and suspicious, for the most part they are forthright warriors and shrewd traders.

Regions: The ancestral home of the gold dwarves is the Great Rift, located in the dry plains of the Shaar. Gold dwarven outposts can also be found in the Smoking Mountains of Unther and in the Giant's Run Mountains west of the Vilhon Reach. The gold dwarf entry on Table 1–4: Character Regions describes characters raised in the Rift.

Racial Abilities: Gold dwarves have all the dwarven racial traits given in Chapter 2 of the *Player's Handbook* except as follows:

- +2 Constitution, –2 Dexterity: Gold dwarves are stout and tough, but not as quick or agile as other races.
- +1 racial bonus on attack rolls against aberrations: Gold dwarves are trained in special combat techniques against the many bizarre creatures that live in the Underdark. (This replaces the attack bonus against orcs and goblinoids.)
- Automatic Languages: Dwarven, Common, home region. Bonus Languages: Giant, Gnome, Goblin, Shaaran, Terran, Untheric.

Gray Dwarves

Long ago, mind flayers conquered the strongholds of clan Duergar of the dwarven kingdom of Shanatar. After generations of enslavement and cruel experimentation at the hands of the illithids, the duergar rose against their masters and regained their freedom. They emerged as a new subrace of dwarf with limited mental powers.

The gray dwarves are an evil and bitter race, but retain the superior skill and workmanship of dwarvenkind. They have found a niche for themselves in the Underdark, creating armor and weapons to trade with the warring races of that realm. They seem to have been denied the Thunder Blessing.

Duergar on the whole are evil, but some turn their backs on their fellows and seek a different sort of life. For some, this means abandoning the evil gods of the duergar and embracing the traditional dwarven pantheon, while for others it is a more practical betrayal, usually involving stealing from other gray dwarves. When discovered, an outcast is typically stripped of his possessions, tattooed on the face and arms to mark him as a criminal, and cast out under penalty of death. Some clans secretly aid their outcasts—or encourage them to leave before they are found out. To return is to die.

This grim fate drives most outcasts to the surface, where they struggle to survive in an unwelcoming world. The surface dwarves hate the duergar because they turned to evil, and no other surface races hold much love for the gray dwarves. Most of the gray dwarves met by surface dwellers are tattooed exiles, although a small number were lucky or smart enough to leave before being discovered.

Male and female duergar are bald, and women do not grow beards. They are much thinner than other dwarves, with severe facial expressions, gray hair, and gray skin.

Faerûnian Names

Faerûn is vast. Among humans alone, its inhabitants bear literally thousands upon thousands of names. Some folk have no surnames, others have a common clan name, and others have a "son/daughter of" appellation. In Tharsult, Tashalar, and the Border Kingdoms, the word "sar" is much used. It means "of the blood of," and denotes a famous ancestor—or falsely claimed ancestor—so that a farmer might be "Baer sar Thardizar," after the famous warlord of centuries ago.

Older usages such as "of the" and the name of a trade or place (such as Ruthrar o' the Forge and Sammert o' the Hollow) are falling out of favor and are now rarely heard. Only wizards and the most haughty adventurers use personal achievements in their names, such as Dastrin of the Three Thunders or Belgaert of the Deadly Stand, and this, too, is dying out. Occupations can be seen within names, however: *Tel* is an old word for "works at" or "works with," *forar* once meant traveler or peddler, *helder* was a guard or warrior on patrol, *turnskull* was a digger, and *turnstone* a miller.

The names given here are by language, since areas sharing a common tongue tend to use the same names.

Aglarondan: *Male:* Aelthas, Courynn, Folcoerr, Gaedynn, Mourgram, Sealmyd, Yuiredd. *Female:* Blaéra, Courynna, Lynneth, Maera, Mourna, Wydda. *Surnames:* Aengrilor, Dulsaer, Gelebraes, Jacerryl, Telstaerr, Uthelienn.

Alzhedo: *Male:* Aseir, Bardeid, Haseid, Khemed, Mehmen, Sudeiman, Zasheir. *Female:* Atala, Ceidil, Hama, Jasmal, Meilil, Seipora, Yasheira, Zasheida. *Surnames:* Basha, Dumein, Jassan, Khalid, Mostana, Pashar, Rein.

Chessentan: *Male:* Aeron, Daelric, Eurid, Nicos, Oriseus, Pharaxes, Thersos, Xandos. *Female:* Ariadne, Cylla, Eriale, Halonya, Idriane, Mera, Numestra, Sinylla. *Surnames:* Aporos, Corynian, Heldeion, Morieth, Nathos, Sphaerideion, Zora.

Chondathan: *Male:* Darvin, Dorn, Evendur, Gorstag, Grim, Helm, Malark, Morn, Randal, Stedd. *Female:* Arveene, Esvele, Jhessail, Kerri, Lureene, Miri, Rowan, Shandri, Tessele. *Surnames:* Amblecrown, Buckman, Dundragon, Evenwood, Greycastle, Tallstag.

Chultan: *Male:* Atuar, Kwalu, Losi, Mezoar, Nsi, Osaw, Selu, Weshtek. *Female:* Azuil, Chuil, Fipya, Isi, Lorit, Mainu, Sana, Tefnek. *Surnames:* None.

Damaran: *Male:* Bor, Fodel, Glar, Grigor, Igan, Ivor, Kosef, Mival, Orel, Pavel, Sergor. *Female:* Alethra, Kara, Katernin, Mara, Natali, Olma, Tana, Zora. *Surnames:* Bersk, Chernin, Dotsk, Kulenov, Marsk, Nemetsk, Shemov, Starag.

Dambrathan: *Male:* Aethelmed, Houn, Rhivaun, Umbril, Waervyn, Xaemar, Zeltaebar. *Female:* Chourm, Glouris, Maeve, Hayaera, Sevaera, Xaemarra, Zraela. *Surnames:* Calaumystar, Lharaendo, Mristar, Talaudrym, Wyndael

Durpari: *Male:* Charva, Duma, Hukir, Jama, Kilimut, Oskut, Pradir, Rajaput, Sikhil. *Female:* Apret, Bask, Erilet, Fanul, Hist, Mokat, Nismet, Ril, Tiket. *Surnames:* Beszrizma, Datharathi, Melpurvatta, Nalambar, Saqarastar, Tiliputakas.

Dwarven: *Male:* Barundar, Dorn, Joyin, Khondar, Roryn, Storn, Thorik, Wulgar. *Female:* Belmara, Dorna, Joylin, Kiira, Sambril, Tace, Umil. *Surnames:* Bladebite, Crownshield, Gordrivver, Horn, Skulldark, Stoneshield.

Elven: *Male:* Aravilar, Faelar, Mourn, Nym, Orlpar, Saevel, Respen, Rhistel, Taeghen. *Female:* Amra, Hacathra, Imizael, Jastra, Jhaumrithe, Quamara, Talindra, Vestele. *Surnames:* Amalith, Braegen, Calaudra, Eveningfall, Laelithar, Moondown, Tarnruth.

Elven (Drow): *Male:* Alak, Drizzt, Ilmryn, Merinid, Pharaun, Rizzen, Tebryn, Zaknafein. *Female:* Akordia, Chalithra, Eclavdra, Jhaelrnya, Nedylene, Qilué, SiNafay, Vlondril. *Surnames:* Abaeir, Coloara, Glannath, Illistyn, Pharn, Seerear, Vrinn, Xiltyn.

Gnome: *Male:* Burgell, Colmarr, Dorgan, Falrinn, Halbrinn, Orlamm, Rondell, Stolig. *Female:* Calanddra, Eriss, Iviss, Jaree, Lissa, Meree, Nathee, Zelazadda. *Surnames:* Blackrock, Blimth, Greatorm, Rivenstone, Tavartarr, Uvarkk, Whitehorn.

Halfling: *Male:* Blazanar, Corkaury, Dalabrac, Halandar, Ombert, Roberc, Thiraury, Wilimac. *Female:* Aloniira, Calathra, Deldiira, Melinden, Olpara, Rosinden, Tara, Weninda. *Surnames:* Aumble, Bramblefoot, Dardragon, Hardingdale, Merrymar, Starnhap.

Halruaan: *Male:* Aldym, Chand, Hostegym, Meleghost, Presmer, Sandrue, Tethost, Uregaunt. *Female:* Aithe, Alaethe, Chalan, Oloma, Phaele, Sarade, Vosthyl. *Surnames:* Avhoste, Darants, Gedreghost, Maurmeril, Stamaraster, Zorastryl.

Lantanese: *Male:* Eberc, Fodoric, Koger, Lambrac, Midoc, Norbert, Samber, Tibidoc. *Female:* Avilda, Bersace, Charissa, Melsany, Phaerilda, Ravace, Umbrasy. *Surnames:* Angalstrand, Decirc, Lamstrand, SeKorc, SeLangstra, SeMilderic.

Illuskan: *Male:* Ander, Blath, Bran, Frath, Geth, Lander, Luth, Malcer, Stor, Taman, Urth. *Female:* Amafrey, Betha, Cefrey, Kethra, Mara, Olga, Silifrey, Westra. *Surnames:* Brightwood, Helder, Hornraven, Lackman, Stonar, Stormwind, Windrivver.

Mulhorand: *Male:* Aoth, Bareris, Ehput-Ki, Kethoth, Mumed, Ramas, So-Kehur, Thazar-De, Urhur. *Female:* Arizima, Chathi, Nephis, Nulara, Murithi, Sefris, Thola, Umara, Zolis. *Surnames:* Ankhalab, Anskuld, Fezim, Hahpet, Nathandem, Sepret, Uuthrakt.

Orc: *Male:* Besk, Durth, Fang, Gothog, Harl, Kesk, Orrusk, Tharag, Thog, Ugurth. *Female:* Betharra, Creske, Edarreske, Duvaega, Neske, Orvaega, Varra, Yeskarra. *Surnames:* Dummik, Horthor, Lammar, Sormuzhik, Turnskull, Ulkrunnar, Zorgar.

Rashemi: *Male:* Borivik, Faurgar, Jandar, Kanithar, Madislak, Ralmevik, Shaumar, Vladislak. *Female:* Fyevarra, Hulmarra, Immith, Imzel, Navarra, Shevarra, Tammith, Yuldra. *Surnames:* Chergoba, Dyernina, Iltazyara, Murnyethara, Stayanoga, Ulmokina.

Shaaran: *Male:* Awar, Cohis, Damota, Gewar, Hapaw, Laskaw, Moktar, Senesaw, Tokhis. *Female:* Anet, Bes, Dahvet, Faqem, Idim, Lenet, Moqem, Neghet, Sihvet. *Surnames:* Cor Marak, Hiaw Harr, Laumee Harr, Moq Qo Harr, Taw Harr, Woraw Tarak.

Tashalan: *Male:* Angwe, Dumai, Gharbei, Indo, Masambe, Morife, Ngongwe, Sepoto. *Female:* Ayesha, Bhula, Lashela, Intingi, Mashai, Shevaya, Shesara, Ushula. *Surnames:* Damarthe, Ghomposo, Ishivin, Jalamba, Konge, Maingwe, Wasatho.

Turmic: *Male:* Anton, Diero, Marcon, Pieron, Rimardo, Romero, Salazar, Umbero. *Female:* Balama, Dona, Faila, Jalana, Luisa, Marta, Quara, Selise, Vonda. *Surnames:* Agosto, Astorio, Calabra, Domine, Falone, Marivaldi, Pisacar, Ramondo.

Uluik: *Male:* Aklar, Hilur, Liruk, Namiir, Selmik, Uknar, Tirmuk, Wariik. *Female:* Chamuk, Iirkik, Kagiik, Lelchik, Nirval, Talchuk, Valiir, Wenvik. *Surnames:* None.

Untheric: *Male:* Azzedar, Chadrezzan, Gibbur, Horat, Kassur, Numer, Samar, Ungred. *Female:* Chadra, Ilzza, Jezzara, Marune, Saldashune, Xuthra, Zeldara. *Surnames:* Seldom used, patronymics preferred.

Regions: The gray dwarven strongholds are all located in the Underdark. The gray dwarf entry on Table 1–4: Character Regions describes the traits of this kind of duergar culture.

Racial Abilities: Duergar have all the dwarven racial traits given in Chapter 2 of the *Player's Handbook* except as follows:

- +2 Constitution, –4 Charisma. Duergar are extremely withdrawn and guarded.
- Darkvision up to 120 feet.
- Immune to paralysis, phantasms, and magic or alchemical poisons (but not normal poisons). Duergar acquired immunity to some illusions and many toxic substances during their servitude to mind flayers.
- +4 racial bonus on Move Silently checks. Gray dwarves excel in stealthy movement.
- +1 racial bonus on Listen and Spot checks.
- Spell-Like Abilities: 1/day—*enlarge* and *invisibility* as a wizard twice the duergar's level (minimum 3rd level). These affect only the duergar and whatever it carries.
- Light Sensitivity: Duergar suffer a –2 circumstance penalty to attack rolls, saves, and checks in bright sunlight or within the radius of a *daylight* spell.
- Automatic Languages: Dwarven, Undercommon, home region. Bonus Languages: Common, Draconic, Giant, Goblin, Orc, Terran.
- Level Adjustment +2: Duergar are more powerful and gain levels more slowly than most of the other common races of Faerûn. See the Powerful Races sidebar for more information.

Shield Dwarves

The sculpted halls and echoing chambers of dwarven kingdoms are scattered through the Underdark like forgotten necklaces of semiprecious stones. Dwarven kingdoms such as Xonathanur, Oghrann, and Gharraghaur taught the less civilized races of Faerûn what it meant to hold and wield power. Unlike the ancient human empires, the dwarves distrusted magic, so they were never seduced to the heights of magical folly that toppled Netheril and Imaskar. Instead, the dwarves became locked in eternal wars with goblin-kind and the other dwellers in the Underdark. One by one, the dwarven empires of the north failed, leaving only scattered survivors in the mountains or unconquered sections of the Underdark.

The clans that survived these battles are the shield dwarves. For many human generations they were divided into two types: the Hidden, given to reclusion and secrecy, and the Wanderers, comfortable with other races and inclined to exploration. Since the Thunder Blessing, the older members of Hidden clans are beginning to change their hearts. Within a few decades the differences between Hidden and Wanderer may become meaningless.

Regions: Shield dwarven holds exist in Damara, Impiltur, the North, the Silver Marches, Vaasa, the Vast, and the Western Heartlands. Citadel Adbar (north and east of Silverymoon, but counted as in that region for these purposes) is the most famous shield dwarven city. Most shield dwarven characters select one of these homelands or the shield dwarf entry on Table 1–4: Character Regions as their native region.

Racial Abilities: Shield dwarves have all the dwarven racial traits given in Chapter 2 of the *Player's Handbook* except as follows:

- Automatic Languages: Dwarven, Common, home region. Bonus Languages: Chondathan, Draconic, Giant, Goblin, Illuskan, Orc.

ELVES

Faerûn is home to six major subraces of elves, which some sages believe were brought to this plane long ago by their gods. The moon elves, sun elves, and wood elves are joined in loose allegiance to the traditions and authority represented by the Elven Court, now located on the island of Evermeet, and in the person of Queen Amlaruil. Most drow elves treat other elves as despised enemies, and the wild elves usually ignore the decrees of the civilized elves of Evermeet. The sea elves are an aquatic people who rarely interact with their surface kindred.

Drow

Descended from the original dark-skinned elven subrace called the Illythiiri, the drow were cursed into their present appearance by the good elven deities for following the goddess Lolth down the path to evil and corruption. Also called dark elves, the drow have black skin that resembles polished obsidian and stark white or pale yellow hair. They commonly have very pale eyes in shades of lilac, silver, pink, and blue. They also tend to be smaller and thinner than most elves. Most drow on the surface are evil and worship Vhaeraun, but some outcasts and renegades have a more neutral attitude.

Drow have a unique language, Drow Sign Language, that allows them to communicate silently with hand gestures at distances of up to 120 feet as long as they can see each other. Drow Sign Language is a bonus language for drow; others have to spend skill points to learn it. It has no alphabet or written form.

Regions: Menzoberranzan, home city of the famed exile Drizzt Do'Urden, is the most famous drow realm. The drow elf entry on Table 1–4: Character Regions describes any character from Menzoberranzan or a similar Underdark city. Drow hailing from Cormanthor or the High Forest may instead choose the wood elf region and its associated feats and equipment.

Racial Abilities: Drow have all the elven racial traits listed given in Chapter 2 of the *Player's Handbook* except as follows:

- +2 Dexterity, –2 Constitution, +2 Intelligence, +2 Charisma. The drow have ruthlessly selected for agility, intelligence, and force of personality over generations.
- Spell-Like Abilities: 1/day—*dancing lights*, *darkness*, and *faerie fire*. These abilities are as the spells cast by a sorcerer of the drow's character level.
- Darkvision up to 120 feet. This replaces elven low-light vision.
- Proficient with either rapier or shortsword; proficient with hand crossbow and light crossbow. This replaces the standard elven weapon proficiencies.
- Light Blindness (Ex): Abrupt exposure to bright light (such as sunlight or a *daylight* spell) blinds a drow for 1 round. In addition, drow suffer a –1 circumstance penalty on all attack rolls, saves, and checks while operating in bright light.
- Spell resistance of 11 + character level.
- +2 racial bonus on Will saves against spells and spell-like abilities.
- Automatic Languages: Elven, Undercommon, home region. Bonus Languages: Abyssal, Common, Draconic, Drow Sign Language, Goblin, Illuskan.
- Favored Class: Wizard (male) or cleric (female).
- Level Adjustment +2: Drow are more powerful and gain levels more slowly than most of the other common races of Faerûn. See the Powerful Races sidebar for more information.

Moon Elves

Moon elves are the most common sort of elves in Faerûn. Also called silver elves, they have fair skin (sometimes tinged with blue) and hair of silver-white, black, or blue. (Humanlike colors

Human   Sun Elf   Wood Elf   Moon Elf   Drow   Wild Elf

LOCKWOOD

Illustration by Todd Lockwood

are rare, but possible.) Their eyes are blue or green, with gold flecks. They are the elven subrace most tolerant of humankind, and most half-elves are descended from moon elves.

Regions: Moon elven domains can be found in the woodlands of the Dalelands (in Cormanthor), Evermeet, the High Forest, the North, Silverymoon, and the Western Heartlands. Evereska, on the

The Retreat, and after

Among the Fair Folk there is a Calling that is a yearning to go west over the sea to Evermeet. It comes to most elves late in their lives, but some feel its tug early, and others are never touched by it at all. Some who have both elven and human blood, as I have, feel it, and others do not. I am so far unmoved by the Calling, and I am beginning to believe I never will be. Simply put, the Calling, which humans and elves alike have termed the Retreat, seems to have come to an end.

No elven council or ruler has decreed an ending to the Retreat. Weary of mortal affairs, exhausted by warfare and care, the Retreat offered elvenkind a hope of lasting peace in a land beyond mortal reach. It is enough to know that for thousands upon thousands of years, as orcs and men spread and raged across Faerûn, elves withdrew by *portal* and ship and far-faring magic westward to Evermeet. Yet now no more ships set sail, no more secret companies steal forth in the shadows never to be seen again. The Retreat is ended. All those Fair Folk who wished to leave have left.

Cormanthor, Ardeep, and other traditional holds stand largely abandoned, fading to pale echoes and shadows of their former splendor. Where once elves abode in easy mastery over unbroken forest, now humans till and rumble in their carts and wagons, and winds howl across bare lands. Elves who remain bide in the shadows, and speak softly; gliding with adroit grace around and among men like silver ghosts in moonlight.

It seems to me that many Fair Folk dwelling in Faerûn today are like fine-cut, glittering gems, or warswords: fair to look upon, but tempered cold and hard of necessity. And abide they do still—ah, yes, know this: the Retreat is ended, and many elves remain. Hear you fey, faerie trumpets in the moonlight, or see impossibly graceful figures dancing in silver armor as free-flowing as any fine gown, long slender fingers curled about harp-strings and pipes and long, curving swords with equal deftness?

The elves are still here—and more than that: Some are returning. They are coming back east with ready sword and wisdom in the ways of humankind. Aye, you may cut down this tree and that, but are you then free of all trees? No, they spring up, in the teeth of your will that such a place be bare of trees. Spring up anew, and endure . . . and when your breath is forever stilled and your bones lie among their roots, the trees will be standing still, covering the ground you hewed them from once more with their shade. Patient and looking down the long years, elves are trees among men. Learn this, if you learn naught else of the Fair Folk.

—*Cambrizym of Candlekeep, Sage Pursuivant*

western edges of Anauroch, is the strongest elven domain remaining in Faerûn. The moon elf entry on Table 1–4: Character Regions describes characters from any small elven forest community.

Racial Abilities: Moon elves have all the elven racial traits given in Chapter 2 of the *Player's Handbook* except as follows:

- Automatic Languages: Elven, Common, home region. Bonus Languages: Auran, Chondathan, Gnoll, Gnome, Halfling, Illuskan, Sylvan.

Sun Elves

Sun elves are less common across Faerûn than moon elves, because most live on Evermeet, where nonelves are not allowed. Also called gold elves, they have bronze skin, golden blond, copper, or black hair, and green or gold eyes. These are seen as the most civilized and haughty elves, preferring to remain separate from nonelven races.

Regions: Aside from Evermeet, where they are most common, sun elves can be found in the woodlands of the North, Silverymoon, and the Western Heartlands. The realm of Evereska is home to a number of powerful sun elven families. The sun elf entry on Table 1–4: Character Regions describes the scions of sun elven families.

Racial Abilities: Sun elves have all the elven racial traits given in Chapter 2 of the *Player's Handbook* except as follows:

- +2 Intelligence, –2 Constitution. Sun elves value study and contemplation over the feats of agility learned by most other elves.
- Automatic Languages: Elven, Common, home region. Bonus Languages: Auran, Celestial, Chondathan, Gnome, Halfling, Illuskan, Sylvan.

Wild Elves

The very rare wild elves are rarely seen by others, because they live in the heart of thick forests and they have incredible skill at keeping hidden. Also called green elves, their skin tends to be dark brown, and their hair ranges from black to light brown, lightening to silvery white with age.

Regions: Wild elves favor warm southern forests and jungles, such as the Chondalwood, the Methwood, the Forest of Amtar, and the Misty Vale. Wild elven characters may use the wild elf entry on Table 1–4: Character Regions or choose the Chondalwood, Chessenta, Chult, or the Shaar as their home region.

Racial Abilities: Wild elves correspond exactly to the wild elves presented in the *Monster Manual*. They have all the elven racial traits given in Chapter 2 of the *Player's Handbook* except as follows:

- +2 Dexterity, –2 Intelligence. Wild elves are hardier than other elves, but favor physical action and feats of athleticism instead of learning to solve problems.
- Automatic Languages: Elven, Common, home region. Bonus Languages: Gnoll, Illuskan, Orc, Sylvan, Tashalan.
- Favored class: Sorcerer.

Wood Elves

Wood elves are reclusive, but less so than the almost feral wild elves. Also called copper elves, they have coppery skin tinged with green, and brown, green, or hazel eyes. Their hair is usually brown or black, with blond and coppery-red occasionally found.

Regions: The High Forest is home to many wood elves. Smaller communities can be found in the forests of the Dalelands (especially Cormanthor), the Great Dale, the North, Tethyr, and the Western Heartlands. The wood elf entry on Table 1–4: Character Regions is appropriate for characters from any of these places.

Racial Abilities: Wood elves are very similar to the wood elves presented in the *Monster Manual*. They have all the elven racial traits given in Chapter 2 of the *Player's Handbook* except as follows:

- +2 Strength, +2 Dexterity, –2 Constitution, –2 Intelligence, –2 Charisma. Wood elves are strong but slight, and tend to be less cerebral and intuitive than other elves.
- Automatic Languages: Elven, Common, home region. Bonus Languages: Chondathan, Draconic, Gnome, Goblin, Gnoll, Sylvan.
- Favored class: Ranger.

GNOMES

The human scholars of Candlekeep refer to the gnomes as the Forgotten Folk, for their willful evasion of the great wars and tragedies that color the history of Faerûn's other races. While the gnomes have been slaves of powerful nations such as Netheril and Calimshan in the past, they have never been conquerors. For the most part, they have lived in out-of-the-way forests and hills, untroubled by the conflicts that occupy human, elven, and dwarven attention.

That has changed as the number of humans in Faerûn has grown. Many gnome youngsters now question the wisdom of attempting to remain completely separate from other societies. Change within gnome communities is slower than in human ones, but more and more young gnomes are leaving home to live as travelers or adventurers.

When Gond, the god of invention, appeared to the world in the form of a gnome, many young gnomes took that as a sign that it was time for gnomes to invent a new way of life. These followers of Gond share the standard gnome distaste for joining organizations that are too big, so they tend to organize themselves into small groups of like-minded inventors rather than trying to remake gnome communities in their own image.

Deep Gnomes

Hidden in the depths of the Underdark live the svirfneblin, or deep gnomes. Reclusive, suspicious, and resentful of intrusion into their cavern homes, the deep gnomes share little of the humor or openness of their surface cousins. Where a rock gnome community bursts with energy, excitement, and laughter, a svirfneblin city is a dull and colorless place of echoing silence and furtive motion in the shadows. All hands are raised against the svirfneblin—or so the deep gnomes believe, anyway.

The deep gnomes may be the world's stealthiest and most elusive folk. Centuries upon centuries of surviving the deadly perils of the Underdark have bred in this race an amazing gift for avoiding attention. In their cavern homes they are nearly undetectable with magic, and even in the strange and threatening (to them) surface world, the deep gnomes' natural stealth makes them difficult to spot or catch.

Svirfneblin have gnarled physiques, brown or gray skin, gray eyes, and gray hair (although males are bald). They tend to be sullen, withdrawn, and suspicious to a fault.

Regions: Very few of the Underdark towns and strongholds of the deep gnomes are known to the surface world. Most svirfneblin characters can be described accurately enough by the deep gnome entry on Table 1–4: Character Regions.

Two years ago, several hundred svirfneblin from the city of Blingdenstone were driven to the surface in the Silver Marches when their city was overrun by drow-summoned demons. These exiles sought refuge in the lands of Silverymoon and are occasionally seen in the North.

Racial Abilities: Svirfneblin have all the gnome racial traits given in Chapter 2 of the *Player's Handbook* except as follows:

- –2 Strength, +2 Dexterity, +2 Wisdom, –4 Charisma. Quick and perceptive, svirfneblin are suspicious and retiring to an extreme.

- Darkvision up to 120 feet. This replaces gnome low-light vision.
- Spell-Like Abilities: 1/day—*blindness*, *blur*, and *change self*. These abilities are as the spells cast by a wizard of the svirfneblin's character level (save DC 10 + spell level). This ability replaces the gnome ability to cast the 0-level spells *dancing lights*, *ghost sound*, and *prestidigitation*.
- Stonecunning: Like dwarves, svirfneblin receive a +2 racial bonus on checks to notice unusual stonework. Something that isn't stone but that is disguised as stone also counts as unusual stonework. A deep gnome who merely comes within 10 feet of unusual stonework can make a check as though actively searching and can use the Search skill to find stonework traps as a rogue can. A svirfneblin can also intuit depth, sensing the approximate distance underground as naturally as a human can sense which way is up.
- Nondetection (Su): Svirfneblin have a continuous nondetection supernatural ability as the spell cast by a wizard of their character level.
- Spell resistance of 11 + character level.
- +4 dodge bonus against all creatures (no special bonus against giants).
- +2 racial bonus on all saving throws.
- +2 racial bonus on Hide checks, which improves to +4 in darkened areas underground.
- Automatic Languages: Gnome, Undercommon, home region. Bonus Languages: Common, Draconic, Dwarven, Elven, Illuskan, Terran.
- Level Adjustment +3: Svirfneblin are more powerful and gain levels more slowly than most of the other common races of Faerûn. See the Powerful Races sidebar for more information.

Rock Gnomes

Rock gnomes are the most common type of gnomes in Faerûn, and are usually just called gnomes, since they are the only sort that surface dwellers ever see. The rock gnomes of Faerûn are nearly identical to the gnomes portrayed in the *Player's Handbook*. They are inquisitive, irrepressible, and at times insincere.

Equipped by nature with keen curiosity and a knack for mechanical workings, gnomes excel at intricate crafts such as gemcutting, toymaking, and clockwork engineering. They happen to be the finest gunsmiths in Faerûn, and they are the most likely of any race to arm themselves with smokepowder firearms.

Regions: If the rock gnomes have a homeland, they would probably count it as the half-mythical island of Lantan. The rock gnome entry on Table 1–4: Character Regions describes mainly these Lantanese gnomes. Other than in Lantan, rock gnomes do not dwell in quantity in any particular country or city. Instead, small communities of a dozen families or so might be found almost anywhere, well hidden in wild terrain or sometimes in their own urban neighborhood. They favor temperate climates, and a number of gnome settlements are known to exist in the Western Heartlands, the Dalelands, and the woodlands of the Great Dale and Thesk.

Racial Abilities: Rock gnomes have all the gnome racial traits given in Chapter 2 of the *Player's Handbook* except as follows:

- Automatic Languages: Gnome, Common, home region. Bonus Languages: Chondathan, Draconic, Dwarven, Goblin, Illuskan, Sylvan, Terran.

HALF-ELVES

Faerûnian half-elves are nearly identical to the half-elves presented in the *Player's Handbook*. The only exception is that their elven parentage gives them distinctive features. Drow half-elves tend to have dusky skin, silver or white hair, and human eye colors. (They have 60-foot darkvision, but they do not gain any other drow traits.) Moon half-elves tend toward pale skin with a tinge of blue around the ears and chin. Sea half-elves tend to blend the flesh tones of their human and elven parents (but cannot breathe water). Sun half-elves have bronzed skin. Wild half-elves have medium-brown skin. Wood half-elves have coppery skin tinged with green.

Regions: Most half-elves are loners because of their unique parentage. However, a few stable communities of half-elves are

orcs and their kin

Every battlefield has its flies and maggots, swarming among the corpses—and the orcs are the flies and maggots of Faerûn. Cunning, they are, and dwell among humans because humans mean coin and ready food and lots of confusion and coming and going. Some even breed with the fierce humans of the North and upland hills, and from them we get "one-tusks" or half-orcs.

Orcs see the need for rules, but hold that the stronger make the rules for the weaker, and that no rule or law need be followed if no one stronger is around to see, or punish. I say all orcs, though I admit some are wiser or more trustworthy than others. But the wise man trusts no orc.

The true, wild orc dwells in mountain caverns—the same homes as dwarves love, which is why the Stout Folk are so few and so grim, these days. In cave-warrens they dwell, snarling and fighting often but seldom to the death, rutting and brawling and delighting in cruelties of trap and pratfall and demeaning tricks, telling tales of great plunder and abundant food in the South.

If times are lean, or the tribe's caves are full with young and reckless warriors, a surging tide of discontent rises and the young warriors fairly roar to be led down on a great raid, to show their worth and seize their fortunes on the ends of their blades. They boil forth, every decade or more, led by canny veterans and either the chief of their tribe (if he's still afire with his own dreams of conquering and pillaging) or a war leader who will never get to be chief save by slaughter that would tear the tribe apart in feuding.

Thus the latest orc horde pours down out of their mountain valleys. Orcs are not subtle folk. Orc hordes seldom pass by any target or foe who waves sword against them, and crash on into battle after battle, a great wave seeking to batter and inundate all before it, rather than sneaking or avoiding or biding in hiding.

Of orc tribes not all shattered or fallen, I can name these handful, of many: Arauthrar, Bale Eye, Braeskull, Cold Bone, Folgorr, Gathatchkh, Haulaeve, Jolruth, Norglor, Oldaggar, Red Talon, Sorok, Tailbold, Wurruvva, and Yultch.

Of orc chieftains great in battle, I know these fallen (or at least vanished when their horde was smashed): Auldglokh, Browhorn, Clamrar, Gulmuth, Hurolk, Irmgrith, Kuthe, Morog, Namrane, Orgog, Rauthgog, Surk, Ulbror, and Yauthlok. And these who may still carry their brawn: Aragh Bloodbanner, Bogdraguth of the Ice, Clarguth Manyheads, Foalorr sug (son of) Fael, Horimbror Ironmask, Korgulk Ibbrin, Mathrankh, Torlor sug Klevven, Umburraglar Bloodtooth, and Zoarkluth.

—*Gulvrin Talamtar, Warrior of Secomber*

Illustration by Todd Lockwood

Human   Half-Orc   Half-Elf   Half-Drow

Ghostwise Halfling   LOCKWOOD

Lightfoot Halfling   Strongheart Halfling

sprinkled around the landscape of Faerûn. Aglarond, Cormyr, the Dalelands, the High Forest, and Silverymoon possess relatively high populations of half-elves and are appropriate homelands for half-elven characters. Half-elves from these areas generally find more acceptance than their solitary counterparts. Half-elves can also select the racial entry of their elven parent on Table 1–4: Character Regions as to represent them if they were raised in a mainly elven culture.

Racial Abilities: Half-elves have all the half-elven racial traits given in Chapter 2 of the *Player's Handbook* except as follows:

- Automatic Languages: Elven, Common, home region. Bonus Languages: Any (except secret languages, such as Druidic).

HALF-ORCS

Even in the tolerant lands of Faerûn, a half-orc's life is hardly ever easy. Some human areas tolerate half-orcs, making their lives no harder than the lives of other settlers in the area. Other human areas despise half-orcs and persecute them, making life in the open with savage orc tribes look survivable by comparison.

Regions: Even more so than half-elves, half-orcs tend to be loners. Most remain among the orc tribes, where their human intelligence and leadership offers a hope of advancement. The half-orc entry on Table 1–4: Character Regions describes a character who strikes out on her own or who is raised primarily among orcs.

Among human lands, Amn, Chessenta, Damara, the Moonsea, the North, Vaasa, and Waterdeep are regions in which half-orcs are commonplace enough to be accepted—within certain limits. Aside from these places, most small cities possess enough of a half-orc population to create a small community of this race.

Racial Abilities: Half-orcs have all the half-orc racial traits given in Chapter 2 of the *Player's Handbook* except as follows:

- Automatic Languages: Orc, Common, home region. Bonus Languages: Damaran, Giant, Gnoll, Goblin, Illuskan, Undercommon.

HALFLINGS

Three major subraces of halfling dwell in Faerûn: the lightfoot halflings, the rare ghostwise halflings, and the strongheart halflings of Luiren in the south. Like the rock gnomes, many halflings live among the Big Folk in the human lands. They are resourceful and quick, perfectly at home among the sprawling human lands or living apart in their own settled communities.

The halflings' name for their race is the *hin*, although most accept "halfling" with a shrug and a smile.

Ghostwise Halflings

These wild, nearly feral halflings rarely leave the confines of the deep forests. Strange and reclusive, they form close-knit communities because of their amazing talents and are uncomfortable with strangers. Like other halflings, they refer to themselves as the *hin*. They do not have a name for their subrace, because their culture is almost entirely cut off from the outside world and their awareness of other kinds of halflings is very low.

Regions: The Chondalwood, south of the Vilhon Reach, is home to a number of ghostwise settlements. Other forests inhabited by these reclusive folk include the Methwood between Chessenta and Unther, and the Forest of Amtar south of the plains of the Shaar.

The ghostwise halfling entry on Table 1–4: Character Regions describes a ghostwise halfling from one of these deep forest communities.

Racial Abilities: Ghostwise halflings have all the halfling racial traits given in Chapter 2 of the *Player's Handbook* except as follows:

- Speak without Sound (Su): A ghostwise halfling, unlike other halflings, can communicate telepathically with any creature within 20 feet, just as if speaking to him or her. The halfling can only speak and listen to one person at a time, and he must share a common language with the person or creature he speaks to telepathically, or the telepathic link fails.
- Ghostwise halflings do not receive the standard halfling +1 racial bonus on all saving throws. They simply are not as lucky as their lightfoot cousins.
- Automatic Languages: Halfling, Common, home region. Bonus Languages: Chondathan, Elven, Gnoll, Shaaran, Sylvan.
- Favored Class: Barbarian.

Lightfoot Halflings

The most common type of halflings seen in the world, the lightfoots are the most likely to give in to their desire to wander. They are at home living side by side with folk of many different races and cultures. Lightfoot halflings are more likely to worship nonhalfling deities than any other halfling subrace.

Regions: Some lightfoot halflings are wandering traders, craftsfolk, and entertainers. A clan of several extended families may settle in a human town for a year or two, working and trading, and then pick up their stakes and move on for reasons known only to themselves. The lightfoot halfling entry on Table 1–4: Character Regions describes a lightfoot halfling of this seminomadic sort.

Many lightfoot halflings prefer a more sedentary existence. The kingdom of Luiren is the ancestral homeland of the halfling race, and some lightfoots live there. Other lightfoots settle permanently in just about any land in which humans live. Any region entry for a human land is acceptable for a lightfoot character.

Racial Abilities: Lightfoot halflings are the standard halflings found in the *Player's Handbook*. They have all the halfling racial traits given in Chapter 2 of the *Player's Handbook* except as follows:

- Automatic Languages: Halfling, Common, home region. Bonus Languages: Chessentan, Chondathan, Damaran, Dwarven, Elven, Illuskan, Goblin.

Strongheart Halflings

While the lightfoot halflings value the experience of travel and the sight of new lands and peoples, the stronghearts are a more organized, orderly, and industrious race. They build to last, and fiercely defend their homelands against threats that their lightfoot kin would simply flee. Northland humans familiar with the easygoing ways of the lightfoot halflings are surprised to learn that some halflings are capable of a warrior tradition and aren't afraid to show a hint of arrogance or confidence in their own abilities and strengths. Strongheart halflings enjoy athletic contests and value exceptional skills of all kinds.

Regions: Strongheart halflings make up most of the population of the land of Luiren. They are uncommon in other lands. The strongheart halfling entry on Table 1–4: Character Regions describes a strongheart halfling from Luiren.

Racial Abilities: Strongheart halflings have all the halfling racial traits given in Chapter 2 of the *Player's Handbook* except as follows:

- Strongheart halflings gain one extra feat at 1st level, because they have a strong drive to compete and many opportunities to practice their skills.

- Strongheart halflings do not receive the halfling racial +1 bonus on all saving throws. They have not experienced the same kind of adversity that the lightfoot halflings have survived.
- Automatic Languages: Halfling, Common, home region. Bonus Languages: Dwarven, Gnoll, Goblin, Halruaan, Shaaran.

PLANETOUCHED

Faerûn is home to many native peoples and has many magic *portals* that lead to distant parts of the world as well as to other worlds. Through these *portals* come visitors from other planes, including outsiders of various sorts, some of whom dally or settle in Faerûn and have children with local humans. Eventually their extraplanar heritage gets diluted over several generations, resulting in a person with a slight bloodline of celestial, infernal, or elemental origin.

These beings, known as the planetouched, have unusual abilities based on the nature of their distant ancestors, but in most ways appear completely human. Because of the widespread *portals*, these planetouched might look like a human from any part of this world, and so may be of Dalelands, Mulhorandi, Turmish, or any other stock. The most common sorts of planetouched are aasimar (descended from celestials), tieflings (descended from demons or devils), and genasi (descended from elemental-related outsiders, such as genies).

The planetouched prefer to blend in with human society and rarely form communities of their own. In this way, they are a more extreme example than the half-elves (who also rarely have their own communities) because of their rarity and varied backgrounds. Some places have a slightly higher frequency of the planetouched because of local circumstances, described in each type's entry.

Native Outsider: Due to the strength of their divine or infernal bloodlines, each of the planetouched races possesses the unusual characteristic of being an outsider native to Faerûn, not a humanoid. This has three principal effects:

First, spells or effects that affect only humanoids, such as a *charm person* or a *dominate person* spell, do not affect planetouched characters.

Second, spells and effects that target extraplanar creatures may affect planetouched characters. For example, the *mace of smiting* and the *sword of the planes* are more effective against outsiders, and are correspondingly more dangerous to a planetouched character. A spell that drives outsiders back to their home planes does not affect planetouched characters, but *banishment*—a spell that removes an outsider from the caster's plane without specifying a return to the outsider's native plane—would work just fine.

Finally, Faerûn's planetouched have lived on Toril long enough for Toril to become, in effect, their native plane. This means that planetouched characters can be *raised* or *resurrected* normally, whereas most outsiders cannot be brought back from the dead without the use of a *miracle* or *wish* spell.

Aasimar

Carrying the blood of a celestial, an aasimar is usually good-aligned and fights against evil in the world. Some have a minor physical trait suggesting their heritage, such as silver hair, golden eyes, or an unnaturally intense stare. Those descended from a celestial minion of a Faerûnian deity often carry a birthmark in the shape of the deity's holy symbol or some other mark significant to that faith.

Regions: Aasimar are relatively common in Mulhorand because the Mulhorandi deities have a legacy of begetting offspring with mortals.

Racial Abilities: Aasimar have the following traits:

- +2 Wisdom, +2 Charisma: Aasimar are blessed with insight and personal magnetism.
- Medium-size.

Illustration by Sam Wood

Aasimar   Tiefling   Fire Genasi   Earth Genasi   Air Genasi   Water Genasi   Human

- Aasimar base speed is 30 feet.
- Acid, cold, and electricity resistance 5.
- *Light* (Sp): Aasimar can use *light* once per day as cast by a sorcerer of their character level.
- +2 racial bonus on Listen and Spot checks.
- Darkvision up to 60 feet.
- Outsider: Aasimar are native outsiders.
- Automatic Languages: Common, home region. Bonus Languages: Any (except secret languages, such as Druidic).
- Favored Class: Paladin.
- Level Adjustment +1: Aasimar are slightly more powerful and gain levels more slowly than most of the other common races of Faerûn. See the Powerful Races sidebar for more information.

Genasi

Genasi are descended from elemental-related creatures, such as efreet, dao, djinn, jann, and marids, among others. Most of them have had no direct contact with their elemental forebears, but the signs of their heritage are apparent. Genasi take great pride in their distinctive features and abilities.

Air Genasi

Air genasi see themselves as the inheritors of the sky, the wind, and the very air of the world. They are most often neutral. They appear mostly human, with one or two unusual traits reflecting their quasi-elemental nature, such as a light blue color to their skin or hair, a slight breeze in their presence at all times, or flesh that is cool to the touch. They care little for their appearance and tend to have wind-tossed hair and much-mended clothes. Their emotions vary quickly between calm reserve and great intensity.

Regions: Air genasi are common in Calimshan, for much of that land was long ago ruled by djinn.

Racial Abilities: Air genasi have the following traits:

- +2 Dexterity, +2 Intelligence, –2 Wisdom, –2 Charisma: Air genasi are quick of hand and sharp of wit, but easily distracted and arrogant.
- Medium-size.
- Air genasi base speed is 30 feet.
- Darkvision up to 60 feet.
- *Levitate* (Sp): Air genasi can use *levitate* once per day as cast by a 5th-level sorcerer.
- Clerical Focus: An air genasi cleric must choose a deity who grants access to the Air domain and select Air as one of her two domains.
- +1 racial bonus on saving throws against all air spells and effects. This bonus increases by +1 for every five class levels the genasi attains.
- Breathless: Air genasi do not breathe, so they are immune to drowning, suffocation, and attacks that require inhalation (such as some types of poison).
- Outsider: Air genasi are native outsiders.
- Automatic Languages: Common, home region. Bonus Languages: Any (except secret languages, such as Druidic).
- Favored Class: Fighter.
- Level Adjustment +1: Air genasi are slightly more powerful and gain levels more slowly than most of the other common races of Faerûn. See the Powerful Races sidebar for more information.

Earth Genasi

Earth genasi are slow to act, ponderous in thought, and set in their ways. They are most often neutral. They appear mostly human, with one or two unusual traits reflecting their quasi-elemental nature, such as earthlike skin, rough facial features, or eyes like black pits. They favor neutral colors and simple clothing, and while some appear to inadvertently collect dirt on their clothes, others keep a neat and polished appearance.

Regions: Earth genasi are more common in the North, near the Spine of the World, where deep caves in the heart of the mountains sometimes manifest *portals* to the plane of Earth.

Racial Abilities: Earth genasi have the following racial traits:

- +2 Strength, +2 Constitution, −2 Wisdom, −2 Charisma: Earth genasi are strong and tough, but somewhat oblivious and stubborn.
- Medium-size.
- Earth genasi base speed is 30 feet.
- Darkvision up to 60 feet.
- *Pass Without Trace* (Sp): Earth genasi can use *pass without trace* once per day as cast by a 5th-level druid.
- +1 racial bonus on saving throws against earth spells and effects. This bonus increases by +1 for every five class levels the genasi attains.
- Clerical Focus: An earth genasi cleric must choose a deity who grants access to the Earth domain and select Earth as one of his two domains.
- Outsider: Earth genasi are native outsiders.
- Automatic Languages: Common, home region. Bonus Languages: Any (except secret languages, such as Druidic).
- Favored Class: Fighter.
- Level Adjustment +1: Earth genasi are slightly more powerful and gain levels more slowly than most of the other common races of Faerûn. See the Powerful Races sidebar for more information.

Fire Genasi

Fire genasi are hot-blooded and quick to anger, proud and unafraid to take action. They are most often neutral. They appear mostly human, with one or two unusual traits reflecting their quasi-elemental nature, such as skin the color of burnt coal, red hair that waves like flames, or eyes that glow when the genasi is angry. They prefer to dress simply and elegantly, although their fashions can be more flamboyant than the most outrageous trend.

Regions: Fire genasi are most common in Calimshan, for much of that land was long ago ruled by efreet. They are also found in Chult, the Lake of Steam, and Unther, which are all lands near volcanoes.

Racial Abilities: Fire genasi have the following racial traits:

- +2 Intelligence, −2 Charisma: Fire genasi have bright minds, but are impatient and quick to anger.
- Medium-size.
- Fire genasi base speed is 30 feet.
- +1 racial bonus on saving throws against fire spells and effects. This bonus increases by +1 for every five class levels the genasi attains.
- Darkvision up to 60 feet.
- *Control Flame* (Sp): Fire genasi can cause a nonmagical fire within 10 feet of them to diminish to the level of coals or flare to the brightness of daylight and double the normal radius of its illumination. This ability does not change the heat output or fuel consumption of the fire source, lasts 5 minutes, and may be done once per day. They use this ability as 5th-level sorcerers.
- Clerical Focus: A fire genasi cleric must choose a deity who grants access to the Fire domain and select Fire as one of his two domains.
- Outsider: Fire genasi are native outsiders.
- Automatic Languages: Common, home region. Bonus Languages: Any (except secret languages, such as Druidic).
- Favored Class: Fighter.
- Level Adjustment +1: Fire genasi are slightly more powerful and gain levels more slowly than most of the other common races of Faerûn. See the Powerful Races sidebar for more information.

Water Genasi

Water genasi are patient and slow to change, preferring to wear away opposition slowly, but are capable of great violence in extreme situations. They are most often neutral. All have one or more traits that reflect their quasi-elemental nature, such as lightly scaled skin, clammy flesh, blue-green skin or hair, or hair that waves as if underwater. They dress sparsely, preferring clothing that won't bind when in the water and ripples like waves when dry.

Regions: Water genasi are most often found in the lands near the Sea of Fallen Stars—the Vilhon Reach, the Dragon Coast, Sembia, Aglarond, and Chessenta—where the extraplanar entities of the sea mingle with mortals.

Racial Abilities: Water genasi have the following traits:

- +2 Constitution, −2 Charisma: Water genasi have high endurance, but are cold and emotionally distant.
- Medium-size.
- Water genasi base speed is 30 feet. They swim at a speed of 30 feet.
- Darkvision up to 60 feet.
- *Create Water* (Sp): Water genasi can use *create water* once per day as cast by a 5th-level druid.
- +1 racial bonus on saving throws against water spells and effects. This bonus increases by +1 for every 5 class levels the genasi attains.
- Water genasi breathe water as an extraordinary ability.
- Clerical Focus: A water genasi cleric must choose a deity who grants access to the Water domain and select Water as one of her two domains.
- Outsider: Water genasi are native outsiders.
- Automatic Languages: Common, home region. Bonus Languages: Any (except secret languages, such as Druidic).
- Favored Class: Fighter.
- Level Adjustment +1: Water genasi are slightly more powerful and gain levels more slowly than most of the other common races of Faerûn. See the Powerful Races sidebar for more information.

Tiefling

Because they are descended from evil outsiders, those who know of their ancestry immediately consider most tieflings evil and untrustworthy. Not all tieflings are evil or untrustworthy, but enough are that the prejudice tends to cling. Some tieflings have a minor physical trait suggesting their heritage, such as pointed teeth, red eyes, small horns, the odor of brimstone, cloven feet, or just an unnatural aura of wrongness. Those descended from an infernal minion of a Faerûnian deity often carry a birthmark of the deity's holy symbol or another trait related to that evil faith.

Regions: Tieflings are most common in Mulhorand because the Mulhorandi deities sometimes beget offspring with mortals. They are also found in Unther and Thay, lands with long, dark traditions of infernal dealings.

Racial Abilities: Tieflings have the following racial traits:

- +2 Dexterity, +2 Intelligence, −2 Charisma: Tieflings are gifted with heightened reflexes and cunning, but tend to disturb people with whom they interact.
- Medium-size.
- Tiefling base speed is 30 feet.
- Cold, fire, and electricity resistance 5.
- *Darkness* (Sp): Tieflings can use *darkness* once per day as cast by a sorcerer of their character level.
- +2 racial bonus on Bluff and Hide checks.
- Darkvision up to 60 feet.
- Outsider: Tieflings are native outsiders.

- Automatic Languages: Common, home region. Bonus Languages: Any (except secret languages, such as Druidic).
- Favored Class: Rogue.

- Level Adjustment +1: Tieflings are slightly more powerful and gain levels more slowly than most of the other common races of Faerûn. See the Powerful Races sidebar for more information.

powerful races

Some of the races available in the FORGOTTEN REALMS campaign setting are significantly more powerful than the races in the *Player's Handbook*. You need your DM's approval before playing a character of such a race. To maintain the balance of power between player characters, adjustments have to be made to characters of these races so that the game remains fair and enjoyable for all involved.

All of these races have a racial trait called level adjustment that is a number between 1 and 3.

When creating a character of this race, add the level adjustment to the character level of the creature. The DM determines how many experience points she lets your new character start with. If a powerful race's minimum experience point requirement is higher than this number, you can't be a member of this race. Your character's beginning equipment is based on his effective level, not his class level. (If the DM wants to bend this guideline and let you play such a character, then that character should start with as many experience points and gold pieces as the DM would normally allow, not the minimum listed here.)

For example, the PC group is 3rd level and 4th, so the DM decides to allow new PCs to start with 2,000 XP rather than 0. A player can therefore play an aasimar but not a drow. If the DM decided to let someone start with a drow, the DM should have that character start with 2,000 XP rather than 3,000 XP. (The player already has the advantage of playing a powerful race. She should not also get the advantage of starting with more experience points than another starting character.) Your DM has the final say on what sort of characters the players can create for his game. Chapter 8: Running the Realms has more advice for DMs on allowing characters of these races as player characters.

Because characters of these powerful races possess a higher level than just their character level alone, they do not gain levels as fast as a normal character. Add your character's level adjustment to your character level to arrive at your effective character level (ECL). From now on, this character uses his ECL to determine how many experience points he needs to reach a new level. These characters begin play with the minimum number of experience points needed to be a normal character of their ECL. You still use the character's actual level for everything else (such as when you acquire feats, skill point acquisition, and so on).

For example, an aasimar has a level adjustment of +1, so Zophas, a 1st-level aasimar paladin, has an ECL of 2 (one character level plus the level adjustment of +1). Because his ECL is 2, Zophas begins play with 1,000 XP, the minimum XP to be a 1st-level aasimar character. He is also treated as a 2nd-level character for purposes of determining how much gold he has to purchase equipment (900 gp, based on Table 2–24 in the *DUNGEON MASTER's Guide*). When he reaches 3,000 XP he gains a level in paladin, and his ECL becomes 3 (two character levels plus the level adjustment of +1). He would pick up a third character level at 6,000 XP, a fourth at 10,000 XP, and so on, always one level behind a human character with the same experience point total.

Another example is Renevelazzon, a 1st-level drow sorcerer from Cormanthor. A drow has a level adjustment of +2, so his ECL is 3 (one character level plus the level adjustment of +2).

Because his ECL is 3, he begins play with 3,000 XP (and 2,700 gp), the minimum experience point total needed to be a 1st-level drow character and the starting equipment recommended for a 3rd-level PC. When he reaches 6,000 XP he gains a level in rogue, and his ECL becomes 4 (two character levels plus the level adjustment of +2). He would pick up a third character level at 10,000 XP, a fourth at 15,000 XP, and so on, always two levels behind a human character with the same experience point total.

This system allows your DM to give you and the other players a set experience point total for your characters, and you can build your characters with any race and class combination and still be about the same power level despite the overall differences between powerful and standard races. For example, your DM could give each player 10,000 experience points and 9,000 gp (from *DUNGEON MASTER's Guide* Table 2–24) to build a character. Michele makes a 3rd-level drow rogue (ECL 5), Duane makes a 4th-level aasimar monk (ECL 5), Julia makes a 5th-level human cleric, and Rich makes a 2nd-level svirfneblin fighter (ECL 5).

The best thing to consider when making a character of one of these races is this question: Is the initial jump in power worth the long-term decrease in the speed your character gains levels?

Essentially, instead of needing your character level × 1,000 to reach the next level, your character needs your ECL × 1,000 to reach the next level. This adjustment is summarized on Table 1–2: ECL Experience Requirements.

TABLE 1–2: ECL EXPERIENCE REQUIREMENTS

XP	ECL = Level (Normal)	ECL = Level +1 (Aasimar, Tiefling, Genasi)	ECL = Level +2 (Drow, Duergar)	ECL = Level +3 (Svirfneblin)
0	1st	—	—	—
1,000	2nd	1st	—	—
3,000	3rd	2nd	1st	—
6,000	4th	3rd	2nd	1st
10,000	5th	4th	3rd	2nd
15,000	6th	5th	4th	3rd
21,000	7th	6th	5th	4th
28,000	8th	7th	6th	5th
36,000	9th	8th	7th	6th
45,000	10th	9th	8th	7th
55,000	11th	10th	9th	8th
66,000	12th	11th	10th	9th
78,000	13th	12th	11th	10th
91,000	14th	13th	12th	11th
105,000	15th	14th	13th	12th
120,000	16th	15th	14th	13th
136,000	17th	16th	15th	14th
153,000	18th	17th	16th	15th
171,000	19th	18th	17th	16th
190,000	20th	19th	18th	17th
210,000	—	20th	19th	18th
231,000	—	—	20th	19th
253,000	—	—	—	20th

classes

Nearly all the information in Chapter 3: Classes in the *Player's Handbook* applies to the character classes of the FORGOTTEN REALMS campaign setting. The entries that follow focus on what is peculiar to Faerûn rather than summarizing the *Player's Handbook*.

Preferred Class Regions: Following the class discussion is a listing of lands or cultures suitable as home regions for characters of that class. For example, Narfell is a land of nomadic horseriders. Barbarians, fighters, rangers, and rogues are well suited to this kind of life, and are commonly found there. Wizards are not. Therefore, the barbarian, fighter, ranger, and rogue class descriptions list Narfell as a region.

You do not have to choose one of the regions listed for your character's class if you do not want to. However, whether your character comes from a region suited for his class affects your ability to choose regional feats and your selection of starting equipment.

BARBARIANS

Free of the comforts and constraints of civilization, barbarians survive in lands that civilized folk only dwell in when they can hide behind high walls. The cosmopolitan nature of some parts of Faerûn is confusing to barbarians, but city folk are used to odd sights and usually accept barbarians without batting an eye.

Most Faerûnian barbarians are humans or half-orcs. They come from places such as the Cold Lands, the North, the High Moors, Rashemen, and tribes ranging across the Western Heartlands. Dwarven barbarians come from icy wastes of the north, the jungles of Chult, and hidden pockets in remote mountains and hills. Elven barbarians are usually wild elves from the warm southern forests, such as the Wealdath or the Chondalwood. The only known barbarian halfling tribes live deep in the Chondalwood, rarely venturing out of the forest's green embrace.

Barbarians of other races are unusual, but not unheard of. Half-elven barbarians are sometimes found among human tribes native to the North or in Western Heartlands, or in the Yuirwood where humans and elves lived together in the wild for generations. Drow, moon elven, sun elven, gnome, or planetouched barbarians are generally individuals who for some reason were raised among barbaric peoples.

Preferred Character Regions: Regions in which barbarians are commonly found include the Chondalwood (ghostwise halflings and wild elves), Chult, the Hordelands, the Moonshaes, Narfell, the Nelanther Isles, the North, Rashemen, Vaasa, and the Western Heartlands. In addition, some shield dwarven, wild elven, wood elven, and half-orc cultures give rise to barbarians.

BARDS

Faerûnian bards are as likely to create their own heroic sagas as they are to sing of others' exploits.

In both the Dalelands and the wilderness of the North, a semisecret society known as the Harpers recruits courageous bards of good alignments to carry on a millennia-old fight against evil. While not all bards are Harpers, the noble deeds of this group have given bards something of a heroic glow that they might not have in other worlds. Good bards who are not Harpers often carry themselves as if they were, a type of self-fulfilling prophecy that frequently causes common folk to look to bards for more than a good song.

Preferred Character Regions: Bards are common in many lands, including Amn, Chessenta, Cormyr, the Dalelands, the Dragon Coast, Evermeet, Luiren, Impiltur, the Moonshaes, Silverymoon, Tethyr, Thesk, Unther, the Vast, Waterdeep, and the Western Heartlands. Gold dwarven, moon elven, sun elven, lightfoot halfling, and strongheart halfling bards are also common.

CLERIC

Faerûnian clerics function as described in the *Player's Handbook*, except that no clerics serve just a cause, philosophy, or abstract source of divine power. The Torilian deities are very real, and events in recent history have forced these divine beings to pay a great deal of attention to their mortal followers.

All clerics in Faerûn serve a patron deity. (In fact, most people in

Faerûnian Instruments

Some bards sing, others orate or dance, and some play familiar instruments such as the mandolin, lyre, dulcimer, and yes, the harp. Still other bards perform on less well-known instruments unique to Faerûn.

Birdpipes: Also known as the shalm, these are pan pipes. They are sacred to Lliira and the satyrs, and popular with wood elven and wild elven bards.

Glaur: A short, curved horn resembling a cornucopia. Fitted with valves, it sounds like a trumpet played in a high wind. Sun elves use them, halflings love them, humans either like them or hate them. Glaurs that lack valves are called gloons, and sound like melancholy horns echoing in fog.

Hand Drum: A double-headed drum, often played at high speed by warriors who wish to demonstrate their prowess without having to beat someone up.

Longhorn: A Faerûnian flute, common only in civilized areas and among the elves.

Shaum: A double-reed instrument, a sort of primitive oboe or bassoon, most popular with gnomes.

Songhorn: A recorder, popular everywhere, unless someone has a hangover.

Tantan: The tambourine, popular with halflings and humans south of the Dalelands, disliked by dwarves, who prefer more honest percussion.

Thelarr: A simple reed instrument also called a whistlecane. An easy instrument to teach and so cheap that some bards give them away as gifts to children.

Tocken: A set of carved, oval, open-ended bells, played like a glockenspiel, particularly in underground civilizations and others whose buildings can maximize the resonant tones.

Wargong: A gong constructed of one or many shields, frequently those of defeated enemies. It is played with mallets, or in extreme cases, with warhammers. The goblins and dwarves make much of alternately constructing huge wargongs or attempting to liberate such shields taken by their foe.

Yarting: A guitar, growing in popularity through Faerûn after coming out of Amn and Calimshan some time in the past forty or fifty years.

Zulkoon: A complex and semiportable pump organ, associated in many minds with the zulkirs of Thay, whose slaves carry such organs in wagons in order to provide the proper music for their masters' spells.

TABLE I—3: FAVORED DEITIES BY REGION

Deity	Regions Favored
Anhur	Chessenta
Auril	The North
Azuth	Calimshan, Chessenta, Halruaa, Lantan, Sembia
Bane	Amn, Moonsea, Thay
Beshaba	Nelanther Isles
Chauntea	Aglarond, Amn, Cormyr, Dalelands, the Moonshaes, Rashemen, Tashalar, Thesk, the Vast
Cyric	Amn, Moonsea, Nelanther Isles
Deneir	Cormyr, the North, Sembia, Silverymoon, Western Heartlands
Dwarven Pantheon	Any dwarf, Calimshan, Lake of Steam, the North, the Shaar, Silverymoon, the Vast, Waterdeep
Drow Pantheon	Drow elf
Eilistraee	Any elf, High Forest, Silverymoon, Waterdeep
Eldath	The North, the Vast, Vilhon Reach
Elven Pantheon	Moon elf, sun elf, wild elf, wood elf, Aglarond, Evermeet, High Forest, Silverymoon, Waterdeep
Faerûnian Pantheon	Lake of Steam, Unther (free), Waterdeep
Gnome Pantheon	Any gnome, Silverymoon, Waterdeep
Gond	Lantan, Mulhorand
Halfling Pantheon	Any halfling, Chondalwood, Luiren, Silverymoon, Waterdeep
Helm	Cormyr, Dragon Coast, Tethyr, Vilhon Reach, Western Heartlands
Hoar	Chessenta
Ilmater	Calimshan, Damara, Impiltur, Tethyr
Kelemvor	Western Heartlands
Kossuth	Thay
Lathander	Chessenta, Cormyr, Dalelands, Sembia, Waterdeep, Western Heartlands
Lliira	Cormyr, Vilhon Reach
Lolth	Drow elf
Loviatar	Moonsea, Sembia
Lurue	The North, Silverymoon
Malar	Cormyr, High Forest, the North, Tashalar, Vilhon Reach
Mask	Dragon Coast, Moonsea, Mulhorand, the Shaar, Thesk

Deity	Regions Favored
Mielikki	Chondalwood, Dalelands, High Forest, the North, Rashemen, Silverymoon
Milil	Cormyr, the North, Silverymoon
Mulhorandi Pantheon	Mulhorand (including Semphar and Murghôm), Unther (occupied)
Mystra	Halruaa, Mulhorand, the North, Rashemen, Sembia, Silverymoon, the Vast
Nobanion	Dragon Coast, Vilhon Reach
Oghma	Dalelands, the North, the Shaar, Silverymoon, Western Heartlands
Orc Pantheon	Half-orc, orc, Moonsea (Thar only)
Red Knight	Chessenta, Mulhorand
Savras	Tashalar
Selûne	Aglarond, Amn, Cormyr, Impiltur, the North
Shar	Amn, Calimshan, the North, the Shaar
Sharess	Calimshan
Shaundakul	Dalelands, the North, Thesk
Shiallia	The North
Siamorphe	Calimshan, Tethyr
Silvanus	Chondalwood, Cormyr, Dalelands, Damara, High Forest, the North, Silverymoon, Vilhon Reach
Sune	Amn, Dragon Coast, Sembia
Talona	Moonsea
Talos	Calimshan, Moonsea, Nelanther Isles, the North, Vilhon Reach
Tempus	Cormyr, Dalelands, Dragon Coast, the Moonshaes, Nelanther Isles, the North, the Shaar, the Vast, Vilhon Reach
Tiamat	Chessenta
Torm	Dalelands, Tethyr, the Vast
Tymora	Cormyr, Dragon Coast, Impiltur, Sembia, the Vast
Tyr	Calimshan, Cormyr, Dalelands, Moonsea, Sembia, Tethyr, Vilhon Reach
Ubtao	Chult
Umberlee	Dragon Coast, Moonsea, Nelanther Isles, the Vast
Uthgar	The North
Valkur	Aglarond, Impiltur
Vhaeraun	Drow elf, High Forest
Waukeen	Amn, Chessenta, Cormyr, Impiltur, Sembia, Tashalar, Thesk, the Vast

Faerûn choose a deity as their patron.) It is simply impossible for a person to gain divine powers (such as divine spells) without one. You may not have more than one patron deity at a time, although it is possible to change your patron deity if you have a change of heart. You cannot multiclass into another class that requires a patron deity unless your previous patron deity is an acceptable choice for the new class. For example, you cannot multiclass as a druid unless your patron deity is a nature deity (since all druids have nature deities as patron deities). You may also bypass this restriction by abandoning your old deity outright (see Changing Deities in Chapter 5: Deities). See the Religion section of this chapter for more information on patron deities.

In some lands, worship of multiple deities takes place in the same temple. For example, many smaller dwarven cities have a single temple for all of the dwarven deities, and the people of Rashemen worship Chauntea, Mielikki, and Mystra in the same locations. The clerics in these temples still choose a single deity as a patron, but not all clerics there share the *same* patron.

Preferred Character Regions: Clerics of different deities are favored in different lands. Consult Table 1–3: Favored Deities by Region.

DRUID

Like clerics, the druids of Faerûn receive their spells from a particular patron deity, always a deity of nature or animals. However, druids do not necessarily see a clear division between nature and the divine forces that run through nature. While many people think only of forests when they think of druids, druids care also for the mountains, deserts, lakes, and even the swamps of Faerûn.

Nature deities include Chauntea, Eldath, Gwaeron Windstrom, Lurue, Malar, Mielikki, Nobanion, Shiallia, Silvanus, Talos, Ubtao, Ulutiu, Umberlee, Anhur, Isis, Osiris, Sebek, Set, Thard Harr, Aerdrie Faenya, Angharradh, Deep Sashelas, Rillifane Rallathil, Baervan Wildwanderer, Segojan Earthcaller, and Sheela Peryroyl.

Mielikki, who is famous for the number of druid/rangers who worship her, has more lenient spiritual oaths than most deities that druids worship in the Realms. Druids of Mielikki can use any of the standard armor or weapons that rangers normally use (all simple and martial weapons, all light and medium armor, and all shields) without violating their spiritual oaths.

Preferred Character Regions: Lands where druids hold sway include Aglarond, the Chondalwood, Chult, the Great Dale, the High Forest, the Moonshaes, the North, the Vast, the Vilhon Reach, and the Western Heartlands. Moon elves, sun elves, wild elves, wood elves, ghost-wise halflings, and lightfoot halflings commonly produce adventuring druids, too.

FIGHTER

Fighters are at home in nearly every society of Faerûn. While they are often over-looked for praise because their skills are so common, great leaders such as Randal Morn, Bruenor Battlehammer, and the late King Azoun IV of Cormyr are very skilled warriors with reputations greater than the reach of their swords. Of course, many have risen to infamy on their fighting skills, such as Gondegal the Lost King, or the notorious assassin Artemis Entreri.

Some countries have famous military or knightly orders. Cormyr is well known for its army, called the Purple Dragons. Tethyr has several knightly orders, the most accessible being the Champions Vigilant (worshiping Helm) and the Knights Kuldar of Barakmordin (worshiping the Triad of Ilmater, Torm, and Tyr).

Preferred Character Regions: Every part of Faerûn produces capable warriors, but the lands of Aglarond, Amn, Anauroch, Calimshan, Chessenta, Cormyr, the Dalelands, Damara, the Dragon Coast, Evermeet, Luiren, the Hordelands, Impiltur, the Lake of Steam, Lantan, the Moonsea, the Moon-shaes, Mulhorand, Narfell, Nelan-ther Isles, the North, Rashemen, Sembia, the Shaar, Tashalar, Tethyr, Thay, Unther, the Vast, the Vilhon Reach, Waterdeep, and the Western Heartlands are renowned for their fighters. In addition, gray dwarves, gold dwarves, shield dwarves, drow, moon elves, deep gnomes, rock gnomes, lightfoot halflings, and strongheart halflings encourage the fighter class.

MONK

Monastic orders usually originate in civilized human lands. Among humans, the earliest monastic orders native to Faerûn seem to have arisen in Amn and Calimshan simultaneously with some orders immigrating from other worlds and the eastern land of Kara-Tur. Unlike clerics and druids, monks do not necessarily have to choose a patron deity (although most do), nor

Tiefling Monk

Illustration by Sam Wood

druid circles

In places where the veneration of wild nature (particularly forests) is threatened, druids abide, working to purge living things of disease, to protect their breeding and feeding, and to slow or halt woodcutting, burning, and the growth of roads. Druids often meet or dwell in clearings, and from that custom has come the name and habit of working together in circles.

Druid circles can even be found in Waterdeep and other large cities, meeting in temples, parks, or in cellars if they can find one that has running water or a natural spring-fed pond or pool, or an earthen floor, or both. Some circles very seldom ever gather all in one place, but communicate by magic or by means of one or more members who travel extensively, serving as go-betweens to their fellows.

The concept of the circle refers also to natural cycles, and to the fact that creatures of varying races, ranks, and capabilities can and should work together. Circles have no official ranks beyond Speaker (spokesperson), though members always have an unofficial pecking order based on age, wisdom, and druidic power. Persons may leave a circle if they disagree with its policies, but the circle as a whole decides on its activities. Many circles include rangers, elves of the forest, and even dryads and treants in their ranks. Most include less than a dozen druids.

Hunters, woodcutters, and steaders intending to clear land or expand existing settlements are advised to consult local clergy of Silvanus, Eldath, Mielikki, and similar deities, or rangers, to learn if a circle is active locally. It is better to work with such a circle than to blunder into its path and end up at war with it.

The Moonshae Isles and the Emerald Enclave lands about the mouth of the Vilhon contain the strongest concentrations of druids. In both places, druids act openly, wielding much power of governance as well as influence, and meet in sacred groves. In contrast, druidic power has been largely shattered in the Dales, where the Circle of Shadowdale and the Battledale Seven were both destroyed in recent decades, and the Circle of Yeven fell long ago.

I only know of a few active circles. The Watchers of Sevreld, who meet in Old Mushroom Grove in the High Forest northeast of Secomber, work to prevent logging roads being cut into the forest. The High Dance, druids who dwell in hidden high valleys of the Thunder Peaks and wander that range, aids the sylvan creatures who tend and guard the Dancing Place. The newly founded Ring of Swords works to cleanse and rejuvenate Neverwinter Wood, drive out gnoll, bugbear, and hobgoblin bands sheltering there, and turn away those seeking tombs and ruins in the leafy heart of the forest. The Flamenar ("Hands Against Flame") works in Amn to recloak its rolling hills in stands of newly planted trees and to drive down the dust storms that have begun to plague the land east of Crimmor and Purskul. And the Starwater Six (named for the tranquil pool where they often meet) are now at work in the northern Forest of Mir, where floods of monsters and strange twisted beasts have been raiding the lands south of the River Ith.

These are but a handful among many, many circles.

Some dismiss them with a sneer as "flower lovers," but I warn such scoffers that few herbs or plant medicines would aid us today were it not for the lore and work of the druid circles of Faerûn.

—Beldrith Tarlelntar, Sage of the Old Ways
House of the Leaning Gate, Scornubel

do monks have to associate themselves with one of the schools listed in the Monastic Orders sidebar. If your monk character belongs to a different monastic group, you and your DM should at least name it and place it in relation to the groups mentioned below.

Most Faerûnian monks are capable of gaining levels in another class before returning to the way of the monk and gaining new levels as monks. This is an exception to the rule in the Ex-Monks section in Chapter 3 of the *Player's Handbook*. The descriptions in the Monastic Orders sidebar specify into which classes an order's members can multiclass freely. The character may add levels of monk and any specified class without penalty. Violating these expanded limits (by multiclassing into a class not on the order's approved list) ends the monk's development as a monk, as described in the normal rules. Some orders place additional restrictions on multiclassing, as brought out in their descriptions. If a monk violates any such restriction, she can no longer advance as a monk.

Preferred Character Regions: Monks are most common in Amn, Calimshan, Damara, Mulhorand, the Lake of Steam, and Silverymoon. Strongheart halflings are also culturally inclined toward becoming monks.

PALADIN

Piergeiron Paladinson, the Open Lord of Waterdeep, might be the most renowned paladin in Faerûn today. Although his adventuring days are behind him, he represents the Lords of Waterdeep with a just and compassionate demeanor and unshakable courage. Many younger paladins model themselves after him.

All paladins of Faerûn are devoted to a patron deity, chosen at the start of their career as paladins. Like paladins of other lands, the paladins of Faerûn must be both lawful and good. The paladin's deity must be lawful good, lawful neutral, or neutral good. For example, both Helm the Vigilant One (lawful neutral) and Chauntea the Earthmother (neutral good) have lawful good paladin worshipers. Sune, the goddess of beauty, love, and passion, is an exception to the alignment rule, for her followers include paladins even though her alignment is chaotic good. Additional information on the paladins of some of Faerûn's religions appears in the Special Paladin Orders sidebar.

Preferred Character Regions: Paladins often come from Cormyr, the Dalelands, Damara, Luiren, Impiltur, Mulhorand, Silverymoon, Tethyr, and Waterdeep.

monastic orders

Dozens of monastic orders exist in Faerûn. Most are small circles of no more than a dozen or so members, living in isolated monasteries in the wilderness. A few orders include hundreds of members and influence events across entire nations. Some of the prominent orders include:

Broken Ones (Good): Of all the popular deities of Faerûn, Ilmater is the deity most associated with an order of monks who act purely in his name. The Broken Ones can freely multiclass as clerics, divine champions, arcane devotees, divine disciples, hierophants, and divine seekers of Ilmater. The Dalelands house no monasteries of great fame, but monks of Ilmater frequently travel through the Dales, sheltering in Ilmater's temples if they cannot find other lodging.

Dark Moon (Evil): Shar is worshiped by a powerful sect of monks who maintain open temples in lands ruled by evil overlords or hide among hills, back alleys, or the Underdark. Most of the Dark Moon monks are human, but occasionally they are joined by a half-orc, shade, or drow. The monks of the Dark Moon can freely multiclass as sorcerers so long as their monk level and sorcerer level stay within two levels of each other.

Hin Fist (Neutral or Good): The halflings of Luiren turn their confidence into belief in the power of a single halfling to master herself and the world. Enterprising Luiren monks sometimes establish monasteries in the north. Although only halflings can study Hin Fist in Luiren, some Hin Fist monasteries outside Luiren accept exceptional gnomes and dwarves. Monks of the Hin Fist order can multiclass as fighters, rogues, or paladins (usually of Yondalla).

Long Death (Evil): The Long Death order worships the principle of death without caring much which deity currently owns the portfolio. They are more than willing to share death and its antecedent, pain, with others. Clerics of the previous god of death, Myrkul, chose to view them as part of their god's long-range plans. Kelemvor (the current god of the dead) views them as enemies, but is at least pleased that they do not actively promote undeath. Velsharoon (the god of necromancy and undeath) wants to woo them, but has not figured out how. Monks of the Long Death may multiclass freely as fighters, assassins, and blackguards. This order is quite strong in Thay, though not with the sanction or cooperation of the Red Wizards.

Old Order (Neutral, Sometimes Good, Rarely Evil): Monks of the Old Order do not worship any deity, but are devoted to the philosophy espoused by a deity who is either now dead or has never existed on the Material Plane of Toril. The monks contradict themselves on this point, but the deity's identity isn't important to them, it's the message they care about. The Old Order never has huge monasteries, but has spread widely throughout Faerûn. Monks of the Old Order can multiclass freely as rogues, sorcerers, and shadowdancers, but must maintain more monk levels than their combined levels of other classes.

Shining Hand (Neutral): The Shining Hand is one of the oldest monk orders of Amn, mixing faith in Azuth and the practice of wizardry with monastic devotions. Amn's crackdown on the practice of wizardry has sent some Shining Hand groups underground and sent others out into the wider world. Monks of the Shining Hand can multiclass freely as wizards so long as their monk level equals or exceeds their wizard level.

Sun Soul (Good or Neutral): The allegiance of this widespread but disorganized sect varies between groups, some following Lathander, others Selûne, and a few devoted to Sune. The Sun Soul order, along with the Old Order, is the most likely to have monasteries hidden in far flung wilderness areas. Members of the Sun Soul order can gain levels in one other class and still progress as a monk as long as their monk level is their highest class level.

Yellow Rose (Good, Neutral): Also known as the Disciples of Saint Sollars, this solitary monastery of Ilmater worshipers in the Earthspur Mountains of Damara is known for loyalty to its allies and destruction to its enemies. Greatly respected on matters of truth and diplomacy, the monks work hard to survive in their harsh remote sanctuary. The monks often travel with Ilmataran paladins, particularly from the Order of the Golden Cup. They may multiclass freely as rangers and shadowdancers.

Shield dwarves sometimes become paladins devoted to deities of the dwarven pantheon, and strongheart halflings often become paladins devoted to deities of the halfling pantheon.

RANGER

Vast areas of Faerûn are covered with ancient forests and populated by fantastic creatures. The rangers of Faerûn, along with the druids, occasional barbarians, and clerics of deities such as Silvanus and Mielikki, are the masters of the "empty" spaces.

Unlike clerics, druids, and paladins, Faerûnian rangers do not have to choose a patron deity until they reach 4th level and acquire divine spellcasting ability (without a patron deity, a ranger cannot cast spells). Many rangers choose a patron deity before then, but others start by devotion to the ranger's way of life instead of to one of the gods. Rangers and druids have similar preferences for deities, although some rangers with odd interests (such as hunting undead) choose different patrons.

Good rangers of the North often find themselves acting in concert with groups such as the Harpers, and some eventually join that organization. However, not all rangers of Faerûn are good, and places such as the forest of Cormanthor and the High Forest are a battleground—good rangers who seek to defend the forest and its inhabitants against evil rangers who follow deities that find it natural to inflict pain on others.

Rangers may select an organization instead of a creature type as a favored enemy. For example, a good ranger might choose to oppose the Cult of the Dragon, and dark Zhentarim rangers often hunt the Harpers. These rangers receive their favored enemy bonus against agents from that organization, regardless of creature type. The bonus applies even if the creature is of the same race as the ranger and the ranger is not evil. The bonus works just like the normal favored enemy bonus, except that it is considered a morale bonus and does not stack with other morale effects.

Preferred Character Regions: Rangers are found on the fringes of civilization in places such as Aglarond, the Chondalwood, Chult, the Dalelands, Damara, Evermeet, the Great Dale, Luiren, the High Forest, the Hordelands, Lake of Steam, Narfell, the North, Rashemen, the Shaar, Silverymoon, Tashalar, Vaasa, Vilhon Reach, and the Western Heartlands. Moon elves, wild elves, wood elves, deep gnomes, lightfoot halflings, strongheart halflings, and half-orcs are often rangers, too.

ROGUE

In Faerûn, rogues are as often diplomats as thieves, a distinction often lost on those who have come out on the losing end of a diplomatic negotiation. Rogues are everywhere in Faerûn, but no one necessarily expects them to be thieves. Depending on their skills and inclinations, rogues may represent themselves as treasure-finders, tomb-breakers, investigators, spies, bounty hunters, thief-catchers, scouts, or—most commonly—as "adventurers."

While it's true that not every rogue is a thief, it's also true that many rogues *are*. Thieves' guilds are common in Faerûn. Some, such as the Shadow Thieves of Amn or the Night Masks of Westgate, are powerful enough to dictate orders to kings and lords, and ruthless enough to enforce their edicts through intimidation, terror, and outright murder. Most guilds are short-lived, local

special paladin orders

Some faiths allow paladins to gain levels in another class and still return to progression as a paladin, exactly as some orders of monks do. Special paladin orders include:

Azuth: Rather than gaining levels as paladins throughout their career, the rare paladins of the High One are more likely to spend some time progressing in that class and then learn wizardry full-time. Azuth's paladins cannot multiclass freely.

Chauntea: Paladins of the Grain Goddess are rare. They value compassion as much as courage, and spend much time helping common folk in rural areas. They may multiclass freely as clerics, divine champions, and divine disciples.

Helm: Paladins of the Watcher prefer to guard against evil or slay it outright rather than work to heal its damages. They seem rigid and uninterested in helping others. They may multiclass freely as fighters, clerics, divine champions, arcane devotees, and Purple Dragon knights.

Ilmater: Paladins of the Broken God guard the weak and use their healing powers on any who need them. They are not shy about fighting evil, but they would rather pause to heal someone who is about to die than sacrifice that life in order to pursue fleeing evil-doers. They may multiclass freely as clerics, divine champions, divine disciples, and hierophants.

Kelemvor: Paladins of the Lord of the Dead devote themselves to hunting and killing undead. Some develop as paladins for their entire career, others begin as paladins but leave that path to progress as rangers and clerics. They cannot multiclass freely.

Lathander: Paladins of the Morninglord are among the best-loved heroes of Faerûn. They are loosely organized (along with other fighters devoted to the god) into a holy order called the Order of the Aster. Within their own church, the paladins are frequently more conservative and concerned with the way things should be done than the clerics, who are often neutral rather than lawful. Paladins may multiclass freely as clerics, divine champions, divine disciples, hierophants, and Purple Dragon knights.

Moradin: The Soul Forger has few paladins, but the dwarves who choose this path often act as champions of the entire dwarven pantheon, blending the virtues of all the dwarven gods. They may multiclass freely as clerics, fighters, divine champions, dwarven defenders, and runecasters.

Sune: Paladins of the Firehair defend things of beauty. They seek out and destroy creatures that are particularly hideous in their evil. They tend to be incredibly self-confident and are particularly effective at destroying undead. They may multiclass freely as divine champions. Paladins may choose Sune as a patron deity despite the fact that she is a chaotic good deity. This is an exception to the normal requirement to select a patron deity whose alignment is no more than one step different from yours.

Torm: Paladins of the True God defend the weak, defeat evil, and uphold the high moral standards required for servants of a god who serves bright and righteous Tyr. They may multiclass freely as one other class.

Tyr: Paladins of the Just God are front-line warriors in the battle against evil and untruth, and often lead military and adventuring groups to further their cause. They may multiclass freely as clerics, fighters, and divine champions.

Yondalla: Paladins of the Protector and Provider are rare, but in halfling-run lands such as Luiren, they serve their fellow citizens with sword and shield. They may multiclass freely as monks.

organizations that rise in a particular city or along a busy trade route, the creation of a charismatic or powerful individual capable of holding such a guild together.

Preferred Character Regions: Rogues are of two general stripes—thieves and brigands. Thieves are common near any large city, and brigands (sometimes charitably referred to as scouts) live in the wild. Rogues are common in Amn, Anauroch, Calimshan, the Dragon Coast, Evermeet, Luiren, Impiltur, the Lake of Steam, Lantan, the Moonsea, the Moonshaes, Mulhorand, Narfell, the Nelanther Isles, Sembia, the Shaar, Tashalar, Thesk, Unther, Vaasa, the Vast, Waterdeep, and the Western Heartlands. Gray dwarves, gold dwarves, shield dwarves, drow, moon elves, sun elves, deep gnomes, rock gnomes, lightfoot halflings, and strongheart halflings are commonly rogues, too.

SORCERER

Sorcerers are (along with wizards) the foremost practitioners of what Faerûnians refer to as the Art, the study and application of arcane magic. The common folk of Faerûn see little difference between the rigorous studies of the wizard and the mysterious ways of the sorcerer, but in some lands a fierce rivalry exists between the two traditions. Many wizards regard sorcerers as inexpert practitioners of the Art and servants of sinister powers better left alone. Some sorcerers see wizards as arrogant and pompous, deliberately cloaking the Art in mummery and obtuse lore.

Some areas of Faerûn are more tolerant than others of the presence of sorcerers. Aglarond, a forest kingdom ruled by the insuperable sorcerer-queen known as the Simbul, is perhaps the best example of such a place. Despite differing regional attitudes toward sorcerers, sorcerous talent seems to be spread nearly evenly through the world and the various races, with the exception of dwarves born before the Thunder Blessing.

True to their tendency toward chaos over law, sorcerers worship all types of deities. Mystra, Oghma, Selûne, and Shar are popular with sorcerers as deities who have something to do with magic. Lathander, Shaundakul, Sune, Tempus, and Tymora are popular with adventuring sorcerers.

In addition to the familiars available in the

A sorcerer casting while he climbs

Player's Handbook, the following creatures are also available as familiars in the FORGOTTEN REALMS campaign setting:

Familiar	Special
Hairy spider†	Poisonous bite, darkvision
Lizard	Master gains a +2 bonus on Climb checks
Octopus	Master gains a +2 bonus on Spot checks

†This creature is described in *Monster Compendium: Monsters of Faerûn.* A hairy spider familiar gains an Intelligence score, becomes a magical beast (not vermin), and loses its immunity to mind-influencing effects.

The Improved Familiar feat (see the next section of this chapter) allows a selection of more powerful familiars.

Preferred Character Regions: Sorcerers are found in Aglarond, Calimshan, the Dragon Coast, the Great Dale, the High Forest, the Lake of Steam, Mulhorand, the Nelanther Isles, the Shaar, Silverymoon, Tethyr, and the Western Heartlands. Gold dwarves, wild elves, and lightfoot halflings display a knack for the sorcerer's arts, too.

WIZARD

Wizards, like other people who can turn a person into a toadstool with a glance, tend to be well respected or simply feared by common folk. The mightiest mortals in Faerûn are powerful wizards such as Elminster, Manshoon, and Szass Tam. Extending their lives for centuries (or, in some cases, choosing the path of lichdom and eternal undeath), these dangerous magic-wielders grow ever wiser and stronger in the ways of the Art as centuries pass by.

Most practicing wizards learned the basics of the Art as apprentices to more experienced wizards. This slow form of education is reliable, and the work an apprentice performs has the advantage of paying for her studies. Other would-be wizards graduated from one of the universities of magic, common in the lands of Lantan and Halruaa in the distant south but uncommon in the northern parts of Faerûn.

North of Halruaa, the best-known university of magic is located in Silverymoon. Smaller universities of magic are known in areas such as Waterdeep, Sembia, Chessenta, the

MAGE RUNES

Every sorcerer or wizard of Faerûn who desires to do so can adopt a personal rune or mage sigil that marks that mage's work. These are sometimes simply marks of ownership or territory, but it is best to assume that every last rune graven on a doorway or boundary stone holds at least one spell waiting to be triggered—usually by handling the item or casting magic upon it. Triggers may be specific as to race, gender, time, and location of the rune-marked item, presence of other substances or magic, and the like.

Spells so hung are usually of a guardian nature, but may do great harm. *Explosive runes, sepia snake sigil, fire trap,* and *symbol* are the most common, and rumors abound of stranger and more

deadly spells that have been devised to guard a mage's rune.

No two mage runes are identical. A design chosen for a rune simply won't function as such if it accidentally resembles one used by another mage (either active or in the past). Most who cast spells in Faerûn choose one rune for their entire lives, never changing.

By the will of divine Mystra herself, the High One visits a heavy curse upon those who falsely use the rune of another creature. As the old apprentice rhyme reminds us:

Whenever magic one doth weave
'Tis never, ever, wise to deceive.

—*Elminster of Shadowdale*

Mage Runes and the Curse of Mystra

All arcane spellcasters create a personal sigil or rune. This rune is used to identify belongings, as a warning, and as a signature. As the goddess of magic, Mystra takes it upon herself to protect powerful spellcasters (above 10th level) maligned by another using their rune with deceitful intent. If anyone (spellcaster or not) willfully copies a sigil with the intent to trick another or usurp the owner's identity, that person must make three DC 15 Will saves to avoid the trifold Curse of Mystra.

If the offender fails the first save, he sustains 2 points of permanent Strength drain.

If the offender fails the second save, he sustains 2 points of permanent Intelligence drain and the effects of a *feeblemind* spell.

If the offender fails the third save, he sustains 2 points of permanent Wisdom drain and loses all bonus spell slots gained from a high ability score for a period of one month.

Vilhon Reach, Impiltur, and Tethyr, with an illusionist's school recently opened in Damara. The methods of education used by the Red Wizards of Thay are equally as effective, even if fully half of those who begin such studies die in their torturous training regimen.

Wizards also have access to the additional familiars listed in the sorcerer entry.

Preferred Character Regions: Lands where wizards are relatively common include Calimshan, Chessenta, Cormyr, Damara, Evermeet, Halruaa, the Lake of Steam, Mulhorand, Rashemen, Sembia, Silverymoon, Tethyr, Thay, Unther, Waterdeep, and the Western Heartlands. Races with similar traditions include drow, moon elves, sun elves, wood elves, and deep and rock gnomes, who frequently specialize as illusionists.

Character Region

A character in the FORGOTTEN REALMS campaign is more than just a class and race. Your homeland determines in part your personality, your outlook, and what sort of abilities you have. In game terms, character regions encourage you to take a class relevant to that region's culture, allow you to learn special feats appropriate to your region, and enable you to start out with some extra equipment based on the way people in that region live. Every character has the opportunity to choose a region during the character creation process.

"Region" is a broad term. In most cases, it refers to a political entity, such as the wizard-ruled nation of Thay. It may also refer to a geographical area that lacks a central government or well-defined borders, such as the barbarian lands of Narfell. Finally, a region can be defined as a racial cultural identity, such as that of the gold dwarves or half-orcs.

A character can only have one homeland, so you cannot get the regional benefits of both Amn and its neighboring nation, Tethyr. However, nonhuman characters are free to designate either their physical homeland or their racial culture as their character region, although they must be a member of a class listed for their race or homeland to select the corresponding regional feats and receive the bonus starting equipment. For example, Vartok the gold dwarf might be from the Smoking Mountains of Unther, but he can choose either gold dwarf or Unther as his native region, and he gains the benefits for the region of his choice if he selects a character class listing the region he chooses as a preferred region.

Table 1–4: Character Regions lists all the regions available to Faerûnian characters and describes automatic languages, bonus languages, regional feats, and bonus starting equipment available in each region.

Automatic Languages: The languages automatically known by all characters from this region, regardless of Intelligence score. Common, though not listed on the table, is always an automatic language unless Undercommon is listed as an automatic language.

Bonus Languages: Characters of exceptional Intelligence (12 or higher) begin play with one bonus language per point of Intelligence bonus, which must be chosen from the list on the table (superseding the *Player's Handbook*). In addition, the following languages are always available as bonus languages to the appropriate characters, regardless of race or region: Abyssal (clerics), Aquan (water genasi), Auran (air genasi), Celestial (clerics), Common, Draconic (wizards), Dwarven, Elven, Gnome, Goblin, Giant, Gnoll, Halfling, Ignan (fire genasi), Infernal (clerics), Orc, Sylvan (druids), Terran (earth genasi), and Undercommon. Druids also know Druidic in addition to their other languages.

In addition, characters can learn any language spoken in Faerûn by spending skill points on the Speak Language skill, regardless of whether the language appears on this list.

Regional Feats: If you choose a home region preferred by your character class, you may select regional feats appropriate to that region. These feats represent the common sorts of talents that people from that region learn.

If you did not choose a character class preferred in your home region, you cannot begin play with one of those regional feats. You are still limited by the number of feats available to your character based on class and race.

You can acquire regional feats later in your adventuring career. With a few exceptions, any regional feats appropriate to your race or homeland that you don't select at 1st level are still available the next time you gain the ability to select a feat.

You may even learn feats from a new region altogether, whether or not you belong to an encouraged class for that region. After 1st level, each 2 ranks in Knowledge (local) pertaining to the new region you have allow you to select feats from a single region (other than your home region, if applicable).

Equipment: Finally, the table lists equipment your character starts with if he chooses a region preferred for his character class. This equipment is in addition to any equipment you get with your starting package or whatever you might buy with your starting money. If multiple choices for bonus equipment are available in a region, you may only choose one of the options listed.

You may choose to sell your bonus equipment at 50% of its listed cost, if you would rather have extra cash instead. (Some particularly wealthy areas offer gold pieces as one of the options. You don't want to sell them.)

Regional Feat Regions

No Associated Region

Hordelands

Rashemen

Narfell

Thay

Mulhorand

Luiren

Damara

The Great Dale

Thesk

Unther

Great Rift

Impiltur

Aglarond

Vaasa

The Vast

Chessenta

Chondalwood

The Shaar

The Ride

Moonsea

Sembia

Vilhon Reach

Hlondeth

Lake of Steam

Halruaa

Anauroch

Dalelands

Cormyr

Dragon Coast

Silver Marches

The North

Western Heartlands

Amn

Tethyr

Calimshan

Tashalar

Silverymoon

The High Forest

Waterdeep

The North

The Moonshaes

Nelanther Isles

Lantan

Chult

TABLE 1–4: CHARACTER REGIONS

Region	Automatic Languages	Bonus Languages	Regional Feats	Equipment
Aglarond	Aglarondan	Chessentan, Damaran, Draconic, Elven, Mulhorandi, Orc, Sylvan	Discipline, Luck of Heroes, Treetopper	(A) Studded leather armor* and 20 arrows* (B) Scrolls of *web* and *protection from arrows* (C) Scrolls of *silence* and *spiritual weapon*
Amn	Chondathan	Alzhedo, Elven, Giant, Goblin, Illuskan, Nexalan, Shaaran	Cosmopolitan, Education, Silver Palm, Street Smart	(A) Thieves' tools*, hand crossbow, 10 bolts* (B) Choice of longsword* or short sword* (C) Light warhorse, bit and bridle, military saddle, and studded leather barding
Anauroch	Midani (or Netherese— shade only)	Chondathan, Damaran, Draconic, Gnoll, Netherese, Orc	Discipline, Survivor	(A) Scimitar* or dagger* (B) Mighty composite shortbow (+1) and 20 arrows*
Calimshan	Alzhedo	Auran, Chondathan, Chultan, Draconic, Ignan, Shaaran, Tashalan	Bloodline of Fire, Mind Over Body, Street Smart, Thug	(A) *Wand of magic missile* (1st) with 20 charges (B) Studded leather armor* and 3 *potions of cure light wounds* (1st)
Chessenta	Chessentan	Aglarondan, Chondathan, Draconic, Mulhorandi, Turmic, Untheric	Arcane Schooling, Artist, Education, Street Smart	(A) Short sword* or longspear* (B) Breastplate* (C) Scrolls of *blur* and *levitate*
Chondalwood	Shaaran	Chessentan, Chondathan, Elven, Halfling, Gnoll, Shaaran, Sylvan, Untheric	Forester, Survivor, Treetopper	(A) Shortbow*, longbow*, or halfspear* (B) 3 doses of blue whinnis poison (C) 2 doses of Medium-size spider venom
Chult	Chultan	Alzhedo, Draconic, Dwarven, Goblin, Shaaran, Sylvan, Tashalan	Foe Hunter, Snake Blood, Survivor	(A) *Potions of hiding* and *sneaking* (B) 2 doses Large monstrous scorpion venom (C) Kukri* or halfspear*
Cormyr	Chondathan	Elven, Damaran, Gnome, Goblin, Halfling, Orc, Turmic	Discipline, Education, Foe Hunter, Saddleback	(A) Longsword* or heavy mace* (B) Banded mail* (C) Scrolls of *flaming sphere* and *endurance*
Dalelands	Chondathan	Elven, Damaran, Giant, Gnome, Orc, Sylvan	Blooded, Forester, Luck of Heroes, Militia, Strong Soul	(A) Mighty composite longbow (+2) (B) Mighty composite shortbow (+2) (C) Longbow*, shortspear*, or quarterstaff* (D) *Potion of cure moderate wounds*
Damara	Damaran	Chondathan, Dwarven, Giant, Goblin, Orc, Uluik	Bullheaded, Foe Hunter, Survivor	(A) Bastard sword* or battleaxe* (B) 2 scrolls of *cure moderate wounds* (C) 300 gp worth of bloodstones
Dragon Coast	Chondathan	Aglarondan, Chessantan, Damaran, Goblin, Halfling, Orc, Turmic	Bullheaded, Silver Palm, Thug	(A) Rapier* or light crossbow* (B) *Potion of protection from arrows* or *blur*
Dwarf, gold	Dwarven	Giant, Gnome, Goblin, Shaaran, Terran, Untheric	Bullheaded, Silver Palm, Smooth Talk, Thunder Twin	(A) Scroll of *bull's strength* and 5 thunderstones (B) Dwarven waraxe* (C) Scale mail* and large steel shield*
Dwarf, gray	Dwarven, Undercommon	Common, Draconic, Giant, Goblin, Orc, Terran	Bullheaded, Daylight Adaptation, Mercantile Background, Resist Poison, Silver Palm	(A) Chain shirt* and 10 bolts* (B) Handaxe* or battleaxe*
Dwarf, shield	Dwarven	Chondathan, Draconic, Giant, Goblin, Illuskan, Orc	Bullheaded, Foe Hunter, Survivor, Thunder Twin	(A) Warhammer* or dwarven waraxe* (B) Breastplate and *potion of cure light wounds*
Elf, drow	Elven, Undercommon	Abyssal, Common, Draconic, Drow Sign, Goblin, Illuskan	Daylight Adaptation, Stealthy, Survivor, Twin Sword Style	(A) Hand crossbow and 20 bolts* (B) Short sword* or dagger* (C) Scrolls of *cat's grace* and *web*
Elf, moon	Elven	Auran, Chondathan, Gnoll, Gnome, Halfling, Illuskan, Sylvan	Education, Forester, Mind Over Body, Strong Soul	(A) Longsword* or rapier* or longbow* (B) Breastplate and 20 arrows* (C) Scrolls of *barkskin* and *cure moderate wounds*
Elf, sun	Elven	Auran, Celestial, Chondathan, Gnome, Halfling, Illuskan, Sylvan	Discipline, Education, Mind Over Body, Strong Soul	(A) Longsword*, longspear*, or longbow* (B) Scrolls of *invisibility* and *levitate* (C) *Wand of color spray* (20 charges)
Elf, wild	Elven	Gnoll, Illuskan, Orc, Sylvan, Tashalan	Forester, Strong Soul, Survivor, Treetopper	(A) Shortspear* or longbow* (B) Studded leather armor* and 20 arrows* (C) Hide armor* and *potion of hiding*
Elf, wood	Elven	Chondathan, Draconic, Gnoll, Gnome, Goblin, Sylvan	Foe Hunter, Forester, Strong Soul, Treetopper	(A) Mighty composite shortbow (+2) (B) Mighty composite longbow (+2) (C) Studded leather armor* and *potion of sneaking*

Region	Automatic Languages	Bonus Languages	Regional Feats	Equipment
Evermeet	Elven	Aquan, Auran, Celestial, Chondathan, Illuskan, Sylvan	Artist, Courteous Magocracy, Education	(A) Scroll of *knock* and *Quaal's feather token* (tree) (B) Studded leather*, 3 *potions of cure light wounds* (C) Longsword* or longbow*
Gnome, deep	Gnome, Undercommon	Common, Draconic, Dwarven, Elven, Illuskan, Terran	Mercantile Background, Strong Soul, Survivor	(A) Dagger* or light pick* or heavy pick* (B) Chain shirt* and 20 bolts*
Gnome, rock	Gnome	Chondathan, Draconic, Dwarven, Goblin, Illuskan, Sylvan, Terran	Artist, Discipline, Strong Soul	(A) Pistol, powderhorn, and 10 bullets†* (B) Studded leather armor*, 3 tanglefoot bags (C) Scrolls of *invisibility* and *minor image*
Great Dale	Damaran	Giant, Goblin, Rashemi, Mulhorandi	Bullheaded, Forester, Silver Palm	(A) Longbow* or shortbow* (B) Healer's kit, 2 antitoxins, and 20 arrows*
Half-elf	Elven, home region	Any (except secret ones)	By region or applicable elven race	(A) By region or applicable elven race
Half-orc	Orc, home region	Damaran, Giant, Gnoll, Goblin, Illuskan, Undercommon	Resist Poison, Stealthy	(A) *Potions of bull's strength, cure moderate wounds* (B) Banded mail with armor spikes (C) Dire flail*, greataxe*, or orc double axe*
Halfling, ghostwise	Halfling	Chondathan, Elven, Gnoll, Shaaran, Sylvan	Forester, Stealthy, Strong Soul, Survivor, Treetopper	(A) Shortbow*, longbow*, or halfspear* (B) 3 doses of blue whinnis poison (C) 2 doses of Medium-size spider venom
Halfling, lightfoot	Halfling	Chessentan, Chondathan, Damaran, Dwarven, Elven, Illuskan, Goblin	Smooth Talk, Strong Soul, Stealthy, Survivor	(A) Light crossbow*, sling*, or shortbow* (B) *Quaal's feather token* (bird) (C) 40 arrows* or bolts*
Halfling, strongheart	Halfling	Dwarven, Gnoll, Goblin, Halruaan, Shaaran	Discipline, Militia, Stealthy, Strong Soul	(A) Short sword* (B) Darkwood shield (C) *Potions of hiding* and *sneaking*
Halruaa	Halruaan	Dambrathan, Elven, Goblin, Halfling, Shaaran, Tashalan	Arcane Schooling, Courteous Magocracy, Magical Training	(A) Arcane scrolls (1 2nd-level and 6 1st-level) (B) Potions totaling 300 gp or less
High Forest	Chondathan	Elven, Gnoll, Goblin, Halfling, Illuskan, Sylvan	Forester, Treetopper	(A) Longsword* or longspear* (B) Mighty composite longbow (+2) (C) *Potion of resist elements*
Hordelands	Tuigan	Damaran, Goblin, Mulhorandi, Rashemi, Shou	Horse Nomad, Saddleback, Survivor	(A) Composite shortbow* (B) Light warhorse, bit and bridle, military saddle, and studded leather barding
Human	Home region	Any (except secret ones)	By region	(A) By region
Impiltur	Damaran	Aglarondan, Chessentan, Chondathan, Dwarven, Giant, Goblin, Mulhorandi, Turmic	Discipline, Mercantile Background, Militia, Silver Palm	(A) Thieves' tools* and studded leather armor* (B) *Potion of Charisma* (C) Bastard sword* or greatsword*
Lake of Steam	Shaaran	Alzhedo, Chondathan, Dwarven, Goblin, Tashalan	Foe Hunter, Mercantile Background	(A) Scimitar*, falchion*, or glaive* (B) *Potion of darkvision* or *invisibility*
Lantan	Lantanese	Alzhedo, Chondathan, Dwarven, Gnome, Ignan, Illuskan, Shaaran	Arcane Schooling, Education, Mercantile Background	(A) Pistol, powderhorn, and 10 bullets†* (B) Heavy crossbow*
Luiren	Halfling, Shaaran	Dwarven, Gnoll, Goblin, Halruaan, Shaaran, Untheric	Discipline, Militia, Smooth Talk	(A) Short sword* (B) Darkwood shield (C) *Potions of hiding* and *sneaking*
Moonsea	Damaran	Chondathan, Chessantan, Draconic, Giant, Goblin, Midani, Orc	Foe Hunter, Silver Palm, Street Smart, Thug	(A) Short sword* or two-bladed sword* (B) Light crossbow* (C) Hand crossbow and 2 doses greenblood oil
Moonshae Isles	Illuskan	Aquan, Chondathan, Elven, Giant, Orc, Sylvan	Bullheaded, Strong Soul, Survivor	(A) Studded leather armor* and 20 arrows* (B) Longbow* (C) Handaxe*, battleaxe*, or greataxe*
Mulhorand	Mulhorandi	Aglarondan, Chessentan, Draconic, Durpari, Goblin, Tuigan, Untheric	Arcane Schooling, Education	(A) Sickle*, scythe*, or falchion* (B) 2 2nd-level divine scrolls (C) *Potion of lesser restoration*
Narfell	Damaran	Goblin, Orc, Rashemi, Tuigan, Uluik	Bullheaded, Saddleback, Survivor	(A) Light warhorse, bit and bridle, military saddle, and studded leather barding (B) Light lance*, longspear*, or kukri*
Nelanther Isles	Chondathan	Alzhedo, Goblin, Illuskan, Lantanese, Orc, Shaaran	Blooded, Bullheaded, Thug	(A) Scimitar* or dagger* (B) Pistol, powderhorn, and 10 bullets†* (C) 3 *potions of cure light wounds* and 150 gp

Region	Automatic Languages	Bonus Languages	Regional Feats	Equipment
The North	Chondathan, Illuskan	Dwarven, Elven, Giant, Goblin, Midani, Orc	Foe Hunter, Saddleback, Survivor	(A) Studded leather armor* and *potion of hiding* (B) Battleaxe*, heavy mace*, or longsword*
Orc	Orc	Damaran, Giant, Gnoll, Goblin, Illuskan, Undercommon	Daylight Adaptation, Resist Poison	(A) *Potions of bull's strength and cure moderate wounds* (B) Banded mail with armor spikes (C) Dire flail*, greataxe*, or orc double axe*
Rashemen	Rashemi	Aglarondan, Damaran, Goblin, Mulhorandi, Tuigan	Bullheaded, Ethran, Survivor	(A) *Potions of jump, cure light wounds, vision* (2 each) (B) *Wand of light* or *wand of detect magic* (C) Spiked chain*, nunchaku*, or sjangham*
Sembia	Chondathan	Chessentan, Damaran, Gnome, Halfling, Mulhorandi, Shaaran, Turmic	Blooded, Education, Mercantile Background, Silver Palm, Twin Sword Style	(A) 300 gp
The Shaar	Shaaran	Alzhedo, Dambrathan, Durpari, Dwarven, Gnoll, Halruaan, Mulhorandi, Tashalan, Untheric	Horse Nomad, Silver Palm, Survivor	(A) Studded leather armor* and *potion of vision* (B) Light warhorse, bit and bridle, military saddle, and studded leather barding
Silverymoon	Chondathan, Illuskan	Dwarven, Elven, Giant, Illuskan, Midani, Orc, Sylvan	Blooded, Education, Smooth Talk, Survivor	(A) Longsword*, rapier*, or longbow* (B) Chain shirt* (C) Studded leather armor* and 2nd-level scroll
Tashalar	Tashalan	Alzhedo, Chultan, Draconic, Illuskan, Orc, Shaaran, Sylvan	Foe Hunter, Mercantile Background, Snake Blood	(A) Hand crossbow and 2 doses greenblood oil (B) Light crossbow* (C) Hide armor* and darkwood shield
Tethyr	Chondathan	Elven, Goblin, Illuskan, Lantanese, Shaaran, Sylvan	Blooded, Foe Hunter, Luck of Heroes, Mercantile Background	(A) *Potion of cure moderate wounds* (B) Scrolls of *protection from arrows* and *blur* (C) Scrolls of *aid* and *lesser restoration*
Thay	Mulhorandi	Chessentan, Damaran, Infernal, Rashemi, Tuigan, Untheric	Discipline, Mind Over Body, Tattoo Focus	(A) Two 2nd-level scrolls (B) One 2nd-level and six 1st-level scrolls (C) Longsword*
Thesk	Damaran	Aglarondan, Chondathan, Giant, Gnoll, Mulhorandi, Rashemi, Tuigan, Turmic, Shou	Mercantile Background, Silver Palm, Smooth Talk	(A) Studded leather armor* and thieves' tools* (B) Studded leather armor* and healer's kit* (C) Studded leather armor* and instrument*
Unther	Untheric	Chessentan, Draconic, Mulhorandi, Orc, Shaaran	Arcane Schooling, Street Smart, Thug	(A) Breastplate* (B) Scale mail* and 20 arrows (C) Scrolls of *detect thoughts* and *misdirection*
Vaasa	Damaran	Abyssal, Giant, Goblin, Orc, Uluik	Blooded, Bullheaded, Foe Hunter, Horse Nomad (the Ride only), Survivor	(A) Splint mail* (B) Heavy mace* or light mace* (C) *Potion of shadow mask*
The Vast	Damaran	Aglarondan, Chondathan, Dwarven, Giant, Goblin, Mulhorandi, Orc, Rashemi, Tuigan, Turmic, Shou	Luck of Heroes, Mercantile Background, Thug	(A) Three *potions of cure light wounds* and 20 arrows* (B) Banded mail with armor spikes
Vilhon Reach	Chondathan, Shaaran**, Turmic**	Chessentan, Damaran, Draconic, Elven, Goblin, Shaaran, Turmic	Silver Palm, Snake Blood (Hlondeth only), Survivor, Thug	(A) Rapier* or dagger* (B) Studded leather armor* and 20 bolts*
Waterdeep	Chondathan	Dwarven, Elven, Giant, Goblin, Illuskan, Orc	Artist, Cosmopolitan, Education, Smooth Talk, Thug, Twin Sword Style	(A) Longsword*, rapier*, or short sword* (B) Any two 2nd-level scrolls (C) 300 gp
Western Heartlands	Chondathan	Elven, Giant, Goblin, Illuskan, Midani, Orc	Bullheaded, Saddleback, Survivor	(A) Bastard sword* or greatsword* (B) Breastplate (C) *Potion of lesser restoration*

*Masterwork armor, weapon, or item.

**Shaaran in Sespech only, and Turmic in Turmish only.

†Renaissance firearms are found in Chapter 6 of the *DUNGEON MASTER's Guide*.

feats

Almost every rogue or fighter from the mythical land of Halruaa knows just a bit of magic. In Sembia, Waterdeep, and the dark cities of the drow, duelists teach the beautiful and deadly twin sword fighting style. Common-born rangers and druids of the Dalelands are known for their oddly fortuitous luck and their perseverance in the face of terrible peril. It seems that any adventurer exploring the deadly ruins and perilous wildernesses of Faerûn possesses a little specialized training or a knack common to the lands in which he grew up.

The feats in this chapter supplement the feats in the *Player's Handbook* and follow all the rules in that book for determining how many may be chosen and how often a character may do so. In addition, some of these new feats possess an additional prerequisite: the appropriate character region, as described in the previous section.

Some of the regional feats are defined as [General, Fighter]. This means a fighter can use his bonus feat to acquire one of those feats. However, the character still needs to qualify for that region in order to take the feat (see Regional Feats in the Character Region section above).

Arcane preparation [General]

You can prepare an arcane spell ahead of time just as a wizard does.

Prerequisite: You must be able to cast arcane spells as a bard or sorcerer before you can select this feat.

Benefit: Each day, you are able to prepare one or more spells as a wizard does. If you are a sorcerer or a bard, this means that you can prepare a spell with a metamagic feat ahead of time, instead of casting it as a full-round action.

Arcane schooling [General]

In your homeland, all who show some skill at the Art may receive training as a wielder of magic. Many characters know something of the ways of the bard, the sorcerer, or the wizard.

Regions: Chessenta, Halruaa, Lantan, Mulhorand, Unther.

Benefit: Choose one arcane spellcasting class. This class is a favored class for you in addition to any other favored class you select. For example, a multiclassed human fighter/rogue could add levels of wizard without incurring any experience penalty for multiclassing in three classes.

Special: You may only take this feat as a 1st-level character.

Artist [General]

You come from a culture in which the arts, philosophy, and music have a prominent place in society.

Region: Chessenta, Evermeet, Waterdeep, rock gnome.

Benefit: You gain a +2 bonus on all Perform checks and to one Craft skill that involves art (your choice) such as calligraphy, painting, sculpture, or weaving.

Blooded [General]

You know what it means to fight for your life, and the value of quick wits and quicker reactions when blades are bared and deadly spells chanted. Enemies find it difficult to catch you off guard.

Regions: Dalelands, Nelanther Isles, Sembia, Silverymoon, Tethyr, Vaasa.

Benefit: You get a +2 bonus on Initiative and a +2 bonus on all Spot checks.

TABLE 1—5: FEATS

General Feats	Prerequisite
Arcane Preparation	Cast arcane spells as bard or sorcerer
Arcane Schooling	Meet regional requirement
Artist	Meet regional requirement
Blooded	Meet regional requirement
Bloodline of Fire	Meet regional requirement
Bullheaded	Meet regional requirement
Cosmopolitan	Meet regional requirement
Courteous Magocracy	Meet regional requirement
Daylight Adaptation	Meet regional requirement
Discipline	Meet regional requirement
Education	Meet regional requirement
Ethran	Female, Cha 11+, spellcaster level 1st+, society approval
Foe Hunter	Meet regional requirement
Forester	Meet regional requirement
Greater Spell Focus	Spell Focus
Greater Spell Penetration	Spell Penetration
Horse Nomad	Meet regional requirement
Improved Counterspell	—
Improved Familiar	Ability to acquire a new familiar, compatible alignment
Innate Spell	Quicken Spell, Silent Spell, Still Spell
Luck of Heroes	Meet regional requirement
Magical Artisan	Any item creation feat
Magical Training	Int 10+, meet regional requirement
Mercantile Background	Meet regional requirement
Militia	Meet regional requirement
Mind Over Body	Meet regional requirement
Resist Poison	Meet regional requirement
Saddleback	Meet regional requirement
Shadow Weave Magic	Wis 13+ or patron deity (Shar)
Signature Spell	Spell Mastery
Silver Palm	Meet regional requirement
Smooth Talk	Meet regional requirement
Snake Blood	Meet regional requirement
Spellcasting Prodigy	—
Stealthy	Meet regional requirement
Street Smart	Meet regional requirement
Strong Soul	Meet regional requirement
Survivor	Meet regional requirement
Tattoo Focus	Specialized in a school of magic, meet regional requirement
Thug	Meet regional requirement
Thunder Twin	Meet regional requirement
Treetopper	Meet regional requirement
Twin Sword Style	Two-Weapon Fighting, meet regional requirement

Item Creation Feats	Prerequisite
Create *Portal*	Craft Wondrous Item
Inscribe Rune	Int 13+, appropriate Craft skill, divine spellcaster level 3rd+

Metamagic Feats	Prerequisite
Delay Spell	Any other metamagic feat
Insidious Magic	Shadow Weave Magic
Pernicious Magic	Shadow Weave Magic
Persistent Spell	Extend Spell
Tenacious Magic	Shadow Weave Magic
Twin Spell	Any other metamagic feat

bloodline of fire [general]

You are descended from the efreet who ruled Calimshan for two millennia. The blood of these fire-spirits runs thick in your veins.

Region: Calimshan.

Benefit: You receive a +4 bonus on saving throws against fire effects. You also add +2 to the DC of saving throws for any sorcerer spells with the fire descriptor that you cast. This benefit stacks with the Spell Focus feat if the spell you cast is from your chosen school.

Special: You may only take this feat as a 1st-level character.

bullheaded [general]

The stubbornness and determination of your kind is legendary. You are exceptionally headstrong and difficult to sway from your intended course.

Regions: Damara, Dragon Coast, the Great Dale, Moonshaes, Narfell, Nelanther Isles, Rashemen, Vaasa, Western Heartlands, gold dwarf, gray dwarf, shield dwarf.

Benefit: You receive a +1 bonus on Will saves and a +2 bonus on Intimidate checks.

cosmopolitan [general]

Your exposure to the thousand forking paths of the city has taught you things you ordinarily would never have uncovered.

Regions: Amn, Waterdeep.

Benefit: Choose a nonexclusive skill you do not have as a class skill. You gain a +2 bonus on all checks with that skill, and that skill is always considered a class skill for you.

Special: You may take this feat multiple times. Its effects do not stack. Each time you take the feat, it applies to a new skill.

courteous magocracy [general]

You were raised in a land where mighty wizards order affairs. Where powerful spellcasters are common, cautious courtesy is the norm and everyone has an eye for magic goods.

Region: Evermeet, Halruaa.

Benefit: You receive a +2 bonus on all Diplomacy and Spellcraft checks.

create portal [item creation]

You have learned the ancient craft of creating a *portal*, a permanent magic device that that instantaneously transports those who know its secrets from one locale to another. Faerûn is riddled with *portals*.

Prerequisite: Craft Wondrous Item.

Benefit: You can create any *portal* whose prerequisites you meet. Crafting a *portal* takes one day for each 1,000 gp in its base price. To craft a *portal*, you must spend 1/25 of its base price in XP and use up raw materials costing half of this base price. See Chapter 2: Magic for details of *portal* creation.

Some *portals* incur extra costs in material components or XP as noted in their descriptions. These costs are in addition to those derived from the *portal*'s base price.

daylight adaptation [general]

Through long exile from the shadowed homelands of your kind, you have learned to endure the painful sunlight of the surface world.

Region: Drow, gray dwarf, orc.

Benefit: If you are a type of creature that suffers circumstance penalties when exposed to bright light (such as a drow or duergar), you no longer suffer those penalties, whether the light comes from natural or magical sources of illumination.

delay spell [Metamagic]

You can cast spells that take effect after a short delay of your choosing.

Prerequisite: Any other metamagic feat.

Benefit: A delayed spell doesn't activate until 1 to 5 rounds after you finish casting it. You determine the delay when casting the spell, and it cannot be changed once set. The spell activates just before your turn on the round you designate. Only area, personal, and touch spells may be affected by this feat.

Any decisions you would make about the spell, including attack rolls, designating targets, or determining or shaping an area, are decided when the spell is cast. Any effects resolved by those affected by the spell, including saving throws, are decided when the spell triggers. If conditions change between casting and effect in such a fashion as to make the spell impossible—for example, the target you designate leaves the spell's maximum range or area before it goes off—the spell fails.

A delayed spell may be dispelled normally during the delay, and can be detected normally in the area or on the target with spells such as *detect magic*. A delayed spell uses up a spell slot three levels higher than the spell's actual level.

discipline [general]

Your people are admired for their single-minded determination and clarity of purpose. You are difficult to distract by spell or blow.

Regions: Aglarond, Anauroch, Cormyr, Impiltur, Thay, strongheart halfling, sun elf, rock gnome.

Benefit: You gain a +1 bonus on Will saves and a +2 bonus on Concentration checks.

education [general]

Some lands hold the pen in higher regard than the sword. In your youth you received the benefit of several years of more or less formal schooling.

Regions: Amn, Chessenta, Cormyr, Evermeet, Lantan, Mulhorand, Sembia, Silverymoon, Waterdeep, moon elf, sun elf.

Benefit: All Knowledge skills are class skills for you. You get a +1 bonus on all skill checks with any two Knowledge skills of your choosing.

Special: You may only take this feat as a 1st level character

ethran [general]

You have been initiated into the secrets of the Witches of Rashemen as a member of the Ethran, the "untried."

Prerequisites: Female, Charisma 11+, spellcaster level 1st+, society approval.

Region: Rashemen.

Benefit: You are a respected member of the Witches of Rashemen. You gain a +2 bonus on Animal Empathy and Intuit Direction checks. When dealing with other Rashemi, you gain a +2 bonus on any Charisma-based skill checks. Acquiring this feat requires the approval of the DM and remaining in good standing with the witches of Rashemen. If you lose their approval, you lose all benefits of this feat.

foe hunter [fighter, general]

In lands threatened by evil nonhumans, many warriors learn ways to fight effectively against these creatures. You have served as a member of a militia or military unit devoted to protecting your home from the fierce raiders who trouble the area.

Regions: Chult, Cormyr, Damara, the Lake of Steam, the North, the Moonsea, Tashalar, Tethyr, Vaasa, shield dwarf, wood elf.

Benefit: Your homeland dictates the type of foe you have trained against. When fighting monsters of that race, you gain a +1 competence bonus on damage rolls with melee attacks and on ranged attacks at ranges of up to 30 feet, and you act as if you had the Improved Critical feat for the weapon you are using. This benefit does not stack with the Improved Critical feat.

Special: In Cormyr, Damara, Tethyr, Vaasa, or as a shield dwarf, your traditional foes are goblinoids—goblins, hobgoblins, and bugbears. In Chult and Tashalar, this feat applies to lizardfolk and yuan-ti. Wood elves train against gnolls. In the Lake of Steam, the North, and the Moonsea, this feat applies to orcs and half-orcs.

You may take this feat multiple times. Its effects do not stack. Each time you take the feat you must qualify for learning regional feats in a land that hunts a different creature from that specified by the regional feat or feats you already have.

Forester [General]

Faerûn's great forests stretch for hundreds of miles across the northlands. You are knowledgeable about the secrets of the forest and wise in its ways.

Regions: Chondalwood, Dalelands, the Great Dale, the High Forest, ghostwise halfling, moon elf, wild elf, wood elf.

Benefit: You receive a +2 bonus on all Heal checks and a +2 bonus on all Wilderness Lore checks.

Greater spell Focus [General]

Choose a school of magic to which you already have applied the Spell Focus feat. Your spells of that school are even more potent than normal.

Prerequisite: Spell Focus.

Benefit: Add +4 to the DC for all saving throws against spells from the school of magic you select to focus on. This overlaps (does not stack with) the bonus from Spell Focus.

Special: You can gain this feat multiple times. Its effects do not stack. Each time you take the feat, it applies to a new school of magic.

Greater spell penetration [General]

Your spells are especially potent, defeating spell resistance more readily than normal.

Prerequisite: Spell Penetration.

Benefit: You get a +4 bonus on caster level checks (1d20 + caster level) to beat a creature's spell resistance. This overlaps (does not stack with) the bonus from Spell Penetration.

Illustration by Todd Lockwood

Improved familiars: imp, pseudodragon, quasit

Horse nomad [Fighter, General]

You have been raised in a culture that relies upon riding and shooting for survival.

Regions: Hordelands, the Shaar, Vaasa (the Ride only).

Benefit: You get Martial Weapon Proficiency (composite shortbow) and a +2 bonus on all Ride checks.

Improved counterspell [General]

You understand the nuances of magic to such an extent that you can counter your opponents' spells with great efficiency.

Benefit: When counterspelling, instead of using the exact spell you are trying to counter, you may use a spell of the same school that is one or more levels higher than the target spell.

Improved familiar [General]

So long as you are able to acquire a new familiar, you may choose your new familiar from a nonstandard list.

Prerequisite: Ability to acquire a new familiar, compatible alignment.

Benefit: When choosing a familiar, the following creatures are also available to you. You may choose a familiar with an alignment up to one step away on each of the alignment axes (lawful through chaotic, good through evil).

The improved familiar is magically linked to its master just like a normal familiar. The familiar uses the basic statistics for a creature of its kind, as given in the *Monster Manual* or Chapter 9: Monsters of this book, with these exceptions:

Hit Points: One-half the master's total or the familiar's normal total, whichever is higher.

Attacks: Use the master's base attack bonus or the familiar's, whichever is better. Use the familiar's Dexterity or Strength modifier, whichever is greater, to get the familiar's melee attack bonus with unarmed attacks. Damage equals that of a normal creature of that kind.

Special Attacks: The familiar has all the special attacks of its kind.

Special Qualities: The familiar has all the special qualities of its kind.

TABLE 1–6: IMPROVED FAMILIARS

Kind of Familiar	Arcane Spellcaster Level Required
Animal, tressym†† [neutral]	5
Beholderkin, eyeball† [neutral evil]	5
Imp [lawful evil]	7
Pseudodragon [neutral good]	7
Quasit [chaotic evil]	7
Night hunter bat† [neutral evil]	5
Formian worker [lawful neutral]	7
Shocker lizard [neutral]	5
Stirge [neutral]	5

†These creatures are described in *Monster Manual Appendix: Monsters of Faerûn.*

††This creature is described in Chapter 9: Monsters.

Saving Throws: The familiar uses the master's base save bonuses if they're better than the familiar's.

Skills: Use the normal skills for a creature of its kind.

Familiar Special Abilities: Use Table 3–19: Familiar Abilities in the *Player's Handbook* to determine additional abilities as you would for a normal familiar.

Innate Spell [General]

You have mastered a spell so thoroughly you can now cast it as a spell-like ability.

Prerequisites: Quicken Spell, Silent Spell, Still Spell.

Benefit: Choose a spell you can cast. You can now cast this spell at will as a spell-like ability, once per round, without needing to prepare it. One spell slot eight levels higher than the innate spell is permanently used to power it. (Note that spell slots above 9th level can be achieved with the rules in the upcoming *Epic-Level Campaigns* book.) If the innate spell has an XP component, you pay the XP cost each time you use the spell-like ability. If the innate spell has a focus, you do not need the focus to use the spell-like ability. If the innate spell has a costly material component (see the spell description), you need an item worth 50 times that cost to use as the focus for the spell-like ability. If the innate spell has a material component with negligible cost, you do not need the material component to use the spell-like ability.

Since an innate spell is a spell-like ability and not an actual spell, a cleric cannot convert it to a *cure* spell or an *inflict* spell, nor can it be converted to a signature spell (see the Signature Spell feat). Divine spellcasters who become unable to cast divine spells cannot use divine innate spells.

Special: You can choose this feat more than once, selecting another spell each time. You have to pay the costs in spell slots, focuses, and material components for each innate spell you acquire.

Inscribe Rune [Item Creation]

You can create magic runes that hold spells until triggered.

Prerequisite: Intelligence 13+, appropriate Craft skill, divine spellcaster level 3rd+.

Benefit: You can cast any divine spell you have prepared as a rune. The caster must have prepared the spell to be scribed and must provide any material components or focuses the spell requires. If casting the spell would reduce the caster's XP total, he pays the cost upon beginning the rune in addition to the XP cost for making the rune itself. Likewise, material components are consumed when he begins writing, but focuses are not. See the Rune Magic section in Chapter 2: Magic for the details of runes and rune magic.

A single object of Medium-size or smaller can hold only one rune. Larger objects can hold one rune per 25 square feet (an area 5 feet square) of surface area. Runes cannot be placed on creatures. The rune has a market price of the spell level × caster level × 100 gp (a 0-level spell counts as 1/2 level). You must spend 1/25 of its market price in XP and use up raw materials costing half this market price. A rune's market value equals its base price.

Insidious Magic [Metamagic]

You can use the Shadow Weave to make your spells harder for Weave users to detect. All creatures employing spells or spell-like abilities are considered to be Weave users unless they possess the Shadow Weave Magic feat.

Prerequisite: Shadow Weave Magic.

Benefit: When a Weave user employs a divination spell, spell-like ability, or magic item (such as *detect magic*) that may detect the magical aura of one of your spells, the Weave user must make a level check (DC 11 + your caster level) to successfully detect your spells. Similarly, a Weave user attempting to use a divination such as *see invisibility* to reveal the effects of one of your spells must make a level check to reveal your spell's effects. The Weave user can check only once for each divination spell used, no matter how many of your spell effects are operating in an area.

This benefit does not extend to spells you cast from the schools of Evocation or Transmutation.

From now on, your ability to detect Weave magic is impaired. Any divination spell you use against a Weave effect is successful only if you make a level check against a DC of 9 + the caster's level. This penalty does not extend to Enchantment, Illusion, or Necromancy effects. (You detect them normally.)

Luck of Heroes [General]

Your land is known for producing heroes. Through pluck, determination, and resilience, your people survive when no one expects them to come through.

Regions: Aglarond, Dalelands, Tethyr, the Vast.

Benefit: You receive a +1 luck bonus on all saving throws.

Magical Artisan [General]

You have mastered the method of creating a certain kind of magic item.

Prerequisite: Any item creation feat.

Benefit: Each time you take this feat, choose one item creation feat you know. When determining your cost in XP and raw materials for creating items with this feat, multiply the base price by 75%.

Special: You may gain this feat multiple times. Each time you take the feat, it applies to a new item creation feat.

Magical Training [General]

You come from Halruaa, a half-legendary land where basic magic is taught to all with the aptitude for it. Every crafter and laborer, it seems, knows a cantrip or two to ease her work.

Prerequisite: Intelligence 10+.

Region: Halruaa.

Benefit: You may cast the 0-level arcane spells *dancing lights*, *daze*, and *mage hand* once per day each. You have an arcane spell failure chance if you wear armor. You are treated as a wizard of your arcane spellcaster level (minimum 1st level) for determining the range at which these spells can be cast.

Special: You may only take this feat as a 1st-level character.

Mercantile Background [General]

Powerful trading costers and craft guilds control the wealth and commerce of Faerûn's lands. You come from a family that excels at a particular trade and knows well the value of any kind of trade good or commodity.

Regions: Impiltur, Lake of Steam, Lantan, Sembia, Tashalar, Tethyr, Thesk, the Vast, deep gnome, gray dwarf.

Benefit: You gain a +2 bonus on all Appraise checks and a +2 bonus on skill checks in the Craft or Profession skill of your choice.

Militia [General]

You served in a local militia, training with weapons suitable for use on the battlefield.

Region: Dalelands, Impiltur, Luiren, strongheart halfling.

Benefit: You get Martial Weapon Proficiency (longbow) and Martial Weapon Proficiency (longspear). In Luiren, this feat applies to Martial Weapon Proficiency (shortbow) and Martial Weapon Proficiency (short sword) instead of longbow and longspear.

mind over body [General]

The arcane spellcasters of some lands have learned to overcome the frailties of the body with the unyielding power of the mind.

Regions: Calimshan, Thay, moon elf, sun elf.

Benefit: At 1st level, you may use your Intelligence modifier instead of your Constitution modifier to determine bonus hit points. (For all ensuing levels, you revert to your Constitution modifier.) You gain +1 hit point every time you learn a metamagic feat.

Special: You may only take this feat as a 1st-level character.

pernicious magic [Metamagic]

You can use the Shadow Weave to make your spells harder for Weave users to counter. Any creature using a spell, spell-like ability, or magic item without the Shadow Weave Magic feat is considered to be a Weave user.

Prerequisite: Shadow Weave Magic.

Benefit: Your spells resist counterspell attempts by Weave users. When a Weave caster tries to counterspell a spell you are casting, he must make a level check (DC 11 + your caster level) to succeed at the counterspell.

This benefit does not extend to spells you cast from the school of Evocation or Transmutation, nor to opponents using *dispel magic* to counterspell (see Tenacious Magic, later in this section).

From now on your ability to counterspell Weave magic is impaired. When you attempt to counter a Weave spell, you must make a level check with a DC of 9 + your opponent's caster level to succeed. This penalty does not extend to Enchantment, Illusion, or Necromancy effects. (You counterspell them normally.) You may attempt counterspells with *dispel magic* normally.

persistent spell [Metamagic]

You make one of your spells last all day.

Prerequisite: Extend Spell.

Benefit: A persistent spell has a duration of 24 hours. The persistent spell must have a personal range or a fixed range (for example, *comprehend languages* or *detect magic*). Spells of instantaneous duration, spells with a range of touch, and spells whose effects are discharged cannot be affected by this feat. You need not concentrate on spells such as *detect magic* and *detect thoughts* to be aware of the mere presence or absence of the thing detected, but you must still concentrate to gain additional information as normal. Concentration on such a spell is a standard action that does not provoke an attack of opportunity. A persistent spell uses up a spell slot four levels higher than the spell's actual level.

resist poison [General]

Over years, some among your people carefully expose themselves to poisons in controlled dosages in order to build up immunity to their effects. A few are thereby weakened, but the strong adjust.

Regions: Gray dwarf, half-orc, orc.

Benefit: You get a +4 bonus on Fortitude saving throws against poison.

Special: You may only take this feat as a 1st-level character.

saddleback [Fighter, General]

Your people are as comfortable riding as walking.

Regions: Cormyr, Hordelands, Narfell, the North, Western Heartlands.

Benefit: You receive a +3 bonus on all Ride checks.

shadow weave magic [General]

You have discovered the dark and dangerous secret of the Shadow Weave.

Prerequisite: Wisdom 13+ or patron deity Shar.

Benefit: From now on, your spells tap the Shadow Weave instead of the Weave. You also can activate magic items that use the Shadow Weave without taking damage.

Add a +1 bonus to the DC for all saving throws of spells you cast from the schools of Enchantment, Illusion, and Necromancy, and spells with the darkness descriptor. You get a +1 bonus on caster level checks to overcome spell resistance for these schools and spells.

The Shadow Weave proves less than optimal for effects involving energy or matter. Your effective caster level for spells you cast from the schools of Evocation or Transmutation (except spells with the darkness descriptor) is reduced by one. (First-level Shadow Weave users cannot cast spells from these schools.) The reduced caster level affects the spell's range, duration, damage, and any other level-dependent variables the spell might have, including dispel checks against you.

You can no longer cast spells with the light descriptor, no matter what your level is. Such spells automatically fail. Your ability to use magic items that produce light effects is also limited—you cannot invoke an item's light power if the item's activation method is spell trigger or spell completion.

From now on, any magic item you create is a Shadow Weave item (see Chapter 2: Magic).

Special: Knowledge of the Shadow Weave has a price. When you acquire this feat, your Wisdom score is immediately reduced by 2 points. If this loss or any future Wisdom loss reduces your Wisdom score to less than 13, you still have the feat. (This is an exception to the general rule governing feats with prerequisites.)

Restorative spells (such as *restoration* or *greater restoration*) do not reverse the Wisdom loss. You can, however, strike a deal with Shar, the goddess who holds sway over the Shadow Weave, to regain your lost Wisdom. You must receive an *atonement* spell from a cleric of Shar. Sharran clerics require the subject to complete a dangerous quest before receiving the *atonement,* and afterward you must choose her as your patron. (The usual quest is to destroy a follower of Selûne whose level is at least as high as yours.) If you later change your patron, you immediately suffer the Wisdom loss. If you take Shar back again as your patron deity, it is not regained.

signature spell [General]

You are so familiar with a mastered spell that you can convert other prepared spells into that spell.

Prerequisite: Spell Mastery.

Benefit: Each time you take this feat, choose a spell you have mastered with Spell Mastery. You may now convert prepared arcane spells of that spell's level or higher into that signature spell, just as a good cleric spontaneously casts prepared spells as *cure* spells.

Special: You may gain this feat multiple times. Each time you take the feat, it applies to a new mastered spell.

silver palm [General]

Your culture is based on haggling and the art of the deal.

Regions: Amn, Dragon Coast, Great Dale, Impiltur, Moonsea, Sembia, the Shaar, Thesk, Vilhon Reach, gold dwarf, gray dwarf.

Benefit: You get a +2 bonus on all Appraise and Bluff checks.

smooth talk [General]

Your people are accustomed to dealing with strangers and foreigners without needing to draw weapons to make their point.

Regions: Luiren, Silverymoon, Thesk, Waterdeep, gold dwarf, lightfoot halfling.

Benefit: You gain a +2 bonus on all Diplomacy and Sense Motive checks.

snake blood [general]

The taint of the yuan-ti runs in your veins. No outward signs give away your heritage, but you are something more—or less—than entirely human.

Regions: Chult, Tashalar, the Vilhon Reach (Hlondeth only).

Benefit: You get a +2 bonus on Fortitude saving throws against poison and a +1 bonus on all Reflex saving throws.

Special: You may only take this feat as a 1st-level character.

spellcasting prodigy [general]

You have an exceptional gift for magic.

Benefit: For the purpose of determining bonus spells and the saving throw DCs of spells you cast, treat your primary spellcasting ability score (Charisma for bards and sorcerers, Wisdom for divine spellcasters, Intelligence for wizards) as 2 points higher than its actual value. If you have more than one spellcasting class, the bonus applies to only one of those classes.

Special: You may only take this feat as a 1st-level character. If you take this feat more than once (for example, if you are a human or another type of creature that gets more than one feat at 1st level), it applies to a different spellcasting class each time. You can take this feat even if you don't have any spellcasting classes yet.

stealthy [general]

Your people are known for their stealthiness.

Regions: Drow elf, half-orc, ghostwise halfling, lightfoot halfling, strongheart halfling.

Benefit: You gain a +2 bonus on all Hide and Move Silently checks.

street smart [general]

You have learned how to keep informed, ask questions, and interact with the underworld without raising suspicion.

Regions: Amn, Calimshan, Chessenta, Moonsea, Unther.

Benefit: You get a +2 bonus on all Bluff and Gather Information checks.

strong soul [general]

The souls of your people are hard to separate from their bodies.

Regions: Dalelands, Moonshaes, deep gnome, ghostwise halfling, lightfoot halfling, moon elf, rock gnome, strongheart halfling, sun elf, wild elf, wood elf.

Benefit: You get a +1 bonus on all Fortitude and Will saves and an additional +1 bonus on saving throws against energy draining and death effects.

survivor [general]

Your people thrive in regions that others find uninhabitable, and excel at uncovering the secrets of the wilderness and surviving to tell the tale.

Regions: Anauroch, Chondalwood, Chult, Damara, Hordelands, Moonshaes, Narfell, the North, the Shaar, Rashemen, Silverymoon, Vaasa, Vilhon Reach, Western Heartlands, deep gnome, drow elf, lightfoot halfling, ghostwise halfling, shield dwarf, wild elf.

Benefit: You get a +1 bonus on Fortitude saves and a +2 bonus on all Wilderness Lore checks.

tattoo focus [special]

You bear the powerful magic tattoos of a Red Wizard of Thay.

Prerequisite: Specialized in a school of magic.

Region: Thay.

Benefit: Add +1 to the DC for all saving throws against spells from your specialized school. You get a +1 bonus on caster level checks (1d20 + caster level) to beat a creature's spell resistance when casting spells from that school.

Special: Only characters with the Tattoo Focus feat can participate in Red Wizards' circles. A character can only select this feat with the help of a Red Wizard who has the scribe tattoo ability.

tenacious magic [metamagic]

You can use the Shadow Weave to make your spells harder for Weave users to dispel. Any magic-wielding creature without the Shadow Weave Magic feat is considered a Weave user.

Prerequisite: Shadow Weave Magic.

Benefit: Your spells resist dispelling attempts by Weave users. When a Weave caster makes a dispel check to dispel one of your spells (including using *dispel magic* to counterspell a spell you are casting), the DC is 15 + your caster level. This benefit does not extend to spells you cast from the schools of Evocation or Transmutation.

From now on your ability to dispel Weave magic is impaired. When you make a dispel check to dispel a Weave spell (or use *dispel magic* to counterspell an opponent's spell), the DC is 13 + the opponent's caster level. This penalty does not extend to Enchantment, Illusion, or Necromancy effects, which you can dispel normally.

thug [general]

Your people know how to get the jump on the competition and push other people around. While others debate, you act.

Regions: Calimshan, Dragon Coast, Moonsea, Nelanther Isles, Unther, the Vast, Vilhon Reach, Waterdeep.

Benefit: You get a +2 bonus on Initiative checks, and a +2 bonus on Intimidate checks.

thunder twin [general]

You are one of the dwarven generation of twins born after Moradin's Thunder Blessing in the Year of Thunder (1306 DR).

Regions: Gold dwarf, shield dwarf.

Benefit: You receive a +2 bonus on all Charisma-based checks. You have a twin brother or sister (fraternal or identical). You may detect the direction of your twin if he or she is alive, on the same plane, and you succeed at an Intuit Direction check against DC 15 (or a Wisdom check if you do not have the skill). A failure on this check gives no information. You may retry once per round as a standard action.

Special: You may only take this feat as a 1st-level character.

treetopper [general]

Your people are at home in the trees and high places, daring falls that paralyze most other folk in abject terror.

Regions: Aglarond, Chondalwood, High Forest, ghostwise halfling, wild elf, wood elf.

Benefit: You get a +2 bonus on all Climb checks. You do not lose your Dexterity bonus to Armor Class or give your attacker a +2 bonus when you are attacked while climbing.

twin spell [metamagic]

You can cast a spell simultaneously with another spell just like it.

Prerequisite: Any other metamagic feat.

Benefit: Casting a spell altered by this feat causes the spell to take effect twice on the target, as if you were simultaneously casting the same spell two times on the same location or target. Any variables in the spell (such as targets, shaping an area, and so on) apply to both of the resulting spells. The target suffers all the effects of both spells individually and receives a saving throw for each.

In some cases, failure of both of the target's saving throws results in redundant effects, such as a twinned *charm person* (see Combining Magical Effects in Chapter 10 of the *Player's Handbook*), although any ally of the target would have to succeed at two dispel attempts in order to free the target from the charm. As with other metamagic feats, twinning a spell does not affect its vulnerability to counterspelling (for example, using an untwinned form of the spell doesn't negate just half of the twinned spell).

A twinned spell uses up a spell slot four levels higher than the spell's actual level.

twin sword style [fighter, general]

You have mastered a style of defense that others find frustrating.

Prerequisite: Two-Weapon Fighting.

Regions: Sembia, Waterdeep, drow elf.

Benefit: When fighting with two swords (dagger, longsword, rapier, scimitar, or short sword, in any combination), you can designate a melee opponent during your action and receive a +2 armor bonus to your Armor Class against attacks from that opponent. This armor bonus stacks with the armor bonus from armor and shield. You can select a new melee opponent on any action. A condition that makes you lose your Dexterity bonus to Armor Class (if any) also makes you lose this bonus.

The benefits of this feat apply only if you are proficient with the weapons you are using.

character Description

In addition to the guidelines given in the *Player's Handbook*, you need to take into account some other considerations when creating a character for the FORGOTTEN REALMS campaign setting.

Religion

The deities of Faerûn are deeply enmeshed in the functioning of the world's magical ecology and the lives of mortals. Faerûnian characters nearly always have a patron deity. Everyone in Faerûn knows that those who die without having a patron deity to escort them to their proper judgement in the land of the dead spend eternity writhing in the Wall of the Faithless, or disappear into the hells of the devils or the infernos of the demons.

The selection of a patron deity does not mean that your character only worships or makes prayers and offerings to one deity. Faerûn is a polytheistic world, not a monotheistic world. At appropriate moments, characters might worship or pay homage to nearly all the deities, even some they could not choose as patron deities. For example, lawful good sailors would never think of choosing Umberlee, the evil goddess of the ocean, as their patron, but it would be hard to find a sailor who had not sacrificed to Umberlee before at least one journey, or made promises to her during a storm. Likewise, an evil follower of Mask, the god of thieves, might make a donation to the temple of Tymora, goddess of luck, before a big heist, even though Tymora is a good goddess.

WHY CHOOSE A PATRON DEITY?

Choosing a patron deity provides you with contacts in the world, particularly if you are known to serve your deity's causes. A character with Helm as her patron is more likely to get assistance—timely healing, a place of refuge, access to divinations and other spells—from the church of Helm in times of need. A bard whose patron is Tymora might have a better chance of convincing a group of Tymora-worshiping bandits to talk peacefully instead of fighting.

Of more concern to most adventurers, a character who dies without a patron deity cannot be raised from the dead by any mortal means short of a *miracle* or *wish*. When such a character dies, he is considered one of the Faithless, and his soul is used to form part of the wall around the realm of Kelemvor, god of the dead. Mortal action cannot reverse this fate, and so unless the character's friends can arrange direct intervention by another deity (or expend a *miracle* or *wish*, spells symbolizing intervention by another deity), that character is unlikely to return to life. (See the Cosmology section of Chapter 5: Deities for more information.)

CHOOSING A PATRON

Having a patron deity implies some true personal attachment to that deity. Given this relationship, it is practically unheard of for a character to have a patron with a radically different alignment than her own. For example, it is essentially impossible for a chaotic good rogue to feel a close personal connection with Bane, the lawful evil god of tyranny and fear.

When choosing a patron if you are a divine spellcaster, you follow the "one-step" rule described in the Alignment subsection of the Cleric section of Chapter 3: Classes in the *Player's Handbook*: Your alignment may be up to one "step" away from your patron's. For example, a chaotic neutral ranger can choose Malar (a chaotic evil god) as his patron, but could not choose Mielikki (a neutral good goddess).

You can only have one patron deity at a time. It is possible to change your patron, but doing so is not a decision made lightly or quickly. If you are a cleric, druid, paladin, or spellcasting ranger (or any other divine spellcaster), this process is described in the Changing Deities section of Chapter 5: Deities. If you are any other character class, changing a patron is a simple matter of deciding to do so that does not require intervention by the church of your new patron (although obtaining its blessing is customary, to show allegiance to the new deity). A character who frequently changes patron deities is likely to gain a reputation of being weak in her faith, and risks being branded as one of the False in the afterlife.

Humans choose a patron deity from the Faerûnian or Mulhorandi pantheons based on the region in which they live or that they grew up in. Nonhumans usually choose a patron from their own pantheon (drow from the drow pantheon, elves from the elven pantheon, and so on). Nonhumans can also select a patron from the human pantheon of the region they live in or grew up in. The most common examples of this are northern halflings, who often choose Tymora, and gnomes, who often choose Gond. Half-orcs choose a patron from the orc pantheon or from the human pantheon of the region they live in or grew up in.. Half-elves choose a patron from the elven or drow pantheon (as appropriate to their nonhuman parent) or from the human pantheon of the region they live in or grew up in. For the most part, creatures choose a patron from their own pantheon, but those that stray from this trend are common enough to be viewed merely as a curiosity rather than as an aberration.

vital statistics

Most characters in the FORGOTTEN REALMS campaign setting use the normal height and weight values given on Table 6–6: Random

Height and Weight in the *Player's Handbook*. However, elves in Faerûn are tall and thin, so all elves except drow use the human height and the half-elven weight, subtracting 10 pounds from the actual weight. Half-elves use the human height and half-elven weight entries. Drow use the elven height and weight entries. The emaciated gray dwarves use the dwarf entries but subtract 30 pounds from their weight result. Aasimars and tieflings use standard human height and weight, and the genasi use that as a base, although air genasi tend to be lighter, earth genasi heavier, fire genasi taller, and water genasi shorter.

prestige classes

Faerûn is home to dozens of secret organizations and elite orders, hundreds of unique adventurers and anointed champions, and thousands of opportunities. A mage might begin her career as a straightforward wizard, but as she gains power and experience, choices confront her. Should she follow the path of the archmage, or plunge into the secret studies of the Red Wizards? Should she seek knowledge in the dark arts of the Shadow Weave, risking life and sanity in pursuit of power, or should she strengthen her ties to her patron deity and serve her chosen church as an arcane devotee?

Characters of any class face similar choices. Many of the most powerful and successful adventurers of Faerûn eventually become embroiled in the struggle of light and dark, assuming the responsibility and the privileges of these unique character classes.

Prestige classes that add to the character's base class for determining the number of spells per day also add to the character's caster level (such as for dispel checks and level checks to overcome spell resistance).

Arcane Devotee

Every major faith numbers sorcerers and wizards among its fervent followers. While some wizards ally themselves with churches close to their own beliefs out of caution and convenience, others are devout representatives of their faith and willingly subordinate their own causes to those of their patron deity, becoming arcane devotees.

Arcane devotees complement the divine magic of a church's clerical leaders and are among the most important and respected members of a deity's following. They provide much of the magical firepower of their faith and collaborate with the church's clerics in the creation of magic items requiring both arcane and divine spells. Arcane devotees provide support for the church's armies in time of war, divine the intentions of the enemies of the faith, and often take the front line to decimate enemy troops or destroy spellcasters of rival faiths.

Arcane devotee of Kossuth

Naturally, arcane devotees are always arcane spellcasters. Sorcerers and wizards are the most common type, but some music-oriented deities tend to have more bard devotees, and a rare few of the more evil deities have been known to have assassin devotees that focus on cruel and terrible forms of death magic.

Hit Die: d4.

REQUIREMENTS

To qualify to become a arcane devotee (Dev) of a particular deity, a character must fulfill all the following criteria.

Spellcasting: Ability to cast 4th-level arcane spells.

Skills: Knowledge (religion) 8 ranks, Spellcraft 8 ranks.

Feats: Enlarge Spell.

Patron: An arcane devotee must have a patron deity, and it must be the deity of which she is a devotee.

CLASS SKILLS

The arcane devotee's class skills (and the key ability for each skill) are Alchemy (Int), Concentration (Con), Craft (Int), Knowledge (all skills taken individually) (Int), Profession (Wis), Scry (Int), and Spellcraft (Int). See Chapter 4: Skills in the *Player's Handbook* for skill descriptions.

Skill Points at Each Level: 2 + Int modifier.

CLASS FEATURES

All the following are class features of the arcane devotee prestige class.

Weapon and Armor Proficiency: Arcane devotees gain no proficiency in any weapon or armor.

Spells per Day: An arcane devotee's training focuses on arcane spells. Thus, when a new arcane devotee level is gained, the character gains new spells per day as if he had also gained a level in whatever arcane spellcasting class he belonged to before he added the prestige class. He does not, however, gain any other benefit a character of that class would have gained (bonus metamagic or item creation feats, bard or assassin abilities, and so on). This essentially means that he adds the level of arcane devotee to the level of whatever other arcane spellcasting class the character has, then determines spells per day and caster level accordingly.

If a character had more than one arcane spellcasting class before he became an arcane devotee, he must decide to which class he adds each level of arcane devotee for the purpose of determining spells per day.

TABLE 1–7: THE ARCANE DEVOTEE

Class Level	Base Attack Bonus	Fort Save	Ref Save	Will Save	Special	Spells per Day
1st	+0	+0	+0	+2	Enlarge Spell	+1 level of existing arcane spellcasting class
2nd	+1	+0	+0	+3	Sacred defense +1, alignment focus	+1 level of existing arcane spellcasting class
3rd	+1	+1	+1	+3	Bonus feat	+1 level of existing arcane spellcasting class
4th	+2	+1	+1	+4	Sacred defense +2	+1 level of existing arcane spellcasting class
5th	+2	+1	+1	+4	Divine shroud	+1 level of existing arcane spellcasting class

Enlarge Spell: The arcane devotee may cast a spell as if it were under the effects of the Enlarge Spell feat. He does not need to prepare this spell in advance, and it does not increase the casting time or use a higher spell slot. This ability can be used a number of times per day equal to 1 + the arcane devotee's Charisma bonus (minimum of once per day).

Sacred Defense: Add this value (+1 at 2nd level, +2 at 4th level) to the arcane devotee's saving throws against divine spells, as well as the spell-like and supernatural abilities of outsiders.

Alignment Focus: A 2nd-level arcane devotee chooses one component of his deity's alignment. He now casts spells of that alignment at +1 caster level. If his deity is neutral, he chooses one component of his alignment for this focus. If the arcane devotee and his deity are neutral, the character chooses chaos, evil, good, or law for his focus.

Bonus Feat: At 3rd level, an arcane devotee can choose any one item creation feat or any feat from the following list: Spell Focus, Greater Spell Focus, Spell Penetration, Greater Spell Penetration, Improved Counterspell, Magical Artisan, or Shadow Weave Magic (devotees of Shar only).

Divine Shroud (Su): Once per day, a 5th-level arcane devotee may surround himself with a shroud of glowing divine power that protects him against enemy spells. The shroud is of a color appropriate to the arcane devotee's patron's alignment: constant blue for law, shimmering white for good, wavering black for evil, or flickering yellow for chaos. The shroud grants spell resistance of 12 + the character's caster level as if he were under the effects of a *spell resistance* spell. This ability can be invoked as a free action and lasts a number of rounds equal to the arcane devotee's Charisma bonus + 5.

Archmage

The highest art is magic—often referred to as *the* Art. Its most advanced practitioners are frequently archmages, bending spells in ways unavailable to other spellcasters. The archmage gains strange powers and the ability to alter spells in remarkable ways, but must sacrifice some of her spell capability in order to master these arcane secrets.

Hit Die: d4.

Illustration by Sam Wood

Archmage Perendra Raslemtar of Tethyr

REQUIREMENTS

To qualify to become an archmage (Acm), a character must fulfill all the following criteria.

Spellcasting: Ability to cast 7th-level arcane spells, knowledge of 5th-level or higher spells from at least five schools.

Skills: Knowledge (arcana) 15 ranks, Spellcraft 15 ranks.

Feats: Skill Focus (Spellcraft), Spell Focus in two schools of magic.

CLASS SKILLS

The archmage's class skills (and the key ability for each skill) are Alchemy (Int), Concentration (Con), Knowledge (all skills taken individually) (Int), Profession (Wis), Scry (Int), Search (Int), and Spellcraft (Int). See Chapter 4: Skills in the *Player's Handbook* for skill descriptions.

Skill Points at Each Level: 2 + Int modifier.

CLASS FEATURES

All the following are class features of the archmage prestige class.

Weapon and Armor Proficiency: Archmages gain no proficiency in any weapon or armor.

Spells per Day: When a new archmage level is gained, the character gains new spells per day as if she had also gained a level in whatever arcane spellcasting class she belonged to before she added the prestige class. She does not, however, gain any other benefit a character of that class would have gained (bonus metamagic or item creation feats, bard or assassin abilities, and so on). This essentially means that she adds the level of archmage to the level of whatever other arcane spellcasting class the character has, then determines spells per day and caster level accordingly.

If a character had more than one arcane spellcasting class before she became an archmage, she must decide to which class she adds each level of archmage for the purpose of determining spells per day.

High Arcana: The archmage learns secret lore unknown to lesser wizards and sorcerers. She gains the ability to select a special ability from among the following by permanently eliminating one spell slot. For example, a 15th-level wizard normally can cast two 7th-level spells per day (not counting bonus spells for specialization or high Intelligence). A Wiz13/Acm2 who chooses the arcane reach ability forfeits one 7th-level spell, and so can only cast one 7th-level spell per day, not counting bonus spells.

The archmage may choose to eliminate a spell slot of a higher level than that required to acquire the high arcana in question, if she so desires.

Arcane Fire (Su): The archmage gains the ability to channel arcane spell energy into arcane fire, manifesting as a bolt of raw magical energy. The bolt is a ranged touch attack with long range (400 feet + 40 feet/level of archmage) and deals 1d6 points of damage per level of archmage plus 1d6 points of damage per level of the spell channeled to create the effect. Therefore, a 5th-level archmage that channels a 7th-level spell into arcane fire deals 12d6 points of damage to the target if it hits. This ability costs one 9th-level spell slot.

Arcane Reach: The archmage can use touch spells on targets up to 30 feet away. If the spell requires a touch attack (melee or ranged), the archmage must make a ranged touch attack. If selected

TABLE 1—8: THE ARCHMAGE

Class Level	Base Attack Bonus	Fort Save	Ref Save	Will Save	Special	Spells per Day
1st	+0	+0	+0	+2	High arcana	+1 level of existing arcane spellcasting class
2nd	+1	+0	+0	+3	High arcana	+1 level of existing arcane spellcasting class
3rd	+1	+1	+1	+3	High arcana	+1 level of existing arcane spellcasting class
4th	+2	+1	+1	+4	High arcana	+1 level of existing arcane spellcasting class
5th	+2	+1	+1	+4	High arcana	+1 level of existing arcane spellcasting class

a second time as a special ability, the range increases to 60 feet. This ability costs one 7th-level spell slot.

Mastery of Counterspelling: When the archmage counterspells a spell, it is turned back upon the caster as if it were fully affected by a *spell turning* spell. If the spell cannot be affected by *spell turning* (for example, if it is an area or effect spell), then it is merely counterspelled. This ability costs one 7th-level spell slot.

Mastery of Elements: The archmage can alter an arcane spell when cast so that it utilizes a different element from the one it normally does. For example, an archmage could cast a *fireball* that does sonic damage instead of fire damage.

This ability can only alter spells with the acid, cold, fire, electricity, or sonic descriptors. The spell's casting time is unaffected. The caster decides whether or not to alter the spell's energy type and chooses the new energy type when she begins casting. This ability costs one 8th-level spell slot.

Mastery of Shaping: The archmage can alter area and effect spells that use the following categories: burst, cone, cylinder, emanation, or spread. The alteration consists of creating spaces within the spell's area or effect that are not subject to the spell. The minimum dimension for these spaces is a 5-foot cube. For example, the archmage could cast a *fireball* and leave a hole where her ally stands, preventing any fire damage. Furthermore, any shapeable (S) spells have a minimum dimension of 5 feet instead of 10 feet. This ability costs one 6th-level spell slot.

Spell Power +1: This ability increases the DC for saving throws against the archmage's arcane spells and caster level checks for her arcane spells to overcome spell resistance by +1. This ability can only be selected once, and stacks with spell power +2 and spell power +3, as well as spell power effects from other sources, such as from the Red Wizard prestige class. This ability costs one 5th-level spell slot.

Spell Power +2: As spell power +1, except the increase is +2 instead of +1. This ability can only be selected once, and stacks with spell power +1 and spell power +3, as well as spell power effects from other sources. This ability costs one 7th-level spell slot.

Spell Power +3: As spell power +1, except the increase is +3 instead of +1. This ability can only be selected once, and stacks with spell power +1, spell power +2, as well as spell power effects from other sources. This ability costs one 9th-level spell slot.

Spell-Like Ability: The archmage can use one of her arcane spell slots (other than the slot expended to learn this high arcana) to permanently prepare one of her arcane spells as a spell-like ability that can be used twice per day. The archmage does not use any components when casting the spell, although a spell that costs XP to cast still does so and a spell with a costly material component instead costs her 10 times that amount in XP. This ability costs one 5th-level spell slot.

The spell-like ability normally uses a spell slot of the spell's level, although the archmage can choose to make a spell modified by a metamagic feat into a spell-like ability at the appropriate spell level. For example, the archmage can make *lightning bolt* into a spell-like ability by using a 3rd-level spell slot to do so, or a maximized *lightning bolt* into a 6th-level spell-like ability.

The archmage may use an available higher-level spell slot to be able to use the spell-like ability more often. Using a slot three levels higher than the chosen spell allows her to cast it four times per day, and a slot six levels higher lets her cast it six times per day. For example, Hezark (Wiz15/Acm2) is a pyromaniac and never wants to be denied the ability to cast *fireball*, so she permanently uses a 9th-level spell slot to get *fireball* as a spell-like ability usable six times per day. She forfeits a 5th-level spell slot to master the ability.

If selected more than one time as a special ability, this can apply to the same spell or to a different spell.

Lady Jeryth Phaulkon of Waterdeep, divine champion of Mielikki

Illustration by Carlo Arellano

divine champion

Divine champions are mighty warriors who dedicate themselves to their deity's cause, defending holy ground, destroying enemies of the church, and slaying mythical beasts and clerics of opposed faiths. For deities that do not count paladins among their followers, divine champions fill the role of the church-sponsored warrior.

Most divine champions come from a combat or military background. Barbarians, fighters, monks, paladins, and rangers are the most common divine champions, but some of the more militant clerics and druids decide to become divine champions. Bards, rogues, sorcerers, and wizards rarely become divine champions unless they are particularly devout and skilled in warfare.

Hit Die: d10.

REQUIREMENTS

To qualify to become a divine champion (Chm) of a particular deity, a character must fulfill all the following criteria.

Base Attack Bonus: +7.

TABLE 1—9: THE DIVINE CHAMPION

Class Level	Base Attack Bonus	Fort Save	Ref Save	Will Save	Special
1st	+1	+2	+2	+0	Lay on hands
2nd	+2	+3	+3	+0	Fighter feat, sacred defense +1
3rd	+3	+3	+3	+1	Smite infidel
4th	+4	+4	+4	+1	Fighter feat, sacred defense +2
5th	+5	+4	+4	+1	Divine wrath

Skills: Knowledge (religion) 3 ranks.

Feats: Weapon Focus in the deity's favored weapon.

Patron: A divine champion must have a patron deity, and it must be the deity of which she is a champion.

CLASS SKILLS

The divine champion's class skills (and the key ability for each skill) are Climb (Str), Craft (Int), Handle Animal (Cha), Jump (Str), Knowledge (religion) (Int), Ride (Dex), Spot (Wis), and Swim (Str). See Chapter 4: Skills in the *Player's Handbook* for skill descriptions.

Skill Points at Each Level: 2 + Int modifier.

CLASS FEATURES

All the following are class features of the divine champion prestige class.

Weapon and Armor Proficiency: A divine champion is proficient with all simple and martial weapons, light armor, medium armor, and shields.

Lay on Hands **(Sp):** As a defender of the faith, a divine champion may lay on hands to heal herself or another creature following the same patron deity as himself. The ability works like a paladin's ability to lay on hands, except the divine champion may heal 1 point of damage per divine champion level times her Charisma bonus. If the divine champion is a paladin, she can combine this healing with her paladin class's *lay on hands* ability.

Fighter Feat: At 2nd level and again at 4th level, a divine champion may choose any one feat (except Weapon Specialization) from the fighter class bonus feat list in Chapter 3 of the *Player's Handbook* or any feat with the [Fighter] designator in this chapter.

Sacred Defense: Add this value (+1 at 2nd level, +2 at 4th level) to the divine champion's saving throws against divine spells, as well as the spell-like and supernatural abilities of outsiders.

Smite Infidel (Su): Once per day, a divine champion may attempt to smite a creature with a different patron deity (or no patron deity at all) with one normal melee attack. She adds her Charisma bonus to the attack roll and deals 1 extra point of damage per divine champion level. If the divine champion accidentally smites someone of the same patron, the smite has no effect but is still used up for that day. If the divine champion is also a paladin, she may use smite evil and this ability separately or combine them into a single strike if the target is evil and of a different faith.

Divine Wrath (Su): The divine champion channels a portion of her patron's power into wrath, giving her a +3 bonus on attack rolls, damage, and saving throws for a number of rounds equal to her Charisma bonus. During this time, the divine champion also has damage reduction 5/—. This ability can be used once per day and is invoked as a free action.

divine disciple

The most zealous, devout, and pious clerics, druids, and paladins possess the ability to serve their deity as intermediaries between the deity's mortal and divine servants. They interpret the divine will, act as teachers and guides to other members of the clergy, and arm the lay followers of their deity with the power of their patron. Eventually they transcend their mortal nature and embody the divine on the face of Toril.

Divine disciples are always divine spellcasters. Clerics and druids are the most common candidates for becoming divine disciples, but paladins and rangers have been known to become divine disciples, and evil deities such as Bane have been known to elevate blackguards as divine disciples in the ranks of their dark faiths.

Hit Die: d8.

REQUIREMENTS

To qualify to become a divine disciple (Dis) of a particular deity, a character must fulfill all the following criteria.

Spellcasting: Ability to cast 4th-level divine spells.

Skills: Diplomacy 5 ranks, Knowledge (religion) 8 ranks.

Patron: A divine disciple must have a patron deity, and it must be the deity of which she is a divine disciple.

CLASS SKILLS

The divine disciple's class skills (and the key ability for each skill) are Concentration (Con), Craft (Int), Diplomacy (Cha), Heal (Wis), Knowledge (arcana), (Int), Knowledge (religion) (Int), Knowledge (nature) (Int), Profession (Wis), Scry (Int, exclusive skill), Spellcraft (Int), and Wilderness Lore (Wis). See Chapter 4: Skills in the *Player's Handbook* for skill descriptions.

Skill Points at Each Level: 2 + Int modifier.

CLASS FEATURES

All the following are class features of the divine disciple prestige class.

Divine disciple of Velsharoon

LOCKWOOD

TABLE 1—10: THE DIVINE DISCIPLE

Class Level	Base Attack Bonus	Fort Save	Ref Save	Will Save	Special	Spells per Day
1st	+0	+2	+0	+2	New domain, divine emissary	+1 level of existing divine spellcasting class
2nd	+1	+3	+0	+3	Sacred defense +1	+1 level of existing divine spellcasting class
3rd	+2	+3	+1	+3	Imbue with spell ability	+1 level of existing divine spellcasting class
4th	+3	+4	+1	+4	Sacred defense +2	+1 level of existing divine spellcasting class
5th	+3	+4	+1	+4	Transcendence	+1 level of existing divine spellcasting class

Weapon and Armor Proficiency: Divine disciples gain no proficiency in any weapon or armor.

Spells per Day: A divine disciple's training focuses on divine spells. Thus, when a new disciple level is gained, the character gains new spells per day as if she had also gained a level in whatever divine spellcasting class she belonged to before she added the prestige class. She does not, however, gain any other benefit a character of that class would have gained (improved chance of controlling or rebuking undead, metamagic or item creation feats, and so on). This essentially means that she adds the level of divine disciple to the level of whatever other divine spellcasting class the character has, then determines spells per day accordingly.

If a character had more than one divine spellcasting class before she became a divine disciple, she must decide to which class she adds each level of divine disciple for the purpose of determining spells per day.

New Domain: The divine disciple may choose a new domain from her deity's available domains. The divine disciple receives the domain's granted power and may choose the domain's spells as domain spells. (The disciple now has three choices each level for domain spells instead of two.)

Divine Emissary: Divine disciples can telepathically communicate with any outsider within 60 feet, as long as that outsider serves the disciple's deity or has the same alignment as the disciple.

Sacred Defense: Add this value (+1 at 2nd level, +2 at 4th level) to the divine disciple's saving throws against divine spells, as well as the spell-like and supernatural abilities of outsiders.

Imbue With Spell Ability (Sp): As the spell, except a divine disciple does not need to use any 4th-level (or higher) spell slots to activate this ability. (She transfers currently prepared spells to her targets on a one-for-one basis without having to use a spell slot for the *imbue with spell ability* spell.) The only limit to the number of spells the divine disciple can transfer is the disciple's available 1st- and 2nd-level spells.

Transcendence: The divine disciple, through long association with her deity's outsider servants and direct intervention by her deity, transcends her mortal form and becomes a divine creature. Her type changes to outsider, which means that she acquires some immunities and vulnerabilities based on her type (see Native Outsider, under the planetouched race description). As a free action she can ward herself with a *protection from chaos/evil/good/law* spell. (She chooses which form to have when she gains the transcendence power and cannot change it thereafter.)

Upon achieving transcendence, the divine disciple's appearance usually undergoes a minor physical change appropriate to her alignment and deity. For example, the eyes of a disciple of Lathander, the Morninglord, might change to glowing gold. Anyone who shares the disciple's patron, including outsider servants of her patron, immediately recognize her transcendent nature, and she gains a +2 bonus on all Charisma-based skill and ability checks in regard to these creatures.

divine seeker

Sometimes a church cannot act openly, either because of political constraints, bureaucracy, or because it doesn't want its presence known in an area. During these times, the abilities of discretion, stealth, and speed are more valuable than the direct manifestation of power. The divine seeker fills this role, infiltrating dangerous places to rescue prisoners, reclaim stolen relics, or eliminate enemy leaders. Quiet and protected by the power of her deity, a divine seeker can often accomplish what a direct assault could not.

Divine seekers may be of any class, though they favor monks, rangers, and rogues. Barbarians and bards often have the skills to become divine seekers, but they tend to be too undisciplined or have abilities that rely on noise. Sorcerers and wizards with subtle and stealthy magic sometimes become divine seekers, but they are rare.

Hit Die: d6.

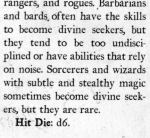

Illustration by Carlo Arellano

Divine seeker of Mask

REQUIREMENTS

To qualify to become a divine seeker (Skr) of a particular deity, a character must fulfill all the following criteria.

Skills: Hide 10 ranks, Knowledge (religion) 3 ranks, Move Silently 8 ranks, Spot 5 ranks.

Patron: A divine seeker must have a patron deity, and it must be the deity of which she is a divine seeker.

CLASS SKILLS

The divine seeker's class skills (and the key ability for each skill) are Bluff (Cha), Climb (Str), Craft (Int), Decipher Script (Int), Diplomacy (Cha), Disable Device (Dex), Intuit Direction (Wis), Jump (Str), Knowledge (religion) (Int), Listen (Wis), Move Silently (Dex), Open Lock (Dex), Pick Pocket (Dex), Profession (Wis), Search (Int), Spot (Wis), Tumble (Dex), and Use Rope (Dex). See Chapter 4: Skills in the *Player's Handbook* for skill descriptions.

Skill Points at Each Level: 6 + Int modifier.

TABLE I—11: THE DIVINE SEEKER

Class Level	Base Attack Bonus	Fort Save	Ref Save	Will Save	Special
1st	+0	+0	+2	+0	Sanctuary, thwart glyph
2nd	+1	+0	+3	+0	Sacred defense +1, sneak attack +1d6
3rd	+2	+1	+3	+1	Locate object, obscure object
4th	+3	+1	+4	+1	Sacred defense +2, sneak attack +2d6
5th	+3	+1	+4	+1	Locate creature, divine perseverance

CLASS FEATURES

All the following are class features of the divine seeker prestige class. All of the divine seeker's spell-like abilities function as if cast by a cleric with a caster level of the divine seeker's class level plus her Charisma bonus.

Weapon and Armor Proficiency: Divine seekers gain proficiency in all simple weapons and light armor.

Sanctuary **(Sp):** Once per day a divine seeker can ward herself with a *sanctuary* spell.

Thwart Glyph: A divine seeker gains a +4 bonus on all Search and Disable Device checks to locate, disable, or bypass magic glyphs, runes, and symbols.

Sacred Defense: Add this bonus (+1 at 2nd level, +2 at 4th level) to the divine seeker's saving throws against divine spells, as well as the spell-like and supernatural abilities of outsiders.

Sneak Attack: As the rogue's ability. This stacks with any sneak attack ability from another class.

Locate Object **(Sp):** Once per day, a divine seeker can use the *locate object* spell.

Obscure Object **(Sp):** Once per day, a divine seeker can use *obscure object*, which prevents her from being tracked by locating a stolen item she carries.

Locate Creature **(Sp):** Once per day, a divine seeker can use the *locate creature* spell.

Divine Perseverance: Once per day, if the divine seeker is brought to –1 or lower hit points, she automatically is cured of 1d8+5 points of damage.

Illustration by Sam Wood

Guild thief

Guild Thief

Guild thieves are thieves who operate in urban areas as part of an organized thieves' guild. They control and manipulate almost all the crime in their home cities. Guild thieves are usually organized into divisions (assassins, beggars, bounty hunters, burglars, con artists and tricksters, cutpurses and pickpockets, enforcers and thugs, racketeers, scouts and spies, and fences, pirates, and smugglers), each of which is led by a guildmaster responsible for crimes of that type. The guildmasters report to a head guildmaster. Guild thieves generally only know their own minions, their coworkers, and their superior. This web of secrecy preserves the organization, because any that are captured can only sell out a few others.

Most guild thieves are rogues, although specialists in some divisions are more likely to be fighters or rangers. Clerics of evil deities (particularly Mask and Shar) take roles in many divisions, and sorcerers and wizards also have important roles, but their prominence is dependent on the land in which they operate. (Some lands have few sorcerers and wizards or discourage them from staying or developing by placing many restrictions on them.) Guild thieves excel at working with others, intimidating common folk, administering punitive beatings, and acquiring important contacts.

Hit Die: d6.

REQUIREMENTS

To qualify to become a guild thief (Gld), a character must fulfill all the following criteria.

Skills: Gather Information 3 ranks, Hide 8 ranks, Intimidate 3 ranks, Move Silently 3 ranks.

Special: Membership in a thieves' guild.

CLASS SKILLS

The guild thief's class skills (and the key ability for each skill) are Appraise (Int), Bluff (Cha), Climb (Str), Craft (Int), Diplomacy (Cha), Disable Device (Dex), Forgery (Int), Innuendo (Wis), Intimidate (Cha), Jump (Str), Knowledge (local), Listen (Wis), Move Silently (Dex), Open Lock (Dex), Pick Pocket (Dex), Profession (Wis), Search (Int), Sense Motive (Wis), Spot (Wis), and Use Rope (Dex). See Chapter 4: Skills in the *Player's Handbook* for skill descriptions.

Skill Points at Each Level: 6 + Int modifier.

CLASS FEATURES

All the following are class features of the guild thief prestige class.

Weapon and Armor Proficiency: Guild thieves gain proficiency in all simple weapons and light armor.

Sneak Attack: As the rogue's ability. This stacks with any sneak attack ability from another class.

Doublespeak: A guild thief gains a +2 bonus on all Bluff, Diplomacy, and Innuendo checks.

Bonus Feat: A guild thief gains a feat from the following list: Alertness, Blind-Fight, Cosmopolitan, Education, Exotic Weapon Proficiency (hand crossbow), Leadership, Lightning Reflexes, Track, Skill Focus (any guild thief class skill), Still Spell, Street Smart, Weapon Finesse, Weapon Focus.

Uncanny Dodge: As the rogue ability. If a guild thief has another class that grants the uncanny dodge ability, add together all the class levels of the classes that grant the ability and determine the character's uncanny dodge ability on that basis.

Reputation: Add this value to the character's Leadership score (see the Leadership feat in Chapter 2 of the *DUNGEON MASTER's Guide*). Most guild thieves with an interest in collecting followers have a permanent base of operations within a city, which gives an additional +2 bonus on their Leadership score according to Table 2–26: Leadership Modifiers in the *DUNGEON MASTER's Guide*.

TABLE 1–12: THE GUILD THIEF

Class Level	Base Attack Bonus	Fort Save	Ref Save	Will Save	Special
1st	+0	+0	+2	+0	Sneak attack +1d6, doublespeak
2nd	+1	+0	+3	+0	Bonus feat, uncanny dodge (Dex bonus to AC)
3rd	+2	+1	+3	+1	Sneak attack +2d6, reputation +1
4th	+3	+1	+4	+1	Bonus feat, reputation +2
5th	+3	+1	+4	+1	Sneak attack +3d6, uncanny dodge (can't be flanked), reputation +3

Harper scout

Harper scouts are members of the Harpers, a secret society dedicated to holding back evil, preserving knowledge, and maintaining the balance between civilization and the wild. Harper scouts learn arcane spells and many skills to help them in their duties of espionage, stealth, and reporting information.

Many Harper scouts are bards, but by no means all. Ranger, rogue, sorcerer, and wizard are common vocations for Harper scouts, since these classes tend to have versatility and mobility. All have some skill at manipulating others, a resistance to outside mental influences, acute abilities of perception, and a talent for solving problems.

Not all Harpers are members of the Harper scout prestige class, and rank within the organization does not depend on a character's level in this or any other class. However, most of the higher-ranked Harpers have at least one level in the Harper scout prestige class.

Hit Die: d6.

REQUIREMENTS

To qualify to become a Harper scout (Hrp), a character must fulfill all the following criteria.

Alignment: Any nonevil.
Skills: Bluff 4 ranks, Diplomacy 8 ranks, Knowledge (local) 4 ranks, Perform 5 ranks, Sense Motive 2 ranks, Wilderness Lore 2 ranks.
Feats: Alertness, Iron Will.
Special: Sponsorship by a member of the Harpers, approval of the High Harpers.

CLASS SKILLS

The Harper scout's class skills (and the key ability for each skill) are Appraise (Int), Bluff (Cha), Climb (Str), Craft (Int), Diplomacy (Cha), Disguise (Cha), Escape Artist (Dex), Gather Information (Cha), Hide (Dex), Intuit Direction (Wis), Jump (Str), Knowledge (all skills taken individually) (Int), Listen (Wis), Move Silently (Dex), Perform (Cha), Pick Pocket (Dex), Profession (Wis), Sense Motive (Wis), Speak Language (Int), Swim (Str), and Tumble (Dex). See Chapter 4: Skills in the *Player's Handbook* for skill descriptions.

Skill Points at Each Level: 4 + Int modifier.

CLASS FEATURES

All the following are class features of the Harper scout prestige class.

Weapon and Armor Proficiency: A Harper scout is proficient with all simple weapons and light armor.

Harper scout Arilyn Moonblade

Spells per Day: Beginning at 1st level, a Harper scout gains the ability to cast a small number of arcane spells. The Harper scout's ability to cast these spells works exactly like a bard's ability to cast spells. (They are Charisma-based and do not need to be prepared.)

A 1st-level Harper scout learns two spells from the Harper scout 1st-level spell list. She learns two new Harper scout spells of any spell level she can cast at each Harper scout level thereafter. There is no limit to the number of these spells the Harper scout can know from this list. She may learn more by studying arcane scrolls or spellbooks.

HARPER SCOUT SPELL LIST

1st level—*change self, charm person, comprehend languages, erase, feather fall, jump, light, message, mount, read magic, scatterspray, sleep, spider climb.*

2nd level—*cat's grace, darkvision, detect thoughts, eagle's splendor, invisibility, knock, locate object, magic mouth, misdirection, see invisibility, shadow mask.*

3rd level—*clairaudience/clairvoyance, nondetection, suggestion, tongues, undetectable alignment.*

Harper Knowledge: Like a bard, a Harper scout has a knack for picking up odds and ends of knowledge. This ability works exactly like the bardic knowledge ability of the bard class. If a Harper scout has bard levels, her Harper scout levels and bard levels stack for the purpose of using bardic knowledge.

Favored Enemy: A Harper scout selects a favored enemy from the following list of evil organizations that oppose the Harpers' goals: the Church of Bane, the Cult of the Dragon, the Iron Throne, the malaugryms, the Red Wizards, or the Zhentarim. This ability works exactly like the favored enemy ability of the ranger class. If a Harper scout with ranger levels chooses a favored enemy that she already has chosen as a ranger, the bonuses stack.

When the Harper scout reaches 4th level, the bonus against her first favored enemy increases to +2, and she gains a new favored enemy at +1.

Deneir's Eye (Su): A Harper scout gains a +2 holy bonus on saving throws against glyphs, runes, and symbols.

Skill Focus: A Harper scout gains the Skill Focus feat for her Perform skill and any one other Harper scout class skill.

Tymora's Smile (Su): Once per day, a Harper scout can add a +2 luck bonus on a single saving throw. This bonus can be added after the die is rolled and after success or failure of the unmodified roll is determined.

Lliira's Heart (Su): A Harper scout gains a +2 holy bonus on saving throws against compulsion and fear effects.

Illustration by Matt Wilson

TABLE 1—13: THE HARPER SCOUT

Class Level	Base Attack Bonus	Fort Save	Ref Save	Will Save	Special	Spells per Day 1st	2nd	3rd
1st	+0	+0	+2	+2	Harper knowledge, 1st favored enemy	0	—	—
2nd	+1	+0	+3	+3	Deneir's eye, Skill Focus	1	—	—
3rd	+2	+1	+3	+3	Tymora's smile	1	0	—
4th	+3	+1	+4	+4	Lliira's heart, 2nd favored enemy	1	1	—
5th	+3	+1	+4	+4	Craft Harper Item	1	1	0

Craft Harper Item: A specialized form of the Craft Wondrous Item feat, this allows a Harper scout to create magic musical instruments, Harper pins, and certain potions (*Charisma, detect thoughts, glibness, tongues,* and *truth*). This ability replaces the need for any other item creation feat for the item. The Harper scout's casting level for these items is her Harper scout level plus all other caster levels from her other spellcasting classes. All the normal requirements for an item (such as race or spells) remain the same. All other rules for creating wondrous items or potions apply.

EX-HARPER SCOUTS

It is possible for a character to violate the code of conduct of the Harpers, endanger other Harpers through negligence or deliberate action, or intentionally turn away from the Harpers. Such an individual quickly gains a reputation among the other Harpers and can no longer progress in the Harper scout prestige class. Furthermore, the former Harper scout can no longer use the Deneir's eye, Lliira's heart, or Tymora's smile abilities. A petition to the High Harpers, a suitable quest decided upon by that group, and an *atonement* spell from a deity chosen by the High Harpers brings the former Harper scout back into good standing, and she can thereafter gain levels in the prestige class.

Hathran

Hathrans comprise an elite sisterhood of spellcasters who lead Rashemen. They are also known as the Witches of Rashemen. Within the borders of Rashemen, their powers are greater than other spellcasters of their level. In Rashemi society, hathrans occupy the place reserved for powerful clerics in most Faerûnian cultures. They heal the sick and wounded, care for the souls of their followers, recruit champions from other planes, and raise the dead. Within the hathran class (which means "learned sisterhood" in the language of Rashemen), 1st-level characters are called blethran ("sisterkin"). The 9th- and 10th-level hathrans are called othlor ("true ones") and have complete authority over all other Witches. Hathrans have the power of life and death over all citizens of Rashemen, although to misuse this authority is a serious offense against the sisterhood. When traveling in Rashemen, hathrans always wear masks. Many are sent outside their homeland to study other cultures and keep watch on important figures.

Illustration by Todd Lockwood

Hathran Lady Thelbruna of Rashemen

To be a hathran requires a certain depth of knowledge in arcane and divine magic. Usually hathrans are cleric/wizards, but some of the sisters have developed their powers as bards, druids, rangers, or sorcerers. The concept of rivalry between spellcasters is considered insane by hathrans, and they share spells with any hathran they deem able to handle the responsibility.

In Rashemi society, the creation of magic items is left to the male spellcasters, and hathrans are not allowed to learn item creation feats. (To do so causes expulsion from the sisterhood and banishment from Rashemen, so great is the social stigma.) The only exceptions are scrolls, which are used to train lesser members in arcane and divine magic. Rashemi wizards who hope to become hathran use their bonus feats for metamagic feats or Spell Mastery.

Hit Die: d4.

REQUIREMENTS

To qualify to become a hathran (Hth), a character must fulfill all the following criteria.

Alignment: Lawful good, lawful neutral, or neutral good.

Race: Human female of Rashemen or Rashemi descent.

Spellcasting: Able to cast 2nd-level arcane spells and 2nd-level divine spells.

Feats: Ethran.

Patron: Chauntea, Mielikki, or Mystra.

Special: Member in good standing of the Witches of Rashemen.

CLASS SKILLS

The hathran's class skills (and the key ability for each skill) are Alchemy (Int), Animal Empathy (Cha), Concentration (Con), Craft (Int), Intuit Direction (Wis), Knowledge (all skills taken individually) (Int), Perform (Cha), Profession (Wis), Scry (Int), Swim (Str), Speak Language, Spellcraft (Int), and Wilderness Lore (Wis). See Chapter 4: Skills in the *Player's Handbook* for skill descriptions.

Skill Points at Each Level: 2 + Int modifier.

CLASS FEATURES

All the following are class features of the hathran prestige class.

Weapon and Armor Proficiency: Hathrans gain Exotic Weapon Proficiency (whip). They gain proficiency in no new armor.

Spells per Day: A hathran's training focuses on arcane or divine

TABLE 1–14: THE HATHRAN

Class Level	Base Attack Bonus	Fort Save	Ref Save	Will Save	Special	Spells per Day
1st	+0	+2	+0	+2	Cohort, place magic	+1 level of existing spellcasting class
2nd	+1	+3	+0	+3		+1 level of existing spellcasting class
3rd	+1	+3	+1	+3	Fear (1/day)	+1 level of existing spellcasting class
4th	+2	+4	+1	+4	Circle leader	+1 level of existing spellcasting class
5th	+2	+4	+1	+4		+1 level of existing spellcasting class
6th	+3	+5	+2	+5	Fear (2/day)	+1 level of existing spellcasting class
7th	+3	+5	+2	+5		+1 level of existing spellcasting class
8th	+4	+6	+2	+6	Fear (3/day)	+1 level of existing spellcasting class
9th	+4	+6	+3	+6		+1 level of existing spellcasting class
10th	+5	+7	+3	+7	Greater command	+1 level of existing spellcasting class

spells. Thus, when a new hathran level is gained, the character gains new spells per day as if she had also gained one level in a spellcasting class (her choice) she belonged to before becoming a hathran. She does not, however, gain any other benefit a character of that class would have gained (improved chance of controlling or rebuking undead, metamagic or item creation feats, and so on). This essentially means that she adds the level of hathran to the level of whatever other spellcasting class the character has, then determines spells per day and caster level accordingly. Since all hathrans are multiclass spellcasters, some choose to expand their skill in the arcane, others the divine, and the remainder strike a balance between the two.

The hathrans also have a short custom spell list. These spells are arcane spells and must be acquired like any other arcane spell. They use spell slots of the appropriate level in the hathran's arcane spellcasting class.

HATHRAN SPELL LIST

1st level—*scatterspray.*
2nd level—*moonbeam.*
3rd level—*flashburst, moon blade.*
5th level—*moon path.*

Cohort: The hathran gains a cohort as if she had the Leadership feat (see Chapter 2 of the *DUNGEON MASTER's Guide*). This cohort is either a Rashemi female with the Ethran feat or a Rashemi male with at least one level of barbarian. This cohort does not count against any cohorts (or followers) the hathran may acquire by taking the Leadership feat.

Place Magic: The hathran's ties to the land of Rashemen are so strong that when in her homeland, she can draw upon the power of the land and its spirits to allow her to cast spells without preparing them. When using place magic, she may cast any arcane spell she knows or any divine spell on her spell list. The spell uses spell slots as normal. Casting with place magic is a full-round action. If the spell has a casting time of 1 action or longer, 1 full round is added to the casting time of the spell. If the hathran wishes to use a metamagic feat she knows on a place magic spell, 1 additional full round is added to the casting time of the spell.

Hierophant of Lathander

Note that when on her home soil, a hathran may use divine spell slots of the appropriate level to cast any of the spells on the hathran spell list, even if she doesn't know the spell as an arcane spell.

Fear (Su): A hathran can cast *fear* as a sorcerer of her highest spellcasting level. The ability is usable once per day at 3rd level, twice per day at 6th level, and three times per day at 8th level.

Circle Leader: The hathran gains the ability to become a circle leader, who is the focus person for hathran circle magic. See Chapter 2: Magic for a description of circle magic.

Greater Command (Su): The hathran can cast a quickened *greater command* once per day as a sorcerer of her highest spellcasting level.

hierophant

A divine spellcaster who rises high in the service of his deity gains access to spells and abilities of which lesser faithful can only dream. The hierophant prestige class is open to powerful divine spellcasters

who are approaching access to the strongest and most difficult divine spells. They delay the acquisition of these greatest gifts in exchange for a deeper understanding of and ability to control the power they channel.

Hit Die: d8.

REQUIREMENTS

To qualify to become a hierophant (Hie) of a particular deity, a character must fulfill all the following criteria.

Spellcasting: Able to cast 7th-level divine spells.
Skills: Knowledge (religion) or Knowledge (nature) 15 ranks.
Feat: Any metamagic feat.

CLASS SKILLS

The hierophant's class skills (and the key ability for each skill) are Concentration (Con), Craft (Int), Diplomacy (Cha), Heal (Wis), Knowledge (arcana) (Int), Knowledge (religion) (Int), Profession (Wis), Scry (Int, exclusive skill), and Spellcraft (Int). See Chapter 4: Skills in the *Player's Handbook* for skill descriptions.

Skill Points at Each Level: 2 + Int modifier.

CLASS FEATURES

All the following are class features of the hierophant prestige class.

Weapon and Armor Proficiency: Hierophants gain no proficiency in any weapon or armor.

Spells and Caster Level: Levels in the hierophant prestige class, even though they do not advance spell progression in the character's base class, still stack with the character's base spellcasting levels to determine caster level.

Special Ability: Every level, a hierophant gains a special ability of his choice from among the following:

Blast Infidel: The hierophant can use negative energy spells to their maximum effect on creatures with a different patron from the hierophant. Any spell with a description that involves inflicting or channeling negative energy (*inflict* spells, *circle of doom, harm*) cast on such creatures works as if under the effect of a Maximize Spell feat (without using a higher-level spell slot). Undead affected by this ability heal the appropriate amount of damage, regardless of their patron (if any).

Divine Reach: The hierophant can use touch spells on targets up to 30 feet away. If the spell requires a melee touch attack, the hierophant must make a ranged touch attack instead. If selected a second time as a special ability, the range increases to 60 feet.

Faith Healing: The hierophant can use healing spells to their maximum effect on creatures with the same patron as the hierophant (including the hierophant himself). Any spell with the heal-

TABLE 1–15: THE HIEROPHANT

Class Level	Base Attack Bonus	Fort Save	Ref Save	Will Save	Special
1st	+0	+2	+0	+2	Special ability
2nd	+1	+3	+0	+3	Special ability
3rd	+1	+3	+1	+3	Special ability
4th	+2	+4	+1	+4	Special ability
5th	+2	+4	+1	+4	Special ability

Illustration by Sam Wood

ing descriptor cast on such creatures works as if under the effects of a Maximize Spell feat (without using a higher-level spell slot). Any creature that falsely claims to be a follower of the hierophant's patron in hopes of gaining extra benefit instead receives none of the effects of the spell and must make a Will save (against the spell's DC) or be stunned for 1 round.

Gift of the Divine: The hierophant may transfer one or more uses of his turning ability to a willing creature. (Hierophants who rebuke undead transfer uses of rebuke undead instead.) The transfer lasts anywhere from 24 hours to a tenday (chosen at the time of transfer), and while the transfer is in effect, the number of turning attempts per day allowed to the hierophant is reduced by the number transferred. The recipient turns undead as a cleric of the hierophant's cleric level but uses her own Charisma bonus.

Mastery of Energy: The hierophant channels positive or negative energy much more effectively, increasing his ability to affect undead. Add a +4 bonus to the hierophant's turning checks and turning damage.

Metamagic Feat: The hierophant can choose a metamagic feat.

Power of Nature: Available only to hierophants with druid levels, this ability allows the hierophant to temporarily transfer one or more of his special druidic powers to a willing creature. The transfer lasts anywhere from 24 hours to a tenday (chosen at the time of transfer), and while the transfer is in effect, the hierophant cannot use the transferred power. He can transfer any of his druidic special abilities except spellcasting and animal companions.

The *wild shape* ability can be partially or completely transferred. For example, he may transfer the ability to *wild shape* once per day to the recipient and retain the rest of his uses for himself. If the hierophant can assume the form of Tiny, Huge, or dire animals, the recipient can as well.

As with the *imbue with spell ability* spell, the hierophant remains responsible to his deity for any purpose the recipient uses the transferred abilities.

Spell Power +2: This ability increases by +2 the DC for saving throws against the hierophant's divine spells and for caster level checks for his divine spells to overcome spell resistance. This ability can be selected multiple times, and stacks with itself and other spell power effects that affect divine spells.

Spell-Like Ability: The hierophant can use one of his divine spell slots to permanently prepare one of his divine spells as a spell-like ability that can be used two times per day. The hierophant does not use any components when casting the spell, although a spell that costs experience points to cast still does so, and a spell with a costly material component instead costs him 10 times that amount in experience points.

The spell normally uses a spell slot of the spell's level (or higher if the hierophant chooses to permanently attach a metamagic feat to the spell chosen). The hierophant can use an available higher-level spell slot to use the spell-like ability more than twice per day. Allocating a slot three levels higher allows him to cast the spell four times per day, and a slot six levels higher lets him cast it six times per day. For example, Lonafin the hierophant is a follower of Velsharoon and

wants to be able to create undead whenever he has the opportunity, so he permanently uses a 9th-level spell slot to get *animate dead* as a spell-like ability usable six times per day.

If selected more than one time as a special ability, this ability can apply to the same spell or to a different spell.

purple Dragon knight

The famous Purple Dragons of Cormyr are regarded across Faerûn as exemplars of disciplined, skilled, loyal soldiers. Their reputation is deserved partly because of the heroic actions of their leaders, the Purple Dragon knights.

Purple Dragon knights develop uncanny skills related to coordinating and leading soldiers. Most are fighters, rangers, or paladins, but a few bards, clerics, and rogues have been known to become Purple Dragon knights. Sorcerers and wizards tend to join the War Wizards, Cormyr's elite brigade of fighting spellcasters, while barbarians are too undisciplined, and druids and monks too "uncivilized" in Cormyr to enter this career.

In general, NPC knight commanders are responsible for leading the troops of the nation of Cormyr. Player character knights either are retirees, special liaisons to the army, or recipients of honorary titles. A character's level in this prestige class is irrelevant to his rank in the military, although higher-ranked knights tend to be of higher level. It is not necessary to have this prestige class to serve in the Purple Dragons at large.

This prestige class can be used as a model for officers in other countries, members of knightly orders, and so on. It is not necessary to have this prestige class to be an officer of the Purple Dragons, but most high-ranking officers do.

Hit Die: d10.

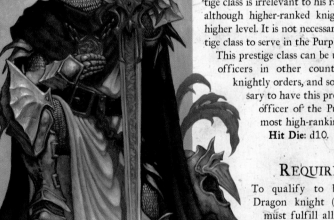
Purple Dragon knight

Illustration by Matt Wilson

REQUIREMENTS

To qualify to become a Purple Dragon knight (Prp), a character must fulfill all the following criteria.

Alignment: Any nonevil and nonchaotic.

Base Attack Bonus: +4.

Skills: Diplomacy or Intimidate 1 rank, Listen 2 ranks, Ride 2 ranks, Spot 2 ranks.

Feats: Leadership, Mounted Combat.

Special: Membership in the Purple Dragons.

TABLE 1–16: THE PURPLE DRAGON KNIGHT

Class Level	Base Attack Bonus	Fort Save	Ref Save	Will Save	Special
1st	+1	+2	+0	+0	Rallying cry, heroic shield
2nd	+2	+3	+0	+0	Inspire courage (1/day)
3rd	+3	+3	+1	+1	Fear
4th	+4	+4	+1	+1	Oath of wrath, inspire courage (2/day)
5th	+5	+4	+1	+1	Final stand

CLASS SKILLS

The Purple Dragon knight's class skills (and the key ability for each skill) are Climb (Str), Diplomacy (Cha), Intimidate (Cha), Jump (Str), Ride (Dex), Swim (Str). See Chapter 4: Skills in the *Player's Handbook* for skill descriptions.

Skill Points at Each Level: 2 + Int modifier.

CLASS FEATURES

All the following are class features of the Purple Dragon knight prestige class.

Weapon and Armor Proficiency: A Purple Dragon knight is proficient with all simple weapons, light armor, medium armor, and shields.

Rallying Cry (Su): The knight can utter a powerful shout (typically "For Cormyr!") that causes all allies within 60 feet to gain a +1 morale bonus on their next attack roll and increases their speed by 5 feet until the knight's next turn. Traditionally, the rallying cry is used when a formation of soldiers is about to charge. This mind-affecting ability may be used up to three times per day.

Heroic Shield: A knight can use the aid another action (see Chapter 8 of the *Player's Handbook*) to give an ally a +4 circumstance bonus to AC instead of the normal +2.

Inspire Courage (Su): This ability has the same effect as the bard ability of the same name. The knight makes an inspirational speech, bolstering his allies against fear and improving their combat abilities. To be affected, an ally must hear the knight speak for a full round. The effect lasts as long as the knight speaks and for 5 rounds after the knight stops speaking (or 5 rounds after the ally can no longer hear the knight). While speaking, the knight can fight but cannot cast spells, activate magic items by spell completion (such as scrolls), or activate magic items by magic word (such as wands). Affected allies receive a +2 morale bonus on saving throws against charm and fear effects and a +1 morale bonus on attack and weapon damage rolls.

Fear (Su): Once per day, a knight can evoke a *fear* effect (DC 13 + the officer's Charisma modifier). His allies are immune to the effect.

Oath of Wrath (Su): Once per day, a knight can select a single opponent within 60 feet and swear an oath to defeat him. For the duration of the encounter, the knight has a +2 morale bonus on melee attack rolls, weapon damage rolls, saves, and skill checks made against the challenged target.

The effect is negated immediately if the knight makes an attack or casts a spell targeted at any creature except the challenged opponent (attacks of opportunity do not count) or if the knight uses a full-round action to move away from the challenged opponent.

Final Stand (Su): Once per day, a knight can inspire his troops to a heroic effort, temporarily increasing their vitality. All allies within 10 feet of the knight gain 2d10 temporary hit points. This ability affects a number of creatures equal to the knight's class level + his Charisma modifier and lasts an equal number of rounds.

red wizard

The Red Wizards are the masters of Thay, the conquerors of that land's native Rashemi, and the would-be magical overlords of Faerûn. They focus on a school of magic more intently than any specialist, achieving incredible mastery of magic within a very narrow focus. Seen as cruel and evil tyrants by people across Toril, a few choose to leave their region, assume secret identities, and practice magic without having to worry about political alliances and possible slave uprisings.

Early in their careers, would-be Red Wizards specialize in a school of magic and acquire the Tattoo Focus feat that prepares them for entry into the full Red Wizard prestige class. All Red Wizards have some skill as a specialist wizard, and most follow that path exclusively, but a few dabble in other sorts of learning (such as combat or divine magic). While it is possible for a sorcerer or bard to become a Red Wizard, such misfits are ridiculed in their homeland and are incredibly rare.

Hit Die: d4.

Zulkir Aznar Thrul, Red Wizard

REQUIREMENTS

To qualify to become a Red Wizard (Red), a character must fulfill all the following criteria.

Alignment: Any nongood.

Race: Human from Thay.

Spellcasting: Ability to cast 3rd-level arcane spells.

Skills: Spellcraft 8 ranks.

Feats: Tattoo Focus and a total of three metamagic feats or item creation feats.

CLASS SKILLS

The Red Wizard's class skills (and the key ability for each skill) are Alchemy (Int), Concentration (Con), Craft (Int), Innuendo (Wis), Intimidate (Cha), Knowledge (all skills taken individually) (Int), Profession (Wis), Scry (Int), Spellcraft (Int). See Chapter 4: Skills in the *Player's Handbook* for skill descriptions.

Skill Points at Each Level: 2 + Int modifier.

CLASS FEATURES

All the following are class features of the Red Wizard prestige class.

Weapon and Armor Proficiency: Red Wizards gain no proficiency in any weapon or armor.

Spells per Day: A Red Wizard's training focuses on arcane spells. Thus, when a new Red Wizard level is gained, the character gains new spells per day as if he had also gained a level in whatever arcane spellcasting class he belonged to before he added the prestige class. He does not, however, gain any other benefit a character of that class would have gained (bonus metamagic or item creation feats, bard or assassin abilities, and so on). This essentially means that he adds the level of Red Wizard to the level of whatever other arcane spellcasting class the character has, then determines spells per day and caster level accordingly.

If a character had more than one arcane spellcasting class before he became a Red Wizard, he must decide to which class he adds each level of Red Wizard for the purpose of determining spells per day.

Illustrated by Todd Lockwood

Enhanced Specialization: Upon becoming a Red Wizard, the character increases his devotion to his wizard school of specialization. In exchange for this, the Red Wizard must sacrifice study in one or more schools. The Red Wizard must choose an additional prohibited school or schools using the rules in Chapter 3 of the *Player's Handbook*. He can never again learn spells from those prohibited schools. He cannot choose the same prohibited schools he chose as a 1st-level wizard. He can still use the prohibited spells he knew prior to becoming a Red Wizard, including using items that are activated by spell completion or spell trigger.

For example, Ghorus Toth is specialized in the school of Transmutation. His prohibited schools are Abjuration and Enchantment (option 3). When he becomes a Red Wizard, he must choose one of the other categories of prohibited schools for Transmutation listed in the School Specialization sidebar the *Player's Handbook*. His options are (1) Conjuration, (2) Evocation, or (4) any three schools. He cannot choose option (3) because there is no way to select that option without selecting schools from which he is already prohibited. If he chooses option (4), he cannot choose Abjuration or Enchantment because those are already prohibited schools for him. He decides to select Conjuration as his additional prohibited school.

Specialist Defense: Add this value to the Red Wizard's saving throws against spells from his specialist school.

Spell Power: For spells involving the Red Wizard's specialist school, add this value to the DC for saving throws and to caster level checks to overcome spell resistance. The value starts at +1 at 1st level and goes up to +2 at 4th level, +3 at 6th level, +4 at 8th level, and +5 at 10th level. This ability stacks with other spell power effects that affect spells from the Red Wizard's specialist school.

Bonus Feat: The Red Wizard can choose an item creation feat, metamagic feat, or Spell Mastery (see Chapter 3 of the *Player's Handbook*).

Circle Leader: The Red Wizard gains the ability to become a circle leader, who is the focus person for Red Wizard circle magic. See Chapter 2: Magic for information on circle magic.

Scribe Tattoo: The Red Wizard gains the ability to place the Thayan wizards' magic tattoos upon qualified novices, allowing them to select the Tattoo Focus feat and inducting them into his circle.

Great Circle Leader: The Red Wizard can be the center of a great circle, which can have up to nine assistants instead of just five. See Chapter 2: Magic for information on circle magic.

Runecaster

Runecaster

A skill originally developed by the dwarves and giants, the ability to create runes of power has spread beyond the hills and mountains. Those that choose to master this ability are runecasters, creating incredibly potent symbols that last for multiple uses and can be triggered without being touched. An established runecaster's goods are usually adorned with many runes, making his equipment very impressive-looking and a true threat to thieves.

Most runecasters are clerics or adepts because a majority of the practitioners of this ability are dwarves and giants. Some rangers and paladins have chosen to become runecasters, particularly since the Thundering has resulted in many young dwarves leaving home to explore the wilderness. A few rare druids have chosen the path of the runecaster as well, although generally only in areas where druids are so scarce that they have to rely on runes to protect a large area. Runecasting clerics and paladins use their abilities to protect their temples and holy items, while ranger runecasters use them to guard trails, lairs of threatened animals, and natural refuges.

Hit Die: d8.

REQUIREMENTS

To qualify to become a runecaster (Rnc), a character must fulfill all the following criteria.

Spellcasting: Ability to cast 3rd-level divine spells.

Skills: Spellcraft 8 ranks, Craft 8 ranks (see the Rune Magic section of Chapter 2: Magic for appropriate Craft skills).

Feats: Inscribe Rune.

TABLE I–17: THE RED WIZARD

Class Level	Base Attack Bonus	Fort Save	Ref Save	Will Save	Special	Spells per Day
1st	+0	+0	+0	+2	Enhanced specialization, specialist defense +1	+1 level of wizard
2nd	+1	+0	+0	+3	Spell power +1	+1 level of wizard
3rd	+1	+1	+1	+3	Specialist defense +2	+1 level of wizard
4th	+2	+1	+1	+4	Spell power +2	+1 level of wizard
5th	+2	+1	+1	+4	Bonus feat, circle leader	+1 level of wizard
6th	+3	+2	+2	+5	Spell power +3	+1 level of wizard
7th	+3	+2	+2	+5	Specialist defense +3, scribe tattoo	+1 level of wizard
8th	+4	+2	+2	+6	Spell power +4	+1 level of wizard
9th	+4	+3	+3	+6	Specialist defense +4	+1 level of wizard
10th	+5	+3	+3	+7	Great circle leader, spell power +5	+1 level of wizard

TABLE I—18: THE RUNECASTER

Class Level	Base Attack Bonus	Fort Save	Ref Save	Will Save	Special	Spells Per Day
1st	+0	+2	+0	+2	Rune craft +1	+1 level of existing divine spellcasting class
2nd	+1	+3	+0	+3	Rune power +1	+1 level of existing divine spellcasting class
3rd	+2	+3	+1	+3	Improved runecasting	+1 level of existing divine spellcasting class
4th	+3	+4	+1	+4	Rune craft +2	+1 level of existing divine spellcasting class
5th	+3	+4	+1	+4	Rune power +2	+1 level of existing divine spellcasting class
6th	+4	+5	+2	+5	Maximize rune	+1 level of existing divine spellcasting class
7th	+5	+5	+2	+5	Rune craft +3	+1 level of existing divine spellcasting class
8th	+6	+6	+2	+6	Improved runecasting	+1 level of existing divine spellcasting class
9th	+6	+6	+3	+6	Rune power +3	+1 level of existing divine spellcasting class
10th	+7	+7	+3	+7	Rune chant	+1 level of existing divine spellcasting class

CLASS SKILLS

The runecaster's class skills (and the key ability for each skill) are Concentration (Con), Craft (Int), Diplomacy (Cha), Heal (Wis), Knowledge (arcana), (Int), Knowledge (religion) (Int), Profession (Wis), Scry (Int, exclusive skill), and Spellcraft (Int). See Chapter 4: Skills in the *Player's Handbook* for skill descriptions.

Skill Points at Each Level: 2 + Int modifier.

CLASS FEATURES

All the following are class features of the runecaster prestige class.

Weapon and Armor Proficiency: Runecasters gain no proficiency in any weapon or armor.

Spells per Day: A runecaster's training focuses on divine spells. Thus, when a new runecaster level is gained, the character gains new spells per day as if he had also gained a level in whatever divine spellcasting class he belonged to before he added the prestige class. He does not, however, gain any other benefit a character of that class would have gained (improved chance of controlling or rebuking undead, metamagic or item creation feats, and so on). This essentially means that he adds the level of runecaster to the level of whatever other divine spellcasting class the character has, then determines spells per day accordingly.

If a character had more than one divine spellcasting class before he became a runecaster, he must decide to which class he adds each level of runecaster for purposes of determining spells per day and caster level.

Rune Craft: Add this bonus to the runecaster's Craft checks made to inscribe runes.

Improved Runecasting: As a runecaster rises in level, he can create runes that function more than once and have different means of being triggered. The extra features increase the cost of the rune, however, as shown on the table below.

Works When Read or Passed: Any attempt to study, identify, or fathom a rune's meaning counts as "reading" the rune. Passing through a portal that bears a rune counts as "passing" the rune. A rune must have an unbroken line of effect to a target to affect that target, and the target must be within 30 feet.

A rune that is triggered when passed can be set to almost any special conditions the runecaster specifies. Runes can be set according to physical characteristics (such as height or weight) or creature type, subtype, or species (such as "drow" or "aberration"). Runes can also be set with respect to good, evil, law, or chaos, or patron deity. They cannot be set according to class, Hit Dice, or level. Runes respond to invisible creatures normally but are not triggered by those who travel past them ethereally. When placing a rune with a "pass" trigger, a runecaster can specify a password or phrase that protects a creature using it from triggering the rune.

Rune Power: For runes created by the runecaster, add this value to the DC of all saves and attempts to erase, dispel, or disable the rune, and to caster level checks to overcome the spell resistance of a target.

Maximize Rune: The runecaster can create runes that are maximized, as if under the effects of a Maximize Spell feat, without altering the level of the spell being used to create the rune. Maximizing a rune adds +5 to the DC of the Craft check required to inscribe it.

Rune Chant: Whenever the runecaster casts a divine spell, he may trace a rune in the air as an extra somatic component for the spell. This allows the runecaster to gain the benefit of his rune power ability for the spell. For spells with a casting time of 1 action, this increases the casting time to 1 full round. All other spells have their casting time increased by 1 round. This ability cannot be used on stilled spells, and it does not function with the maximize rune ability.

shadow adept

Some spellcasters who discover the existence of the Shadow Weave are cautious, altering their magic slowly. Others are more reckless, and hurl themselves into the abyss of the Shadow Weave, immediately acquiring all the gifts available to the casual student and discovering secrets unavailable to all but the most dedicated. These spellcasters are the shadow adepts, who make great sacrifices in some aspects of the Art in order to reap greater benefits elsewhere.

Most shadow adepts are sorcerers or wizards, and they gain the greatest power from this path. However, any spellcaster can tap the Shadow Weave, and a few bards, druids, and rangers have been known to make this choice. Among clerics, only the followers of Shar are common in the ranks of the shadow adepts.

Hit Die: d4.

Number of Uses/Trigger	Runecaster Base Price	Level**
One	Spell level* × caster level × 50 gp	—
Charges†	Spell level* × caster level × charges × 50 gp	3
Charges per day†	Spell level* × caster level × charges × 400 gp	8
Permanent (until dispelled)††	Spell level* × caster level × 2,000 gp	8
Works when touched	Base cost	—
Works when read or passed	Base cost × 2	3

*A 0-level spell counts as 1/2 level.

**The minimum runecaster level to inscribe a rune of this type. "—" indicates the default ability granted by the Inscribe Rune feat.

†If the spell has a component or XP cost, add that cost times the number of charges to the base price of the rune.

††If the spell has a component or XP cost, add 100 times that cost to the base price of the rune.

REQUIREMENTS

To qualify to become a shadow adept (Sha), a character must fulfill all the following criteria.

Alignment: Any nongood.

Spellcasting: Ability to cast 3rd-level arcane or divine spells.

Skills: Knowledge (arcana) 8 ranks, Spellcraft 8 ranks.

Feats: Shadow Weave Magic and any metamagic feat.

CLASS SKILLS

The shadow adept's class skills (and the key ability for each skill) are Bluff (Cha), Concentration (Con), Craft (Int), Disguise (Cha), Hide (Dex), Knowledge (all skills taken individually) (Int), Profession (Wis), Scry (Int), Spellcraft (Int). See Chapter 4: Skills in the *Player's Handbook* for skill descriptions.

Skill Points at Each Level: 2 + Int modifier.

CLASS FEATURES

All the following are class features of the shadow adept prestige class.

Weapon and Armor Proficiency: Shadow adepts gain no proficiency in any weapon or armor.

Spells per Day: A shadow adept's training focuses on magic. Thus, when a new shadow adept level is gained, the character gains new spells per day as if he had also gained a level in whatever spellcasting class he belonged to before he added the prestige class. He does not, however, gain any other benefit a character of that class would have gained (improved chance of controlling or rebuking undead, metamagic or item creation feats, and so on). This essentially means that he adds the level of shadow adept to the level of whatever other spellcasting class the character has, then determines spells per and caster level accordingly.

If a character had more than one spellcasting class before he became a shadow adept, he must decide to which class he adds each level of shadow adept for the purpose of determining spells per day.

Shadow Feats: A shadow adept gains the Insidious Magic, Pernicious Magic, and Tenacious Magic feats.

Low-Light Vision (Su): A shadow adept gains low-light vision if he doesn't already have it.

Shadow Defense: Add this value to a shadow adept's saving throws against spells from the schools of Enchantment, Illusion, and Necromancy, and spells with the darkness descriptor.

Shadow adept Aeron Morieth

Illustration by Sam Wood

Darkvision (Su): A shadow adept can see in the dark as though he were permanently affected by a *darkvision* spell.

Metamagic Feat: The shadow adept can choose any one metamagic feat.

Spell Power: Add this value to the DC for saving throws and to caster level checks to overcome spell resistance for spells the shadow adept casts from the schools of Enchantment, Illusion, or Necromancy, and spells with the darkness descriptor. This stacks with other spell power effects that affect the specified spells.

Shield of Shadows (Su): A shadow adept can create a mobile disk of purple-black force as a standard action. The shield of shadows has the effects of a *shield* spell and also provides three-quarters concealment (30% miss chance) against attacks from the other side of the shield. As with the *shield* spell, the shadow adept can change the defensive direction of the shield of shadows as a free action once per round on his turn. The shadow adept can see and reach through the shield, so it does not provide cover or concealment to opponents.

The shield of shadows lasts 1 round per caster level per day and need not be used all at once. Creating or dismissing the shield of shadows is a standard action.

At 8th level, the shield also grants spell resistance of 12 + the character's shadow adept level on attacks against the shadow adept that originate from the other side of the shield, as if the shadow adept were under the effect of a *spell resistance* spell.

Shadow Walk (Sp): A shadow adept can cast the *shadow walk* spell once per day.

Shadow Double: Once per day, a shadow adept can use a standard action to create a double of himself woven from shadowstuff. The double has the ability scores, base AC, hit points, saves, and attack bonuses as its creator, but no equipment. (Any apparent clothing or equipment is nonfunctional.) The double can attack the creator's enemies if given a weapon or items (since it can use anything its creator can) or function as the target of a *project image* spell, duplicating the creator's actions and acting as the origin of the creator's spells when it is within a direct line of sight. Mentally commanding the double is a free action. Using it as the originator of a spell counts as an action for the creator and the double. Causing the creator or the double to leave the plane they share dismisses the double.

The double lasts 1 round per caster level. The death of the double does not affect the shadow adept or vice versa. The double still lasts to the end of its duration if its creator dies.

TABLE 1–19: THE SHADOW ADEPT

Class Level	Base Attack Bonus	Fort Save	Ref Save	Will Save	Special	Spells per Day
1st	+0	+0	+0	+2	Shadow feats	+1 level of existing class
2nd	+1	+0	+0	+3	Shadow defense +1, low-light vision	+1 level of existing class
3rd	+1	+1	+1	+3	Spell power +1	+1 level of existing class
4th	+2	+1	+1	+4	Shield of shadows	+1 level of existing class
5th	+2	+1	+1	+4	Metamagic feat, shadow defense +2	+1 level of existing class
6th	+3	+2	+2	+5	Spell power +2	+1 level of existing class
7th	+3	+2	+2	+5	Shadow walk, darkvision	+1 level of existing class
8th	+4	+2	+2	+6	Shadow defense +3, greater shield of shadows	+1 level of existing class
9th	+4	+3	+3	+6	Spell power +3	+1 level of existing class
10th	+5	+3	+3	+7	Shadow double	+1 level of existing class

Magic

The exact nature of the Weave is elusive because it is many things simultaneously. The Weave is the body of Mystra, the goddess of magic. Mystra has dominion over magic worked throughout Toril, but she cannot shut off the flow of magic altogether without ceasing to exist herself. The Weave is the conduit spellcasters use to channel magical energy for their spells, both arcane and divine. Finally, the Weave is the fabric of esoteric rules and formulas that comprises the Art (arcane spellcasting) and the Power (divine spellcasting). Everything from the texts of arcane spellbooks to the individual components of spells is part of the Weave. Magic not only flows from source to spellcaster through the Weave, the Weave gives spellcasters the tools they need to shape magic to their purposes.

Whenever a spell, spell-like ability, supernatural ability, or magic item functions, the threads of the Weave intertwine, knit, warp, twist, and fold to make the effect possible. When characters use divination spells such as *detect magic*, *identify*, or *analyze dweomer*, they glimpse the Weave. A spell such as *dispel magic* smooths the Weave, attempting to return it to its natural state. Spells such as *antimagic field* rearrange the Weave so that magic flows around, rather than through, the area affected by the spell.

Areas where magic goes awry, such as wild magic zones and dead magic zones, represent damage to the Weave.

The world of Toril is literally a magical place. All existence is infused with magical power, and potential energy lies untapped in every rock, every stream, every living creature, even the air itself. Raw magic is the frozen stuff of creation, the mute and mindless will of *being*, suffusing every bit of matter and present in every manifestation of energy throughout the world.

Magic permeates the peoples of Faerûn as well as the lands. Every town is home to mighty temples venerating the deities and housing clerics who call upon divine power to heal injury, ward against evil, and defend the lives and property of the faithful. Subtle and astute wizards stand by (and sometimes behind) the throne of every land, turning their formidable powers to the service of their lords. Aberrations made by ancient magic seethe and hunger in the dark spaces beneath the world's surface, awaiting the chance to feed. Even the most unimaginative fighter or most brazen rogue quickly learns to respect the power of magic, or sees her career as an adventurer come to a spectacular and ghastly end.

Wild Magic

In some areas of Toril, the Weave is so warped or frayed that magic does not function reliably. This damage may be due to some magical disaster, such as those that were common during the Time of Troubles in 1358 DR, or due to some powerful effect that distorts the Weave, such as a *mythal* (see Elven High Magic, below). Most zones of wild magic created during the Time of Troubles have since disappeared, but small pockets of wild magic remain, especially underground and in wilderness areas.

DETECTING WILD MAGIC ZONES

Wild magic zones are generally unnoticed until they make some spell or effect go awry. A character who views a wild magic zone with a *detect magic* spell detects the presence of magic on the first round and the existence of a wild magic zone on the second. If the character studies the area for 3 rounds, he can attempt a Spellcraft check (DC 25) to determine the exact borders of the affected area.

Some clever wizards use existing wild magic zones to defend their towers or strongholds. With careful study, they chart the boundaries of the wild magic effect and then use this information to best advantage when fighting on their home ground against enemy spellcasters.

The Weave

Mortals cannot directly shape raw magic. Instead, most who wield magic make use of the Weave. The Weave is the manifestation of raw magic, a kind of interface between the will of a spellcaster and the stuff of raw magic. Without the Weave, raw magic is locked away and inaccessible—an archmage can't light a candle in a dead magic zone. But, surrounded by the Weave, a spellcaster can shape lightning to blast her foes, transport herself hundreds of miles in the blink of an eye, even reverse death itself. All spells, magic items, spell-like abilities, and even supernatural abilities such as a ghost's ability to walk through walls, depend on the Weave and call upon it in different ways.

EFFECTS OF WILD MAGIC ZONES

Any spell or spell-like ability whose caster is within a wild magic zone is vulnerable to the effects of wild magic. (Wild magic does not affect supernatural, extraordinary, or natural abilities.) The caster must roll a caster level check (DC 15 + spell level). For a magic item, use its caster level for the caster level check.

If the caster level check fails, roll on Table 2–1: Wild Magic Effects to determine if the spell actually goes awry, and if so, how. Spells or spell-like abilities cast from outside a wild magic zone at targets inside the zone are not affected by the zone, nor are mobile effects brought into a wild magic zone. Only magic originating inside the zone is affected.

TABLE 2–1: WILD MAGIC EFFECTS

d%	Effect*
01–10	The spell rebounds on the caster with normal effect. If the spell cannot affect the caster, it fails.
11–25	The spell affects a random target or area. The DM should randomly choose a different target from among those in range of the spell or relocate the point of origin of the spell to a random place within range of the spell. To generate the direction in which the point of origin is moved randomly, roll 1d8 on the Grenadelike Weapons diagram in Chapter 8 of the *Player's Handbook*. To generate how far the point of origin is moved from its intended position randomly, roll 3d6. Multiply the result by 5 feet for close-range spells, 20 feet for medium-range spells, or by 80 feet for long-range spells. It is possible for the spell effect to extend outside the wild magic zone; however, its point of origin cannot exceed its range. If the result generated would do that, adjust the point of origin to the limit of the range in the randomly generated direction. Spells whose range is personal or touch simply fail.
26–40	Nothing happens. The spell does not function. Any material components are used up. The spell or spell slot is used up, and charges or uses from an item or spell-like ability are used up.
41–50	Nothing happens. The spell does not function. Any material components are not consumed. The spell is not expended from the caster's mind. (Thus, a spell slot or prepared spell can be used again.) An item does not lose charges, and the use does not count against an item's or spell-like ability's use limits.
51–55	The spell functions, but shimmering colors swirl around the caster in a 30-foot radius for 1d4 rounds. Consider this a *glitterdust* effect with a save DC of 10 + spell level of the spell that generated this result.
56–85	The spell functions normally.
86–95	The spell functions normally, but any material components are not consumed. The spell is not expended from the caster's mind. (Thus, a spell slot or prepared spell can be used again.) An item does not lose any charges that would have been expended, and the use does not count against an item's or spell-like ability's use limits.
96–100	The spell functions at increased strength. Saving throws against the spell suffer a –2 penalty. The spell is maximized as if with the Maximize Spell feat. If the spell is already maximized, this result has no further effect.

SUPPRESSING WILD MAGIC

Through hard-earned experience, Faerûn's spellcasters have stumbled across a couple of methods for dealing with a wild magic zone. An area dispel use of *dispel magic* cast into a wild magic zone causes magic in the area covered by the spell to function normally for 1d4 minutes. An area dispel use of *greater dispelling* causes magic to work normally for 1d4×10 minutes. A *wish* or *miracle* spell permanently repairs all wild magic zones in a 30-foot-radius area (or a 30-foot-

mystra and the weave

Open any three books describing the magic and mage lore of Faerûn, and you're apt to find three conflicting accounts of the origins and true nature of magic. Some of this apparent contradiction is deliberate falsehood designed to restrict the mastery of magic to those beings properly trained. Much of the rest of it arises from strange views or outright mistakes often unwittingly reproduced by later scholars.

Hear now the truth of things, as best it is understood. To speak simply, all known worlds and planes swarm with ever-present energies. Large and small, free-flowing or bound by physical barriers or magical effects (themselves merely energies shaped and designed to restrict or hold other energies); these surges and dissipations of energy give light and life and movement to everything. They are the stuff of life itself, and they would be present even if all living and once-living things on Toril were stripped away to bare rocks.

What some folk refer to as magic and wizards speak of as the Art is the means by which some beings can call on the ever-present energies and wield them to create effects. Sorcerers do this instinctively through an innate gift and the incredible force of their personalities. Bard songs waken echoes of the songs of beginning, the music of creation itself. Wizards construct processes—spells—enabling them to bend the Weave to their will in order to do what they desire. The divine power infusing any cleric holding the spells of her god or goddess can do the same, shaping the Weave through the holy (or unholy) power granted her.

Many types of magic—rune magic, shadow magic (not to be confused with the Shadow Weave), gem magic, elemental magic, even the elven high magic of old—have been spoken of down the years, but these are all merely different processes or paths to the same mastery of natural energies. This endless, ever-shifting web of forces is known as the Weave. Humans refer to the entity or awareness that is bound to the Weave of Toril as Mystra, and worship her as their goddess of magic.

The present Mystra is a recently ascended mortal woman, who took over from her exhausted predecessor during the Time of Troubles. Mystra exists to give magic to all creatures and to control its use. In ancient times, the archmages of Netheril ignored the dictates of Mystryl, goddess of magic at the time. One, the wizard Karsus the Mad, tried to seize divinity by the casting of mighty spells that would have wrecked Toril's Weave. Mystryl sacrificed herself to save the Weave. Her successor Mystra decreed that no mortals would be allowed to wield such terrible magic again—and that decree holds to this day.

Mystra wards the Weave against those powerful or reckless enough to damage it further. Until the world changes or the divine powers themselves lay down their guardianship over human affairs, the high and perilous magic of the past remains locked away under Mystra's eye.

radius portion of a larger wild magic zone). None of these spells, however, are effective against wild magic effects caused by a *mythal*.

dead magic

In some areas of Toril, the Weave is absent altogether. The Weave has a tear or hole, and the area effectively has no magic at all. Like the rare wild magic zones, many regions of dead magic were created during the Time of Troubles and have since faded or retreated. Dead magic zones often persist in places where extreme concentrations of magical power were abruptly scattered or destroyed—in the vicinity of a shattered *mythal*, at the spot where an artifact was broken, or at the scene of a god's death.

DETECTING DEAD MAGIC

Spellcasters and creatures with spell-like or supernatural abilities immediately notice when they enter a zone of dead magic. Spellcasters are attuned to the Weave, and they feel uneasy and uncomfortable in dead magic zones. A Weave user can take a move-equivalent action to note the exact boundary of a dead magic zone. Shadow Weave users are not attuned to the Weave and experience no such unusual sensations in regions of dead magic.

Any spellcaster, Weave or Shadow Weave, can use a *detect magic* spell to delineate the extent of any dead magic within the spell's range. Naturally, a Weave user must be outside the affected area in order to employ this tactic.

EFFECTS OF DEAD MAGIC

A dead magic zone functions in most respects as an *antimagic field* spell, except that it does not impede the spells or spell-like abilities of Shadow Weave users, nor does it interfere with the operation of Shadow Weave magic items. Divination spells cannot detect subjects that are within dead magic zones. Finally, it isn't possible to use a teleportation effect to move into or out of a dead magic zone.

A dead magic area cannot temporarily be returned to normal function. A *wish* or *miracle* spell permanently repairs all dead magic zones in a 30-foot-radius area (or a 30-foot-radius portion of a larger dead magic zone).

spellfire

Spellfire is the raw energy of the Weave. It can be manipulated in two ways. Mystra gives the silver fire ability to her Chosen and certain other favored servants. The spellfire ability—the wielding of true spellfire—is by far the more powerful of these rare and precious talents. It is a random gift bestowed upon only a handful of women and men in a generation.

Spellfire in any form is refined, controlled raw magic. In beneficent manifestations, it is a font of silver light and healing energy. In battle, it is a searing blue-white jet of all-consuming radiance.

SILVER FIRE

This powerful supernatural ability is unique to the Chosen of Mystra. Manifesting as a beautiful silver-white flame that surrounds the wielder and fills the area into which it is projected, silver fire can be used for different effects. It can act as a *ring of warmth* or a *ring of mind shielding*, allow the user to breathe water, or banish all external magical compulsions upon the user as if a *greater dispelling* spell were cast upon her. Only one of the above effects can be used at any time.

The user can call upon silver fire to revitalize her, allowing her to function without food or drink for up to seven days. (This function can only be used once a tenday.) Once every 70 minutes she may unleash silver fire as a blast of flame. This blast may be in an area 5 feet wide and up to 70 feet long, breaking through barriers as a *lightning bolt* would and overcoming magical barriers and spell resistance automatically. This blast deals 4d12 points of fire damage (Reflex half DC 23). Alternately, the silver fire can be unleashed in a 70-foot cone, dealing no damage but permanently restoring dead magic zones within the cone to normal and dispelling (as a *greater dispelling* spell) any *antimagic field* effects that contact the cone. This cone effect is draining on the Weave, and Mystra discourages its use except for emergencies.

All effects function as if cast by a 20th-level sorcerer.

SPELLFIRE

Persons gifted with the spellfire ability can do amazing things, dependent upon their skill, talent, and the amount of magical energy they have within them at the time. In general, spellfire can be used to heal, create blasts of destructive fire, or absorb magical effects it contacts, although the exact effects vary by circumstance and user. Talented wielders can release multiple blasts at once or even fly using the ability.

A spellfire wielder can ready an action to absorb spells targeted at her as if she were a *rod of absorption*. She gets one level of spellfire energy for every spell level absorbed and can store a number of spellfire energy levels equal to her Constitution score.

The story of spellfire

Right or wrong, legends hold that only one person in all Faerûn is gifted with true spellfire at a time. Gossip identifies that one person today as the lass Shandril Shessair, an orphaned kitchen-maid from a tavern in Highmoon of Deepingdale.

Shandril has spellfire, yes, and a hundred mages hound her for it, Zhentarim and Thayans and Cult of the Dragon and independents, slaughtering each other in their ruthless pursuit of her power. Learn this, if you heed nothing else in this book: Legends lie.

Mystra's Chosen wield lesser spellfire, if they care to call on it, and some among them command true spellfire.

A mage hiding in the Border Kingdoms possesses true spellfire, and a cruel and arrogant noble of Chessenta, and the wizard R— but I'm sure you grasp my point.

In the early Sword Coast North, the ranger Haelam Sunder-stone undoubtedly possessed spellfire. He stood alone against an orc horde pouring south past the Coldwood—and turned them into smokes and scorch scars.

I could go on. So can anyone who cares to spend the years in study at Candlekeep that I did before I chose to flee to this nameless backwater keep and cloak myself in squalor and obscurity.

Why did I spend my fortune and my eyesight, and then steal away to here, to grow wizened and ugly and bent?

Why? Well, because I have true spellfire too, of course. Come looking for me, and I will blast you to dust, and then lay waste to all your descendants, ancestors, and the realm you came from, every last tree and stone of it. Why? Well, it's what I usually do.

—*Baerendra Riverhand, Sage of Spandeliyon*

As a standard action, she may expend these spellfire energy levels as a ranged touch attack (maximum range 400 feet), dealing 1d6 points of spellfire damage per level expended (Reflex half DC 20). Spellfire damage is half fire damage and half raw magical power, just like the damage of a *flame strike* spell is half fire and half divine energy. Creatures with immunity, resistance, or protection against fire apply these effects to half the damage.

A spellfire wielder can also heal a target by touch, restoring 2 hit points per spellfire energy level expended for this purpose.

Unlike most supernatural abilities, spellfire is affected by spells and magic items that affect spell-like abilities, such as a *rod of absorption* or a *rod of negation* (if pointed at the manifestation rather than the wielder). It can be thwarted or counterspelled by *dispel magic*, and theoretically a spellfire wielder could counterspell another's spellfire. However, spellfire is a supernatural ability and does not provoke an attack of opportunity when used, nor is it subject to spell resistance.

secret Lore

Since the days when elves, dwarves, giants, and dragons ruled a Faerûn of trackless forest and unspoiled wilderness, those who could manipulate the Weave have sought deeper understanding, greater power, and hidden knowledge in the hope of gaining an advantage over their enemies. The early human empires were no different. The Imaskari mastered the lore of *gates* and *portals*, transporting thousands of hapless slaves from other worlds to serve their arcane might. The Netherese studied the art of devising magic devices, creating marvels and terrors that still slumber under the sands of Anauroch. The Raumathari blighted Faerûn forever by summoning hordes of orc warriors to serve in their war against old Narfell and then losing control of their own warriors.

Wizards dream of secret schools of magic, paths of spells made possible by a new understanding of the Art, and forbidden studies leading to awesome new powers. Dozens of paths to power and understanding have been tried and abandoned, and new research—some founded in meticulous study, some inspired by fevered flights of horror—routinely unveils some new methodology of arcane spellcasting or results in spells never before seen in Faerûn.

Stories abound of the legendary spells of old Netheril and the vanished elven realms, spells whose power dwarfed that of the mightiest *wish* possible today. Wizards have unlocked the secrets of a dark Weave unfettered by Mystra's power, clerics and adepts draw potent spells

with runes, and the wreckage of ancient dweomers lie scattered across the land in the form of a *portal* network riddling the fabric of space.

The shadow weave

During the course of her eternal war with the goddess Selûne, the goddess Shar created the Shadow Weave in response to Selûne's creation of Mystra and the birth of the Weave. If the Weave is a loose mesh permeating reality, the Shadow Weave is the pattern formed by the negative space between the Weave's strands. It provides an alternative conduit and methodology for casting spells.

Shar, being the goddess of secrets, has mostly kept the secret of the Shadow Weave to herself. Over the millennia some mortals, mainly her servants, have been allowed to discover the Shadow Weave or have stumbled across it in their researches.

Shadow Weave users enjoy several advantages. First, they ignore disruptions in the Weave. A Shadow Weave effect works normally in a dead magic or wild magic zone. (An *antimagic field*, which blocks the flow of magic, remains effective against Shadow Weave magic, as does spell resistance.) Skilled Shadow Weave users are able to cast spells that are extraordinarily difficult for Weave users to perceive, counter, or dispel.

Shadow Weave users also suffer some disadvantages. First, Shar has full control over the Shadow Weave and can isolate any creature from it or silence it entirely without any harm to herself. Second, the secrets of the Shadow Weave are disquieting and injurious to the mortal mind. Without assistance from Shar, a Shadow Weave user loses a bit of his or her mind. Third, while the Weave serves equally well for any kind of spell, the Shadow Weave is best for spells that sap life or muddle the mind and senses, and is unsuited to spells that manipulate energy or matter—and cannot support any spell that produces light. (See the Shadow Weave Magic feat in Chapter 1: Characters for details.)

Finally, the more familiar a mortal becomes with the secrets of the Shadow Weave, the more divorced she becomes from the Weave. An accomplished Shadow Weave user can work spells that Weave users find difficult to detect, dispel, or counter, but the Shadow Weave user also becomes similarly unable to affect spells worked through the Weave.

SHADOW WEAVE MAGIC ITEMS

Magic items created by those who use the Shadow Weave are rare and dangerous. Only the clergy of Shar and Shar's few arcane devotees create any number of Shadow Weave items. Shadow adepts unal-

The Magister

At any time in Faerûn, one wizard is anointed by Mystra and Azuth as the Magister. Most believe that this office is usually gained through competition (seizing it from the incumbent in an often fatal spell duel). Holding it confers special powers on its owner. It also imperils its holder by making him or her the target of many ambitious and powerful mages all over Faerûn.

The Magister is the personal champion of Mystra. This doesn't mean the Magister fights on Mystra's behalf, but rather that the office is intended to further the influence and power of Mystra by making magic more available to any who would seek to know its secrets. Magisters often goad or teach other wizards to develop new spells, improve old ones, and increase their own magical powers as pupils or challengers of the Magister.

A Magister gains special powers and access to many spells

unknown to normal wizards and sorcerers. Mages who come from competitive lands such as Thay inevitably see ascension to Magister as a way to become the most powerful wizard in Faerûn. They crave the special powers of the office to use them to slay old foes and potential rivals and to seize any magic that interests them. The violent history of the office reflects the ambitions of such deadly and selfish wizards. However, Magisters who allow themselves to be guided by higher purposes are taught, cajoled, and guided personally by the god Azuth, and given tasks that spread magic.

To most mortals of Faerûn, a serving Magister is someone who appears without warning to bestow magic, issue a warning, or hurl or prevent a spell. Why create Magisters, and have them behave thus? As the old wizards' maxim says: "Gods work in mysterious ways, and magic is the greatest mystery of all."

lied to Shar's church are rare and reclusive enough that only a handful of magic items are manufactured as Shadow Weave items.

Shadow Weave items are nearly identical to items created by Weave users, but the differences are profound.

Spell-like effects generated from Shadow Weave items have the same benefits and limitations that a Shadow Weave spellcaster has: Effects from the schools of Enchantment, Illusion, and Necromancy gain a +1 bonus on their save DCs and a +1 bonus on caster level checks to overcome spell resistance. The same benefits apply to effects with the darkness designator. Effects from the schools of Evocation and Transmutation have their caster levels reduced by one (though their costs are based on the original caster level). The reduced caster level affects the spell's range, duration, damage, and any other level-dependent variables the effect might have. The effect's save DC is reduced by −1 and caster level checks to overcome spell resistance suffer a −1 penalty. The DC to dispel Evocation or Transmutation effects from a Shadow Weave item is 11 + the reduced caster level. In general, Shadow Weave users do not bother to create items that include Evocation or Transmutation effects.

Shadow Weave items cannot generate effects with the light designator.

Shadow Weave items can pose a serious danger to users who are not familiar with the mysteries of the Shadow Weave. Activating a Shadow Weave item through spell completion, spell trigger, or command word deals 1d4 points of temporary Wisdom damage to the user unless the user has the Shadow Weave Magic feat. A use-activated Shadow Weave item deals 1 point of temporary Wisdom damage the first time it is used each day unless the user has the Shadow Weave Magic feat. If the item functions continuously, the temporary Wisdom damage occurs at dusk each day or when the user takes off or puts aside the item, whichever comes first.

Elven High Magic

In ancient times, before the Weave took on its present form, the rules of magic were different. Many beings experimented with powerful dweomers that produced larger and much more potent effects than are possible today. Many minor and major artifacts date back to these times.

Just as one can find ancient artifacts scattered across Faerûn, one also can find ancient and powerful magical effects still lingering (and usually functioning erratically) today. The most famous of these is the *mythal* of Myth Drannor (see the section on the forest of Cormanthor in Chapter 4: Geography). A *mythal* is an ancient form of elven magic created by a group of spellcasters working together to create a lasting magical effect over a large area. *Mythals* that remain today usually are beginning to fail but resist attempts to dispel them. They can produce any number of bizarre effects, including wild magic (see the Wild Magic section above). The exact nature of such effects varies with each *mythal*.

Rune Magic

In the snowbound mountains of the North, dwarves and giants have dwelled for uncounted years as rivals and enemies, and their deeds are only rumored in human lands. In the lore of the shield dwarves, runes—carefully inscribed symbols from the secret characters of the dwarven alphabet—can be carved to hold spells of great potency.

LEARNING THE RUNES

In order to use rune magic, a character must learn the Inscribe Rune feat (see Chapter 1: Characters). Rune magic is strongly tied to the dwarven and giant deities and is thus the province of divine spellcasters. Some students of rune magic choose to virtually abandon the normal practice of magic in order to concentrate on their chosen medium, becoming runecasters of great power.

CREATING RUNES

If you know Inscribe Rune, any divine spell you currently have prepared can instead be cast as a rune. A rune is a temporary magical writing similar to a scroll. It can be triggered once before it loses its magical power, but it lasts indefinitely until triggered. A rune written or painted on a surface fades away when expended, erased, or dispelled. A rune carved into a surface remains behind as a bit of nonmagical writing even after its magic is expended.

Inscribing a rune takes 10 minutes plus the casting time of the spell to be included. When you create a rune, you can set the caster level at anywhere from the minimum caster level necessary to cast the spell in question to your own level. When you create a rune, you make any choices that you would normally make when casting the spell.

You must provide any material components or focuses the spell requires. If casting the spell would reduce your XP total, you pay this cost upon beginning the rune in addition to the XP cost for making the rune itself.

Inscribing a rune requires a Craft check against a DC of 20 + the level of the spell used. The Craft skill you use is anything appropriate to the task of creating a written symbol on a surface (metalworking, calligraphy, gemcutting, stonecarving, woodcarving, and so on). You paint, draw, or engrave the rune onto a surface and make the check. (Dwarves usually engrave their runes in stone or metal in order to take advantage of their racial affinity for these items.)

If the check fails, the rune is imperfect and cannot hold the spell. The act of writing triggers the prepared spell, whether or not the Craft check is successful, making the spell unavailable for casting until you rest and regain spells. That is, the spell is expended from your currently prepared spells, just as if it had been cast.

A single Medium-size or smaller object can hold only one rune. Larger objects can hold one rune per 25 square feet (an area 5 feet square) of surface area. Runes cannot be placed on creatures. The rune has a base price of the spell level × caster level × 100 gp (a 0-level spell counts as 1/2 level). You must spend 1/25 of its base price in XP and use up raw materials costing half this base price. A rune's market value equals its base price.

TRIGGERING RUNES

Whoever touches the rune triggers the rune and becomes the target of the spell placed in it. The rune's creator may touch the rune safely without triggering it, or deliberately trigger it if he so desires. (Runemakers often carry healing or restorative runes for just this purpose.) The rune itself must be touched in order to trigger it, so an object with a rune may be handled safely as long as care is taken to avoid contacting the rune. If the spell only affects objects, then an object must trigger the rune. Triggering a rune deliberately is a standard action.

As with a *symbol* spell, a rune cannot be placed upon a weapon with the intent of having the rune triggered when the weapon strikes a foe.

Unlike the spell *glyph of warding*, the rune spell is not concealed in any way and is obvious to anyone inspecting the object holding the rune. A *read magic* spell allows the caster to identify the spell held in a rune with a successful Spellcraft check (DC 15 + the spell's level).

DISARMING RUNES

Runes can be disarmed or deactivated in several ways. A successful *erase* spell deactivates a rune (DC 15 + your caster level). Touching the rune to erase it does not trigger the rune unless the *erase* spell fails to deactivate the rune.

A *dispel magic* spell targeted on an untriggered rune can dispel its magic if successful (DC 11 + your caster level). Untriggered runes are not subject to area dispels. Finally, a rogue can use her Disable Device skill to disable runes (DC 25 + the spell's level), like any magic trap.

circle magic

Some of the most powerful and spectacular spells worked across Faerûn are cast in the form of circle magic. Circle magic is a type of cooperative spellcasting that allows the spellcaster leading the circle to increase her caster level significantly and achieve results otherwise unavailable to the spellcasters composing the circle. The Red Wizards of Thay and the Witches of Rashemen make frequent use of circle magic. Stories of other forms of circle magic abound in Faerûn.

PARTICIPATION

The ability to participate in circle magic requires the selection of a character feat—Tattoo Focus for a Red Wizard or Ethran for a Witch of Rashemen.

One spellcaster, usually the most powerful or experienced character present, stands at the center of the circle. This character is the circle leader. A hathran must be at least 4th level in the hathran prestige class to be a circle leader. A Red Wizard cannot be a circle leader unless he is at least a 5th-level Red Wizard.

A circle requires a minimum of two participants plus the circle leader. Up to five participants can aid a circle leader in a standard circle, but a Red Wizard of 10th level can lead a great circle containing up to nine participants.

All participants in a circle must stand within 10 feet of the circle leader, who stands in the center.

CIRCLE POWERS

The first use of circle magic is to empower the circle leader with the strength of all the participants. This requires 1 full hour of uninterrupted concentration on the part of all participants and the circle leader. Each participant casts any single prepared spell, which is consumed by the circle and has no effect other than expending the prepared spell. The spell levels expended by the circle participants are totaled as circle bonus levels. Each bonus level may be used to accomplish the following effects:

- Increase the circle leader's caster level by one for every bonus level expended (maximum caster level 40th).
- Add Empower Spell, Maximize Spell, or Heighten Spell metamagic feats to spells currently prepared by the circle leader. Each bonus level counts as one additional spell level required by the application of a metamagic feat to a spell. The circle leader may add the feats listed to a spell even if he does not know the feat or if the addition of the feat would raise the spell level past the circle leader's normal maximum spell level (maximum spell level 20th).
- Increase the circle leader's level by one for level checks (dispel checks, caster level checks, and so on) for every bonus level expended (maximum level 40th).

These effects last for 24 hours or until expended. Circle bonus levels may be divided up as the circle leader sees fit. For example, the Red Wizard Hauth Var leads a circle in which four participants each cast 2nd-level spells. Hauth Var chooses to use three circle bonus levels to maximize his *cone of cold* spell, three to increase his caster level from 10th to 13th level for all level-based variables in his spells, and two to add a +2 bonus to any level checks he needs to make. The maximized spell is used up whenever he casts his *cone of cold*, and the other two effects remain for the next 24 hours. Many high-level Red Wizards lead circles on a daily basis to exact magical power from their apprentices.

portals

Magic *portals* link many places across Toril. A *portal* is simply a permanent teleportation effect that safely whisks its user to a predetermined place. Most *portals* lead from one place on Toril to another, but a few lead to other planes or other celestial bodies in the skies of Toril.

qualities of portals

Hundreds of archmages, high priests, secret circles, monstrous races, and dark cabals had a hand in creating the multitude of hidden doorways riddling Faerûn. Magic of this sort is unusually durable, and often survives for centuries—or millennia—after its creators have vanished into history or lost any use for their handiwork. Accordingly, the workings of *portals* are mysterious and unpredictable. Each one is built for a reason, but all too often these reasons are lost when the creator passes into history or obscurity.

Portals share some common features and qualities. All *portals* are two-dimensional areas, usually a circle with a radius of up to 15 feet, but sometimes square, rectangular, or another shape. The *portal* itself is intangible and invisible.

Portals often come in pairs or networks. A single *portal* is a one-way trip. There must be a matching *portal* at the destination to return. Some *portals* are attuned to several potential destinations, each equipped with a matching *portal*, but most are simply two-way doors between one point and another far distant. Once created, a *portal* cannot be moved.

DETECTING PORTALS

An archway or frame of some kind usually marks a *portal*'s location so it can be found when needed and so that creatures don't blunder into it accidentally. *Detect magic* can reveal a *portal*'s magical aura. If the *portal* is currently functioning (ready to transport creatures), it has a strong aura. If the *portal* is not currently able to transport creatures (usually because it has a limited number of uses, and they are currently exhausted), it has a weak aura. Strong or weak, a *portal* radiates transmutation magic.

The *analyze portal* spell can reveal even more about a *portal*.

PORTAL OPERATION

Creatures who touch or pass through the area of the *portal* are instantly teleported to the locale the *portal*'s builder has specified. (The teleportation effect is similar to *teleport without error* cast by a 17th-level caster, except that interplanar travel is possible.) It is not possible to poke one's head through a *portal* to see what's on the other side. A *portal* can only transport creatures that can fit through the *portal*'s physical dimensions.

If a solid object blocks the destination, the portal does not function. Creatures, however, do not block *portals*. If a creature already occupies the area where a *portal* leads, the user is instead transported to a suitable location as close as possible to the original destination. A suitable location has a surface strong enough to support the user and enough space to hold the user.

Unattended objects cannot pass though a *portal*. For example, a character can carry any number or arrows through a *portal*, but he cannot fire an arrow through a *portal*. An unattended object that hits a *portal* simply bounces off.

Unless the builder has preset some limit, any number of creatures can pass through a *portal* each round. A creature using a *portal* can take along up to 850 pounds of gear. In this case, gear is anything a creature carries or touches. If two or more creatures touch the same piece of equipment, it counts against both creatures' weight limits.

This active portal gives a glimpse of what awaits on the other side.

KEYED PORTALS

Portal builders often restrict access to their creations by setting conditions for their use. Special conditions for triggering a *portal* can be based on the possession of a *portal key*, the creature's name, identity, or alignment, but otherwise must be based on observable actions or qualities. Intangibles such as level, class, Hit Dice, or hit points don't qualify.

A keyed *portal* remains active for 1 full round. Any creature who touches the activated *portal* in the same round also can use the *portal*, even if such creatures don't have a key themselves.

Many *portal keys* are rare and unusual objects that the creature using the *portal* must carry. Some *portals* are keyed to work only at a particular time, such as sunrise, sunset, the full moon, or midnight. Spells can serve as *portal keys*, as can the channeling of positive or negative energy. When the *portal* is the target of the specified spell or within the spell's area or touched by its effect, the spell is absorbed and the *portal* is activated. Any form of the spell works to activate the *portal*, including spell-like effects of creatures or magic items and spells from scrolls.

SEALING PORTALS

A *portal* cannot be destroyed by physical means or by spell effects that destroy objects (such as *disintegrate*). A successful targeted *dispel magic* (DC 27) causes a *portal* to become nonfunctional for 1d4 rounds. *Mordenkainen's disjunction* destroys a *portal* unless it makes a Will save (a *portal*'s Will save bonus is +10). The spell *gate seal* (described later in this chapter) locks a *portal* and prevents its operation.

unusual portals

Things are never certain in the many lands of Faerûn, and *portals* are not always entirely reliable. *Portal*-makers have created through design or mischance *portals* with many insidious and dangerous characteristics.

RANDOM PORTALS

These *portals* can only be activated at random times. They may or may not require a key for activation when they are working. A fairly common random pattern is a *portal* that works until 1d6+6 creatures use it, then shuts down for 1d6 days. Other patterns are possible.

VARIABLE PORTALS

These *portals* are hazardous in the extreme for those who are unfamiliar with their quirks. Creatures using these *portals* are transported to any one of several preset locations. The destination sequence may follow a set pattern or may be random.

Some variable *portals* have keys that allow users to choose a specific destination served by the *portal*. Others function by transporting users to a default location—an inescapable dungeon, the innards of a volcano, or some particularly hostile outer plane—*unless* the user presents the proper key.

CREATURE-ONLY PORTALS

These *portals* transport only the creatures that use them, not the creatures' clothing and equipment. Such *portals* are often used defensively to render intruders vulnerable after they use the *portals*. A rare and more difficult variation on this type of *portal* transports creatures to one area and their equipment to another.

MALFUNCTIONING PORTALS

The other types of unusual *portals* are generally created through careful effort by their makers. Malfunctioning *portals*, on the other hand, are almost always unintended.

Over the centuries, prodigious forces have swept over Toril, profoundly affecting magic. Because of decades (or centuries or millennia) of magical wear and tear or the strength of the cataclysmic forces to which they have been exposed, many ancient dweomers have gone slowly awry. *Portals* are no exception.

A malfunctioning *portal* is usually at least one hundred years old, but many are far older. Using one can have many different results. Roll once on Table 2–2: Portal Malfunction each time a malfunctioning *portal* is activated. If such a *portal* functions continuously, the effect indicated lasts 1d10 rounds, and anyone using the *portal* during that time is subject to that effect.

TABLE 2–2: PORTAL MALFUNCTION

d%	Effect
01–05	The *portal* does not function, but draws magical power from the user in an attempt to power itself. The user is affected as though struck by a targeted dispel effect of a *greater dispelling* spell cast at 17th level.
06–10	The *portal* does not function, but draws magical power from the user's items in an attempt to power itself. A random number of items (1d10) are struck by an effect similar to a targeted *greater dispelling* cast at 17th level. Use Table 10–1: Items Affected by Magical Attacks, in the *Player's Handbook* to determine which items are affected. Successful dispelling suppresses permanent magic items for 1d4 rounds. Charged or limited-use items lose 1d4 charges or uses as if they had been used to no effect and are suppressed for the same number of rounds (if still magical).
11–20	The *portal* does not function. The user is hurled away as though struck by the violent thrust of a *telekinesis* spell cast at 17th level. The user is entitled to a Will save (DC 17) to negate the effect and takes 1d6 points of damage if hurled against a solid surface.
21–25	The *portal* does not function. Instead, a wave of negative (50%) or positive energy (50%) emanates from the *portal* in a 30-foot radius. Negative energy acts just like an *inflict serious wounds* spell cast at 17th level (3d8+15 points of damage, Will half DC 14). Positive energy acts just like a *cure serious wounds* spell cast at 17th level.
26–40	The *portal* functions, but it sends the user to the wrong destination. To determine where the user ends up, use the table in the *teleport* spell description (Chapter 11 of the *Player's Handbook*) and roll 1d20+80 as on the "false destination" line.
41–50	Nothing happens. The *portal* does not function.
51–100	The *portal* functions normally.

Building a portal

Any character can build a *portal* if she knows the Create Portal feat and either the *teleport, teleport without error, teleportation circle,* or *gate* spell. The *portal* can lead to any locale the builder has personally visited at least once. The *portal* fails if the builder chooses a destination that cannot safely hold her (such as inside a solid object or into thin air). The *portal* also fails if the destination is a locale where astral travel is blocked (see the *teleport* spell description).

Base Cost: The builder must spend 50,000 gp on raw materials to create a single, continuously active one-way *portal* covering an area up to 10 feet in radius (about 300 square feet). The market value of a *portal* is twice its cost in raw materials. Crafting a *portal* requires one day for each 1,000 gp in its market price, and 1/25 of the market price in XP (one hundred days and 4,000 XP for the base *portal*).

The builder can create a second *portal* at the destination point, making a two-way *portal,* for half price (25,000 gp, fifty days, 2,000 XP).

Larger and Smaller Portals: A *portal* can be crafted as small as 1 square foot (about a 6-inch radius), but this does not reduce the cost. The smallest *portal* usable by a Medium-size creature is 12 square feet (roughly a 2-foot radius). Small creatures can use *portals* as small as 7 square feet (an 18-inch radius), and Tiny creatures can pass through *portals* of 2 square feet (a 10-inch radius). Diminutive and Fine creatures are the only beings who can pass through *portals* of 1 square foot.

Larger *portals* add 100% to the base cost for each extra 300 square feet of area or fraction of 300 square feet. Large and Huge creatures can pass through a standard *portal,* but Gargantuan and Colossal creatures generally need double- or triple-sized *portals.*

Special Properties: Some special properties add significantly to the cost of creating a *portal.*

Keyed Portals: Keyed *portals* may be created at no extra cost. The key must be designated during the creation of the device and cannot be changed after that.

Random Portals: Random *portals* may be created at no extra cost. The conditions must be designated during the creation of the *portal* and cannot be later changed.

Variable Portals: Variable *portals* add 25% to the base price per extra destination after the first included in the device. For example, a continuously active *portal* with two variable destinations costs 62,500 gp to make. A continuously active *portal* with three variable destinations costs 75,000 gp to make.

Creature-Only Portals: Creature-only *portals* cost twice as much to make as standard *portals.* If the *portal* sends intruders' belongings to some place different from the users' destination, it is considered a variable *portal* with one extra destination.

Limited Use: The prices and construction times noted above are for *portals* that operate constantly, transporting anyone who passes through them at any time. If the *portal* can be used only four times per day or less, the base costs are reduced.

The materials and XP cost of a limited-use *portal* are based on the number of uses available. The materials cost is 10,000 gp × a *portal's* uses per day, and the experience point cost is 800 XP × a *portal's* uses per day. (The second *portal* in a two-way pair costs half this amount.) The market value is twice the materials cost. The construction time is one day per 1,000 gp of market value.

A *portal* usable five times per day or more is just as expensive as a continuously active *portal*. *Portals* usable less than once per day can be created by using the appropriate fraction. For example, a *portal* usable once per four days effectively has 1/4 a use per day, costs 2,500 gp in materials, and 200 XP. The minimum cost of a limited-use *portal* is 1,000 gp and 80 XP for a *portal* usable once per ten days. (The *portal* builder can choose to have a *portal* operate even less often—once a year, for instance—but this does not reduce the cost or XP expenditure any further.)

Each activation of a limited-use *portal* lasts 1 round. Once activated, a limited-use *portal* can transport as many creatures as can touch it that round.

Spells of faerûn

Almost every faith of Faerûn harbors secret divine spells, prayers and invocations known only to the initiated clergy. Hundreds of reclusive wizards and sinister circles devise new arcane spells, seeking a purer understanding of the Art or a simple weapon other spellcasters lack. The temples of fallen deities and the ruins of ancient cities hold scrolls of powerful and dangerous spells, forgotten by the lesser clerics and wizards who populate Faerûn today.

The spells and domains described in the *Player's Handbook* form the common knowledge of Faerûn's bards, clerics, druids, paladins, rangers, sorcerers, and wizards. Any character may acquire these spells in the usual fashion. The domains and spells described here represent the secrets and special knowledge available to certain groups and individuals, plus a few Faerûnian spells that have become common parlance among the land's spellcasters.

cleric domains

In addition to the domains described in the *Player's Handbook*, various deities of Faerûn permit clerics to choose from the additional domains presented here. These new domains follow all the rules presented for domains in the description of the cleric class in the *Player's Handbook*. A cleric chooses any two domains listed for his deity (see Chapter 5: Deities).

In the descriptions that follow, granted powers and spell lists are given for domains that are presented in this book. If a domain description here lacks an entry for granted powers and spells, refer to the *Player's Handbook* for that information. In the listings of domain spells, a dagger (†) preceding a spell name signifies a spell described in this book.

AIR DOMAIN

Deities: Aerdrie Faenya, Akadi, Auril, Set, Shaundakul, Sheela Peryroyl, Valkur.

ANIMAL DOMAIN

Deities: Aerdrie Faenya, Baervan Wildwanderer, Chauntea, Fenmarel Mestarine, Gwaeron Windstrom, Lurue, Malar, Mielikki, Nobanion, Sebek, Shiallia, Silvanus, Thard Harr, Ulutiu, Uthgar.

CAVERN DOMAIN

Deities: Callarduran Smoothhands, Dumathoin, Geb, Ghaunadaur, Grumbar, Gruumsh, Luthic, Segojan Earthcaller, Shar.
Granted Power: You gain the dwarven ability of stonecunning. If you already have stonecunning, your racial bonus for stonecunning increases from +2 to +4 on checks to notice unusual stonework.

Cavern Domain Spells

1 Detect secret doors	6 Find the path
2 Darkness	7 Maw of stone
3 Meld into stone	8 Earthquake
4 Leomund's secure shelter	9 Imprisonment
5 Passwall	

CHAOS DOMAIN

Deities: Aerdrie Faenya, Angharradh, Anhur, Bahgtru, Beshaba, Corellon Larethian, Cyric, Deep Sashelas, Dugmaren Brightmantle, Eilistraee, Erevan Ilesere, Fenmarel Mestarine, Finder Wyvernspur, Garagos, Ghaunadaur, Gruumsh, Haela Brightaxe, Hanali Celanil, Kiaransalee, Labelas Enoreth, Lliira, Lolth, Lurue, Malar, Nephthys, Rillifane Rallathil, Sehanine Moonbow, Selûne, Selvetarm, Sharess, Shargaas, Sharindlar, Shaundakul, Shevarash, Solonor Thelandira, Sune, Talona, Talos, Tempus, Thard Harr, Tymora, Umberlee, Urdlen, Uthgar, Valkur, Vhaeraun.

CHARM DOMAIN

Deities: Eilistraee, Finder Wyvernspur, Gargauth, Hanali Celanil, Lliira, Milil, Oghma, Sharess, Sharindlar, Sheela Peryroyl, Sune.
Granted Power: You can boost your Charisma by 4 points once per day. Activating this power is a free action. The Charisma increase lasts 1 minute.

Charm Domain Spells

1 Charm person	6 Geas/quest
2 Calm emotions	7 Insanity
3 Suggestion	8 Demand
4 Emotion	9 Dominate monster
5 Charm monster	

CRAFT DOMAIN

Deities: Callarduran Smoothhands, Dugmaren Brightmantle, Dumathoin, Flandal Steelskin, Garl Glittergold, Geb, Gond, Laduguer, Moradin, Thoth.
Granted Power: You cast creation spells at +1 caster level and gain Skill Focus (a +2 bonus) in the Craft skill of your choice.

Craft Domain Spells

1 Animate rope	6 †Fantastic machine
2 Wood shape	7 Major creation
3 Stone shape	8 Forcecage
4 Minor creation	9 †Greater fantastic machine
5 Wall of stone	

DARKNESS DOMAIN

Deities: Lolth, Mask, Set, Shar, Shargaas.
Granted Power: Free Blind-Fight feat.

Darkness Domain Spells

1 Obscuring mist	6 Prying eyes
2 Blindness/deafness	7 Nightmare
3 †Blacklight	8 Power word, blind
4 †Armor of darkness	9 Power word, kill
5 †Darkbolt	

DEATH DOMAIN

Deities: Jergal, Kelemvor, Osiris, Urogalan, Velsharoon, Yurtrus.

DESTRUCTION DOMAIN

Deities: Bane, Cyric, Garagos, Ilneval, Istishia, Kossuth, Lolth, Talona, Talos, Umberlee, Yurtrus.

DROW DOMAIN

Deities: Eilistraee, Ghaunadaur, Kiaransalee, Lolth, Selvetarm, Vhaeraun.
Granted Power: Free Lightning Reflexes feat.

Drow Domain Spells

1 †Cloak of dark power	6 Greater dispelling
2 Clairaudience/clairvoyance	7 Word of chaos
3 Suggestion	8 Greater planar ally
4 Discern lies	9 Gate
5 †Spiderform	

DWARF DOMAIN

Deities: Abbathor, Berronar Truesilver, Clangeddin, Deep Duerra, Dugmaren Brightmantle, Dumathoin, Gorm Gulthyn, Haela Brightaxe, Laduguer, Marthammor Duin, Moradin, Sharindlar, Thard Harr, Vergadain.
Granted Power: Free Great Fortitude feat.

Dwarf Domain Spells

1 Magic weapon	6 Stone tell
2 Endurance	7 Dictum
3 Glyph of warding	8 Protection from spells
4 Greater magic weapon	9 Elemental swarm
5 Fabricate	(earth spell only)

EARTH DOMAIN

Deities: Callarduran Smoothhands, Chauntea, Dumathoin, Geb, Gond, Grumbar, Luthic, Moradin, Segojan Earthcaller, Urdlen, Urogalan.

ELF DOMAIN

Deities: Aerdrie Faenya, Angharradh, Corellon Larethian, Deep Sashelas, Eilistraee, Erevan Ilesere, Fenmarel Mestarine, Hanali Celanil, Labelas Enoreth, Rillifane Rallathil, Sehanine Moonbow, Shevarash, Solonor Thelandira.
Granted Power: Free Point Blank Shot feat.

Elf Domain Spells

1 True strike	6 Find the path
2 Cat's grace	7 Liveoak
3 Snare	8 Sunburst
4 Tree stride	9 Antipathy
5 Commune with nature	

EVIL DOMAIN

Deities: Abbathor, Auril, Bahgtru, Bane, Beshaba, Cyric, Deep Duerra, Gargauth, Ghaunadaur, Gruumsh, Ilneval, Kiaransalee, Laduguer, Lolth, Loviatar, Luthic, Malar, Mask, Sebek, Selvetarm, Set, Shar, Shargaas, Talona, Talos, Tiamat, Umberlee, Urdlen, Velsharoon, Vhaeraun, Yurtrus.

FAMILY DOMAIN

Deities: Berronar Truesilver, Cyrrollalee, Eldath, Hathor, Isis, Lliira, Luthic, Yondalla.

Granted Power: Once per day as a free action, you may protect a number of creatures equal to your Charisma modifier (minimum one creature) with a +4 dodge bonus to AC. This supernatural ability lasts 1 round per level. An affected creature loses this protection if it moves more than 10 feet from you. You may affect yourself with this ability.

Family Domain Spells

1 Bless	6 Heroes' feast
2 Shield other	7 Refuge
3 Helping hand	8 Protection from spells
4 Imbue with spell ability	9 Prismatic sphere
5 Rary's telepathic bond	

FATE DOMAIN

Deities: Beshaba, Hathor, Hoar, Jergal, Kelemvor, Savras.

Granted Power: You gain the uncanny dodge ability of a 3rd-level rogue. If you have another class that grants the uncanny dodge ability, treat your level in that class as three higher for determining your uncanny dodge ability.

Fate Domain Spells

1 True strike	6 Geas/quest
2 Augury	7 Vision
3 Bestow curse	8 Mind blank
4 Status	9 Foresight
5 Mark of justice	

FIRE DOMAIN

Deities: Gond, Kossuth, Talos.

GNOME DOMAIN

Deities: Baervan Wildwanderer, Baravar Cloakshadow, Callarduran Smoothhands, Flandal Steelskin, Gaerdal Ironhand, Garl Glittergold, Segojan Earthcaller, Urdlen.

Granted Power: You cast all illusion spells at +1 caster level.

Gnome Domain Spells

1 Silent image	6 †Fantastic machine
2 †Gembomb	7 Screen
3 Minor image	8 Otto's irresistible dance
4 Minor creation	9 Summon nature's ally (earth
5 Hallucinatory terrain	elementals or animals only)

GOOD DOMAIN

Deities: Aerdrie Faenya, Angharradh, Anhur, Arvoreen, Baervan Wildwanderer, Baravar Cloakshadow, Berronar Truesilver, Chauntea, Clangeddin, Corellon Larethian, Cyrrollalee, Deep Sashelas, Deneir, Dugmaren Brightmantle, Eilistraee, Eldath, Flandal Steelskin, Gaerdal Ironhand, Garl Glittergold, Gorm Gulthyn, Gwaeron Windstrom, Haela Brightaxe, Hanali Celanil, Hathor, Horus-Re, Ilmater, Isis, Labelas Enoreth, Lathander, Lliira, Lurue, Marthammor Duin, Mielikki, Milil, Moradin, Mystra, Nephthys, Nobanion, Osiris, Rillifane Rallathil, Segojan Earthcaller, Sehanine Moonbow, Selûne, Sharess, Sharindlar, Shiallia, Solonor Thelandira, Sune, Thard Harr, Torm, Tymora, Tyr, Valkur, Yondalla.

HALFLING DOMAIN

Deities: Arvoreen, Brandobaris, Cyrrollalee, Sheela Peryroyl, Urogalan, Yondalla.

Granted Power: You gain the ability to add your Charisma modifier to your Climb, Jump, Move Silently, and Hide checks. This extraordinary ability is a free action that lasts 10 minutes. It can be used once a day.

Halfling Domain Spells

1 Magic stone	6 Move earth
2 Cat's grace	7 Shadow walk
3 Magic vestment	8 Word of recall
4 Freedom of movement	9 Foresight
5 Mordenkainen's faithful hound	

HATRED DOMAIN

Deities: Bane, Ghaunadaur, Gruumsh, Set, Urdlen.

Granted Power: Once per day, as a free action, choose one opponent. Against that opponent you gain a +2 profane bonus on attack rolls, saving throws, and Armor Class. This supernatural ability lasts 1 minute.

Hatred Domain Spells

1 Doom	6 Forbiddance
2 Scare	7 Blasphemy
3 Bestow curse	8 Antipathy
4 Emotion (hate effect only)	9 Wail of the banshee
5 Righteous might	

HEALING DOMAIN

Deities: Berronar Truesilver, Ilmater, Lurue, Luthic, Sharindlar, Torm.

ILLUSION DOMAIN

Deities: Akadi, Azuth, Baravar Cloakshadow, Cyric, Mystra, Sehanine Moonbow.

Granted Power: You cast all illusion spells at +1 caster level.

Illusion Domain Spells

1 Silent image	6 Mislead
2 Minor image	7 Project image
3 Displacement	8 Screen
4 Phantasmal killer	9 Weird
5 Persistent image	

KNOWLEDGE DOMAIN

Deities: Angharradh, Azuth, Deep Sashelas, Deneir, Dugmaren Brightmantle, Dumathoin, Gond, Gwaeron Windstrom, Labelas Enoreth, Milil, Mystra, Oghma, Savras, Sehanine Moonbow, Shar, Siamorphe, Thoth, Tyr, Waukeen.

LAW DOMAIN

Deities: Arvoreen, Azuth, Bane, Berronar Truesilver, Clangeddin, Cyrrollalee, Deep Duerra, Gaerdal Ironhand, Gargauth, Garl Glittergold, Gorm Gulthyn, Helm, Hoar, Horus-Re, Ilmater, Jergal, Kelemvor, Laduguer, Loviatar, Moradin, Nobanion, Osiris, Red Knight, Savras, Set, Siamorphe, Tiamat, Torm, Tyr, Ulutiu, Urogalan, Yondalla.

LUCK DOMAIN

Deities: Abbathor, Beshaba, Brandobaris, Erevan Ilesere, Haela Brightaxe, Mask, Oghma, Tymora, Vergadain.

MAGIC DOMAIN

Deities: Azuth, Corellon Larethian, Hanali Celanil, Isis, Laduguer, Mystra, Savras, Set, Thoth, Velsharoon.

MENTALISM DOMAIN

Deity: Deep Duerra.
Granted Power: You can generate a mental ward, a spell-like ability to grant someone you touch a resistance bonus on her next Will saving throw equal to your level +2. Activating this power is a standard action. The mental ward is an abjuration effect with a duration of 1 hour that is usable once per day.

Mentalism Domain Spells

1	Random action	6	Rary's telepathic bond
2	Detect thoughts	7	Antipathy
3	Clairaudience/clairvoyance	8	Mind blank
4	Modify memory	9	Astral projection
5	Mind fog		

METAL DOMAIN

Deities: Dumathoin, Flandal Steelskin, Gond, Grumbar, Laduguer.
Granted Power: Free Martial or Exotic Weapon Proficiency and Weapon Focus with your choice of hammer.

Metal Domain Spells

1	Magic weapon	6	Blade barrier
2	Heat metal	7	Transmute metal to wood
3	Keen edge	8	Iron body
4	Rusting grasp	9	Repel metal or stone
5	Wall of iron		

MOON DOMAIN

Deities: Eilistraee, Hathor, Malar, Sehanine Moonbow, Selûne, Sharindlar.
Granted Power: Turn or destroy lycanthropes as a good cleric turns or destroys undead. You can use this ability a total number of times per day equal to three + your Charisma modifier.

Moon Domain Spells

1	Faerie fire	6	Permanent image
2	Moonbeam	7	Insanity
3	†Moon blade	8	Animal shapes
4	Emotion	9	†Moonfire
5	†Moon path		

NOBILITY DOMAIN

Deities: Horus-Re, Lathander, Milil, Nobanion, Red Knight, Siamorphe.
Granted Power: You have the spell-like ability to inspire allies, giving them a +2 morale bonus on saving throws, attack rolls, ability checks, skill checks, and weapon damage rolls. Allies must be able to hear you speak for 1 round. Using this ability is a standard action. It lasts a number of rounds equal to your Charisma bonus and can be used once per day.

Nobility Domain Spells

1	Divine favor	6	Geas/quest
2	Enthrall	7	Repulsion
3	Magic vestment	8	Demand
4	Discern lies	9	Storm of vengeance
5	Greater command		

OCEAN DOMAIN

Deities: Deep Sashelas, Istishia, Ulutiu, Umberlee, Valkur.
Granted Power: You have the supernatural ability to breathe water as if under the effect of a *water breathing* spell, for up to 10 rounds per level. This effect occurs automatically as soon as it applies, lasts until it runs out or is no longer needed, and can operate multiple times per day (up to the total daily limit of rounds).

Ocean Domain Spells

1	Endure elements	6	Otiluke's freezing sphere
2	Sound burst	7	†Waterspout
3	Water breathing	8	†Maelstrom
4	Freedom of movement	9	Elemental swarm
5	Wall of ice		(cast as a water spell only)

ORC DOMAIN

Deities: Bahgtru, Gruumsh, Ilneval, Luthic, Shargaas, Yurtrus.
Granted Power: You gain the smite power, the supernatural ability to make a single melee attack with a damage bonus equal to your cleric level (if you hit). You must declare the smite before making the attack. It is usable once per day. If used against a dwarf or an elf, you get a +4 bonus on the smite attack roll.

Orc Domain Spells

1	Cause fear	6	Eyebite
2	Produce flame	7	Blasphemy
3	Prayer	8	Cloak of chaos
4	Divine power	9	Power word, kill
5	Prying eyes		

PLANNING DOMAIN

Deities: Gond, Helm, Ilneval, Red Knight, Siamorphe, Ubtao.
Granted Power: Free Extend Spell feat.

Planning Domain Spells

1	Deathwatch	6	Heroes' feast
2	Augury	7	Greater scrying
3	Clairaudience/clairvoyance	8	Discern location
4	Status	9	Time stop
5	Detect scrying		

PLANT DOMAIN

Deities: Angharradh, Baervan Wildwanderer, Chauntea, Eldath, Fenmarel Mestarine, Gwaeron Windstrom, Mielikki, Osiris, Rillifane Rallathil, Sheela Peryroyl, Shiallia, Silvanus, Solonor Thelandira, Thard Harr, Ubtao.

PORTAL DOMAIN

Deities: Eilistraee, Shaundakul.
Granted Power: You can detect an active or inactive *portal* as if it were a normal secret door (DC 20).

Portal Domain Spells

1	Summon monster I	6	Banishment
2	†Analyze portal	7	Etherealness
3	Dimensional anchor	8	Maze
4	Dimension door	9	Gate
5	Teleport		

PROTECTION DOMAIN

Deities: Angharradh, Arvoreen, Baravar Cloakshadow, Berronar Truesilver, Chauntea, Corellon Larethian, Deneir, Dumathoin, Eldath, Gaerdal Ironhand, Garl Glittergold, Geb, Gorm Gulthyn, Hanali Celanil, Helm, Kelemvor, Laduguer, Lathander, Marthammor Duin, Moradin, Nephthys, Rillifane Rallathil, Selûne, Shaundakul, Silvanus, Sune, Tempus, Torm, Tymora, Ubtao, Ulutiu, Urogalan, Valkur, Waukeen, Yondalla.

RENEWAL DOMAIN

Deities: Angharradh, Chauntea, Finder Wyvernspur, Kossuth, Lathander, Shiallia, Silvanus.

Granted Power: If you fall below 0 hit points, you regain a number of hit points equal to 1d8 + your Charisma modifier. This supernatural ability functions once per day. If an attack brings you to −10 hit points or less, you die before this power takes effect.

Renewal Domain Spells

1 Charm person
2 Lesser restoration
3 Remove disease
4 Reincarnate
5 Atonement
6 Heroes' feast
7 Greater restoration
8 Polymorph any object
9 Freedom

RETRIBUTION DOMAIN

Deities: Hoar, Horus-Re, Kiaransalee, Loviatar, Osiris, Shevarash, Tyr, Uthgar.

Granted Power: If you have been harmed by someone in combat, you may make a strike of vengeance with a melee or ranged weapon against that individual on your next action. If this attack hits, you deal maximum damage. You may use this supernatural ability once per day.

Retribution Domain Spells

1 Shield of faith
2 Endurance
3 Speak with dead
4 Fire shield
5 Mark of justice
6 Banishment
7 Spell turning
8 Discern location
9 Storm of vengeance

RUNE DOMAIN

Deities: Deneir, Dugmaren Brightmantle, Jergal, Mystra, Thoth.
Granted Power: Free Scribe Scroll feat.

Rune Domain Spells

1 Erase
2 Secret page
3 Glyph of warding
4 Explosive runes
5 Lesser planar binding
6 Greater glyph of warding
7 Drawmij's instant summons
8 Symbol
9 Teleportation circle

SCALYKIND DOMAIN

Deities: Finder Wyvernspur, Sebek, Set, Tiamat, Ubtao.
Granted Power: Rebuke or command animals (reptilian creatures and snakes only) as an evil cleric rebukes or commands undead. Use this ability a total number of times per day equal to three + your Charisma modifier.

Scalykind Domain Spells

1 Magic fang
2 Animal trance*
3 Greater magic fang
4 Poison
5 Animal growth*
6 Eyebite
7 Creeping doom
  (composed of tiny snakes)
8 Animal shapes*
9 Shapechange
*Affects ophidian and reptilian creatures only.

SLIME DOMAIN

Deity: Ghaunadaur.
Granted Power: Rebuke or command oozes as an evil cleric rebukes or commands undead. Use this ability a total number of times per day equal to three + your Charisma modifier.

Slime Domain Spells

1 Grease
2 Melf's acid arrow
3 Poison
4 Rusting grasp
5 Evard's black tentacles
6 Transmute rock to mud
7 Destruction
8 Power word, blind
9 Implosion

SPELL DOMAIN

Deities: Azuth, Mystra, Savras, Thoth.
Granted Power: You get a +2 bonus on Concentration and Spellcraft checks.

Spell Domain Spells

1 Mage armor
2 Silence
3 †Anyspell
4 Rary's mnemonic enhancer
5 Break enchantment
6 †Greater anyspell
7 Limited wish
8 Antimagic field
9 Mordenkainen's disjunction

SPIDER DOMAIN

Deities: Lolth, Selvetarm.
Granted Power: Rebuke or command spiders as an evil cleric rebukes or commands undead. Use this ability a total number of times per day equal to three + your Charisma modifier.

Spider Domain Spells

1 Spider climb
2 Summon swarm
3 Phantom steed
  (has a vermin shape)
4 Giant vermin
5 Insect plague
6 †Spider curse
7 †Stone spiders
8 Creeping doom
9 †Spider shapes

STORM DOMAIN

Deities: Aerdrie Faenya, Anhur, Auril, Isis, Istishia, Talos, Umberlee.
Granted Power: You gain electricity resistance 5.

Storm Domain Spells

1 Entropic shield
2 Gust of wind
3 Call lightning
4 Sleet storm
5 Ice storm
6 Summon monster VI
  (air spell only)
7 Control weather
8 Whirlwind
9 Storm of vengeance

STRENGTH DOMAIN

Deities: Anhur, Bahgtru, Clangeddin, Garagos, Gruumsh, Helm, Ilmater, Lathander, Loviatar, Malar, Tempus, Torm, Ulutiu, Uthgar.

SUFFERING DOMAIN

Deities: Ilmater, Jergal, Kossuth, Loviatar, Talona, Yurtrus.
Granted Power: You may use a pain touch once per day. Make a melee touch attack against a living creature, which bestows on that creature a −2 enhancement penalty to Strength and Dexterity for 1 minute on a successful attack. This spell-like ability does not affect creatures immune to critical hits.

Suffering Domain Spells

1 Bane
2 Endurance
3 Bestow curse
4 Enervation
5 Feeblemind
6 Harm
7 Eyebite (sicken effect only)
8 Symbol (pain effect only)
9 Horrid wilting

SUN DOMAIN

Deities: Horus-Re, Lathander.

TIME DOMAIN

Deities: Grumbar, Labelas Enoreth.
Granted Power: Free Improved Initiative feat.

Time Domain Spells

1	True strike	6	Contingency
2	Gentle repose	7	Mass haste
3	Haste	8	Foresight
4	Freedom of movement	9	Time stop
5	Permanency		

TRADE DOMAIN

Deities: Abbathor, Nephthys, Shaundakul, Vergadain, Waukeen.
Granted Power: You may use *detect thoughts* once per day as a spell-like ability, affecting one target and lasting a number of minutes equal to your Charisma bonus. Activating this power is a free action.

Trade Domain Spells

1	Message	6	True seeing
2	†Gembomb	7	Mordenkainen's magnificent
3	†Eagle's splendor		mansion
4	Sending	8	Mind blank
5	Fabricate	9	Discern location

TRAVEL DOMAIN

Deities: Akadi, Baervan Wildwanderer, Brandobaris, Fenmarel Mestarine, Gwaeron Windstrom, Hoar, Istishia, Kelemvor, Lliira, Marthammor Duin, Mielikki, Oghma, Sehanine Moonbow, Selûne, Sharess, Shaundakul, Tymora, Vhaeraun, Waukeen.

TRICKERY DOMAIN

Deities: Abbathor, Akadi, Baravar Cloakshadow, Beshaba, Brandobaris, Cyric, Erevan Ilesere, Gargauth, Garl Glittergold, Lolth, Mask, Oghma, Sharess, Shargaas, Vergadain, Vhaeraun.

TYRANNY DOMAIN

Deities: Bane, Tiamat.
Granted Power: Add +2 to the saving throw DC of any compulsion spell you cast.

Tyranny Domain Spells

1	Command	6	Geas/quest
2	Enthrall	7	Bigby's grasping hand
3	Discern lies	8	Mass charm
4	Fear	9	Dominate monster
5	Greater command		

UNDEATH DOMAIN

Deities: Kiaransalee, Velsharoon.
Granted Power: Free Extra Turning feat.

Undeath Domain Spells

1	Detect undead	6	Create undead
2	Desecrate	7	Control undead
3	Animate dead	8	Create greater undead
4	Death ward	9	Energy drain
5	Circle of doom		

WAR DOMAIN

Deities: Anhur, Arvoreen, Clangeddin, Corellon Larethian, Deep Duerra, Gaerdal Ironhand, Garagos, Gorm Gulthyn, Gruumsh, Haela Brightaxe, Ilneval, Red Knight, Selvetarm, Shevarash, Solonor Thelandira, Tempus, Tyr, Uthgar.

WATER DOMAIN

Deities: Auril, Deep Sashelas, Eldath, Isis, Istishia, Sebek, Silvanus, Umberlee.

spell descriptions

The spells presented here follow all the rules presented in Chapter 10: Magic and Chapter 11: Spells in the *Player's Handbook*.

AGANAZZAR'S SCORCHER

Evocation [Fire]
Level: Sor/Wiz 2
Components: V, S, F
Casting Time: 1 action
Range: Close (25 ft. + 5 ft./2 levels)
Area: 5-ft.-wide path to close range (25 ft. + 5 ft./2 levels)
Duration: Instantaneous
Saving Throw: Reflex half
Spell Resistance: Yes

A jet of roaring flame bursts from your outstretched hand, scorching any creature in a 5-foot-wide path to the edge of the spell's range. *Aganazzar's scorcher* deals 1d8 points of damage per two caster levels, to a maximum of 5d8 points of damage.
Focus: A red dragon's scale.

ANALYZE PORTAL

Divination
Level: Brd 3, Portal 2, Sor/Wiz 3
Components: V, S, M/DF
Casting Time: 1 minute
Range: 60 ft.
Area: A quarter circle emanating from you to the extreme of the range
Duration: Concentration, up to 1 round/level (D)
Saving Throw: See text
Spell Resistance: No

You can tell if an area contains a magic *portal*. If you study an area for 1 round, you know the sizes and locations of any *portals* in the area. Once you find a *portal*, you can study it. (If you find more than one *portal*, you can only study one at a time.)

Each round you study a *portal*, you can discover one property of the *portal*, in this order: any key or command word needed to activate the *portal*, any special circumstances governing the *portal's* use (such as specific times when the *portal* can be activated), whether the *portal* is one-way or two-way, any of the usual properties listed in the Building a Portal section earlier in this chapter, and finally, a glimpse of the area where the *portal* leads. You can look at the area where the *portal* leads for 1 round. *Analyze portal* does not allow other divination spells to extend through the *portal*. For example, you cannot also use *detect magic* or *detect evil* to study the area where the *portal* leads while viewing the area with *analyze portal*.

For each property, you make a caster level check (1d20 + caster level) against DC 17. If fail, you can try again the next round. *Analyze portal* has only a limited ability to reveal unusual properties of *portals*, as follows:

- Random *Portals:* The spell reveals only that the *portal* is random, and whether it can be activated now. It does not reveal when the *portal* starts or stops functioning.

- Variable *Portals:* The spell reveals only that the *portal* is variable. If the caster studies the *portal*'s destination, the spell reveals only the destination to which the *portal* is currently set.
- Creature Only *Portals:* The spell reveals this property. If the caster studies the *portal*'s destination, the spell reveals where the *portal* sends creatures. If it is the type of *portal* that sends creatures one place and their equipment another place, the spell does not reveal where the equipment goes.
- Malfunctioning *Portals:* The spell reveals only that the *portal* is malfunctioning, not what sort of malfunction the *portal* produces.

Arcane Material Components: A crystal lens and a small mirror.

Illustration by Carlo Arellano

ANYSPELL

Transmutation
Level: Spell 3
Components: V, S, DF (and possibly M, F, and XP)
Casting Time: 15 minutes
Range: Personal
Target: You
Duration: Instantaneous

Anyspell allows you to read and prepare any arcane spell of up to 2nd level. You must have an arcane magical writing (a scroll or spellbook) on hand to cast *anyspell*. During the spell's 15-minute casting time, you can scan the spells available and choose one to read and prepare.

Once you choose and prepare an arcane spell, you retain it in your mind. The prepared spell occupies your 3rd-level domain spell slot. If you read the spell from a spellbook, the book is unharmed, but reading a spell from a scroll erases the spell from the scroll.

When you cast the arcane spell, it works just as though cast by a wizard of your cleric level except that your Wisdom score sets the save DC (if applicable). You must have a Wisdom score of at least 10 + the arcane spell's level to prepare and cast it. Your holy symbol substitutes for any noncostly material component. If the spell has a costly material component (one to which a gold piece value is assigned), you must provide it. If the spell has another focus, you must provide the focus. If the spell has an XP component, you must pay the experience point cost.

ARMOR OF DARKNESS

Abjuration [Darkness]
Level: Darkness 4
Components: V, S, DF
Casting Time: 1 action
Range: Touch
Target: Creature touched
Duration: 10 minutes/level
Saving Throw: Will negates (harmless)
Spell Resistance: Yes (harmless)

Claws of darkness

The spell envelops the warded creature in a shroud of flickering shadows. The shroud can, if the caster desires, conceal the wearer's features. In any case, it grants the subject a +3 deflection bonus to Armor Class plus an additional +1 for every four caster levels (maximum bonus +8). The subject can see through the armor as if it did not exist and is also afforded darkvision with a range of 60 feet. Finally, the subject gains a +2 saving throw bonus against any holy, good, or light spells or effects.

Undead creatures that are subjects of *armor of darkness* also gain +4 turn resistance.

BLACKLIGHT

Evocation [Darkness]
Level: Darkness 3, Sor/Wiz 3
Components: V, S, M
Casting Time: 1 action
Range: Close (25 ft. + 5 ft./2 levels)
Area: A 20-ft.-radius emanation centered on a creature, object, or point in space
Duration: 1 round/level (D)
Saving Throw: Will negates or none (object)
Spell Resistance: Yes or no (object)

You create an area of total darkness. The darkness is impenetrable to normal vision and darkvision, but you can see normally within the blacklit area. Creatures outside the spell's area, even you, cannot see through it.

You can cast the spell on a point in space, but the effect is stationary unless you cast it cast on a mobile object. You can cast the spell on a creature, and the effect then radiates from the creature and moves as it moves. Unattended objects and points in space do not get saving throws or benefit from spell resistance.

Blacklight counters or dispels any light spell of equal or lower level, such as *daylight.* The 3rd-level cleric spell *daylight* counters or dispels *blacklight.*

Material Component: A piece of coal and the dried eyeball of any creature.

CLAWS OF DARKNESS

Illusion (Shadow)
Level: Sor/Wiz 2
Components: V, S
Casting Time: 1 action
Range: Personal
Target: You
Duration: 1 round/level (D)
Saving Throw: Fortitude partial
Spell Resistance: Yes (see text)

You draw material from the Plane of Shadow to cause your hands and forearms to elongate and change shape into featureless claws of inky blackness. Starting on your next action, you may use the claws to make unarmed attacks as if they were natural weapons. (You attack with one claw and can use the other claw for an off-hand attack. If you have multiple attacks you use them normally when attacking with the claws.) Attacks with the claws are melee touch attacks. Each claw deals 1d4 points of cold damage. If you grapple an opponent, you deal claw damage with each successful grapple check, and the grappled target is under the effect of a *slow* spell for as long as you maintain the grapple unless the opponent makes a Fortitude save.

You can extend the claws up to 6 feet, which gives you natural reach of 10 feet, or retract them as a free action.

When the spell is in effect, you may not cast spells with anything other than verbal components, nor may you carry items with your hands. Any magic items worn on your hands are temporarily absorbed and cease functioning while the spell is active.

CLOAK OF DARK POWER

Abjuration
Level: Drow 1
Components: V, S
Casting Time: 1 action
Range: Touch
Target: Creature touched
Duration: 1 minute/level
Saving Throw: Will negates (harmless)
Spell Resistance: Yes (harmless)

Cloak of dark power creates a dusky haze around the subject. The haze does not interfere with vision, but the subject and anything she wears or carries is protected from the effects of full sunlight, even under the open, daytime sky of the surface world. A drow subject suffers no blindness or bright light combat penalties while under the effects of a *cloak of dark power*.

The subject also gains a +4 resistance bonus on saves against light or darkness spells or effects.

CREATE MAGIC TATTOO

Conjuration (Creation)
Level: Sor/Wiz 2
Components: V, S, M, F
Casting Time: 10 minutes
Range: Touch
Target or Area: Creature touched
Duration: 1 day
Saving Throw: None
Spell Resistance: Yes (harmless)

Create magic tattoo creates a single magic tattoo. The caster determines the exact type of tattoo, though the selection of possible tattoos is limited by caster level. The caster of *create magic tattoo* must have a modicum of artistic talent to sketch the desired tattoo—at least one rank of Craft (drawing), Craft (painting), Craft (calligraphy), or a similar Craft skill. Inscribing a magic tattoo requires a Craft check. The DC varies with the kind of tattoo, as noted below.

A caster of 3rd to 6th level can inscribe the following tattoos (DC 10):

- +2 resistance bonus on one type of saving throw (Fortitude, Reflex, or Will).
- +1 luck bonus on attack rolls.
- +1 deflection bonus to AC.

A caster of 7th to 12th levels can inscribe the lower-level tattoos, plus the following (DC 15):

- +2 resistance bonus on all saving throws.
- +2 competence bonus on attack rolls.
- The ability to recall one cast 0-level, 1st-level, or 2nd-level spell (just as though the subject were using a *pearl of power*). The caster chooses the spell level.

A caster of 13th level or higher can inscribe all of the above tattoos plus the following (DC 20):

- Spell resistance of 10 + 1 per six caster levels.
- +2 enhancement bonus to any one ability score.
- +1 level of casting ability. This increases the subject's effective level, but not the total number of spells. An 11th-level caster raised in casting ability in this manner casts spells as a 12th-level caster in terms of range, area, effect, and so on, but this tattoo does not provide any extra spells.

A single creature can have only three magic tattoos at a time. Once a creature has three magic tattoos operating, any additional magic tattoos fail.

A successful *erase* spell removes a single magic tattoo. A successful *dispel magic* spell can remove multiple magic tattoos if targeted on the creature bearing the tattoos (see the *dispel magic* spell in the *Player's Handbook*).

Material Components: Tattoo inks in appropriate colors.
Focus: Tattoo needles.

DARKBOLT

Evocation [Darkness]
Level: Darkness 5
Components: V, S
Casting Time: 1 action
Range: Medium (100 ft. + 10 ft./level)
Effect: One ray/2 caster levels (maximum seven)
Duration: Instantaneous (see text)
Saving Throw: Will partial
Spell Resistance: Yes

You unleash beams of darkness from your open palm. You must succeed at a ranged touch attack to strike your target. You can hurl one *darkbolt* for every two caster levels you have (maximum seven bolts). You can hurl all the bolts at once, or you can hurl one bolt per round as a free action, starting on the round when you cast the spell. You do not have to hurl a bolt every round, but if you don't hurl the bolt you were entitled to that round, it is lost. If you hurl all the bolts at once, all your targets must be within 60 feet of each other.

A *darkbolt* deals 2d8 points of damage to a living creature, and the creature is dazed for 1 round unless it makes a Will save (a creature struck by multiple bolts during the same round is dazed for a maximum of 1 round, no matter how many times it fails its save). Undead take no damage, but are dazed if they fail their saves.

EAGLE'S SPLENDOR

Transmutation
Level: Brd 2, Hrp 2, Sor/Wiz 2, Trade 3
Components: V, S, M/DF
Casting Time: 1 action
Range: Touch
Target: Creature touched
Duration: 1 hour/level
Saving Throw: Will negates (harmless)
Spell Resistance: Yes (harmless)

The transmuted creature becomes more poised, articulate, and personally forceful. The spell grants an enhancement bonus to Charisma of 1d4+1 points, adding the usual benefits to Charisma-based skills. Sorcerers and bards who receive *eagle's splendor* do not gain extra spells, but the save DCs for their spells increase.

Arcane Material Component: A few feathers or a pinch of dung from an eagle.

ELMINSTER'S EVASION

Evocation
Level: Sor/Wiz 9
Components: V, S, M, F, XP
Casting Time: At least 10 minutes (see text)
Range: Personal
Target: You
Duration: Until discharged

This powerful variant of the *contingency* spell automatically transfers you and everything you carry or touch (except for other creatures or objects that weigh more than 50 pounds) to a locale you name.

When casting *Elminster's evasion,* you must specify the locale and detail up to six specific conditions that trigger the spell. When any of these situations occurs, your body, mind, and soul are whisked away to the location. The location can be any place you have visited, even on another plane. Also when casting the spell, you cast *teleport without error* and one or two other spells that are to take effect when you arrive at your destination. The 10-minute casting time is the minimum total for all castings. If the companion spells have combined casting times longer than 10 minutes, use the combined casting times instead. The *teleport without error* spell whisks you through the Astral Plane to your destination, so anything that prevents astral travel also foils *Elminster's evasion.*

The spells to be brought into effect by the *evasion* must be ones that affect your person (*feather fall, levitate, fly, teleport,* and so on) and be of a spell level no higher than one-third of your caster level (maximum 6th level).

The conditions you specify to bring the spell into effect must be clear, although they can be general (see the *contingency* spell, in Chapter 11 of the *Player's Handbook*).

The spell pulls together your mind, body, and soul if they have been separated. For example, if your soul is trapped in a *magic jar* when the *evasion* is triggered, your soul returns to your body. (This breaks the *magic jar* spell.) If your body or soul has been magically trapped (for example with a *binding, imprisonment,* or *trap the soul* spell), you must succeed at a caster level check (DC 11 + the caster level of the person who cast the trapping spell). If you succeed, the trapping spell is broken and the *evasion* works. If you fail, the *evasion* fails. If you're dead when you arrive at your destination, your soul immediately departs just as though you died at your destination.

Material Components: Those of the companion spells, plus quicksilver; an eyelash of an ogre mage, ki-rin, or similar spell-using creature; and some of your own blood, freshly drawn. Drawing the blood deals 1d4 points of temporary Constitution damage.

Focus: A statuette of you carved from ivory and decorated with gems (worth at least 1,500 gp). You must carry the focus for the *evasion* to function.

XP Cost: 5,000 XP.

FANTASTIC MACHINE

Illusion (Shadow)
Level: Craft 6, Gnome 6
Components: V, S, DF
Casting Time: 1 action
Range: Medium (100 ft. + 10 ft./level)
Effect: A 10-ft. machine
Duration: 1 minute/level (D)
Saving Throw: None
Spell Resistance: No

Fantastic machine creates an illusory, many-armed, noisy mechanical construct of impressively massive appearance. You can command the machine to perform any simple, physical task that you can describe in 25 words or less. You can order the machine to perform the same task over and over, but you can't change the task. You must specify the task when you cast the spell. The machine always acts on your turn in the initiative order. (It can act during the turn you cast the spell.)

The machine functions as a Large (tall) animated object (see the *Monster Manual*). It trundles over the ground at a speed of 40 feet. It can swim or fly at a speed of 10 feet (clumsy maneuverability). It has 22 hit points, an Armor Class of 14 (–1 size, +5 natural), and a hardness of 10. Its saving throw modifiers are Fortitude +1, Reflex +1, Will –4.

A light load for the machine is up to 230 pounds, a heavy load is 231–460 pounds, and a heavy load is 461–700 pounds. The machine can fly or swim only when lightly loaded.

The machine can lift a weight of up to 1,400 pounds to a height of 15 feet. It can push or drag 3,500 pounds. It can excavate 7,000 pounds of loose rock each minute (which is sufficient to clear a 5-by-5-by-5-foot space in 3 rounds). It can excavate sand or loose soil at twice that rate.

The machine has an attack bonus of +5 and can make one slam attack each round that deals 1d8+4 points of damage. It deals triple slam damage (3d8+12) against stone or metal. The machine can hurl Small rocks (if any are at hand) with an attack bonus of +3. Its range increment is 150 feet, and it can throw a rock up to 10 range increments. A thrown rock deals 2d6+4 points of damage.

FIRE STRIDE

Transmutation [Teleportation]
Level: Sor/Wiz 4
Components: V, S
Casting Time: 1 action
Range: Personal
Target: You
Duration: 10 minutes/level or until expended (see text)

You gain the ability to step into fires and move from fire to fire. The fires you enter and move between must be at least as big around as you are. Fire elementals and other fire creatures are not "fires" for purposes of *fire stride,* nor are sources of great heat such as pools of lava.

Once in a fire, you can transport yourself to any other sufficiently large fire within long range (400 ft. + 40 ft./level), and you instantly know the locations of all suitable fires within range. Each transport counts as a full move action. With each casting of the spell, you can transport yourself one time per caster level. If a fire's location doesn't offer enough space for you (for example, a fire contained inside a furnace too small to hold you or a fire already occupied by a big cauldron), it is not a viable destination and you don't sense its location. If a fire rests on a surface that can't support you, it is still a viable destination and you suffer the appropriate consequences if you transport yourself to it. For example, if you transport yourself into a fire burning in a pit full of oil, you fall into the oil when you arrive there.

The spell provides no protection against fire, so it is advisable to obtain such protection before using the spell.

FLASHBURST

Evocation [Fire]
Level: Hth 3, Sor/Wiz 3
Components: V, S, M/DF
Casting Time: 1 action
Range: Long (400 ft. + 40 ft./level)
Area: A 20-ft.-radius burst
Duration: Instantaneous (see text)
Saving Throw: Will partial
Spell Resistance: Yes

Flashburst creates a blinding, dazzling flash of light. Sighted creatures within the area are automatically dazzled for 1 round (–1 penalty on attack rolls), and possibly blinded for 2d8 rounds (Will negates). Creatures outside the area, but within 120 feet of the burst, can be blinded if they have line of sight to the burst (Will negates). The spell does not dazzle creatures outside the burst area.

In addition to the obvious effects, a blinded character suffers a 50% miss chance in combat (all opponents have full concealment), loses any Dexterity bonus to AC, grants a +2 bonus on attackers' attack rolls (they are effectively invisible), moves at half speed, and suffers a –4 penalty on most Strength- and Dexterity-based skill checks.

Arcane Material Component: A pinch of sulfur or phosphorus.

FLENSING

Evocation
Level: Sor/Wiz 8
Components: V, S, M
Casting Time: 1 action
Range: Close (25 ft. + 5 ft./2 levels)
Targets: One corporeal creature
Duration: Up to 4 rounds (see text)
Saving Throw: Fortitude partial (see text)
Spell Resistance: Yes

You literally strip the flesh from a corporeal creature's body.

Each round, the target suffers pain and psychological trauma that literally undermines the spirit. The assault deals 2d6 points of damage and 1d6 points of temporary Charisma and Constitution damage. A Fortitude save negates the temporary Charisma and Constitution damage and reduces the normal damage by half. The target can make a saving throw each round to reduce the damage in that round.

Flensing has no effect on creatures in gaseous form or on incorporeal creatures.

Material Component: An onion.

GATE SEAL

Abjuration
Level: Brd 6, Clr 6, Drd 6, Sor/Wiz 6
Components: V, S, M
Casting Time: 1 action
Range: Close (25 ft. + 5 ft./2 levels)
Target: One *gate* or *portal*
Duration: Permanent
Saving Throw: None
Spell Resistance: No

You permanently seal a *gate* or *portal*. *Gate seal* prevents any activation of the *gate* or *portal*, though the seal may be negated by a successful *dispel magic* cast upon the spell. A *knock* spell does not function on the *gate seal*, but a *chime of opening* dispels the spell.

Material Component: A silver bar worth 50 gp.

GEMBOMB

Conjuration (Creation) [Force]
Level: Gnome 2, Trade 2
Components: V, S, M
Casting Time: 1 action/bomb
Range: Touch
Targets: Up to 5 touched gems worth at least 1 gp each
Duration: 10 minutes/level or until used
Saving Throw: Reflex half (see text)
Spell Resistance: Yes

You turn up to five gems into bombs you (and only you) can lob at enemies. You must hold the gems in your hand when casting the spell.

Together, the bombs are capable of dealing 1d8 points of force damage per two caster levels (maximum of 5d8), divided up among the gems as you wish. A 10th-level cleric could create one 5d8 bomb, a 3d8 and 2d8 bomb, five 1d8 bombs, or any combination of five dice of damage and up to five gems.

You can toss the bombs up to 100 feet with a range increment of 20 feet. A ranged touch attack roll is required to strike the intended target. A creature struck can attempt a Reflex save for half damage.

Tossing a *gembomb* counts as an attack for you, so you usually cannot toss one during the turn that you cast the spell. You can only toss one bomb at a time, but you can toss more than one each round if you have multiple attacks.

Material Components: Up to five gems worth at least 1 gp each

GREAT SHOUT

Evocation [Sonic]
Level: Brd 6, Sor/Wiz 8
Components: V, S, F
Casting Time: 1 action
Range: Close (25 ft. + 5 ft./2 levels)
Area: See text
Duration: Instantaneous
Saving Throw: See text
Spell Resistance: Yes (object)

You emit a thunderous, devastating yell. The primary area affected is 5 feet high and 5 feet wide, extending out from you to the limit of the spell's range. Stone, crystal, and metal objects in the area take 20d6 points of damage. Creatures holding vulnerable objects can attempt Reflex saves to negate the damage. Objects that survive the spell's primary effect are not subject to the secondary effect.

The spell's secondary effect is a cone of sound. Creatures within the cone take 10d6 points of damage, and are stunned for 1 round and deafened for 4d6 rounds. A successful Fortitude save negates the stunning and halves both the damage and the duration of the deafness. Any brittle or crystalline object or crystalline creature takes 1d6 points of damage per caster level (maximum 20d6). Creatures holding fragile objects can negate damage to them with successful Reflex saves.

The *great shout* spell cannot penetrate the spell *silence*.

Focus: A small metal or ivory horn.

GREATER ANYSPELL

Transmutation
Level: Spell 6
Components: V, S, DF (and possibly M, F, and XP)
Casting Time: 15 minutes
Range: Personal
Target: You
Duration: Instantaneous

As *anyspell*, except you can read and prepare any arcane spell of up to 5th level, and the prepared spell occupies your 6th-level domain spell slot.

GREATER FANTASTIC MACHINE

Illusion (Shadow)
Level: Craft 9
Components: V, S, DF
Casting Time: 1 action
Range: Medium (100 ft. + 10 ft./level)
Effect: A 10-ft. machine
Duration: 1 minute/level (D)
Saving Throw: None
Spell Resistance: Yes

Greater fantastic machine creates an illusory, many-armed, noisy mechanical construct of impressively massive appearance.

You can concentrate on controlling the machine's every action or specify a simple program, such as collect all the logs in an area and stack them in a neat pile, plow a field, drive piles, or the like. The machine can perform only fairly simple physical tasks. Directing the machine's actions or changing its programmed movement is a standard action for you. The machine always acts on your turn in the initiative order. (It can act during the turn you cast the spell.)

Except where noted below, the machine functions as a Large (tall) animated object (see the *Monster Manual*) constructed from adamantine. It trundles over the ground at a speed of 60 feet. It can swim or fly at a speed of 20 feet (poor maneuverability). It has 16 HD, 88 hit points, an Armor Class of 20 (−1 size, +11 natural), and a hardness of 20. Its saving throw modifiers are Fortitude +5, Reflex +5, and Will +0.

Greater fantastic machine

The machine has a Strength score of 22. A light load for the machine is up to 520 pounds, a medium load is 521 to 1,040 pounds, and a heavy load is 1,041 to 1,560 pounds. The machine can fly or swim only when lightly loaded.

The machine can lift a weight of up to 3,120 pounds to a height of 15 feet. It can push or drag 7,800 pounds. It can excavate 20,000 pounds of loose rock each minute (which is sufficient to clear a 5-by-5-by-5-foot space in 1 round). It can excavate sand or loose soil at twice that rate.

The machine makes slam attacks with an attack bonus of +17/+12 for 1d8+9 points of damage. It deals triple slam damage (3d8+27) against stone or metal. The machine can hurl Small rocks (if any are at hand) with an attack bonus of +12/+7. Its range increment is 150 feet, and it can throw a rock up to 10 range increments. A thrown rock deals 2d6+9 points of damage.

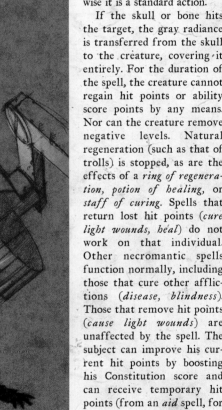

GRIMWALD'S GRAYMANTLE

Necromancy
Level: Sor/Wiz 5
Components: V, S, M
Casting Time: 1 action
Range: Medium (100 ft. + 10 ft./level)
Targets: One creature
Duration: 1 round/level
Saving Throw: Fortitude negates
Spell Resistance: Yes

You imbue a skull or bone with a pale gray radiance and then hurl (or touch) the skull or bone to hit a target creature. You can attack with the skull on the round you cast the spell, but otherwise it is a standard action.

If the skull or bone hits the target, the gray radiance is transferred from the skull to the creature, covering it entirely. For the duration of the spell, the creature cannot regain hit points or ability score points by any means. Nor can the creature remove negative levels. Natural regeneration (such as that of trolls) is stopped, as are the effects of a *ring of regeneration*, *potion of healing*, or *staff of curing*. Spells that return lost hit points (*cure light wounds*, *heal*) do not work on that individual. Other necromantic spells function normally, including those that cure other afflictions (*disease*, *blindness*). Those that remove hit points (*cause light wounds*) are unaffected by the spell. The subject can improve his current hit points by boosting his Constitution score and can receive temporary hit points (from an *aid* spell, for example).

Upon the expiration of the spell, automatic healing abilities and items such as a *ring of regeneration* or a troll's regeneration ability begin to function again.

Material Component: The skull or bone used.

LESSER IRONGUARD

Abjuration
Level: Sor/Wiz 5
Components: V, S, M
Casting Time: 1 action
Range: Touch
Target: Creature touched
Duration: 1 round/level
Saving Throw: Will negates (harmless)
Spell Resistance: Yes (harmless)

Illustration by Carlo Arellano

You or a creature you touch becomes immune to nonmagical metal. Metal items (including metal weapons) simply pass through you, and you can walk through metal barriers such as iron bars. Magic metal affects you normally, as do spells, spell-like abilities, and supernatural effects. Attacks delivered by metal items (such as poison on a dagger) affect you normally. If the spell expires while metal is inside you, the metal object is shunted out of your body (or you away from the metal, if it is an immovable object such as a set of iron bars). You and the object each take 1d6 points of damage as a result (ignoring the object's hardness for determining damage to it).

Because you pass through metal, you may ignore armor bonuses from metal armor on opponents you attack with unarmed attacks.

Material Component: A tiny shield of wood, glass, or crystal.

MAELSTROM

Conjuration (Creation)
Level: Ocean 8
Components: V, S, DF
Casting Time: 1 full round
Range: Long (400 ft. + 40 ft./level)
Effect: A whirlpool 120 ft. wide and 60 ft. deep
Duration: 1 round/level
Saving Throw: Reflex negates (and see text)
Spell Resistance: No

Maelstrom causes a deadly vortex to form in water. A body of water at least 120 feet wide and 60 feet deep must be present, or the spell is wasted.

Waterborne creatures or objects within 50 feet of the vortex (below and on all sides) must make successful Reflex saves or be sucked in. Trained swimmers can attempt Swim checks instead if their skill modifier is higher than their Reflex save bonus. Waterborne vessels avoid being sucked in if their operators make Profession (sailor) checks against the same DC as the spell's saving throw. These creatures take 3d8 points of damage upon being sucked in.

Once inside, creatures and objects take 3d8 points of battering damage each round. They remain trapped for 2d4 rounds. Subjects of Large or smaller size are ejected from the bottom of the vortex. Larger subjects are ejected from the top.

MAW OF STONE

Transmutation
Level: Cavern 7
Components: V, S, DF
Casting Time: 1 action
Range: Close (25 ft. + 5 ft./2 levels)
Effect: One cave mouth or natural chamber up to 15 ft. high and wide
Duration: 10 minutes/level (D)
Saving Throw: None
Spell Resistance: No

You cause a single natural opening or natural chamber to become animated. The opening or chamber cannot move, but it can attack. You can order it to attack any creature, or a specific type of creature. You also can order it to attack under a specific circumstance, such as when creatures try to leave or when they touch something.

An animated opening can only attack creatures that try to move through it. An animated chamber can attack every creature inside. Only one *maw of stone* can be in effect on a particular opening or chamber at a time.

The animated opening or chamber has a Strength score of 30 and an attack bonus equal to your level + your Wisdom modifier + 7 for its Strength. If it has any single dimension (height, length, or width) of 8 feet or more, it has a –1 size penalty on attack rolls for being Large.

An animated opening can make one grapple attack each round against a creature passing through. If it succeeds with its grab attempt, it makes a grapple check and deals 2d6+10 points of normal damage with a successful hold. A Large opening gains a +4 special size modifier and deals 2d8+10 points of damage.

An animated chamber works the same way, except that it can make a separate attack against every creature inside.

The animated stone has an Armor Class of 15, or 14 if Large (–1 size), and a hardness of 8. An opening has 40 hit points (60 if Large). A chamber has 60 hit points (90 if Large).

MOON BLADE

Evocation
Level: Hth 3, Moon 3
Components: V, S, M/DF
Casting Time: 1 action
Range: 0 ft.
Effect: A swordlike beam
Duration: 1 minute/level (D)
Saving Throw: None
Spell Resistance: Yes

A 3-foot-long, blazing beam of moonlight springs forth from your hand. Anyone who can cast *moon blade* can wield the beam with proficiency. However, if you are proficient with any type of sword, you can wield the beam as if it were any type of sword and thus gain the benefits of any special sword skill you might have, such as Weapon Focus.

Attacks with the *moon blade* are melee touch attacks. Its strike saps vitality or life force, causing no visible wounds but dealing 1d8 points of damage plus 1 point per two caster levels (to a maximum of +15) to any type of creature except undead. Undead are visibly wounded by a *moon blade*. Their substance boils away from its touch, and they take 2d8 points of damage plus 1 point per caster level (to a maximum of +30) per blow. The blade is immaterial, and your Strength modifier does not apply to the damage.

A successful *moon blade* strike temporarily scrambles magic. On the target's next turn after a hit from a *moon blade*, the creature must make a Concentration check to use any spell or spell-like ability. The DC is 10 + points of damage dealt + spell level. (An opponent hit by a *moon blade* while casting a spell must make the usual Concentration check to avoid ruining the spell in addition to the check on its next turn.)

The *moon blade* spell has no connection with the magic items known as *moonblades* borne and made by some elves.

Arcane Material Component: A small candy made with wintergreen oil.

MOON PATH

Evocation [Force]
Level: Hth 5, Moon 5
Components: V, S, M/DF
Casting Time: 1 action
Range: Medium (100 ft. + 10 ft./level)
Effect: A variable-width, glowing white stair or bridge of translucent force up to 15 ft./level long (see text)
Duration: 1 minute/level (D)
Saving Throw: None (see text)
Spell Resistance: No

Moon path allows you to create a stair or bridge from one spot to another. The effect is a railless ribbon of glowing white translucent force like a glass strip. The strip can be from 3 to 20 feet wide as you decide. (You can vary the width over the ribbon's length if you want.) It sticks to its endpoints unshakably, even if these endpoints are in midair.

At the time of casting, you designate up to one creature per caster level to receive extra protection while standing on or moving along the *moon path*. Protected creatures gain the benefits of a *sanctuary*. This works exactly like the 1st-level spell *sanctuary* except that the save DC is 15 + your Wisdom modifier, and any subject of the spell who attacks breaks the *sanctuary* effect for all subjects. Protected creatures also stick to the top of the *moon path* as though they have received *spider climb* spells. A creature loses both benefits immediately when it leaves the path.

Unlike a *wall of force*, a *moon path* can be dispelled. It is otherwise similar to a *wall of force* in that it needs no supports and it is immune to damage of all kinds. A *disintegrate* blasts a hole 10 feet square, leaving the rest of the path intact. (If the moon path is 10 feet wide or less, this merely creates a 10-foot gap.) A hit from a *rod of cancellation*, a *sphere of annihilation*, or *Mordenkainen's disjunction* destroys a *moon path*. Spells and breath weapons cannot pass through a *moon path*, although *dimension door, teleport*, and similar effects can bypass the barrier. It blocks ethereal creatures as well as material creatures. Gaze attacks cannot operate through the *moon path*.

A *moon path* must be straight, continuous, and unbroken when formed. If its surface is broken by any object or creature, the spell fails. The bridge version of the spell must be created flat. The stair version cannot rise or descend any more sharply than 45 degrees.

Arcane Material Component: A white handkerchief.

MOONBEAM

Evocation [Light]
Level: Hth 2, Moon 2
Components: V, S, M/DF
Casting Time: 1 action
Range: Close (25 ft. + 5 ft./2 levels)
Area: Cone
Duration: 1 minute/level (D)
Saving Throw: None or Will negates (see text)
Spell Resistance: No

A cone of pale moonlight springs from your hand. On your turn each round, you can change the direction the cone points.

Light from a moonbeam does not adversely affect creatures that are sensitive to light, but lycanthropes in humanoid form caught in the cone must make Will saves to avoid involuntarily assuming their animal forms. Lycanthropes in animal form can change out of it on their next turn (spending a round in animal form). However, if they are still in the area of the spell, they must succeed at a Will save to do so. Once a lycanthrope successfully saves against *moonbeam*, it is not affected by any more of your *moonbeam* spells for 24 hours.

Moonbeam penetrates any darkness spell of equal or lower level, but does not counter or dispel it. Darkness spells of higher level block a *moonbeam*.

Arcane Material Component: A pinch of white powder.

MOONFIRE

Evocation [Light]
Level: Moon 9
Components: V, S, DF
Casting Time: 1 action
Range: Close (25 ft. + 5 ft./2 levels)
Area: Cone
Duration: Instantaneous (see text)
Saving Throw: Reflex half (see text)
Spell Resistance: Yes

A cone of fiery, white moonlight springs from your hand. Living creatures in the area feel an unnatural chill and take 1d8 points of damage per two caster levels, to a maximum of 10d8. Undead and shapechangers take double damage. This application of the spell allows a Reflex save for half damage.

All magical auras within the cone glow with a faint blue light for 1 round per caster level. Disguised, shapechanged, or polymorphed creatures and objects in the spell's area at the time the spell is cast must make Will saves or immediately return to their normal forms. Even if the save succeeds, they remain covered in ghostly white outlines that show their true forms for 1 round per caster level.

The entire area covered by the cone glows silver white for 1 round per caster level. This radiance is as bright as the light of a full moon and negates electricity for 1 round per caster level unless the creature generating it makes a caster level check against a DC equal to the caster's level. If an electricity effect is generated outside the glowing cone, the cone blocks the electricity effect if the caster level check fails. If an electricity effect is generated inside the glowing cone, the cone completely negates the electricity effect if the caster level check fails.

SCATTERSPRAY

Transmutation
Level: Hrp 1, Hth 1, Sor/Wiz 1
Components: V, S
Casting Time: 1 action
Range: Close (25 ft. + 5 ft./2 levels)
Target: Six or more Diminutive or Fine objects, all within 1 ft. of each other, whose total weight does not exceed 25 lb.
Duration: Instantaneous
Saving Throw: None (see text)
Spell Resistance: No

You can point to a collection of little, unsecured items and cause them to fly off in all directions simultaneously. The spray of items makes a burst with a 10-foot radius. If the items are fairly hard or sharp (such as stones, sling bullets, coins, or the like), creatures in the burst take 1d8 points of damage. A successful Reflex save negates this damage. Eggs, fruit, and other soft objects can be used, but the damage then dealt is subdual damage.

SHADOW MASK

Illusion (Shadow)
Level: Hrp 2, Sor/Wiz 2
Components: V, S, M
Casting Time: 1 action
Range: Personal
Target: You
Duration: 10 minutes/level (D)

You cause a mask of shadows to form around your face. It does not impede your vision, cannot be physically removed, completely hides your features, and protects you against certain attacks. You receive a +4 bonus on saving throws against light or darkness spells and any spells that rely on bright light for damaging effects, such as the *flare* spell or the fireworks effect of *pyrotechnics*. You also gain a 50% chance each round to avoid having to make a saving throw against gaze attacks, just as if you averted your eyes. If you avert your eyes while using *shadow mask*, you get to check twice to see if you avoid having to make the saving throw.

When the spell's duration ends, the *shadow mask* fades over the course of 1d4 rounds (rather than immediately), giving you time to keep your face hidden via other means. A successful *dispel magic* cast against a *shadow mask* effectively ends the spell and causes the same slow fading.

Material Component: A mask of black cloth.

SHADOW SPRAY

Illusion (Shadow)
Level: Sor/Wiz 2
Components: V, S, M
Casting Time: 1 action
Range: Medium (100 ft. + 10 ft./level)
Area: 5-foot radius burst
Duration: 1 round/level
Saving Throw: Fortitude negates (see text)
Spell Resistance: Yes

You cause a multitude of ribbonlike shadows to instantaneously explode outward from the target point. Creatures in the area take 2 points of temporary Strength damage, are dazed for 1 round, and suffer a −2 morale penalty on saving throws against *fear* spells and effects. The *fear* penalty ends when the *shadow spray* spell does, but the temporary Strength damage is instantaneous.

Material Component: A handful of black ribbons.

SNILLOC'S SNOWBALL SWARM

Evocation [Cold]
Level: Sor/Wiz 2
Components: V, S, M
Casting Time: 1 action
Range: Medium (100 ft. + 10 ft./level)
Effect: 10-ft.-radius burst
Duration: Instantaneous
Saving Throw: Reflex half
Spell Resistance: Yes

A flurry of magic snowballs erupts from a point you select. The swarm of snowballs deals 2d6 points of cold damage to creatures and objects within the burst. For every two caster levels beyond 3rd, the snowballs deal an extra die of damage, to a maximum of 5d6 at 9th level or higher.

Material Component: A piece of ice or a small white rock chip.

SPIDER CURSE

Transmutation [Mind-Affecting]
Level: Spider 6
Components: V, S, DF
Casting Time: 1 action
Range: Medium (100 ft. + 10 ft./level)
Target: 1 humanoid of Medium-size or smaller
Duration: 1 day/level
Saving Throw: Will negates
Spell Resistance: Yes

You turn a humanoid into a driderlike creature that obeys your mental commands.

The transmuted subject gains a spider's body with a humanoid head, arms, and torso, just like a drider.

The subject has a drider's speed, natural armor, bite attack, and poison (but see below). The subject gains a +4 bonus to its Strength, Dexterity, and Constitution scores.

The subject retains its Intelligence, Wisdom, and Charisma scores, level and class, hit points (despite any change in Constitution score), alignment, base attack bonus, and base saves. (New Strength, Dexter-

ity, and Constitution scores may affect final Armor Class, attack, and save bonuses.) The subject's equipment remains and continues to function as long as it fits a drider's body shape. Otherwise it is subsumed into the new form and ceases to function for the duration of the spell. Retained items include anything worn on the upper body (head, neck, shoulders, hands, arms, and waist). Nonfunctioning items include anything worn on the legs, feet, or the whole body (armor, robes, vestments, and boots).

The subject's bite delivers a poison with a Fortitude save DC of 16 + your Wisdom bonus. Initial and secondary damage is 1d6 points of temporary Strength damage.

Your control over the subject is like that provided by a *dominate person* spell. (You telepathically control the creature so long as it remains within range.)

Although *spider curse* is similar to *polymorph other*, it does not heal damage or cause disorientation.

SPIDER SHAPES

Transmutation
Level: Spider 9
Components: V, S, DF
Casting Time: 1 action
Range: Close (25 ft. + 5 ft./2 levels)
Targets: One willing creature/level, all within 30 ft. of each other
Duration: 1 hour/level (D)
Saving Throw: None (see text)
Spell Resistance: Yes (harmless)

As *polymorph other*, except you polymorph up to one willing creature per level into a monstrous spider of any size from Tiny to Huge as you decide (see Appendix 2 in the *Monster Manual*). All the creatures you transmute must become spiders of the same size. The spell has no effect on unwilling creatures.

Subjects remain in the spider form until the spell expires or you dismiss the spell for all subjects. In addition, an individual subject may choose to resume her normal form as a full-round action. Doing so ends the spell for her and her alone.

Parts separated from the resulting spiders do not revert to their original forms, so the resulting spiders have poisonous bites.

Creatures polymorphed by *spider shapes* don't suffer the disorientation penalty that those transformed by *polymorph other* often do. Subjects of *spider shapes* regain hit points as though they had rested for a day.

SPIDERFORM

Transmutation
Level: Drow 5
Components: V, S, DF
Casting Time: 1 action
Range: Personal
Targets: You
Duration: 1 hour/level (D)

You can polymorph into a drider or Tiny, Small, Medium-size, or Large monstrous spider (see the *Monster Manual*). You regain lost hit points as if you rested for a day on the initial transformation. The spell lasts until you decide to resume your normal shape.

You acquire the physical and natural abilities of the creature you polymorph into, including natural size, Strength, Dexterity, and Constitution scores, armor, attack routines, and movement capabilities.

Unlike *polymorph self*, you acquire the poisonous bite and web-spinning ability of whichever spider form you choose. You do not suffer any disorientation.

You retain your Intelligence, Wisdom, and Charisma scores, level and class, hit points (despite any change in Constitution score), alignment, base attack bonus, and base saves. (New Strength, Dexterity, and Constitution scores may affect final attack and save bonuses.) You can cast spells and use magic items if you choose drider form, but no other spider form is capable of spellcasting or manipulating devices.

If you choose drider form, your equipment remains and continues to function as long as it fits a drider's body shape. Retained items include anything worn on the upper body (head, neck, shoulders, hands, arms, and waist). Otherwise your equipment is subsumed into the new form and ceases to function for the duration of the spell.

STONE SPIDERS

Transmutation
Level: Spider 7
Components: V, S, DF
Casting Time: 1 full round
Range: Close (25 ft. + 5 ft./2 levels)
Targets: 1d3 pebbles or 1d3 vermin, no two of which can be more than 30 ft. apart
Duration: 1 round/level (D)
Saving Throw: None
Spell Resistance: No

You transform 1d3 pebbles into stone constructs that resemble monstrous spiders. The constructs can be any size from Tiny to Huge as you decide, but all the constructs you create must be the same size. The constructs have the same statistics as monstrous spiders (see Appendix 2 in the *Monster Manual*) of the appropriate size, except as follows:

Their natural armor increases by +6.

They have damage reduction 30/+2.

Their poison has a Fortitude save DC of 17 + your Wisdom modifier. Initial and secondary damage is 1d3 points of temporary Strength damage.

If the constructs can hear your commands, you can direct them not to attack, to attack particular enemies, or to perform other actions. Otherwise, they simply attack your enemies to the best of their abilities.

Alternatively, you can cast *stone spiders* on 1d3 vermin of any type or size. The affected vermin gain the benefits of a *stoneskin* spell (damage reduction 10/+5) for 1 round per caster level.

THUNDERLANCE

Evocation [Force]
Level: Sor/Wiz 4
Components: V, S, M
Casting Time: 1 action
Range: 0 ft.
Effect: A spearlike beam
Duration: 1 round/level (D)
Saving Throw: None
Spell Resistance: Yes

A faint, gray, shimmering force in the general shape of a staff or spear springs from your hand. You can freely make the force retract or grow to any size from 1 foot to 20 feet, but it always remains a straight lance of force. This gives you natural reach of 20 feet. You can use the *thunderlance* to make powerful melee attacks.

The *thunderlance* strikes as a Huge longspear, dealing a base 2d6 points of damage (crit ×3). You only need one hand to wield the *thunderlance,* and you suffer no nonproficiency penalties if you do not have Martial Weapon Proficiency (longspear). The *thunderlance* strikes with a Strength score equal to 12 + your caster level (maximum +15) which replaces your own Strength score when you make attack and damage rolls with the spell.

If you successfully strike a target protected by any force effect of 3rd level or lower, such as a *shield* or *mage armor* spell, the *thunderlance* may dispel the force effect in addition to damaging the target. Make a dispel check against the caster who created the effect. If you succeed, the effect is dispelled. The *thunderlance* remains whether you succeed or fail at this check.

You can choose to attack objects or to use the Strength score of the *thunderlance* for Strength scores involving breaking or damaging items.

Material Component: A small metal spear.

WATERSPOUT

Conjuration (Creation)
Level: Ocean 7
Components: V, S, DF
Casting Time: 1 full round
Range: Long (400 ft. + 40 ft./level)
Effect: A cylinder 10 ft. wide and 80 ft. tall
Duration: 1 round/level
Saving Throw: Reflex negates
Spell Resistance: No

Waterspout causes water to rise up into a whirling, cylindrical column. A body of water at least 10 feet wide and 20 feet deep must be present, or the spell is wasted. If the waterspout encounters insufficient depth after it has formed, it collapses.

The waterspout moves at a speed of 30 feet and must remain over water. You can concentrate on controlling the waterspout's every movement or specify a simple program, such as move straight ahead, zigzag, circle, or the like. Directing the waterspout's movement or changing its programmed movement is a standard action for you. The waterspout always moves during your turn in the initiative order. If the waterspout exceeds the spell's range, it collapses and the spell ends.

The waterspout batters creatures and objects it touches, and it often sucks them up. Any creature or object that comes in contact with the waterspout must succeed at a Reflex save or take 3d8 points of damage. Medium-size or smaller creatures who fail their save are sucked into the spout and held suspended in its powerful currents, taking 2d6 points of damage each round with no save allowed. Trapped creatures remain inside for 1d3 rounds before the waterspout ejects them out the top of the spout, and they fall back to the surface (taking falling damage) 1d8×5 feet from the base of the waterspout.

Waterborne creatures or objects within 10 feet of the spout (below and on all sides) also must make successful Reflex saves or be sucked into the spout if they are Medium-size or smaller. Anything sucked into the spout takes 3d8 points of damage and is then trapped for 1d3 rounds as explained above.

Only the smallest canoes, kayaks, or coracles can be sucked into the spout. The occupant of any such craft may make a Profession (sailor) check instead of a Reflex save (his choice) to avoid being sucked up.

Life in Faerûn

Nomadic hunters wander the icy barrens of the Great Glacier and the trackless jungles of Chult. Soot-covered armorers hammer away in the dwarven forges of the Great Rift and the stinking smelters of Baldur's Gate. Heavily guarded merchant caravans wind through Calimshan's harsh deserts and along the roads of the Heartlands. An adventurer's road leads through many lands and even more cultures, customs, and locales.

Most of Faerûn's humans labor as peasants, farmers, and simple craftsfolk, living in countless tiny thorps and villages. Over this vast sea of simple folk rule the wealthy and the privileged, in whatever form wealth and privilege take in a particular land. In some lands the common people are ruthlessly shackled and exploited by their cruel overlords, but by and large Faerûn is populated by folk content with their lot in life. This chapter covers many aspects of life in Faerûn.

Time and seasons

Almost every people or race of Faerûn marks the passage of days, seasons, and years in some fashion. In Cormyr and a dozen other kingdoms, royal astrologers carefully tend the Roll of Years. Even the war-heralds of the unlettered orc-tribes compose harsh chants that record the days and deeds of their fierce chieftains.

Day and Night

Faerûn's days are 24 hours long, divided into night and day by the rising and setting sun. In southern lands such as Halruaa, the length of the night does not vary much with the season, and 12 hours of light and 12 of dark is the rule year-round. In the north, the days are markedly longer in summer and shorter in winter. Midwinter day in Silverymoon sees little more than 8 hours of daylight, and Midsummer almost 16.

Ten days comprise a Faerûnian week, also known as a tenday or, less commonly, a ride. The individual days of the tenday do not have names. Instead, they're referred to by number: first-day, second-day, and so on. Most folk start counting using their thumb as first-day, but halflings are famous for using their pinkies to count first-day, so much so that the phrase "counting like a halfling" means that someone is being different just to be difficult.

The Hours of the Day

Timepieces are very rare, and most people break up the day into ten large slices—dawn, morning, highsun (or noon), afternoon, dusk, sunset, evening, midnight, moondark (or night's heart), and night's end. Dozens of conventions for naming these portions of the day exist, and cause no little confusion for travelers in foreign lands.

These customary divisions are only approximations, and one person's late afternoon might be another's early dusk. Local customs dictate the general length of each portion of the day. Each of these customary periods lasts anywhere from 1 to 4 hours, so highsun is generally accounted to be noon and an hour or so on either side.

Few Faerûnians have cause to measure an hour (or any length of time shorter than a day) with any great precision. People are accustomed to gauging time by intuition, the movement of the sun, and the activity around them. Two merchants might agree to meet at a particular tavern at dusk, and chances are both will show up within 15 or 20 minutes of each other.

In large cities, the tolling of temple bells replaces the more casual accounting of the day's passage. Several major faiths attempt to measure time more accurately. The priests of Gond treasure their mechanical clocks and delight in sounding them for all to hear. Lathanderians assign acolytes to watch sundials, carefully adjusted by years of observation of the sun's movements in the sky. Traditionally, the hours are numbered 1 to 12 twice, and the bells sound once for each hour on the hour. "Twelve bells" is virtually interchangeable with "midnight"—or "highsun," depending on the context.

The Calendar of Harptos

Most of Faerûn uses the Calendar of Harptos, named after the long-dead wizard who invented it. Few bother to refer to Harptos by name, since the calendar is the only calendar they know.

Each year of 365 days is divided into 12 months of 30 days, and each month is divided into three tendays. Five special days fall between the months. These annual holidays mark the seasons or the changing of the seasons. The months of Faerûn roughly correspond to the months of the Gregorian calendar.

TABLE 3-1: THE CALENDAR OF HARPTOS

Month	Name	Common Name
1	Hammer	Deepwinter
Annual holiday: Midwinter		
2	Alturiak	The Claw of Winter
3	Ches	The Claw of the Sunsets
4	Tarsakh	The Claw of the Storms
Annual holiday: Greengrass		
5	Mirtul	The Melting
6	Kythorn	The Time of Flowers
7	Flamerule	Summertide
Annual holiday: Midsummer		
8	Eleasis	Highsun
9	Eleint	The Fading
Annual holiday: Highharvestide		
10	Marpenoth	Leaffall
11	Uktar	The Rotting
Annual holiday: The Feast of the Moon		
12	Nightal	The Drawing Down

SEASONAL FESTIVALS

Five times a year the annual holidays are observed as festivals and days of rest in almost every civilized land. Each seasonal festival is celebrated differently, according to the traditions of the land and the particular holiday.

Midwinter: Nobles and monarchs greet the halfway point of winter with a feast day they call the High Festival of Winter. Traditionally it's the best day to make or renew alliances. The common folk enjoy the celebration a bit less—among them it's called Deadwinter Day, noted mainly as the halfway point of winter, with hard times still to come.

Greengrass: The official beginning of spring is a day of peace and rejoicing. Even if snow still covers the ground, clerics, nobles, and wealthy folk make a point of bringing out flowers grown in special rooms within temples and castles. They distribute the flowers among the people, who wear them or cast them upon the ground as bright offerings to the deities who summon the summer.

Midsummer: Midsummer night is a time of feasting and music and love. Acquaintances turn into dalliances, courtships turn into betrothals, and the deities themselves take a part by ensuring good weather for feasting and frolicking in the woods. Bad weather on this special night is taken as an omen of extremely ill fortune to come.

Highharvestide: This holiday of feasting to celebrate the autumn harvest also marks a time of journeys. Emissaries, pilgrims, adventurers, and everyone else eager to make speed traditionally leave on their journeys the following day—before the worst of the mud clogs the tracks and the rain freezes into snow.

The Feast of the Moon: The Feast of the Moon celebrates ancestors and the honored dead. Stories of ancestors' exploits mix with the legends of deities until it's hard to tell one from the other.

SHIELDMEET

Once every four years, Shieldmeet is added to the Faerûnian calendar as a "leap day" immediately following Midsummer night. Shieldmeet is day of open council between the people and their rulers. It is a day for making or renewing pacts and for proving oneself in tournaments. Those not seeking advancement treat the elite's tournaments, duels, and trials of magical prowess as welcome additions to the holiday's theatrical and musical entertainments.

In the Dales, a great Shieldmeet celebration is planned in the town of Essembra in Battledale this year. Other regions of Faerûn have planned festivals ranging from the somber to the outrageous.

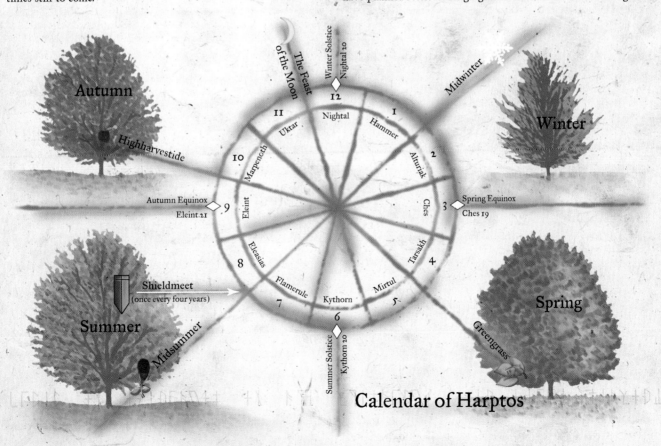

Calendar of Harptos

marking the years

Almost every land and race has its own preferred system for marking the passing years. The ancient realm of Mulhorand begins its calendar at the founding of Skuld, the City of Gods, more than 3,500 years ago. Cormyrians reckon years from the foundation of House Obarskyr almost 1,350 years ago. Some draconic calendars are reputed to stretch back more than 10,000 years, although few dragons care about something as mundane as the scholarly accounting of events that even the oldest dragons alive today do not remember.

DALERECKONING

The calendar against which most others are compared is Dalereckoning (DR), marked by the raising of the Standing Stone and the pact between the elves of Cormanthor and the first human settlers of the Dalelands. Dalereckoning was the first human calendar the Elven Court reconciled with its own ages-old calendar, and thus became widespread anywhere elves and humans lived in peace.

THE ROLL OF YEARS

Very few of Faerûn's common folk bother with musty calendars and meaningless numbers. Instead, years are known by names. For example, 1372 DR—the current year—is called the Year of Wild Magic. People refer to births, deaths, weddings, and other events by the name of the year. Children learn the order of the years from bards' songs, artistic designs in the great temples, and the teachings of their elders.

The naming of a year is not random, nor does it necessarily commemorate any great event or occurrence. Many centuries ago the Lost Sage Augathra the Mad wrote out thousands of years and named them in the great library of Candlekeep. It's a rare year that doesn't see some event that seems clearly connected with its name, and most folks view Augathra's names as mysterious portents of the years ahead.

1372 DR	The Year of Wild Magic (current year)
1373 DR	The Year of Rogue Dragons
1374 DR	The Year of Lightning Storms
1375 DR	The Year of Risen Elfkin
1376 DR	The Year of the Bent Blade
1377 DR	The Year of the Haunting
1378 DR	The Year of the Cauldron
1379 DR	The Year of the Lost Keep
1380 DR	The Year of the Blazing Hand

lore of the land

Toril is a large world, and Faerûn one of its largest continents. Thanks to diligent sages and scribes over centuries, the details and characteristics of many lands have been recorded. But in all that time, only a small part of Faerûn has been described in any detail.

To most folk who dwell in it, climate is a matter of harsh basics: when the seasons come, how the growing season (and therefore the available food supply) fares, and how severe the weather is the rest of the time. In general, the kingdoms of Faerûn produce more than enough food to feed their people and the various beasts that roam them. But localized shortages and the perils of lack of water, blistering heat, exposure, and freezing keep folk from complacency.

climate

The lands of Faerûn encompass extremes from the frigid arctic to the steamy tropics. Few have conducted any real study of the continent's weather patterns. A farmer in the Heartlands knows only that winters are too long and cold, spring and fall too long and wet (with lingering frosts and too much mud), and the too-short summer is too hot. Perhaps the weather is better over the next hill.

CHARACTERISTICS

Two chief characteristics describe a particular region's climate: its latitude and its precipitation. Of course, many local conditions can affect climate. High elevation, for example, has much the same effect as high latitude, so snow-capped mountains are not unheard of even in the tropics. Large bodies of water tend to moderate temperatures in the lands nearby. The ever-present strivings of the deities to bring about the kind of weather that pleases them is a factor of great importance in Faerûn. As often as not, it snows because Auril or Talos wants it to snow. Finally, great magical curses and spells can affect the weather over vast reaches—such as the Anauroch Desert.

The following survey of Faerûn begins at the Sword Coast and proceeds counterclockwise.

THE NORTHWEST

In its northernmost reaches, the Sword Coast is a forever frozen, wind-blasted waste that becomes the Endless Ice Sea overlying the continent as far east as one can go and still find land. A mountain range, the Spine of the World, holds back this polar ice cap from cloaking the Sword Coast North, but only onshore breezes make frozen Icewind Dale habitable at all—and that settlement lacks a growing season entirely.

South of the mountains is the crag- and lake-studded "Savage Frontier" of the North. These alpine valleys know only a short, fierce summer, and see icy water, chilling mists, and ice-capped mountains year-round. A little farther south, in the lower valley of the Dessarin, or the vales of the Gray Peaks, the land is rich and blessed with a long enough growing season to support great cities.

The northwest portion of Faerûn is generally well watered and humid, with heavy snowfalls in the winter and a great deal of rain in the spring and fall. Along the Sword Coast, folk exaggeratedly complain that it never stops raining.

As one travels south, the land warms until one can find dust, sand, and scorching heat around Scornubel and the southern reaches of the Anauroch Desert.

THE SOUTHWEST

True temperate conditions hold sway from about the River Chionthar (Baldur's Gate) southward, and the land grows warmer and hotter until both true deserts and steamy temperatures are the rule in southernmost Tethyr and Calimshan. Sea breezes cool Nimbral, Lantan, and Tashalar, but volcanism makes the Lake of Steam area uncomfortable to most civilized inhabitants, and combines with latitude and warm sea-damp to make Chult and Mhair endless jungle steam baths.

The southwest, like the northwest, is very humid and receives a great deal of precipitation from the western seas. The cooling, moisture-holding properties of forests play a part in keeping Tethyr and the Border Kingdoms moderate in climate and pleasant places to live.

THE SOUTHEAST

The Great Sea south of Halruaa is warm, and Rethild, Dambrath, Luiren, and the lands about the Golden Water are all warm to hot places of sweat, many insects, long summers, and short, stormy winters. The prevailing winds carry rainfall to the coastlands, but the mountain chains following the coastline (the Toadsquat and Gnollwatch mountains) create a rain shadow in the interior of this corner of Faerûn. The Shaar is an arid grassland that sometimes goes months without rain.

The great windblown plains of the Shaar, Raurin, and the Plains of Purple Dust are also far from the moderating effects of lakes and seas. Summers are extremely hot and dry, while winters can be perversely cold—the Shaar routinely experiences winter cold unknown in the southern reaches of the Sword Coast, more than a thousand miles to the north.

THE NORTHEAST

The icily aggressive cold of the Great Glacier affects most of the lands north and east of the Sea of Fallen Stars. This is an arid region, and forests do not flourish here. The Moonsea tends to be chilly year-round, and winds blowing south from the northern ice make Thar fiercely cold most of the year.

THE INTERIOR

If the Sea of Fallen Stars (also called the Inner Sea) did not exist, the center of Faerûn would most likely be a vast desert far from the rainfall and moderating temperatures of the coast. The Sea of Fallen Stars provides rainfall and moderate temperatures to the surrounding lands. Relatively shallow and affected in places by seabed volcanism, the Inner Sea warms the lands all around it, while at the same time keeping them damp (and therefore verdant, the Vilhon Reach in particular).

The winds and weather that derive from the Inner Sea make Cormyr, Sembia, and the Dales quite pleasant places to live—despite cool mountain winds and harsh winters that often make the Wyvernwater and the coasts of the Moonsea, the Dragon Reach, and the Dragonmere freeze over.

THE OCEANS

The warmth felt by sailors on the eastern Great Sea speaks of the strength of warming ocean currents. They are the reason Zakhara enjoys moderate temperatures for a greater span of distance southward from the equator than the Sword Coast region does to the north, and also the reason why so much of Kara-Tur and the known part of Maztica have warm climates.

Evermeet, the island kingdom of the elves far to the west of the Sword Coast, enjoys a far gentler climate than the Moonshaes, which are much closer to mainland Faerûn. A warm current sweeps northwest out of the Great Sea and curves past eastern Evermeet on its way toward the Icepeak and Icewind Dale, accounting for Evermeet's sunny climes.

flora and fauna

The vegetation and wildlife of an area are governed first and foremost by its weather. In northern, humid regions, evergreen forests are quite common. Temperate areas have deciduous forests. Toril is a large world, and Faerûn is only part of it—and even druids and rangers and explorers of long years in the wild do not claim to know all the kinds of forests or types of animals that may be found in Faerûn.

TREES AND SHRUBS

Travelers who have ventured into other planes and worlds claim that the same oak, ash, maple, chestnut, spruces, and pines among Faerûn's trees are also found in those distant places. Here follow a few of the most dramatic, plentiful, or useful trees and shrubs found only in Faerûn.

Blueleaf: Recognizable by the eerie, gleaming blue color of their many-pointed leaves, blueleafs (not "blueleaves") bend in winds or under ice rather than breaking, often forming snow tunnels that shelter winter travelers. Blueleafs grow close together in thick stands, reaching 40 feet in height but rarely attaining thick trunks.

Blueleaf wood is durable, and the sap and crushed leaves yield a vivid blue dye much favored in cloakmaking in the North. When burned, it yields beautiful leaping blue flames (prized in inns and taverns as "mood" illumination for tale-tellers and minstrels).

Blueleaf is found in humid temperate and subarctic latitudes north of Amn.

Helmthorn: A vinelike ground shrub that sometimes cloaks other bushes and dead trees, helmthorn has dark, waxy green leaves and bristling black thorns. As long as human hands, these sharp, durable thorns are often used as crude needles or dart points. Helmthorn berries are indigo in hue, edible (tart in flavor), and often harvested even when frozen or withered for use in winemaking.

Helmthorn is very hardy and grows throughout Faerûn, providing food for many.

Shadowtop: The soaring giants of Faerûnian forests, shadowtops can grow 2 feet a year and top out at 90 feet. A full-grown shadowtop flares out to a diameter of 10 feet or more at its base, its trunk surrounded by many pleatlike ridges. Shadowtops are named for the dense clusters of feathery leaves at the tops of their trunks. Shadowtop leaves are irregular in shape and have copper undersides and deep green upper surfaces.

Shadow-wood is fibrous and tough, but unsuitable for carving or structural work because under stress it splits down its length into splayed fibers. These fibers are valued in ropemaking (a few added to the twist improves the strength and durability of a completed coil) and burns slowly but cleanly, generating a very hot fire with little smoke. This makes it ideal for cooking.

waterdeep's climate

Waterdeep lies slightly above the 45 degree north latitude line on Toril. The ocean's proximity moderates the more severe aspects of the northern climate, so rain falls as commonly as snow in fall and spring, changing roads to rivers of mud. Prevailing winds blow from the west to the east.

A vast southward-moving current, usually called the Southern Drift by sailors, lies immediately offshore from Waterdeep. This current is the tail end of a gigantic clockwise rotating current in the northern Trackless Sea between Máztica and Faerûn, encircling the Moonshaes and Evermeet. Interesting debris from across the sea sometimes floats past Waterdeep on the current.

Arctic winds often sweep down over Waterdeep in late fall and winter, moving from the northwest to the southeast, carrying ferocious storms, snow, hail, and freezing rain. Icebergs are rarely seen here because of the warm offshore current, but ice often forms along the shore in winter and may clog Waterdeep's harbor. Icy roads are easier to travel over than muddy ones, which is why the spring thaw is regarded with glum favor by travelers, merchants, and soldiers.

Shadow-wood is much used in the making of magical staffs, rods, and wands.

Shadowtops are found in all humid areas across Faerûn.

Suth: Suth are graybark trees with olive-green leaves. They grow almost horizontally and then double back to angle in another direction. If a few suth trees grow together, their branches intertwine until they are inextricably entangled, forming a screen or wall barring passage to all things that can't fly over the tangled trees or scuttle under their lowest branches. Suth leaves are long, soft, and fluffy, but spike-ended.

Suth-wood is very hard and durable, so hard that it's difficult to work without the finest tools. Thin sheets of this wood retain astonishing strength for decades, and thus are favored for use in book covers. Suth is also the preferred wood for shields since it never shatters and doesn't catch fire if soaked in water before battle. A crushing blow might crack a suth-wood shield but won't cause it to fly apart.

The name of this tree may be a corruption of the word "south." Suth are found along the edges of the Shaar, in the woods of Chondath, and farther south in Faerûn.

Weirwood: Weir trees resemble oaks but have leaves that are brown (with a silver sheen) on their uppers and velvety black beneath. If undisturbed, weir trees grow into huge, many-branched forest giants. Weirwood won't ignite in normal (non-magical) fire and is resilient and durable. It's favored in the making of musical instruments because of the unmistakable warm, clear tone it imparts.

Weirwood can be used as a replacement for oak or holly in any spell. It grows throughout Faerûn but is very rare. Most trees are now found deep in large forests and actively protected by dryads, treants, druids, and rangers.

Zalantar: Often called blackwood in the North because of its jet-black wood and bark, the zalantar tree has a central root and eight or more trunks that branch out from the root at ground level like the splayed fingers of a hand. The trees may reach 60 feet in height, but are usually half that. Their leaves are white through beige.

Zalantar wood is strong yet easily worked and sees much use in southern buildings and the making of wagons, litters, and wheels. Southern wizards and sorcerers use durable and handsome zalantar wood almost exclusively in the making of rods, staffs, and wands.

This subtropical species is rarely seen north of the Shaar. It is plentiful along the shores of Chult and the southern coasts of Faerûn and seems to grow in any terrain short of mountainous.

WILD AND DOMESTIC ANIMALS

Given the vast distances they travel, adventurers in Faerûn understand the value of a reliable mount. Those who seldom travel outside a city may care nothing about mounts, and instead think of avoiding, fighting, or eliminating guard beasts owned by others.

For humans, horses and mules are the most popular mounts for almost all purposes. In unusual situations such as aerial travel, Underdark travel, and extreme climates, folk favor griffons or pegasi, riding lizards, and camels in deserts or ghost rothé in frozen wastes.

Beasts of burden are usually valued for their strength, endurance, and temperament, with oxen at the head of the list and horses considered the most nimble (again, with adjustments for climate and nature of travel). Beyond that, most folk have little care for the wildlife around them except as it competes for their viands (wolves, foxes, and rats), offers them direct peril (poisonous snakes), or is easily snared or slain in the hunt for use on the table (rabbits, deer, grouse, and river fish that can be drag-netted or caught in a weir).

Dragons and other large predators that require great amounts of food often survey beasts around them very much as humans do—prizing herd animals grazing in the open as the easiest food to take.

The same endless wheel of eat-and-be-eaten governs life in Faerûn as in a dozen worlds. Folk who live close to the land (rangers, hunters, foragers, and farmers) know well that the little chipmunklike rodent they call the berrygobbler is as important in the scheme of things as the wolf that eats the creature that ate the creature that devoured a luckless berrygobbler. They also know that dying berrygobblers signals some taint or fell magic or disease upon the land.

In the Heartlands, mice, rats, berrygobblers, rabbits, hares, raccoons, and squirrels are familiar scurriers underfoot. In Calimshan and Tashalar, the warmer climes see mice, rats, slinks (very swift black-furred berrygobblers), skradda (darting, sticky-tongued lizards that eat insects and small frogs), and sardrant (armadillolike plant-chewers, slow-moving, shaggy, and semiarmored, with edible meat).

Fish leap out of the oceans and rivers: bluefin and silverfin, the brilliant, tiny, inedible silver jewelfish, and the splar (winged eels that can leap but not really fly).

The shaggy, buffalolike rothé dwells in both hot and cold climes. The North has the ghost or snow rothé. The brown rothé ambles across the Heartlands and the South, becoming lighter in hue and less shaggy as latitudes become warmer. The deep rothé inhabits the Underdark.

Only foolish adventurers or city-dwellers ignore the lesser fauna of Faerûn. As the adventurer Steeleye once noted, "Rabbits fall easily into the stewpot, but downing, butchering, and cooking your dragon is a task that can take up your whole day."

Home and Hearth

Wood elves make their homes in graceful pavilions under the stars in forest clearings, rarely remaining in the same place for more than a day or two. Shield dwarves carve workshops and mines from the hearts of mountains, fortifying their homes. Goblins and orcs favor warrens of burrows in the wilderness. Human homes run the gamut from a herder's yurt in the Endless Waste to a prince's palatial townhouse along Waterdeep's richest street. Any experienced traveler soon comes to appreciate that there are as many different ways of life in Faerûn as there are kinds of people.

Orc-infested mountain ranges, troll-haunted wastelands, wild woods guarded by secretive and unfriendly fey creatures, and sheer distance divide Faerûn's nations from each other. Faerûn's city-states and kingdoms are small islands of civilization in a vast, hostile world, held together by tenuous lines of contact.

Government

The most common forms of government in the Heartlands are feudal monarchies, generally found in the larger realms and more isolated lands, and plutocratic monarchies, common among city-states and realms dominated by trade. In either case, a hereditary lord, king, monarch, or potentate holds the power to make laws, dispense justice, and manage foreign affairs. The monarch's power is checked to a greater or lesser degree by the powerful feudal lords or wealthy merchant princes who owe him allegiance.

Since the nobles or great merchants are ruled only by their own consent, many Heartlands city-states and kingdoms are realms of weak central authority and strongly independent nobility. A monarch who pushes a willful noble too far might drive that noble to open revolt—and in many cases the noble's strength-of-war is nearly the match of the overlord's, so quelling a rebellious province is hardly an easy undertaking. Worse yet, a monarch may be forced to solicit the support (or at least neutrality) of other nobles of the realm as he goes about suppressing one of their peers. This support usually comes at a price, further eroding royal authority.

Strong thrones may be rare, but they do exist. The Cormyr of King Azoun Obarskyr was a shining example of the good that can come of a strong monarchy in the hands of a wise and courageous leader. Unfortunately, the death of Azoun and the plague of evils that descended on that land have left Cormyr's fate uncertain. Azoun's daughter, the Regent Alusair, must chart a careful course among the realm's nobility as she attempts to retain the power her father held.

Civil warfare in the mercantile city-states of the Inner Sea is rare, but the lords and princes who rule these small realms must contend with merchant-nobles every bit as willful and haughty as a feudal lord in his castle. In the walls of a city-state, a wealthy noble thinks carefully before defying the ruler, since he lacks the safety of miles of roads and empty lands between his demesne and his ruler's army. But it also means that any noble's own private army is only an hour's march from the seat of power. Powerful lords deal with overmasters they don't like through palace coups, feuds, and assassinations.

city and countryside

In the Heartlands, a very basic division separates people into two distinct groups: townsfolk and rural folk. The dividing line is blurry at times—a large village or small town blends many of the characteristics of rural and urban life. The division is not exclusive. Even in Faerûn's largest cities, farmers and herders till crops and tend livestock within the shadow of the city walls.

In most lands, nine people live in the countryside for every city-dweller. Large cities are hard to sustain, and in Faerûn's Heartlands, most people are compelled to work the land in order to feed themselves. Large towns and cities can only flourish in places that enjoy easy access to farmlands and resources producing a surplus of food.

RURAL LIFE

In painting a picture of the average Faerûnian, an observer discovers that the most ordinary, unremarkable, and widespread representative of Faerûn's incredible diversity is a simple human farmer. She lives in a small house of wood, sod, or thatch-roofed fieldstone, and she raises staple crops such as wheat, barley, corn, or potatoes on a few dozen acres of her own land.

In some lands the common farmer is a peasant or a serf, denied the protection of law and considered the property of whichever lord holds the land she lives on. In a few harsh lands, she is a slave whose backbreaking work is rewarded only by the threat of the lash and swift death should she ever defend herself from the overseers and lords who live off her endless toil. But in the Heartlands she is free if somewhat poor, protected from rapacious local lords by the law of the land, and allowed to choose whatever trade or vocation she has a talent for in order to feed her family and raise her children.

The common farmer's home is within a mile or so of a small village, where she can trade grain, vegetables, fruit, meat, milk, and eggs for locally manufactured items such as spun cloth, tools, and worked leather. Some years are lean, but Faerûn's Heartlands are rich and pleasant, rarely knowing famine or drought.

A local lord guards the common farmer from bandits, brigands, and monsters. He is a minor noble whose keep or fortified manor house watches over her home village. The noble appoints a village constable to keep order and might house a few of the king's soldiers or his own guards to defend against unexpected attack. Within a day's ride, a more powerful noble whose lands include one or two dozen villages like the typical commoner's has a castle manned by several dozen soldiers. In dangerous areas, defenses are much sturdier and trained warriors more numerous.

CITY LIFE

Typical townsfolk or city-dwellers are skilled crafters of some kind. Large cities are home to numbers of unskilled laborers and small merchants or storeowners, but the most city-dwellers work with their hands to make finished goods from raw materials. Smiths, leatherworkers, potters, brewers, weavers, woodcarvers, and all other kinds of artisans and tradesfolk working in their homes make up the industry of Faerûn.

The city-dweller lives in a wood or stone house, shingled with wooden shakes or slate, that sits shoulder-to-shoulder with its neighbors in great sprawling blocks through which myriad narrow streets and alleyways ramble. In small or prosperous towns, his home might include a small plot of land suitable for a garden. Many relations, boarders, or whole families of strangers share his crowded home. If he isn't married, he might live as a boarder with someone else.

In some cities he may be required to join great guilds of craftsfolk with similar skills, or risk imprisonment. In others, agents of the city's ruling power closely monitor his activities and movements, rigidly enforcing exacting laws of conduct and travel. But in most cases, he is free to pack up and leave or change trades whenever he likes.

He purchases food from the city's markets, which sometimes means that he is stuck with whatever fits within his budget. A prosperous man can work hard and comfortably feed his family, but in lean times the poorer laborers must make do with stale bread and thin soup for weeks on end. Every city depends on a ring of outlying villages and farmlands to supply it with food on a daily basis. Most also possess great granaries against times of need, and many provisioners and grocers specialize in stocking nonperishable foodstuffs at times of the year when fresh food is not available in the city's markets.

A city of any size is probably protected by a city wall, patrolled by the city watch, and garrisoned by a small army of the soldiers of the land. Rampaging monsters or bloodthirsty bandits don't trouble the average city-dweller, but he rubs elbows every day with rogues, thieves, and cutthroats. Even the most thoroughly policed cities have neighborhoods where anybody with a whit of common sense doesn't set foot.

WEALTH AND PRIVILEGE

Just as nine out of ten Faerûnians live in small villages and freeholds in the countryside, roughly nineteen out of twenty people are of common birth and ordinary means. They rarely accumulate any great amount of wealth—a prosperous innkeeper or skilled artisan might be able to set her hands on a few hundred gold pieces, but most common farmers and tradesfolk are lucky if they have more than forty or fifty silvers to their name.

In many lands, common-born people are bound by law to defer to their betters, the lords and ladies of the nobility. Even if the law does not require deference, it's usually a good idea. Nobles enjoy many protections under the law and in some cases can escape punishment for assault, provocation, or the outright murder of a commoner.

The typical noble is a rural baronet or lordling whose lands span only a few miles, ruling over a few hundred common folk in the king's name. She collects taxes from the villagers and farmers and is vastly more wealthy than all but the most prosperous entrepreneurs in her lands. With her wealth and power come certain responsibilities, of course. She is answerable to her own feudal masters for the lawkeeping and good order of her lands. She can be called upon to provide soldiers and arms for her lords' causes. And, most important, most nobles feel some obligation to protect the people in their charge against the depredations of monsters and banditry. To this end, most nobles frequently deal with companies of adventurers, retaining their services to clear out troublesome monsters and hunt down desperate outlaws.

class and station

As Cormyr's recent troubles prove, the Heartlands of Faerûn are not always stable or safe. Incursions of monstrous hordes of orcs, ogres, or giants can easily overrun even stoutly defended cities. Would-be kings continually challenge the powers of the land from within, seeking to unseat the ruler. Proud and arrogant foreign powers watch warily for any sign of weakness, always ready to annex a province or sack a city. Magical disasters, plagues, and flights of raging dragons can lay low even the most peaceful and secure lands.

To fend off these dangers, most realms of the Heartlands have developed an enlightened feudal system over centuries of strife and warfare. Lords hold lands in the name of their king, raising armies and collecting taxes to defend the realm. They are expected to answer their king's call to arms and to defend his interests to the best of their ability. This reasonably effective system supports independent warbands in the defense of far-flung territories.

THE PEASANTRY

As previously noted, common farmers and simple laborers make up most of the human population of Faerûn's kingdoms and cities. The lowest class across all of the Heartlands, the peasantry forms the solid base upon which the power structures of nobles, merchants, temples, and kingdoms all rest.

Most Heartlands peasants are not bound to the lands they work and owe no special allegiance to the lord who rules over them, other than obeying his laws and paying his taxes. They do not own their farmlands but instead rent croplands and pastures from the local lord, another form of taxation normally accounted at harvest time.

In frontier regions such as the Western Heartlands, many common farmers own and work their own lands. These people are sometimes known as freeholders if no lord claims their lands, or yeomen if they are common landowners subject to a lord's authority.

TRADESFOLK AND MERCHANTS

A step above the common peasantry, skilled craftsfolk and merchants generate wealth and prosperity for any city or town. The so-called middle class is weak and disorganized in most feudal states, but in the great trade cities of the Inner Sea, strong guilds of traders and companies of craftsfolk are strong enough to defy any lord and protect themselves from the monarch's authority by the power of their coffers.

The wealthiest merchants are virtually indistinguishable from mighty lords. Even if born from peasant stock, a merchant whose enterprises span a kingdom might style himself "lord" and get away with it.

CLERGY

Existing alongside the feudal relationship of a rural province or guild organization of a trading city, the powerful temples of Faerûn's deities parallel the king's authority. The lowest-ranking acolytes and mendicants are rarely reckoned beneath the station of a well-off merchant, and any cleric or priest in charge of a temple holds power comparable to that of a baronet or lord. The high priests of a faith favored in a particular land are equal to the highest nobility.

Many of Faerûn's temples are implacable enemies or bitter rivals. In most rural regions, folk tend to follow one or two deities who are particularly active or actively supported in their immediate locale. If a powerful and benevolent temple of Tempus happens to stand just outside a small town, many townspeople will worship Tempus, even if farmers are generally more inclined to the teachings of Chauntea and merchants might otherwise follow Waukeen.

LOW NOBILITY

Descended from warriors who won land to rule (or valuable hereditary positions with handsome stipends) in service to their homeland or king, the low nobility is the backbone of the feudal realm. From their sons and daughters are drawn the knights and officers of the king's armies, and from their house guards and vaults come the manpower and gold necessary to field the kingdom's fighting power. They administer the king's justice within their demesnes and collect his taxes.

Low nobles hold court to settle disputes that occur on their land or under their responsibility, and are expected to try cases of low justice—just about any crime short of murder or treason. They claim a tithe of any wealth in food or gold generated by the commoners who work their land, and may levy local taxes as long as they do not interfere with the monarch's taxes. In return, they are expected to see to the defense and prosperity of their fiefs. Regrettably, more than one local lord is nothing more than a thief in a castle, wringing every copper he can from the people he rules.

A new breed of low noble is rising in prosperous lands such as Sembia and Impiltur—the so-called merchant prince. A merchant establishes an enterprise or industry of great and lasting value, and

titles and forms of address

Most realms across Faerûn have some form of nobility, and many also have ruling royalty. All have officials who sport titles, from a simple "Master of the . . ." to such mouthfuls as "His Most Exalted and Terrible, Beloved of the Gods and Venerable Before All His People, Hereditary and-may-his-line-prosper-forever. . . ." Many long and involved tomes at Candlekeep outline the intricacies of the various systems of titles, their ranks and precedence. Here's a brief overview.

Position	Male	Female
Commoner	Goodman	Goodwife or Maid
Knight, Officer	Sir	Lady or Lady Sir
Mayor, Warden, Commander, Seneschal	Lord	Lady or Lady Lord
Baron, Count	Milord	Milady
Duke, Viscount, Marquis	High Lord	High Lady
Grand Duke, Prince,	Highness	Highness
King, Queen, Archduke	Majesty	Majesty

General titles for nobility of uncertain rank include "Zor/Zora" in Mulmaster, "Syl" in Calimshan, and "Saer" (for both genders) almost everywhere else. This latter term also applies to children of nobility too young or low-ranking to have been awarded titles of their own.

In general Heartlands usage, if the head of a noble house is "Lord Grayhill," his children are all "Saer [name] Grayhill." His widowed or aged parents, or older uncles and aunts living but bypassed in precedence are "Old Lord (or Lady) Grayhill."

Various Faerûnian professions and races have popular verbal greetings and farewells, but "Well met" for both is almost universal. Oloré ("oh-LOR-ay") serves the same purpose around the Sea of Fallen Stars, and human nobles are adopting the elven "Sweet water and light laughter until next we meet." Merchants of all races often use the terse dwarven "I go."

then passes it to his heirs. Over time these upstarts may hope to purchase with gold the noble title otherwise won only by valor in days long past.

Knights, lords, baronets, and barons are accounted low-landed nobles. Lord-mayors, sheriffs, commanders, wardens, and seneschals are low nobles who hold titles but no lands.

High Nobility

Frequently related by blood or marriage to the ruling family, high nobles are those who are due allegiance from some number of low nobles. Unlike low nobles, who frequently carry noble titles without lands, high nobles are usually landed, commanding great fiefs that could be considered small kingdoms in their own right.

High nobles hear disputes that lower nobles cannot settle, and dispense justice for all but the most heinous of crimes. Like low nobles, they collect taxes in the ruler's name and levy additional taxes as they see fit. They maintain personal armies sometimes numbering in the hundreds and use them to vigorously police and patrol their lands.

The high counselors of a kingdom or realm are often accounted high nobles, even if they are not rewarded with lands. The stipends and royalties associated with their titles make them some of the wealthiest people in a kingdom.

Counts, viscounts, dukes, earls, and marquises are high-landed nobles. Lord-governors and high counselors are high-titled nobles. Grand dukes, archdukes, and princes are considered royalty, even if they are not immediately related to the ruling house.

Families

As a rule, adventurers do not choose to begin families while they actively pursue their careers—lich lords and raging dragons tend to make a lot of widows and orphans. But for the common folk of the land and even the great lords, the most important thing in the world is their family. Parents carefully train their children in the trades they follow and secure their property for the day they pass their homes and businesses to their children.

The Heartlands of Faerûn are generally enlightened and liberal regarding gender roles. Women are as free as men to own property, run businesses, and run off to become adventurers. Many of Faerûn's most powerful heroes are women. Some societies observe strict codes of gender conduct (some matriarchal, not patriarchal), but this is not the case in most of Faerûn.

Marriage

In almost every society, human and nonhuman, marriage ceremonies are celebrated with feasting, dancing, song, and stories. The exact customs vary wildly from land to land, but in any Heartlands village a marriage is an excuse to set aside work for a day and celebrate.

Among nobles, arranged marriages are not unusual, but very few commoners marry against their will. Marriages for love are far more common. Divorce is rare, particularly since standards of marital fidelity are decidedly relaxed in some lands. It's not unknown for a man or woman to have more than one spouse at the same time, but such arrangements are rare and usually reserved for those who have enough money or power to do whatever they like.

Children

Children are regarded as a blessing and a treasure throughout the Heartlands. Large families are quite common, especially in relatively safe and prosperous regions. The careful attention of clerics, healers, and divine healing magic makes childbirth reasonably safe in most civilized lands.

In parts of Faerûn, particularly in rural areas dependent on agriculture, responsibilities and tasks come to children early. Children from urban areas begin to learn their parents' trades at a similarly early age. By eight to ten years of age, most children are well on their way to acquiring the knowledge necessary to continue in their parents' work. The children of nobles and wealthy merchants are formally schooled and enjoy significantly more leisure time until their mid-teens.

Ironically, children from nomadic and "savage" groups may enjoy the happiest childhood, since they're encouraged to develop the skills that will serve them as adults by playing in the wilds. This is not to say that children are allowed to roam free without supervision from discreet guards—life in Faerûn is too dangerous to allow innocents to wander completely unguarded.

Old Age

Common laborers, farmers, and peasants work until the day they die, unless they have strong and dependable children who can take over the family enterprise and care for them. A life without work is usually only an option for the wealthy, including the few adventurers who live to middle age to enjoy their loot in peace. On the bright side, the blessings of the gods and the beneficial prayers and spells of clerics and healers avert many of the worst ravages of old age. Elderly folk rarely suffer extended infirmities or disabling illness until just before death.

Learning

Formal schooling is the exception rather than the rule in the Heartlands. Only the children of wealthy or highborn parents receive any real education. Even so, most Faerûnians of civilized lands are literate and understand the value and the potential power of the written word.

Most people learn to read and write from their parents or from clerics of Oghma or Deneir. Very few schools exist. Those that do are expensive, exclusive, private schools or academies that spend as much time teaching riding, courtly manners, and swordplay as they do on true academic matters. Most young nobles or merchant scions acquire their education from personal tutors, bards, heralds, and noble counselors retained specifically for that purpose by their parents.

True scholarly learning is the preserve of sages, scribes, clerics, and wizards. The nonhuman races of Faerûn, particularly the elves, are a notable exception to that statement, as are human cities or nations that encourage citizens to study with the clergy of deities who promote knowledge and learning.

Adventurers

Any heroic adventurer breaks many of the rules and norms associated with the feudal hierarchy. She is often the champion of the common folk, yet granted access to the highest halls of power as an agent of her lord or king. Generations of good-hearted adventurers have helped make Faerûn a safer and better place to live, and any ruler knows that the best way to solve a sticky problem often involves finding the right adventurer for the job.

By definition, adventurers are well armed and magically capable beings who are incredibly dangerous to their enemies . . . and not always healthy to be around, even for their friends. Lords and merchants tread carefully around adventurers and take steps to defend themselves against a powerful adventurer who suddenly develops a crusading zeal or an appetite for power—typically by retaining skillful and well-paid bodyguards to discourage sudden violence.

ADVENTURER COMPANIES

Groups of adventurers sometimes form communal associations that share treasure, responsibility, and risk. Adventuring companies stand a better chance of receiving official recognition and licenses from kingdoms, confederations, and other principalities that prefer formalized relations with responsible adventuring parties to unlicensed freebooting by random adventurers. In rare cases, adventuring companies can receive exclusive rights to specific areas, making it legal for them to "discourage" their competition.

Chartered adventurers are considered officers of the realm they serve, with some powers of arrest and protection against the interference of local lords guaranteed by the terms of their charter. For example, most strangers entering a city might be required to surrender or at least peacebond their weapons, but chartered company members are allowed to retain their arms and armor as long as they remain on their good behavior.

ADVENTURERS IN SOCIETY

Most residents of the Dales, Cormyr, the Western Heartlands, and the North are well disposed toward adventurers of good heart. They know that adventurers live daily with risks they would never be willing to face themselves. The common folk eagerly seek news of travelers regarding great deeds and distant happenings, hoping to glean a hint of what the future might hold for them as well.

An adventurer willing to ally himself with a lord whose attitudes and views coincide with his own gains a powerful patron and a place in society commensurate with the influence and station of his patron. Adventurers inclined to threaten or intimidate the local ruler simply invite trouble. Those who abuse their power are thought of as nothing but powerful bandits, while adventurers who use their power to help others are blessed as heroes. Adventurers are exceptional people, but they live within societies of everyday people living commonplace lives.

Language

Common language and culture defines a state just as much as borders, cities, and government do. Each major nonhuman race speaks its own language, and humans seem to generate dozens of languages for no other reason than their lands are so widespread and communications so chancy that language drift occurs over time. Hundreds of human dialects are still spoken daily in Faerûn, although Common serves to overcome all but the most overwhelming obstacles to comprehension.

The oldest languages spoken in Faerûn are nonhuman in origin. Draconic, the speech of dragons, may be the oldest of all. Giant, Elven, and Dwarven are also ancient tongues. The oldest known human languages date back some three to four thousand years. They come from four main cultural groups—Chondathan, Imaskari, Nar, and Netherese—that had their own languages, some of which survive today in altered forms after centuries of intermingling and trade.

THE COMMON TONGUE

All speaking peoples, including the humans of various lands, possess a native tongue. In addition, all humans and many nonhumans speak Common as a second language. Common grew from a kind of pidgin Chondathan and is most closely related to that language, but it is far simpler and less expressive. Nuances of speech, naming, and phrasing are better conveyed in the older, more mature languages, since Common is little more than a trade language.

The great advantage of Common, of course, is its prevalence. Everybody in the Heartlands speaks Common well enough to get by in any but the most esoteric conversations. Even in remote areas such as Murghôm and Samarach, just about everybody knows enough Common to speak it badly. They might need to point or pantomime in a pinch, but they can make themselves understood. Natives of widely separated areas are likely to regard each other's accents as strange or even silly, but they still understand each other.

The Concerns of the Mighty

There comes a time when every student and many a passing merchant, farmer, and king, too, demands the same answer of me: Why, O meddler and mighty mage, do ye not set the crooked straight? Why not strike directly against the evils that threaten Faerûn? Why do not all mighty folk of good heart not simply make everything right?

I've heard that cry so many times. Now hearken, once and for all, to my answers as to why the great and powerful *don't* fix Toril entire every day.

First, it is not at all certain that those of us with the power or the inclination can even accomplish a tenth of the deed asked of us. The forces arrayed against us are dark and strong indeed. I might surprise Manshoon or old Szass Tam and burn him from the face of Toril—or he might do the same to me. It's a rash and short-lived hero who presses for battle when victory is not assured.

Second, the wise amongst us know that even gods can't foresee all the consequences of their actions—and all of us have seen far too many instances of good things turning out to cause something very bad, or unwanted. We've learned that meddling often does far more harm than good.

Third: Few folk can agree on what is right, what should be done,

and what the best end result would be. When ye consider a mighty stroke, be assured that every move is apt to be countered by someone who doesn't like the intended result, is determined to stop it, and is quite prepared to lay waste to you, your kingdom, and anything else necessary to confound you.

Point the fourth: Big changes can seldom be effected by small actions. How much work does it take just to build one house? Rearrange one room? How many simple little actions, then, will it take to destroy one kingdom and raise another—with name, ruler, and societal order of your choice—in its place?

Finally: D'ye think we "mighty ones" are blind? Do we not watch each other, and guess at what each is doing, and reach out and do some little thing that hampers the aims of another great and mighty? We'll never be free of this problem, and that's a good thing. I would cower at the thought of living in any Faerûn where all the mighty and powerful folk agreed perfectly on everything. That's the way of slavery and shackles and armed tyranny . . . and if ye'd like to win a bet, wager that ye'll be near the bottom of any such order.

Right. Any more silly questions?

—*Elminster of Shadowdale*

ALPHABETS

The human and humanoid languages of Faerûn make use of six sets of symbols for writing: Thorass, a human symbology; Espruar, a script invented by the elves; Dethek, runes created by the dwarves; Draconic, the alphabet of dragons; Celestial, imported long ago through contact with good folk from other planes; and Infernal, imported through those outsiders of a fiendish bent.

A scribe whose name is lost to history invented the set of symbols that make up the Thorass alphabet. Thorass is the direct ancestor of today's Common tongue as a spoken language. Though no one speaks Thorass anymore, its alphabet survives as the alphabet of Common and many other tongues.

Espruar is the moon elven alphabet. It was adopted by sun elves, drow, and the other elven peoples thousands of years ago. Its beautiful weaving script flows over jewelry, monuments, and magic items.

Dethek is the dwarven runic script. Dwarves seldom write on that which can perish easily. They inscribe runes on metal sheets or carve in stone. The lines in all Dethek characters are straight to facilitate their being carved in stone. Aside from spaces between words and slashes between sentences, punctuation is ignored. If any part of the script is painted for contrast or emphasis, names of beings and places are picked out in red while the rest of the text is colored black or left as unadorned grooves.

The three remaining scripts, Draconic, Celestial, and Infernal, are beautiful yet alien, since they were designed to serve the needs of beings with thought patterns very different from those of humanoids. However, humans with ancient and strong cultural ties to dragons (and their magic) or beings from far-off planes have occasionally adapted them to transcribe human tongues in addition to the languages they originally served.

LIVING LANGUAGES

Scholars at Candlekeep recognize over eighty distinct active languages on Toril, not including thousands of local dialects of Common, such as Calant, a soft, sing-song variant spoken in the Sword Coast, Kouroou (Chult), or Skaevrym (Sossal). Secret languages such as the druids' hidden speech are not included here, either.

A character's choice of race and region determines her automatic and bonus languages. The information on Table 1–4: Character Regions supersedes the automatic and bonus language information in the *Player's Handbook*. However, the following languages are always available as bonus languages to characters, regardless of race or region: Abyssal (clerics), Aquan (water genasi), Auran (air genasi), Celestial (clerics), Common, Draconic (wizards), Dwarven, Elven, Gnome, Goblin, Giant, Gnoll, Halfling, Ignan (fire genasi), Infernal (clerics), Orc, Sylvan (druids), Terran (earth genasi), and Undercommon. Druids also know Druidic in addition to their other languages.

If a character wishes to know a language other than her automatic and bonus languages determined by race, region, and the above list, she must spend skill points on Speak Language to learn it.

DEAD LANGUAGES

Scholars and researchers of the obscure can name a number of dead languages. These languages are often the antecedents of one or more modern languages, but the original language is so different that it is usually incomprehensible to one fluent in the modern tongue. None of these languages has been a spoken, living language in thousands of years, and it is doubtful that anyone in the world knows their proper pronunciation.

Language	Alphabet	Notes
Aragrakh	Draconic	Old high wyrm
Hulgorkyn	Dethek	Archaic orc
Loross	Draconic	Netherese noble tongue
Netherese	Draconic	A precursor of Halruaan
Roushoum	Imaskari	A precursor of Tuigan
Seldruin	Hamarfae	Elven high magic
Thorass	Thorass	Old Common

These languages can be recognized by anyone who knows how to read the alphabet the language is written in, but the words are gibberish unless the character used the Speak Language skill to buy the ability to comprehend the dead language or succeeds on a Decipher Script check against DC 25. Because Thorass is archaic Common and still somewhat comprehensible to those who know Common, the DC to read it is only 20. The only way to read something written in Roushoum or Seldruin is to use a *comprehend languages* spell or to succeed on a Decipher Script check against DC 30, since the alphabets of these languages are no longer in use at all.

TABLE 3—2: LIVING LANGUAGES

Regional Language	Spoken in . . .	Alphabet
Aglarondan	Aglarond, Altumbel	Espruar
Alzhedo	Calimshan	Thorass
Chessentan	Chessenta	Thorass
Chondathan	Amn, Chondath, Cormyr, the Dalelands, the Dragon Coast, the civilized North, Sembia, the Silver Marches, the Sword Coast, Tethyr, Waterdeep, the Western Heartlands, the Vilhon Reach	Thorass
Chultan	Chult	Draconic
Common	Everywhere on Faerûn's surface (trade language)	Thorass
Damaran	Damara, the Great Dale, Impiltur, the Moonsea, Narfell, Thesk, Vaasa, the Vast	Dethek
Dambrathan	Dambrath	Espruar
Durpari	Durpar, Estagund, Var, Veldorn	Thorass
Halruaan	Halruaa, Nimbral	Draconic
Illuskan	Luskan, Mintarn, the Moonshaes, the Savage North (uncivilized areas), Ruathym, the Uthgardt barbarians	Thorass
Lantanese	Lantan	Draconic
Midani	Zakhara*, the Bedine	Thorass
Mulhorandi	Mulhorand, Murghôm, Semphar	Celestial
Mulhorandi (var.)	Thay	Infernal
Nexalan	Maztica*	Draconic
Rashemi	Rashemen	Thorass
Serusan	Inner Sea (aquatic trade language)	Aquan
Shaaran	Lake of Steam, Lapaliiya, Sespech, the Shaar	Dethek
Shou	Kara-Tur*	Draconic
Tashalan	Black Jungle, Mhair Jungle, Samarach, Tashalar, Thindol	Dethek
Tuigan	Hordelands	Thorass
Turmic	Turmish	Thorass
Uluik	Great Glacier	Thorass
Undercommon	Underdark (trade language)	Espruar
Untheric	Unther	Dethek

*These other lands on Toril are not in Faerûn.

Dethek

Espruar

Thorass

coin and commerce

If one single reason explains how humans have come to dominate so much of Faerûn compared to older, wiser races, it might be this: Humans are Toril's best merchants. The great ports of the Inner Sea spin gold like a spider spins silk. Dwarves excel at pure industry and craftsmanship, and elves command ancient magic conceived long before humans walked Faerûn, but humans command a different and perhaps more powerful magic—the magic of gold.

The growth of human prosperity and influence in lands that were once wilderness is the single greatest development in the Heartlands of Faerûn over the last thousand years or so. Human settlers carve out freeholds and villages from the virgin wilderness, often fighting for their lives and property against the monsters (or sometimes the elves, fey folk, or forest creatures) who dwell there. From the new settlements flow raw materials such as timber, furs, valuable ores, and perhaps fish or meat. More humans come to harvest the waiting riches, and new cities are born. Eventually a city is surrounded by farmland instead of forest, and the process repeats in some other trackless forest or mountain valley.

Labor

Hard work is a way of life throughout the Heartlands. As in the medieval society modeled in the *Dungeon Master's Guide*, the standard wage for a day laborer is a single silver piece. In agricultural regions, most people work from sunrise to sundown, with breaks for meals and naps.

Common folk working for the daily silver piece might resent adventurers, whose economy functions at an entirely different level as detailed in the price lists in the *Player's Handbook* and *Dungeon Master's Guide*. But common folk seldom risk death and dismemberment on a daily or hourly basis. Given the number of adventurers who wind up dead long before their day-laboring relatives, the adventuring lifestyle is viewed as an occupation for those who like to gamble with their lives for potentially great rewards.

WORK AND REST

Common folk, artisans, merchants, and even the nobility routinely work tenday after tenday until a religious holiday, local festival, or one of the annual holidays rolls around to give them a day off. Some parts of the Heartlands have gradually accepted the idea that people who do not want to work every day, and whose duties and responsibilities allow it, can take the tenth day of the week off. There is no standard name for this nonholiday day of rest. In the Dalelands, for reasons no one knows, they call it the "elf day." In Cormyr they call it "dragon-rest," saying, "Even a dragon has to rest."

In any given town, hamlet, or city, some folk choose to work through the tenday. But the day of rest has become common enough that nearly everyone associates the tenth day with some form of avoiding one's duty. Raising both open palms, showing all one's fingers, and waving them back and forth has become visual slang for "just taking it easy, not doing anything much."

SLAVERY

Few of the human kingdoms and cities of the Heartlands permit slavery within their borders. Indentured servitude and serfdom are relatively common practices that approach the hopelessness and brutality of slavery in some lands, but even the most wretched serf or servant is considered a human being, not property.

This does not prevent slavers from other regions or races from seeking their quarry in these lands. Orcs and goblins sweep down from their mountain strongholds, carrying off unfortunates to brutal thralldom in their mines and fields. Pirates of the Inner Sea frequently sell their victims into captivity in the eastern lands of Mulhorand or Thay. Parties of Zhentarim slavers brazenly ply their trade almost anywhere in the Heartlands, deterred only by the most vigorous and aggressive defenses. Thayan enclaves in many of the more dangerous or lawless cities openly trade magic devices for slaves, and are rumored to deal in slaves secretly in cities where they are not allowed to do so openly.

Outside the Heartlands, slave-owning societies are much more common. Zhentil Keep and Mulmaster in the Moonsea make extensive use of slave labor. The societies of the eastern lands—Thay, Mulhorand, and Unther—are founded on the ceaseless toil of millions of state-owned and privately held slaves. In these lands, a free peasant or small common-born farmer simply does not exist. All lands are worked and all menial tasks performed by slaves. A strong, healthy slave costs between 50 and 100 gold pieces in lands where slavery is common.

Conditions of slavery vary wildly between different lands. Slaves in Mulhorand outnumber the free citizens—and, not surprisingly, the life of a slave in Mulhorand is little worse than the life of a peasant in most other lands. Slaves in Thay and Unther endure far harsher treatment, both by callous masters and a society that considers them to be nonentities. Anyone unfortunate enough to fall under the cruel dominion of orcs or goblins rarely lives out a year of abject misery before succumbing to overwork, malnutrition, and various slave-baiting "games."

Regardless of the conditions, most Heartlands humans find slavery extremely distasteful at the very least, and more than a few consider it an abomination in the sight of the gods.

Agriculture and Industry

With the exceptions of the gnomes and perhaps the Lantanese, the people of Faerûn possess few machines more complicated than a waterwheel mill and no engines capable of replacing a team of strong horses or a good stiff breeze. Every endeavor from plowing to harvesting, from woodcarving to the refining of valuable ores, is accomplished by human hands, human backs, and human minds—or dwarven, elven, goblin, halfling, or orc labor, depending on the realm in question.

Farms worked by more than an extended family and perhaps a hired hand or two are extremely rare, although the slave fields of Mulhorand and Thay break that rule. Workshops or smelters requiring more than a half-dozen trained workers are also very rare. Every carved chair or table is the unique creation of a skilled craftsman, every apple is handpicked, every wheel of cheese or smoked haunch of meat handmade.

Crop Farming

The principal crops in the Heartlands of Faerûn are grains (wheat, barley, rye, and others), corn, and a great variety of vegetables. Orchards and vineyards are also common in climes favorable to fruit trees and grapes. Planting usually takes place in early or mid-spring, some time in the month of Ches or in Tarsakh. The principal harvesting generally occurs in Eleint. Most civilized areas in the Heartlands farm with iron plows, often single-bladed. All other work is done by hand and with hand tools.

Most rural areas grow all their own food, but many of Faerûn's larger cities import vast quantities of grain, produce, fruit, or other types of food that their land and economy are ill-suited for. Minor magic can help keep food fresh for as much as two or three days longer than normal, but few traders carrying perishables dare travel farther than that.

Livestock

Lands too steep, arid, or dangerous to farm are often suitable for animal husbandry. Herds of sheep or goats can flourish on rocky hillsides, boggy tundra, high mountain pastures that are snow-free for only a couple of months of the year, or in regions subject to monster raids or banditry—provided the shepherds are wary enough to remove their livestock from harm's way.

Grazing herds of domestic animals is not a particularly efficient way to feed large numbers of people. It takes ten times as much land to produce a pound of meat as it does a pound of grain. But herd animals also provide milk, cheese, bone, leather, and even manure for fertilizing crops.

In the Heartlands, the most common domestic animals are cattle, chickens, goats, pigs, and sheep. Any farmer keeps a small number of these animals on whatever land he can spare. In the southern plains of the Shaar, Dambrath, and Estagund, great herds of cattle are the primary source of livelihood for most people. In the cold and rocky hills of the north, goatherds and shepherds raise small flocks in every mountain pass and dale. Of course, Faerûn's numerous large, dangerous predators and monsters account for high losses. Most shepherds go about their work armed with slings and spears at the very least. More commonly, a goatherd arms himself with a pair of ferocious and well-trained wolfhounds and a sturdy crossbow.

Mining and Metalwork

Steel weapons and armor don't grow on trees, nor do tin cups, copper kettles, iron pots, or gold and silver jewelry. Valuable ores are mined wherever they are found in all lands of Faerûn, excepting only the most primitive and remote regions. Iron, copper, lead, tin, and zinc are the most commonly mined and smelted ores. Coal, guano, and peat are quarried or cut as well.

Dwarves and elves have held the secret of steelmaking for thousands of years. Most human kingdoms of the Heartlands work in steel as well. Beyond the Heartlands, steelwork is much less common. In Unther and Mulhorand, these extremely conservative cultures eschewed technological innovation for centuries after the western humans learned the secret of iron. Before the decline of their empires, the bronze-armored soldiers of Unther and Mulhorand conquered almost half the known world despite their technological backwardness, bolstered by highly organized states, the direct leadership of their deities, and the zealous use of magic. Bronze armor is symbolic of former glory in both lands, although Mulhorand's legions wear iron now, and even the most obstinate of Unther's warlords have abandoned the old ways.

In the lands of the Unapproachable East, steelwork is rare as well. The arms of Narfell and Rashemen are made of cold-wrought iron. The more advanced tribesfolk of the Chultan jungles make spearheads and arrow points of copper, trading for iron blades whenever possible.

The masters of both mining and metalwork are, of course, the dwarves. The shield dwarves work principally in the base metals—lead and iron. Their steel weapons and armor are the best of Faerûn. Gold dwarves excel at more decorative work, although their arms and armor are nearly the match of their northern cousins' work.

Papermaking and Bookbinding

Most of Faerûn relies on well-trained scribes to copy volumes by hand. This tedious work drastically limits the number of copies of a manuscript. It's an unusual book indeed that exists in more than a dozen copies, each hidden away in a noble's library or in a temple sanctum. The Lantanese build simple, hand-operated printing presses under the auspices of Gond, but to date have kept them secret from the trading powers of the Sword Coast.

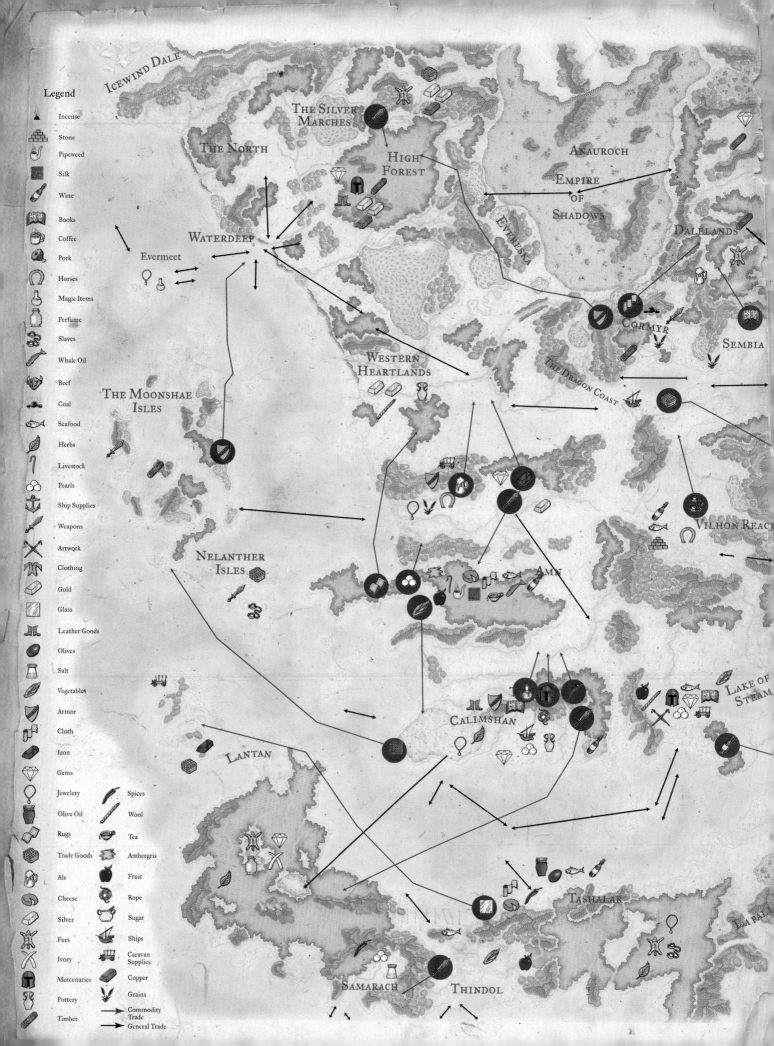

Legend

- Incense
- Stone
- Pipeweed
- Silk
- Wine
- Books
- Coffee
- Pork
- Horses
- Magic Items
- Perfume
- Slaves
- Whale Oil
- Beef
- Coal
- Seafood
- Herbs
- Livestock
- Pearls
- Ship Supplies
- Weapons
- Artwork
- Clothing
- Gold
- Glass
- Leather Goods
- Olives
- Salt
- Vegetables
- Armor
- Cloth
- Iron
- Gems
- Jewelery
- Olive Oil
- Rugs
- Trade Goods
- Ale
- Cheese
- Silver
- Furs
- Ivory
- Mercenaries
- Pottery
- Timber

- Spices
- Wool
- Tea
- Ambergris
- Fruit
- Rope
- Sugar
- Ships
- Caravan Supplies
- Copper
- Grains
- Commodity Trade
- General Trade

ICEWIND DALE

THE SILVER MARCHES

THE NORTH

HIGH FOREST

ANAUROCH

EMPIRE OF SHADOWS

EVERESKA

DALELANDS

WATERDEEP

Evermeet

CORMYR

SEMBIA

THE DRAGON COAST

WESTERN HEARTLANDS

THE MOONSHAE ISLES

VILHON REACH

NELANTHER ISLES

AMN

LAKE OF STEAM

LANTAN

CALIMSHAN

LA PAL

TASHALAR

SAMARACH

THINDOL

VAASA

NARFELL

HORDELANDS

DAMARA

RASHEMEN

Moonsea

THE GREAT
DALE

DALELANDS

THAY

IMPILTUR

THESK

THE
SEMBIA

AGLAROND

MURGHOM

TURMISH

CHESSENTA

VILHON REACH

UNTHER
(FREE)

MULHORAND

CHONDATH

SESPECH

UNTHER
(OCCUPIED)

LAKE OF STEAM

THE BORDER KINGDOMS

ESTAGUND

LUIREN

LAPALIYA

HALRUAA

DAMBRATH

The most common writing surface is parchment made from the skins of sheep, goats, or calves. Parchment sheets can be laboriously scraped clean and reused. More than one priceless ancient text has been destroyed by a careless scribe desperate for parchment to write on. True paper made from wood pulp is rare, occasionally created as a result of alchemical processes rather than technological methods. Books of spells and other important books are often written on vellum, parchment made from the skin of newborn calves. Vellum is not as sturdy as parchment but provides a higher-quality writing surface.

All books are bound by hand, and the pages are sometimes stitched to leather sheets and protected by covers of leather-covered wood. In eastern lands, books are more likely to be assembled by stitching pages side to side to create a long, continuous scroll that is then wound onto two wooden handles and protected by a snug-fitting leather scroll tube.

Travel

Although many folk are tied to the land and seldom travel far from home, a surprising number of others crisscross the continent for years at a time for business and trade. The paramount travelers are merchants, peddlers, mercenaries, and drovers, all of them moving goods or services (their own) from one place to another.

Travel by barge on an inland waterway is easiest and cheapest—either drifting downstream steered by oar and pole, or working upstream, sometimes aided by beasts towing from shore. Sea travel is faster and less costly in terms of manpower when hauling bulk goods—hence the string of seaport cities up and down the coasts of Faerûn.

Air travel by steed or device (such as *flying carpets* or Halruaan sky-ships) features often in tavern tales, but in personal experience is almost unknown to the common Faerûnian. Dragons, storms, and other perils of the air restrict such travel to military uses, or to individuals who are either personally powerful (mages) or need to move far and fast, such as messengers conveying vital information or items of great worth. Wizards' *teleport* spells and *portals* that convey anyone from one spot across great distances to another also provide unusual modes of transport.

Most travel on the surface of Faerûn is by foot. The walking traveler often leads a pack mule or train of pack mules, tows a travois, or drags or pushes a small cart. She might ride in a wagon or cart, go alone by horseback, or travel afoot with whip or staff, guiding an oxcart. In some southern lands she might travel by palanquin, carried by sturdy bearers.

Most of the roads of Faerûn are dusty tracks between cities and outposts, wide enough for one wagon and a horse passing in the opposite direction. Major trade routes such as the Trade Way running from Waterdeep to Baldur's Gate can fit three or even four wagons across at the same time. Paved roads are nearly unknown, but the largest trade routes consist of hard-packed dirt and grass over sunken cobblestones so that caravans escape the dust and mud plaguing smaller tracks.

Cities tend to have the best travel surfaces, streets of cobbles or gravel or hard-packed earth that turns to mud in wet weather. These tend to be choked with traffic and obstacles such as vendors' stalls, wagons, and stacked goods at all hours, restricting the fastest movement to the walking traveler.

The lone walker can usually hide more readily than other travelers, but she is more vulnerable to the dangers of the road. Southern Cormyr, coastal Calimshan near its large cities, and some areas of Sembia and the Dales are exceptions—but even then, cutpurses, crooked innkeepers, and other travelers threaten the lone traveler.

In a world abundantly supplied with brigands and predatory monsters, protecting caravans of wagons with mounted guards is almost a requirement. Caravans tend to be of two sorts: the closed or coster caravan (a highly disciplined group of employees working together, often in uniform) and the open or road caravan of mixed-owner wagons and other travelers, who pay a fee to a caravan master to travel under his or her protection. These can vary widely in size, fighting strength, and resources.

Any road caravan with a competent master will have at least two spare gear wagons loaded with arms and armor, spare harnesses, replacement wagon wheels and axles, tow ropes and chains, firewood and kindling, tents and repair tools and materials, and four or more food wagons. These spare wagons can be pressed into service as replacements for wagons that must be abandoned or are lost to fire, attacks, crashes, or irreparable damage along the way. Injured beasts of burden are typically sold or butchered and eaten on the road.

Almost every inn has mounts and beasts of burden that can be purchased by passing travelers (even if a tired or injured beast is "traded in," innkeepers tend to want a coin or two as well). Many sell gear abandoned or left as payment by previous travelers as well. Caravan centers such as Assam, Iriaebor, Ormpetarr, Riatavin, Scornubel, Silverymoon, Teziir, Uthmere, and Waterdeep can replace anything a traveler desires. So can almost all major seaports.

Successful caravan masters tend to be veteran guards who've survived the life for decade or more (though a few are veteran merchants), and both they and the mercenaries they hire have trade agents, usually called factors, in every settlement of trading worth in the areas in which they operate. Factors serve as spies, sources of information (about water sources, camping places, and perils), and local arrangers of storage, meetings with smiths, wheelwrights, alchemists and other useful crafters, and hiding places.

Trade

The lifeblood of Faerûn, trade ties together lands and peoples who might otherwise meet only as enemies—or not at all, depending on the distance between them. The shield dwarves trade their matchless arms and armor for vast quantities of grain, beef, ale, and other foodstuffs hard to come by in their forbidding mountains. The Red Wizards of Thay trade their priceless magic devices for slaves, steel, silk, and rivers of gold. Elven woodcarvings fetch handsome prices in the most expensive stores of Waterdeep, while bolts of good Dalelands linen are carried as far south as the Lake of Steam. Even the fierce goblin tribes of the Cloven Mountains trade coal, iron, and quarried stone to the human lands of the Vilhon Reach.

Trade roads, trails, and sea routes bring the goods and materials of distant lands to civilized folk. Most regions produce their own staple items such as basic foodstuffs and clothing, but even the most mundane commodity can be produced cheaper and faster in some lands than others. See the accompanying map, which details the largest trade routes.

MERCHANT COMPANIES

Great merchant companies dominate the trade of the Heartlands and the Inner Sea. A merchant company buys raw materials or manufactured goods at their point of origin, transports them to the markets in which the goods will fetch the best price, and sells them through company-owned emporiums or through local merchants. Typically, a merchant company's greatest asset lies in the trade routes and markets it controls. A powerful company won't hesitate to use ruthless tactics or outright violence to prevent a rival from attempting to supply a prized market with a competing product.

Wherever possible, merchant companies exert their muscle to force the lowest possible prices on their suppliers and monopolize particular goods in their chosen markets in order to command the best price possible. Laws and regulations that might control such practices are virtually unheard of in Faerûn. With a tangled web of city-states, freeholds, and kingdoms competing with each other, merchant companies can run their businesses in any manner they choose. If a particular city or land attempts to force a powerful company to compete fairly, there's always some other market waiting for the same goods and willing to pay the company's price.

COSTERS

The term "coster" properly applies to an alliance of small independent traders or merchants who band into shared caravans for safety in travel. The coster itself is a business that survives by selling caravan space to other merchants, who naturally have a say in how their goods are transported to market.

Costers frequently hire adventurers and mercenaries to make up shortfalls in caravan guards. It's not especially glamorous, but a character can usually negotiate a fee of 1 to 20 gold pieces per level per day to guard a caravan through dangerous territory. The fee varies widely with the skill and reputation of the character, the condition of the road, and the coster's financial situation.

Most Faerûnian cities with dangerous country nearby have many costers—and they employ more adventurers, and more often, than any other group in Faerûnian society. Coster hires soon learn the unwritten code of the industry: "Break nothing, and admit less!"

coinage

Barter and sworn "I owe you" declarations may suffice for trade on the frontier, but portable wealth in the form of hard currency is mandatory for any kind of stable exchange over long distances and strange lands. While barter, blood notes, and similar "letters of trade" are common enough in Faerûn, metal coins and trade bars are the everyday currency of trade.

Like the baseline economy detailed in Chapter 6 of the *DUNGEON MASTER's Guide*, Faerûn's economy works on the silver and gold standard. Other metals, including copper and platinum, are used in specific nations and cities, but silver and gold coins are accepted throughout most of the trading communities of the Heartlands no matter which kingdom, city state, or elder race stamped them. Paper currency is almost unknown, though Cormyr, Sembia, and Archendale recognize IOU notes signed in the blood of the parties to the contract and affixed with the seal of a royal agent appointed to watch over trade.

Coins come in a bewildering variety of shapes, sizes, and materials. They're minted here, there, and everywhere—though most countries simply use whatever coinage passes by. Except in special situations where a local coin or token may have an unvarying, artificially supported worth, coins are valued for the metal they're made of, not age, rarity, or whose face they bear. For this reason, platinum pieces, minted only in a few lands and regarded with suspicion in many places, have fallen out of favor. Nonetheless, they remain in circulation.

A coin's value is expressed firmly in terms of how it relates to a gold piece—a "standard" gold coin, circular and unpierced, about an eighth-inch thick and an inch-and-a-quarter across. "Shaved" coins, deliberately cut or worn thinner, are worth less. The current standard is: 10 coppers = 1 silver; 10 silvers or 100 coppers = 1 gold; and 10 gold = 1 platinum.

COMMON COINAGE

Thanks to the ambitious traders of Sembia, its oddly shaped coins can be found everywhere throughout Faerûn. Many other human nations and city-states mint their own coins. Few achieve widespread distribution, but nearly all are accepted by everyone except those looking to pick a fight with a stranger.

In Waterdeep, *the* bustling cosmopolitan center of trade, coppers are called nibs, silvers are shards, gold pieces are dragons, and platinum coins are suns. The city's two local coins are the toal and the harbor moon. The toal is a square brass trading-coin pierced with a central hole to permit it to be easily strung on a ring or rope, worth 2 gp in the city and nothing outside Waterdeep. The harbor moon is a flat crescent of platinum with a central hole and an electrum inlay, worth 50 gp in Waterdeep and 30 gp elsewhere.

Iron steelpence replace copper coins in rich and bustling Sembia. Silvers are ravens, gold pieces are nobles, and platinum coins are unknown. All coinage is accepted in Sembia (including copper pieces from elsewhere). Sembian-minted coins are square if they're iron, triangular if silver, and five-sided if gold.

In Cormyr, coppers are called thumbs, silvers are silver falcons, gold pieces are golden lions, and platinum coins are tricrowns. In Southern lands, coppers are bits, silvers are dirham, and golds are dinars.

Folk of some lands (notably Thay and Halruaa) use the currencies of other realms when trading abroad because their own coins and tokens are feared to be magically cursed or trapped, and so are shunned by others.

Conversely, the coins of long-lost legendary lands and centers of great magic are honored, though persons who find them are wise to sell them to collectors rather than merely spending them in markets. Particularly famous are the coins of Cormanthyr: thalvers (coppers), bedoars (silvers), shilmaers (golds), and ruendils (platinum). These coins are fine, numerous, and sometimes still used in trade between elves.

TRADE BARS

Large numbers of coins can be difficult to transport and account for. Many merchants prefer to use trade bars, ingots of precious metals and alloys likely to accepted by virtually anyone. Trade bars are stamped or graven with the symbol of the trading coster or government that originally crafted them. A 1-pound trade bar of silver has a value of 5 gp, a 1-pound gold bar is valued at 50 gp, and heavier bars are worth proportionally more. Trade bars typically come in 1-, 2-, 5-, and 10-pound weights.

The city of Baldur's Gate mints large numbers of silver trade bars and sets the standard for this form of currency. Damaged bars are virtually worthless, but bars issued by defunct costers and fallen countries and rulers are usually worth face value. The city of Mirabar issues black iron spindle-shaped (with squared ends) trade bars weighing about 2 pounds each, worth 10 gp in that city but only 5 gp elsewhere.

Gold trade bars are very rare. Only the wealthiest and most powerful merchants and nobles smelt these bars, since only the largest transactions require a currency with such a high face value.

ODD CURRENCY

Coins and bars are not the only form of hard currency. Gond bells are small brass bells worth 10 gp in trade, or 20 gp to a temple of Gond. Shaar rings, pierced and polished slices of ivory threaded onto strings by the nomads of the Shaar, are worth 3 gp per slice.

Some undersea races typically use pearls as currency, particularly those who dwell in the shallows and trade with surface races. The value of a pearl varies by size—a quarter-inch diameter is the standard—rarity, and quality (freedom from flaws). In the Sea of Fallen Stars, a white pearl or seyar is worth 1 cp "below the wave" and averages 2 sp in value ashore. A yellow hayar pearl is 1 sp undersea and averages 2 gp ashore, a green tayar is 1 gp and 20 gp respectively, and a blue nuyar is 5 gp "wet" and 100 gp "dry." The most prized pearls of all are olmars, the 7-inch-long, 3-inch-wide diamond-shaped olive pearls of great clams, worth 500 gp among the aquatic races and over 2,000 gp ashore.

magic in society

From the smoking foundries of Luskan to the wondrous cities of Halruaa, Faerûnians live in a world populated by practitioners of magic both arcane and divine. Magic has changed the world more than once in the past—the deserts of Raurin and Anauroch now mark the places where the highly magical empires of Imaskar and Netheril once stood. The great river of history is directed and redirected by magically powerful people acting out of both malice and benevolence. Even so, magic still rarely touches the life of the common Faerûnian.

the Art

Wielders of arcane magic—also known as the Art—are rare in most Heartlands societies. No more than one person in a hundred or so is likely to have any ability as a wizard or sorcerer. Half of those are dilettantes and dabblers—a merchant who's studied a little wizardry to protect himself on the road, or a noble who received an unusual education. In some lands and among some races, of course, the incidence of arcane magic use is much higher. Everyone is reputed (incorrectly) to be a wizard in mythical lands such as Halruaa or Nimbral. Sun elves, moon elves, and rock gnomes take to the Art with such ease that mages might be more than ten times as common in their lands as elsewhere.

WIZARDS AND SORCERERS

Wizards and sorcerers are both known as mages in many places. Most people in the Heartlands simply don't know the difference. Both sorcerers and wizards have mysterious powers, strange demeanors, frighteningly intelligent pets, and frequently do things such as turn invisible, fly through the air, and blast lightning out of their fingertips. After that, any differences are purely cosmetic to the common folk.

In some cities or lands, the rivalry between wizard and sorcerer becomes deadly. In Thay, for instance, sorcery is regarded as corruption of the Art, while wizardry is respected as a studious and academic pursuit—largely due to the reactionary leaders of that land.

If it's possible to accomplish a task without magic, then in most places and in most circumstances the mundane methods are employed. Even powerful wizards easily capable of flying or teleporting are inclined to walk on their own two legs from one town to the next. The reason for this is simple: It's prudent to reserve one's magic for when it's *really* needed. A wizard who expends a portion of his magical strength flying everywhere he goes might one day be short a *lightning bolt* or a *dispel magic* when it might save his life.

COMMON FOLK AND MAGES

Mages are regarded with suspicion, fear, and respect wherever they go. In any land, the affairs of wizards and sorcerers are the topic of endless gossip and speculation. Over tankards of ales, locals compare stories of the deeds of this mage or that, and wonder aloud which might win in a duel of magic.

Any mage not well known by the local people is regarded as a dangerous unknown quantity until he shows by action, word, and manner that he means no harm. The local people are careful not to give offense, and the local authorities quietly observe any such person with as much discretion as possible.

masters and apprentices

Wizards who have already mastered high magic can further their own powers by experimentation, though this is a slow and painstaking road compared to searching out spells crafted by earlier mages. Novice wizards, however, don't know how to direct their experimentation to have the slightest hope of success, or even to avoid poisoning themselves or perishing in explosions they cause. For the inexperienced wizard, there's truly no substitute for a teacher in the ways of magic.

This means apprenticeship—a term of service during which the novice serves a master under whatever conditions the two of them agree upon in return for being taught magic. Usually the terms are stipulated in a contract made before a local ruler, mage guild, or temple of Mystra or Azuth.

Being an apprentice often involves a lot of drudgery and humiliation—from doing the master's laundry to cooking and mending and even serving as the master's stand-in, body-slave, or guard in dangerous situations. Many apprentices grow to hate their masters, and some masters use either spells or physical restraints (literal chains, or confinement in towers or dungeon cells) to prevent apprentices from slaying them, stealing from them, or betraying them during battles with rival mages, monster attacks, or business dealings.

On the other hand, some apprentices grow to love their masters, serving them life-long and continuing their work after they die. Some spend years seeking to rescue or avenge their masters, while others willingly house the minds of their masters in their own bodies when the old wizards lose their own bodies or desire to escape dying, diseased, or crippled forms.

Traditionally, the apprenticeship arrangement is rarely more complicated than "Well, you'll help me in my work, and learn by seeing and doing alongside me—and the spells you get will be those you pick up as we go." Apprentices of some personal wealth or station in society may be able to exact a formal promise of teaching and bestowal of agreed-upon spells, although penniless aspirants must accept whatever they can get.

There are few rules of thumb regarding length and conditions of service versus spells taught, because wizards are highly secretive. Generally, teaching the casting (and providing a copy) of a 1st-level spell or lesser magic might involve a month of service during which at least one important task is successfully completed, or at least three months of drudge service. Spells of higher levels require greater tasks and payments. Once apprentices know enough magic not to kill themselves in their first battle, many of these tasks take the form of missions or ventures to further the master's goals and research by retrieving lost bits of lore or rare spell components.

Assuming a novice wizard has the wits to wield magic at all and the master has sufficient components and spell writings and the like at hand, the teaching of a spell shouldn't require more than three or four days of intensive casting, practice, observation of effects, and more practice. If the nature of the spell is such that its use doesn't require a lot of practice, or the mage hasn't the time for niceties but has a pressing need to blast something, learning a new spell can take mere hours.

No wizard is obligated to teach except by local law, guild rule, or personal decree of Azuth, Mystra, or another divine power. Many mages dislike teaching, which involves giving up their time and surrendering their personal safety and privacy. Willing teachers are apt to be few, and many who do tutor are lazy, less than capable, or very frail and elderly.

A mage who settles downs somewhere, or who visits an area often enough to become well known, almost always becomes an important and respected member of the community. If trouble breaks out, especially magical trouble, the nearest good-hearted spellcaster is one of the first sources of help for the locals. Even a reclusive or downright malevolent mage might be approached for help in extreme cases, if the locals placate their dangerous neighbor with gifts and shows of respect.

MAGE FAIRS

Any town or city with a population of more than a dozen wizards and sorcerers is likely to host an annual mage fair. These gatherings offer an opportunity for business, bluster, and socializing between otherwise reclusive magicians. Business usually consists of territorial agreements, research pacts, and sales of spells, items, and information. Bluster follows close upon business's heels as rival mages show off for their peers or challenge each other to duels. Socializing takes all forms, from wizards who seek new apprentices to spellcasters playing semifriendly pranks upon each other to magically empowered drinking games.

Mage fairs are usually held in out-of-the-way places, no more than a day or two from a big city. The occasional exceptions to that rule tend to be remembered forever. Sorcerers are welcome to attend, but may be treated with some condescension if they are not considered powerful practitioners.

RELIGION

Across all of Toril, people respect and fear the divine powers. The deities of Faerûn take an active role in the world, promoting the causes they favor, watching over the domains for which they are responsible, and constantly seeking to increase (or at least defend) their temporal power by protecting their worshipers and encouraging the active expansion of their faiths.

Mortals who deny the deities who made the world and govern its basic forces are rare indeed, although a few powerful beings such as the enigmatic sharns and phaerimms acknowledge no entity as their superior. Human (and humanoid) souls who refuse the gods come to a bad end after death, lacking a deity to speak for them upon the Fugue Plane. What befalls primal creatures such as the sharns, no one can say.

Some Faerûnians zealously follow one deity. Others make sacrifices to many deities, while upholding one as their personal patron. Still others sacrifice to as many deities as possible, shifting allegiances as their circumstances and needs warrant. It's a rare Faerûnian who hasn't occasionally hoped to avert the baleful influence of an evil deity with a propitious gift, or thanked a good power for an unexpected blessing. The belief system of most Faerûnians generally centers on a particular deity whose interests and influences are most likely to affect them, but acknowledges other gods as significant and important, too.

DIVINE INFLUENCES

Divine magic can play a significant role in society, but not always through the direct intercession of a cleric or druid wielding divine spells. Deities of prosperity and plenty such as Chauntea answer their worshipers' prayers with abundant harvests and fair weather. Gods of plague and famine—Talona, primarily—demand placation and send all manner of blights and epidemics against those foolish enough to deny their power. These supernatural influences tend to balance each other, with the extremes of bounty and famine generally unlikely to occur. Chauntea finds a way to bring forth some sustenance in even the worst blights, and Talona manages to mar even the most plentiful harvest in some small way.

TEMPLES AND CLERICS

All of the clerics, soldiers, shrines, churches, abbeys, temples, and holy sites dedicated to a particular deity are collectively referred to as the Temple, or Faith, of that power. Neither term is exactly accurate, since the Temple of Tyr includes many temples to Tyr, and the Faith of Tyr refers both to that deity's followers and the system of beliefs they hold.

The Temples of the great powers—Bane, Chauntea, Tyr, and a handful of others—are as powerful as small kingdoms. A dozen major temples in great cities across Faerûn house hundreds of clerics and soldiers dedicated to the deity. Hundreds of small temples and shrines in the towns and villages of countless lands serve thousands upon thousands of worshipers. A militant faith can gather an army of crusaders, while a mercantile faith holds lands and properties of staggering expanse. Almost all faiths sponsor high-level clerics, champions, devotees, and secular agents who look after the faith's interests and defend it against those who resent its power.

Most of a Temple's clergy are not clerics. They're experts, aristocrats, even commoners who serve as advisors and counselors to the faithful and officiate at routine observances. A cleric usually leads any particular temple, shrine, or order, judiciously using her spells to aid sick or injured followers and assist the local authorities in maintaining law and order in the community as it suits the deity in question.

HEALING

Temples and shrines to some number of deities stand in virtually every thorp and hamlet of Faerûn. Most of these are under the supervision of a low- to mid-level cleric of the appropriate deity. Frequently, these parish priests and shrine-keepers possess healing abilities unavailable to low-level adventurers.

The degree to which a local cleric may make her healing spells available to adventurers in the town varies greatly with the tenets of her faith, the demands of the town, and her own best judgment. Clerics obviously prefer to aid fellow followers of their patron deity, and if healing resources are limited, the faithful will be aided before people devoted to other gods. Naturally, the followers of deities antithetical to the clerics' own deity are extremely unlikely to be helped in any circumstance.

Same Patron Deity: If the character or characters requiring healing follow the same patron deity as the local cleric, they stand the best chance of receiving help.

Characters of the same faith brought before the cleric in a dying state (hit points between 0 and –10) will be stabilized, often without any expectation of compensation. Any person who is not dying is not likely to find free healing. After all, people heal with time, and most clerics prefer to retain their spell power rather than give it away.

Adventurers can purchase routine healing spells at the normal prices for purchasing spellcasting. Some clerics may be moved to heal a follower of the same faith at no cost, but only if it is clearly an immediate need of the faith to get the injured person back into top form as soon as possible.

Disease, level loss, blindness, or other conditions besides hit point loss are more complicated. The adventurer may be healed at no cost if he has served his faith well. Otherwise, he might be healed in exchange for a special donation (20% to 50% of the normal spellcasting cost) or a special service for the temple.

Raising or resurrecting the dead is never undertaken lightly. In general, the friends of a dead character should expect to pay the normal spellcasting cost. In some very rare instances, a dead character might be raised by clerics of his own faith regardless of whether he or his comrades can meet the spellcasting cost. This only happens when the deceased has been an exemplary servant of the faith, and the cleric in question has cause to believe that it is absolutely imperative to the faith to restore the dead character to life. Even then, the raised character might be charged with a *geas/quest* to serve the faith in a specific task to justify the effort and expense of his resurrection.

Allied Patron Deity: A local cleric devoted to a deity allied to the adventurer's patron deity, or a local cleric who simply wishes to support like-minded adventurers who advance his own cause by advancing theirs, is the next best thing to a cleric of a hero's own faith. Again, characters of the allied faith who arrive in a dying state will be stabilized, often without any expectation of compensation. Adventurers can purchase routine healing spells at the normal prices for purchasing spellcasting. Some allied clerics may heal an adventurer at a reduced cost (20% to 50% of the normal spellcasting cost), but only if it is clearly advantageous to get the adventurer back on his feet fast.

The adventurer may be healed of disease or other conditions for the normal spellcasting cost. Again, if it is clearly a good idea for the local cleric to aid the adventurer, he might be healed in exchange for a special donation (20% to 50% of the normal spellcasting cost) or a special service for the temple.

Neutral Patron Deity: If the local cleric's patron deity is not particularly friendly or hostile to the patron deities of the adventurers, the decision to aid them or not is much more mercenary and situational. Any good-aligned cleric is likely to stabilize a dying character brought before her unless that character is clearly an agent of evil. Other than that, any healing spells are available at the normal spellcasting costs, but only if the neutral cleric has reason to believe that aiding the adventurer in question won't cause any harm or risk to followers of the cleric's faith.

Magic Items

Magic is not technology. Wizards and clerics do not manufacture levitating elevators or mass-produce magic *portals* for simple convenience or crude commerce. These things do exist, but they are almost always built somewhere for a very good reason, since they take a great deal of time and money for a highly skilled and uncommonly gifted spellcaster to create.

Most magic items fall into one of two broad categories—gimmicks and adventuring magic. Gimmicks are commonplace because they're not hard to make and not very expensive. They amuse, delight, and entertain, and on occasion do something useful in a small way. Adventuring magic is not anywhere near as commonplace, and it is useful for increasing one's personal power and capabilities to deal with the sorts of problems adventurers often face.

Nearly all Faerûnians, no matter how humble or removed from the adventuring lifestyle, have seen minor magic gimmicks at some point in their lives. Fewer actually own such treasures, but it's not unheard of for well-off merchants or low nobles to save their money for minor trinkets such as a pot that can make itself hot, or a broom that can sweep itself. *Real* magic—wands and rings, magic arms, and wondrous devices—is relegated to the wealthy, the powerful, and those adventurers who stumble across such items in the course of their journeys and battles.

In Faerûn, magic items come from one of four principal sources. The first is the distant past. Ruined cities, forgotten treasure vaults, the hoards of dragons, and similar dangerous places often hold powerful items lost, buried, or stolen long ago. On occasion, adventurers have discovered to their chagrin that legal heirs to some of these old heirlooms still live and expect the return of their ancestors' property. More commonly, news of a valuable item recovered from some particularly dangerous spot invites the attention of rogues or mages more inclined to steal than to negotiate.

The second source is the powerful temples of Faerûn. Clerical hierarchies are wealthy, well organized, and inclined to invest in producing magic devices to assist their chosen agents in their duties. Many magic weapons and armors are created at the forges of Moradin, Tempus, and Tyr.

Independent wizards working for whatever mysterious purpose happens to move them are the third major source of magic items. Mercantile wizards (or wizards in the employ of merchants) create much of the gimmick-type magic for specific purposes or markets.

Finally, the last major source is the Red Wizards of Thay. The Red Wizards have always been magical artificers of great skill. In walled enclaves throughout the Inner Sea, mercantile Red Wizards sell their goods with whispered urgings and overly generous lines of credit—which entice the foolish to buy more than they can afford. It is a very bad thing to be indebted to the Red Wizards, and the fate of those who seek to cheat the Thayans is rumored to be horrible beyond imagining.

Craft and Engineering

With a few exceptions, Faerûn is a land without heavy industry, steam power, or firearms. For millennia magic, not technology, has been the path to understanding and true power. Hundreds of wizards develop new spells, create new magic items, or uncover new fields of magical lore with each passing year, but the number of savants who advance the boundaries of mundane knowledge is much smaller. Just as wizards are inclined to closely guard their magical secrets, many great architects, engineers, and inventors hoard their learning and rarely pass it on to the world at large.

While technology is sometimes viewed as a somewhat inelegant and weak compared to true magical power, most folk of the Heartlands have a passing familiarity with simple machines such as waterwheels and building principles such as the arch. Magic often serves as an adjunct to any large construction process, not a replacement for good engineering and months or years of heavy labor. The design of a city's new bridge is likely to come from an expert architect, who consults with various wizards regarding the use of magic to strengthen, reinforce, and preserve the work after it is complete. The strongest and most enduring structures make use of both sound construction and potent magic without relying entirely on either.

Fortifications

Keeps, castles, watchtowers, and walls are the best way to fortify a town or stronghold, despite the prevalence of magic and powerful monsters. It takes an adult dragon at the height of its vigor and determination to contemplate a single-handed attack on a well-built and well-defended castle. No wizard of less than 15th level or so commands enough magical power to raze a keep. Hundreds of tons of stone and iron doors with double locks prove surprisingly resistant to any destructive spell short of *disintegrate* or *earthquake*, and even then numerous castings may be required to achieve the outright destruction of a stronghold.

That said, surface fortifications work best against human-sized attackers who possess limited access to magic. Attackers who can tunnel or fly are best fought off by magic-capable defenders, earth elementals, or mounted aerial troops. Savvy defenders who prefer not to rely on magic for defense employ crenellated walls, nets, and aerial ballistae against fliers, and use preset deadfalls, gas traps, or other buried mechanical devices against tunnelers.

Since the most dangerous threats to fortifications come from powerful spells and monsters with potent magical abilities, the largest and most impressive fortifications also tend to have built-in magical wards and protections. Lead sheeting incorporated into the

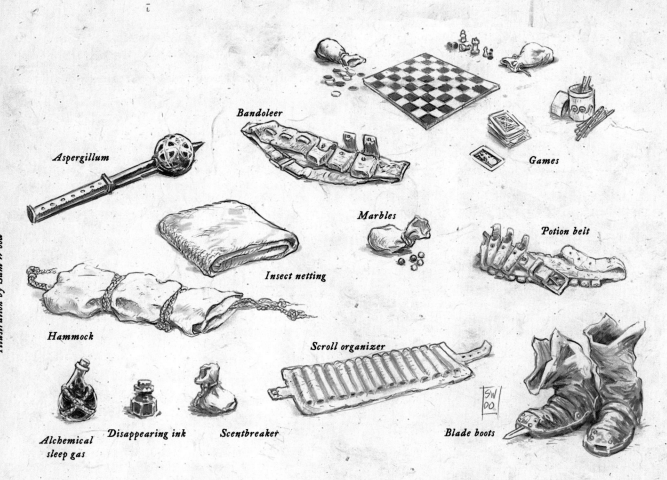

Illustration by Sam Wood

Aspergillum

Bandoleer

Games

Insect netting

Marbles

Potion belt

Hammock

Scroll organizer

Alchemical sleep gas

Disappearing ink

Scentbreaker

Blade boots

walls and doors blocks many divination spells. A *forbiddance* spell can stop hostile creatures from teleporting into a stronghold or passing its walls ethereally.

The main gate of a fortress is most likely toughened with *resist elements* and extra hardness and hit points, making it nearly impenetrable. Some wizards assume that static fortifications are merely noble vanity and pay little attention to them, but more than one overconfident mage has met his end in an attempt to assault a castle.

Ships

Vessels of all different types and technology levels coexist on Faerûn's seas and rivers. Most seagoing vessels on the western seas—the Trackless Sea and the Sea of Swords—are sailing ships such as cogs and caravels. The Northmen of Ruathym and the Moonshaes build longships with both oars and sails. The great trading powers of Waterdeep and Amn are famed for their greatships, or carracks, towering vessels that seem more like floating castles than seagoing craft. The lightly built galleys favored in more sheltered waters do not fare well in the winds and storms of the Sword Coast.

In the Sea of Fallen Stars, oared galleys and dromonds are as common as sailing ships. Most warships of the Inner Sea are galleys capable of ramming and boarding enemy ships with overwhelming manpower. Sailed ships fleet enough to escape such galleys exist, and can survive rough weather better than the galleys, but the deadly ram of a galley puts a sailing ship at a distinct disadvantage in most fights.

The elven fleets of Evermeet are made up of swift frigates and sloops that represent the pinnacle of the shipwright's craft on Toril. No human warship can overhaul an elven vessel under sail—or escape it if the elves are inclined to seek battle.

Equipment

All items described in Chapter 7 of the *Player's Handbook* are available in Faerûn, provided one looks for them in a city of the appropriate size. In addition to the standard equipment available, characters in the FORGOTTEN REALMS campaign setting have access to a number of special items.

Starting Cash and Bonus Equipment: Characters who chose a home region in which their character class is encouraged gain a special benefit at 1st level. The character receives the bonus equipment specified for her region, *plus* her normal allocation of starting cash. If the character chooses to take extra cash instead of her bonus equipment, she may sell the equipment for half its normal value and add that amount to her starting cash.

MUNDANE ITEMS

These items have proven popular with adventurers throughout Faerûn. Prices for the items described here are listed on Table 3–3: Mundane Items.

Aspergillum: This lightweight metal device looks like a small club or a light mace. Each contains a reservoir that can hold up to 3 pints (three flasks) of holy water. By shaking the aspergillum as a standard action, you can sprinkle one flask of holy water on a target within melee reach. This action is a ranged touch attack (which does not provoke an attack of opportunity). An aspergillum does not require any proficiency to use. Many adventurers prefer using an aspergillum to dispense holy water rather than throwing or pouring out the contents of a flask.

Bandoleer: This leather belt has loops or pouches for carrying small items (up to dagger size). It is usually worn across the chest. It holds eight items.

TABLE 3—3: MUNDANE ITEMS

Item	Cost	Weight
Aspergillum	5 gp	3 lb.†
Aspergillum (silver)	50 gp	3 lb.†
Bandoleer	5 sp	1/2 lb.
Bandoleer, masterwork	50 sp	1/2 lb.
Chess set (common)	2 gp	4 lb.
Chess set (fine)	25 gp	7 lb.
Draughts set	1 gp	2 lb.
Hammock	1 sp	2 lb.
Insect netting	5 gp	1 lb.
Old men's bones set	2 sp	1 lb.
Potion belt	1 gp	1 lb.
Potion belt, masterwork	60 gp	1 lb.
Scroll organizer	5 gp	1/2 lb.
Talis deck	2 gp	1/4 lb.

†These items weigh one-quarter this amount when made for Small characters.

Bandoleer, Masterwork: This well-crafted bandoleer holds twelve items.

Games: Some games of skill are detailed below, but games of chance are also popular. Wagering on any sort of game is also a favorite pastime.

Chess: Faerûnian chess game pieces include kings, queens, priests (bishops), knights-errant (knights), rooks (castles), and pawns. Sets often use famous figures, such as rulers or deities, as kings. A set consists of thirty-two pieces and a board in a wooden case. A fine set has ebony and ivory pieces and a marble board. A common set is made from more humble materials, such as carved and dyed wood.

Draughts: Draughts is similar to the modern game of checkers. A set consists of twenty-four clay or stone pieces and a board of alternating light and dark squares in a wooden case. The board is the same as a chessboard in pattern.

Old Men's Bones: This game is similar to the modern game of pick-up sticks. The object is to remove the bones from the pile you have dumped them into one at a time without toppling the pile. The set has "sticks" made from bones (usually those of a fowl) and a leather or metal canister for carrying them.

Talis Deck: A deck of seventy-eight cards, typically made of lacquered paper or parchment, in a wooden case. The deck is similar to a tarot deck.

Hammock: An innovation from the land of Maztica, a hammock is a hemp or linen blanket with sturdy cords woven into it so that it can be strung up between two trees or other vertical supports.

Insect Netting: These sheets of fine mesh are made of silk from Kara-Tur. When draped around a sleeper in a bedroll or hammock, insect netting keeps away normal insects (Fine vermin, but not magical effects that employ such creatures such as *insect plague* or *creeping doom*).

Marbles: About two dozen assorted glass, flawed rock crystal, or clay spheres in a leather pouch. Commonly used as a toy, but also useful for checking the slope in a dungeon corridor (just set one down and see which way it rolls), or as a nondamaging alternative to caltrops. One bag covers an area 5 feet square. Creatures moving through or fighting in the area must make Balance checks (DC 15) or be unable to move for 1 round (or they may fall; see the Balance skill description in the *Player's Handbook*).

Potion Belt: This sturdy leather belt similar to a bandoleer has pockets shaped to hold potion vials and is fitted with ties or flaps to keep the potions from falling out. It holds six potions. Retrieving a potion from a potion belt is a free action once per round.

Potion Belt, Masterwork: This extremely well-made potion belt holds ten potions. Retrieving a potion from a potion belt is a free action once per round.

Scroll Organizer: This long strip of leather has an overlapping series of fifteen pockets sewn along one side, each large enough to hold a scroll of a single spell. When slipped into a pocket, only the top of a scroll shows, allowing you to scan the scrolls' titles.

SPECIAL ITEMS

Prices for the items described here are given on Table 3–4: Special Items.

Alchemical Sleep Gas: This liquid evaporates quickly when exposed to air, creating a temporary, mildly toxic cloud that puts living creatures to sleep. You can throw a flask of sleep gas as a grenadelike weapon. It has a range increment of 10 feet.

On a direct hit (splashes have no effect because the gas dissipates instantly), a living target must succeed on a Fortitude save (DC 15) or fall asleep for 1 minute. After 1 minute, the target must make another Fortitude save (DC 15) or sleep 1d4 additional minutes. The sleep gas affects creatures that are immune to magical sleep effects but not creatures that are immune to poison. Spells and effects that cancel or counter poisons (such as *neutralize poison*) are effective against the gas.

The gas affects only one creature of Small or larger size. The gas affects all creatures of Tiny or smaller size in the 5-foot square where it strikes.

Note: A sleeping creature is helpless. Slapping or wounding awakens the creature, but normal noise does not. Awakening the creature is a standard action.

The Alchemy DC to make alchemical sleep gas is 25.

Disappearing Ink: After being used to write a message, this blue or red ink vanishes from view at the end of an hour (though ink can be made, at greater expense, that will disappear after longer periods, such as a day, a tenday, or a month). Heat (such as a candle flame) applied to the writing surface makes the ink appear again. A Spot or Search check (DC 20) reveals traces of the writing.

The Alchemy DC to make disappearing ink is 15.

Herb, Cassil: Cassil is a small shrub similar to a mustard plant. Its seeds are ground into a fine, tasteless powder that suppresses male fertility. Men who want to avoid fathering children use this herb. A male humanoid who eats about a teaspoon of cassil is rendered infertile for a period of 3d4 days, although it requires about an hour before the herb takes effect.

Stories abound of disloyal courtiers dosing their kings or lords in order to prevent the conception of a royal heir. Using either the Heal skill or Profession (herbalist), the effects can be detected with a DC 15 check and countered with a DC 20 check.

Herb, Nararoot: Nararoot is a black, woody tuber with a licorice-like flavor. Shavings steeped in hot water make a strong tea that renders a woman infertile for d4+2 days. Chewed raw, the root tastes unpleasant, but the effects are more potent, lasting 2d4+4 days. Women who do not wish to become pregnant use nararoot. Using either the Heal skill or Profession (herbalist), the effects can be detected with a DC 15 check and countered with a DC 20 check.

Powderhorn: This waterproof horn holds 2 pounds of *smokepowder*.

Powderkeg: This is a normal wooden keg that holds 15 pounds (240 ounces) of *smokepowder*.

Scentbreaker: This small bag contains either a collection of aromatic herbs or a strongly scented alchemical mixture. Either version can confound any creature's sense of smell. You can toss the bag as a grenadelike weapon with a range increment of 10 feet, or you can scatter the contents someplace where a creature tracking by scent will come across it. (It covers an area 5 feet square.) Once scattered, the contents remain potent for 1 hour.

A creature can sniff the bag's contents from a direct hit, from a splash, or from sniffing the area where the contents were scattered. If struck by a direct hit, the creature must succeed at a Fortitude save (DC 18) or lose its scent ability for 1 minute. After the minute is up, the creature must make a second Fortitude save (DC 18) or lose its scent ability for another hour. Being splashed or sniffing the scattered contents has the same effect, but the save DC is 15. A direct hit or splash affects only one creature of Small or larger size. The contents affect all creatures of Tiny or smaller size in the 5-foot square where a bag of scentbreaker strikes.

Note: The Alchemy DC to make scentbreaker is 15. If you have 5 or more ranks in Profession (herbalist), you get a +2 synergy bonus on checks to craft it.

TABLE 3—4: SPECIAL ITEMS

Item	Cost	Weight
Alchemical sleep gas	30 gp	1 1/4 lb.
Disappearing ink	5 gp	—
Herbs		
Cassil (1 dose)	1 gp	—
Nararoot (1 dose)	2 sp	—
Powderhorn (32 shots)	35 gp	2 lb.
Powderkeg (240 shots)	250 gp	20 lb.
Scentbreaker	5 gp	—

MUNDANE WEAPONS

Longswords and crossbows are just as common in Faerûn as they are in any fantasy world. In addition to the weapons described in the *Player's Handbook*, various weaponmakers of Faerûn forge a few items especially prevalent in (or unique to) various lands. Refer to Weapon Categories and Weapon Qualities in Chapter 7 of the *Player's Handbook* for descriptions of the various entries on Table 3–5: Weapons.

Firearms exist in Faerûn, but use smokepowder instead of gunpowder. They are especially common in the island nation of Lantan and among the rock gnomes, but are available throughout Faerûn for those who can afford them. Refer to Renaissance Weapons in Chapter 6 of the Dungeon Master's Guide. Smokepowder is a magical alchemical substance, and therefore does not work in an antimagic field or dead magic area.

Creating smokepowder requires the Craft Wondrous. Item feat and 9 ranks in the Alchemy skill, and produces 1 pound (16 ounces) of smokepowder with a market price of 16 gp. One ounce of smokepowder is needed to fire a bullet.

Blade Boot: Custom-fitted to the wearer's boot, this device consists of a sturdy sole assembly concealing a spring-loaded dagger. The buyer can add one blade to either of his boots at the given cost, or buy a matched set for double the amount.

The wearer's movement is not impaired when the blades are retracted. With one or both blades extended, the wearer cannot run or charge. A monk using a blade boot can strike with his unarmed base attack, including his more favorable number of attacks per round, for normal blade boot damage. The Weapon Finesse feat can be applied to blade boots.

A character proficient with the blade boot can attack with a single blade boot as his primary weapon, or with two blade boots as if attacking with two weapons, provided he makes no attacks with his hands. He can choose to attack with a weapon in his primary hand and use a single blade boot as his off-hand weapon, but in this case he cannot attack with an off-hand weapon in his secondary hand. A character cannot attack with a primary weapon, an off-hand weapon, and a blade boot in the same round unless he knows the Multiweapon Fighting feat described in the *Monster Manual*.

A character wearing blade boots gains a +4 bonus on Escape Artist checks made to escape from rope bonds.

Chakram: The chakram is a throwing disk or quoit about 1 foot in diameter, with a sharpened outer rim.

Claw Bracer: Popular with sorcerers and wizards of the Cult of the Dragon, a claw bracer is a metal armband with three steel claws projecting from the top, extending about 4 inches beyond the tip of the wearer's extended fingers. The wearer can cast spells normally while wearing the bracer, and cannot be disarmed.

Cutlass: The cutlass is a short, heavy, slightly curved blade useful for both stabbing and slashing. It is popular with many sailors. Its heavy basket hilt gives the wielder a +2 circumstance bonus on any checks to resist being disarmed.

Khopesh: The famed sword of Mulhorand, the khopesh looks like a normal longsword whose blade suddenly turns sickle-shaped about a foot from the hilt. You can use the khopesh to make trip attacks due to its hooklike blade.

Maul: The maul is simply a two-handed warhammer of enormous size. It is favored by dwarves.

Saber: A weapon of the Tuigan and the Nars, the saber is a long, heavy sword specialized for the long cuts used in mounted combat. You gain a +1 circumstance bonus on your attack rolls when you use a saber while mounted.

Scourge: A scourge is a multitailed, barbed whip. The scourge is often dipped in a poison delivered via injury (such as greenblood oil, Medium-size spider venom, or Large scorpion venom). With a scourge, you get a +2 bonus on your opposed attack roll when attempting to disarm an enemy (including the roll to avoid being disarmed if you fail to disarm your enemy).

You can also use this weapon to make trip attacks. If you are tripped during your own trip attempt, you can drop the scourge to avoid being tripped.

TABLE 3—5: WEAPONS
Martial weapons—melee

Weapon		Cost	Damage	Critical	Range Increment	Weight	Type
Small	Cutlass	15 gp	1d6	19–20/×2	—	3 lb.	Slashing and piercing
Medium-size	Saber	20 gp	1d8	19–20/×2	—	4 lb.	Slashing and piercing
Large	Maul	15 gp	1d10	×3	—	20 lb.	Bludgeoning

Exotic weapons—melee

Weapon		Cost	Damage	Critical	Range Increment	Weight	Type
Tiny	Blade boot	15 gp	1d4	19–20/×2	—	1 lb.	Piercing
	Claw bracer	30 gp	1d4	19–20/×2	—	2 lb.	Piercing
Medium-size	Khopesh	20 gp	1d8	19–20/×2	—	12 lb.	Slashing
	Scourge*	20 gp	1d8	×2	–	2 lb.	Slashing

*See the description of this item for special rules.

Exotic weapons—ranged

Weapon		Cost	Damage	Critical	Range Increment	Weight	Type
Small	Chakram	15 gp	1d4	×3	30 ft.	2 lb.	Slashing

GEOGRAPHY

Seeing every kingdom, every city-state, every mountain range and forest and ruined castle of Faerûn would be the journey of a dozen human lifetimes. Faerûn is a continent of extremes, in climate, terrain, and human geography. Almost anything can be found somewhere within its vast wilds and myriad cultures, which collectively are home to more than sixty-eight million inhabitants. Towering mountains and oceans of grassland, blasted deserts and lush forests, barbarians in iron and furs or decadent city-folk in silk and perfume . . . all of these things and many, many more exist in this wide and wondrous land.

Exploring Faerûn

A company of adventurers can find countless places to go and things to do in the dozens of kingdoms, hundreds of cities, and thousands of ruins, lairs, and wild places of Faerûn. Heroes are the great travelers and explorers of Toril, the privileged few who see new lands with every sunrise and face new challenges every day.

The map on pages 100 and 101 shows the major political boundaries that divide Faerûn into its dozens of regions.

The Heartlands

While every realm and important city-state of Faerûn is at least touched on in the rest of this chapter, the center of them all is the Heartlands, the region that includes Cormyr, the Dalelands, and Sembia.

The nations of the Heartlands share a common language, and their cultural heritage and social order are similar. They are not necessarily the most populous, dangerous, or powerful states of Faerûn, but they are perhaps the most representative. Travelers from one part of the Heartlands generally find the same kind of villages, the same kind of merchants, and the same kind of overlords in other parts of the Heartlands as they are accustomed to at home. Beyond the Heartlands, people seem strange and lands are wild, uncivilized, decadent, or ancient beyond belief.

Many adventurers lead long and successful careers without setting foot outside the Heartlands. There is no shortage of dangerous monsters, mysterious ruins, and murderous dungeons within these lands. Sinister powers such as the drow, the Zhentarim, the Cult of the Dragon, the Red Wizards of Thay, and now the proud archwizards of Shade all seek to extend their dominion over the human kingdoms of these lands. Only the courage of bold and resolute adventurers stands between Faerûn and a very dark future.

For the Dungeon Master

You are about to be introduced to hundreds of adventure ideas and settings, all couched as an overview of the lands and peoples of the FORGOTTEN REALMS Campaign Setting. This chapter outlines most of the lands, peoples, and perils of Faerûn, but it's also your guide to an entire world of adventures.

The descriptions in this chapter are organized first of all by major region—the Chultan Peninsula, the Old Empires, or the Unapproachable East, for example—and then by realms, city-states, cantons, or tribal lands within that area. To locate a particular place description, refer to the Table of Contents or the Index.

HOW TO READ A REGION ENTRY

Each kingdom or subregion listed in this chapter begins with a short block of data, featuring the following points of information.

Capital: The capital city of the kingdom or realm, if one exists. In some cases, a city is not recognized as the seat of a throne, but it is clearly the power center of the domain. These are marked as capitals, too.

Population: The total number of all sentient humanoids counted as citizens of that land. The percentages indicate how the population is distributed by race. Just because a particular race isn't represented in the population breakdown doesn't mean that none of its members live in that kingdom—they're simply too low in number to come close to 1% of the kingdom's population. Note that the total population percentages equal 99% rather than 100% to account for this scattering of "other races."

Nearby humanoids do not appear in population figures unless they are actually residents of the land in question. For example, Cormyr's Storm Horns and Thunder Peaks are home to thousands of orcs and goblins, but these creatures are not residents of Cormyr and do not appear in its population total.

Government: The form of government over that land. Refer to the definitions in Chapter 6 of the *Dungeon Master's Guide*. Some small realms ruled by hereditary nobles are not large enough to be called true monarchies, so instead they are referred to as lordships.

Religions: Deities whose temples or worshipers are particularly common in that land. Deities not listed in this block may have small numbers of worshipers in the land, but they are not well organized or sanctioned by the state.

Imports: Goods commonly carried to the land by foreign merchants.

Exports: Goods or products produced in abundance and sold to other lands.

Alignment: The general alignment tendency of people within the land, beginning with the most common. At least one of the towns and cities in the region that are power centers usually follows the most common alignment.

Anauroch

Capital: Shade (none for the Bedine)
Population: 114,048 [not including the city of Shade] (humans 77%, asabi 17%, gnolls 5%)
Government: Magocracy (city of Shade); tribal (the Bedine)
Religions: Beshaba, Elah (Selûne), Kozah (Talos), N'asr (Kelemvor), place spirits, Shar
Imports: Livestock, wooden goods
Exports: Salt, spices
Alignment: NE, CE, CG

Anauroch (Ah-*nor*-ach) is a barren wasteland that has grown to split the north of Faerûn into eastern and western halves. Also known as the Great Desert or the Great Sand Sea, Anauroch swallowed the ancient empire of Netheril more than fifteen centuries past, then devoured the shining kingdoms that rose in its wake. For generations Anauroch's relentless encroachment has destroyed realms and driven monsters into the neighboring lands.

Anauroch is the greatest of Faerûn's deserts, but far from empty. A nomadic race of noble barbarians known as the Bedine roams its wastes. Zhentarim garrisons and patrols hold down a line of oases along the Black Road, the trade route that winds west from the ruins of Teshendale to Llorkh under the eaves of the Graypeak Mountains. Finally—and most significantly—the Empire of Shadows has settled over the anvil once known as the Shoal of Thirst. Shade, a city of Netheril that escaped that land's fall by removing itself to the Plane of Shadow, has now returned to Faerûn, and its masters contemplate the current shape of the world and consider what conquests to undertake next.

LIFE AND SOCIETY

The Bedine, human nomads who survive by raiding and leading caravans through the hidden passes, make their homes on the surface of the wastes. They are divided into dozens of small tribes led by sheiks, whose wealth is measured by the size and well-being of their herds. The Bedine roam from oasis to oasis, rarely staying long in any one place.

The Zhentarim have spent decades seeking a safe caravan route across Anauroch. The northern routes across the High Ice are plagued by monsters too numerous to fight, and the southern routes are bedeviled by humanoid raiders and subject to interference from the Dales and Cormyr. Through years of painstaking work the Zhents created a chain of caravanserais at oases in the Sword, the sandy southern portion of Anauroch. The Zhentarim marauders and garrisons fought for years against the Bedine, but they hold only the land on which they stand at any given moment.

As in many deserts, the secret life of Anauroch takes place below the surface. Only the most learned scholars know that the race of evil creatures known as the phaerimms were imprisoned in a magical bubble beneath the Great Desert. The phaerimms, once all-powerful within the confines of their desert prison, are scattered and broken now. A race of evil lizardlike humanoids, called the asabis, also dwells below the desert sands.

The new masters of Anauroch are the archwizards of Shade. Their black citadel—a whole city-state capable of shifting from one place to another or through the barriers between dimensions—rests near the desert's center. The Shade-folk have a regimented society, and they are devoted to their city and loyal to the city's princes, the most powerful mages of the realm. They have ignored the other desert-dwellers as beneath their notice.

MAJOR GEOGRAPHIC FEATURES

Although outsiders think of the Great Desert as a single gigantic waste, it is in fact a succession of different types of deserts: sere dust-bowls turn to wind-scoured rocky steppes that give way to frozen tundra, inhospitable mountains, and finally the gigantic glacier known as the High Ice. Anauroch can be divided into three broad regions: The High Ice, the Plain of Standing Stones, and the Sword.

Azirrhat: These cloven, rocky spires rise on the east side of At'ar's Looking Glass. The deep crevices in the rocks lead down to caverns infested with aggressive asabi tribes, which plague the desert for dozens of miles about.

Saiyaddar: Not far from the Shoal of Thirst lies the Saiyaddar, a region of arid grasslands home to wild grazing animals. It is the hunting ground of the Bedine tribes—a hundred miles of plenty in the middle of the Sword.

Scimitar Spires: These dark, obelisklike rocky spires separate the Shoal of Thirst from the stony waste known as At'ar's Looking Glass. The black, jagged blades of stone rise out of dusty sand without foothills, ravines, or any trace of vegetation. Two passes, the Gap of Skulls and the Road of Jackals, break the mountains.

The Shadow Sea: Formerly this was the Shoal of Thirst, a great basin stretching for miles in all directions, a salt flat completely devoid of water. With the return of the city of Shade, some great magic has been worked here, for a clear, cool lake perpetually shrouded in dark clouds and fog now lies where thousands of square miles of the most forbidding terrain on Toril once existed. The city of Shade rests at the lake's northern edge.

The Sword: The Sword is a region dominated by sandy desert and great dune seas. Its heart is the Quarter of Emptiness, where not even the Bedine choose to go.

IMPORTANT SITES

No travel in Anauroch is truly safe. Dust storms, blistering heat, and freezing cold in winter can kill even those hardened to difficult journeys.

City of Shade (Metropolis, 25,000+?): Early in the Year of Wild Magic, a mysterious flying city of black walls and high spires materialized above the Dire Wood. Shortly thereafter, it came to rest near the Scimitar Spire mountains in southern Anauroch. Its appearance coincided with the flooding of the Shoal of Thirst. The inhabitants of the newly arrived city are the descendants of Netherese wizards who slipped into the Plane of Shadow to escape the destruction of Netheril. Legions of dark-armored wizard-warriors patrol the city's streets and new surroundings, and a circle of

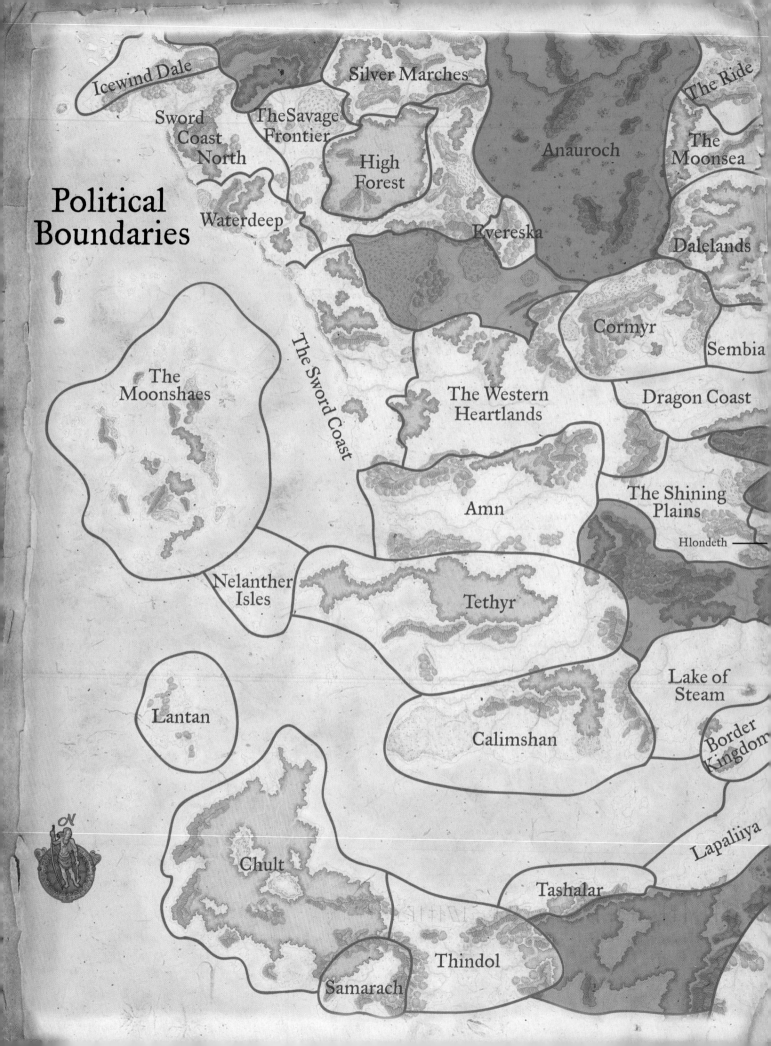

Political Boundaries

Icewind Dale

Silver Marches

The Ride

Sword Coast North

TheSavage Frontier

Anauroch

The Moonsea

High Forest

Waterdeep

Evereska

Dalelands

The Sword Coast

The Moonshaes

The Western Heartlands

Cormyr

Sembia

Dragon Coast

Amn

The Shining Plains

Hlondeth

Nelanther Isles

Tethyr

Lake of Steam

Lantan

Calimshan

Border Kingdom

Chult

Lapaliiya

Tashalar

Thindol

Samarach

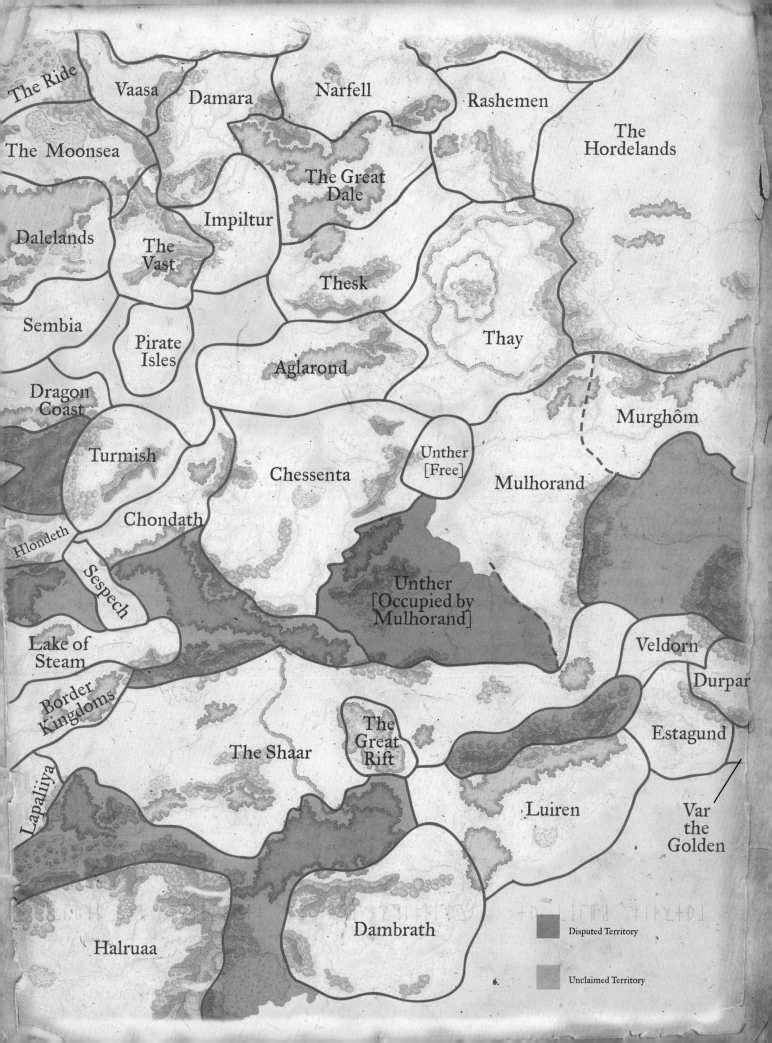

The Ride

The Moonsea

Vaasa

Damara

Narfell

Rashemen

The Hordelands

Dalelands

Impiltur

The Great Dale

The Vast

Sembia

Pirate Isles

Thesk

Thay

Dragon Coast

Aglarond

Murghôm

Turmish

Chessenta

Unther [Free]

Mulhorand

Chondath

Hlondeth

Sespech

Unther [Occupied by Mulhorand]

Veldorn

Lake of Steam

Durpar

Border Kingdoms

Estagund

Lapaliiya

The Shaar

The Great Rift

Luiren

Var the Golden

Dambrath

Halruaa

Disputed Territory

Unclaimed Territory

archwizard shades infused with the power of shadowstuff leads the city, just as the Netherese mage-princes ruled these lands in olden times. The city of Shade represents one of the most potent concentrations of arcane might on the face of Toril, and its unexpected arrival troubles the councils of the wise and the powerful across Faerûn.

Hlaungadath: About forty miles east of the ruined city of Ascore on the northwestern border of the desert, another abandoned city rises from the sands. Old but largely intact, the ruins are home to a powerful and arrogant clan of lamias. The lamias prowl nearby oases in search of careless Zhent caravans or unwary Bedine, but Hlaungadath has an evil reputation among the desert-dwellers, and they give it a wide berth. The lamia leader is said to be a mighty sorcerer.

REGIONAL HISTORY

Anauroch is the work of the phaerimms, a race of powerful nonhuman wizards who rose in the Underdark beneath the heart of Netheril thousands of years ago. As Netheril reached the zenith of its power, these secret enemies created terrible *lifedrain* magic, a curse that desiccated the lands of Netheril and drove the mighty archwizards into a dozen different lands.

The phaerimms attempted to eliminate all life on Faerûn; fortunately, they succeeded only in wiping out Netheril. To contain the damage they had caused, another primordial race, the sharns, imprisoned all but a few of the phaerimms underneath the ruins of the Netherese empire.

After the fall of Netheril's great wizards and the flight of its people, three successor states arose in the borderlands of the old empire in regions unblighted by the phaerimm curse. The cities of Anauria, Asram, and Hlondath survived for centuries after Netheril had vanished. But the desert continued to encroach on these lands, fed by the unhuman fury of the phaerimm. Hlondath, the last to fail, did not vanish until almost three hundred years after the raising of the Standing Stone in Cormanthor, but now all three of the Buried Realms, as they are known, have been abandoned for more than a thousand years. Their folk became wanderers in the wastelands of Anauroch and mixed with the Bedine, who had been magically transported here from Zakhara, producing a hybrid culture.

The Bedine were left alone in their desert home for many years, since few invaders could tolerate Anauroch's wrath. Until early this year, the phaerimms were still imprisoned beneath the sands of Anauroch, honing their wizardly skills and searching for a way out, but the coming of Shade has shattered the Sharn Wall. That would be good news for the phaerimms, except that the shades are their worst foes. This year may see a major battle in the depths of Anauroch. Divinations concerning the outcome of the battle yield nothing but shadows.

PLOTS AND RUMORS

Adventurers have come to Anauroch for generations in search of the magical might of fallen Netheril and the fabulous treasures of the Buried Realms. It remains to be seen whether the soldiers and wizards of the city of Shade will take note of this activity and move to stop it . . . or, for that matter, what the shades are likely to do next.

Desert Deadline: At the end of one of their adventures, the PCs recover a map to a fabulous treasure buried in the Great Desert of Anauroch, a map drawn by a Zhent agent and intercepted on its way to Zhentil Keep. Curiously, the map is attached to another document, a selection of prophecies from Alaundo of Candlekeep, who believed that some large-scale magical catastrophe was going to hit the Great Desert some time in 1372 DR.

The map's creator was principally concerned that Zhentil Keep would not have enough time to put together a powerful party capable of retrieving the treasure. This, in fact, has turned out to be true, since the Zhents no longer have the map. But the PCs have time. Don't they?

Hadrhune

Illustration by Sam Wood

HADRHUNE

Male shade Wiz10/Sha10: CR 22; Medium-size outsider; HD 10d4+10 plus 10d4+10; hp 77; Init +9; Spd 30 ft.; AC 25 (touch 15, flat-footed 20); Atk +11/+6 melee (1d6+1/+1d10 cold, *Hadrhune's dark staff*) or +15/+10 ranged touch (by spell); SQ Shadow adept abilities; SR 17; AL NE; SV Fort +12, Ref +18, Will +23; Str 10, Dex 20, Con 13, Int 21, Wis 14, Cha 14. Height 6 ft.

Skills and Feats: Alchemy +15, Bluff +12, Concentration +24, Craft (woodcarving) +8, Diplomacy +4, Disguise +12, Hide +15, Intimidate +4, Knowledge (arcana) +25, Knowledge (the planes) +25, Listen +7, Scry +25, Search +9, Spellcraft +25, Spot +7; Combat Casting, Craft Staff, Craft Wondrous Item, Improved Initiative, Iron Will, Insidious Magic, Lightning Reflexes, Pernicious Magic, Quicken Spell, Scribe Scroll, Shadow Weave Magic, Silent Spell, Spell Penetration, Spellcasting Prodigy, Tenacious Magic.

In Darkness or Shadows: hp 97; Spd 50 ft.; AC 29 (touch 19, flat-footed 24); Atk +13/+8 melee (1d6+3/+1d10 cold, *Hadrhune's dark staff*) or +17/+12 ranged touch (by spell); SQ Shade abilities, shadow adept abilities; SR 31; SV Fort +17, Ref +22, Will +27; Str 10, Dex 20, Con 17, Int 21, Wis 14, Cha 18.

Skills in Darkness or Shadows: Bluff +13, Concentration +25, Diplomacy +5, Disguise +13, Hide +23, Intimidate +5, Listen +11, Move Silently +13, Spot +11.

Special Qualities: Shade Abilities: Control light, fast healing 2, invisibility, shadesight, shadow image, shadow stride, shadow travel. Shadow Adept Abilities: Darkvision, low-light vision, shadow defense +3, shadow double, shadow walk, shield of shadows 10 rounds per day, spell power +3.

Spells per Day: 4/6/6/5/5/5/4/4/4. Base DC = 19 + spell level, 20 + spell level for enchantment, illusion, necromancy, and darkness spells.

Spellbook: As one of the most powerful and influential wizards of the city of Shade, Hadrhune has a vast library of spells, including all spells in this book and the *Player's Handbook* from the schools of Enchantment, Illusion, and Necromancy, as well as those with the darkness descriptor.

Possessions: Hadrhune's dark staff (+1 icy burst quarterstaff with energy drain, Grimwald's graymantle, project image, shadow spray, 33 charges), black robe of the archmagi, gloves of Dexterity +6, boots of speed, amulet of natural armor +5, cloak of resistance +5, pearl of power (7th level), arcane scrolls of dominate monster, horrid wilting, mass charm, wail of the banshee, and weird.

Cold, calculating, and evil, Hadrhune fought his way to the top of the hierarchy of the city of Shade with talent, determination, and manipulation of his enemies. He stands at the right hand of Most High Telamont, the ruler of Shade, functioning as his personal emissary and agent.

A powerful wizard unafraid to create magic items to complement his spells or use as bribes, Hadrune spies on his underlings and rivals, feeding information to other persons of power to guard his interests and eliminate threats to himself. Hadrhune is very curious about the state of the world and frequently uses scrying magic and other divinations to learn about the nearby lands. He is probably the best informed of the shades about the happenings in the Heartlands, and it was he who proposed eliminating nearby cities that might discover the shades' return, for he understands the threat that modern-day spellcasters and adventurers pose to the plans of his people. His agents in Faerûn search for rumors of Netherese ruins and information on known spellcasters of power.

Ever an ambitious man, when the shades conquer Faerûn Hadrhune plans to have himself appointed governor of Thay or the North so that he may explore the magic of the Red Wizards or the hidden treasures of Undermountain. Still relatively young, he intends to pursue the path of the undead when his body begins to fail him.

Hadrhune's characteristic magic item is his dark staff, which he uses to punish incompetent minions and fend off attacks from envious princes. Although he is very quiet and reserved in his manner, when agitated he grinds his thumbnail against the handle of the staff, which has worn a groove in it. The staff sometimes "leaks" harmless black energy from this point.

chultan peninsula

Considered by most to be a backward, unsettled land of monsters, jungles, disease, and savages, the Chultan peninsula boasts several distinct cultures and relatively stable governments that date back hundreds of years. These lands' reputations derive from their isolation from the rest of the world, the magical concealment of key cities, and the fever-induced rants of old sailors.

The Chultan peninsula encompasses the land from the Mhair Jungles westward, including the Black Jungles, the jungles of Chult, and the countries of Tashalar, Samarach, and Thindol.

chult

Population: 440,640 (humans 60%, goblins 20%, lizardfolk 10%, wild dwarves 5%, pterafolk 4%)
Government: Tribal (rural areas); theocracy (in the city of Mezro)
Religions: Eshowdow (an aspect of Shar), Tharrd Harr, Ubtao
Imports: Food, jewelry, weapons
Exports: Furs, gems, ivory, perfume
Alignment: LN, CE, LG

Located at the westernmost end of the Chultan peninsula, Chult is a mountainous jungle of savage beasts, hulking dinosaurs, and disease-ridden swamps. Reclusive human tribes, fierce goblins, and strange monstrous folk haunt this dangerous land. Nevertheless, Chult draws adventurers who search for its legendary riches.

Faith in the many aspects of the deity Ubtao holds dominion in this land, for the divine powers of Faerûn awarded Ubtao the land of Chult in exchange for his vigilance over the threat from under the Peaks of Flame.

LIFE AND SOCIETY

The humans of Chult live in small tribal villages of ten to fifteen family units, moving yearly when the poor soil becomes depleted. They use weapons that don't require much metal, such as handaxes, bows, clubs, halfspears, bolas, knives, and shortspears. Iron and steel are too rare for the Chultans to produce metal armor in any quantity, so their warriors wear hide breastplates and carry large, oval-shaped hide shields.

Tribal custom restricts the practice of sorcery and wizardry among the rural clans, although people with an aptitude for magic are as common in Chult as they are anywhere else. Only one wielder of arcane magic is permitted to practice his or her craft in any given clan or village. These sorcerers and wizards participate in hunting ceremonies and brew potions to aid the warriors. Renegade mages hide in the jungle and study magic in secret, or abandon their home villages to travel to the college in Mezro.

The Chultans distrust power and wealth, preferring to live simply and trading excess valuables for useful goods. Other than the humans, intelligent creatures living in large numbers in Chult include the Batiri (tribes of green-skinned goblins skilled at tracking), wild dwarves, lizardfolk, pterafolk, and yuan-ti. Less common are aarakocras, chuuls, hydras, nagas, troglodytes, trolls, and wyverns. The natives greatly respect the dinosaurs, which have a special place in local mythologies and are sometimes worshiped as aspects of Ubtao.

chultan weapons

Many wealthy warriors or chiefs own weapons of good steel acquired from northern traders, but weapons made of stone, wood, obsidian, or copper are not uncommon in Chult. Weapons made of inferior materials suffer a -2 attack and damage penalty (with a minimum damage of 1).

No Chultan armorers work in heavy metal armors, due to the scarcity of iron and steel and the hot, humid conditions of the peninsula. Any character wearing armor that has an armor check penalty of -5 or worse for more than an hour becomes fatigued as if she had slept in armor (-2 penalty to Strength and Dexterity, cannot charge or run). She remains fatigued as long as she wears the armor and for 1 full hour after she removes it.

Chultan hide breastplates are equivalent to leather armor and hide shields are equivalent to large wooden shields.

MAJOR GEOGRAPHICAL FEATURES

The famous jungles cover most of the western end of the Chultan peninsula. Only the highest mountains rise clear of the verdant growth, although great, marshy clearings and grasslands surround large lakes in the interior.

The Jungles of Chult: If one listens to tavern tales told across the rest of Faerûn, it's hard to escape the conclusion that the jungles of Chult are the deadliest places on all Toril. Every bush and vine is a strangling, poisonous, flesh-eating, or blood-sucking monster—and under every bush lurk a thousand scaled, taloned, fanged monsters.

These tales aren't far wrong. The heat and humidity is incredible, and the insects are everywhere, clinging and stinging, their noise unceasing. The trackless jungles are home to strange tribes of dwarves and scaly folk found nowhere else. Land leeches, carnivorous plants, and giant slugs are all too common, and every serpent seems to be armed with deadly venom.

Disease is the deadliest killer of Chult. It is carried in plants with stabbing spines, or in any of the hundreds of insect bites suffered in a typical day, or even borne by jungle mists. Those who drink unboiled jungle water are almost certain to acquire some sort of disease or parasite before long.

Travel in the "deep canopy" jungle is easiest, though not without danger. Here giant solifugids, ants, spiders, carrion crawlers, and purple worms slither and scuttle in the everlasting, vine-hung, fungus-filled gloom beneath the hundred-foot-tall trees, where the sun never reaches. At least the undergrowth is sparse, and the alert traveler can see hungry death coming.

Yet explorers from elsewhere in Faerûn enter Chult again and again in search of its fabled veins of gold, gems as large as a man's palm, exotic plants prized by collectors in Amn, Calimshan, Sembia, Tethyr, Thay, and Waterdeep (and sources of poisons, perfumes, and medicines by the score), huge jungle timbers, and even rubber trees.

Chult's riches are not exaggerated in the slightest. Satraps of Calimshan send a constant stream of slaves into the jungles to carve roads through the fast-growing vines and creepers and reach known mines and ruined cities. Most perish, but a few escape to tell colorful tales of extensive caves underlying the jungles haunted by gigantic bats or cloakers, and of ruined cities choked with coins and gems and lurking monsters, where only vines hold up the crumbling stones and weird six-headed snakes slither and even fly. They speak of the fabled city of Mezro, where the Chultan priest-kings dwell, worshiping strange deities . . . and of the eerie creatures known as deepspawn that vomit forth living duplicates of creatures they've devoured before.

Peaks of Flame: Home to salamanders and other fiery creatures, the Peaks of Flame stand over a pair of iron doors that lead to the realm of the dead. When the doom of the world approaches, Dendar the Night Serpent (a terrible monster that feeds on the unremembered nightmares of all creatures) will break down these doors and escape into Toril.

Valley of Lost Honor: A place surrounded by the thickest parts of the jungle, this valley was the last refuge of the Eshowe (see Regional History, below) before they were destroyed. The entire wealth of the Eshowe may be hidden in caves here, but other legends say that the evil deity Eshowdow (Shar in another guise) resides here, recruiting followers and planning for revenge. The surrounding jungle teems with great numbers of Batiri and natural predators.

Wild Coast: The rocky, inhospitable stretch of Chult's southwestern coastline creates a hazard for ships. Sailors give it a wide berth, for whirlpools, shifting gale-force winds, and aquatic monsters are all common, and above, flying dinosaurs battle giant eagles for supremacy of the skies. Brave or foolish folk explore the caves along the coast, hoping to find tunnels leading to the rich mines that lie under the jungle.

IMPORTANT SITES

Despite the dangers from the jungles, determined folk still manage to carve out civilized areas for themselves and for visitors to the country.

Fort Beluarian (Hamlet, 313): This outpost belongs to the Flaming Fist, a mercenary company based in Baldur's Gate. Its membership includes rangers, wizards, clerics, and a large number of fighters who hire themselves out for any venture that doesn't serve an evil purpose. They are well supplied and familiar with the jungle, and they even let desperate adventurers stay in the fort for the night if in great need.

Mezro (Metropolis, 28,126): Mezro is the largest civilized area in Chult. In past years, a magic wall surrounded the city, preventing it from being seen and causing *confusion* in those who approached too closely. This protection was lowered in 1363 DR after a victorious battle against the Batiri goblins. It is now a safe haven for explorers battered by the jungle.

Mezro is a holy city to the Chultan tribes, and it is generally peaceful, with few people carrying weapons other than utilitarian knives. Any chronic lawbreaker is tattooed with a blue triangle on the forehead and exiled. Ubtao's undying baras, six paladinlike Chosen who exist to protect the city from all harm, rule Mezro.

The city has its own college of wizardry, although it is generally closed to non-Chultans. After studying at Mezro for several years, wizards generally go back to their native tribes. Only rarely do Chultan mages travel to the other regions of Faerûn to find their fortunes.

Port Nyanzaru (Small City, 9,375): The major trading center in Chult, this port town's harbor was designed with defense as its first priority, since many pirates roam these waters. It is rumored that the harbormaster pays tribute to a powerful dragon turtle that drives away all other sea monsters.

REGIONAL HISTORY

Millennia ago, the deity Ubtao created the jungle and populated it with creatures. Four thousand years ago he built the city of Mezro with his own hands and empowered the baras—his Chosen—to defend it. Eventually Ubtao tired of the constant demands of the people in the city and retreated, allowing the baras to rule Mezro in his stead.

Realizing that the act of creation had distanced him from mortals, Ubtao imbued a portion of his essence in the land, creating nature spirits and inadvertently drawing the attention of a dark shadow. A tribe of humans called the Eshowe freed this shadow-creature, Eshowdow, who attacked Mezro only to be driven back after causing great destruction. In retaliation, a bara called Ras Nsi hunted down and killed the entire Eshowe people. Most Chultans have forgotten the Eshowe and Ras Nsi's ancient crime.

Several years ago, the undying King Osaw (LG male human Pal15, Chosen of Ubtao) opened Mezro to the outside world again. Trade goods now flow back and forth to the rest of Faerûn.

PLOTS AND RUMORS

As noted above, unimagined treasure waits in the jungles of Chult . . . and mortal peril, too. Choosing to search for the one despite the risk of the other is what separates adventurers from the common folk.

Dragons of the Coast: Dragon turtles lurk in the sea near the river outlets, seeking prey and tribute. Local interests hire heroes to kill or distract some of these creatures so that valuable shipments can escape unhindered. To sweeten the pot, certain wizards require dragon turtle parts for exotic spells or magic items and would pay dearly for carcasses.

Fallen Champion: The renegade bara Ras Nsi was exiled long ago for his ruthless extermination of the Eshowe. He still maintains a twisted devotion to Mezro and violently disagrees with Osaw's opening of the city. Driven by determination to save Mezro from its misguided rulers, Ras Nsi has raised an army of undead to throw down his former fellows and drive all outlanders out of Chult.

Tashalar

Capital: Tashluta
Population: 889,920 (humans 94%, lizardfolk 4%, yuan-ti 1%)
Government: Merchant oligarchy
Religions: Chauntea, Malar, Savras, Waukeen
Imports: Beef, fruit, silver, slaves
Exports: Cheese, dyed fabric, glass, olive oil, olives, seafood, spices, wine
Alignment: CN, N, NE

More civilized than Chult and more friendly than Calimshan, Tashalar is an exotic land of strange food, beautiful people, and great wealth. The skilled craftsfolk make excellent crossbows and fast ships. The accomplished hunters keep trophies of their most dangerous kills. The people of Tashalar live on the strip of friendly coastline along the southern Shining Sea, avoiding the Black Jungles and entering the Hazuk Mountains only occasionally to mine for gold and iron.

Tashalaran grapes are so perfect that even the worst vineyard produces wines worth a hundred gold pieces in Waterdeep. Overshadowing this wealth and splendor are the Rundeen consortium that puts a chokehold on trade and the evil yuan-ti that haunt the jungles.

LIFE AND SOCIETY

The larger towns of Tashalar (small city-states, really) are home to wealthy and ostentatious merchant families. The "princes" of these families control the merchant consortiums that rule the country. Those common folk who don't make their living in the fields, groves, or vineyards work as sailors, shipwrights, sailmakers, and provisioners.

Hunting is a popular sport, with the bravest hunters seeking out the deadly denizens of the jungle. Spicy food and strong wine are the typical dining fare. The folk of Tashalar obsess over the future, and every adult owns at least one set of cards or plaques used for per-

sonal divinations. (Wealthier folk own ones made of silver or ivory.) The people see the hand of Savras the All-Seeing in their daily card readings, numerology, and astrology.

MAJOR GEOGRAPHICAL FEATURES

Tashalar is a warm but breezy country, with open land covered in vegetable gardens, olive groves, and vineyards.

Black Jungles: These jungles are home to three large tribes of yuan-ti, one of which has allied with the Rundeen consortium. The Sesehen tribe provides exotic herbs and poisons to the Rundeen in exchange for slaves and transport of pureblood spies to northern ports. The jungle has connections to the Underdark, and one temple to the snake god of the yuan-ti contains a *portal* to a similar place in Hlondeth in the Vilhon Reach.

Hazuk Mountains: These mountains produce enough gold and iron to support Tashalar's economy. Civilized but short-tempered stone giants live in the remote peaks in enormous rock mansions, trading gems for fine wine and knowledge for dragon turtle meat.

Mhair Jungles: Remnants of an old yuan-ti empire still live in isolated pockets of these vast, sparsely settled jungles. Bloodflower, a rare herb extinct everywhere else in Faerûn, is harvested here to be made into a potent healing salve. The jungles also hold wandering groups of wild dwarves (survivors of a lost kingdom) who trade enormous green spinel gems, but carefully guard the secret of where they find them.

IMPORTANT SITES

The city of Tashluta is the largest of the Tashalar city-states and the most welcoming to visitors to the nation.

Tashluta (Metropolis, 51,522): The capital of Tashalar is the common port for visitors, as only here do the locals make any effort to learn the other languages of Faerûn. They enjoy playing jokes on foreigners, usually involving incredibly spicy food. The city has a ban on snakes of all sorts, and the Tashlutans kill any that are discovered.

REGIONAL HISTORY

Long ago, a great mercantile empire called Tashtan ruled the central part of the Chultan peninsula. As a result of many battles with Calimshan and jungle plagues, Tashtan dissolved into smaller

A Jungle Legend: The Uluu Thalongh

Of all the legends whispered about the monster-infested, swamp-riddled jungles of Chult, the most eerie is that of the Uluu Thalongh, a name whose meaning has been lost along with the tribe that bestowed it.

The Uluu Thalongh is a huge, ancient, and malevolent flesh-eating beast. A weird, tuneless piping always marks its approach. The sound reduces intelligent jungle creatures to headlong flight or mortal fear.

When it closes on its intended prey, the Uluu "goes within" jungle plants and trees, causing them to ripple and bulge. These swellings move swiftly to branches, from which they burst forth as huge jaws at the end of tentacles—eyeless jaws that see prey perfectly, snapping and tearing until all creatures nearby have died or fled.

If a jaw is "killed," the Uluu leaves the area, but it is never itself slain. Even cabals of wizards casting fiery and explosive spells that

obliterate miles upon miles of jungle have failed to destroy the Uluu Thalongh.

More frightening is the tendency of this mysterious predator to lure prey to itself by causing beings to speak for it. To create a "speaker," the Uluu first "stings" a jungle creature or even a human by driving a rootlet into the target. Through this, the Uluu sucks out all nutrients (leaving its speaker to crumple into dust, an empty husk). The Uluu can then convey its own thoughts and mental control through the speaker. Even creatures that don't normally speak can hoarsely whisper words in an attempt to lure humans to its jaws. Sometimes speakers plead for help or shout mock cries for aid from afar—but more often they pose as aides or companions whom the Uluu has already slain.

Who or what the Uluu Thalongh truly is remains a deadly mystery.

Illustration by Sam Wood

Hunters take on a nest of yuan-ti in the thick jungle.

nations, the northernmost being the collection of city-states now known as Tashalar.

A strong mercantile kingdom, Tashalar protects its borders with fleets of strong ships, most of which have fallen under the influence of a consortium of aggressive traders known as the Rundeen. The Rundeen reaches into Calimshan through a partnership with the Knights of the Shield, an organization of spies active in Amn, Calimshan, and Tethyr. Tashalaran vessels now sail to ports in Calimshan and the Lake of Steam, bringing unusual goods to eager recipients elsewhere in Faerûn.

PLOTS AND RUMORS

Adventures in Tashalar generally begin in the city of Tashluta, though the uncharted reaches of the mountains and jungles may entice adventurers looking for places not often explored.

Fighting for the Crown: Assassinations and blackmail of the ruling families' princes are believed to be the work of someone wishing to install a single noble as figurehead-ruler of Tashalar. Most think members of the Rundeen or the yuan-ti are involved, along with several less-influential merchant families. All sides have begun hiring mercenaries and adventurers for protection and to make counterattacks on their suspected enemies.

Risen: A long-sunken ship, festooned with seaweed, its crew no more than slumped heaps of coral-encrusted bones, rose from the sea bottom outside Tashluta's harbor and sailed into the docks, causing much terror. Tashlutan authorities towed the ship to a private dock and refused to announce its contents. The next morning all of the skeletal crew were gone, and several people have since been found dead in the streets.

samarach

Little is known about this kingdom, since it is separated from the rest of the peninsula by thick jungle and rugged mountains. Explor-

ers from Tashalar claim it is populated by cowards who barricade themselves in walled cities at night. The natives cloak the paths to their cities and the passes through the mountains with illusions.

thindol

Expanses of tall grass cover this land, home to a race of humans similar to the Chultans but renowned as incredibly fleet of foot. In the hills and mountains live gold dwarves, their caverns ringing with the sound of weapons being forged to fight the hordes of kuo-toa that live in the waterlogged tunnels underground. The kuo-toa are allied with yuan-ti that have the traits of swimming snakes.

cold Lands

The region called the Cold Lands consists of the territories adjacent to or near the Great Glacier, namely Damara, Narfell, Sossal, and Vaasa. Their inhospitable climates are largely due to the glacier's influence. This collection of nations is erroneously called the Bloodstone Lands by many, but that title actually refers only to Damara and Vaasa. Sparsely inhabited but rich in mineral wealth, these lands draw foreigners looking to strike it rich quickly. Most, however, quickly become daunted by the hostile environment and aggressive tribesfolk.

Damara

Capital: Heliogabalus
Population: 1,321,920 (humans 87%, dwarves 6%, halflings 4%, half-orcs 2%)
Government: Monarchy
Religions: Ilmater, Silvanus, Tempus (barbarians)
Imports: Food, livestock, wood
Exports: Gems, gold, iron, silver
Alignment: LN, N, NE

North of Impiltur and east of the Moonsea lies the once-mighty realm of Damara, now rebuilding from decades of war against its neighbors and the orcs and gnolls of the mountains. Tolerant of all races and most religions, the country is friendly to visitors, especially those who have skill in slaying monsters. Those interested in politics and adventure can find plenty of opportunities here.

Damara maintains friendly relations with its neighbors and has a thriving gem trade based on its bountiful chalcedony (known as "bloodstone" for its red flecks) mines. However, the leaders of Damara keep a wary eye on the neighboring land of Vaasa and stay prepared for any strange threat that may arise from there.

LIFE AND SOCIETY

The hardy people of Damara have worked hard to rebuild their land. Although many are grim and bitterly lament the loss of their former way of life, the worship of Ilmater gives them strength in the face of hardship and high hopes for the future. Paladins of the Crying God (particularly from the Order of the Golden Cup) are a common sight, as are monks of that faith from the Monastery of the Yellow Rose near the Glacier of the White Worm.

Despite the travails of their recent history, Damarans are proud of their country, which is home to peacefully coexisting humans, dwarves, halflings, and half-orcs. Their mines produce enough metals and gems to pay for needed repairs, and the svirfneblin colony under Bloodstone Pass has recently opened a school for illusionist magic.

MAJOR GEOGRAPHICAL FEATURES

Damara's few roads are generally impassable in the wintertime, but rivers link the remote country with the capital. In warm months, keelboats and barges ply the cold, swift waters, and in winter, the river ice serves as a road for horse-drawn sleds and sledges.

Bloodstone Pass: This is the only true pass through the Galena Mountains. Whoever controls Bloodstone controls the trade between Vaasa and Damara and can stop armies with ease. The pass contains Bloodstone Gate (large city, 13,233) a small forest, and a high mountain lake.

Earthwood: This small, thick forest is amazingly resilient, growing back whatever is cut from it in only a few years. Legends say that long ago a great druid enspelled the wood in defiance of the glacier, and that since that time it has never been covered in ice. Monsters generally avoid the wood.

Galena Mountains: These jagged, broken peaks are laced with ice and snow and inhabited by thousands of goblins and giants as well as other humanoid monsters. The residents of four major dwarven settlements—the Bloodstone Mines (village, 500), Hillsafar Hall (small town, 1,500), Ironspur (small town, 1,000), and a new settlement of gold dwarves, Firehammer Hall (hamlet, 300)—mine the Galenas for iron, silver, and bloodstone. Well-armed dwarf patrols keep the monsters at bay. The Underdark is close by, and the inhabitants of drow, derro, and duergar cities also mine deep veins under these mountains. The cities of Melvaunt and Mulmaster sponsor fortified mining camps in the western foothills.

IMPORTANT SITES

With a government still finalizing the bounds of its responsibilities after an invasion by the hordes of an evil lich, Damara is a land ideally suited for adventurers.

The Gates: These two large fortress-walls guard the ends of Bloodstone Pass. The Gates contain stockpiles of food in case of an invasion and are regularly patrolled. The Damaran Gate is three miles long, thirty feet high, and studded with ballista-defended towers at regular intervals. A castle stands at either end. The Vaasan Gate is half a mile long and 60 feet high, with similar towers but no end castles. Many adventurers camp within the Vaasan Gate, using it as a base for monster hunting within that land.

Heliogabalus (Metropolis, 44,111): This is the old seat of Damara's throne, now reclaimed for the new monarchy. A prosperous trading city, it is literally the end of the road for merchants traveling north from other areas of Faerûn. Heliogabalus supplies all of Damara with foreign goods and is influenced by independent merchants' guilds.

Until five years ago the city had no army, only mercenaries controlled by the guilds. The new king ordered the guilds to disperse their mercenaries, and older paladins of Ilmater now lead young recruits in protecting the city.

Trailsend (Large City, 14,116): This barony capital is built around a huge, heavily fortified castle. The city and barony maintain a friendly relationship with the nation of Impiltur. Baron Donlevy the Young (LN male human Ftr3/Rog3) who survived the reign of the Witch-King in hiding, leveraged that alliance to endorse King Dragonsbane. Now a wealthy noble, Baron Donlevy is the king's primary liaison to Impiltur.

As Trailsend is usually the first city that visitors to Damara see,

glacier of the white worm

From the peaks of the Earthspur Mountains (see the entry for Impiltur, below), a frozen river of ice spills from a high cliff into the Moonsea at one end and into Lake Icemelt between Impiltur and Damara at the other. The Glacier of the White Worm is named for the white remorhazes that roam it, often in herds of a dozen or more and reputedly led by a "king" worm of giant size. Adventurers tell of fleeing from snow spiders of gigantic size, or remorhazes whose heads were fringed with long, reaching tentacles. The glacier is also home to many lesser creatures.

Old histories claim that this glacier was once part of the Great Glacier that covered all these lands. Modern sages warn of something sinister at work in or under this high ice. The glacier is too far south and at too low an altitude to persist without cold-based magic of great power, they suggest, and the safety of

all Faerûn might hinge on learning who works such magic, and why—or at least learning the true nature and powers of the "white worms."

Overlooking the glacier, built into the jagged side of one of the tallest peaks in the Earthspurs, is the Citadel of the White Worm. This sprawling fortress of balconies, windows, and turrets includes tunnels into the rock below it, plus endless rooms, passages, and catacombs of great age. The citadel is better known as the Monastery of the Yellow Rose, a holy house of Ilmater. Monks here venerate the Suffering God, make blueberry wine, keep extensive archives of the Bloodstone Lands, and preserve the work of the Ilmatari faithful in a spectacular museum of art and handiwork. The monks of the Yellow Rose also gather and record local news from Damara, Impiltur, Narfell, and Vaasa.

several businesses cater solely to finding unusual employment for adventurers.

REGIONAL HISTORY

Damara was founded almost three hundred years ago under the Bloodfeathers dynasty. Formerly a wealthy trading kingdom enriched by its iron, silver, and bloodstone (traded in 25-gp value trade bars now regarded as unlucky "cursed money"), Damara fell from greatness in a twelve-year war against invaders from Vaasa, the land to the northwest.

Vaasa's Witch-King led armies of giants, goblins, orcs, and undead into Damara and eventually triumphed over King Virdin Bloodfeathers at the Ford of Goliad. The fell creatures of Vaasa occupied northern Damara, but fled and scattered after the Witch-King's power was broken by a local band of adventurers. Gareth Dragonsbane was able to cement key alliances with lesser nobles through the support of the common folk, and was crowned king of Damara in 1359 DR.

Since the unification of Damara, King Dragonsbane (LG male human Pal20/Clr5 of Ilmater) has worked hard to rebuild his nation's economy and strength of arms. Damara has recovered from the war with Vaasa and watches at the Gates to guard against future invasion from its northern neighbor. Trade relations with Impiltur are positive, and acceptance of the bloodstone tradebars is increasing.

King Dragonsbane is trying to attract adventurers to his land by building upon Damara's reputation for adventuring. His agents cite mineral-rich mountains, proximity to monster-heavy Vaasa, the deep gnomes' school of illusion magic, and opportunities for land grants. Dragonsbane has even offered minor noble titles to folk of law and good who are willing to build homes and swear allegiance to Damara. These incentives are working, and there is now a steady flow of adventurers into Damara.

PLOTS AND RUMORS

Heroes can find plenty of opportunities in the monster-infested mountains and northern lands. Those who come here can earn prestige for themselves in the aftermath of this nation's political turmoil.

Legacy of the Witch-King: Bandit activity in the Galena Mountains and northern Damara may be tied to the Citadel of Assassins, the evil organization that supported the Witch-King. Bolstered by spells cast by the evil wizard Knellict (LE male human Wiz15/Asn4), the bandits have been hard to track and very effective in their raids. Capturing some of the bandits could lead to a break in discovering the location of the Citadel and rooting out the last vestige of Zhengyi's power.

Underground Connections: Recently miners in the Earthspurs broke through to a previously unsuspected section of the Underdark. The large cavern they discovered contains an icy lake and is thought to connect to several known evil cities underground. Parties of adventurers are assembling to explore these areas and chart the myriad passages and caverns below.

Narfell

Capital: Bildoobaris (summer only)
Population: 36,720 (humans 99%)
Government: Tribal
Religions: Lathander, Tempus, Waukeen
Imports: Clothing, jewelry
Exports: Horses
Alignment: CN, CG, CE

A country where only the strong survive, Narfell is a land of infertile soil that supports only scraggly grass. The people of Narfell are tribal folk called the Nars, fierce horse-riders who believe that all people are judged by their actions. Their motto, "Deed, not blood," shows their disregard for those who expect deference because of "noble" birth. Some of the tribes are hostile to outsiders, but all set aside their differences once a year for their great trademeet.

In addition to the riders, Narfell is home to tundra yeti (dire apes) and hordes of hobgoblins in the mountains. Ancient Narfell was a powerful, wizard-ruled state that was destroyed in wars against the now-fallen empire of Raumathar. The barbaric folk living here today remember little of their civilized past, but the Nars occasionally find buried cities within their land, each containing great items of battle-magic.

LIFE AND SOCIETY

This dry, flat grassland is home to vast herds of reindeer and wild oxen—and the nomadic horsefolk who feast on them. The Nars move with their food, erecting "waymeets" (temporary tent villages) wherever nightfall finds them. They gather annually at Bildoobaris for a tenday-long Trade Fair to meet outlander merchants in a massive tent city.

At the Trade Fair, the twenty-seven Nar tribes determine common policy for external matters such as wars and meet with outlander trade delegations. During the rest of the year, fast-riding messengers maintain communications between tribal chiefs as needed.

The Nars are loosely united in a tribal council led by the largest tribe, Harthgroth. The Harthgroth, who can muster four thousand riders under the grizzled old warrior Thalaman Harthgroth (N male human Bbn5/Ftr11), regard outlanders as sources of trade-wealth rather than foes to be robbed or slain. Other tribes are far more hostile—notably the Creel, who attack outlanders and other Nars on sight. The Var tribe, however, welcomes outlanders, and its people strive to become more like them. The Dag Nost are as civilized as folk in Impiltur.

Nar tribes don't use badges, uniforms, specific colors, or identifying banners. An outlander who doesn't look like a Nar—tanned skin, long black hair braided in a horsetail, gaudy clothes, superbly skilled at riding—always travels in peril. Nar horses are tall, tough, strong, and can endure great hardship. They are the chief wealth and primary trade-goods among the Nars, who love to barter and buy, having a weakness (the men in particular) for jewelry and bright-colored clothing.

MAJOR GEOGRAPHICAL FEATURES

The flat plains of Narfell boast few features of note. More lies under the surface, however, including remnants of the ancient empire that once thrived here.

Icelace Lake: Formed of runoff from the Great Glacier, this lake boasts pure water and plenty of fish. The water is so cold that it can kill a swimmer within 10 minutes. Home to unusual aquatic creatures, the lake is also known for the aggressive dire bears that live on its shores.

IMPORTANT SITES

The "cities" of Narfell consist primarily of simple towns where the nomads congregate.

Bildoobaris (Metropolis, 33,048, summer only): For a tenday each summer, the tribes of Nars gather to form a massive tent city. Miles of animal-skin tents cover the land, and the natives welcome merchants from other countries for a brief time, exchanging horses and items taken from ruins for clothing, jewelry, dried meats, weapons, and quality barding.

Illustration by Carlo Arellano

Trademeet in Narfell

REGIONAL HISTORY

The country of Narfell dates back nearly as far as the Orcgate Wars that broke the back of Mulhorand. The mercenaries who were hired to fight the invading orcs established the nation of Narfell. Both they and their enemies from Raumathar claimed portions of Mulhorand's northern empire. Eventually these two nations went to war, and while both asked Mulhorand and Unther for aid, neither country gave it, fearing prophecies that such a war would end in mutual destruction.

The last battle between Narfell and Raumathar involved demons, dragons, and great magic that burned entire cities. When the smoke cleared, both nations were dead, their people scattered into small tribes and enclaves on the blasted land. Narfell has survived ever since in this form, greatly humbled and ignorant of its former glory. Certain legacies remain in the great weapons and heroic names some of the Nars carry, which date back a thousand years to the great kingdom of Narfell.

PLOTS AND RUMORS

Adventuring in Narfell means dealing with the native tribes. Assuming that the heroes encounter Nars who don't simply attack them outright, they may still have to "prove" themselves to win a fair hearing.

Staking a Claim: King Gareth Dragonsbane of Damara has established a friendly relationship with Thalaman Harthgroth, obtaining permission for the people of Damara to mine the Narfell side of the Giantspire Mountains in exchange for a tithe of gems and jewels. Now the barons of Damara need people to find suitable mining locations and secure these areas against attacks by hostile humanoids.

Vaasa

Capital: None
Population: 145,440 (humans 60%, dwarves 30%, orcs 9%)
Government: None (formerly dictatorship)
Religions: Dwarven pantheon, orc pantheon
Imports: Food, weapons
Exports: Furs, gems
Alignment: CE, LN, N

This untamed wasteland of frozen moors and tundra was the seat of power for the evil lich Zhengyi the Witch-King until his defeat by a band of adventurers. Vaasa is once again a lonely land dotted with scratch farms and inhabited by evil humanoids and other monsters. What the land lacks in hospitality it makes up for in untapped wealth, as the mountains of Vaasa are rich in metals and gems, particularly bloodstone. Miles of mountainside go unclaimed by any civilization, and many well-armed prospectors make the trip to Vaasa hoping to find gems as large as a grown man's fist—and survive long enough to sell them.

LIFE AND SOCIETY

Vaasa is a cold, dreary place with poor soil, inadequate for large settlements without magical help. During the brief summer the frozen earth turns to thick mud, making travel more difficult than it is in the wintertime, when dogsleds and skis are a common sight. Numerous bands of humanoids hunt the plains and mountains in search of game, mainly caribou and small herbivores. Other humanoids resort to consuming the dead of enemy tribes.

Local settlements of humans are well protected or in isolated places where they are likely to go undiscovered. Life is hard and the people are tough, quiet, and stern. People of the flatlands speak a mixture of Common and Dwarven, while the inhabitants of remote mountain settlements (and those close to Palischuk) use many Orc words.

MAJOR GEOGRAPHICAL FEATURES

Bordered by mountains and the Great Glacier, Vaasa is virtually isolated from the rest of Faerûn.

Bottomless Bogs: These large, sometimes hard-to-spot areas of mud and rotting scrub plants are deadly traps for the unwary, for they can drag even a strong person down with a grip as powerful as a giant's. A few form around hot springs, which some say are fed by a magical source. Water from these springs can reputedly enhance abilities, heal wounds, or grant even more powerful magic.

Great Glacier: Formed from the magic ice necklace of the deity Ulutiu, this glacier has been consistently retreating for centuries. Until three hundred years ago, it covered Damara and Vaasa. Tribes of humans (Ulutiuns) live in the remote parts of the glacier, occasionally traveling to the "hot lands" for meat and iron weapons. Within the territory covered by the glacier is the Novularond mountain range, a region said to hold lost cities strangely free of the ice.

The Glacier is home to white dragons, remorhazes, snowflowers (edible plants that tumble about in icy winds), iceflowers, "ice worms" (white-furred things as long as a man's arm that live on meltwater and snowflowers), "ghost" or white rothé, and even roaming gelugons. These are the "Icy Claws of Iyraclea," servants of the ancient and mighty human priestess who styles herself "the Ice Queen."

Iyraclea (NE female human Clr15/Dis5/Hie5 of Auril) is the mistress of the Great Glacier. From her realm beneath the ice she spell-snatches young, vigorous mages for some unknown but doubtless sinister purpose. Iyraclea worships Auril the Frostmaiden and commands magic of awesome power, including spells of her own devising, such as *icerazor*, *ice fist*, and *cold claws*. Few see her castle of sculpted ice and live to tell the tale.

IMPORTANT SITES

Despite its hazards, Castle Perilous is the most impressive and visited site in Vaasa, a land now largely empty.

Castle Perilous: Vaasa became a cauldron of evil decades ago when, through the labors of demons, a dark stone fortress arose in a single night. The Castle Perilous on the shores of the Lake of Tears was the seat of the lich Zhengyi, who styled himself the Witch-King of Vaasa. With the aid of his demons, he assembled hosts of dire

Castle Perilous

wolves, giants, goblins, orcs, and undead to conquer Damara.

The ironbound castle is a crumbling ruin today, roamed by lurking monsters and hopeful adventurers seeking Zhengyi's magic. The castle collapsed when Gareth Dragonsbane led heroes into Vaasa to break the lich's power.

Dragons often lair atop Castle Perilous, only to be slain or driven out by adventurers or a lurking, terrible *something* that evidently feeds on things even as large and powerful as great wyrms.

Darmshall (Small City, 5,333): The Tenblades adventuring band founded this fortress-village in southwestern Vaasa, hard by the southern Galenas peaks. It withstood Zhengyi's rise and fall, and today it is the center of a small but growing territory of farms and cattle ranches.

Walled Darmshall boasts huge underground granaries, armories, and a weapons-muster of almost five hundred capable soldiers, under the rule of the tireless warrior Gelgar Talonguard (LN male human Rgr15 of Helm). Women are few in Darmshall, and Gelgar has sent recruiters to the Dragon Reach, Telflamm, and Impiltur, seeking wives for the men of Darmshall.

Delhalls and Talagbar: Recent melts along the edge of the Ice Run glacier have revealed these two long-frozen dwarven mines that hold rich bloodstone, emerald, and ruby deposits, as well as some workable iron and copper veins.

Palischuk (Small City, 9,211): This town to the east of Castle Perilous is a larger but less grand fortress, a ruined city rebuilt by half-orcs. The half-orcs worked hard to befriend nearby settlements—and succeeded. They trade peacefully and honorably with Bloodstone Gate, Darmshall, and neighboring dwarves, though humans continue to regard Palischuk warily.

REGIONAL HISTORY

For most of its existence, Vaasa has been a frozen land barely capable of supporting civilized folk. For centuries nothing more than humanoid tribes and scattered hunters, trappers, and farmers inhabited the land. The arrival of Zhengyi and the creation of his fortress in 1347 DR turned Vaasa into a military nation of goblinoids, orcs, giants, undead, demons, bandits, and skilled assassins, all intent on conquest.

The armies of Vaasa attacked and defeated the people of Damara, dividing that nation into petty baronies. The so-called Witch-King disappeared for a time, and a group of heroes rose to defeat the demonic minions and eventually the lich himself, which caused Castle Perilous to collapse. The Vaasa of today has reverted to its old ways, with bands of monsters running loose and no central authority. However, bandits and assassins are still thought to be hiding somewhere in the country, plotting revenge.

PLOTS AND RUMORS

Great magic means great treasure—adventurers hope, anyway. The Witch-King may be gone but his works still remain, from the ruins of Castle Perilous to the creatures that served him.

Monster Hunt: King Dragonsbane of Damara is concerned with the large numbers of humanoids that live in the mountains and plains of Vaasa. He has increased the bounty on goblins, bugbears, and giants to 5 gp, 15 gp, and 200 gp respectively in hopes of convincing adventurers to stake claims here. Increased numbers of these humanoids have been gathering around the ruins of Castle Perilous, perhaps in service to some newly rising evil power.

sossal

This remote realm far to the north of Narfell has little contact with the rest of Faerûn. Once or twice a year (generally in the summer), visitors from Sossal arrive in Damara, bringing furs, seal meat from the Great Glacier, beautiful items of shaped wood, and gold. They leave with dwarven weapons, silver, and various kinds of meat to trade with the people of the glacier.

Some Sossrim have natural powers akin to druidic magic and can bend plants to their will, pass through growth impenetrable to others, or even transport themselves from one tree to another. In fact, the ornate and smoothly shaped Sossar furniture sold so steeply in Sembia is not carved at all, but sculpted by the minds of Sossrim "carvers."

cormyr

Capital: Suzail
Population: 1,360,800 (humans 85%, half-elves 10%, elves 4%)
Government: Monarchy
Religions: Chauntea, Deneir, Helm, Lathander, Lliira, Oghma, Malar, Milil, Selûne, Silvanus, Tempus, Tymora, Waukeen
Imports: Glass, ivory, spices
Exports: Armor, carved ivory, cloth, coal, food, swords, timber
Alignment: LG, LN, NG

Founded over a thousand years ago, the kingdom of Cormyr benefits from an enlightened monarchy, hard-working citizens, and an advantageous location. Cormyr is a civilized land surrounded by mountains, forests, and settlements of evil humanoids. Known for its well-trained military and its active group of government-sanctioned spellcasters, Cormyr boasts fine food, honest people, strange mysteries, and abundant contacts with other parts of the world.

Recently challenged by treacherous noble families, armies of goblins and orcs, famine, a marauding ancient red dragon, and the death of its beloved monarch, Cormyr is now struggling to maintain its holdings. With one of its cities in ruins and great numbers of evil humanoids still roaming the countryside, this nation is in need of resourceful individuals willing to defend the crown and confront its enemies.

LIFE AND SOCIETY

Though there are strong reasons why it shouldn't be, Cormyr is a steadfast and prosperous land. Despite an often-violent past, constant armed vigilance against beasts and border perils, and frequent treasonous intrigues, Cormyrians remain loyal, content, prosperous, and peace-loving folk. While the serious reverses of the last two years have shaken the kingdom, Cormyrians expect better days ahead and are willing to work to achieve that goal.

The Obarskyr family rules Cormyr, assisted by wise Royal Mages. The long reign of Azoun IV, aided by former Royal Magician Vangerdahast, gave the realm a legacy of stability and prosperity that's the envy of much of Faerûn.

Beneath the royal family is a wealthy, sophisticated, often fractious group of noble families of long lineage, influence, and demonstrated loyalty to the crown. The War Wizards—a force of battle-mages under the command of thoughtful wizards such as Caladnei—temper both royal and noble excesses. As the sage Bradaskras of Suzail put it, the Obarskyrs, the nobility, and the War Wizards "form three legs of a stool on which the common folk sit."

Most Cormyrians are farmers, ranchers, horse-breeders, foresters, or craftsfolk. The country also maintains a large, capable army, the Purple Dragons—not to be confused with Azoun IV, the king who was called the Purple Dragon, or the Purple Dragon Thauglor, long the largest and mightiest wyrm of the Dragon Reach.

MAJOR GEOGRAPHICAL FEATURES

The Forest Kingdom is a rolling, green, and pleasant land, flanked by mountains and well fed by its own farms and ranches. Old, deep, and lush forests dominate the landscape and national character. The dragon, the stag, and the unicorn characterize the land in Cormyrian folk tales, ballads, and heraldry: The wyrm represents the land's old, never-quite-tamed wildness; the stag stands for royal (and noble and wealthy) sport, plus the bounty of the land for all; and the unicorn symbolizes the hidden mysteries and serenity at the heart of the forests—and the shelter those green fastnesses have always offered Cormyrians in peril. Even the nation's kings took advantage of this shelter in the realm's darkest days.

Farsea Marshes: A fallen civilization that predated the elves rests in this ugly marsh. Its only remnants are ornate buildings made of glass as strong as steel. Those who have seen these structures seldom live long, however, for the swamp is thick with pestilence and plague. The ruins hold gold and strange creatures, which draw adventurers despite the dangers.

Hullack Forest: Once a part of the forest of Cormanthor, the Hullack used to define the eastern border of Cormyr. Over the prosperous reign of Azoun IV, people heavily settled the forest verge and cut it back substantially. The Hullack is the most primeval forest in Cormyr, with dark valleys and hidden vales that have gone unseen for decades. Ghostly creatures and odd monsters pepper the local folklore, and orcs and goblins are frequent visitors from the Thunder Peaks. Cormyrian wardens often direct adventurers to the Hullack in the hope of taming this wood.

King's Forest: This is the westernmost fragment of Cormanthor, long abandoned by the elves to humankind. With little undergrowth, a wealth of wildlife, and a high canopy, the King's Forest is entirely the property of the crown and used to be a pleasant place to ride. Now, however, it is inhabited by the orcs who were driven from Arabel. The King's Forest contains no known ruins and fell creatures had never been known to lair here until the orcs moved in.

Marsh of Tun: Sister to the Farsea Marshes, the Marsh of Tun holds a similar ancient civilization. Old stories say that the two city-states quarreled and unleashed foul magic upon each other, both on the advice of an old woman who may have been an agent or manifestation of an evil deity. Bands of humans who raid caravans leaving Cormyr live in the portions of the swamp not tainted by sickness, under the rule of bandit lord Thaalim Torchtower (LE male human Ftr10).

Stonelands: A band of wide, rocky desolation between the Storm Horns and Anauroch, this region is inhabited by small groups of military-minded goblins, gnolls, orcs, and evil humans, all of which are referred to as "border raiders." For decades, Cormyr's rulers have offered generous land grants to adventurers willing to tame these lands and carve out human holdings. The Zhentarim, on the other hand, actively marshal the goblin bands as raiders, but have had only erratic success in recruiting them.

Storm Horns: These forbidding mountains are massive and sharp, forming a high wall broken only near High Horn Pass and Gnoll Pass, which are guarded by Castle High Horn and Castle Crag. The Storm Horns protect Cormyr from attack but also limit expansion to the north and west. Although humanoid tribes live in the mountains, their power was broken long ago. They pose a threat only when a shaman or charismatic barbarian manages to pull them together for raids. Some of the tribes are learning to trade peacefully, exchanging iron ore and furs for food and gold. Other tribes deeper within the Storm Horns resent the flatlanders and prepare ambushes for explorers. A number of orc survivors from the attack on Arabel have fled to the eastern Storm Horns, and many roam the flatland between the mountains and the city. The mountains are also home to rogue dragons, which often wake up hungry after resting from their last great flight.

The Storm Horns have two permanent human settlements. Eagle Peak (hamlet, 153) is built on a large outcropping and is a popular caravan stop, while Skull Crag (hamlet, 270) is a mining community overshadowed by a large rock dedicated as a shrine to Kelemvor.

Thunder Peaks: Named for the sudden and devastating storms that batter them all year, these wild and unsettled mountains are home to tribes of orcs and goblins that bear no love for Cormyr, Sembia, or the Dales. The humanoids raid settlements constantly despite Cormyrian patrols, and travelers are advised to go armed and wary. The mountain passes are blocked in the winter by snow. The inclement weather makes large-scale mining operations difficult, although solitary prospectors sometimes return with silver nuggets the size of fists. Many never return at all, however, having encountered Aurgloroasa the Sibilant Shade, a dracolich that lairs in the abandoned dwarven city of Thunderholme.

Vast Swamp: This region of marsh forms the border between Cormyr and Sembia, as neither country wishes to claim it and both disregard the area unless its monsters wander into their territories. Home to gnolls, hobgoblins, lizardfolk, and trolls, the swamp is also known to shelter a few small black dragons, a mad beholder or two, will-o'-wisps, and stranger things. This is probably the deadliest region within the country, but since the creatures usually remain in the swamp and the people of Cormyr have no reason to enter it, they are content to ignore it.

Wyvernwater: This clean, clear, star-shaped lake produces abundant fish, crabs, and eels every year. In the morning the water is covered in a thick fog, and fisherfolk who rise early to fish the lake are known as mistfishers. Connected to the Dragonmere by the Wyvernflow River, the Wyvernwater provides access to the Sea of Fallen Stars.

IMPORTANT SITES

Cormyr has become a land of chivalrous knights, fractious nobles, and wealthy and verdant farms. Its freedom-loving, often independent citizens are proud to live under the Purple Dragon banner—but they remain quick to complain about injustice, corruption, and decadence.

Ancient ruins of glass in the Farsea Marshes

Illustration by Carlo Arellano

Arabel (Metropolis, 30,606): During the goblin war, Arabel was evacuated to Suzail with the help of magic, and the city was occupied for several months by an army of orcs and goblins. The trading company outposts were looted, the mercenary groups that were not slain fell back to other cities, and the great temple to Tymora was burned (as were the shrines to Chauntea, Deneir, Helm, Lliira, Tempus, and Waukeen). Arabel's lord, Myrmeen Lhal (NG female human Rgr12 of Tymora), known as the Lady Lord, swore to reclaim her city. Despite the loss of her left arm and its subsequent restoration by powerful magic, she spent the last few months collecting mercenaries, rangers, scouts, and adventuring bands for that purpose, then forced the orcs from the city. The orcs fled to the Hullack, King's Forest, eastern Storm Horns, and the plains to the north of Arabel. While routing the humanoids from the open farmlands may go easily, clearing the forests of their presence will be far more difficult.

Castle Crag: Built to defend Cormyr's northern border against dangers from the Stonelands, Castle Crag houses five hundred Purple Dragons and a detachment of five War Wizards. The stiff-necked commander Bren Tallsword (LN male human Ftr10) calls for frequent drills and inspections. Adventurers are not welcome here; those who arrive are sent on their way as quickly as possible.

Dhedluk (Small Town, 936): This community in the King's Forest is home to farmers and woodcarvers; cutting live wood has been forbidden for several years. Surrounded by a stockade, the village is now threatened by the orc raiders driven out of Arabel. Dhedluk's lord Thiombar (NG male human Ftr8) has a talent for reading people and a reputation for knowing everyone in Cormyr. A two-way *portal* on the outskirts of town connects to a spot near the entrance to the Royal Court in Suzail.

Eveningstar (Small Town, 954): Eveningstar is a crossroads settlement. It serves the nearby farms, a small number of craftsfolk who rely on the farmers' goods, and the adventurers who travel this way. Lord Tessaril Winter (CG female human Wiz12/Ftr6) is a quick and efficient ruler. The village maintains a temple to Lathander but is mainly known for its proximity to many ruins, notably the Haunted Halls of Eveningstar (see Chapter 8, "Known Dungeons of Faerûn"). The winged cats known as tressym are common in this area, making Eveningstar a popular place for anyone who would have one as a familiar (as Tessaril does). A *portal* created by a cleric of Mielikki connects a blueleaf tree here with another in the royal gardens of Suzail. The quiet pace of life here was interrupted by Myrmeen Lhal, who used the city as a mustering-point in her battle to reclaim Arabel, and the place has had to fend off occasional orc raids ever since.

Immersea (Small Town, 1,170): This community is home to the Wyvernspur and Thundersword noble families, who inhabit several of the manors on the southwest end of town. Visitors are warned to respect anyone dressed in finery or displaying arrogance, since the families are powerful and not afraid of proving it.

Immersea is a stop on the trade road. Its Five Fine Fish inn produces ale famous throughout Cormyr. There are no temples here, but a large open-air shrine to Selûne is maintained by a cleric of that faith. The lord of Immersea is Culspiir (LN male human Rog3), former herald of the previous lord.

Marsember (Metropolis, 36,007): The second-largest city in Cormyr, Marsember is a seaport constructed on a series of islands connected by bridges and cut with canals. Originally built on a swamp, Marsember grew to include nearby terrain, but it still often smells like a marsh. Known as the City of Spices for the local trading companies that procure those goods from far nations, the city relies on trade. Small boats crowd the canals, and many dealings are done in secret to avoid the law.

Flat, hard ground is hard to find here, and only the wealthy can afford large paved areas, usually on top of buildings. Marsember's single large temple is to Lathander, though it also has small shrines to Tymora, Umberlee, and Waukeen. Bledryn Scoril (LG male human Ftr9) has taken over as lord of the city since the untimely demise of the previous lord. A twelve-ship detachment of the imperial navy is stationed here.

Suzail (Metropolis, 45,009): The royal capital and richest city in Cormyr, Suzail is home to the important nobles and merchant houses of the country. The center of the city is the royal palace, which is surrounded by gardens and the buildings of the Royal Court.

The city maintains a large barracks for the Purple Dragons, plus stockyards, shipyards, and dozens of inns, taverns, and festhalls. Tymora's is the most prominent temple, though shrines to Lliira, Oghma, Malar, Milil, Tempus, and Waukeen are also found here. The famous ivory carvers of Suzail buy exotic ivory from many lands, shape it into new and decorated forms, and export it at a greatly increased value.

The lord of the city is Sthavar (LG male human Ftr10/Prp5), a confident and loyal man who also commands the Purple Dragons. The presence of the Purple Dragons and War Wizards has been more visible since the death of Azoun, as the Princess Regent wishes to assure the common people of their safety and simultaneously be prepared for riots or rebellious activities instigated by contrary nobles. She makes regular appearances with the heir in order to make herself available to the people and to show that she is not afraid for her life or for Cormyr's future.

Thunderstone (Small Town, 1,800): Named for the nearby Thunder Peaks, this logging and fishing town has become a haven for adventurers preparing to explore the Hullack Forest. A group of gnome alchemists has set up shop here, selling alchemical items to adventurers and making quite a profit. Popular items include acid, tanglefoot bags, and (of course) thunderstones. A garrison of one hundred Purple Dragons guards the pass to Sembia and occasionally has to rescue adventurers fleeing the forest with monsters on their tails. The town has no lord, but the Purple Dragons enforce

Cormyr's laws as directed by their commander, Faril Laheralson (LG male human Ftr7/Rgr3).

Tilverton (formerly Small City, 9,002; now empty): This city was occupied for many years and was formally absorbed into the nation of Cormyr last year. Once a valuable piece of territory overlooking one of the three passes through the Thunder Peaks, Tilverton suffered an attack of unknown origin in Mirtul of 1372 DR. Now all that is left is a dark, concave space filled with shadows and flitting regions of deeper darkness. A force of fifty Purple Dragons has been stationed nearby to ward off visitors, for those who enter the area become dim and eventually vanish, never to return.

A triad of wizards from Waterdeep has been studying the site from a distance, but so far has reported only that a great deal of powerful magic has been used in the area. It has caused a disruption in the Weave to such an extent that it greatly limits their ability to investigate further. A dirt road has been cleared around the strange ruin to allow caravan traffic passing through the area.

Waymoot (Small Town, 1,980): Waymoot was built in a five-mile-diameter artificial clearing inside the King's Forest. The town has a large keep, but because of the general safety of this forest, the outlying buildings are not protected by the walls.

A trader's town, Waymoot breeds quality horses and creates and repairs wagons. Its lord is Filfar "Trollkiller" Woodband (LG male human Ftr10), a very strong man somewhat uncomfortable with his well-deserved title (gained when he helped repel a troll attack when he was younger). The town has a small temple to Tymora and one to Lliira.

Wheloon (Small City, 6,661): Known for its vibrant green slate roofs, Wheloon grew up around the ferry traffic on the Wyvernflow river. The roofs' color is derived from the stone of a large and monster-haunted quarry due north of the town.

Most of the locals are craftsfolk, making boats, baskets, sails, and pottery. Their lord is Sarp Redbeard (NG male human Ftr9), a headstrong man who disagrees with court policy on many matters and is liked by the locals for his attitude, which they suspect keeps the Purple Dragons out of their daily lives. The town has a temple to Chauntea and a shrine to Silvanus.

REGIONAL HISTORY

In ancient times, the Forest Country between the Thunder Peaks and Storm Horns mountain ranges was the domain of dragons, including "the" Purple Dragon, the mighty wyrm Thauglorimorgorus. Elves who settled here found themselves at war with the dragons. This ongoing strife ended in a Feint of Honor duel in which the elf Iliphar Nelnueve, Lord of Scepters, defeated Thauglor. Even as the elves displaced the dragons, humans from Impiltur and Chondath eventually pushed back the elves from the coast of the future Cormyr.

As strife between elves and humans grew and humans cleared forests to establish farms, the wisest elves saw that they could not stop or defeat the human intruders. Judging the settler Ondeth Obarskyr to be the most influential human leader, they selected the human wizard Baerauble Etharr (consort to the elf Alea Dahast) to be their agent in guiding Ondeth. In this way the elves hoped to slow settlement, keep peace, and retain the best stretches of forest. Ondeth's farm ultimately grew into the great city of Suzail, named for Ondeth's wife Suzara. Ironically, she hated Cormyr and the frontier life so much that she eventually left him.

Ondeth was a just and honorable man, and although Baerauble was reluctant to leave elven society, he became the first of the famous guiding Royal Magicians of Cormyr. When Ondeth died, the elves convinced his son Faerlthann to become the first king of the human realm they'd shaped—and so, in the Year of Opening Doors (26 DR), Cormyr was founded.

Through the efforts of Baerauble and his successors, as well as the vigor and wits of Cormyr's royal family, the throne has been held by the Obarskyrs for over a thousand years. During that time, the Forest Kingdom has grown prosperous and strong, survived several invasions, absorbed the realms of Esparin and Orva, claimed the still-wild Stonelands, and crushed repeated rebellions in the cities of Arabel and Marsember. Despite several challenges to the throne and internal uprisings, the Obarskyrs have remained in control of Cormyr, assisted and directed by wise and forward-looking wizards.

Cormyr reached its zenith under the rule of King Azoun IV, who was crowned in 1336 DR. Years of prosperity under his capable rule, bolstered by the wisdom of the Royal Magician Vangerdahast, made Cormyr stronger. Its might and influence waxed, its population grew, and Cormyrians became successful merchants and shopkeepers, each generation achieving more wealth and learning than the last.

During Azoun's time the westernmost marches were settled in earnest, Sembia was rebuffed in border disputes, forays were mounted against the growing Zhentarim power in the Stonelands, Tilverton was occupied as a protectorate, and overtures of lasting alliance were made to the Dales. Though never a match for the glittering wealth of neighboring Sembia, Cormyr was widely envied for its strength and security.

Cormyr's peace finally failed in the last two years of Azoun's reign. A blight fell upon the land, orcs and goblins invaded in numbers not seen in Cormyr for centuries, and old foes of the Obarskyrs, risen through evil magic as ghazneths (magic-draining winged creatures of great power), tore at the realm. Cormyr roused itself to war, only to suffer defeat after defeat. Goblin castles arose in the northern reaches, Vangerdahast disappeared, and the ghazneths were joined in the skies by a huge wyrm, the "Devil Dragon," Nalavarauthatoryl the Red.

Azoun and his warlike younger daughter, Alusair the Steel Princess, fought the goblinkin but tasted more defeat. The city of Arabel was besieged, evacuated, and lost to goblin armies. Some nobles committed outright treason, and others openly defied the Crown Princess, revealing that many among Cormyr's nobility no longer felt any loyalty to the crown beyond their personal respect for Azoun.

By the end of the crisis, the Devil Dragon and Azoun IV had slain each other on the battlefield, and a great number of the realm's mightiest warriors, officials, soldiers, War Wizards, and highest nobility were lost. Crown Princess Tanalasta defeated the ghazneths but died soon after in childbirth, giving the land a new king: the infant Azoun V.

Today Princess Alusair rules Cormyr as regent, ably assisted by the Dowager Queen Filfaeril. The ailing wizard Vangerdahast has chosen a successor, the battle-sorcerer Caladnei, and hidden himself away from the eyes of the world. Many nobles are on the sword's edge of rebellion, others seek to claw their way back from exile, and Sembian interests are trying to covertly take control of Cormyr or at least gain substantial influence. As the land rebuilds, it offers new opportunities—and new dangers.

PLOTS AND RUMORS

The Regent has more to do than resources to do it with. Alusair has always been favorably inclined toward fellow adventurers, and she is turning again to bold companies and freebooting bands of heroes to help her restore order to the land. Unfortunately, some of Cormyr's high nobles perceive this as yet another sign of weakness in Suzail.

Baron of the Stonelands: Now that the Zhentarim control the Moonsea area, they are again turning their eyes to the southwest, hoping to enter Cormyr through the Stonelands. King Azoun maintained a standing offer to grant the title of Baron of the Stonelands to any claimant who dwelled there, built a castle, and policed the area. Alusair honors this policy, so a clever and powerful adventurer could take advantage of this offer, clearing the area of monsters, bandits, and Zhentarim agents. Once titled, the character could establish a stronghold and ensure noble titles and a permanent place in Cormyr's history.

The Quiet War: With the disruptions to the lands of the nobles and the royal house, and Sembia looming aggressively on the horizon, intrigue is in season among the nobles of Cormyr. The houses try to win new lands, influence, titles, and positions at court by choosing their words carefully and backing the popular factions. Sembia takes advantage of its merchant power, exiled nobles try to force their way back into politics, rising families pressure Alusair, and the War Wizards argue for spying on every noble household to prevent treason. Adventurers can support or thwart any of the factions and may be rewarded for their efforts and fealty with titles and plots of land.

Alusair Obarskyr

Illustration by Matt Wilson

ALUSAIR OBARSKYR

Female human Ftr 7/Rgr 1/Prp 2: CR 10; Medium-size humanoid; HD 10d10+30; hp 85; Init +3; Spd 20 ft.; AC 28 (touch 16, flat-footed 25); Atk +17/+12 melee (1d8+8/17–20, +3 vorpal longsword); SQ favored enemy (orcs +1), fight with two weapons, Purple Dragon Knight abilities; AL NG; SV Fort +13, Ref +5, Will +5; Str 16, Dex 16, Con 16, Int 14, Wis 13, Cha 14. Height 5 ft. 6 in.

Skills and Feats: Climb +4, Diplomacy +6, Handle Animal +7, Intimidate +8, Jump +4, Listen +7, Profession (sailor) +2, Ride (horse) +10, Search +5, Sense Motive +4, Spot +7, Wilderness Lore +4; Endurance, Improved Critical (longsword), Iron Will, Leadership (12), Mounted Combat, Ride-By Attack, Spirited Charge, Track, Weapon Focus (longsword), Weapon Specialization (longsword).

Special Qualities: Purple Dragon Knight Abilities: Heroic shield, inspire courage 1/day, rallying cry.

Possessions: +3 vorpal longsword, mithral dwarven full plate (human-sized), +2 large metal shield (bears Azoun's standard, a purple dragon on a black field), royal Cormyrian signet ring (allows Caladnei to communicate telepathically with her and know her location), ring of proof against detection and location (worn only when necessary, because it negates the powers of the signet ring), ring of freedom of movement, ring of protection +3.

Named the Steel Regent of Cormyr upon the death of her father Azoun IV, Princess Alusair Nacacia Obarskyr now rules the kingdom for her infant nephew, Azoun V.

Once a rebellious tomboy, the hot-tempered, impulsive youngest child of Azoun and Filfaeril won the hearts of commoners for her valiant battles against the Tuigan horde. Accomplished in battle, strategy, hard living, and mastery of horses, Alusair spent her life fighting and riding the Stonelands with other young noble-born knights, who admiringly dubbed her the Steel Princess for her battle prowess and spirit. She is Cormyr's best battlemaster—more at ease in raids and skirmishes than in matters of diplomacy.

Alusair hates court life, gossip, and endless revels. Her anger at her role makes her precise, clear, and cold in diplomatic dealings, but the wise advice of Caladnei and Filfaeril, coupled with her own battlefield experience, means that she misses very few nuances in the games of the court.

She aims to rebuild Cormyr's morale and military strength by reclaiming and resettling all lost territory, replanting crops, and rebuilding steads. At the same time she denies investors from Sembia and Westgate who want to gain firm holds in Cormyr—and rebuffs all their attempts to control and influence Cormyrian affairs.

As long as she can pour out her rage in short, savage sword-bouts against the Blades (the young nobles she rode with and trusts), Alusair will be an efficient regent, and an increasingly contented one. She's good at ruling, and her father's death—a fate he embraced, she believes, because he would not flee his duty—makes her determined to preserve the realm for the next Azoun. She'll avoid being goaded by clever-tongued envoys into doing anything that's not best for Cormyr.

CALADNEI

Female human Sor11/Ftr4: CR 15; Medium-size humanoid; HD 11d4+14 plus 4d10+4; hp 67; Init +7; Spd 30 ft.; AC 20 (touch 15, flat-footed 17); Atk +13/+8 melee (1d8+5/ 19–20, *+2 longsword*) or +12/+7 ranged touch (by spell); AL NG; SV Fort +10, Ref +7, Will +12; Str 12, Dex 16, Con 13, Int 14, Wis 14, Cha 18. Height 5 ft. 3 in.

Skills and Feats: Alchemy +5, Climb +4, Concentration +11, Craft (blacksmithing) +4, Diplomacy +6, Handle Animal +9, Intimidate +7, Jump +3, Knowledge (arcana) +12, Knowledge (Cormyr local) +3, Knowledge (geography) +3, Listen +5, Ride (horse) +10, Scry +7, Search +4, Spellcraft +12, Spot +5, Swim +6; Arcane Preparation, Craft Wondrous Item, Enlarge Spell, Great Fortitude, Improved Initiative, Iron Will, Maximize Spell, Toughness, Weapon Focus (longsword), Weapon Specialization (longsword).

Spells Known (6/7/7/7/7/4; base DC = 14 + spell level): 0—*daze, detect magic, detect poison, disrupt undead, ghost sound, light, mending, ray of frost, read magic;* 1st—*feather fall, mage armor, mount, shield, true strike;* 2nd—*bull's strength, detect thoughts, invisibility, Melf's acid arrow, protection from arrows;* 3rd—*dispel magic, displacement, flame arrow, fly;* 4th—*enervation, scrying, stoneskin;* 5th—*cone of cold, teleport.*

Possessions: +2 longsword, staff of charming, ring of protection +2, bracers of armor +5, minor cloak of displacement, winged boots, brooch of shielding.

Caladnei

Raised in Turmish by her Cormyrian father and Turmian mother, Caladnei (Kah-*lad*-nay) left home to join an adventuring company. Traveling far via *portals* her group discovered, she became acquainted with the people and cultures of other parts of the world. She trained with fighters in Waterdeep, exchanged spells with Halruaan wizards, and learned to forge metal with the gold dwarves of the Great Rift. She came to Cormyr to tend to her ailing father, who returned to his homeland after Caladnei's mother drowned in a storm at sea, and supported herself as a local mercenary spellcaster and crafter of minor magic items.

Caladnei attracted the attention of Vangerdahast, the Royal Magician of Cormyr, when she single-handedly wiped out an orc raiding party from the Thunder Peaks. The fact that this powerful sorcerer was content to lead a life without fame impressed him. Her refusal to accept the knighthood he arranged for her cemented his interest. In subtle ways he began

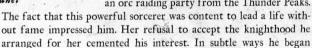

the purple Dragon

Hearken now to one of the deepest secrets of the realm . . . aye, lean close and listen low, for some slay to learn this, and others to keep it secret.

You've heard, I doubt not, that somewhere in Cormyr, skulking in the Stonelands or the Storm Horns or the green forest deeps, there's always one Purple Dragon.

Aye, a wyrm whose scales are purple, that can hide in the semblance of a human, though its eyes burn like purple flames. None know all the powers of the Purple Dragon, but it hates too much tree-felling and too many laws and grasping greed, and loves wild things and the beauty of the land. It wants its folk to be free and daring in their dreams and deeds.

The Purple Dragon walks alone and stands apart, and none know its mind. It can be kind and caring, or fell and deadly, res-cuing a lost child one moment and tearing proud and cruel knights out of their armor bone by bloody bone the next.

The purple comes from elven magic that entered the blood of dragons here long ago, none know or dare to ask. It lets the creature take man-shape and do other great and terrible things besides.

It is said that when the last Purple Dragon dies, then so too will Cormyr. Some there are who say that day is not so far off now. Others—enemies of the crown—seek the Purple Dragon, meaning to slay it and so bring about the end of the Forest Kingdom. For my own part, I hope they find what they seek. It's a hard thing to kill a dragon, after all, and that would be one less Zhent or Thayan or haughty high lord to worry about.

—An old Cormyrian forester

Illustration by Matt Wilson

training her for work under the royal banner of Cormyr, and when Vangerdahast decided to retire after the recent troubles, he named her as his successor. Humbly, she accepted.

Despite her typical humility, Caladnei is feisty and opinionated, which makes dealing with court intrigue difficult for her at times. Fortunately for her, the Regent Alusair is of similar temperament, and the two can discuss matters of state in a direct fashion. Caladnei prefers to remain a silent figure in the background, but she is slowly being pushed into the limelight by Alusair as the Steel Regent seeks time to herself away from the gossip and infighting.

The Dalelands

Capital: None
Population: 602,640 (humans 80%, drow 6%, half-elves 5%, elves 4%, halflings 2%, gnomes 1%, dwarves 1%)
Government: Varies by dale; Dales Council loosely unifies all dales
Religions: Chauntea, Lathander, Mielikki, Silvanus, Tempus, the Triad (Ilmater, Torm, Tyr)
Imports: Armor, books, glass, jewelry, metalwork, paper, textiles, weapons
Exports: Ale, bread, cheese, fruit, grain, hides, timber, vegetables
Alignment: CG, NG, N

The Dales are broad forest vales with rolling farmlands, linked by narrow trade roads running through beautiful woods. Blessed with fertile soil and a temperate climate (aside from the extremely harsh winters), the Dales are the breadbasket of the Heartlands. The Dales' independent spirit and age-old alliance with the elves of Cormanthor have made them the historic birthplace or favored home of many of Faerûn's greatest heroes.

Eleven separate dales exist today, each with its own territory, government (or lack of it), militia, trading pacts, ambitions, and character. Archendale and Harrowdale value trade over all else. Tasseldale values industry and craftsmanship. Daggerdale stands alone against a powerful enemy, while Scardale struggles to

recover its independence after years of occupation. Meanwhile, the other dales respect the old Dales Compact and prefer to be left alone.

The Dalelands Character

Although they share common traditions, cultural practices, and religious allegiances, the Dalelands are not a unified kingdom like Cormyr or Sembia. Instead, they are an enigma to the rest of Faerûn. How can small and disorganized groups of stubborn, backwoods farmers and craftsfolk maintain control of the coveted lands surrounding the great elven forest?

In the past, the forest itself was a major reason for the Dales' continued existence, as the presence of the Elven Court deterred most foes. Now that the elves are a secondary power in Cormanthor, Dalesfolk rely upon the gifts they've always had: heroism, self-reliance, and a strong, almost clannish sense of community.

To an outsider, Dalesfolk seem close-mouthed, suspicious, and reserved. Until newcomers are identified as friends or foes, or vouched for by a trusted friend, Dalesfolk prefer civil silence to empty pleasantries. Once a person is accepted, Dalesfolk are generally open and giving, especially in the common defense. Once accepted by Dalesfolk as a friend, a stranger is expected to contribute to the defense of the community.

Most dales maintain at least an informal militia. The training levels and professionalism of such groups varies, but all are capable of providing some training with a melee weapon and a good Dales longbow. The archers of the Dales might be the finest human archers of Faerûn, which gives would-be invaders pause.

The Dales Compact

The Dales were once deep woods hunted only lightly by the dragons, for these creatures preferred to make meals of ogres, deer, bears, and rothé available in the open Stonelands to the west. As the wyrms declined and elven might grew, the elven realm of Cormanthyr flourished.

The Lost Dales

Bards tell colorful tales of dales that are no more—overgrown ruins deep in the forest, their treasures waiting to be found. Much of this talk of dancing ghosts, stalking monsters, and lost riches is poetic fancy, but kernels of truth exist in every story. All Dalesfolk know the names of the dales lost most recently: Moondale, Sessrendale, and Teshendale. Dales have fallen before, and dales will fall again.

Moondale: Far from the great forest and too close to Sembia, Moondale abandoned the Dalelands and joined the young merchant kingdom hundreds of years ago. Ordulin, Sembia's capital, was built on the site of old Moondale. Dalesfolk take Moondale's transformation as a warning against growing too close to the power to the south. Tasseldarrans are the exception, sometimes viewing Moondale's history as a plan instead of a warning.

Sessrendale: Sessrendale, the "Dead Dale," was founded in 880 DR. It lay between the eastern face of the Thunder Peaks and the westernmost verge of Semberholme, from Thunder Gap in the south to Tilver's Gap in the north. The southern half lay close to Archendale, which also claimed Thunder Gap, and that sealed Sessrendale's doom.

A land of shepherds, masons, traders, and miners, Sessrendale

was ruled by a Dusk Lord who was accused by Archendale of fell sorceries. The Dusk Lord fell when Archendale's army invaded in 1232 DR. The Archenfolk slew or drove off Sessrendale's citizens and destroyed all its buildings, fields, and mines. Then the Archenfolk sowed Sessrendale's fields with salt to ensure that Sessrenfolk families that had fled to Battledale and Deepingdale would never resettle their lands. Only a few trappers and woodcutters venture into haunted Sessrendale now.

Teshendale: Teshendale occupied the lands along the Tesh, within the shadow of Zhentil Keep. As Zhentil Keep transformed from an independent trading city into a hive of evil, Teshendale's days became numbered. Daggerdale has survived its bouts with Zhentil Keep relatively intact, but Teshendale succumbed to orc hordes recruited by the Zhents in 1316 DR. Teshwave and Snowmantle, former Teshendale towns, still figure in the Zhents' plans for the Dales.

The Dales Council keeps a seat open for the elder who used to represent Teshendale, partially as a reminder of what happens to those who underestimate the Zhents, and partially as a reminder that the Dales do not always manage to support each other as quickly as they ought.

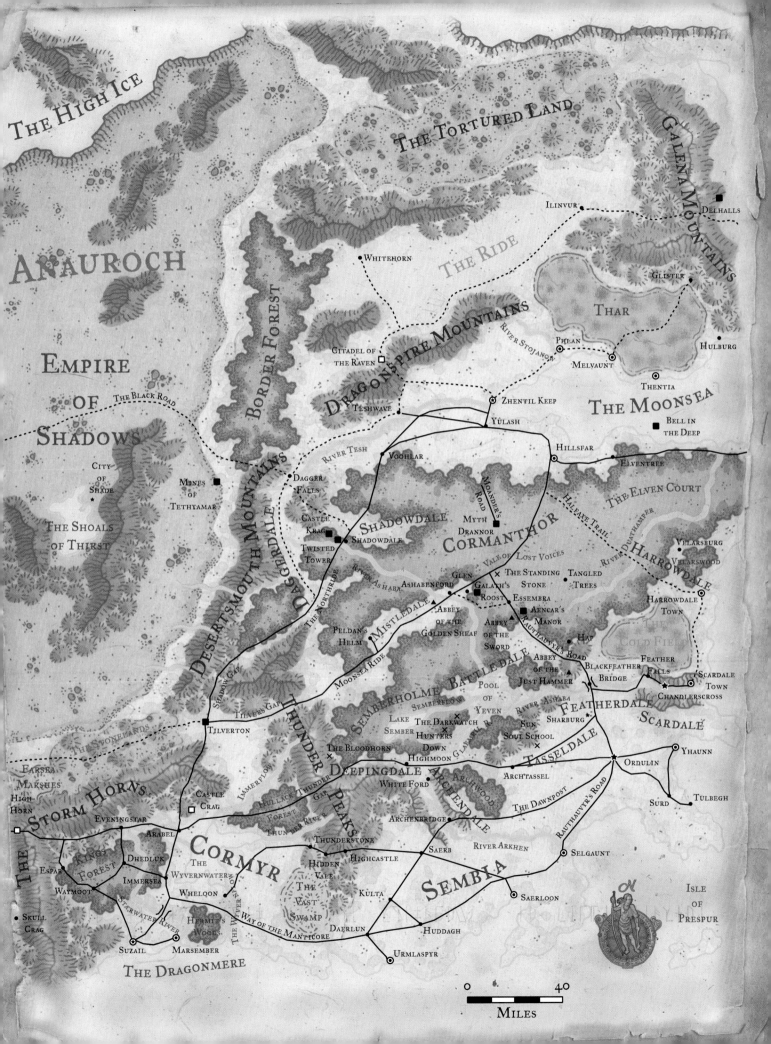

THE HIGH ICE

ANAUROCH

THE TORTURED LAND

GALENA MOUNTAINS

ILINVUR

DELHALLS

EMPIRE OF SHADOWS

THE BLACK ROAD

WHITEHORN

THE RIDE

GLISTER

THAR

HULBURG

DRAGONSPIRE MOUNTAINS

RIVER STOJANOW

PHLAN

CITADEL OF THE RAVEN

MELVAUNT

THENTIA

THE MOONSEA

CITY OF SHADE

BORDER FOREST

TESHWAVE

ZHENTIL KEEP

YÛLASH

BELL IN THE DEEP

MINES OF TETHYAMAR

RIVER TESH

VOOHLAR

HILLSFAR

ELVENTREE

THE SHOALS OF THIRST

DAGGER FALLS

SHADOWDALE

MOANDER'S ROAD

CORMANTHOR

THE ELVEN COURT

HALFAXE TRAIL

VELARSBURG

CASTLE KRAG

SHADOWDALE

MYTH DRANNOR

VELARSWOOD

DESERTSMOUTH MOUNTAINS

DAGGERDALE

TWISTED TOWER

RIVER ASHABA

VALE OF LOST VOICES

TANGLED TREES

RIVER DUATHAMPER

HARROWDALE

THE NORTHRIDE

GLEN

ASHABENFORD

THE STANDING STONE

HARROWDALE TOWN

MISTLEDALE

GALATH'S ROOST

ESSEMBRA

AENCAR'S MANOR

HAP

PELDAN'S HELM

ABBEY OF THE GOLDEN SHEAF

ABBEY OF THE SWORD

RAUTHAUVYR'S ROAD

COLD FIELD

MOONSEA RIDE

SEMBERHOLME

BATTLEDALE

ABBEY OF THE JUST HAMMER

BLACKFEATHER BRIDGE

FEATHER FALLS

SHADOW GAP

SEMBERFLOW

POOL OF YEVEN

SCARDALE TOWN

TILVER'S GAP

THE DARKWATCH

SHARBURG

CHANDLERSCROSS

THUNDER PEAKS

TILVERTON

THE STONELANDS

LAKE SEMBER

HUNTERS DOWN

RIVER ASHABA

SUN SOUL SCHOOL

FEATHERDALE

SCARDALE

TASSELDALE

EARSEA MARSHES

HIGH HORN

THE BLOODHORN

HIGHMOON

GLAEMRIL

DEEPINGDALE

ARCHWOOD

ARCHENDALE

ORDULIN

YHAUNN

STORM HORNS

CASTLE CRAG

IMMERFLOW

WHITE FORD

ARCHTASSEL

THE DAWNPOST

SURD

TULBEGH

EVENINGSTAR

ARABEL

BULLACK THUNDER FOREST

THUNDER GAP

THUNDER RIVER

ARCHENBRIDGE

RAUTHAUVYR'S ROAD

SELGAUNT

KING'S FOREST

CORMYR

THE WYVERNWATER

THUNDERSTONE

SAERB

HIGHCASTLE

RIVER ARKHEN

ISLE OF PRESPUR

ESPAR

DHEDLUK

IMMERSEA

HIDDEN VALE

SEMBIA

SAERLOON

WALMOOT

WHELOON

THE VAST SWAMP

KULTA

SKULL CRAG

STARWATER RIVER

HERMIT'S WOODS

THE WYVERNFLOW

WAY OF THE MANTICORE

DAERLUN

HUDDAGH

SUZAIL

MARSEMBER

URMLASPYR

THE DRAGONMERE

N

0   40
MILES

Humans hailing from lands known today as Chondath and Impiltur settled the edges of that great forest. These migrations attracted folk from other regions of Faerûn: exiles, fugitives from justice, and adventurers who saw a land of bright promise. Scattered human farmsteads and hamlets began to appear at the fringes of Cormanthor around −200 DR. Elven defenses hampered woodcutting, so human settlements were scattered and isolated instead of sprawling across wide-open farmland, as they did in the lands that would become Cormyr to the west and Sembia to the south.

Foreseeing the eventual doom of his people if they tried to fight off increasingly numerous human settlers, the elven coronal Eltargrim arranged the Dales Compact between the elves of the forest empire of Cormanthyr and the humans who would become known as Dalesfolk. Human and elven wizards together raised the Standing Stone in the center of Cormanthor as a symbol of unity between the two races. In return for promising not to cut deeper into the Cormanthor forest, the ancestors of the current Dalesfolk were allowed to settle around the forest's edges or in places where the great trees did not grow.

While the early dales struggled to survive, the elves of Cormanthor grew strong and confident. In 220 DR, the elven coronal allowed humans to enter his kingdom. In 261 DR, he made the fateful decision to welcome them into its very heart, transforming the elven city then known as Cormanthor into the open city of Myth Drannor. All races were welcome in Myth Drannor, which enjoyed a golden age that lasted nearly five centuries. Myth Drannor reached heights of arts, crafting, and culture unsurpassed since, and the city brought human, halfling, dwarven, and gnome trade, travel, and settlement to the Dragon Reach lands.

Myth Drannor's rise allowed the Dales to survive their troubled infancy. The city's fall in 714 DR gave the Dales the chance to flourish in ways that would have been impossible if elven might had remained intact. Few survivors of Myth Drannor's collapse escaped the demons, devils, and dragons that flocked to the ruins, but these survivors took the scraps of their wealth, magic, and learning to the nearby dales.

Although the Compact stands no more, most of the Dales still abide by its terms. Tradition has replaced elven might as the principal motivation for adhering to the Compact, but for now it is sufficient to preserve Cormanthor's borders as they stand.

The Dales Council

Each year at Midwinter, every dale sends a delegate to a selected Dalelands town for the Dales Council. Delegates debate issues affecting all the dales, such as maintenance of trade routes, defense pacts against Zhent or Sembian aggression, border squabbles between neighboring dales, and matters relating to the great forest of Cormanthor.

Two serious attempts have been made to unify the Dales. The first was under the legendary Aencar the Mantled King, who sought to forge the Dales into one realm but was slain in 1044 DR. His dream died with him. The second would-be unifier rose and fell in 1356 DR. Lord Lashan of Scardale overran Battledale, Featherdale, and Harrowdale, proclaiming his intention of conquering all the Dales. Lashan vanished after his defeat in the great battles in Mistledale and Shadowdale, but his legacy initiated a string of bad luck that has plagued Scardale to this day.

A Sea of Troubles

In the current year, 1372 DR, the Dales face a number of terrible threats. The enemy they know best broods to the north in Zhentil Keep. An unsuspected enemy has just arrived to create the Empire of Shadows in the wastes of Anauroch. And in their Retreat to Evermeet, the elves left the great forest of Cormanthor open to exploitation by another great foe, the drow.

The drow might not be the worst enemy the Dales face. The Dales Compact is fraying. For over thirteen centuries, this treaty has survived treachery (usually human), magical disasters (usually elven), and pressure from would-be colonizers (Sembians) and conquerors (folk of the Moonsea). With the elves of Cormanthor now in Evermeet, what remains of the Dalelands' agreement to preserve the forest by cultivating only land that was already cleared by natural forces? The people of some dales, such as Archendale, have already welcomed the chance to log and exploit the elven woods. Residents of other dales, such as Deepingdale, did all they could to encourage elves to stay in the forest.

At the next Dales Council meeting of 1373 DR, the two most pressing topics are likely to be the drow occupation of Cormanthor and the fate of Scardale. The drow press hard upon the holdings of those dales nearest Cormanthor. Other dales have yet to be affected by the fight. One of these is Daggerdale, the site of next year's Council meeting (still half a year away). Daggerdale's worst enemies are the Zhents, who helped create Scardale's miserable situation. It remains to be seen if the dales can agree on actions against either of these enemies.

Archendale

Capital: Archenbridge
Population: 92,300 (humans 92%, half-elves 3%, gnomes 2%, halflings 2%)
Government: Autocratic rule by the Swords
Religions: Chauntea, Lathander, Tempus (Mielikki, Selûne, Silvanus)
Imports: Exotic metalwork, silks, spices
Exports: Produce, ores, timber
Alignment: NG, LN, N

Most of the dales are free-form republics or enlightened feudal states, but Archendale is ruled by three masked autocrats who call themselves the Swords. Over the past couple hundred years, the Swords have consistently played on Archenfolk's militaristic instincts, insisting that the dale needs to be stronger than its neighbors.

Key to the Dales

The Dales are tiny places compared to most of the realms detailed elsewhere in this chapter. Two entries for the Dales have slightly different meanings than the same entries as applied to large kingdoms such as Sembia or Cormyr.

Religions: This entry lists those faiths that actually have temples in the dale. Faiths that have only shrines in the dale appear in parentheses.

Imports and Exports: Nearly all dales import and export the goods mentioned earlier in the Dalelands statistics block that opened this section, in addition to any listed here.

The Swords' devotion has paid off. Archendale's defenders, ten squadrons (each consisting of sixty mailed riders) are the largest and best-equipped military force fielded by any of the Dales. These Archenriders, as they are called, clatter up and down the excellent roads on either side of the River Arkhen, looking for spies from other dales or the south, cultists from Thay, or random passersby who look like they need a lesson in Archendale justice.

In Archendale's defense, it's usually acknowledged that the dale owes its wealth to ruthless mercantilism rather than military adventurism. Unlike other dales that farm first, hunt second, and trade third, Archendale is a merchant's haven. Archenfolk in the capital, Archenbridge, cherish the life of the wealthy merchant. Archenbridge is a hub of trade for all the Dales, and it is the first stop for Sembian caravans wending their way north.

LIFE AND SOCIETY

For all Archendale's posturing, it *is* a dale. Archendale's common folk and its merchants and soldiers (though not all of its nobility and warrior elite) respect fair play and decency. Given Archendale's warlike attitude, it's not surprising that the dale maintains a major temple to Tempus in the keep of Swordpoint. Other popular deities of the region include Chauntea (revered by the country folk who tend their small farms without undue interest in the wheeling and dealing of the city) and Lathander (whom the townsfolk of Archenbridge have chosen as their patron deity). Devotion to Chauntea in particular comforts those who wish to clear as much as possible of Arch Wood and other elven woods, as clearing land for Chauntea's sacred croplands can be phrased as a noble aim.

MAJOR GEOGRAPHICAL FEATURES

Archendale's waterfalls, quick rivers, and forested northern slopes place it among the most picturesque landscapes in the Dales, next to the forests and hills of Deepingdale.

Arch Wood: Arch Wood stands on the northern flank of Archendale, south of Deepingdale and west of Tasseldale. The wood figures prominently in the economic, social, and political life of all three communities.

Though not technically part of Cormanthor, Arch Wood has largely escaped cutting because of its proximity to that great forest. In fact, Cormanthor and Arch Wood blend together around Highmoon's tree-shaded lanes and in the forest gardens in Deepingdale.

The people of Archendale have always wanted to log the forest. After squabbling with the Dales Council in 1370 DR, they went ahead with plans to log the sections of the wood closest to its borders. A year later, Archendale's logging of the Arch Wood stopped so quickly that folk in the next dale could hear the axes dropping. Archendale's rulers did not reveal the reason for their decision. In truth, the logging uncovered ancient ruins that the Swords of Archendale determined were better left undisturbed.

Arkhen Falls: The largest and most beautiful waterfall of the Dales flows from a natural spring on Mount Thalagbror, then plunges hundreds of feet into the valley below. On sunny days, worshipers of Chauntea and Mielikki walk to the falls, hoping to see pegasi frolicking in the spray.

Arkhen Vale: The long valley created by the River Arkhen forms the land occupied by Archendale. The valley is enclosed on both sides by high banks that can be climbed on foot but not on horseback. Two paths to the outside world, one on either end of the valley, are accessible to a mounted warrior or a trader's wagon. These are the road north from White Ford and the road south from Archenbridge.

Mount Thalagbror: Dalesfolk tend to rename geographic features originally named after evil beings, once those villains are safely dead. But Archenfolk still refer to this mountain using the

name of an ogre mage who once terrorized the valley, until he was slain by heroes whose names were forgotten. Far up the slope, near the ogre mage's cavern lair, a great spring forms the origin of the River Arkhen.

IMPORTANT SITES

Archenbridge, the capital, is the only urban area of any size in Archendale. Most significant locations within this dale are in its capital.

Archenbridge (Small City, 8,179): Archendale's capital is the largest city in the Dales and the only town with more than two thousand inhabitants in all of Archendale. Archenbridge's proximity to the official border of Sembia explains how Sembian connections help fuel Archendale's thriving markets, merchant houses, and investments. Simultaneously, fear of Sembia's military fuels Archendale's martial stance. The Swords have convinced Archenfolk that success in trade and military strength are inseparable pieces of their dale's national character.

The result is a bustling but uneasy city that constantly sprawls out of its rebuilt walls. Its inner core is as loud and bustling as the markets of Waterdeep. Its nobility and rich merchants build high townhouses in the center of the city to catch all the action. Townhouses feature barred windows and hidden inner holds equipped with arrow slits and nastier defenses.

Bounty of the Goddess: Archenbridge's temple to Chauntea is a richly painted tithing barn. Worshipers enter through an arched door between two pillars carved to look like giant stalks of wheat, past a beautiful fountain. The legend says that if a priest of Chauntea is slain in Archendale, the fountain's water turns into blood capable of healing diseases, wounds, and even lycanthropy. The priests of Chauntea discourage the spread of this tale.

Swordpoint: From a rocky outcropping above Archenbridge, Swordpoint dominates Arkhen Vale to the north, the Dawnpost trading road from Ordulin, and the water route down the River Arkhen. The massive fortress bristles with ballistae, catapults, and other engines of war meant to destroy would-be besiegers. The walls themselves are old and crumbling in places, having improved little since the days they were built by a notorious robber baron named Sangalar the Crag, but they make up in thickness what they lack in quality.

Swordpoint is the capitol building of Archendale, the home of the Swords, and the headquarters of their warriors, the Archenriders. Three sixty-member units of the Archenriders remain on duty or on local patrols here.

Despite what other Dalesfolk view as the nasty suspicion and arrogance of the Archendale military, morale inside Swordpoint is high. A shrine to Tempus within the walls assures the soldiers that their god is with them. The secret tunnels into and out of Swordpoint don't concern them as long as their commanders remain aware of them, and any prisoners screaming in the dungeons no doubt deserve their fate.

White Ford (Small Town, 1,052): The Archenfolk dumped boulders into the river to construct a trustworthy ford at a whitewater rapids in the fast-running River Arkhen, downstream from Arkhen Falls. The sleepy town of White Ford grew up around the ford, caring for passing merchants without working hard to attract their business or compete with Archenbridge to the south. Its inhabitants are woodcarvers, farmers, mushroom-pickers, or members of the Archenriders, who always have one or two sixty-member units defending a ditch-and-stone ring stronghold named Arch Hold. A larger wall called the Wolfwall encircles the entire community in a wide oval. Its gates are usually open, but they can be closed in times of trouble or in the winter to keep beasts from stealing into the village for food.

REGIONAL HISTORY

Archendale's history revolves around conflicts with Sembia over their shared but undefined border. Ironically, Archendale's recent military improvements were financed by a wartime settlement in which every year Sembia paid the Swords an amount in gems worth hundreds of thousands of gold pieces. Over time, these payments became a form of protection money paid to Archendale so that it did not interfere with Sembian trade.

The new Sembian Overmaster, Kendrick Selkirk, has judged correctly that Archenbridge is now far too dependent on that same trade to interfere with Sembia's merchants, so the payments have stopped. The border conflicts have not.

PLOTS AND RUMORS

Adventurers aren't always welcomed in Archendale. The folk of the dale are generally content with the prosperity and good order kept by the Swords, and in turn the Swords don't allow chaotic things like adventures to take place within their domain. Of course, adventures have a way of happening despite the rulers' intent.

The Sessren Curse: Throughout Archendale prominent citizens begin dying at the hands of a powerful and deadly ghost, reputed to be the spirit of none other than the Dusk Lord of Sessrendale. Fearful rumors hold that the ghost will not stop until it slays one descendant of each soldier who marched on Sessrendale a century ago—or at least one person from each of hundreds of Arkhen families. The hundredth anniversary of the bitter fighting has arrived, and folks fear the ghost's vengeance.

Of course, it isn't clear if the murdered citizens are actually descendants of the cursed families, or even that a ghost is responsible for the deaths. If the truth of the matter is not what people say, then who is killing Archenfolk, and why is he or she doing it?

Battledale

Capital: Essembra
Population: 32,714 (humans 87%, half-elves 5%, halflings 4%, gnomes 2%, dwarves 1%)
Government: Lordship
Religions: Gond, Tempus (Chauntea, Corellon Larethian, Silvanus)
Imports: Clothing, fine metalwork, oil, rope, spices
Exports: Ale, cheese, fruit, grain, meat, livestock, wool
Alignment: CG, NG, N

Battledale's fierce name isn't a reflection on its character or its foreign policy—it's an indication of the dale's geographic position in the middle of the best invasion routes through the Dalelands. Historically, the biggest local battles have been fought in Battledale's rolling meadows.

Not all outlanders who arrive in Battledale come to fight. Over the centuries, Battledale has grown into its role as a meeting place and refuge for an odd mix of warriors, adventurers, and traders from all over Faerûn.

LIFE AND SOCIETY

For its size, Battledale is nearly as diverse as Waterdeep. Merchants of Turmish settle in the country, then raise children who move out into the Belt or join the local militia. Refugees from the wars in Tethyr come to Battledale to serve as hunters for a Sembian estate-lord and stay on after their Sembian employer passes away, sending messages to Tethyr to bring their other relatives.

On the other hand, Battledale's children leave as adventurers, traders, or travelers, many of whom never return. The dale is large, but its population is relatively small. In some areas, overgrown ruins outnumber lived-in cottages. Battledale's biggest town, Essembra, isn't even in the dale. It rests about thirty miles north, inside the elven woods.

Essembra is the closest thing Battledale has to a capital, but Ilmeth, the lord of Essembra, has little authority over the rest of the dale. Nor does Battledale possess any formal system of laws. Neighbors usually enforce law and order themselves. Serious matters such as banditry, arson, or murder are taken to Ilmeth if they can't be handled locally, but he is under no official obligation to deal with problems outside Essembra. In practice, since Ilmeth is a good and just lord, Battledarrans listen to his advice.

MAJOR GEOGRAPHICAL FEATURES

To most outsiders, "Battledale" means the pleasant meadows and fields alongside Rauthauvyr's Road. In fact, this dale has several disparate regions.

The Belt: This region of open rolling farmland by Rauthauvyr's Road is pleasant country, consisting mainly of small walled orchards, fenced-in farms, and large expanses of sheep-grazing land. The country folk live in walled cottages or palisades, since banditry and dangerous beasts from Cormanthor are constant problems here.

Streams and ponds full of fish are sprinkled through the Belt, often alongside small shrines to Chauntea or Silvanus. Chauntea's shrines are stone tables that travelers and Belt-dwellers heap with offerings of food meant to be consumed by hungry travelers. Silvanus's shrines consist of small bells hung above pools or woodland springs.

Three Rivers Land: The lands where the Semberflow and the Glaemril join the River Ashaba northwest of the Pool of Yeven are fertile and beautiful but sparsely settled. Burnt-out ruins of now-

---

Between Shieldmeets

In the four years since the last Shieldmeet festival (in 1368 DR), the list of the potential attendees of this year's Dalelands Shieldmeet has changed wildly. Randal Morn has retaken Daggerdale from the Zhents. Plague decimated Scardale and its occupying forces. The Red Wizards of Thay built a trade enclave in the shattered port of Scardale. South of the Dales, a vigorous new Overmaster dominates Sembia. Drow, some of whom erupted from Underdark *portals* within Battledale itself, build strongholds in Cormanthor. Zhentil Keep looms to the north, boding worse for the future now that Bane has returned to bolster the power of the Zhentarim priests.

On the bright side, moon elves, wood elves, and a few sun elves who left for Evermeet are filtering back into the Dales through Evereska, Deepingdale, and their own forest pathways. Battledale's elven allies promise that they will attend this year's Shieldmeet, cheering those who missed the grace and beauty lent by the elves of the Court to the festival.

Illustration by Carlo Arellano

The drow invasion of Battledale

dead adventurers' keeps and manors testify to the viciousness of the owlbears, lycanthropes, and other magical beasts that occasionally plague Three Rivers.

Yevenwood: This ancient wood has plentiful game, no dangerous inhabitants, and a delicious edible mushroom, the relshar. It has held a dozen names over the centuries, including the Wood of Many Names. It was also called Battlewood (during the years when it was forcibly cleared of monsters), Satyr's Run (after a famous satyr sorcerer who eventually disappeared into the Underdark), and Forester's Freehold (after the years when the wood was occupied by emigrants from Aglarond who weren't yet certain they wanted to be part of Battledale).

IMPORTANT SITES

Unlike those dales that consist of one interesting town and an assortment of mundane cottages and orchards, Battledale is known for dangerous locations within a half-hour's walk of places that are relatively safe.

Abbey of the Sword: Fourteen years ago, during the Time of Troubles, Tempus appeared on the battlefield of Swords Creek in Mistledale. An Amnian priest named Eldan Ambrose traced Tempus's path to the battlefield and discovered that the god had arrived in Faerûn in the shell of a shattered castle in Battledale. Ambrose established a temple, the Abbey of the Sword, in a rebuilt portion of the castle. About fifty to one hundred worshipers of Tempus took it upon themselves to guard the temple and the numerous *portals* in its subcellars and in the local Underdark tunnels.

In 1371 DR, a strong force of Vhaeraunian drow, the vanguard of the Auzkovyn clan, attacked the Abbey. The drow came up through an unwatched *portal* in a nearby deep cavern and smashed past the Abbey's defenders. Eldan Ambrose himself perished in the assault, devoured by a demon after he had destroyed the *portal*. His actions prevented the whole strength of the Auzkovyn from descending on an unguarded Battledale.

Unfortunately for the defenders of the Abbey, the drow vanguard slipped away into the forests despite fierce fighting. The Auzkovyn later managed to open another *portal* somewhere in the forests north of Battledale, bringing the rest of their people to Cormanthor. The defenders of the Abbey of the Sword no longer have enough warriors to guard all of the *portals* below, and even *true resurrection* spells cannot bring back Ambrose until the demon that devoured him is permanently slain.

Aencar's Manor: Four miles south of Essembra, in plain view of Rauthauvyr's Road, stands one of the most deceptively inviting ruins in Faerûn. Unlike many haunted estates, Aencar's Manor still looks like a splendid and stately home, albeit the home of a warlord, judging from the relief carvings of mounted knights covering the outside of the manor. Indeed, the outer gardens and environs of Aencar's Manor are safe enough to serve as the site of the great Battledale Shieldmeet festivals.

The manor's interior is another matter. It's certain that the manse is haunted, but the wraiths do not disturb everyone who comes in. The Cult of the Dragon has a secret stronghold in one of the building's cellars, which is accessible through tunnels from the Underdark.

Essembra (Large Town, 2,804): Battledale's largest town does not demand respect like Archenbridge, or impress visitors with its beauty like Highmoon. Deep within the elven woods, Essembra is a long lane of well-spaced cottages on both sides of Rauthauvyr's Road. The road is dotted with watchposts—small wooden archers' towers outfitted with road-blocking equipment that are usually left unmanned. Only a few cross-streets lead between these cottages to other cottages in the woods—and those paths are more trails than alleys.

Toward the center of Essembra, the great walled courtyard of Battle Court leads to the only part of the town that city folk think of as a town, a grouping of fifty or so residences, taverns, shops, a temple to Gond, and one official building, Ilmeth's Manor. The temple, known as the House of Gond, is quite impressive, but visitors accustomed to Gondar enthusiasm for new ways of doing things may be disappointed. Clerics who favor Gond's aspect as a god of crafts-folk, not inventiveness, staff Gond's Battledale temple.

Ghost Holds: For every estate owned by a Sembian nobleman, there are two or three more that went to ruin and were overgrown by the forest. With all the attention focused on confronting the drow of Cormanthor, Battledale's roads and countryside are not as safe as they used to be. Bandits have taken to occupying these ruined estates for days at a time. Ilmeth is seeking companies of reputable adventurers to clean out the "ghost holds," since the few soldiers under his command have been busy patrolling against drow raids.

Hap (Village, 467): This spot of twelve permanent buildings and many outlying farms has a blacksmith, a sawyer, a tavern, a shrine to Lathander, and a permanent guard of five to fifteen of Ilmeth's Lord's Men. The guards spend their time hunting, gambling, or practicing at arms, but they also keep an eye on the traffic along Rauthauvyr's Road and another eye cocked warily up Haptooth Hill.

Haptooth Hill: An old wizard's tower crowns this granite hill overlooking Hap. Not so long ago, it was occupied by a Red Wizard named Dracandros. Adventurers slew him and dealt with his drow allies, who had built up some hidden strength in the passages riddling the hill. Now that drow have returned to Cormanthor, the folk of Hap fear that some of these new invaders may seek to reoccupy their old stronghold beneath the wizard's tower.

Ilmeth's Manor: The present Lord of Battledale lives in a moated keep inside the greater enclosure of Battle Court, the walled east side of Essembra. Ilmeth (LN male human Ftr8/Chm3 of Helm) is a fair man, but grim and somewhat obsessed with his responsibilities. Chief among these is command of Battledale's small army, a hundred-warrior squadron known as the Lord's Men. If adventurers stay out of Ilmeth's way (and most especially stay out of his manor!), he grudgingly tolerates them as useful scouts and extra swords that he does not have to feed, arm, or heal.

REGIONAL HISTORY

Battledale began as pieces of older dales, stitched together when their governments proved untrustworthy and the people decided to settle their affairs themselves.

Essembra, Battledale's most influential settlement, has a better-known story. The town is named after a red-haired adventurer, a woman who carved a name for herself with a sword and a fierce wit. Essembra the adventurer spurned an elf lord, strangled a dwarven king with her bare hands in a wrestling match, and finally revealed her true song dragon nature by marrying a silver dragon. Some say that descendants of Essembra's part-dragon children still live near the town that bears her name. It's certain that modern Essembra produces far more than its share of skilled sorcerers, humans and half-elves whose magical talents flow free instead of fitting into the harness of wizardry.

Slightly over three hundred years ago, Battledale gave the Dale-lands the closest thing they have had to a High King. Aencar became warlord of Battledale in the year 1030 DR. He took the title of the "Mantled King" and began a campaign to unify the Dales. After some early success, the man who would be High King accepted an invitation to a feast in Essembra that turned out to be a trap. Aencar was slain by a dracolich summoned by one of his enemies. Shadowdale and the other dales owed Battledale itself nothing; their

Aencar, the Mantled King

Dalesfolk admire heroes who resemble themselves: modest, hard-working, and enduring. They rally swiftly after defeat, rebuild rather than whine, and stand up for what is right, without bluster. "I fear you'll have to strike me down first," is the quiet warning made popular by the first man to unite the Dales, Aencar the Mantled King.

Aencar (ay-AN-kar) Burlisk was a warrior of Battledale who grew up with local elves, from whom he learned forest lore, military skills, and wisdom, along with patience and empathy for others. As a young man, he left the Dales to adventure with Sembian acquaintances who called themselves the Mailed Mantle.

The warriors of the Mantle enjoyed great success as mercenaries, serving one Sembian employer after another. Inevitably, though, they were marked for death by Sembian foes and fearful employers. The Mantle warriors chose to make themselves scarce in Sembia and returned to Battledale.

There, Aencar and his comrades found corrupt local merchants taking advantage of poor neighbors through usury and hired thugs. The Mantle ended such practices, and Aencar, the group's leader, was hailed as Lord of Battledale. Aencar tended the safety and prosperity of his people as diligently as a good farmer tends his livestock, and the other members of the Mantle settled into comfortable roles patrolling the dale. For nine years, Aencar made

Battledale ever stronger. Traders from other dales took their measure of him, liked what they saw, and told him of monsters and oppressive rulers elsewhere.

In 1038 DR, Aencar decided to make himself King of the Dales. In the winter months he persuaded the folk of Shadowdale and Tasseldale to join with Battledale under his rule. In spring he burst forth like an angry storm against the other dales, striking swiftly and leaving the folk of the Mantle in his wake as either lords or "swordmasters." In one season, the Mantle banner rose over all the dales except Archendale and High Dale. Within two years, Dalesfolk came to love their king and saw his rule as rightful.

Unfortunately, Aencar reigned for only six summers as King of the Dales, and accounts of his "fifteen-year-rule" include his time as Lord of Battledale. During that time, Aencar seldom rested from fighting monsters, brigands, agents of Archendale and Sembia, and evil wizards. After one wizard cursed Aencar with a rotting disease, he concealed his wasting flesh behind a red hood and mask, becoming the Mantled King.

In 1044 DR, Aencar was slain by a dracolich during a feast. His lieutenants destroyed the bone dragon and its summoners (evil wizards, notably Alacanther of Arrabar), and burned Aencar in his manor house. The ruined manor with its many towers still stands just east of Rauthauvyr's Road.

allegiance had been to Aencar, so the dream of a united Dales died with the Mantled King.

A descendant of Aencar's chief swordcaptain still rules Essembra. Chancellor Ilmeth, Essembra's current lord, is a brooding warrior who serves as Battledale's delegate to the Dales Council.

Along with Deepingdale, Battledale is heavily committed to combating the drow now occupying parts of Cormanthor. Essembrans in particular have always been good friends of the elves of Cormanthor, and they feel strongly about the drow invaders since the attack at the Abbey of the Sword.

PLOTS AND RUMORS

The greatest threats to the security of Battledale are the House Jaelre drow (see Cormanthor, below), who see an opportunity to overthrow a weak dale while they gather their strength to deal with better defended or better organized dales. Skirmishes against the drow concern the Battledarrans greatly because of the quadrennial Shield-meet festival to be held outside Aencar's Manor at Midsummer. The Lord of Essembra seeks loyal and competent adventurers to help him secure Battledale's borders before the festival begins.

A Strange Visit: A Red Wizard walks peacefully into Battledale, telling all who ask that he intends to visit Dracandos's Tower on Haptooth Hill. He journeys on to Hap and enters the tower—but doesn't come out. Strange lights and sounds around the tower convince the locals that this is a job for adventurers. The heroes are asked to find out what became of the Red Wizard and to determine what he wanted with the old tower in the first place.

cormanthor

Capital: Myth Drannor (see text)
Population: 154,223 (drow 47%, elves 30%, half-elves 10%, humans 10%, halflings 2%)
Government: None
Religions: Corellon Larethian, Eilistraee, Mielikki, Mystra, Silvanus, Vhaeraun
Imports: None
Exports: Furs, magic items looted from Myth Drannor, meat
Alignment: All

The abandoned Elven Court of Cormanthor

Illustration by Todd Lockwood

Walking beneath Cormanthor's giant maples, looming shadowtops, and towering oaks, humans soon realize that they have entered a world that does not need them. The great forest is a living testament to a forgotten green age, a time in which humans were an afterthought instead of the dominant society.

During the Elven Retreat, more than 90% of the elves who called Cormanthor home left for Evermeet or moved west to Evereska. A few remained, particularly in the Semberholme area near Lake Sember and in the communities of Bristar and Moonrise Hill in Deepingdale. Others, who had human mates, human friends, or half-elf children, stayed on in other parts of the Dales.

As the elves left Cormanthor, they set traps and magic wards to discourage humans and others from moving into their ancestral lands. The defenses were particularly strong in the area surrounding the former Elven Court. Queen Amlaruil's followers must have known that their efforts would not keep nonelves out forever. But it is doubtful that they guessed that their ancient enemies, the drow, would be the first to slip past the defenses and claim the forest.

LIFE AND SOCIETY

The formal life of the Elven Court has given way to the hunting of the ranger and the steps of the druid. Though Cormanthor is still beautiful, and still very much a high forest worthy of bards' songs and poets' flights of fluttering adjectives, it now shudders at the felling of trees in its fringe and the sounds of stealthy battle in its heart.

War is brewing in Cormanthor as humans, elves, drow, and gnolls struggle to carve their settlements from the green fastness and establish strongholds and borders they can defend against their rivals. The old Elven Woods stretch for hundreds and hundreds of miles. They may prove expansive enough for all the competing powers and settlements. The drow, the elves, and the occasional human settlers can go days and even tendays within the forest without running into signs of each other's existence. But even Cormanthor might not be large enough for all of these races to share.

MAJOR GEOGRAPHICAL FEATURES

Cormanthor itself is the dominant feature of the entire region. Once the great forest extended all the way to the Dragon Reach, covering the lands that are now Sembia and Cormyr. Even after thousands of years of human encroachment, the great woods of the Elven Court are the mightiest forestland in this part of Faerûn.

Lake Sember: This beautiful lake in south Cormanthor is the heart of the elven community of Semberholme. Full humans are seldom welcome near the lake's waters, which are regarded as the heart of elven life here.

IMPORTANT SITES

The elves created most of the forest's wonders, but humans and mad deities have left permanent scars.

Elven Court: The Court covered a wide area. Elves like living space, so they leave enough room to allow the creatures of the forest to pass naturally between elven tree-homes without feeling trapped in a city. The Court influenced the entire northwest quarter of Cormanthor, even if it was only to create a series of cunningly landscaped glades linked by beams of sunlight and miniature stepping-stone *portals*.

Even though the moon and sun elves of the Court dismantled their greatest structures during the Retreat, the shaped tree-homes of the former Elven Court still offer the most comfortable and defensible habitation in Cormanthor for surface drow, who have decades of practice dismantling elven defenses and overcoming green warders.

Of the drow, those of House Jaelre spend the largest part of their time establishing themselves in the area of the Court. Unlike previous plunderers, they avoid the elven barrows beneath the home trees, as the drow would rather not waste time fighting elven guardian spirits until they have a secure hold upon the forest.

Moander's Road: Moander, a deity of corruption and rot, had been thought dead since the days of Myth Drannor's glory. In truth, Moander slept in the ruins of Yûlash, north of the Dales. In 1357 DR, Alias of the Azure Bonds unintentionally woke the old deity, who arose and plowed a course of devastation toward the ruins of Myth Drannor, intending to absorb other magical energies still sleeping in that perilous site. Alias and her companions managed to stop Moander after he destroyed a wide swath of forest.

The damage to the forest has regrown poorly. The "road" now is afflicted with strange fungi, loathsome oozes, and plant monsters. This does not prevent Zhent agents from using the road as a quick (and, for them, safe) path to Myth Drannor, but they avoid the high hill that is the dead god's corpse.

Myth Drannor: Myth Drannor is arguably the richest and most dangerous adventuring site in all of Faerûn. It's actually dozens of sites in roughly the same location, the ruined remains of the huge elven and human city that was once the greatest magical place in the world.

Myth Drannor was the seat of an incredibly powerful civilization, and gold, magic items, and other worthwhile debris still rest everywhere here along with their magical guardians and invading creatures. Human, nonhuman, and monstrous adventurers who enter the ruins frequently leave their possessions, their corpses, and even their souls behind, new pickings for the next vile cult, ambitious magician, or adventuring party that comes by.

In centuries past, a form of elven high magic known as a *mythal* protected the ruins of Myth Drannor. When the elves moved to Evermeet, the *mythal* weakened. The laws of magic vary inside Myth Drannor, but most of the space- and time-distortion effects created by the *mythal* have faded out.

Semberholme: The oaks and maples fed by Lake Sember's pure waters soar high above the rest of the forest, creating a cathedral-like retreat for elves who wanted to escape from the politics and whirl of the Elven Court. The limestone caves that formerly provided the elves with a perfect refuge now supply the surface drow with splendid hideouts. Given the proximity of Bristar and Moonrise, and the area's historic importance as one of the three main elven communities of Cormanthor, Semberholme could be sorely contested in times to come.

Standing Stone: The huge plinth of glossy gray rock, erected to commemorate the Dales Compact between the Elven Court and the new Dalesfolk, still stands proudly in the forest. The stone magically repairs all damage to itself, so the elven runes winding around its base, outlining the particulars of the treaty, can be clearly read 1,372 years after the plinth's creation. Originally, the Standing Stone was not as accessible to humans. When Rauthauvyr of Sembia forced his road through the forest, threatening war if he was not allowed to build, the elves routed the road within sight of the Standing Stone. It pointed out that humans who were the elves' friends did not need to resort to violence to achieve what they wanted.

Tangled Trees (Small Town, 1,168): After the Elven Court and Semberholme, the Tangled Trees was the third great community in Cormanthor. It was largely populated by youngsters, warriors, adventurers, half-elves, and rogues who did not join the Retreat.

Tangled Trees would be the largest elven community in the forest, but many of its residents are elsewhere at any given time. The Elven Court and Semberholme consist mainly of widely spaced family dwellings and some common areas, but the Tangled Trees is known for its interlocked trails, webbing, platforms, and tree forts occupied by the community's eclectic group of elves, half-elves, and occasional human friends or lovers. In winter, when the wanderers come home and the patrols decrease, the actual population of the Tangled Trees is double that listed above.

Vale of Lost Voices: The Vale of Lost Voices cuts across Rauthauvyr's Road between the Standing Stone and Essembra. In truth, the Vale came first, and it was Rauthauvyr's bad luck to forge his road across its ancient elven burial grounds. Travelers who stay on the road are safe enough. Humans who stray off the road into the forest in the Vale of Lost Voices risk encounters with elven ghosts and guardian spirits that take years off their lives or slay them outright. The area is sacred to elves, who occasionally visit it alone but never in groups. Elves do not build or settle in the area. The drow avoid the area even more assiduously than humans do.

REGIONAL HISTORY

There was a time when deep, green forest stretched unbroken from the Sea of Fallen Stars north to the Tortured Land, west through the Thunder Peak passes, and around the Stonelands to the Storm Horns. Trees cloaked both shores of the Dragon Reach, broken only by occasional peaks, deadfall glades where huge trees plunged to earth, and the burned scars of lightning-strike fires.

Then came the elves, the first gardeners of the forest. They found haunting, sacred beauty around Lake Sember. They saw the works of their high gods farther north, near Elventree. They settled in the latter place, still known as the Elven Court today, and tended the woods as carefully as any royal gardener. The elves broke the "evershade" beneath the trees by creating magical glades. Great and terrible beasts were largely slain or driven off in eldritch hunts.

The kingdom of Cormanthyr in the great forest of Cormanthor was founded approximately four thousand years before the creation of the Dales and the start of Dalereckoning. For a time, the elves lived freely in their great forest, but the millennia of elven rule were over once humans entered Faerûn. The elves watched with increasing anger as humans clawed at the borders of the once-endless wood, cutting it ever smaller, forcing roads and trails through undisturbed forest. Woodcutters, adventurers, and homesteaders who penetrated too boldly into the green vastness of the old elven forest often met their ends under elven arrows.

Yet humans came in waves, as numerous as gnats. Oak after oak fell to their axes, then the shadowtop and duskwood trees, and they brought swords and wizards of their own to contend with elven arrows. Farsighted elven leaders saw that the heart and strength of the elves would be worn away if they fought humans at every turn. Such battle would only leave them weak before orc hordes, drow forays from the realms below, and strokes from the divine powers, such as merciless "wolf winters" and flights of dragons.

So they welcomed humans as allies and even gave passage and settlement room to gnomes, dwarves, and halflings. These were the early years of the Dales Compact that created the Dales. The elves sought to make peace with the humans rather than fighting against them, but remained wary of their neighbors. To guard themselves and a vestige of their original realm, the elves raised great areas of magic called *mythals* within the borders of Cormanthor.

Each *mythal* was the product of an elven high magic ritual that created a magical field governing various conditions within its confines. Some *mythals* protected the forest by inhibiting fires and explosive magic; others increased the power of spells drawing upon the elven deities or elven scrolls while suppressing nonelven magic.

As the centuries rolled on, the elves of Cormanthor layered the forest with *portals*, invisible hideaways, and wards. Thus, the elves made the woods alive with magic. Unfortunately, elven high magic has a steep price. Riddled with *portals*, the great forest was more open to *portals* created by others, threatening the realm with attacks from its enemies and dooming the *mythals* to eventual decay. Today, the once-bright city of Myth Drannor is a fiend-roamed, haunted ruin. The rest of Cormanthor is not nearly as dangerous as Myth Drannor, but centuries of magical wards, *portals*, and summonings have turned certain parts of the forest into areas that only the skilled, wood-wise, or magically gifted can expect to survive without harm.

THE CORMANTHOR DROW

For many years, the fiends and decaying high magic of Myth Drannor were widely held to be the greatest peril of the Elven Wood, but now an even greater danger has appeared—the return of drow to the surface world. As the last few decades of the Elven Retreat left vast portions of the Elven Court and its surrounding forests virtually unoccupied, some drow factions in the Underdark—particularly those who owe their allegiance to Vhaeraun rather than to Lolth—contemplated a return to the surface world. First as small scouting parties, then as larger warbands, and finally as conquerors with trains of slaves and belongings, the drow have established themselves in the deep places of Cormanthor.

The drow have not been present in Cormanthor for long, but they've made themselves known with raids against Archendale, Battledale, Deepingdale, and Mistledale. Incessant raiding and murders in the forest may not be the worst the drow have to offer Dalesfolk. The Great Druid of Cormanthor went missing near Myth Drannor shortly after the drow invaded. The story passed on to druids through the animals of the forest is that he perished in a great battle with a demon summoned by drow newly arrived in Myth Drannor. The only consolation for Dalesfolk is that the druids say that the Great Druid killed his demonic attacker as well.

Even more alarming than the prospect of a war in Cormanthor's shadow is the drow interest in the abandoned realm's ancient *mythals*. The drow seek to twist Cormanthor's ancient *mythals* into shapes that please them. Elven high magic effects that please such beings, however, are likely to demoralize and enfeeble humans and elves. The drow could never create powerful *mythals* on their own, but with time and study, they may master the magic of the Elven Court and permanently darken the great forest. Those elves who have returned from Evermeet know this and work constantly to conceal old magic from the drow or defend sites too large to hide with the most powerful guardians they can find.

Although it is not widely known, the drow who have moved into Cormanthor are divided into several factions. Several groups of drow compete and even cooperate to turn Cormanthor into their new fortress home. The main factions are described here, with brief notes on other drow forces in Cormanthor.

Auzkovyn Clan (3,505 drow): For centuries the Auzkovyn drow (so called after the long-dead founder of their clan) wandered in the uppermost reaches of the Underdark and occasionally took up residence on the surface. About two hundred years ago, the Auzkovyn carved out a small fastness in the heart of the High Forest, determined to forge a surface homeland despite the wealth of enemies present in that location.

While the Auzkovyn wore away their strength in constant warfare, the wood elves of the High Forest—never proponents of the Elven Retreat—grew stronger and more vigorous, intent on reestablishing the ancient elven kingdom of Eaerlann. The surface drow of the High Forest recognized the growing strength of the wood elves and realized that they had little but incessant warfare to look forward to.

After long and secret effort, the High Forest drow created a *portal* that led into Cormanthor—specifically into the Underdark near the Abbey of the Sword. Although the Tempus-worshipers deflected the Auzkovyn assault by destroying this first *portal*, the rest of the High Forest drow quickly forged a second to join their vanguard in the forests north of Battledale.

Unlike House Jaelre, the Auzkovyn clan does not wish to settle into old elf havens such as the Elven Court. The Auzkovyn feel most comfortable as woodland nomads. At various times, they range in large or small groups over nearly the whole of Cormanthor, setting up temporary camps on the ground, in the treetops, and sometimes in cave entrances to the Underdark.

Most of the Auzkovyn drow offer sacrifices to Vhaeraun, even if not all worship him as their patron deity. Unlike the other surface drow who've invaded Cormanthor, the Auzkovyn are willing to accept elves, half-elves, and possibly even Vhaeraun-worshiping humans into their clan, which may work to their advantage in the long run.

As Vhaeraun worshipers who aren't set on occupying specific territory, the Auzkovyn drow get along fairly well with House Jaelre. Of course, for evil drow factions, "getting along well" means they don't slit each other's throats after they've hit each other with sleep-inducing arrows.

House Jaelre (7,945 drow): Decades ago, a house of Vhaeraun worshipers lost a civil war in Menzoberranzan. Calling themselves House Jaelre, they wandered the deep Underdark, too weak to retake their home city. Around the same time as the Auzkovyn clan came through the *portal* beneath the Abbey of Swords, House Jaelre drow found *portals* in the ruined gnome city of Blingdenstone that led into sections of Cormanthor once inaccessible thanks to Myth Drannor's powerful *mythal*.

Unlike the Auzkovyn clan, House Jaelre drow seek to occupy the elves' original homes, particularly the area around the Elven Court. They're motivated in part by the hope that they can take over the elves' original *mythals* and wards, then use the elven magic to keep out both the elves and their own drow enemies.

A crafty drow sorcerer-rogue named Jezz the Lame heads the forces of House Jaelre charged with creating distractions in the Dales. These events help to keep the Dalesfolk's attention away from developments in the old Elven Court. At the moment, Jezz is having great success slashing into Mistledale.

Spider-kissers (1,168 drow): This term is a catchall for Lolth-worshiping drow who splintered off the other groups or came into Cormanthor through other Underdark ways. They have no intention of permanently settling the surface. Rather, they plot to retake their home cities using the traditional drow engine of social change: civil war. The Lolth-worshipers (Ssinssriggorbb) prefer to cluster around entrances to the Underdark, even if that does make them vulnerable to raiders from the Underdark cities.

Underdark Raiders: The Blingdenstone *portals* that allowed the House Jaelre drow to enter Cormanthor have also enabled ambitious Menzoberranzan commanders to follow. Menzoberranzan raiders switch between raiding their former comrades and raiding Dalesfolk. (The latter action has the bonus of being blamed by victims on the drow settling Cormanthor.)

PLOTS AND RUMORS

Drow raiders, human bandits, and all manner of wild and dangerous forest creatures make Cormanthor a dangerous place to visit. At the heart of the forest, the failing *mythal* around Myth Drannor protects untold wealth and power, while trapping unspeakable evil within.

Elven Armory: The characters find a map to an elven treasure cache that appears to be located near the fringes of the former

Elven Court. If the map's annotations can be trusted, the hidden cavern contains several suits of powerful magic armor that fit anyone who dons them and give to wearers potent battle-spells and embedded powers. The catch is that the map is laid out in a manner that frustrates even elves, with references to trees of a particular type and the shadows they cast at particular times of day as guideposts.

When the PCs figure the map out, they discover that the real catch is that drow of the House Jaelre group frequent the forest in that area. If the PCs manage to overcome all obstacles and obtain the armor, they can use *read magic* to read the fine elven runes printed on it. The final problem is that each suit comes with strange magical *geases* to complement its powers, laying tasks and obligations on its wearers. Some suits even take their wearers on unforeseen journeys to strange ruins elsewhere in Faerûn.

Jezz the Lame

Male drow Rog6/Sor6: CR 14; Medium-size humanoid (elf); HD 6d6 plus 6d4; hp 36; Init +9; Spd 30 ft.; AC 24 (touch 17, flat-footed 24); Atk +14/+9 melee (1d4+2/15–20, *+2 keen kukri*) or +12 ranged (1d8/19–20, light crossbow); SA Sneak attack +3d6; SQ Drow traits, evasion, familiar benefits, locate traps, uncanny dodge (can't be flanked, Dex bonus to AC); SR 23; AL NE; SV Fort +4, Ref +12, Will +9; Str 10, Dex 20, Con 11, Int 16, Wis 14, Cha 19. Height 5 ft. 3 in.

Skills and Feats: Balance +11, Bluff +9, Climb +5, Concentration +10, Diplomacy +12, Disguise +8, Hide +17, Intimidate +11, Knowledge (arcana) +8, Knowledge (Dalelands local) +8, Listen +15, Move Silently +27, Ride (horse) +7, Search +10, Sense Motive +8, Spellcraft +13, Spot +15, Swim +1, Tumble +9, Use Magic Device +6, Use Rope +10, Wilderness Lore +4; Alertness, Daylight Adaptation, Exotic Weapon Proficiency (kukri), Improved Initiative, Stealthy, Weapon Finesse (kukri).

Special Qualities: Familiar Benefits: Grants Jezz Alertness when within reach, share spells, empathic link (1 mile), familiar may deliver touch spells, scry on familiar, speak with familiar.

Spells Known (6/7/6/4; base DC = 14 + spell level; 10% chance of spell failure): 0—*detect magic, detect poison, ghost sound, mage hand, mending, ray of frost, read magic;* 1st—*change self, feather fall, obscuring mist, shield;* 2nd—*cat's grace, invisibility;* 3rd—*fly.*

Possessions: +2 keen kukri, +5 silent moves leather armor, ring of protection +2, glove of storing, Keoghtom's ointment, Murlynd's spoon, rope of climbing, stone salve (2 doses).

Keheneshnef: Male viper familiar; CR 1/2; Tiny magical beast; HD 1/4 d8 (12 HD); hp 18; Init +3; Spd 15 ft., climb 15 ft., swim 15 ft.; AC 20 (touch 15, flat-footed 17); Atk +12 melee (poison, bite); Face/Reach 2 1/2 ft. by 2 1/2 ft. /0 ft.; SA Poison (initial and secondary damage 1d6 temporary Con, DC 11, onset time 1 minute); SQ Improved evasion, scent; AL NE; SV Fort +4, Ref +10, Will +8; Str 6, Dex 17, Con 11, Int 8, Wis 12, Cha 2.

Skills and Feats: Balance +11, Climb +12, Hide +18, Listen +15, Spot +15; Weapon Finesse (bite).

Jezz the Lame

Illustraation by Matt Wilson

Jezz the Lame is one of the leaders of House Jaelre, commanding the drow who make raids on the Dales to divert attention from those who now reside in the old elven sites of Cormanthor. Jezz scouted for his tribe while they wandered the Underdark. His leg was badly broken during a fight with an umber hulk in which a cavern ceiling collapsed. His companions thought him dead, but he managed to drag himself into their camp a tenday later. One of the clerics was able to snap the healing bone and reset it in a normal position, but the old injury still pains him from time to time, and he wears a special brace and shoe to help him walk more easily.

Young and confident, Jezz knows how hard he can push the Dalesfolk before they become so enraged that they descend upon the forest in great numbers. He prefers to keep his band small and his followers ready to move on short notice. Given his charisma and the respect his followers have for him, if House Jaelre does manage to obtain a permanent foothold in the forest, Jezz may be presented as a speaker to the outside world.

Daggerdale

Capital: Dagger Falls
Population: 28,041 (88% humans, 5% dwarves, 3% half-orcs, 2% gnomes, 1% halflings)
Government: Lordship
Religions: Lathander (Mielikki, Silvanus, Tempus)
Imports: Armor, books, glass, jewelry, metalwork, paper, textiles, weapons
Exports: Furs, meats, ores
Alignment: LG, NG, N

Daggerfolk are known to be hard, grim, and unforgiving, largely because Zhentil Keep has been trying to claim their land for decades, seeking to rule this dale as a client state or smash it as Teshendale was ruined. In fact, Zhent agents ruled the dale for nearly thirty years, driving Randal Morn—the dale's rightful lord—into an outlaw's life in his own land.

Three years ago, Randal Morn (NG male human Ftr6/Rog4) overthrew the Zhent occupiers in his homeland and reclaimed his ancestors' seat. Barely holding his war-torn community together in the face of Zhent aggression, Randal Morn is in no shape to help other dales with their problems.

Of all the dales, Daggerdale is the most likely to offer contracts and support to adventuring parties willing to fight Zhents, clean out monster-infested mines, rescue hostages taken by bandits, kill those same bandits, or travel into the mountains after predatory vampires. If Daggerdale is to survive, Randal Morn's followers and hired agents must pacify the dale's wildlands and drive out local monsters.

Life and Society

The years of Zhentarim occupation forced Daggerfolk farmers to put aside their plows and become hunters or herders. Venison and goats could be hidden from Zhent tax agents; fields planted with winter wheat and hardy cabbages could not.

Most Daggerdale communities keep their gates locked, opening them only to trusted friends or people vouched for by someone inside. Some still behave as if they were at war with the Zhents. It's possible that the roughness of current Daggerdale society will smooth out over time, but Daggerfolk might also make themselves as ruthless as the Zhents in order to survive.

MAJOR GEOGRAPHICAL FEATURES

Most of the land is rolling wooded hills broken by labyrinthine rocky valleys. It's good grazing country for livestock, but large farms are confined to the region around Dagger Falls.

Border Forest: The Border Forest is the frontier connecting four different regions of Faerûn: Daggerdale and the Dalelands to the south, the Moonsea and the Zhents' Citadel of the Raven to the east, Anauroch to the west, and the Tortured Land to the north. The forest's native inhabitants are fey, such as satyrs, pixies, grigs, and dryads. In part because of their constant fight with Zhent loggers working out of Snowmantle, Border Forest fey tend toward cruelty and violence instead of the lighthearted capriciousness typical of fey farther south.

Dagger Falls: The waterfalls above Dagger Ford, which give the town of Dagger Falls its name, are not navigable by boats. Unlike Feather Falls along the Ashaba, Dagger Falls' sheer drop is too much for salmon returning from the Sea of Fallen Stars to overcome.

Dagger Hills: Some parts of the thick bracken of the Dagger Hills are not bandit country. Unfortunately, such areas *are* monster country—wolves, leucrottas, owlbears, lycanthropes, and even beholders hunt through the thick underbrush. In the years of Zhent occupation, cleared farmlands were reclaimed by nature—not by the forests to the south, but by the dense thickets and thorn fields of the northern hills. These plants are as resistant to fire as they are to human intrusion.

Desertsmouth Mountains: These rough mountains form the western border of the Dalelands and tower over the hills of Daggerdale. Now that the city of Shade stands in the Shoals of Thirst, the Desertsmouth Mountains shield the Dales from more than just the harsh winds of Anauroch.

The great dwarven kingdom of Tethyamar once occupied the Desertsmouths. Several hundred years ago, it fell to orcs, ogres, evil wizards, and fiends, and some of the last still lurk in the peaks. The last king of Tethyamar, Ghellin, died of old age in 1369 DR in Cormyr, still dreaming of retaking his lost realm.

IMPORTANT SITES

The town of Dagger Falls is the cornerstone of Daggerdale. Most of the region's important sites are in or near that town.

Constable's Tower: Rebuilt many times over the past few centuries, this fortress near Dagger Falls is now so imposing that Randal Morn wishes to take it over as the new seat of his government. He is prevented by an ongoing magical cataclysm within the structure—a tempest of *lightning bolt, fireball, disintegrate,* and *meteor storm* spells occurring in alternating cycles with powerful magic that repairs the damage to the keep itself. Fools who step into the tower suffer from the damaging spells but are not helped by the repairing spells. Randal Morn would pay 5,000 gp and give land and a title to anyone who could make the keep livable.

Dagger Falls (Large Town, 2,804): They're not pretty, but to the inhabitants of Daggerdale, the stone walls of Dagger Falls are the surest haven in a troubled land. The walled town sits just northwest of Dagger Ford, where the Tethyamar Trail crosses the River Tesh beneath the falls. The stone construction and steep slate roofs of the town's buildings allow them to survive heavy winter snows.

Dagger Falls began as a storage site for dwarven metals being shipped down from the mountains to the southern lands. After all these years it's still a frontier town, a place where everyone wears weapons and occasionally has cause to draw them in the public good (as well as in the pursuit of private quarrels).

Eagles' Eyrie: Rising above Dagger Falls, this rocky knoll houses altars sacred to the Brightblade clan of dwarves, who sometimes return to make sacrifices. Any favors that can be done for the dwarves make Randal Morn happy, because his family's prior relations with them amounted to a blood feud. He can't afford this type of conflict if he wants to keep the town out of the hands of the Zhentarim.

Lathander's Light: The temple to Lathander in Dagger Falls still smells of smoke from the fires that ruined it during the Zhent occupation. The Daggerfolk rebuilt the temple as a sign of their determination to heal the scars of the occupation. Lathander's clergy are well-loved, not least because a sizable number of young priests from around the Dales come to Daggerdale to spread the Dawn Lord's light where it's most needed.

REGIONAL HISTORY

Daggerdale began as the happy community of Merrydale. The community's peace and prosperity ended bloodily during an infestation of vampires. People forced to stake their undead children found little merry about the dale from that point, and over a few years the appellation fell out of use. Daggerdale—a translation of the valley's original name in the dwarven tongue—eventually supplanted the name of Merrydale.

Daggerdale prospered for a long time as a trading partner to the dwarven realm of Tethyamar. When that kingdom fell, Daggerdale came on hard times. Its bustling trade vanished, and Daggerdale became a rustic backwater, little troubled by events elsewhere in the Dalelands.

That changed in 1336 DR. Two decades after Teshendale fell to the Zhents, Daggerdale met the same fate. Randal Morn, the hereditary ruler of Daggerdale, was driven into exile in the hills. For years, he fought a grim campaign against Zhent forces occupying the dale's biggest town, Dagger Falls.

In 1353 DR, Randal Morn and his friends succeeded in killing Malyk, the puppet ruler the Zhents had installed to give the dale a show of autonomy. This only increased Zhentil Keep's determination to keep the dale beneath its boot. The Zhents installed a series of constables and hired unsavory locals for the constabulary as an auxiliary to the Zhent garrison. The fight against Randal Morn's guerillas in the hills appeared to go in the Zhents' favor, so the constables made the most of their opportunities to lord it over their fellow Dalesfolk.

Morn's personal war turned into an all-out battle in 1369 DR, when he succeeded in retaking the town of Dagger Falls, killing or driving off all the Zhents. The long battle left many scars—the war in Daggerdale was often a civil war, pitting Dalesfolk against Dalesfolk.

PLOTS AND RUMORS

Zhentil Keep's numerous setbacks and factional infighting over the last five years provided Randal Morn with a narrow window of Zhent apathy in which to free his land. That window has now closed. The Zhents control virtually all of the Moonsea. Some among the Black Network are looking southward again, and Daggerdale may not have the strength to shake off Zhent rule a second time.

Dark Deeds, Bright Relic: When the Zhentarim burned the temple of Lathander, they also looted its altars. One of the temple's holy relics, a magic torc that radiates light capable of dispelling *darkness* spells, turns out not to have been taken back to Zhentil Keep. Divination spells cast by the priests have determined that the torc is located somewhere within Eagle's Eyrie, possibly in the areas that are sacred to the Brightblade dwarves.

It's a delicate mission, because the Brightblade dwarves have their own sacred relics in the Eyrie that need to be left alone. Only adventurers considered trustworthy by Randal Morn or the temple of Lathander will be considered for the job.

Deepingdale

Capital: Highmoon
Population: 50,239 (humans 70%, half-elves 20%, elves 9%)
Government: Republic with elected lord
Religions: Corellon Larethian, Oghma
Imports: Cotton, fine manufactured items, silk, textiles, wool
Exports: Fur, meat, timber
Alignment: LG, NG, CG

Situated along the contested route between Cormyr and Sembia, Deepingdale could have gone down the road of the sword, the militaristic path chosen by Archendale and Scardale. But although its folk are battle-ready and its rulers are no strangers to combat, Deepingdale avoided Scardale's obsession with conquest and Archendale's preoccupation with power. Instead, Deepingdale remains true to its founding vision, the original Dalelands compact with the elves of Cormanthor, in which Dalesfolk were guests of the elves and joint custodians of the mighty trees of the forest.

Other Dalesfolk and even some elves refer to Deepingdale as the Dale of the Trees. Unlike the farmers of other dales who thrive by clearing land, the folk of Deepingdale practice forestry in order to maintain the land's original thick green blanket of vegetation. The woods of the human-occupied portions of Deepingdale are as well managed as the farms of Featherdale. Careful harvesting and cultivation of hedges, timberland, native game, and the land's rich streams and rivers have turned the dale into a forest garden.

LIFE AND SOCIETY

Of all Dalesfolk, the inhabitants of Deepingdale are probably the most tolerant and quietly welcoming. They tend to judge people by their actions rather than their words or looks, so adventurers who present themselves well can often make good friends in Deepingdale. On the other hand, adventurers who play games with the truth, or who persist in cutting trees or hunting where they should not, learn that the Deepingfolk can afford to be tolerant because they trust their ability to deal with people they view as threats. A large number of the Deepingfolk muster for the local militia.

Most adventuring Deepingfolk choose the ranger's path, and even human members of the militia are skilled at moving silently through their native woods. Nonhuman members of the militia include elven archers from Moonrise Hill and sorcerer-rangers from Bristar.

MAJOR GEOGRAPHICAL FEATURES

More than any other dale, Deepingdale is woven into and around Cormanthor itself. The inhabitants of Deepingdale live in the shadow of the trees and in the lighter growth at the outskirts of the great forest.

The Blood Horn: Standing above the ruins of vanished Sessrendale like a great red tooth, this striking mountain is presently the home of a young adult red dragon named Thraxata. It is Deepingdale's misfortune to be the closest dale to her lair. Thraxata usually hunts south and west toward Cormyr, but she has also looted and ravaged several caravans on the East Way. The dragon becomes ever more aggressive as her strength and power grow with the years.

Glaemril and Wineflow: Deepingdale is comprised of the lands around these streams and rivers. Both of them run swift and strong and have abundant salmon runs that nourish forest creatures as well as the people of Highmoon. Any outsider who fishes for more than one salmon for his or her own meal is considered a bandit.

Lake Eredruie: This enchantingly beautiful pool is the headwaters of the Glaemril. Residents of Deepingdale, particularly the moon elves of Bristar who guard the waters from intruders, refer to this large-sized pond as a lake because its supernatural powers are far greater than its size. It is sacred to the elven deity Labelas Enoreth. Vials of the lake water function as *cure light wounds* spells (in potion form) for elves and half-elves only. The potency of the water lasts for up to a day after it is removed from the lake, although no one individual can benefit from more than three such draughts in a tenday—additional drinks have no effect.

IMPORTANT SITES

Human settlements dot the busy road known as the East Way, from the Glaun Hills almost to the borders of old Sessrendale. The heart of this community, though, lies in the forests and glades on either side of the road.

Bristar (Village, 701): Just south of Lake Eredruie, the moon elf village of Bristar weathered the years of the Retreat by affirming its ties to Deepingdale instead of joining the nearby community of Semberholme in allegiance to the Elven Court. Now that the Retreat has ended, Bristar is one of the largest elven communities remaining in Cormanthor. Bristar contributes a company of archers to the Deepingdale militia while patrolling vigorously against drow scouts and raiders.

Darkwatch: North of the Glaemril, deep enough in the forest that only elves have good cause to stumble upon it, lies a long, dark rift in the forest floor marked by blackened and twisted trees. As far as the Elven Court and the magicians of the Dales can ascertain, at one time the rift was the prison of an enormously evil deity of decay and corruption. It is not known whether it was the now-dead god Moander in one of its early forms or some other evil being. Neither is it known if the monster is still within its prison, for none have dared descend into the unnatural darkness between the rift's steep sides.

What's certain is that the rift is a nexus for evil spirits and dark gods. Madness infects forest creatures and magical beasts that stray into the area, sometimes driving them into a killing frenzy. Priests of Cyric, the Prince of Lies, relish the energies swirling around the rift. They visit the Darkwatch as a sort of unholy invigoration, though none stay for long. Even the Vhaeraunian drow shun the Darkwatch.

Highmoon (Large Town, 3,505): After Silverymoon in the far north, Highmoon is the most integrated human, elven, and half-elven town in Faerûn. The city is only three hundred years old and growing fast. Before the advent of the Vhaeraunian drow, plans to expand the city's walls bogged down because of a lack of support for military preparedness against hypothetical enemies. Now that the Auzkovyn drow of the High Forest haunt the southern reaches of Cormanthor, expansion and fortification of Highmoon's walls is proceeding apace.

Leaves of Learning: Rising even higher than Lord Ulath's Tower of the Rising Moon, this temple to Oghma in Highmoon contains one of the finest libraries of Faerûn. The temple library eschews all books upon magic in favor of subjects unconnected to the Art. Consequently the temple's collection has grown without suffering unduly from the attentions of overly inquisitive wizards.

Outsiders may examine books for 15 gp per volume—a stiff price, but a better bargain than it might appear because the library has an excellent index, the unique vision of its high priest, Danali the Indexer (LG male human Clr9 of Oghma). As a result, a researcher can usually identify right away the book or books he needs, without having to pay to look at volumes that don't have the information he wants. Clerics and initiates of Oghma pay only 1 gp per volume, a price that applies only to themselves and not to inquisitive friends.

Moonrise Hill (Village, 818): Like the folk of Bristar, the elves of this village that lies just a few miles northeast of Lake Eredruie serve in the Swords of Deepingdale, the Dale's unofficial and seldom-gathered militia. The Moonrise Hill elves are more stand-offish than the elves of Bristar. Adventurers are not welcome visitors to Moonrise Hill and should practice their arrow-dodging skills.

Rhauntides's Tower: Until 1371 DR, this small hexagonal tower on the top of Spell Hill in Highmoon was the home of the sage of Deepingdale, the renowned wizard Rhauntides. He died of old age, leaving his possessions to Theremen Ulath (NG male moon half-elf Ftr7), the ruler of Highmoon. Ulath has moved them to strongrooms in the Tower of the Rising Moon. Shaunil Tharm, the apprentice of Rhauntides, took the wizard's magic *belt of stars* and set off on a secret mission, and she has not been seen since.

To everyone's surprise, Rhauntides bequeathed the tower itself to an energetic Waterdhavian monk he befriended when the latter was passing through Deepingdale as an adventurer. The monk, Teesha Than (LG female human Mnk11/Exp1), has started a small monastery in Rhauntides's Tower. It is the first monastery of the Old Order in the Dalelands. The locals were wary at first, but they now realize that the monks training with Teesha are good neighbors.

Tower of the Rising Moon: Lord Theremen Ulath's black-walled stronghold graces the high ground within Highmoon's walls. As a fortress that has never had to fight off a serious attack, it is known more for the good humor of its lord, the marvels of its interior architecture, and the joys of its splendid feasts than for any martial strength.

This is just as Ulath wishes it. Lulled by tales of the tower's wonders (hanging plants in an atrium open to the stars but somehow shielded from heavy rain, and a stunning map of the Dalelands carved into a huge wooden table in the central Starfall Chamber), attackers might underestimate the fortress's capabilities. It was built in 1022 DR by the half-elf hero Aglauntaras and conceals unusual defenses and weaponry, most nonmagical.

REGIONAL HISTORY

Deepingdale was founded by the half-elf sorcerer Imryll Eluarshee. Known as the Deeping Princess, Imryll forged a society in which humans, half-elves, and elves could join in a common vision centered on the elven ways and lore of living in the great forest without destroying it in human fashion.

Deepingdale's relationship with the elves and the Elven Court has always been cordial and has gotten better over the centuries. Half-elf ancestry is a point of pride among the Deepingfolk. Even during the peak of the elven Retreat, Ulath and the other half-elves and humans of Deepingdale maintained excellent relations with the elven communities of Bristar and Moonrise Hill.

Unlike other Dalesfolk leaders who have mixed feelings about the end of the Retreat, Lord Ulath extends a warm welcome to elves who wish to settle in Deepingdale or fight against the Vhaeraunian drow for their ancestral homes in Cormanthor. Ulath even welcomes drow worshipers of Eilistraee, judging that they may have the best access to magic capable of turning back the followers of Vhaeraun and Lolth.

Access to potent magic is a special concern of Ulath's since the passing of his trusted advisor, the wizard Rhauntides. Skillful and wise magicians can find employment with Ulath while he searches for Rhauntides's successor.

PLOTS AND RUMORS

Like several other peaceful dales, Deepingdale is now threatened by a dangerous and determined enemy. The southwest corner of the forest retained the largest population of elves during the Retreat,
but the Auzkovyn view Deepingdale and its elven allies as the greatest obstacle to their domination of the forest.

The Storm King: Somewhere in the mountains south of Thunder Gap stands the black keep of the Storm King, a chaotic evil cloud giant sorcerer who commands the loyalty of several ogre bands and numerous goblin tribes. The Storm King has demanded tribute from the folk of Highmoon, threatening to lay waste to the land between the Arkhen and the East Way if he is not placated. With the accelerated effort to build Highmoon's walls, Lord Ulath has neither the gold nor the inclination to pay the tribute. He also does not have warriors to spare to guard against an attack from the mountains.

A company or two of experienced adventurers might suffice to drive off any raiding force the Storm King sends into Deepingdale. It might even be possible for a dedicated and powerful band to eliminate the problem altogether by striking at the Storm King directly, before he marshals an army of goblins and ogres to his cause.

featherdale

Capital: None
Population: 14,020 (84% humans, 11% halflings, 2% half-elves, 2% gnomes)
Government: Democracy
Religions: Lathander (and Cyric)
Imports: Armor, fine manufactured goods, weapons, oil
Exports: Cheese, corn, grain, salted meat, vegetables
Alignment: NG, N, CG

Featherdale survives as a relatively innocent pastoral farmland while more powerful dales around it crumble into anarchy or arm themselves for war. Occupying the lowlands north of the Ashaba between Blackfeather Bridge in the west and Feather Falls in the east, Featherdale has muddled through all the eras of Dalelands history without possessing a ruler, capital, standing army, or sizable town.

The Featherdarrans' chief virtues are resilience, common sense, brawn, and a natural aptitude for farming. Sembians, in particular, think that these qualities qualify Featherdarrans as ideal fellow citizens, but Sembia has failed to annex Featherdale three times and has turned its attention elsewhere.

LIFE AND SOCIETY

Most Featherdarrans are farmers. The young folk of the dale seem content to settle alongside their parents without ever going forth to see the world other than an occasional visit to Essembra, Shadowdale, or, for the daring, what's left of Scardale.

The Featherdarrans' only political gatherings are infrequent four- or five-day meetings called Dalemeets. These free-for-all debate sessions are held in Feather Falls to settle disputes or problems that affect Featherdale's inhabitants. Anyone can participate in a Dalemeet.

Featherdarrans are known to hold grudges. Few in Featherdale suffer a Red Wizard to walk unmolested through their dale, because ten years ago two Red Wizards murdered Featherdale's resident wizard. On the other hand, if Featherdarrans held a grudge against every group that had done them wrong, they'd be an extremely surly lot. For the most part, they don't hold Sembia's occasional attempted coups against individual Sembians, or pin responsibility for Lashan of Scardale's invasion of Featherdale on Scardalefolk.

Featherdarrans settle personal disputes in time honored fashion, usually by talking in the presence of respected elder farmers. Around sixty years ago, blood feuds rippled across this valley as several families became embroiled in a bitter dispute over contested land. The families involved in the feuding exhausted themselves until the surviving members were run off toward the Moonsea by a local family of bards and sorcerers who'd had enough.

MAJOR GEOGRAPHICAL FEATURES

Featherdale isn't technically a dale, since it is lowland and not a valley like other Dalelands. Featherdale occupies rich farming lands within the sweep of the River Ashaba as it flows east toward the Sea of Fallen Stars. Unlike other Dalesfolk, Featherdarrans have little to do with the elven woods.

Feather Falls: This waterfall is the eastern border between Featherdale and Scardale. The water cascades in a series of drops from the Featherdale flood plain down into the Scar, the gorge that gives Scardale its name. Boats and barges can't go up or down the falls, but the salmon that spawn far up the River Ashaba can reach the top of the falls after a day-long struggle through all the small drops and eddying pools that comprise its jumbled face.

River Ashaba: This great river flows out of the Storm Horns near Daggerdale, through Shadowdale, and onward toward the Sea of Fallen Stars through Cormanthor, Mistledale, Battledale, Featherdale, and finally the Scar and Scardale itself.

Featherdale's social and economic life centers on the River Ashaba. Transportation and communication across the dale usually go by the river, in small keelboats manned by men and women who make their living poling up and down the Ashaba. In centuries past, the river's spring floods overwhelmed the dale's farmlands, but elaborate dikes and long-practiced magic now prevent these floods from doing much damage.

IMPORTANT SITES

All of Featherdale's citizens put together amount to a small town in Sembia or Cormyr. For the most part, Featherdale is a region that citizens of the Heartlands know only as a wide and pleasant stretch of road in between regions of greater significance.

Blackfeather Bridge (Village, 818): The rapidly growing settlement of Blackfeather Bridge surrounds a bridge of the same name across the River Ashaba. The bridge, like the growing town, has been updated considerably since its first incarnation as a ramshackle wooden span painted black to increase travelers' confidence in its sturdiness. It's now a stone bridge, guarded occasionally by self-appointed Featherdarran youths on the lookout for Red Wizards and Cyricists. Should any be spotted, the young folk are prepared to ride into the hills for help. Featherdarrans know that priests of Cyric view the bridge as a sacred site, but few know why. (It's because here, the deity of murder killed Leira, the former goddess of illusion.) Cyric's priests visit the bridge to pray and make auspicious sacrifices.

Cholandrothipe's Tower: The wizard Cholandrothipe wielded powerful spells that allowed him to shrink entire boats and move them around Feather Falls without carrying their cargo over the portage. A few years ago, Red Wizards of Thay slew Cholandrothipe, possibly because he refused to share his spells or because they wanted any treasure he had accumulated in his tower.

The Thayans entered the slender tower near Feather Falls, but magical guardians and traps sent them fleeing for their lives. Since then, adventurers entering the Tower have reported extensive underground passages and grisly laboratories that indicate that Cholandrothipe was less benevolent than the people of Feather Falls had believed.

Feather Falls (Village, 584): This town by the waterfall used to be the largest settlement in Featherdale, but that title is now held by Blackfeather Bridge. Feather Falls is the standard mooring point for the small keelboats that ply the Ashaba. Now that Cholan-

drothipe is dead, boatloads of cargo are carried up or down the portage beside the falls.

Temple Beneath the Falls: Depending on who you ask, the secret grottoes beneath the water and boulders of Feather Falls are either stories to entertain children and credulous adventurers, or actual lairs for traveling cultists, smugglers, and sorcerous outlaws. Some locals pronounce "Temple Beneath the Falls" in portentous tones as a joke, but others don't find the idea funny.

REGIONAL HISTORY

Like Mistledale, Featherdale has enjoyed a slightly charmed existence. Whereas Mistledale has entirely avoided occupation by hostile forces, Featherdale's luck consists of surviving such episodes relatively unscathed. When Lashan of Scardale conquered Featherdale, the Featherdarrans laid low for months and counted on their carefully cultivated friendships with other Dalesfolk to save them in the end. As long as Featherdarrans remain generous to their neighbors and reliable members of the Dales Council, their numerous family ties with militarily stronger dales may be sufficient to keep them from being overtaken by a power such as Sembia.

PLOTS AND RUMORS

Featherdale is rarely plagued by monsters and has little banditry or brigandage—there just aren't many spots for a predatory gang to lie low.

The Price of Freedom: A Sembian wizard seeks support for a new magically augmented portage around Feather Falls. He repeatedly attempts to call a Dalemeet to discuss funding and operation of such a project. Unfortunately, the so-called Sembian is a Zhent slaver with no higher motive than drawing as many Featherdarrans into Feather Falls as possible. When he succeeds in calling a Dalemeet, he intends to bring several vicious slaving parties through *portals* and Underdark passageways to carry off hundreds of Dalesfolk from relatively undefended lands.

Harrowdale

Capital: Harrowdale Town
Population: 42,061 (humans 90%, half-elves 5%, elves 4%)
Government: Republic (plutocracy)
Religions: Chauntea, Mystra, Oghma, Tymora (Malar, Mielikki, Silvanus)
Imports: Glassware, lace, ore, paper, silk, spices, tools, weapons
Exports: Ale, beef, cheese, fruit, furs, lumber, mutton, wool
Alignment: LG, LN, NG

As the oldest surviving dale, Harrowdale has learned to tend to its own affairs, respect its neighbors, and care for its land—both the cleared lands of its farmers and the woodlands it considers borrowed from the elves. Until recently, Dalesfolk would have described citizens of Harrowdale as conservative country folk, much like the Featherdarrans to the south. Harrowdale Town's growth into a large port has changed that image.

LIFE AND SOCIETY

Scardale's misfortunes have transformed neighboring Harrowdale in the space of only ten short years. Harrowdale Town can now claim to be the best, if not quite the largest, port into the Dales. The folk of Harrowdale Town are more worldly than their parents and more interested in entertaining visitors from the outside world. Unlike the opportunists of Archenbridge, the new entrepreneurs of Harrowdale Town have not fallen far from their dale's core values, preferring a well-measured plan to risky speculation.

The country folk have changed little. Like the Deepingfolk, the Harrans of the countryside often live among the trees. Harrans are not as connected to the Elven Court as the Deepingfolk, but they are sympathetic to druids, rangers, and others who share the elves' bond with the land.

Harrowdale's rulers are the Council of Seven Burghers, the seven wealthiest folk of the dale. A Burgher holds his or her position for life, and upon a death in the Council, the Harrans appoint the wealthiest non-Burgher to fill the seat.

MAJOR GEOGRAPHICAL FEATURES

Harrowdale's borders can't be missed: Cormanthor to the north, the Dragon Reach to the east, and the Cold Field to the southwest. The dale itself is mostly farmlands, which turn to orchards closer to the sea and to the Velarswood at its center.

The Cold Field: South of Harrowdale and north of Scardale, this treeless moor is haunted by the spirits of warriors who fell in dozens of battles here. In summertime, shepherds of Harrowdale and rural Scardale graze their sheep along the high grass, since the sheep care less than the shepherds about the spirits sleeping restlessly in the unmarked graves beneath the hills. In winter, only fools venture into the Cold Field's confines.

Velarswood: Harrowdale's woodcutters and loggers stay on the fringes of this ancient wood. Cloakers, trolls, stirges, bonebats, and more dangerous predators hunt the interior of the forest, and they are hunted in turn by worshipers of Eilistraee who have a hidden temple in the wood's northern reaches. The drow who worship the Dark Maiden spend much of their time in Cormanthor now, fighting against the Vhaeraunian drow, but they don't leave the temple unguarded.

IMPORTANT SITES

The significant sites in Harrowdale are in Harrowdale Town on the coast of the Sea of Fallen Stars.

Halvan's Keep: The former residence of Harrowdale Town's hated tyrant, this burnt-out ruin on the outskirts of Harrowdale Town clings stubbornly to its secrets, including Halvan's supposed treasure trove. It's an open secret that the 50-gp fine assessed by the town watch to anyone coming out of the ruin does nothing but keep young Harrans from venturing into the old castle's grounds for a lark. Secret organizations, dark brotherhoods, monkish sects, monster summoners, and adventurers are still drawn to the ruined keep like rats to darkness.

Harrowdale Town (Large Town, 4,206): It's a testament to the Harrowdale way of doing business that the bustle of new activity in this port town's harbor hasn't been allowed to overshadow the village's other charms. Some of Harrowdale's noteworthy buildings are left over from the town's previous era of prosperity, six to seven hundred years ago.

The Council of the Seven Burghers runs a tight ship. The constabulary is run by Ellarian Dawnhorn (LG female sun elf Ftr5/Wiz4). She has little love for adventurers and even less love for Sembian adventurers. Adventurers who can stay out of Ellarian's way have more luck at the town's temples and with the general populace. Harrans have nothing against adventurers, as long as the latter solve problems instead of create them.

House of Mystra: All three temples in Harrowdale Town frequently sponsor or aid adventurers. The clerics of the temple to Tymora enjoy gambling on adventurers' luck, sponsoring numerous groups to find relics blessed by the goddess. The temple to Oghma helps adventuring groups for a fee. The House of Mystra wishes to attract the goodwill of adventuring companies. Sadly for the temple's high priest, Llewan Aspenwold (NG female human Clr11 of Mystra), Harrowdale has turned out to be a poor site for a temple to Mystra. The old Harrans do not trust wizards or other practitioners of the Art, and the younger generation lacks magical aptitude—few Harrans possess the basic talents required for successful study of the Art. The temple relies on the patronage of travelers, merchants, other outsiders, and customers of the Fall of Stars tavern.

REGIONAL HISTORY

In the first centuries of the Dalelands, Harrowdale was named Velarsdale after its founder, whose name also graces the Velarswood. In those days, Velarsdale was ruled by chaotic lords and was every bit as disorganized as modern Featherdale. A tyrant named Halvan taught the Velarsfolk that disorganization could cost them their freedom. After Halvan's mad (and fatal) quest to carve Halfaxe Trail into the heart of the Elven Court, the folk of the dale renamed themselves and instituted their current form of self-government, a ruling council comprised of the seven richest merchants of Harrowdale Town.

Within the last twenty years, Scardale's career through disaster after disaster has opened the way for Harrowdale to become a major Dalelands port. The resulting economic boom is tempered by several factors. Several of the Seven Burghers aren't keen on encouraging other Harrans to become richer than they are. Nor are they keen on blatantly exploiting new economic opportunities for their own gain. Hence, Harrowdale's economic policies emphasize sustainable and wise growth instead of quick profits. This suits the Harrans, who are happy to have more gold in their pockets but less keen on sharing their space with the Sembian opportunists, Moonsea con artists, and Archenfolk who sniff down the trail of bigger profits.

PLOTS AND RUMORS

The corner of the Elven Court that lies east of the River Duathamper is one of the wildest and most desolate portions of the forest, inhabited by dire animals, magical beasts, and dangerously cunning bands of gnolls who wandered into the region from the Vast. Small freeholds and homesteads in the northern part of Harrowdale are constantly plagued by wild animal attacks and harassed by gnolls.

The Black Trade: A cleric of Tyr begins a campaign to keep Zhent trade goods out of Harrowdale. The Council of Seven is mildly embarrassed that the Zhents move so much of the trade flowing through Harrowdale. They'd like the cleric to turn his attention to stopping Zhent attacks rather than focusing on Zhent trade, but the cleric continues his tirades until an assassin tries to kill him. Are the Zhents striking back, or has a misguided Harran merchant resolved to shut him up?

HIGH DALE

Capital: Highcastle
Population: 8,179 (humans 86%, gnomes 10%, half-elves 3%)
Government: Republic with elected High Constable
Religions: Gods of the Dancing Place
Imports: Armor, books, metalwork, paper, textiles, weapons
Exports: Copper
Alignment: LG, LN, NG

Those who were born in High Dale swear by its crisp air, its splendid views of the Thunder Peaks between Cormyr and Sembia, and its citizens' self-sufficient, self-determined lifestyles as shepherds, small farmers, craftsfolk, or stonecutters. Those not born in High Dale regard it as nothing more than a convenient or strategic mountain pass just barely below the tree line.

LIFE AND SOCIETY

The people of High Dale have one huge advantage over their lowland cousins: Except for their land's strategic importance as a pass between Cormyr and Sembia, they don't have anything anyone else wants.

The Highdalefolk live relatively free of the political intrigues and mercantile competition that frequently intrude in the lowland Dales. Vigilance against monsters that don't care about politics and economics is always necessary, but if simple lives are happy lives, the people of High Dale are happy.

High Dale's peacefulness may be nearing an end, though. During the Time of Troubles, Zhent mercenaries occupied the dale. More recently, several powerful Sembian merchant-princes have taken note of Cormyr's troubles and entertain ideas of invasion. If this should come to pass, High Dale is a perfect route by which a flanking army might penetrate Cormyr and trap any forces committed to defending the plains south of the Vast Swamp.

MAJOR GEOGRAPHICAL FEATURES

Some maps fail to note High Dale's existence, tucked as it is just below the main section of the Thunder Peaks and just north of the splinter of that range that runs alongside the Vast Swamp of Cormyr to the west. The main area of High Dale is a high plateau suitable for farming. The Highdalefolk supplement the land of the plateau by carving terraces into the mountains alongside.

High Dale's pass has three hidden valleys branching off to its sides: Copper Gulp, the Dancing Place, and Hidden Vale. Casual travelers seldom see these lands, which are not much settled by Dalesfolk. The Dancing Place, though, has some powerful human and nonhuman inhabitants.

Copper Gulp: Copper delvings riddle this small valley. Roughly half are still actively mined. If any of the copper mines intersect with the Underdark, the miners don't know it yet.

Hidden Vale: Centuries ago, with the blessing of the Highdalefolk, gnomes settled in this difficult-to-find valley. Depending on the season, humans who pass through the valley are too taken by its innumerable alpine wildflowers (late summer and fall) or its swirling fogs (other seasons) to notice the gnomes' homes, tucked back among the trees and boulders of the vale's walls. The gnomes participate in the life of High Dale, but until the Time of Troubles they had little to do with the world beyond the dale. After Gond manifested as a gnome during the Time of Troubles in 1358 DR, several of the younger gnomes of the Vale left its comforts to seek adventure. Friends left behind often try to coax news of their friends from traveling adventurers.

Wyvernfang: North and east of the rest of the dale, this mighty spur of the Thunder Peaks is a notoriously dangerous wyvern roost. More than a dozen wyverns of varying ages lair upon the mountain. At least one of them possesses above average intelligence and organizational skills. The wyverns keep lookouts posted for aerial intruders. Even stranger, small herds of ill-kept sheep can be found hidden in pockets of the Thunder Peaks that are accessible only by air. Monster slayers speculate that the wyverns provide themselves with a renewable food source by allowing some of the animals they steal to breed in isolated mountaintop pens. They also speculate on the disposition of the treasure belonging to the hundreds of wyvern victims ambushed along the Thunder Way.

IMPORTANT SITES

High Dale lays claim to one shining spot on the great map of Faerûn: the Dancing Place, a valley sacred to the major gods who ask their worshipers to make the world a better place.

Arrowpoint: The Pegasus Archery Company, a mercenary band from outside the dale, built this earthen strongpoint just outside the town of Highcastle. As a condition of basing themselves in High Dale, the members of the company had to agree to be magically bound not to take up arms against the dale or attempt to rule it. Given the Company's remote location, it pays low rates to those who wish to join, but its members can provide excellent training.

The Dancing Place: The third of the hidden valleys of High Dale, just a few miles north and west of Highcastle, is preserved as a sacred garden by clerics of Mielikki, Mystra, Oghma, Selûne, and Silvanus. The site is sacred to humans and elves; more than a dozen human and elven deities manifested here in 720 DR to inspire the founding of the Harpers. Elves and Harpers come to the Dancing Place as pilgrims, though the agreements they made with their gods prevent them from staying here long. Other agreements related to the Dancing Place call upon Cormyr to defend High Dale if it is threatened.

Highcastle (Village, 818): Only a few of the shops and taverns in High Dale's biggest settlement stay open all through the winter, since most travelers have enough sense to avoid Thunder Way in bad weather. Highcastle endured hard times during the brief Zhent occupation, losing the few riches its wealthier citizens had accumulated.

High Castle: This castle with the same name as the town it guards is partly ruined by rocks rolling down from the mountains above it. The castle's ballistas and catapults still command excellent fields of fire down upon Thunder Way and the rest of the dale. The Zhent attack in 1358 DR bypassed the castle's defenses by coming in through a magical *portal*.

Thunder Way: This wagon track cuts from Thunderstone in Cormyr up into High Dale, then down again to the small city of Saerb in Sembia. Few travel the Thunder Way, which is rougher and less direct than the preferred route through Daerlun to the south or Thunder Gap to the north, but it's the closest thing High Dale has to a major trade route.

REGIONAL HISTORY

Compared to Archendale, Battledale, and Shadowdale, High Dale has had little to do with pivotal moments in the history of the Dalelands. High Dale is noteworthy for what has *not* taken place within its borders. Despite occasional posturing and skirmishes, Cormyr and Sembia have not fought a war over control of this dale's high pass through the Thunder Peaks.

Historians outside High Dale judge only two events in its history as worthy of mention: the manifestation of over a dozen of Faerûn's mightiest deities at the Dancing Place, six centuries in the past, and the recent occupation of High Dale by the forces of Zhentil Keep during the Time of Troubles. Elminster and the Rangers Three eliminated the Zhents before they could do lasting harm, and Highdalefolk are happy to leave history's stage and return to the quiet lives they love.

PLOTS AND RUMORS

Just as the forces of the giant Storm King menace Deepingdale, so is High Dale threatened. The mountains north of High Dale are virtually impassable, but the goblin servants of the evil cloud giant have subterranean passages leading from the Storm King's black keep into the upper reaches of the Copper Gulp and the Hidden Vale.

Hunting the Hunters: The magical defenses of the Dancing Place are too powerful for all but the mightiest villains to assault directly, but are the pilgrims who trek in secret to the blessed spot so well defended? Evil druids and the People of the Black Blood have ear-marked these pilgrims for cruel death in the badlands between Thunder Gap and High Dale.

mistledale

Capital: Ashabenford
Population: 27,807 (humans 87%, dwarves 5%, gnomes 3%, half-lings 2%, half-elves 2%)
Government: Republic
Religions: Chauntea, Moradin, Silvanus, Tyr
Imports: Manufactured items, oil, ores, textiles
Exports: Ale, beets, cheese, grain, hay, meat, potatoes, vegetables
Alignment: LG, NG, CG

Thousands of years ago, the heavens ensured Mistledale's future prosperity when a falling star plowed a hundred-mile-long, thirty-mile-wide swath through the elven woods. The trees never regrew in the scar where the star had fallen, but the land proved amazingly fertile once Dalesfolk put it to the plow. Mistledale has always been the lucky dale—blessed with fertile land, protected from foes such as the Zhentil Keep and Sembia by intervening dales or the Elven Court, and occupying excellent trade routes between larger areas like Cormyr and the Moonsea.

LIFE AND SOCIETY

Life is good in Mistledale, or at least it was until the present struggle against the drow of the forest. The dale has no lord; instead, six elected Councilors serve as its governing body. The Council of Six chooses a seventh Mistran who serves as the high councilor, bears a black rod as a sign of office and commands the Riders of Mistledale. The present high councilor is Haresk Malorn (LG male human Exp6/Ftr2), a quiet merchant known more for his wisdom and compassion than his martial skill. Haresk is doing an excellent job of keeping his people calm in the face of danger, but he worries that he might have to step down to make room for a true warrior.

Mistledale is a widely spread dale. Its small settlements can see each other across the gently rolling hills, except in the mornings and evenings when mist from the river rises to fill the valley. For communication across the dale, each hamlet is equipped with special bells designed to penetrate the fog. Each bell carries different messages of alarm or inquiry. These sounds are understood by long-term residents of the dale but a mystery to outsiders.

MAJOR GEOGRAPHICAL FEATURES

Mistledale occupies the clear valley along both sides of the Moonsea Ride, east of Peldan's Helm and west of the spot where the forest closes in some three miles before the Standing Stone. The River Ashaba cuts across the center of the dale, crossed by the Moonsea Ride at the excellent natural ford at Ashabenford.

Of all the Dales, Mistledale is closest to the ancient ruins of Myth Drannor. Forest trails, somewhat dangerous at times, lead to Shadowdale and to Essembra to the east.

The Barrowfields: Located at the western end of the dale, the Barrowfields earn their name from the dead warriors buried in the long lines of low, grass-covered hills throughout the area. The ancient Netherese wizard-warrior corpses here have a disturbing tendency to manifest unusually deadly undead powers.

Beast Country: The western end of Mistledale has always been dangerous, thanks to a seemingly indestructible population of bugbears, orcs, goblins, and other obnoxious creatures coming down out of the Thunder Peaks into the softer climate of the Dales. It's a great spot for rangers and other skillful hunters, but less of an attraction to normal folk. The arrival of the House Jaelre drow has not improved the country's reputation.

IMPORTANT SITES

Fiercely independent homesteaders and freeholders occupy most of Mistledale. Hundreds of small farmsteads dot the vale, but there are few real villages.

Abbey of the Golden Sheaf: Like Goldenfields in the Sword Coast North, this temple to Chauntea doubles as a walled farm. The Abbey of the Golden Sheaf is not as large as Goldenfields, covering only three square miles, but its twelve segmented fields yield the greatest harvests per acre in all of human Faerûn. It's said that the Abbey has enough stored food to feed all the Dales for years. The clerics of Chauntea who oversee the Abbey wield great power and influence throughout Mistledale.

Ashabenford (Small Town, 1,869): Ashabenford is the largest town in Mistledale, the market center for its widespread farmers, and as generally pleasant a place as anyone could hope to visit. The House Jaelre drow of Cormanthor have begun a campaign of fast raids and skirmishing to weaken the folk of Ashabenford and distract them from the new drow strongholds rising in the Elven Court. The cottages, homes, and businesses along the east bank of the River Ashaba weren't built for defense—and defense is what Ashabenford needs most now.

The map of Ashabenford on the following page illustrates a typical Dalelands village. Numbered locations are described below.

1. White Hart Inn: Under the proprietorship of the retired adventurer Holfast Harpenshield (NG male human Ftr9), this inn serves all folk of good heart passing through Ashabenford. Holfast is especially fond of good adventurers and gladly shares information and advice with any who seek it. He's also not above throwing a Sembian or Moonsea merchant out on the street if he decides he doesn't like the visitor's looks or manners. Lodgings cost 1 gp per night.

2. Thorm's Mill: Thorm Ubler (NE male human Exp3) is a miserly man who gladly lines his pockets as the owner of the only mill in Mistledale. Heldo and Parvus, his two good-for-nothing sons, are the town braggarts and bullies (both CE male human War5), although they have somehow avoided being caught at anything serious enough to get themselves run out of town or worse.

3. Kaulvaeras Stables: At one of the better stables in the Dalelands, Kaulvaeras Greymantle (LN male moon half-elf Exp2/Ftr2) maintains a fine selection of riding horses and ponies. He also trains and breeds warhorses, although he only has 1d4–2 light warhorses and 1d4–3 heavy warhorses for sale in his stable in any given tenday.

4. Lhuin's Fine Leathers: Lhando Lhuin (NG male human Exp2) is an outstanding worker of leather. His goods are unusually inexpensive but well made, averaging about 10% less than the listed cost in the *Player's Handbook*.

5. The Velvet Veil: This small taproom and festhall is hardly worth the appellation when compared to the perfumed dens of such large cities as Waterdeep or Suzail. The entertainers and servants here pick up news from all corners of the Dalelands from whoever happens to be passing through.

6. Temple of Tyr: Raised only three years ago, this large and impressive temple marks Ashabenford as a more important community than the traveler might expect. The High Priest Nerval Watchwill (LG male human Clr7 of Tyr) distrusts adventurers, and he is currently spending his time and effort aiding the Riders in defending the town against the Cormanthor drow raids.

7. The Ashabenford Arms: Older and more ostentatious than the White Hart, the Arms charges 1 gold and 6 silvers per night, but provides luxurious service by Dalelands standards.

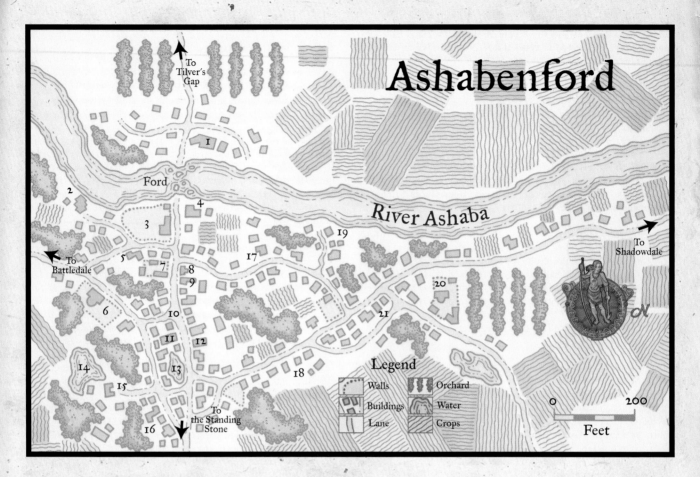

Ashabenford

Legend

Walls	Orchard
Buildings	Water
Lane	Crops

0   200
Feet

8. Shrine to Chauntea: Now somewhat dwarfed by the newer and larger temple of Tyr, this small shrine is maintained by a priest named Jhanira Barasstan (NG female human Clr6 of Chauntea).

9. Arhlo's Fine Flasks: A brewery and distillery of some local note and exceptional quality, this business is run by a quiet, self-effacing man named Arhlo of Arabel (LG male human Exp4).

10. Multhimmer the Merchant: Multhimmer (CN male human Rog7) runs a general trading post, buying and selling almost anything. He occasionally deals in stolen goods, although he is careful not to traffic in goods stolen from locals.

11. Braunstar Wheelwright: The epitome of the stolid, thoughtful Dalesman with a tremendous store of common sense, Braunstar (LN male human Ftr1/Exp6) makes and repairs all kinds of wagons and carts.

12. Jarwain's Imports: Specializing in silks, spices, cottons, and lace imported from Cormyr, this small store is run by Jarwain (CE male moon half-elf Exp3) himself, a handsome fellow with fiery eyes and a soft-spoken manner. Jarwain's goods have steadily climbed in price of late, due to the unrest and disruption of trade in war-torn Cormyr.

13. Horsewater Pool: An open well serving all passersby, the Horsewater Pool is a local gathering place for neighborly gossip.

14. Haresk's Pool: Local legends hold that a bandit captain of old hid a great treasure at the bottom of this pool. Every so often someone tries to dredge it up and finds nothing more interesting than muck and weeds.

15. House of the High Councilor: High Councilor of Mistledale Haresk Malorn owns a general store in the town and considerable lands nearby. He is no warrior or great lord, but he's an honest and wise merchant who is well liked by folk in the town. Haresk's house is the largest in Ashabenford, so the dale's Council of Six uses it as a

seat of government. Plans to build a separate council building or hall have gathered dust for years, since no one really wants to pay for an expensive public building.

16. Black Eagle Coster: Iletian Blackeagle (LN male human Ftr3) buys local grain, cheese, ale, and barrels of salted meat for sale in Hillsfar and Harrowdale.

17. Almaes the Alchemist: Almaes (NG male gnome Wiz3/Exp3), more properly known as Almaestaddamir Auldcastle, produces and sells a variety of useful alchemical mixtures, including tanglefoot bags, sunrods, acid, antitoxin, and the occasional batch of smokepowder. He cheerfully proposed to build a machine for flinging kegs of smokepowder into battle as a surprise for the next band of drow troublemakers, but High Councilor Haresk politely declined.

18. Jhaer Brightsong's House: A restless traveler, Jhaer Brightsong (CG female moon elf Brd6) is very rarely at home. She is known as the best minstrel in Mistledale, but she spends her time wandering all the Dales, and some of the nearby lands as well. She delights in stories of old magic and doom averted, and sometimes aids adventurers who share their tales with her.

19. Noristuor the Mage: Renowned for his habitual sour manner, sharp tongue, and frightening appearance, the wizard Noristuor (N male tiefling Wiz8) took up residence in Ashabenford to avoid stupid interruptions in his researches—which he explains loudly and in profane terms to anyone causing said interruptions. The folk of Ashabenford don't like Noristuor, but he keeps to himself and on rare occasions consents to work magic for the town's benefit.

20. Barracks of the Riders: This walled compound is the headquarters of the Riders of Mistledale. The Riders train Ashabenford's militia in the courtyard and use the small keephouse as the town jail.

Troublemakers are likely to be imprisoned here until the High Councilor decides what to do with them.

21. Arvien's House: This is the home of Arvien Blackhair (LE female human Exp2/Rog4), a tin and pewtersmith with a reputation as the nosiest person in town. Arvien is actually a Zhent spy who carefully watches the activities of the council and the movements of the Riders. She is very good at her job, and the townsfolk, ignorant of her duplicitous mission, have suggested she might make a good Councilor.

The Dark Road: This little-traveled forest path cuts through Cormanthor to Essembra. It would be traveled more often by nonelves if it didn't come so close to the Vale of Lost Voices. For the Mistrans, the only consolation about the proximity of the Vale of Lost Voices is that the place is even harder on drow than on humans. Luring drow pursuers into the Vale wouldn't be a bad tactic if the fleeing person cared more about hurting the drow than saving his or her own skin.

Galath's Roost: Some fifteen miles from Glen, a couple miles inside Cormanthor, this ruined bandit's keep is rumored to hold great treasure. The tales are enough to draw occasional adventuring parties. None have found the great treasure said to lie somewhere in the flooded tunnels beneath the keep, but more than one has had to fight against villains and monsters searching for something themselves.

Glen (Village, 701): This dwarven village of stone-and-thatch cottages has a secret. The "Deep Mine" on the outskirts of town isn't a mine at all, but a tunnel into the Underdark. It allows the dwarves of Glen to trade with their fellows as far away as the Great Rift, via an amazing Underdark tunnel called the Long Road that runs south under the entire length of the Sea of Fallen Stars.

The secret of Deep Mine has started to leak into the general Mistledale community. Mistrans might be more concerned about the Underdark connection if they weren't already fighting off the Auzkovyn and House Jaelre drow. At least Glen's dwarves do a good job of policing their Underdark passageways, unlike some worshipers of Tempus in Battledale that the Mistrans could name.

Peldan's Helm (Hamlet, 210): This tiny village of stone-walled cottages is humanity's foothold in the Beast Country at Mistledale's western end. Hunters from Sembia, Cormyr, and elsewhere in Faerûn come here to track magnificent prizes. Some hunters end up as prey themselves.

REGIONAL HISTORY

Though sometimes overlooked by those who keep an eye on the armed strength of the Dalelands, the Mistrans are anything but soft. As recently as 1356 DR, the Riders of Mistledale (with a little help) defeated Lashan of Scardale and his army. In war, as in peace, Mistledale has had a charmed career.

In the current year, some say that Mistledale's luck may have finally run out. Of all the Dales, Mistledale is suffering the most from pressure brought to bear by the Vhaeraunian drow in Cormanthor. It used to be that only the western side of Mistledale was subject to monstrous incursions, but now the entire dale is on edge, never knowing where the next fight with the drow may flare up.

The Riders who turned back the Zhents' seven-thousand-strong warrior army during the Time of Troubles have had less success against the drow. Unlike the Zhents, the drow are fighting a campaign of stealth and sudden retreat. Mistledale's defenders do not yet know that several different groups of drow live in Cormanthor, or that their principal antagonists are the drow under the command of Jezz of House Jaelre.

PLOTS AND RUMORS

More than anything else, the High Councilor and the Riders under his command want to determine where the drow raiders are coming from and just how many of them there are, and then strike back. So far, efforts to locate the Vhaeraunian drow and drive them away from Mistledale have failed.

The Black Network: A Sembian merchant is killed on the Moonsea Ride by a party of drow raiders who are quickly driven off by Riders of Mistledale. On the body the Riders discover a sealed letter in code that, on translation, turns out to be a detailed description of Haresk's efforts to bolster Ashabenford's defenses. Apparently, a Zhent spy in Ashabenford dispatched the report with the Sembian. Who is the spy, and what else has he or she learned? Do the Zhents have plans to strike at Mistledale?

scardale

Capital: Chandlerscross
Population: 125,015 (94% humans, 3% half-orcs, 2% halflings)
Government: Republic (anarchy)
Religions: Tempus, Tymora
Imports: Illicit substances, manufactured goods, oil
Exports: Ale, grain, vegetables
Alignment: LN, N, CE

Shattered by wars it started, occupation by its enemies, and a horrible plague, Scardale might have gone the way of Teshendale. Scardalefolk, though, are made of sturdy stuff. In order to put their dale back on its feet, they have washed their hands of their former capital, the port of Scardale Town where the Ashaba empties into the Sea of Fallen Stars.

Scardale Town is in virtual anarchy, but the other major towns of the dale—Scarsdeep and Chandlerscross—are recovering from the disasters that beset Scardale over the last fifteen years and are slowly rebuilding the dale's strength. Meanwhile, the Sembians and the Zhents are the most powerful factions in Scardale Town.

LIFE AND SOCIETY

The port of Scardale Town has yet to recover from the triple blows of the defeat in Mistledale, the occupation, and the plague. Power has shifted away from the port town to the farming and mercantile communities of the interior, especially since many common folk fled Scardale Town to live with relatives farther inland.

The present government of the dale is a nine-person council. The nominal head of the council is Provisional Governor Khelvos Dermmen (LN male human Ftr4/Clr4 of Torm), a priest chosen to replace the previous lord Myrian Beechwood on his resignation. Four members apiece are chosen from the two towns of Chandlerscross and Scarsdeep, and an additional member is chosen at random from among the farms along the Ashaba. Until the Scardale plague drove the garrisons from Scardale Town, the council numbered thirteen and included the Sembian, Zhent, Hillsfarian, and Dalelands garrison commanders from Scardale Town, although in practice the garrison commanders rarely bothered to attend the Scardale Council and frequently ignored its edicts.

MAJOR GEOGRAPHICAL FEATURES

Scardale's three significant geographical features are the River Ashaba, which runs through the dale from west to east; the Sea of Fallen Stars at the river's mouth; and the great gorge named the Scar, which gives the dale its name.

Illustration by Carlo Arellano

Four Dolphins Fountain, Scardale

The Scar: According to legend, this high-sided gorge is the result of an errant blow from the sword of Corellon Larethian as he fought the orc god Gruumsh. The wound is still deep but has healed well, and the River Ashaba runs swiftly through the Scar on its final leg to the sea. The Scar is fifteen to twenty miles wide for most of its length. Feather Falls marks the gorge's west end, and Scardale Town is at the east end where the Ashaba empties into the Sea of Fallen Stars.

Scardale Town's decline has led to the rise of a new port farther up the Ashaba, the town of Chandlerscross within the Scar. Ocean-going ships cannot proceed all the way to Chandlerscross. Even small boats have to unload and seek portage at Feather Falls.

IMPORTANT SITES

Scardale Town lost its preeminence as the balance of power shifted to the towns and country folk of the interior.

Chandlerscross (Large Town, 4,790): The chaos that overcame Scardale Town has no hold on Chandlerscross. The town is clean, the paint on the wooden houses is fresh, and the city watch—consisting entirely of Scardalefolk, with no foreign troops to run things—is quietly competent. Though not mindful of the original Dalelands charter, the citizens of Chandlerscross generally feel that cooperation with the rest of the Dales could be a fine thing, as long as the other Dales keep their troops out of Scardale and their spies in Sembia and Cormyr.

In partnership with the nearby town of Scarsdeep, Chandlerscross serves as the seat of Scardale's government. Provisional Governor Khelvos Dermmen administers the dale from a small keep overlooking the Ashaba, and for routine business the Scardale Council meets here.

Scardale Town (Large Town, 4,440 [formerly Small City, 11,099]): Before the plague, Scardale Town had more than 10,000 occupants, making it the largest and most powerful city of the Dales. Even so damaged, it's still big by Dales' standards. The population has recovered somewhat since the plague. For every honest citizen who fled the city, one or two rogues or bandits moved in, finding life in Scardale more appealing than life on the run in the Dalelands forests.

Only the bravest, strongest, or most evil merchants bring their cargoes in through Scardale's formerly flourishing port. Even so, the port is at least as busy as it was during the years of the occupation, which says something about how many brave and unscrupulous merchants roam the Sea of Fallen Stars.

Since no larger governments were willing to take a chance on occupying Scardale after the plague, the city runs itself by the laws of anarchy, the obligations of power politics, and the double-edged knives of friendship. In Scardale's present topsy-turvy condition, the only things that matter are the identity and intentions of the groups presently struggling to gain control over the city.

One site in Scardale Town deserving of mention is Four Dolphins Fountain. Somehow, this beautiful statue of four leaping dolphins survived Scardale's turmoil. The courtyard surrounding it is in the center of Scardale Town's port district. Not only is it beloved by folk for its calm and beauty, it is also valued by those who want privacy and discretion because it generates a magical effect that prevents all scrying and eavesdropping magic from working in the courtyard.

Whenever possible, members of the Thayan enclave arrange their deals at Four Dolphins Fountain. They wish to give Dalesfolk the sense that they can shop for precious magic items without having to worry about being watched by prying wizards from other dales.

REGIONAL HISTORY

After inheriting the throne from his father Uluf, Lord Lashan Aumersair set about building Scardale's power and wealth, intending to conquer all the southern dales. In 1356 DR, he conquered Harrowdale, Featherdale, and, for a time, Battledale. He then moved against Mistledale and its ally Shadowdale, but was soundly defeated by a hasty alliance of several dales and foreign powers who had no wish to see the region united under a single, powerful leader like Lashan.

After Lashan's fall, Scardale was occupied by an uneasy coalition of troops from Cormyr, Sembia, the other dales, and even Zhentil Keep. Lashan's actions had threatened the security of the entire Heartlands region, so all the great powers of the Heartlands needed to play a part in seeing that the threat was not repeated. In truth, the Sembians and Zhents wanted to keep Scardale for themselves, so they instructed their garrisons to work to those ends.

By 1370 DR, Sembia felt ready to assert its power. The Cormyrian and other Dalelands forces had already left, Hillsfar's troops had been bribed, and no one would protest overmuch if the Sembians drove the Zhents from the dale. Before the Sembians could act, Scardale suffered its second great disaster, the Shaking Plague. The Sembian garrison was particularly hard hit: Only three members survived. The towns and countryside of Scardale were hurt far less by the plague.

What's left of Scardale Town is a lawless area fought over by gangs, agents of the various realms, cultists and religious leaders. The other dales talk about establishing a new interim government to control Scardale Town and prevent things from getting any worse, but Governor Khelvos and his Scardale Council are opposed to continuing the occupation in any guise. Given the other dales' troubles with the Zhents and the arrival of the Cormanthor drow, few are willing to push ahead against the sullen resistance of the Scardalefolk.

While Khelvos and the rest of the Council work hard to put the countryside back on its feet and consider the question of how to reestablish the rule of law in their largest city, a growing number of Scardalefolk openly hope for the return of the Aumersair family. No Aumersair heirs have come forward, and Lashan's fate is still not known, but a document discovered recently has jolted the Provisional Council and sent a shock of alarm through the other dales. Lashan's will and testament, discovered in Scardale Town months after the plague, identifies the Zhent knight Scyllua Darkhope (see her entry in the Moonsea, below) as Lashan's illegitimate daughter and names her as his heir.

The news that the "rightful" heir of the Aumersair family is a Zhent champion received mixed reactions in the dale. Some Scardalefolk believe that Scyllua would make a fine lord and openly support the return of Aumersair rule in any form. Most think that Scardale Town and its former ruling line are problems that their dale would be better off without. In any event, Scyllua has not come to Scardale to assert her claim, although it's not clear what exactly would happen if she did.

FACTIONS IN SCARDALE

While Scardale Town is ungoverned at the moment, it isn't completely lawless. Several factions all work to enforce their own sort of order on the chaos of the city.

The Dancers: These halfling fighter-rogues generally arm themselves with magically enhanced kukris. They seem to be nothing more than common brigands looking for an opportunity to wring as much gold as possible from the chaos in the city. The Dancers are quick to assert their strength with blade and bolt. Their boast: "One dance with a Dancer is all you get."

The Long Death: Monks of the Long Death have taken advantage of Scardale's dissolution to establish a school in old warehouses of the port district. Their existence isn't exactly public, but the players on the political landscape hope to use the monks for their own ends instead of making enemies of them.

The Silver Ravens: Official Sembian policy is to leave Scardale alone until the mystery of the Shaking Plague is solved. The Silver Ravens follow Miklos Selkirk (see Sembia, below), not the Sembian government, and Miklos has no intention of watching the Zhents steal the prize that Sembia had in its grasp. Miklos's fondest hope is to reform Scardale Town as a free port on the Sea of Fallen Stars that pays lip service to the Dales Compact. He thinks that "Silverdale" has a nice ring to it.

Thayan Enclave: The Red Wizards of Thay have a medium-sized enclave operating in Scardale Town. As usual, they sell magic items to anyone who pays their eminently fair prices. The Red Wizards operating in Scardale are of neutral alignments, and consequently, the Thayans are among the most trustworthy power groups operating in Scardale. Even the Harper agents in the area treat them with some forbearance, since the Red Wizards in Scardale scrupulously avoid slaving.

Zhentil Keep: The Dalesfolk are weighing what to make of Scyllua's right to the throne of Scardale—assuming that the whole thing isn't a Zhent ruse. Zhentarim agents in the town are laying the groundwork for Scyllua's eventual bid for power, but old habits die hard, and some Zhent agents engage in their usual routines of sabotage, kidnapping, extortion, and murder.

PLOTS AND RUMORS

The great questions troubling Scardale are easily asked, and not so easily answered. Is the occupation over? Who rules in Scardale Town?

For the first question, the answer would seem to be yes, provided Scardale Town is not included. The folk of Scardale are running their own affairs and have done so for years. But sooner or later the Provisional Governor must be replaced with a lord, a high councilor, or some kind of permanent position, and it's unclear how Khelvos Dermmen's successor will be chosen. Factions of Scardalefolk, some aided and abetted by foreign powers and interests, are beginning to maneuver for the upper hand when the time comes to declare Scardale's independence again. Some of this maneuvering involves quiet threats, the building-up of armed forces, and large bribes and sordid doings of all kinds.

Regarding the rule of Scardale Town, the first power to land a couple of hundred troops in the harbor is likely to claim the city—unless the other powers are willing to dispute the issue with troops of their own.

shadowdale

Capital: Shadowdale
Population: 14,020 (humans 78%, half-elves 8%, elves 6%, gnomes 4%, halflings 3%)
Government: Elected lordship
Religions: Chauntea, Lathander, Tymora (Mielikki, Silvanus)
Imports: Jewelry, manufactured items, ore
Exports: Ale, looted magic items, produce
Alignment: CG, NG, CN

Shadowdale is the best known of all the Dales because of its history of successful battles against drow, Zhents, and would-be conquerors

Spiderhaunt Woods

Illustration by Carlo Arellano

such as Lashan of Scardale. Although small, Shadowdale makes up in quality what it lacks in quantity of citizens. The dale is notorious as a home for adventurers who now prefer a quieter life but are capable of exerting extreme force when necessary.

LIFE AND SOCIETY

Though not quite as spread out as Battledale, Shadowdale's population lives beyond town walls or village fences, in small farms and cottages that may be within eyesight of a neighbor's chimney but not within earshot of that neighbor's disputes.

The folk of Shadowdale have a history of choosing their lords by popular acclaim. The last two lords were suggested by Khelben "Blackstaff" Arunsun of Waterdeep, but the tradition still holds, marking Shadowdale's proud refusal to be ruled by anyone but the most deserving heroes. The town of Shadowdale is the center of the dale's civic life and the home of its heroes, its lord, and the lord's militia.

MAJOR GEOGRAPHICAL FEATURES

Unlike Mistledale to the west, which was swept clean by a meteorite, Shadowdale alternates patches of cleared land with small forests and thick brush. The Northride between Cormyr and the Moonsea runs south to north through the dale, and the River Ashaba cuts west to east. The town of Shadowdale and the looming presence of the Old Skull dominate the forested area where the Northride and the Ashaba cross.

Old Skull: When the drow ruled Shadowdale, this white granite promontory located on the north side of the Northride and just east of the River Ashaba loomed over the town like a message from the

grave, a sign of bad things to come. Now that the dale is free and has proven itself against many enemies, its folk think of the big white dome fondly. Shepherds herd their sheep from town into the hills beyond the Skull, which keeps its sparse vegetation from getting any thicker.

Beneath the surface, Old Skull tells a different tale. The Twisted Tower was only the tip of the drow's power in the dale. Old Skull's depths descend to the Underdark itself. Nowadays, Old Skull's monstrous inhabitants seldom trouble the townspeople, particularly not since 1350 DR, when Elminster took up residence in an abandoned windmill on the south side of the hill. Adventurers who insist on finding routes into the old volcanic dome pass beyond Elminster's zone of protection and must rest their hopes for survival upon their wits. Every few years, adventuring groups confide that they have cleaned Old Skull out once and for all, but an equal number of Old Skull's Underdark residents can boast that they taught the Shadowdale fools the price for trespassing.

Shadow Gap: This pass through the Desertsmouth Mountains south of Shadowdale marks several borders. First, Shadow Gap is the place where the Desertsmouth Mountains give way to the Thunder Peaks. Second, Shadow Gap separates the eastern lands controlled by the Dales from the western lands controlled by Cormyr. Third, now that Tilverton is a smoking black pit, Shadow Gap marks the point where travelers from the north gird themselves to pass by that magical ruin.

Spiderhaunt Woods: Sorcerers and wizards whose spell components call for the webs, eggs, or fangs of giant spiders have cause to venture into this dark forest. All others are well advised to keep a wary eye on the tree line as they ride along the Northride Trail toward Shadowdale or Shadow Gap. Ettercaps and chitines are known to swarm out of the woods to seize captives and drag them away.

IMPORTANT SITES

Most noteworthy sites in the dale cluster in or around the town of Shadowdale in the forest at the valley's western end.

Druid's Grove: Just outside Shadowdale's town limits to the northwest, one of Faerûn's most powerful druidic circles previously met to conduct rituals to increase the strength of the forest. The circle disbanded some time after the Time of Troubles. Powerful druids who may have been members of the Circle occasionally visit the old clearing and its circle of ancient menhirs, but none comment upon the Circle's current whereabouts.

The grove is undoubtedly a place of power. The ancient standing stones hold many secrets, some of which could be used to help fight the battle against the drow of the forest.

Elminster's Tower: If Elminster is not the most powerful mortal being in Faerûn, it's not clear who is. He lives in an unpretentious tower that looks like an old silo or windmill on the south side of the Old Skull. He doesn't encourage visitors.

Morningdawn Hall: Even Lathander might blush at the ostentation of his temple in the town of Shadowdale. The building is a miracle of unbreakable rose-tinted glass blown into the shape of a giant phoenix, its wings outstretched to greet the dawn. Bane himself destroyed the first version of Morningdawn Hall during the Time of Troubles. Lathander's zealous clergy then recreated it in every detail—to the private dismay of Shadowdale's residents, who think highly of Lathander himself but not so well of the priests who have twice raised this gaudy monstrosity in their town.

Old Skull Inn: The inn at the base of Old Skull is around one hundred years old. It's known throughout the Heartlands as one of the finest adventurer lairs in Faerûn, so much so that in lands outside the Dales, adventurers use "oldskull" as an adjective to describe an excellent place to drink. The proprietor, Jhaele Silvermane (NG female human Exp2/Ftr4), has a no-nonsense approach that endears her to her regular patrons and rids her quickly of skulkers and layabouts. Many adventurers hint that the tavern's cellars have secret passageways into the Underdark beneath Old Skull itself, a rumor that seems so obviously true to anyone with the least bit of experience in these matters that whispers to this effect are enough to mark someone as a novice.

Shadowdale (Small Town, 1,402): Shadowdale's sleepy appearance and the retiring ways of its people have lulled half a dozen would-be conquerors into underestimating their target. Inside these sturdy wood and stone buildings, built to survive winters that send Sembians trotting back to the warm plains, Dalesfolk maintain a curious balance between commonplace lives and unshakeable courage and determination.

Unlike the folk of other Dalelands towns situated along trade routes, Shadowdale's people don't go out of their way to cater to merchants, nor do they turn caravan folk aside. They just refuse to orient their civic life around the needs of traders who are just passing through.

Twisted Tower: If the ability to withstand overwhelming powerful Zhent invasions is an indicator, the helix-shaped Twisted Tower is the strongest fortress in the Dales. The tower earned its name because of its off-balance appearance. The lord of Shadowdale, Mourngrym, rules from this former drow stronghold. The tower's garrison is nearly a hundred members strong. The tower is presently used as a landing site for hippogriffs that serve as aerial mounts for several of the Tower's guards.

REGIONAL HISTORY

Before the founding of Shadowdale, Lolth-worshiping drow took advantage of the fall of Myth Drannor to conquer the area known as the Land Under Shadow. Humans and elves fought the drow for nearly two centuries, until the great water wizard Ashaba drove the dark elves from the Twisted Tower in 906 DR. For his trouble, the people of Shadowdale proclaimed Ashaba their first lord.

In the four centuries since Shadowdale's founding, the Pendant of Ashaba, the magical symbol signifying Shadowdale's lordship, was passed to good men, great men (Aencar the Mantled King), and a couple of false kings. The worst of the lot, a deceiver named Jyordhan, became lord of Shadowdale in 1339 DR, ruling first in secret, then openly, on behalf of the Zhents. Jyordhan was killed six years later by the wizard Khelben of Waterdeep, who later supported a new candidate for lordship, an adventurer named Doust Soulwood.

The present lord, Mourngrym Amcathra (NG male human Ftr8) was suggested by Khelben when Soulwood retired. For services rendered to Lord Soulwood and the dale, the people acclaimed Mourngrym as lord. He wed a Cormyrian agent named Shaerl Rowanmantle (LN female human Rog8), who soon renounced her allegiance to Cormyr to work for the good of her adopted people. The couple has a fourteen-year-old son, Scotti. Mourngrym has raised the boy as if he is to inherit the lordship from his father, a proposition that may test the dale's resolve to avoid hereditary rulers.

Given Shadowdale's history as a battle zone between humans and drow, it's ironic that Lord Mourngrym has thus far kept his military out of the struggle against the Vhaeraunian drow. The surface drow settling into Cormanthor have chosen not to raid or infiltrate Shadowdale. Other dales accuse Mourngrym of turning his back on the Dalelands' common plight. The truth is probably that Mourngrym is more worried about other threats that he does not discuss out loud for fear of distressing the anxious delegates to the Dales Council.

PLOTS AND RUMORS

Adventurers come to Shadowdale for three reasons: to explore the Underdark caverns below the Old Skull, to mount forays into the Elven Court, or to pester Elminster for some tiny glimmer of his knowledge. Few of those who come to Shadowdale for the third reason leave with much satisfaction, although on occasion they learn something.

Not from Around Here: A curious group of adventurers accumulates in the Old Skull Inn over the period of a fortnight. Although they drift in from all different roads, they know each other and share a military bearing, even the magicians. As they gather supplies and make plans, it becomes clear that they intend to explore Castle Krag (see Chapter 8, "Known Dungeons of Faerûn") in force. The group could be Silver Ravens from Sembia, or a War Wizard party from Cormyr. In any case, they appear to have a line on information that has eluded the PCs—for one thing, they seem far more competent than necessary for simple exploration of Castle Krag.

If the PCs simply turn their back on the problem, the military group succeeds and takes semipermanent possession of Castle Krag, or fails spectacularly, releasing a gibbering evil upon Shadowdale. Elminster and similar pillars of the community are waging larger battles, forcing the PCs to sort out the mess.

STORM SILVERHAND

Female human (Chosen of Mystra) Rog1/Ftr4/Sor12/Brd8/Hrp3: CR 32; Medium-size humanoid; HD 1d6+8 plus 4d10+32 plus 12d4+96 plus 3d6+24; hp 226; Init +8; Spd 30 ft.; AC 28 (touch 16, flat-footed 24); Atk +18/+13/+8 melee (1d8+9/19–20, *+1 luck longsword*) or +16/+11/+6 ranged touch (by spell); SA Sneak attack +1d6; SQ Bardic music, bardic knowledge +10, Chosen immunities, Chosen spell-like abilities, detect magic, enhanced Constitution, favored enemy (Zhentarim +1); Harper abilities, Harper knowledge, epic-level benefits, electricity immunity, locate traps, silver fire, spell healing; AL CG; SV Fort +18, Ref +15, Will +18; Str 18, Dex 18, Con 26, Int 15, Wis 16, Cha 18. Height 6 ft. 2 in.

Skills and Feats: Balance +9, Bluff +6, Climb +8, Concentration +23, Decipher Script +6, Diplomacy +12, Disable Device +6, Disguise +6, Gather Information +9, Heal +10, Hide +18, Jump +5, Knowledge (arcana) +12, Knowledge (the Dales local) +6, Knowledge (religion) +6, Listen +15, Move Silently +24, Open Lock +8, Perform (dance, sing) +16, Pick Pocket +8, Profession (herbalist) +8, Ride (horse) +9, Scry +12, Search +8, Sense Motive +9, Spellcraft +17, Spot +11, Tumble +8, Use Magic Device +9, Use Rope +8, Wilderness Lore +6; Alertness, Blind-Fight, Combat Casting, Craft Wondrous Item, Dodge, Endurance, Improved Initiative, Iron Will, Luck of Heroes, Weapon Focus (longsword), Weapon Specialization (longsword).

Special Qualities: Bardic Music: Countersong, fascinate, inspire competence, inspire courage, suggestion; Chosen Immunities: Storm is unaffected by attacks that duplicate these effects: *charm person, circle of death, disintegrate, fear, feeblemind, fireball, maze, meteor swarm, misdirection, prismatic spray.* Chosen Spell-like Abilities: 1/day—*detect thoughts, identify, legend lore, Simbul's synostodweomer* (converts prepared spells into 2 hit points of healing per spell level), *stoneskin, teleport, water breathing.* Detect Magic (Su): Line of sight. Electricity Immunity: Storm is immune to natural forms of electricity such as lightning. Enhanced Constitution: The Chosen of Mystra template adds +10 to Storm's Constitution. Epic-level Benefits: Five effective levels of bard and three of Harper scout (included in the above totals). Harper Abilities: Deneir's eye (+2 holy bonus against glyphs, runes and symbols), Skill Focus (Perform), Skill Focus (Sense Motive), Tymora's smile (+2 luck bonus on one saving throw each day). Silver Fire (Su): See Chapter 2 for details. Spell Healing: These spells give her temporary hit points (expiring after 1 hour) instead of causing harm: *magic missile, lightning bolt, ice storm, chain lightning.*

Bard Spells Known (3/4/4/2; base DC 14+ spell level; arcane spell failure 20%): 0—*dancing lights, daze, flare, open/close, read magic, resistance;* 1st—*charm person, cure light wounds, feather fall, identify;* 2nd—*cure moderate wounds, daylight, invisibility, suggestion;* 3rd—*blink, cure serious wounds, scrying.*

Sorcerer Spells Known (6/7/7/7/5/3; base DC 14+ spell level; arcane spell failure 20%): 0—*arcane mark, detect magic, disrupt undead, ghost sound, light, mage hand, mending, ray of frost, read magic;* 1st—*cause fear, comprehend languages, jump, magic missile, spider climb;* 2nd—*arcane lock, cat's grace, mirror image, see invisibility, web;* 3rd—*dispel magic, fly, hold person, tongues;* 4th—*charm monster, dimension door, minor creation;* 5th—*hold monster, teleport;* 6th—*antimagic field.*

Harper Spells Known (2/1; base DC 14+ spell level; arcane spell failure 20%): 1st—*change self, charm person, comprehend languages, erase, feather fall, jump, light, message, mount, read magic, scatterspray, sleep, spider climb;* 2nd—*cat's grace, darkvision, detect thoughts, eagle's splendor, invisibility, knock, locate object, magic mouth, misdirection, see invisibility, shadow mask.*

Possessions: Amulet of natural armor +5, +2 elven chainmail, cloak of elvenkind, boots of elvenkind, ring of protection +2, ring of spell storing, amulet of proof against detection and location, tiara of major fire resistance, +1 luck longsword (1 wish remaining), 2 potions of cure serious wounds (10th), buckle of feather falling and warmth. Through her Harper connections, Storm has access to many other items given sufficient time.

The famous Bard of Shadowdale is known for her merry manner and her bold adventures as a leader of the Harpers. She approaches life with endless high spirit and gusto, has little personal arrogance, and spends much time training young Harpers, protecting Shadowdale against its foes, and aiding unhappy youngsters. About all that upsets Storm is the unhappiness of good folk; working to make others happy drives her through the days.

Folk of Shadowdale see her as their local healer, midwife, herbalist, and a fellow farmer who'll pitch in to help them at harvesttide, bringing along several willing Harpers to serve as unpaid, somewhat skilled "hands." They bring their injured and sick to her—and no matter what the hour, Storm greets them all with a smile and a gentle hand. Children love her, the common folk adore her, and the elves of Evereska awarded her with high noble titles never before given to a human.

The stupidity of rulers causes her exasperation—but deliberate misuse of authority infuriates her. Storm's grim, get-even temper leads her to arrange "poetic justice" (punishment fitting the crime) for swindlers, thieves, arsonists and vandals, and tyrants—and she'll combat such foes with no thought for her personal safety, but a deep regard for what danger her actions may bring upon others. Rulers whom she thinks can be "rescued" by education or guidance, she'll work with. The Harpers regard her as their most valuable member. Others may be more powerful or wiser, but Storm is the perfect teacher and inspiration. She's also a personal favorite of the goddess Mystra, who several times whisked her away from certain death (though Storm never expects or counts on such aid).

Storm Silverhand

Illustration by Todd Lockwood

Tasseldale

Capital: Tegal's Mark
Population: 14,020 (humans 94%, halflings 2%, gnomes 2%, half-elves 1%)
Government: Republic
Religions: Tyr
Imports: Gold, jewels, silver, tin
Exports: Fine manufactured goods, pottery, textiles
Alignment: LG, LN, N

Tasseldale sits north and east of the Arch Wood, southwest of Featherdale, and just barely north of Sembia. Tasseldale is a dale of craftsfolk and tradesfolk, heavily influenced by Sembia. Archenfolk and members of the Dales Council express surprise that Sembia hasn't formally annexed Tasseldale. The truth is that Sembia prefers having Tasseldale as an independent buffer state to the north. Sembia won't annex Tasseldale the way it turned Moondale into Ordulin until it can also take over the dales that truly matter to the north.

"Tassel" is the local word for town. The twelve tassels in Tasseldale shelter a bit over half of the dale's inhabitants. The tassels would pass for hamlets only in other lands.

LIFE AND SOCIETY

The Tassadrans are for the most part a contented lot, an orderly collection of craftsfolk, small farmers, traders, and artists who see themselves as Sembia's friends rather than Sembia's clients.

Despite the disdain that some Dalesfolk heap upon them, the Tassadrans tend to be a brave, cool-headed lot who defend their interests when they have need. Unlike other Dalesfolk, they also excel at arranging situations in which they do not have to defend themselves constantly.

A sizable minority of Tassadrans don't particularly care for the life of the free-crafter. Such citizens migrate to other dales for a time, or hunt and trap in the Arch Wood. As if to compensate for the complacency of the rest of their dale, Tassadran woodsfolk have a reputation for hotheadedness that rivals that of the Archenfolk.

MAJOR GEOGRAPHICAL FEATURES

Like Sembia to the south, Tasseldale is largely flat, open land, perfect for farming. Arch Wood to the west provides fur, timber, and hunting for Tassadrans who can't bear to work the loom or plow.

Dun Hills: The Dun Hills run diagonally across the north part of the dale, separating it from Battledale in the north, Deepingdale in the west, and Featherdale's portion of the River Ashaba to the north. Wild ponies are more common than roving goblins here, so the Tassadrans treat the hills as safe land.

Glaun Bog: Southwest of the Dun Hills, the Glaun Bog presents travelers new to the area with obstacles including quicksand, carnivorous plants, and malicious will-o'-wisps. Local Tassadrans know how to pick their way through the Bog to harvest its peat and mine its iron ore without disturbing the undead spirits living in the barrows at its center.

IMPORTANT SITES

Some would argue that Tasseldale has no important sites. Only a Tassadran would argue with them.

Abbey of the Just Hammer: This abbey dedicated to Tyr bears the responsibility for the taming of the Dun Hills. Situated near the River Ashaba, the abbey emphasizes the "justice" aspect of Tyr's portfolio, dispensing free legal education to all who care to journey there for instruction. Given the problems with drow just to the north in Battledale, the abbey is short-staffed. Its former defenders prefer traveling north and fighting in the cause of justice to patrolling the already pacified Dun Hills. Many former defenders have failed to survive their forays into the forest, causing the abbey to soften its hard-line disapproval of adventurers.

Sharburg: Located above Tegal's Mark, the Sharburg is an ancient elven fort converted into the military headquarters of the mounted marshairs (a local variant of "marshals") who police the Dale. If rumors of hidden elven magic within the Sharburg's walls aren't just wishful thinking, it's certain that the Tassadrans have never chosen to summon them up.

Sun Soul Order: Further contributing to the pacification of the Dun Hills, monks of the Sun Soul order refurbished a ruined freehold and turned it into one of the Dalelands' few active monasteries. The order accepts well-qualified students of all nationalities and races, but is exceptionally hard upon would-be monks of Sembian descent.

Tegal's Mark (Small Town, 1,402): The so-called capital of Tasseldale is named after an ancient swordsmith's mark. Citizens of Tegal's Mark are proud of their city's crafts. The quickest way to cause trouble here is to sell inferior merchandise or, worse, inferior merchandise with the claim that it was produced in Tegal's Mark.

REGIONAL HISTORY

The rivalry between the foresters of Archendale and those of certain Tasseldale hamlets such as Archtassel turned violent in 1368, after several Tassadran hunters were murdered by unknown assailants. The citizens of Archendale and Tasseldale now fight a peculiar type of limited war in the Arch Woods.

The Woodsman's War battle depends on the willingness of youths, toughs, soldiers and rangers to wear their side's colors into the Arch Wood. Archenfolk wear black and silver and Tassadrans wear blue and yellow. Those who are beaten senseless or surrender have their colors stripped off and a few bones broken, but they are generally left alive. Several inns in both dales cater to this game by displaying the colors taken from the opposing side.

Female fighters and rangers of the two dales normally avoid involvement in this silly fight, but those women who do participate take it extremely seriously. The phrase "bring a woman to the Woodsman's War" has come to mean that a situation may turn deadly, as female adventurers from both dales have killed rival Woodsmen within the past year.

Dragon Coast

Capital: No unified nation, no capital
Population: 820,800; (humans 92%, halflings 3%, half-elves 2%, gnomes 2%)
Government: Independent city-states and pirate holds
Religions: Helm, Sune, Tempus, Tymora, Umberlee
Imports: Food, precious metals, slaves, trade goods for export
Exports: Ships, trade goods from other nations
Alignment: N, NE, LE

The Dragon Coast consists of the lands and islands on the south shore of a branch of the Sea of Fallen Stars. It's more of a way of life than a geographical area for the three powerful city-states, seven or so major thieves' guilds, dozen pirate bands, and agents of Faerûn's darkest secret societies who live and work here.

To outsiders who don't know how to play the game, the Dragon Coast is a nest of vultures and thieves located in the center of too many otherwise-ideal trading routes. To the initiated (canny Sembian merchants, shrewd rogues, and caravan masters who aren't afraid to grease a palm), the Dragon Coast is a perfect place to get things done . . . to get *anything* done. As the Sembians say, "Everyone has a price. But the price is more reasonable on the Dragon Coast."

No one sneers at anyone else—but no one trusts anyone else, either.

LIFE AND SOCIETY

The veteran caravanmaster Gulkyn Drouthe of Reddansyr once described the Dragon Coast as "Waterdeep without guilds or Watch, and Westgate with its sinister powers reduced to the same swift blades and underhanded spells as the rest of us." A visitor here can expect to meet all kinds of beings, from drow and illithids to beholders and lizardfolk—and the usual poisonous array of unscrupulous mages for hire, doppelgangers and other shapechangers, and anyone on the run from justice elsewhere.

There is no central government. Throughout much of the Dragon Coast there is no government at all, or any law enforcement beyond hireswords and a general, unwritten code of conduct enforced by anyone who cares to take the time to do so. Few do unless they witness an offense that might be directly harmful to them: someone poisoning a well, for example, or using magic to destroy warehouses.

All manner of goods constantly flow through the Dragon Coast. Only three groups of people command universal respect: the healers-for-hire (usually priests of Lathander, Shaundakul, or Waukeen); the Waukeenar-sponsored moneychangers who are forbidden to practice swindles and deceptions; and the coopers and master shippers who craft containers for trade goods and pack them against heat, cold, wet, hard blows, and long falls.

The most important Coast structures—and the only ones likely to be made of stone (aside from the walled cities)—are the warehouses. These are typically fortresses with watchtowers, slate roofs to discourage fire, and (to inhibit thieves' tunneling) concentric stone ring-walls. Many warehouses have undead guards (typically zombies, skeletons, and monster skeletons) activated by opening the closets that confine them. A few boast sleep gas, spike-lined pit traps to capture intruders, and mimics or similar beasts among the stored goods.

Like everything else in regions where coinage is king, there's a clear scale of warehouses from the massive, heavily-guarded stone fortresses down to small hideaway compartments behind sliding walls and within window-sills in even the rudest of dwellings. It's been said that not a hovel in the Sword Coast lacks its hidden storage chamber. Many of these contain goods long-forgotten, left behind when owners were slain or just never returned.

MAJOR GEOGRAPHICAL FEATURES

The natural geography of the Dragon Coast both isolates it and makes it an essential part of Faerûn-wide trade.

Dragonmere: Also known as the Lake of Dragons, this pinched-off arm of the Sea of Fallen Stars serves as the Dragon Coast's quick-access trade route to Cormyr and Sembia. At its widest point, the Dragonmere is almost one hundred miles wide. Its narrowest point, the stretch between Westgate and Urmlaspyr in Sembia, is still ten miles across. Few lakes have the Dragonmere's problems with piracy, sea dragons, and ocean storms, so sailors advise newcomers to treat the voyage with respect.

Giant's Run Mountains: As far as the human inhabitants of the Dragon Coast can remember, the Giant's Run Mountains have never had more than their standard share of hill and stone giant marauders. Obviously, some great civilization of giants occupied the mountains at one time, since dozens of peaks are carved with long spiral staircases (each step of which is four feet high). They also boast rough-hewn palaces scaled for fifty-foot-tall humanoids,

though these are now often occupied by roosting perytons, and gigantic benches positioned for the best view. Humans usually avoid the mountains, which is just as well, given the truth about the region. (See Cairnheim in the Underdark section, below.)

Gulthmere Forest: This wide, tangled forest divides the Dragon Coast from the Vilhon Reach. It is a sprawl of rising uplands dotted with cedars and pines, eventually giving way to the Orsraum Mountains to the south. Gulthmere is noted for rich loads of mineral-bearing rock, particularly topazes and rubies, throughout its length. Prospectors and dwarven miners roam the wooded hills and challenge the native monsters and tribesfolk for the riches within.

The lion-god Nobanion ceaselessly roams the wood to protect it. All the tribes of Gulthmere venerate Nobanion and call on the deity to halt invasions by greedy northerners.

Pirate Isles: The Pirate Isles are a collection of rocky spurs dotting the sea some one hundred miles from the coast of Sembia. A great mountain known as the Dragonspur dominates the largest of the Isles, the Dragonisle (pop. 2,000). The Dragonspur shelters two excellent natural harbors that have been fortified, destroyed, and then fortified again by generations of pirates. Three other secure anchorages are scattered around the island.

At any given time, between twenty and sixty pirate vessels anchor here. Of these, 10% to 20% are beached, docked, or in drydock for repairs.

The pirates of the Isles lack the strength and unity to attack Sembia's ports directly, though they speak of such an operation constantly, encouraged by the legend of Immurk. The pirate king ruled from 1164 DR until 1201 and put Sembian cities to the torch even after they had paid him tribute.

Sea of Fallen Stars: Also known as the Inner Sea, this huge body of water connects the east and west of Faerûn. Through the River Lis, the Inner Sea also connects with the Moonsea to the northeast. The Sea of Fallen Stars was the original migration route for the Chondathan humans who spread out from the Vilhon Reach and settled the center and north of Faerûn.

Cormyr, Sembia, and to some extent the Impilturans maintain powerful navies on the Inner Sea, but for the most part these are merchants' waters rather than warships' domains. Undersea kingdoms of aquatic elves, merfolk, and sahuagin populate the Sea, but surface dwellers have little to do with them aside from violent flare-ups like the sahuagin attacks that battered the coastal human cities of both the Inner Sea and the Trackless Sea in 1369 DR.

The Dragons of the Dragon Coast

A dozen Coasters, if asked what the Dragon Coast's named for, will deliver a dozen different, often scathing, replies. Who has time for such foolishness . . . and how much coin is an answer worth to you, anyway?

Pay a dozen sages to reveal the origin of the term "Dragon Coast"—and you'll reap another dozen different replies!

Most answers begin with mention of the dragon Kisonraath-jisar, slain by Saldrinar of the Seven Spells in −349 DR. (Some tales say Saldrinar imprisoned the wyrm in a scepter, to call forth its powers at will.) Saldrinar founded Westgate on the dragon's lair and proclaimed himself its king. But the list only begins there.

Many identify "the" Purple Dragon of Cormyr, Thauglor, as the inspiration. Others speak of Kuldrak the Many-Taloned, a red wyrm of mountainous size who laired amid the southernmost Thunder Peaks before Thauglor was hatched—and was vanquished

by Rauthstokh "Redbones," the sire of the god-dragon Tchazzar.

Still others favor the fang dragon Arauvrim, a small, vicious predator known for flying low over the water and plucking sailors and fisherfolk from vessels. He preyed fearlessly along the coasts in a ten-season reign of terror that ended when Arauvrim was petrified by a shipborne mage and plunged under the waves, never to be seen again.

Perhaps the most fearsome wyrm of all is Larithylar, who may still live in several possessed bodies (just as she may earlier have possessed some of the dragons described above). A lamia sorceress who devised magic to give herself human, humanoid, and draconic forms, she learned to possess and control true dragons. Until she faked her own death, centuries ago, she was briefly notorious as "the Chameleon Dragon." She may dwell in Westgate, seeking the specific magic items for some dark scheme.

IMPORTANT SITES

Aside from the major cities, other communities are either too tiny (fishing villages, barbarian strongholds in the hills, or small farming settlements) or too transitory (smugglers' strongholds, pirate hideouts, pirate cities, and floating cities made of temporarily lashed-together pirate ships) to be jotted on a map. The Pirate Isles on the eastern edge of the Dragon Coast are thick with freebooters of all stripes, ranging from evil marauders who leave no victim unscarred to swashbucklers who wage personal wars against Thayan or Zhent shipping.

Cedarspoke (Small City, 6,080): This quiet, independent city lies in the heart of the Gulthmere Forest and is more often associated with the Vilhon Reach than the Dragon Coast. The Cedar River flows through the city and splits it in two. The city's inhabitants are druids or people seeking a simple, natural life. The druids of Cedarspoke are not part of the Emerald Enclave (see the Vilhon Reach below and Chapter 7: Organizations for more information), but they seldom oppose the Enclave's activities. The city's most notable landmark is Earthome College, a seat of druidic learning and a repository for perhaps the best collection of historical documents relating to the Vilhon Reach. Zalaznar Crinios (N male human Drd17 of Silvanus) is the undisputed ruler of Cedarspoke, but he is an even-handed and popular tyrant.

Elversult (Small City, 9,728): Elversult is a rich community located south of the Dragonmere at the junction of many trading roads, including the Overmoor Trail and the Trader's Road. Although Elversult is not a port itself, its warehouses are the branching point for trade north to Cormyr and west to the Sword Coast.

Elversult is the least Dragon Coast-ish city on the Dragon Coast. Its present ruler, a former adventurer named Yanseldara (NG female human Ftr11/Sor8) led a brilliant rebellion against the previous necromantic regime. Centuries of smuggling and intrigue cannot be undone in a decade, but those seeking dishonest deals now think twice before taking their business to Yanseldara's city, particularly since she leaves law enforcement to her consort and adventuring companion, Vaerana Hawklyn (CG female human Rgr20 of Mielikki).

That does not mean that assassins, slavers, Banites, and cultists completely avoid Elversult—they simply cloak their movements with magic or operate under the cover of darkness. The Cult of the Dragon in particular has refused to relinquish the city as one of its staging points for operations to the south. Harpers and other adventurers frequently become entangled in thwarting the Cult's assassination schemes, drug running, and poison manufacturing—all of which are means toward their true goal of seeing Faerûn ruled by undead dragons.

Ilipur (Large Town, 2,432) and Pros (Small Town, 1,824): These small ports serve as the loading and unloading points for Elversult. Neither town compares with the true ports of Westgate and Teziir, since shipments need to be loaded onto flat barges and poled out to waiting ships or into shore. Each town has its own Council of Burghers and mayor. "You can't smell the fish for the graft," grumble the merchants of Elversult, who have no choice but to pay the burghers what they want. The alternative is to let their cargoes fall completely into the hands of thieves' guilds such as the Purple Masks and Tide Flowers, or bandit-slavers such as the Men of the Basilisk.

Proskur (Large City, 13,984): Proskur lies just outside Cormyr and the Stormhorn Mountains on the Overmoor Trail. Like most Dragon Coast trading cities, Proskur is run by a merchant council. Unlike other Dragon Coast councils, Proskur's rulers are confessed thieves, former thieves' guild bosses who realized that they could become richer if they became the government instead of always

fighting the government. Ironically, Proskur is now known as a fairly honest region, in the sense that its ruling thieves are up front and efficient. Other covert operatives have difficulties evading its authorities, who have done it all before. The long-time leader of the Proskur council is a brilliant swindler named Leonara Obarstal (NG female human Rog12/Gld3).

Reddansyr (Village, 608): A small town on the road leading to Starmantle, Reddansyr is known as an information clearing-house for adventurers. One might think that the town's fair-sized temple to Oghma would be responsible for this reputation, but the truth is that Oghma's priests are more tight-lipped than usual. Apparently, they resent the ongoing free information exchange that takes place at the Giant's Folly, a festhall located inside an overturned boat that was hauled inland by a fire giant who wanted to win a bet.

Starmantle (Small City, 6,080): For centuries, Starmantle and Westgate have competed for trade moving across the Sea of Fallen Stars. Despite the cities' efforts to crush each other, neither has fallen. In fact, the competition has helped them both, since their price wars have increased the volume of trade moving through the Dragon Coast. Starmantle is somewhat less corrupt than Westgate, but it is deeply aligned with the pirates of the Isles.

Teziir (Small City, 10,944): Built on the ruins of the previous city of Teziir, this city was founded in 1312 DR by a group of merchants who disapproved of Westgate's wickedness and wanted a port on the Dragonmere they could control themselves. The council of merchants continues to rule, maintaining power mostly because its members reward competent employees and terminate business relationships with those who fail them.

Teziir subsidizes construction of temples and shrines to nonevil Faerûnian deities, believing that pilgrims, tithes, and occasional divine miracles are good for business. Consequently, the city has more than its share of temples and minor shrines, and clerics of nearly any of the divine powers can be found somewhere here. Teziir is also plagued by a thieves' guild known as the Astorians which has as many as seven hundred members and has been infiltrated by the Night Masks of Westgate.

Westgate (Metropolis, 29,184): Westgate is the major trading city of the southern coast. It wields enough economic clout to make it the third major trading power of the Inner Sea after Sembia and Cormyr.

The "anything goes and everything has a price" reputation of the Dragon Coast is directly attributable to Westgate, whose citizens are not ashamed of its reputation. On the contrary, they pride themselves on Westgate's status as an open city—open to all races, open to all faiths, and open to all coins. Westgate's noble rulers, all descended from rich merchant houses, believe that personal ethics may be fine for private life but have no place in business.

Willingness to cut any deal has helped the city grow into a major economic power, but it has also created an environment in which thieves view their activities as extensions of normal business by other means. A thieves' guild known as the Night Masks controls nearly as much of Westgate as its official rulers do. The Night Mask assassins, extortionists, enforcers, and spies are for sale to any, meaning that the noble houses who ostensibly oppose the thieves' guild frequently are their best clients.

Temples or shrines to evil deities, including Beshaba, Malar, Shar, and Talona, are sometimes "unmentionable" in polite Westgate society, depending on the fashion of the moment, but there's no doubt that they exist. They have as many devotees as the aboveground temples of Ilmater, Gond, Talos, Mask, and Loviatar (a favorite of several of the decadent noble houses).

The newest addition to Westgate's parade of novelties is a gladiatorial enterprise named the Quivering Thumb, which fled from the collapse of Unther to the city whose rulers would pay the best for bloody circuses. The Quivering Thumb's new sandpit arena is popu-

Westgate arena

lar with nobility, merchants, commoners, and even with slaves, because the Thumb promises freedom and a thousand gold pieces to any slave who can survive a year in the pit. The Thumb is regarded as a "fair-fight" enterprise, in which no side of any given battle is meant to be massacred.

REGIONAL HISTORY

Humans began to settle the Dragon Coast about a thousand years before the beginning of Dalereckoning, emigrating from the realms of Chondath and the Vilhon Reach. Settlements of one sort or another have existed at the sites of the region's towns and cities ever since that long-ago time. The largest of these was Westgate, a human town ruled cruelly by the great dragon Kisonraathiisar.

In −349 DR, the wizard Saldrinar of the Seven Spells destroyed the dragon and became the first human king of Westgate. He and his immediate successors set the city on the road to growth and power, but in −286 DR, Westgate was taken over by Orlak, the Night King. Orlak was a powerful vampire who ruled the city for more than a hundred years until the adventuring paladin Gen Soleilon overthrew him. Orlak died, but his vampire minions fled into the catacombs and selected a new Night King to rule the city's dark underworld. As Westgate's surface rulers changed with the passing years, so too did the Night King's line continue, even to the present day.

More and more folk came to lands along the Sea of Fallen Stars, founding cities and realms. The Pirate Isles were settled by lawless cutthroats and corsairs who owed fealty to no king. In 257 DR, the pirates descended on Westgate and unseated its king, beginning nearly two hundred years of rule by the city's notorious Pirate Kings.

Mulsantir Illistine, a Chondathan mercenary, overthrew the last of the Pirate Kings of Westgate in 429 DR. Mulsantir himself was overthrown in 452 DR by a Shoon wizard called Myntharan the Magus. Over and over again the lordship of Westgate changed hands, while the other free cities of the area grew and failed. The most notorious of Westgate's kings during this time was none other than Iyachtu Xvim the Baneson, who led an army of tief-lings and demons against the city and ruled it in tyranny for twenty-odd years before the rightful heir, Farnath Ilistar, drove him in 734 DR.

In the Pirate Isles, small numbers of corsairs plagued the Inner Sea year after year, but none of these were of any great note until the rise of the first great pirate leader. Immurk began his career in 1164 DR. He fearlessly pillaged all of the powers on the Inner Sea and built up a corsair flotilla of more than a dozen ships. Immurk's agents spied out rich prizes in every major port on the Sea of Fallen Stars and fomented unrest across the region. Immurk died at the helm of his *Sea-Scorpion* in 1201 DR, fighting a Sembian warship.

The growing power of the pirate fleets forced the great realms of the Inner Sea—Cormyr, Sembia, Impiltur, and others—into a temporary alliance in 1209 DR. The united fleets smashed the pirates in a great sea battle that left the Pirate Isles virtually empty for a century.

Westgate's succession of troubled kings culminated in the rule of Verovan, the city's last king. After his death, the nobles decided that Westgate had not flourished under its monarchs and established an elected lord called the Croamarkh as the city's leader. In 1353 DR, the powerful thieves' guild known as the Night Masks arose in Westgate, quickly becoming the rulers of the city in all but name. The guild suffered badly at the hands of adventurers in 1368 DR, but it has recovered from these setbacks. As of the current day, the Night Masks are the strongest power on the Dragon Coast.

In the Pirate Isles the corsairs have slowly rebuilt their strength. Dozens of pirate factions exist in and around the Dragonisle today, preying upon the commerce of the Inner Sea. But no other great

Illustration by Carlo Arellano

leader emerged until the rise of a captain named Samagaer Silverblade in 1364 DR, the Year of the Wave.

Samagaer appeared to be following in Immurk's footsteps, occupying the Dragonisle's largest harbor and gathering as many as a hundred ships beneath his banner. But in 1368 DR Silverblade disappeared, just in time to miss the disastrous battles with undersea creatures that hit the pirates of the Isles nearly as hard as it hit the ports of Sembia. There are rumors that Samagaer Silverblade's lieutenants, who still control half of his original fleet, take orders from him from wherever he is hiding. Only a handful know that Samagaer Silverblade is also the man who would be king of Sembia, the Silver Raven. The Raven makes much of his career as an adventurer, but only his most trusted associates have any idea that he was more successful than he has so far admitted, and that the Pirates of the Isles might be brought to his cause when he judges the time is right.

PLOTS AND RUMORS

It's a rare day when the Dragon Coast isn't crawling with plots and rumors. The Night Masks assassinate, intimidate, sabotage, and murder virtually at will throughout the region. The Fire Knives, members of an assassins' guild exiled from Cormyr, plot to retake the throne held by the Regent Alusair. And Sembian merchants smuggle and scheme in the ports of the region, hoping to make some fast gold in cities where few rules apply.

Princes of the Night: A rash of vampire attacks plagues the powerful merchants and nobles of Westgate. The inner circle of Night Masks has taken a dark and perilous step indeed, and these predatory thieves have now become predators of another sort. The secret leader of the organization is clearly a powerful vampire wizard, supported by a cadre of vampire servitors who can strike anywhere in the city. The rank and file of the organization dare not protest, and the folk of the city can hardly move against the powerful and pervasive guild without provoking a bloodletting of ghastly proportions.

The Hordelands

Capital: None
Population: 133,488 (humans 85%, gnolls 8%, centaurs 5%, dwarves 1%)
Government: Tribal
Religions: Etugen (Grumbar), Teylas (Akadi), local spirits, aspects of Eldath, Malar, and Selûne
Imports: Coffee, metals, paper, rice, sugar, tea
Exports: Gems, leather, livestock, wool
Alignment: CN, CG, N

Often considered a completely barren region, the Hordelands features sparse vegetation, rare oases, and the quarreling tribes of the Tuigan. These horse-riding nomads are best known for their invasion of Faerûn more than a decade ago. Fierce riders expert with their composite shortbows, the nomads are divided among at least ten tribes, living in tents and surviving on meat and milk. Their few permanent settlements center around oases, for water is their most precious commodity.

The superstitious local people are distrustful of strangers, especially after their defeat by the western armies. It will be at least a generation before the Tuigan again pose a significant threat to Faerûn. Dismissed as inconsequential for years, the Hordelands now see increased trade activity between Faerûn and the Kara-Turan empire of Shou Lung far to the east. Traders carry exotic goods to and from each locale, making many rich along the way.

LIFE AND SOCIETY

Life in the Hordelands is harsh, with cold winters, hot summers, poor soil unsuitable for farming, and frequent violent storms. The nomads are forced to wander to survive, letting their tough steppe ponies forage on the sparse vegetation and feeding themselves on livestock, horse milk, and the creatures of the Endless Waste (only part of the vast Hordelands). The Tuigan culture is egalitarian, with children of both sexes trained to ride and use the bow, although men are expected to become warriors while women assume a powerful role in the household. Small dwarven settlements dot the slopes of the Sunrise Mountains, but the two races avoid each other due to language and cultural barriers.

MAJOR GEOGRAPHICAL FEATURES

The great feature of the Hordelands is really a lack of features at all. The Endless Waste and the regions beyond are flat steppelands, shading toward tundra on the northern flank and cold, rocky desert to the south. The land is scoured by fiercely cold winds blowing off the Great Ice Sea in the wintertime, and blasted by dry furnace heat and billowing duststorms in the summer. The great herds of grazing animals represent the wealth of the land, a resource of food, clothing, and shelter that the Tuigan follow from one end of the land to the other in a perpetual migration, season after season.

North of the Endless Waste lies the Great Ice Sea, known to the Tuigan as Yal Tengri. This body of water is frigid and icebound in the winter, inhabited by cold-loving creatures and a wealth of fish and marine life. Though it clears of ice in the summer, in springtime icebergs dot its surface, some of them moving about contrary to winds and currents.

IMPORTANT SITES

The Endless Waste features no permanent cities, few ruins, and even fewer settlements or centers of civilization. The roaming camps of the barbaric Tuigan are the closest thing to civilization that this region knows.

The Dragonwall: Too far east to be seen on Faerûnian maps, past the enormous Quoya Desert, this lengthy wall of brick and stone was built by the Shou to protect their western border. The spirit of a mighty dragon acts as its mortar, and nonmagical weapons do not harm it. The dragon was tricked into this service and can be freed a section at a time with the proper sacrifice. Any communication magic enables talk with the dragon, who gladly tells how to free it. When it pulls itself free, the wall crumbles in that area and the Shou must rebuild it with mundane materials.

The Golden Way: Perhaps the most famous of Faerûn's trade routes, the Golden Way runs from the city of Telflamm on the Easting Reach, through Thesk and Rashemen around the Sunrise Mountains, and then across the Hordelands all the way to Shou Lung. While there is little need for a road or even a beaten trail in the steppes, the Golden Way is marked by a series of encampments and caravanserai providing safe haven and shelter for those merchants who dare the months-long journey.

Winterkeep: This ruin shows little on the surface but cracked pillars and stacks of stone. Once the winter palace of Raumatharan kings, its underground levels are richly appointed, and rumors tell of hidden treasure vaults, armories, and granaries. It is not known what remains, as no one has made an extensive exploration of its interior.

REGIONAL HISTORY

Thousands of years ago, this area was once part of the Imaskar empire, ruled by powerful wizards. Since that time a succession of great empires have claimed the Hordelands, including Mulhorand, Raumathar, and Shou Lung. Few of these claims meant much, for none bothered to settle or fortify the area. For centuries now the Endless Waste has been ignored by other nations, leaving the Tuigan nomads to do as they wish in their native land, which they call Taan.

After the Time of Troubles, an ambitious Tuigan noble named Yamun killed his father to assume leadership of his tribe. With charisma, force, and strategy, he united the tribes of the Endless Waste and formed them into an army three hundred thousand strong, claiming the title Yamun Khahan. The great chieftain invaded Faerûn and Kara-Tur in 1360 DR. The horde fought against Rashemen, Thay, and Thesk, and was finally stopped later that year by an alliance of Faerûnian powers including Cormyr, Zhent orcs, dwarves from the Earthfast Mountains, Sembian mercenaries, and Dalesfolk. Reduced to less than seventy thousand capable warriors, the Tuigan people returned to the Taan to lick their wounds and rebuild their strength.

PLOTS AND RUMORS

For most people, simply surviving a few days of travel across the Hordelands is an adventure, albeit a boring, exhausting, and miserable one.

City of the Dead: A ruined city has been discovered in the wastes. The nomads avoid it, citing evil spirits and many curses, but those on the caravan route from Kara-Tur say the city holds magic and treasure from Netheril, Raumathar, or Imaskar itself. The ruins are pushing themselves upward from the ground, as if rebuilding themselves for their old inhabitants.

The Tuigan Scouts: A new leader among the nomads seeks information about the lands to the west and has been sending eager young ones on journeys of knowledge. These travelers avoid Thay and Rashemen, entering through Narfell to the Inner Sea, where they study everyone they meet, bring back interesting items and found valuables, and (some say) avenge the death of Yamun by assassinating one noble or influential person in Cormyr. These last rumors are again turning public opinion against the Tuigan, even though they have caused no trouble for more than ten years.

island kingdoms

Capital: Various
Population: See individual entries
Government: Varies by island kingdom
Religions: Varies by island kingdom
Main Imports: Varies by island group
Main Exports: Varies by island group
Alignment: Varies, all possible

The great island kingdoms of the western seas have little to do or with each other. Nor, for that matter, do they have much to do with the rest of Faerûn. Each of them has its own people, history, and way of life, ranging from the shifting arrays of magical power surrounding the Elven Court on Evermeet to the brutal raiders of the Nelanther Isles.

Evermeet

Capital: Leuthilspar
Population: 1,658,880 (sun elves 50%, moon elves 30%, sea elves 10%, wood elves 9%)
Government: Monarchy
Religions: Corellon Larethian and the rest of the Seldarine
Imports: Elven items retrieved from Faerûn, otherwise self-sufficient
Exports: Elven adventurers, jewelry, some exotic or magic items given as gifts
Alignment: CG, CN, NG

Originally populated by sun elves, Evermeet is now the refuge for the Elven Court that has withdrawn from Faerûn. Moon elves, sun elves, and some wood elves followed Queen Amlaruil when she moved the center of elven life out of its ages-old home in the forest of Cormanthor. Evermeet is a defensible location far removed from human power centers such as Cormyr and Zhentil Keep.

The magical kingdom of the elves lies eighteen hundred miles to the west of Faerûn in the Trackless Sea. Elven high magic, sea elves,

The seas of Faerûn

Three great seas—the Sea of Swords, the Trackless Sea, and the Great Sea—bound Faerûn's western and southern coasts. A fourth, the Shining Sea, divides the peninsula of Chult from the shores of Calimshan and the Lake of Steam. Seafarers from Faerûn venture on all four bodies of water, but only the most confident and skilled mariners leave the coastal waters behind and strike out across the open seas.

The Great Sea: South of Chult lies the Great Sea. Somewhere in the vast sweep of ocean beyond the jungle peninsula, the Great Sea and the Trackless Sea become one; it's hard to say where one stops and the other begins. The Great Sea is a wedge of water almost two thousand miles long and nearly as wide at its western base, narrowing toward the east, where Faerûn and Zakhara meet. Zakharan corsairs plague its eastern reaches.

The Sea of Swords: Between the Sword Coast and the Moonshae Isles lies the Sea of Swords, a cold and storm-wracked gulf hundreds of miles across and more than a thousand long, reaching

from the Nelanther Isles of the south to Waterdeep in the north. Few harbors break the cliffs of the Sword Coast north of Amn or the rugged shores of the Moonshaes, and the pirates of the Nelanther threaten all who seek to pass Asavir's Channel and the Race to reach Faerûn's southern seas and the rich ports there.

The Shining Sea: Between Chult and Calimshan extends an arm of the sea more than a thousand miles long and hundreds of miles wide. Of all the waters described here, the Shining Sea has the most merchant traffic and trade, almost comparable to the Sea of Fallen Stars in the center of Faerûn.

The Trackless Sea: The western ocean extends from the western coast of Faerûn to the distant continent of Maztica, which lies more than three thousand miles west by southwest of Amn. This mighty expanse of water has barely been explored by the boldest of Faerûn's mariners. Even the elves of Evermeet, the greatest seafarers and shipwrights of Toril, can only guess at what wonders and terrors the remotest regions of the Trackless Sea might hold.

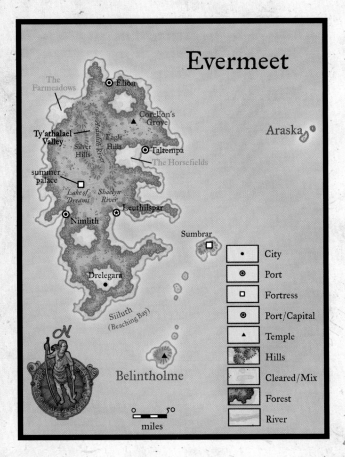

Evermeet

(Map labels:)
The Farmeadows
Elion
Corellon's Grove
Ty'athalael Valley
Eagle Hills
Silver Hills
Taltempa
The Horsefields
Araska
summer palace
Lake of Dreams
Shaelyn River
Leuthilspar
Nimlith
Sumbrar
Drelegara
Siiluth (Beaching Bay)
Belintholme

Symbol	Legend
•	City
◉	Port
□	Fortress
◉	Port/Capital
▲	Temple
🌿	Hills
	Cleared/Mix
	Forest
	River

0   50
miles

vigilant wizards, and a powerful navy guard the island. Few approach Evermeet who are not already the elves' guests.

LIFE AND SOCIETY

The dignified and gracefully evolving life of the Elven Court pivots around the carefully smoothed passage of the seasons, giving life on Evermeet a stately cadence in which the decades blur into centuries of contemplative serenity. Nothing in human Faerûn compares to it.

For the most part, the moon elves and sun elves form a single culture, though the noble houses, family lines, and clan relationships color associations between individuals. The wood elves hold themselves somewhat apart, preferring a quieter relationship with the forest and its spirits, but individual wood elves frequently blend into the life of the Court. The sea elves are welcome to participate in the life of the Court, but few do so for long. The handful of wild elves who opted to join the Court on Evermeet either carry themselves as the other elves of the court or live among the wood elves and forest spirits.

MAJOR GEOGRAPHICAL FEATURES

To a nonelf, Evermeet looks essentially like a single huge forest. Elves can distinguish between the forest's regions, moods, and realms by reading the messages left over centuries of symbiotic relationships between trees and their elven wardens. Humans can only see the type of geography they're accustomed to—Evermeet's occasional wide meadows, fair rivers, and some impressive hilly ranges.

Eagle Hills: From Thalikaera Rock, the highest peak of the range, lookouts can see all the way to the island of Sumbrar to the southeast. Using magic, they can see much farther.

The Farmeadows and the Horsefields: The two largest meadows on Evermeet are representative of the dozens of smaller glades tucked in among the trees. Centaurs run free through the long grasses alongside moon-horses, the intelligent horses native to the island who serve and are served by the elves.

River Ardulith: Few humans penetrate the interior of Evermeet, much less ride a leaf boat from the River Ardulith's source high in the Silver Hills down to where it joins the River Shaelyn to flow into the sea in view of the queen's palace in Leuthilspar.

Silver Hills: Like the Eagle Hills, these three-thousand-foot, conifer-lined peaks tower over the rest of the island. Lookouts keep watch from the peaks and tend to their giant eagle mounts in nests on the crags.

IMPORTANT SITES

Evermeet brims with wonders. No human land comes close to its integration of natural beauty and supernatural splendor. The elves compose wondrous songs describing and praising the ever-changing marvels of the island. The few humans welcomed to Evermeet's shores likely only see Queen Amlaruil's crown city.

Corellon's Grove: The high temple of the chief deity of the elven pantheon can be found in the forest in the north of the island. It would be proper to say that the north quarter of the island *is* the high temple to Corellon, since it's impossible to know where the "normal" forest ends and the space holy to the great deity begins. More than any other place, Corellon's Grove is the heart of elven life on Toril.

Leuthilspar (Metropolis, 50,269): The capital of Evermeet is a radiant example of the elves' organic architecture, in which buildings are grown rather than built. Even the coarsest dwarven miner would catch his breath at his first glimpse of Queen Amlaruil's palace. Crystals as tall as mighty trees are riddled with spiral passageways and glass-floored living quarters. Trees grow into citadels, linked bole to bole by fluting branches. Soaring arches and shimmering fields of magical force support airy palaces that seem too fragile to exist even in a dream. Eternally vigilant warriors and mages in armor of gleaming glass guard the tranquil city.

Sumbrar: Sumbrar, a small island fifty miles to the east, serves as Evermeet's military and naval headquarters. The island is a series of interwoven magical fortresses. A thousand wizard-warriors stand ready there with their pegasus and eagle mounts. An armada of ships remains magically prepared for launch, secure in hidden sea caves. Deep below the island, the last twelve dragons of Evermeet lie sleeping alongside their riders, waiting for a threat worth their power. Uninvited vessels are warned off sternly—or, should that fail, destroyed.

REGIONAL HISTORY

The overall history of the elves of Faerûn is detailed elsewhere in this volume, particularly in the description of Cormanthor (see The Dalelands). Evermeet was settled by sun elves thousands of years ago. Over the last century the elves of Cormanthor and other realms chose to remove themselves to this idyllic land, far from the ever-growing human empires and remorseless humanoid hordes that had destroyed so many elven realms on Faerûn's mainland.

Yet now the Elven Retreat is at an end. All who were willing to abandon their lands in Faerûn have done so, and no more elves come to Evermeet to forget the human world. Although Queen Amlaruil's reign is just and fair, many elves—some of whom have been on Evermeet for centuries—find themselves dissatisfied with their withdrawal from the rest of the world.

Unlike the elves loyal to the Elven Court, both the wild elves and the drow remained on the mainland. Instead of being overrun by the humans, both subraces have flourished in recent years, thanks in part to opportunities afforded them by the emigration of the other elves to Evermeet.

No one, least of all the Elven Court, has proclaimed an end to the Retreat or stated a determination to return. But more and more elves are choosing to return to Faerûn each year. Some intend to settle in Faerûn permanently or fight for ancestral lands taken by drow and other outsiders. Others intend to simply walk for a time in the lands they love, using secret *portals* to come or go as they please. Finally, Queen Amlaruil has quietly dispatched a number of agents and scouts to reestablish diplomatic ties with other friendly kingdoms. Evermeet no longer stands apart from events in Faerûn.

Evermeet is not as safe as its "impregnable" magical defenses might indicate. In recent years, the drow have dared to strike at Leuthilspar through magical *portals*, as if to remind Amlaruil that no haven is perfect. Forty-three years ago—a mere blink of the eye to an elf—Amlaruil's husband King Zaor was murdered in the heart of his palace, surrounded by all the strength and splendor of his realm.

PLOTS AND RUMORS

A serene land guarded vigilantly by powerful forces offers little to interest the typical adventurer . . . but *reaching* Evermeet is a journey of epic proportions. A company of adventurers might be charged by a lord or high priest to carry tidings, gifts, a plea for help, or a warning to Amlaruil's realm. It would be an adventure indeed to search for undefended *portals* or to cross the Trackless Sea, eluding those forces anxious to follow the heroes to Evermeet in order to spy out a route to the elven homeland, and then convince the isle's defenders to allow them to proceed.

A gnome of Lantan

Lantan

Folk hear tales of Lantan, "where Gond is worshiped and magic shunned." Most know very little more beyond the hearsay that Lantan is a strange and dangerous place where clockwork machines and infernal devices work great wonders and terrors at their makers' direction. Common wizardry pales in comparison.

The humans and gnomes of the island of Lantan pioneer technological solutions to problems that citizens of Faerûn solve with magic. The faith of Gond rules the pleasant island realm, and its inhabitants farm, craft things, and experiment endlessly. The Lantanese inventors constantly create new "small wonders" for the greater glory of Gond, and sometimes sell or trade these devices for glass, charcoal, and other odd ingredients their clients require.

Some Lantanese devices popular on mainland Faerûn include wagon suspensions and repairable sectioned wagon wheels; self-filling oil lamps that never go out as long as an oil tank is kept filled; various light-beam and tripwire intruder alarms; intricate hinges, chains, clockwork time-release devices, hasps, locks, and castings with special features (such as "stabbing pins" that can be poisoned to deter thieves, key-hiding cavities, catches that can ring chimes to

announce the opening of a portal, and so on). The Lantanese have also created wind-driven fans, "snap-together" weapons, grapnels that can be disassembled and concealed in clothing, and a variety of intricate needles and tools for sewing and surgical uses.

moonshae isles

Capital: Caer Callidyrr
Population: 680,400 (human 89%, halflings 4%, elves 3%, dwarves 2%, half-elves 1%)
Government: Monarchy
Religions: Chauntea (in an aspect as the Earthmother) among the Ffolk, Tempus among the Northlanders
Imports: Coal, horses, minor magic items, ore, parchment, silk
Exports: Armor, timber, weapons
Alignment: NG, N, NE

A cold cluster of rocky islands cloaked in mists and deep woods and sprinkled with abundant beasts, bogs, and soaring mountains, the Moonshae Isles are shared by two dominant races of human folk. The northern section of the islands is dominated by seafaring Northlanders descended from the raiders of Ruathym. A darker-haired and darker-skinned human race known as the Ffolk, the islands' longer-term residents, control the southern part. The Ffolk thrive in a dozen petty kingdoms ruled over by a High Queen.

In previous years the Northlanders and the Ffolk spent much of their time at each other's throats, particularly because of the Northlanders' penchant for bloody raiding. The rise of High King Tristan Kendrick unified the two peoples of the Moonshaes. Tristan's daughter, High Queen Alicia, has held her kingdom together through the usual small wars between petty lords. Compared to the nations of mainland Faerûn, the Moonshaes have enjoyed several decades of relative peace.

LIFE AND SOCIETY

All Moonshavians are shaped by the rugged, striking landscape and harsh weather. The Ffolk revere the land (and the deity who *is* the land), long aware of the divine power present in the rushing streams, secret pools, and mist-wreathed forests of their isles. The Ffolk adore their home with a deep and abiding love hard for other humans to understand.

The Northlanders are less moved by the landscape. Their hearts are turned to the sea, and they tend to be boisterous and outgoing compared to their neighbors. Relations between the two peoples are often strained, even if they are better now than ever before.

The Ffolk do not often welcome outlanders. To farmers, outlanders are trouble: brigands and thieves who imperil families, belongings, stock, and crops. To local lords and warriors, outlanders are rivals. If they abide by local laws, they are respected but watched: There's no telling what trouble will erupt if foreign sword-swingers run amok. News from the Sword Coast travels fairly well to the Moonshaes, so the previous deeds and reputation of arrivals color their reception. Heroes may be fully accepted by warriors of the Ffolk as one of their own. The Northlanders have a stronger tradition of sea trade and travel and tend to be simply curious about visitors from the rest of Faerûn.

Outlanders are most likely to find employment as sellswords in the service of feuding lords, or as guards aboard Moonshavian vessels running to and from Sword Coast ports. The Nelanther Isles are all too close for comfort, and the pirates grow bolder with each passing year. In every Moonshavian port tavern, one may hear a dozen colorful tales about narrow escapes.

MAJOR GEOGRAPHICAL FEATURES

The Moonshaes consist of a handful of major islands and hundreds of smaller isles. Among the noteworthy ones are the following.

Alaron: Ruled from the city of Caer Callidyrr, the island of Alaron is the most powerful of the Moonshae's kingdoms. The rugged Fairheight Mountains to the north of Caer Callidyrr separates the traditional lowland homes of the Ffolk in the south from the homes of the Northlanders. Intermarriage between the two peoples is slowly eliminating the divide between their customs.

Gwynneth: The largest of the southern islands, its northern half was settled by Northlanders from Oman's Isle and the southern part (which became the city of Caer Corwell) by the Ffolk. Nelanther pirates have made some landings on the island's southern coast, but no large-scale raids have been reported.

Moray: The westernmost of the major Moonshae islands is also the wildest of the southern isles. Since the peace between the Northlanders and the Ffolk, Northlanders have taken to raiding the monsters of the Orcskull Mountains that run down the island's spine. Consequently, Moray is a safer place to live and has attracted Ffolk and Northlander settlers.

Ruathym: This rugged, barren island is not properly part of the Moonshaes at all, lying more than two hundred miles north of the island chain. Ruathym is the ancestral home of the Northlanders, the barbarians who colonized the northern Moonshaes and Luskan. Scattered steadings and villages cluster around the isle's fjords and inlets. The largest settlement is the town of Ruathym, a city of five thousand. The Northlanders here have a long-standing feud with the folk of Luskan on the Sword Coast.

IMPORTANT SITES

Most of the Moonshae Islands boast at least one or two small villages. The major islands are home to dozens of settlements each, often divided by large stretches of wild and rugged terrain. Large towns are rare.

Caer Callidyrr (Large City, 21,486): Caer Callidyrr is a leftover of a previous civilization's peak, a mighty castle built on the island of Alaron above a sprawling port city. The Kendrick family now rules the kingdom of the same name in addition to their ancestral holdings on Gwynneth. The wizards and sorcerers who directly serve the High Queen live in the castle at Callidyrr instead of going south to Caer Corwell.

Unlike the rest of the Moonshaes, Caer Callidyrr is accustomed to the presence of visitors and merchants from other parts of Toril.

Caer Corwell (Small City, 11,459): The home region of the Kendrick family, occupying the south half of the island of Gwynneth, was the land first settled by the Ffolk. Its rocky shores and high moors make it an excellent place for strong-minded individualists who prefer space to neighbors, or for druids who seek to worship in the temple of the wild.

Iron Keep (Small City, 5,730): The strongest fortress of the Northlanders perches upon the northern shore of Oman's Isle. Iron Keep was formerly the most feared and violent of the Northlanders' kingdoms. It's still a warlike realm, but its inhabitants' aggressions are spent on other Northlander kingdoms, particularly the isle of Ruathym.

Myrloch Vale: The land sacred to the Earthmother occupies the central portion of the island of Gwynneth to the north of the Myrloch, the island's central lake. Unlike the aspect of Chauntea known throughout the rest of Faerûn, the Earthmother of the Moonshaes treasures unspoiled wildlands more than cleared farmland. Only druids and elves walk without fear in this place. The lands' primary occupants are centaurs, pixies, sprites, and the elves of the Moonshaes, known as the Llewyrr. Few of the Llewyrr joined the Retreat to Evermeet, owing nothing to the Elven Court and preferring their life in Myrloch Vale. Though the Vale is sacred to the Ffolk, Northlanders still fear it as a place of dangerous magic.

REGIONAL HISTORY

For centuries, the cycles of history in the Moonshaes pivoted around struggles between the invading Northlanders and the Ffolk. Early in the 1300s DR, the islands' conflicts took on greater significance. The evil deities Bhaal, Malar, and Talos attempted to take possession of the Moonshaes from the Earthmother.

The evil deities were thwarted largely through the heroism of the Kendrick family and their friends and lovers. The Kendricks ascended to become a new dynasty of High Kings and Queens, expanding the High Throne's hold upon the islands and convincing the Northlanders to accord them fealty alongside the Ffolk.

The last three decades of rule by High Queen Alicia Kendrick (NG female human Ftr6/Drd7 of the Earthmother) and her consort High King Keane (NG male human Wiz18) have been largely peaceful. Alicia and Keane have raised worthy heirs and appear to have founded a successful dynasty. The islands' only significant problem at this time is a growing conflict with pirates from the Nelanther Isles, who are ranging north in search of better haunts. The Northlanders have proven to be excellent allies against the Nelanther pirates, but adventurers from the mainland can sometimes find employment fighting the pirates' deadly wizards.

PLOTS AND RUMORS

Although much of the vast Moonshae woodlands is little visited, there's a claim on every foot of land. Outlanders must seek permission from local druids before felling trees, or face attack. Dwarves already occupy the best sites for mountain strongholds, and giants and other monsters imperil the wilder reaches of the mountains. Nevertheless, the Moonshaes possess abundant wilderness where the strong can carve out holdings for themselves. Eager adventurers are reminded that founding a realm can take a lifetime, and is never safe or easy.

The Wolf Still Has Fangs: The heroes are hired to accompany a merchant convoy bound for Amn that is too heavily laden to make good speed. They expect to be attacked by Nelanther pirates, and they are given one-use magic items to help them destroy their attackers, since the point of the trip is to draw a pirate attack and then smash it.

The true predators on the convoy's route are Northlanders, whose Tempus-inspired battle frenzies and fast ships make them more dangerous than Nelanther pirates. Despite the Northlanders' peace with the Ffolk, some still raid Moonshae's neighbors at will. Worse yet, Northlanders captured or slain in the battle carry the colors of Iron Keep. Was Iron Keep framed for the attack? Or, if that city is responsible, would an attempt to enforce the High Queen's justice on the unruly Northlanders of Oman's Isle drive them into open rebellion and rekindle the old wars?

nelanther isles

Capital: None
Population: 2,822 (orcs 30%, humans 20%, half-orcs 15%, lizard-folk 15%, ogres 10%, humanoids 9%)
Government: Armed anarchy
Religions: Beshaba, Cyric, Talos, Tempus, Umberlee
Imports: Anything natives can steal, loot, or salvage
Exports: Slaves, stolen and salvaged goods of all types
Alignment: NE, CE, CN

The Nelanther Isles are a widely scattered chain of nearly a thousand islands sprinkled from Amn into the Trackless Sea. More than half the islands lack water and are fit only for wrecking ships upon. The hundreds of islands that have drinkable water and can support life are fought over by seagoing pirates who prey upon the shipping of Amn, Calimshan, the Sword Coast, and the Moonshae Isles.

Aside from their dependence on violence and larceny, the Nelanthers have surprisingly little in common with the Pirate Isles of the Dragon Coast. The Pirate Isles are predominantly human, while the Nelanthers' pirates are nonhumans such as orcs, lizardfolk, ogres, and minotaurs. The various races and factions of Nelanther pirates war on each other as often as they war on outsiders.

LIFE AND SOCIETY

The raiders of the Nelanther Isles live by the winds that fill their sails on the Sea of Swords and die by the gales that smash them to Umberlee's depths. Unlike the swashbucklers of the Pirate Isles who sometimes observe strange forms of chivalry, the Nelanther reavers torture their victims and leave them to hideous deaths. The pirates here are born into the society's violent cycle and escape only by dying, usually while young. Nearly all able-bodied adults fight aboard ships, while the weak, crippled, and surviving children are left ashore to make repairs or salvage wrecks.

MAJOR GEOGRAPHICAL FEATURES

Aside from the sea itself and the innumerable rocky islands of the Nelanther Isles, there are no particularly notable features. No single island is large enough or densely settled enough to deserve special mention.

IMPORTANT SITES

Instead of erecting permanent settlements, the pirates of the Nelanther Isles live in their ships or in huts that can be abandoned at a moment's notice. The only permanent structures in the area were built long before the arrival of the pirates.

The Sea Towers: High towers made of hard stone jut out of several of the islands and occasionally straight out of the sea. The sea towers of Irphong and Nemessor are leftovers of a previous civilization or civilizations. Most are magically locked and warded against intrusion by simple bandits (including Nelanther raiders who have tried to get in). Others have become the homes of monsters such as ogre magi or Bane-worshiping gargoyles. In either case, the Sea Towers have a bad name among the Nelanther pirates, who avoid them with superstitious dread.

REGIONAL HISTORY

Tethyr's Velen peninsula and the Nelanther archipelago have always divided Faerûn's northern seafarers from its southern waters. With the rise of the mercantile powers of the northern waters— Amn, Waterdeep, and the cities of the North—traffic through the

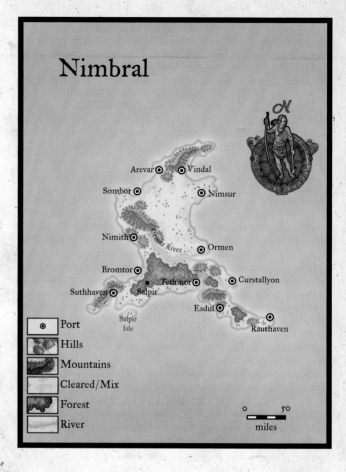

Nelanther Isles burgeoned into a rich stream of trade. And that activity, of course, attracted pirates like a battlefield draws crows. For centuries now, the Nelanther Isles have been more or less as they are today.

The Sea Towers tell a different tale, though. The furnishings, scrolls, and tomes discovered within newly breached towers indicate that there was a time when the islands of the Nelanther were home to other than cruel tyrants and vicious buccaneers. Much of the history of this vanished civilization has been lost to the tides.

PLOTS AND RUMORS

Adventures in the Nelanther nearly always end up dealing with pirates. Wealthy merchants of Amn and the Sword Coast cities frequently outfit punitive expeditions to locate and destroy particularly successful or cruel pirate bands. Heroes from these lands cut their teeth chasing corsairs in the Nelanther.

A Cell with a View: A one-way *portal* used to escape a villain's fortress leads to the top of one of the Sea Towers. While the heroes search for another way off the island, the pirate ships that "watch" the island for the villain sail up, ready to transport their ally to the island containing her other *portals*. If the PCs decide to hole up in the wizard's tower instead of confronting the pirates, they'll soon learn the dangers of living within a functional tower without knowing the proper spells and passwords that keep the tower's defenses from activating.

nimbral

Nimbral the Sea Haven is a fabled and seldom visited land that lies off the western coast of Faerûn, southwest of Lantan. It is a small realm of mountains, high meadows, and deep green forests. Little farms and spired, fairytale castles dot the countryside. The small coastal cities serve as fishing ports and docks for infrequent visitors. Many believe the land to be a mere legend.

The reclusive folk of Nimbral have a well-deserved reputation as great wizards. An enclave of studious, introverted, and extremely powerful archmages called the Nimbral Lords rule the place. The lords keep to themselves and split their time between governing and magical research. There are reputed to be more than two dozen of these lords and half as many apprentices, and they form a tight-knit, loyal family. They guard their secrets jealously, fearing attacks from groups such as the Red Wizards, the Arcane Brotherhood, the Cult of the Dragon, and the Twisted Rune.

Nimbral is also known as the land of the Flying Hunt. Aerial knights mounted on pegasi and clad in armor of glass patrol the skies and waters of the island, seeking out flying monsters and keeping pirates and raiders away from Nimbral's shores. These knights follow the highest ideals of romantic chivalry, though some (mostly Calishite slavers) revile them as raiders and bandits.

Lake of Steam

Capital: None (largely independent city-states)
Population: 1,745,280 (humans 90%, halflings 9%; higher proportions of nonhumans in the Border Kingdoms)
Government: Varies
Religions: Any
Imports: Grain, horses, livestock, small ships, soldiers, stone, wood (varies by region)
Exports: Cast brass and bronze, chains, dyed wool, dyes, fruit, gems, ink, magic items, mercenaries, mirrors, pearls, seafood, sheepskins, spellbooks, sturdy books, vegetables, wagons, weapons, wine (varies by region)
Alignment: Any

With independent city-states on the north shore and a succession of small countries founded or conquered by people of many races, faiths, and agendas to the south, the Lake of Steam is a hodgepodge of varying interests, bustling trade, and frequently changing boundaries. Most of the cities on the north shore were part of Calimshan in the past and retain their parent's desire for wealth, comfort, and influence, as well as a strong desire to remain independent. The intrigues brewing around these cities led observers to dub the northern shore the Moonsea of the South.

The Border Kingdoms on the southern shore are the homes of powerful adventurers of many types, each seeking to carve out a piece of land and rule it in the manner he or she feels is best . . . at least until the next would-be ruler decides to take over. Wizard towers, monasteries, fortresses, and temples dot the Border Kingdoms, only to have their owners replaced time and again.

South of the Lake of Steam on the eastern shores of the Shining Sea lies the fractious kingdom of Lapaliiya, a crossroads land between the Shaar plains, the Chultan jungles, and the verdant Lake of Steam.

LIFE AND SOCIETY

The northern shore of the Lake of Steam, with its strong historic ties to Calimshan, reflects the materialistic attitude of that nation. However, the people of the lake have a fierce independent streak and rarely tolerate slavery. In the Border Kingdoms on the chaotic southern shore of the lake, the people have had little opportunity to develop any sort of national identity. What they do have in common is a stoic determination to get on with their lives regardless of who

claims to be their king, overlord, theocrat, high wizard, grand guildmaster, or supreme musician that year.

MAJOR GEOGRAPHICAL FEATURES

The lake itself and the Shining Sea to the south are the primary features of the area, along with the forests that surround the lake.

Duskwood: This tangled haunt of stirges, predatory trees, giant spiders, and enormous snakes is still widely visited for many kinds of rare plants prized by herbalists, spellcasters, and alchemists. The wood is also known for several pools said to be capable of repairing magic items. The Vauntagar, a magical binding-ward, keeps a cycle of monsters alive to guard the pools. When the active monster is severely injured, it shifts to an extradimensional space where the others live, and a fresh creature is sent to take its place in the wood. Aside from the Vauntagar creatures, at least one beholder haunts the forest.

Jundarwood: Spiders of all kinds inhabit this tall forest, both normal and giant-size. Rumors abound that intelligent spiderlike beings, either ettercaps or araneas, also lair here. Evidence is scarce, so if they do exist, they have been living in tunnels underground or high in the forest canopy. The eastern end of the Jundarwood sports a volcanic hill known as the Jundarmount, which releases small amounts of lava and a great mass of cinders at least once a month, often setting portions of the wood on fire if the wind is right.

Lake of Steam: Despite its name, the Lake of Steam (also called Arnaden) is a saltwater bay of the Shining Sea. Its stinking yellow waters give off clouds of steam due to volcanic activity beneath the waves, so its waters are always warm and cloaked with impenetrable mists on cold nights. Shallow as a pan, the lake is less than two hundred feet deep at its deepest, and only a few dozen feet in depth for most of its eastern arm.

The warm, iron-strong, undrinkable waters are rich in minerals that spur weeds, shellfish, and fish to grow to great size; the lake has been called "the Breadbasket of the Seas." Predators here grow very large, too, from birds and otters to dragon turtles. Dolphins are common, and sharks and leeches (some as large as rowboats, and given to hunting ashore during wet nights) are frequent, outnumbering more fearsome aquatic monsters. The lake is also known for the greenish pearls of its oysters.

The islands in the Lake of Steam change as volcanic stacks collapse and rise, but tend to be concentrated at Arnaden's western end. The Arnrock is an active volcano that exploded about a thousand years back, and is now a low, wide, open-topped dome with a cauldron filled with woods and always active hot springs and fumaroles. It's the abode of a small settlement of strongheart halflings who call themselves the Arn. They fish, farm, and do a little copper-casting using volcanic rifts at the cauldron's heart.

Great numbers of wild beasts roam the island of Olodel. The place was once the private hunting preserve of the Lords of Olodel, eccentric Calishite merchants who brought a number of deepspawn hence and fed them deadly monsters, from tigers to manticores and chimeras. Several beholders slew the Lords and now rule Olodel. The island of Felmer's Keep looks like a castle but is actually a steep-sided extinct volcano, its outer flanks rocky ramparts, and its heart a verdant meadow.

The Strait of Storms (also known as the Suldolphor Strait or the Wide Water) links Arnaden with the Shining Sea, and waters flow through it dangerously fast. To voyage north into the lake, ships wait on strong winds and favorable tides, sometimes for days.

Qurth Forest: This forest is thick almost to the point of being impassable. Long ago a Calishite sorcerer cursed one of the local rulers that monsters would overrun his realm, and while the curse died with the offending ruler, the offspring of those monsters still thrive here. Owlbears, intelligent fungi, and giant spiders are common, and an occasional naga can be found. Ruined, overgrown cities still exist in the interior of the forest, long abandoned when monsters drove out the inhabitants.

Thornwood: This forest is one of the most dangerous in southwestern Faerûn. It is inhabited by evil humanoids, dangerous plants, and at least one beholder. Wood elves, druids, and treants struggle to hold back the tide of evil. Legends tell of the Green's Sword, a green blade that sprouts from a particular grove every ten years; the sword can be claimed to fight evil by one who is worthy. The grove is encircled by brambles and is otherwise only remarkable for the sword-shaped leaves of the plants where the sword appears.

Winterwood: This lush forest's canopy allows little direct sunlight to penetrate. The ground is often shrouded in white mist that resembles snow. Green elves, orcs, and intelligent mold-based creatures fight for territory. The forest is also home to Foilsunder, an old male green dragon with druid powers.

IMPORTANT SITES

The volcanism of the lake has discouraged dwarves and other delving races from settling in the area, and human realms have been shattered by Calimshan's armies and by successive waves of beholder rule. Eye tyrants lurking in the mountains west and north of the lake still occasionally burst forth with charmed servitor creatures from cavern strongholds to descend on caravans and encampments. Brigands fleeing Calishite justice also infest the shores.

Ankhapur (Metropolis, 33,514): This city was ruled for many years by an undead king. The current King Janol Famisso (N male human Rog10) destroyed the old ruler and set about opening up the city for trade. He has decreased merchant taxes and compensated for the loss by increasing the taxes on nobles, which has made him popular with the former and less so with the latter. For unknown reasons, all the tressym within the city disappear on the day before Highsummer and return three days later.

The Border Kingdoms (9,485 inhabitants): This stretch of coast is dotted with villages and towns like any other part of Faerûn. The main difference in the Border Kingdoms is that the people here are used to frequent changes in leadership, precipitated by powerful adventurers who decide to carve out a small kingdom and rule for a while. With a limited number of prime locations for bases, battles between would-be rulers are frequent. These changes make it difficult to record accurately anything about the current state of this region, although the commoners have an enduring and pragmatic attitude. Local towns such as Beldargan, Derlusk, Themasulter, Theymarsh, and Yallash have populations of between one thousand and two thousand and survive by logging, mining, and fishing.

Dalelost: These ruins once contended with Yhep for the largest share of the pearl trade, but a series of unremembered calamities left the place ruined and abandoned over a period of a decade. It is now home to a cabal of clerics of Bane who are being controlled by the Twisted Rune. The Banites have a small temple and command some lesser undead, although more powerful undead are believed to lair beneath the city.

Innarlith (Metropolis, 48,691): Anything can be bought in this fortified city for the right price, including illegal goods such as poison and narcotics. The city's leader, the Ransar Pristoleph (CE male fire genasi Sor8/Dev5 of Cyric) discourages clerics of benevolent faiths and ruthlessly persecutes thieves, but welcomes an enclave of Red Wizards with open arms. The genasi unseated the previous ransar and his Black Firedrakes in a bold coup last year, at the same time driving his rival Mandalax out of the city.

Pristoleph is a secret devotee of Cyric, and with his tacit assistance the priests of the Black Sun are infiltrating the city's merchant houses and subverting key civic leaders to their sinister cause. The

Cyricists dream of transforming Innarlith into the Zhentil Keep of the south, a stronghold in which the followers of the Prince of Lies wield supreme power.

Mintar (Large City, 21,500): This city, along with the former Tethyrian town of Kzelter, were conquered by an army of the church of Xvim (now Bane) led by Teldorn Darkhope (LE male human Clr9 of Bane). Now everything in the city serves the army and the church, which is also backed by Fzoul Chembryl of the Zhentarim. Remnants of the Academy of the Drawn Sword school have allied with others in Saelmur and are preparing raids against outlying camps of the Banite army. Here Darkhope and Chembryl forged the *Scepter of the Tyrant's Eye,* the first relic of Xvim and now rededicated to the church of Bane.

Because Mintar lies nearly six hundred miles from Innarlith, the unpleasant developments in these two cities are unlikely to affect each other.

Saelmur (Metropolis, 25,294): Once called the cleanest city on the lake, Saelmur is now overcrowded with refugees from Mintar. The city is the home of many arcane spellcasters and the Master of the Blade school. Magic items and spell components are easily found here. The churches of Helm, Torm, and Tyr are locked in constant debate over how to deal with the Banite threat in Mintar.

Yhep (Small City, 5,691): Yhep is famous for the vivid red pearls found in its oyster beds. Part of the town rests on stilts, underneath which are oyster farms. The Yhepan shipwrights build wondrous ships with levitation magic and skilike runners that skim across water, mud, and sandy flats like darting birds. The minions of Vaxall, a beholder of Thornwood and ally of the Banites in Mintar, are influencing certain nobles in town.

REGIONAL HISTORY

The city-states on the Lake of Steam have all been part of Calimshan's empire or were founded by people working for or fleeing it, including rival nobles and empowered generals. Calimshan lost pieces of its eastern holdings on several occasions due to wars with elves, beholders, and drow (including an extended period when beholder cults were prevalent), and the city-states have remained independent for several hundred years.

The cities of the Lake of Steam have access to their trading partners through the area and overland to the Vilhon Reach. These city-states are prosperous and rich but lack strong leadership. Gold rules these lands, and powerful merchant princes have toppled more than one city lord for interfering with the pursuit of private wealth.

PLOTS AND RUMORS

The Border Kingdoms are always bubbling with wars, feuds, and power-hungry adventurers seeking thrones. On the northern shore, fierce competition for trade and the military forces of Bane's church in Mintar now pose a threat to the tenuous stability of the other city-states.

A Rare Find: Ilmur Baraskro, a merchant of Ankhapur, claims to have found a mysterious magic item that enables its possessor to create multiple bodies and move his intellect from one to another freely. He is offering it for sale to any interested person for two million gold coins, and has survived three assassination attempts to date, each of which slew one of his spare bodies.

Some sages say his item may be the fabled *Thringal's Gorget*—of which it is said that creating too many bodies with it can drive the possessor insane, one of the bodies must wear the *Gorget* at all times, and damage done to one body weakens all the others. Interested parties are hunting for Baraskro, most posing as potential buyers.

Demon Hunt: A demon summoned just before the conquest of Mintar broke free of its confining magic circle, causing much havoc among the Banite troops before flying southward. The Banites want the demon captured or destroyed, while others want to bribe the demon to continue attacking the minions of the Black Hand. The demon itself plans to claim a land among the Border Kingdoms.

ARRK

Male troll Ftr2: CR 7; Large giant; HD 6d8+30 plus 2d10+10; hp 78; Init +2; Spd 30 ft.; AC 22 (touch 11, flat-footed 20); Atk +12/+7 melee (2d6+10/19–20 plus spell, *+1 spell storing greatsword*) or +8/+3 ranged (1d6+6, throwing axe); Face/Reach 5 ft. by 5 ft./10 ft.; SQ Darkvision 90 ft., regeneration 5, scent; AL CN; SV Fort +13, Ref +4, Will +4; Str 22, Dex 14, Con 20, Int 9, Wis 10, Cha 6. Height 8 ft.

Skills and Feats: Hide –4, Listen +7, Spot +6, Swim +8; Alertness, Iron Will, Power Attack, Weapon Focus (greatsword).

Possessions: +1 spell storing greatsword (currently holding an *inflict serious wounds* spell, bears an odd curse drawback that it drips blood when unsheathed), *Arrk's gold necklace* (acts as a *ring of feather falling*), chain shirt, 2 masterwork throwing axes.

Smaller but smarter than most of his kind, Arrk abandoned his tribe after years of fighting to survive among his cruel kin. Leaving the Neth Stand where he was born, he convinced a band of brigands to lend him a sword and let him join them. He took to the work exceptionally well but found the rewards insufficient. Arrk eventually left the bandits and joined a mercenary company, where he became rather successful, was able to travel, and was expected to give in to bloodlust from time to time.

Illustration by Matt Wilson

Arrk

Arrk is now a relatively well-known figure in the Lake of Steam region, although hardly a popular one. He sells his services to anyone with money as long as the job doesn't take more than a tenday, for Arrk has a short attention span and tires of other people quickly. He has the unnerving habit of licking his bleeding sword when he grows bored or nervous, and his hygiene is no better than that of a common troll, so civilized folk can't tolerate him for long.

Despite these faults, Arrk can be counted on to hold up his end of a bargain. Given that he tends to eat people who steal from him or refuse him his pay, other folk deal with him honestly. Arrk commonly works as a caravan escort or personal bodyguard through hostile territories but also hires on as additional muscle for adventuring parties.

Lapaliiya

The city-states along the southeast shore of the Shining Sea together form a league or confederation known as Lapaliiya. The folk of this land are zealous warriors and industrious merchants who place a tremendous value on personal honor and propriety. Duels and feuds over slights that folk of other lands might hardly notice are common.

Each city in the Lapal League takes one deity as its patron, glorifying that faith above all others. Ilmater, Kelemvor, Selûne, Talos, and Waukeen are the civic deities of the five largest Lapal cities. Other faiths are actively discouraged in a particular city, and relations between cities tend to mirror the alliances and enmities of the gods themselves.

The Lapal people were formerly a widespread tribal folk who settled a broad swath of territory from the southern coasts of Chult, where the Lapal Sea still bears their name, to the borders of the Shaar. Barbaric and warlike, they harried the frontiers of Calimshan's great empires until the mage-kings of the Shoon Dynasty conquered and civilized them. The cities are still ruled by satraps claiming descent from the Shoon rulers of old.

Lands of Intrigue

South of the Western Heartlands and west of the Vilhon Reach are the Lands of Intrigue: Amn, Calimshan, and Tethyr. Tied to each other by geography and a long history of invasions, conquest, and competition, the people of these countries have survived by wits and sword, learning to guard their true feelings and present a pleasant face to their enemies.

All three of these large, populous nations rely heavily on trade, particularly with distant countries. Their lands contain a wide variety of terrain, making them home to an equally wide variety of monsters.

Amn

Capital: Athkatla
Population: 2,963,520 (humans 83%, halflings 15%, half-orcs 1%)
Government: Plutocracy
Religions: Bane, Chauntea, Cyric, Selûne, Sune, Waukeen
Imports: Exotic goods (from Maztica), magic items, mercenaries, pearls, siege weaponry
Exports: Ale, armor, beer, caravan items (wagons, wheels), gems, gold, grain, horses, iron, jewelry, weapons
Alignment: LN, LE, NG

Amn is a nation of merchants, a place where caravans start and end and ships leave for exotic ports and return laden with gold and strange items. The Shadow Thieves have their hand in everything, and the rulers are an anonymous group known only as the Council of Six. Divine spellcasters are respected if their work brings money to Amn, while arcane spellcasters are universally reviled and feared.

Amn maintains a large colony on the distant tropical continent of Maztica and has profited greatly from its trade. The government's disregard for the humanoids in its southern mountains has come back to haunt the country; two ogre mage leaders forged an army and took over much of southern Amn, including its secondary port city. Now Amn struggles to retake its territory while maintaining its trade routes and dominance in Maztica.

LIFE AND SOCIETY

The people of Amn are obsessed with wealth. Unlike their southern neighbors, who pursue wealth for the comfort it brings, Amnians desire wealth for its own sake and for power, using the money they acquire to create more riches for themselves. Also in contrast to Calimshan, the wealthy in Amn make a great show of donating money to charities and the needy. Large donations demonstrate that a person can afford to be generous. Everything a citizen does should be done for money; doing something unprofitable is considered foolish and wasteful.

Amn's economy is supported by strong guilds, controlled by powerful merchant families who have a great deal of wealth and political clout. Every aspect of trade or craft is covered by a guild.

Major Geographical Features

Amn is a great plain between two parallel mountain ranges. Four broad, slow rivers wind across its lowlands, laden with trade goods.

The Cloud Peaks: These mountains mark the northern border of Amn. Despite being home to white dragons and remorhazes, they are mined for iron, precious metal, and even some gems. A pair of steep crags known as the Fangs guards the Trade Way leading to the Sword Coast lands.

Lake Esmel: This dark blue lake plummets to unknown depths in the central, southern, and eastern portions. Hot mineral springs flow in the western shallows, making it a popular vacation spot and health resort for the wealthy. Rumors speak of an aquatic monster in the lake, but most dismiss them as sightings of Balagos the Flying Flame, a red great wyrm legendary for his gigantic size, temper, and recklessly hurled spells.

Shilmista: The elven king of this area, also known as the Forest of Shadows, has declared that no more trees or elves of his realm shall die, and slays any who violate his order. Only one tribe of elves remains, and its members prefer to stay in small, hard-to-find camps rather than in larger settlements. The tribal leaders have established a tenuous contact with the rulers of Tethyr that may ease their paranoia.

The Small Teeth: This range of mountains was considered a nuisance because of the number of evil humanoids and giants living here, but now it is the backbone of the Sythillisian Empire, an area of conquered Amnian territory ruled by two ogre mages. The peaks are home to Iryklathagra "Sharpfangs," a blue wyrm that awakens about once a century, and the Twin Towers of the Eternal Eclipse, two fortifications dedicated to the church of Cyric.

Snakewood: This place's name comes from the black and green snakes that live here. Clerics of Eldath inhabit the central woods despite isolated pockets of monstrous spiders, giant snakes, beholders, and lycanthropes. An ambitious green dragon named Ringreemeralxoth lairs in the northeastern portion.

Troll Mountains: Rich in gems and full of mysteries, these mountains are mostly unexplored due to the predations of the monsters from which they take their name. The trolls here are unusually clever and well organized, and once ruled a small kingdom of their kind. The mountains are also home to the red dragon Balagos the Flying Flame, a temple of Talos that is struck by lighting daily, and the fortified gnome mining village of Quarrelshigh.

An enormous vertical slab of rock four thousand feet high in the western portion of the mountains is carved to resemble a dwarf. Known as the Wailing Dwarf because of the noise of the wind blowing through its hollow eyes, ears, and mouth, it marks the site of a fallen dwarven city and is now inhabited by trolls and other monsters.

Important Sites

Amn is heavily settled, especially along its great rivers and around Lakes Esmel and Weng. Inns and taverns catering to the Trade Way traffic line the road for the length of its passage through the country.

Athkatla (Metropolis, 118,304): This city is the seventh busiest port in all Faerûn. Any sort of nonmagical good can be found here for a price. Because this is Amn's only remaining free port, ships from the western land of Maztica dock here, bringing back exotic vegetables, fruits, jewelry, and large amounts of gold. The city's marketplace is twice the size of Waterdeep's. Above the bay is Goldspires, a temple to Waukeen nearly as large as a small town.

Crimmor (Metropolis, 35,491): The caravan capital of Amn, this fortified city is the mustering point for practically all trade heading northward by land. The Shadow Thieves forbid any thievery in this town as payment of a favor owed to a powerful family. Crimmor has many inns, taverns, and festhalls to serve the numerous caravanners and adventurers who pass this way.

Eshpurta (Large City, 24,252): Although the rich in Athkatla consider this city a backwater, Eshpurta is proud of its status as Athkatla's main military city. It has more business devoted to the military (including the manufacture of arms and armor) than most other cities in Faerûn. The city also mines iron from the southern foothills of the Troll Mountains. Eshpurta has a quiet temple to Ilmater, an oddity in Amn.

Keczulla (Metropolis, 47,322): Settled hundreds of years ago when gold and iron were found nearby, the town fell on hard times two centuries later when those mines were depleted, only to rise again fifty years ago when gems were discovered. The city houses a secret cabal of benevolent mages, who keep their skills hidden from all but each other.

Murann (Metropolis, 43,773): The secondary port town of Amn, Murann is now fully in the hands of two ogre mages and their minions. The city's alchemists' guild remains intact, its members creating alchemical items and potions for the armies of the Sythillisian Empire. The humanoid armies seized the gold-laden ships and are now quite wealthy, and the Nelanther pirates and the Tashalar-based Rundeen use the place as a safe haven in exchange for defending it against naval attacks. The church of Selûne crusades relentlessly to see the city reclaimed, since they have a large temple here.

Purskul (Metropolis, 27,210): A granary city, Purskul is a significant caravan stop. Orcs were enslaved here over a hundred years ago, with the hardest workers earning their freedom. The half-orc population (15% of the total population) works as mercenaries and caravan guards. Purskul's temple to Chauntea remains empty after its resident clerics died of sickness two years ago.

Regional History

Humans have inhabited Amn for thousands of years, but only with the rise of the Shoon Empire did the place become a unified nation, reaching its current borders in 768 DR. During the rise of Shoon, most of the elves in Amn's forests were killed or enslaved, a fact that has not been forgotten by the elves living here today.

With independence, Amn became a center of trade, and its people became wealthy and prosperous. A series of plagues and monsters released by certain schools of wizards has led Amnian citizens to hold a very poor opinion of arcane spellcasters.

Amn is ruled by the Council of Six, anonymous overlords who share their identities only with each other. The Council of Six made an accord with the Shadow Thieves, an exiled Waterdhavian guild of thieves and assassins, and the two organizations have prospered since then (in fact, a member of the Council leads the Shadow Thieves). Mercenaries in the employ of Amnian merchants discovered Maztica in 1361 DR, sparking a veritable gold rush whose effects continue to grow with each passing year.

In 1370 DR, two ogre mages named Sythillis (LE male ogre mage Sor12) and Cyrvisnea (LE female ogre mage Ftr12) gathered an army of goblins, kobolds, ogres, and hill giants (backed by worshipers of Cyric) to attack the southern cities of Amn, with the ultimate goal of acquiring Maztican gold from docked ships in Murann. They succeeded and have since held the southern portions of Amn despite various efforts by the Council and adventuring groups to dislodge them. At nearly the same time, two southern Amnian cities defected to Tethyr, seeking better treatment and more freedom.

PLOTS AND RUMORS

Only a year ago, folk would not have thought of Amn as a land in great need of adventurers. With the rise of the monster-lords in the south of the land and the pervasive influence of the Shadow Thieves in all aspects of Amnian trade, that is no longer true.

The Masked Prisoner: One of the Council of Six was in Murann when the city fell to monsters and has not been seen since. He is presumed to be the prisoner of the ogre mages and perhaps is being tortured for information. Anyone who rescues the missing leader would be well received by the rest of the Council and become a national hero in Amn.

The Overlords of Murann: The monster army in Murann is too powerful for a direct assault by anything but another army, but some factions believe that key assassinations within the monsters' organization (particularly the ogre mages themselves) would destabilize it enough to cause a collapse.

SAHBUTI SHANARDANDA

Male human Mnk6/Sor4/Shd3: CR 13; Medium-size humanoid; HD 6d8+6 plus 4d4+4 plus 3d8+3; hp 62; Init +2; Spd 50 ft.; AC 20 (touch 16, flat-footed 20); Atk +11/+6 melee (1d10+3/19–20, masterwork bastard sword [two-handed]) or +12/+9 melee (1d8+3, unarmed strike) or +10/+5 ranged touch (by spell); SA Flurry of blows, stunning attack 6/day (DC 16); SQ Darkvision, evasion, haste (1/day, *monk's belt*) hide in plain sight, purity of body, slow fall 30 ft., shadow companion, shadow illusion (as *silent image*, 1/day), still mind (+2 on saves against enchantment spells), uncanny dodge (Dex bonus to AC); AL LE; SV Fort +8, Ref +11, Will +13; Str 14, Dex 14, Con 12, Int 12, Wis 16, Cha 12. Height 6 ft.

Skills and Feats: Balance +9, Climb +7, Concentration +7, Escape Artist +5, Hide +15, Jump +12, Knowledge (arcana) +3, Listen +11, Move Silently +14, Perform (dance) +6, Search +4, Spellcraft +5, Spot +8, Swim +5, Tumble +11, Use Rope +5; Combat Reflexes, Deflect Arrows, Dodge, Improved Trip, Martial Weapon Proficiency (bastard sword, two-handed), Mobility, Spring Attack, Weapon Focus (unarmed strike).

Special Qualities: Shadow Companion: Sahbuti is served by a loyal undead shadow (Shemnaer).

Spells Known (6/7/3; base DC = 11 + spell level): 0—*dancing lights, detect magic, detect poison, mage hand, ray of frost, read magic;* 1st—*shield, shocking grasp, true strike;* 2nd—*bull's strength.*

Possessions: armcloths of armor +4 (as *bracers of armor*), *monk's belt,* masterwork bastard sword. Sahbuti also has a permanent *magic fang* spell on each of his hands and feet, a gift from another follower of Shar.

Shemnaer: Shadow companion; CR 3; Medium-size undead (incorporeal); HD 3d12; hp 19; Init +2; Spd 30 ft., fly 40 ft. (good); AC 13 (touch 13, flat-footed 11); Atk +3 melee touch (1d6 temporary Strength, incorporeal touch); SQ Cannot be turned, create spawn, incorporeal, undead immunities; AL LE; SV Fort +1, Ref +3, Will +4; Str —, Dex 14, Con —, Int 6, Wis 12, Cha 13. Height 5 ft.

Skills and Feats: Hide +8, Intuit Direction +5, Listen +7, Spot +7; Dodge.

Sahbuti Shanardanda

Sahbuti is a member of the Dark Moon order of monks. These monks seek out the enemies of the dark deity Shar and are dedicated foes of the followers of Selûne. Terse, straightforward, and sure of himself, Sahbuti accepts no criticism of his skills and is quick to accept any reasonable challenge of a duel.

Born and raised in Amn, Sahbuti now travels from Waterdeep to Calimshan for the order and the church of Shar. He is likely to turn up anywhere Shar's work needs to be done. Aided by his loyal shadow Shemnaer, he guards shipments of goods valuable to the church, escorts important officials from his order, and acts as an assassin from time to time.

Sahbuti loves nothing and no one. Indoctrinated in the worship of Shar at an early age, he nurses a cold bitterness and loneliness, which he believes will abate when he dies and his awareness is extinguished by the Mistress of Night.

calimshan

Capital: Calimport
Population: 5,339,520 (humans 94%, half-orcs 2%, halflings 2%, half-elves 1%)
Government: Autocracy
Religions: Anachtyr (Tyr), Azuth, Bhaelros (Talos), Ibrandul (dead god, now an aspect of Shar), Ilmater, Shar, Shassess
Imports: Food, slaves, wizards
Exports: Armor, books, gems, jewelry, leather goods, mercenaries, minor magic items, pearls, pottery, rare herbs, rope, ships, silk, spices, weapons, wine
Alignment: LN, N, NE

Calimshan is a land obsessed with wealth and unimpressed by magic. Its people are heirs to an old empire founded by genies, and now fear such creatures and ban them from their lands. Familiar with displays of magic, they see the Art as any other skill that can be learned. Some say the blood of the efreet runs in some Calishites, giving them sorcerous powers and a talent for fire magic.

Calimshan is renowned for its chauvinism, exotic markets, thieves' guilds, decadent harems, desert landscape, and wealthy ruling class, as well as its enormous population and many slaves.

LIFE AND SOCIETY

Most Calishites rely upon mercantilism for their livelihood. The cutthroat politics of Calimshan involve backstabbing, layers of deception, and numerous advisors. The current ruler, Syl-Pasha Ralan el Pesarkhal (NE human male Wiz7/Rog12), reached his current position through lies, murder, and blackmail. Calishites are obsessed with titles and status, and an inappropriate look or remark from a person of lower station results in severe punishment.

The people of Calimshan seek wealth not for wealth itself, but for the comforts and status it brings. Calishites believe that wealth is the reward for a life of work, and they look down upon those who rely upon charity or "adventuring" to support themselves.

Arcane magic is relatively common here, to the extent that half of the imperial guard are wizards. However, despite a reputation for being a land of genies, Calishites avoid evocation magic (except for the efreet-descended sorcerers), planar magic, and teleportation, preferring conventional methods such as flying carpets.

The business underworld comprises an important aspect of Calishite culture. Because a person's power on the surface and her influence in the underworld are considered two separate things, titles and ranks may vary greatly. The underworld is the only place in Calimshan where women are treated as equals to men. The rules for negotiations and meetings between underworld rivals are complex and delicate, involving proper forms of address, lying, and courtesy to the host.

MAJOR GEOGRAPHICAL FEATURES:

Calimshan extends along the northern coast of the Shining Sea for more than five hundred miles and includes all land south of the River Agis and the Marching Mountains.

Calim Desert: This expanse of sand, salt, and rocks is not a natural desert, but the blasted battleground of two powerful imprisoned genies. When the minds of the genies become active, the desert rages with violent sandstorms. The sands hide the ruins of great cities, which are said to still hold ancient treasures.

Forest of Mir: This forest grows on rough, hilly terrain and is dense with a variety of monsters. Large numbers of evil goblinkin and smaller giants live here, establishing petty fiefdoms and occasionally raiding to the north or south. In the northern part of the forest, a decaying *mythal* around Myth Unnohyr guards magical treasures, but the *mythal* turns helpful magic into harmful effects. Three Vhaeraunian drow settlements exist just under the surface near the foothills of the Marching Mountains.

Marching Mountains: This forested mountain range has protected Calimshan's northern border for centuries, although its resident orcs and ogres organize large raids every few years. Groups called the Janessar have military outposts in the mountains, using them as bases for their activities, most of which involve the betterment of the common folk of Calimshan, particularly the freeing of slaves.

Spider Swamp: This hot, fetid swamp was formed when a great marid (water genie) was slain near two sluggish rivers. Inhabited by monstrous spiders, aranea (who trade for fine silk and rare herbs), bullywugs, and lizardfolk, the swamp is avoided by all but the most foolhardy. In the northern part of the swamp is Lost Ajhuutal, a submerged aranea city. A third of the three hundred aranea living here worship Zanassu (an aspect of the drow deity Selvetarm) and tend toward neutral evil alignment and aggressive tendencies.

IMPORTANT SITES

Calimshan is unthinkably ancient, the oldest of all human lands still in existence. Ancient ruins and magical palaces can be found in many places in Calimshan, now forgotten.

Almraiven (Metropolis, 43,652): This port city is home to the country's largest shipbuilding facility. Aside from its whirlwind of mercantile and guild activity, wizards and sorcerers know Almraiven best as the premier center for magical study within Calimshan, a role the city has held for over three thousand years.

Calimport (Metropolis, 192,795): In addition to its huge population of permanent free citizens, Calimshan draws large numbers of seasonal residents and transient traders. One of the oldest continuously populated cities in Faerûn, it contains two great arenas, large palaces, and impressive examples of just about any sort of building found elsewhere, including auction houses for slaves.

Memnon (Metropolis, 29,101): Founded by the army of the efreet, Memnon is a garrison city, fishing port, trade stop, and the secondary port for the country's navy. Memnon's warships and soldiers defend Calimshan from northern aggression and any evils that dig themselves free from ruined Memnonnar across the river. The city's outer walls are made of a dark, smooth rock that absorbs heat and shrugs off wear.

Suldolphor (Metropolis, 143,687): A wealthy and intrigue-ridden city, Suldolphor is almost independent of Calimshan's rule, grudgingly paying taxes so its citizens may be left alone. Located on the strait connecting the Shining Sea to the Lake of Steam, the city is important to both Calimshan's trade and defense.

REGIONAL HISTORY

Calimshan has long been the dominant power of southwest Faerûn, with a tumultuous recorded history spanning nine thousand years. It has always been a hot, damp, verdant land, suitable for growing olives and dates and grazing by huge herds of livestock. Its forests are filled with fragrant carving-woods, and its sandbars and coastal shoals bristle with oysters, crabs, edible fish, and rocks harboring both gems and metals. In short, Calimshan has always been a land worth fighting for—and so there has been much fighting for it.

In ancient times, the great forest Keltormir cloaked the region and was home to warring giants and elves. Humans also lurked in hiding among the trees, and the dwarves founded Deep Shanatar and flourished beneath the earth.

Then came the mighty djinn from "otherwhere," geniekin and their halfling and human slaves led by the djinni Calim. They founded the Calim Empire, clearing trees from the lands south and west of the Marching Mountains, slaughtering or driving out dragons, and establishing a domain whose borders correspond with the Calimshan of today.

The djinni ruled over humans in the Calim Caliphates for a thousand years before an efreeti of great power, Memnon, arrived from another "otherwhere" and established the realm of Memnonnar. The two empires broke into all-out war in the Era of Skyfire, a protracted struggle that so damaged the land that the elves used a form of great high magic to bind the spirits of Calim and Memnon into the ground and air, leaving them to struggle to this day in the sandy waste of their endless battle: the Calim Desert.

Humans and dwarves overthrew the few remaining geniekin in mere decades. Coram the Warrior founded the realm of Coramshan over the ruins of the genie empire. Riddled by intrigues and dynastic strife, it soon fell under the sway of evil human priests, but arose again as the reunited realm of Calimshan.

Ylveraasahlisar the Rose Dragon conquered Calimshan and ruled for over a century before being slain—whereupon beholders seized power. Humans drove the beholders out and established colonies across western Faerûn, but plagues weakened their empire. Tethyr and the Vilhon Reach shook off Calimshan's rule and became independent.

Human power in Calimshan peaked under the Shoon dynasty of a thousand years past. In more recent times, Calimshan has seen a Rage of Dragons (1018 DR), a Black Horde of orcs that slew its ruling Syl-Pasha (1235 DR), and the Time of Troubles (1358 DR), when the criminal underworld of Calimport was rocked by the death of all Bhaal-worshiping assassins.

The current ruler of Calimshan, Syl-Pasha Persakhal, has made an alliance with Tethyr. He hopes to study its ways—and then annex the land.

PLOTS AND RUMORS

Old magic, cruel slavers, forgotten ruins, and dangerous hinterlands make Calimshan a perilous and exciting place. Outlander adventurers would be wise to choose their enemies carefully.

The Secret Masters: Events and alliances in Calimshan have long been influenced by the Twisted Rune, a group of powerful undead spellcasters (including a blue dracolich) that meddles with mortal affairs for power and amusement. These spellcasters control *portals* leading to places across Faerûn and have hundreds of agents, most of whom don't know their ultimate masters.

The Unseen Hand: Originating in Tashalar, the Rundeen is an association of merchants and traders that controls most of the shipping in Calimshan, using piracy to sabotage rivals. The Rundeen dabbles in slavery and fiercely opposes the Harpers, who have made several successful attacks against the group. Its primary motivation is profit, and the organization sponsors adventurers who aren't selective in their causes to assist in profitable ventures.

tethyr

Capital: Darromar
Population: 3,771,360 (humans 76%, halflings 20%, elves 3%)
Government: Feudal monarchy (free commoners)
Religions: Helm, Ilmater, Siamorphe, Torm, Tyr
Imports: Magic items, mercenaries, spices, weapons
Exports: Ambergris, carpets, cheese, cloth, fish, fruit, livestock, nuts, pearls, pipeweed, rugs, silk, tea, vegetables, wine, whale oil
Alignment: CG, N, LG

Tethyr recently emerged from a decades-long civil war with two new monarchs. The strong rule of Queen-Monarch Zaranda Star Rhindaun and King Haedrak III (who for years served as scribe in Shadowdale to the great wizard Elminster under the name Lhaeo) is beginning to restore hope to a cynical, suspicious, war-torn land.

Tethyr is now growing, establishing ties with hesitant neighbors, and driving monsters from its lands. Its political situation still involves much intrigue, and the people distrust organizations that admit to meddling in others' affairs (such as the Harpers). The forest elves remain wary of the new rulers, for the last three kings sought to tame the great forest with axe, fire, and sword. The pirates living in the Nelanther Isles to the west plague the kingdom's maritime commerce, including trade with far-off Maztica.

LIFE AND SOCIETY

Tethyr is an old, often fragmented land that lies between the economic powerhouses of Amn and Calimshan. It is a dry, hot, and yet fertile realm of pride and mounted knights, forests and farms, herds and wealth, with two peninsulas thrusting out into the Sea of Swords. The huge Wealdath Forest, still inhabited by elves, stands as its northern wall. The interior is a largely empty region of rolling grasslands. Most Tethyrians dwell along the Murann–Riatavin and Zazesspur–Saradush trade routes, and one in five is a halfling (with almost all others being human).

Most of the well-made furniture, chests, and coffers in use in the Heartlands is Tethyrian or made in imitation of Tethyrian work. The realm is widely known for its superb wares, and Tethyrian guilds strive to promote excellence rather than controlling markets as they do elsewhere. Each of Tethyr's prosperous merchant families dedicates itself to a particular craft or trade good.

Land equals status in Tethyr; the nobles either earned their land themselves or inherited it. The common folk are ruled by counts, who appoint local sheriffs from among the commoners to administer laws, muster militias, collect taxes, and support local magistrates. The counts in turn answer to dukes, and the dukes to the Queen. She is advised by the Royal Privy Council of the monarch, her heir or crown regent, eight dukes, and five religious and racial emissaries: the Archdruid of Mosstone, the Treespeaker of the Wealdath (elves), the Hills' Voice (halflings), the Shield Brother of the remaining Starspire dwarves, and the Samnilith, a spokesperson for the gnomes.

The Queen directly oversees the standing army and judiciary. She has made Darromar the new capital of the realm, and it has risen swiftly to join Myratma, Riatavin, Saradush, and Zazesspur as an important Tethyrian city.

Tethyr has many knightly orders sponsored by Ilmater, Torm, Tyr, and Helm. The most prestigious is the Order of the Silver Chalice, followed by the Champions Vigilant who worship Helm. Intrigue and opportunity have sprouted of late as Tethyr recovers its prosperity and grows larger—the cities of Riatavin and Trailstone seceded from Amn and declared allegiance to the throne of Tethyr in 1370 DR.

Travelers are warned that the number five is considered very unlucky in Tethyr.

MAJOR GEOGRAPHICAL FEATURES:

In terms of land area, Tethyr is one of the largest of Faerûn's realms. Much of this vast expanse of plains and forests is settled only sparsely.

Omlarandin Mountains: Barely higher than the foothills around them, these mountains are legendary for omlar gems that are very suitable for magical uses. Only a few rare omlars have been discovered in centuries, but those have fetched princely sums from wizards. Wyverns and displacer beasts inhabit the area.

ghost ships

The Sword Coast is famed for brutal battles between rival navies, pirates and merchants, sailors and the monsters of the deeps seeking to drag them down—and dragons pouncing from the skies, seeking to smash and sink or slay. Such strife never ceases.

Over the centuries, thousands of vessels have been lost at sea . . . and not all of them lie quietly beneath the waves. Wherever sailors in taverns talk of the sea, they mention Those Who Sail Forever, then duck their heads and make warding circles with their thumbs to keep the undead from hearing and coming for them.

While some pirates and slavers use the cloaks of night, fog, and bobbing skull-masks to pose as "ghost ships," true ghost ships do sail the waters of Faerûn. Spells on the hull or tainted and corrupted magical energies used on the cargo keep some such ships afloat. They sail empty, or with skeletons or zombies as crew.

They may ride the waves with or without sails rigged, or wallow along waterlogged, with decks awash yet refusing to sink. Others are true phantoms: wraithlike clouds that are the images of their former selves.

It's said that the evil sea deity Umberlee uses ghost ships to bring long-drowned magic items back into the hands of those who'll take them ashore, or bear treasure tales into port to draw the greedy out into her clutches.

Famous ghost ships include *Red Prow* of Calimport, a slave ship that sank under the weight of the gold and gems it carried. It now houses wraiths and "weirder things" that ride folk like steeds. Perhaps most feared is *Ravager* of the pirate Gonchklas, a wallowing wreck of a caravel with tattered sails and a zombie and skeleton crew who storm and board every vessel they encounter.

Starspire Mountains: These low mountains contain treacherous and winding peaks. A few small clans of dwarves live here, enjoying their privacy despite the local perytons, displacer beasts, goblin tribes, ogres, and werewolves. The easternmost mountain is Mount Thargill, a long-dead volcano that is a secondary home to the red dragon Balagos the Flying Flame. Balagos has imprisoned two dragons, a brown and a black, to act as guards.

The Wealdath: Home of the two surviving local tribes of elves, the Suldusk and the Elmanesse, this forest also contains fey creatures that vigorously defend it against encroachers. Gnolls, lycanthropes, giant spiders, wyverns, and dragons (two greens, a bronze, and a gold) pose occasional dangers, although they have learned to avoid the elves. *Portals* leading to the plane of the lythari (elven shapechangers) exist in the forest, although only the lythari know how to open them.

IMPORTANT SITES

The castles of Tethyrian nobles—some now in ruins from the recent war—dot the plains and river valleys of the countryside.

Darromar (Metropolis, 68,520): The new capital city and home of the queen and consort, Darromar has become the premier city of Tethyr. It boasts well-trained troops and draws many mercenaries, both for training and employment as brigand and monster hunters. A small academy here harbors sorcerers and wizards who have no intention of going south to Calimshan.

Mosstone (Small Town, 1,713): This walled town is significant for its location along the Trade Way, its collective government (ruled by townsfolk and nearby druids), and its proximity to the grove of powerful druids. The nearly two hundred druids associated with the grove work with the townsfolk to protect the forest and instruct those using the Trade Way how not to anger the elves of the Wealdath.

Myratma (Metropolis, 51,390): This walled city is more like Calimshan than any other city in Tethyr. It is the port through which the country's agricultural products flow, and it is fighting to reclaim its honor after being the home of a rebellious noble family. Myratma has a paucity of sorcerers and wizards (most find employment in Calimshan), but the place is remarkable for the Jaguar Guard, a group of noble warriors brought over from the exotic land of Maztica to the west.

Riatavin (Metropolis, 85,650): Crucial in the flow of trade to and from the Sea of Fallen Stars, Riatavin gained little benefit from Amn's Maztican colonization. Largely ignored by Amn's Council of Six, Riatavin seceded to Tethyr in 1370 DR. Previously hidden sorcerers and wizards have revealed themselves to the city leaders to show their support for the decision and aid in defending against reprisals from Amn.

Velen (Large City, 14,389): Many ghosts haunt this fortified city, although the people are so happy and vibrant that visitors believe the hauntings to be greatly exaggerated. Important as a naval outpost against the Nelanther pirates, Velen is also a valuable fishing port. Seafaring adventurers are quite welcome here.

Zazesspur (Metropolis, 116,485): An amalgam of Tethyrian, Calishite, and other cultural and architectural influences, Zazesspur is a former capital of Tethyr and consists of two sections separated by the mouth of the Sulduskoon River. Ruled by a council of lords, the city resents its loss of prestige to the new capital of Darromar. Few wizards or sorcerers live here, because those fleeing Amn usually travel farther than Zazesspur; the city's proximity to Calimshan means those with arcane powers are quickly hired for a comfortable salary and life in the south.

REGIONAL HISTORY

Once a great forest populated by elves, the land now known as Tethyr has been overrun by giants, dragons, and djinn, given rise to a great dwarven kingdom, fallen to the Calishites, harbored escaped slaves, and suffered through numerous political turmoils. The most recent of those was a civil war a generation ago that killed hundreds of thousands of people and resulted in the secession of one of its provinces.

Two long-forgotten scions of the noble line have been placed on the throne and, with the secret backing of powerful foreign wizards, have established order again. But certain people in power have ties to foreign interests and hostile powers, making the job of Queen-Monarch Zaranda Star Rhindaun (CG female human Ftr7/Wiz6) and King Haedrak III (NG male human Ftr2/Wiz6) that much more difficult. The new nobility, especially those not of Tethyrian blood, must still win the respect of their people.

PLOTS AND RUMORS

Tethyr's extensive wilds and unsettled lands are home to brigands, evil humanoids, magical beasts, and all other sorts of troubles requiring the attention of adventurers.

Old Shanatar: At the height of the dwarven kingdom of Shanatar, the cities that are now Darromar, Memnon, Myratma, and Zazesspur were dwarven cities with extensive underground tunnels. The entrances to the tunnels have been lost or forgotten; no human has set foot in any of them since the kingdom's fall, and they probably hold great treasures. However, old dwarven traps and constructs are sure to guard whatever riches are buried there.

ARTEMIS ENTRERI

Male human Rog4/Rgr1/Ftr12/Asn1: CR 18; Medium-size humanoid; HD 4d6+8 plus 1d10+2 plus 12d10+24 plus 1d6+2; hp 121; Init +9; Spd 30 ft.; AC 22 (touch 18, flat-footed 22); Atk +20/+15/+10/+5 melee (1d8+7/17–20 plus wounding, *+3 longsword of wounding*) and +21/+16 melee (1d4+7/17–20, *+4 defending dagger*); SA Death attack (Fort DC 14), fight with two weapons, sneak attack +3d6; SQ Evasion, favored enemy (human +1), locate traps, poison use, uncanny dodge (Dex bonus to AC); AL LE; SV Fort +13, Ref +15, Will +8; Str 14, Dex 20, Con 15, Int 16, Wis 16, Cha 13. Height 5 ft. 5 in.

Skills and Feats: Balance +14, Bluff +6, Climb +12, Decipher Script +6, Diplomacy +5, Disable Device +5, Disguise +9, Escape Artist +8, Forgery +6, Gather Information +4, Handle Animal +6, Hide +13, Intimidate +6, Intuit Direction +6, Jump +12, Knowledge (the North local) +6, Listen +8, Move Silently +13, Open Lock +10, Pick Pocket +13, Read Lips +6, Ride (horse) +11, Search +8, Sense

Artemis Entreri

Illustration by Matt Wilson

The Unseen Hand: Originating in Tashalar, the Rundeen is an association of merchants and traders that controls most of the shipping in Calimshan, using piracy to sabotage rivals. The Rundeen dabbles in slavery and fiercely opposes the Harpers, who have made several successful attacks against the group. Its primary motivation is profit, and the organization sponsors adventurers who aren't selective in their causes to assist in profitable ventures.

Tethyr

Capital: Darromar
Population: 3,771,360 (humans 76%, halflings 20%, elves 3%)
Government: Feudal monarchy (free commoners)
Religions: Helm, Ilmater, Siamorphe, Torm, Tyr
Imports: Magic items, mercenaries, spices, weapons
Exports: Ambergris, carpets, cheese, cloth, fish, fruit, livestock, nuts, pearls, pipeweed, rugs, silk, tea, vegetables, wine, whale oil
Alignment: CG, N, LG

Tethyr recently emerged from a decades-long civil war with two new monarchs. The strong rule of Queen-Monarch Zaranda Star Rhindaun and King Haedrak III (who for years served as scribe in Shadowdale to the great wizard Elminster under the name Lhaeo) is beginning to restore hope to a cynical, suspicious, war-torn land.

Tethyr is now growing, establishing ties with hesitant neighbors, and driving monsters from its lands. Its political situation still involves much intrigue, and the people distrust organizations that admit to meddling in others' affairs (such as the Harpers). The forest elves remain wary of the new rulers, for the last three kings sought to tame the great forest with axe, fire, and sword. The pirates living in the Nelanther Isles to the west plague the kingdom's maritime commerce, including trade with far-off Maztica.

LIFE AND SOCIETY

Tethyr is an old, often fragmented land that lies between the economic powerhouses of Amn and Calimshan. It is a dry, hot, and yet fertile realm of pride and mounted knights, forests and farms, herds and wealth, with two peninsulas thrusting out into the Sea of Swords. The huge Wealdath Forest, still inhabited by elves, stands as its northern wall. The interior is a largely empty region of rolling grasslands. Most Tethyrians dwell along the Murann–Riatavin and Zazesspur–Saradush trade routes, and one in five is a halfling (with almost all others being human).

Most of the well-made furniture, chests, and coffers in use in the Heartlands is Tethyrian or made in imitation of Tethyrian work. The realm is widely known for its superb wares, and Tethyrian guilds strive to promote excellence rather than controlling markets as they do elsewhere. Each of Tethyr's prosperous merchant families dedicates itself to a particular craft or trade good.

Land equals status in Tethyr; the nobles either earned their land themselves or inherited it. The common folk are ruled by counts, who appoint local sheriffs from among the commoners to administer laws, muster militias, collect taxes, and support local magistrates. The counts in turn answer to dukes, and the dukes to the Queen. She is advised by the Royal Privy Council of the monarch, her heir or crown regent, eight dukes, and five religious and racial emissaries: the Archdruid of Mosstone, the Treespeaker of the Wealdath (elves), the Hills' Voice (halflings), the Shield Brother of the remaining Starspire dwarves, and the Samnilith, a spokesperson for the gnomes.

The Queen directly oversees the standing army and judiciary. She has made Darromar the new capital of the realm, and it has risen swiftly to join Myratma, Riatavin, Saradush, and Zazesspur as an important Tethyrian city.

Tethyr has many knightly orders sponsored by Ilmater, Torm, Tyr, and Helm. The most prestigious is the Order of the Silver Chalice, followed by the Champions Vigilant who worship Helm. Intrigue and opportunity have sprouted of late as Tethyr recovers its prosperity and grows larger—the cities of Riatavin and Trailstone seceded from Amn and declared allegiance to the throne of Tethyr in 1370 DR.

Travelers are warned that the number five is considered very unlucky in Tethyr.

MAJOR GEOGRAPHICAL FEATURES:

In terms of land area, Tethyr is one of the largest of Faerûn's realms. Much of this vast expanse of plains and forests is settled only sparsely.

Omlarandin Mountains: Barely higher than the foothills around them, these mountains are legendary for omlar gems that are very suitable for magical uses. Only a few rare omlars have been discovered in centuries, but those have fetched princely sums from wizards. Wyverns and displacer beasts inhabit the area.

Ghost Ships

The Sword Coast is famed for brutal battles between rival navies, pirates and merchants, sailors and the monsters of the deeps seeking to drag them down—and dragons pouncing from the skies, seeking to smash and sink or slay. Such strife never ceases.

Over the centuries, thousands of vessels have been lost at sea . . . and not all of them lie quietly beneath the waves. Wherever sailors in taverns talk of the sea, they mention Those Who Sail Forever, then duck their heads and make warding circles with their thumbs to keep the undead from hearing and coming for them.

While some pirates and slavers use the cloaks of night, fog, and bobbing skull-masks to pose as "ghost ships," true ghost ships do sail the waters of Faerûn. Spells on the hull or tainted and corrupted magical energies used on the cargo keep some such ships afloat. They sail empty, or with skeletons or zombies as crew.

They may ride the waves with or without sails rigged, or wallow along waterlogged, with decks awash yet refusing to sink. Others are true phantoms: wraithlike clouds that are the images of their former selves.

It's said that the evil sea deity Umberlee uses ghost ships to bring long-drowned magic items back into the hands of those who'll take them ashore, or bear treasure tales into port to draw the greedy out into her clutches.

Famous ghost ships include *Red Prow* of Calimport, a slave ship that sank under the weight of the gold and gems it carried. It now houses wraiths and "weirder things" that ride folk like steeds. Perhaps most feared is *Ravager* of the pirate Gonchklas, a wallowing wreck of a caravel with tattered sails and a zombie and skeleton crew who storm and board every vessel they encounter.

Starspire Mountains: These low mountains contain treacherous and winding peaks. A few small clans of dwarves live here, enjoying their privacy despite the local perytons, displacer beasts, goblin tribes, ogres, and werewolves. The easternmost mountain is Mount Thargill, a long-dead volcano that is a secondary home to the red dragon Balagos the Flying Flame. Balagos has imprisoned two dragons, a brown and a black, to act as guards.

The Wealdath: Home of the two surviving local tribes of elves, the Suldusk and the Elmanesse, this forest also contains fey creatures that vigorously defend it against encroachers. Gnolls, lycanthropes, giant spiders, wyverns, and dragons (two greens, a bronze, and a gold) pose occasional dangers, although they have learned to avoid the elves. *Portals* leading to the plane of the lythari (elven shapechangers) exist in the forest, although only the lythari know how to open them.

IMPORTANT SITES

The castles of Tethyrian nobles—some now in ruins from the recent war—dot the plains and river valleys of the countryside.

Darromar (Metropolis, 68,520): The new capital city and home of the queen and consort, Darromar has become the premier city of Tethyr. It boasts well-trained troops and draws many mercenaries, both for training and employment as brigand and monster hunters. A small academy here harbors sorcerers and wizards who have no intention of going south to Calimshan.

Mosstone (Small Town, 1,713): This walled town is significant for its location along the Trade Way, its collective government (ruled by townsfolk and nearby druids), and its proximity to the grove of powerful druids. The nearly two hundred druids associated with the grove work with the townsfolk to protect the forest and instruct those using the Trade Way how not to anger the elves of the Wealdath.

Myratma (Metropolis, 51,390): This walled city is more like Calimshan than any other city in Tethyr. It is the port through which the country's agricultural products flow, and it is fighting to reclaim its honor after being the home of a rebellious noble family. Myratma has a paucity of sorcerers and wizards (most find employment in Calimshan), but the place is remarkable for the Jaguar Guard, a group of noble warriors brought over from the exotic land of Maztica to the west.

Riatavin (Metropolis, 85,650): Crucial in the flow of trade to and from the Sea of Fallen Stars, Riatavin gained little benefit from Amn's Maztican colonization. Largely ignored by Amn's Council of Six, Riatavin seceded to Tethyr in 1370 DR. Previously hidden sorcerers and wizards have revealed themselves to the city leaders to show their support for the decision and aid in defending against reprisals from Amn.

Velen (Large City, 14,389): Many ghosts haunt this fortified city, although the people are so happy and vibrant that visitors believe the hauntings to be greatly exaggerated. Important as a naval outpost against the Nelanther pirates, Velen is also a valuable fishing port. Seafaring adventurers are quite welcome here.

Zazesspur (Metropolis, 116,485): An amalgam of Tethyrian, Calishite, and other cultural and architectural influences, Zazesspur is a former capital of Tethyr and consists of two sections separated by the mouth of the Sulduskoon River. Ruled by a council of lords, the city resents its loss of prestige to the new capital of Darromar. Few wizards or sorcerers live here, because those fleeing Amn usually travel farther than Zazesspur; the city's proximity to Calimshan means those with arcane powers are quickly hired for a comfortable salary and life in the south.

REGIONAL HISTORY

Once a great forest populated by elves, the land now known as Tethyr has been overrun by giants, dragons, and djinn, given rise to a great dwarven kingdom, fallen to the Calishites, harbored escaped slaves, and suffered through numerous political turmoils. The most recent of those was a civil war a generation ago that killed hundreds of thousands of people and resulted in the secession of one of its provinces.

Two long-forgotten scions of the noble line have been placed on the throne and, with the secret backing of powerful foreign wizards, have established order again. But certain people in power have ties to foreign interests and hostile powers, making the job of Queen-Monarch Zaranda Star Rhindaun (CG female human Ftr7/Wiz6) and King Haedrak III (NG male human Ftr2/Wiz6) that much more difficult. The new nobility, especially those not of Tethyrian blood, must still win the respect of their people.

PLOTS AND RUMORS

Tethyr's extensive wilds and unsettled lands are home to brigands, evil humanoids, magical beasts, and all other sorts of troubles requiring the attention of adventurers.

Old Shanatar: At the height of the dwarven kingdom of Shanatar, the cities that are now Darromar, Memnon, Myratma, and Zazesspur were dwarven cities with extensive underground tunnels. The entrances to the tunnels have been lost or forgotten; no human has set foot in any of them since the kingdom's fall, and they probably hold great treasures. However, old dwarven traps and constructs are sure to guard whatever riches are buried there.

Artemis Entreri

Illustration by Matt Wilson

ARTEMIS ENTRERI

Male human Rog4/Rgr1/Ftr12/Asn1: CR 18; Medium-size humanoid; HD 4d6+8 plus 1d10+2 plus 12d10+24 plus 1d6+2; hp 121; Init +9; Spd 30 ft.; AC 22 (touch 18, flat-footed 22); Atk +20/+15/+10/+5 melee (1d8+7/17–20 plus wounding, *+3 longsword of wounding*) and +21/+16 melee (1d4+7/17–20, *+4 defending dagger*); SA Death attack (Fort DC 14), fight with two weapons, sneak attack +3d6; SQ Evasion, favored enemy (human +1), locate traps, poison use, uncanny dodge (Dex bonus to AC); AL LE; SV Fort +13, Ref +15, Will +8; Str 14, Dex 20, Con 15, Int 16, Wis 16, Cha 13. Height 5 ft. 5 in.

Skills and Feats: Balance +14, Bluff +6, Climb +12, Decipher Script +6, Diplomacy +5, Disable Device +5, Disguise +9, Escape Artist +8, Forgery +6, Gather Information +4, Handle Animal +6, Hide +13, Intimidate +6, Intuit Direction +6, Jump +12, Knowledge (the North local) +6, Listen +8, Move Silently +13, Open Lock +10, Pick Pocket +13, Read Lips +6, Ride (horse) +11, Search +8, Sense *power*, 5th level), *boots of speed*, rune necklace (usually holds 4 runes of *cure critical wounds* and 2 of *raise dead*).

Cleric Spells per Day: 6/6/6/5/3/2. Base DC = 13 + spell level. Domains: Evil (cast evil spells at 10th spell level), Storm (electricity resistance 5).

Daughter of frost giant jarl Orel the Grayhand, Gerti worships Auril the Frostmaiden, a domineering and oppressive deity. She will inherit the leadership of the tribe since her father has no sons, and her strength and allies will help her keep it. Her cleric powers are great, and because she teaches rune magic to clerics in nearby tribes, she has strong support within her own tribe and in others.

Gerti uses her runes to ward the narrow passes that lead to her tribe's caves in the Spine of the World, create objects of healing for the tribe's warriors and hunters, and protect the tribe's valuables. With her wisdom and skill at negotiation, she is called upon to arbitrate disputes between tribes. She preaches that the frost giants are the chosen people of Auril, for of the creatures that thrive in the cold, only they have hands and minds to direct them in the service of the Frostmaiden.

The Grayhand is old, and is expected to die within the next year or two. When Gerti assumes the mantle of leadership, she likely will send more raids into the lowlands or try some great collective magic with the other frost giant clerics of the mountains to bring a great winter of storms to the nearby lands. Gerti is a capable leader and not averse to allying with other kinds of giants if she thinks it would serve her needs and the needs of her deity.

silver marches

Capital: Silverymoon
Population: 1,090,800 (humans 40%, dwarves 20%, elves 20%, half-elves 10%, halflings 5%, gnomes 2%, half-orcs 2%)
Government: Confederation of lords headed by Alustriel of Silverymoon
Religions: Corellon Larethian, Helm, Lathander, Lurue, Mielikki, Moradin, Mystra, Oghma, Selûne, Sune, Tymora
Imports: Armor, books, manufactured goods, pottery, spices, wine
Exports: Dwarven and elven craftwork, furs, heroes, precious metals
Alignment: LG, NG, CG

Silverymoon is the Gem of the North, a city built as a center of learning and a symbol of the greatness that once shone out of the elven capital of Myth Drannor. Three years ago, the ruler of Silverymoon, High Lady Alustriel, reached out to the rulers of other human, elven, and dwarven strongholds north of the High Forest, west of the Evermoors, and south of the great mountains. After much debate, the diverse dwarfholds, human and half-elven settlements, and human cities decided to ally in a mutual defense pact headed by Alustriel, who stepped down as ruler of Silverymoon in order to oversee the new confederacy of the Silver Marches.

The present member settlements of the Silver Marches include Citadel Adbar, Citadel Felbarr, Deadsnows, Everlund, Jalanthar, Mithral Hall, Quaervarr, Silverymoon, and Sundabar.

LIFE AND SOCIETY

The folk of the Silver Marches are confident, hopeful, and content. All around stands a wide and beautiful land, a promise of growth and prosperity for generations to come. Acting with care and respect, the humans hope to reap the riches of the forests and mountains without destroying what they touch, learning from elves and dwarves how to live with the land instead of bending the land to human whim. All people are free, all people may own land, and no one is guaranteed rights and privileges that are denied to others under the law. The Silver Marches represent the unfolding of a dream, a chance to forge a better Faerûn, and everyone from the poorest woodcutter to the richest city merchant senses the beginning of something extraordinary.

That said, the new confederation is not perfect. Just because humans, elves, and dwarves have set aside their differences in a few small cities in the North doesn't mean that the barbarians, orcs, gnolls, giants, and dragons of this forbidding landscape feel constrained to join them. Deadly enemies surround Alustriel's league and plot its downfall. The orc hordes of the high mountains grow strong again and arm for war. The drow of Menzoberranzan threaten the fledgling realm from the depths of the earth. And, as in most other places of Faerûn, the wreckage of ancient realms and the remnants of magical disasters wait under the forests and snows of the realm. Plagues and evils untold await those foolish enough to disturb them.

The new settlers

In the long history of the settled lands of the North, few civilized humans have dared to establish permanent dwellings outside walled cities and towns such as Silverymoon and Everlund. That has begun to change in the first few years of peace brought by the creation of the Silver Marches. Immigrants from all over Faerûn have moved into the north lands, drawn by the new alliance that promises to stand strong against the orcs.

To the surprise of the citizens of the Silver Marches, the new immigrants include retired Zhent soldiers and their families. They've been cashed out of active service with the Zhent forces, provided with enough gold to buy seed, a plow, and possibly even some land, and asked to move somewhere far away from the Moonsea. Most of the Zhent retirees can't wait to move as far away from Zhentil Keep as possible, since few of them wish to risk being called back to active service. Or at least that's the story they tell the citizens of the Silver Marches.

The Zhent retirees group together in newly established stockade communities of between one hundred and three hundred souls. They know that the cities in the Silver Marches alliance view them with suspicion. Even so, they have brought their families and their dreams of a better life and ask only to be allowed to contribute to the area's growth and peace. The new communities have chosen simple names such as Newfort, Hilltop, and Winter Edge, names calculated to sound friendly instead of threatening. As a group, they refer to themselves as the Free Towns. As of 1372 DR, the Free Towns' total population numbers around four thousand.

Roughly one third of the newcomers are evil in alignment, some 10% are good, and the rest (more than 50%) are neutral. The degree of Zhentarim involvement in the newcomers' lives remains to be seen. Few of the retirees care passionately for the Zhent cause, but covert agents, religious obligations, old feuds, and untrustworthy leaders could embroil them in conflicts with the other inhabitants of the Silver Marches and with each other.

MAJOR GEOGRAPHICAL FEATURES

The Silver Marches generally includes the lands west of Anauroch, east of the River Surbrin, and north of the River Rauvin. Vast stretches of the forests and mountains within these borders are unsettled wilds.

The Cold Wood: A pine, birch, and spruce forest unmarked by civilized settlers or foresters, the Cold Wood is home to some Uthgardt tribes, who never cut down living trees. Snow tigers, orcs, and ettins roam the wood.

The Moonwood: The large forest north of Silverymoon is blessedly free of orcs and other goblinoids. Unfortunately, this state of affairs has little to do with the efforts of Silverymoon's rangers and much to do with the fearsome reputation of the lycanthropes who inhabit the forest's northern quarter. Many of these evil lycanthropes are members of the People of the Black Blood, a sect of Malar-worshiping werebeasts who resent the civilizing influence of Silverymoon.

Nether Mountains: Silverymoon may be civilized, but its people will never grow soft as long as they have to contend with the yearly tides of monsters that tire of the hard life in the mountain snows and look to the lowlands for plunder. The pass between Silverymoon and Sundabar is closed about six months of the year by heavy snows.

Rauvin Mountains: Goblin kingdoms and orc warrens infest these mountains. The River Rauvin passes through the peaks in a steep-sided, mist-filled gorge of roaring white water. A perilous trail climbs along the shoulder of the gorge through Dead Orc Pass to the north side of the Rauvins, but most travelers choose to pass around the mountains to the east, since the pass is the home of a particularly strong and aggressive orc tribe.

IMPORTANT SITES

The heart of the Silver Marches is the upper and lower valley of the River Rauvin. Winding for hundreds of miles in the shadow of the Nether Mountains and the Evermoors, the Rauvin marks a narrow ribbon of civilization and security in an otherwise inhospitable land. Along the Rauvin lie the farmsteads and settlements that feed Silverymoon and Everlund, and its swift cold waters carry trade from Sundabar all the way to Waterdeep.

Beorunna's Well (Large Town, 2,139): The ancestral home of the Uthgardt Black Lion tribe, this is a huge pit containing their ancestor mound. The rough village of the Black Lions lies nearby. The Black Lions have abandoned their traditional ways and settled to farm, herd, and hunt the nearby forests.

Citadel Adbar (Large City, 19,962): The dwarves who populate this militarily powerful fortress live underground in miles of twisting, dwarf-sized corridors. Adbar's aboveground citadel may be the mightiest fortress north of Amn, having withstood nearly a hundred major orc attacks over the centuries. Reaching Adbar is difficult: Merchant caravans generally travel through the Underdark from Mithral Hall or Mirabar. And caravans do come, to supply the dwarves with fruits and surface-grown vegetables and return with metals or fine dwarven craftworks.

Humans and elves find Citadel Adbar a difficult place to relax in: It's too cramped and too cold, and the stench of the metalworks (placed aboveground instead of below, where the dwarves live) reminds the elves, at least, of nothing less than an orc siegeworks.

Citadel Felbarr (Small City, 6,987): A former dwarven citadel given over to humans when the dwarves retreated into deeper holds, Felbarr fell to orcs three hundred years ago. Renamed the Citadel of Many Arrows by its new masters, it stood as an example of how orcs could conquer the weaker folk of the south.

Centuries later, in 1367 DR, a huge orc horde moving south against the settled cities paused in front of the orc citadel, held by a chief calling himself King Obould. Instead of pressing on to the human lands, the horde besieged their fellows inside. After a four-month siege, the invaders broke down the gates and entered the main keep, but a strong dwarven force fell on both tribes and seized the citadel out from under the orcs' tusks.

King Emerus Warcrown (LG male shield dwarf Ftr16) took control of the citadel, hanging on through the first bitter winter until six hundred shield dwarf reinforcements could march up from the south to join his forces. Warcrown's people are now well established and determined not to lose their citadel again.

Meanwhile, north in the Spine of the World, Obould, who escaped the fall of his citadel, is gathering forces for another assault upon the lands he once mastered. He is aware of the Silver Marches defense pact and is attempting to determine how best to strike through the alliance's weak spots.

Everlund (Large City, 21,388): A walled city of humans, elves, half-elves, and halflings, Everlund is a caravan trading city and a solid ally of Silverymoon. Its Council of Six Elders is part of the Lords' Alliance.

Everlund faces threats from all sides. The trolls who used to occupy the Evermoors could be counted on to be stupid and predictable. Not so the giants who have replaced them. To the city's south, the huge trees of the High Forest are growing closer and closer to Everlund's walls. The great treant Turlang is expanding the High Forest to the north, ostensibly in order to bury the remains of Hellgate Keep off to the east. No one thinks that taking an axe to the trees is a good idea, but urban human pursuits are substantially less relaxed in the shadow of the great trees.

Jalanthar (Hamlet, 314): Jalanthar is a collection of two hundred or so human trappers, hunters, and rangers who inhabit both the ruins of their former village and a network of caves in the hills. At first glance, visitors assume that Jalanthar is a dying community, crushed by its wars with the orcs. Nothing could be further from the truth. By both necessity and aptitude, the locals have become expert orc fighters, trackers, and guides. Instead of sticking to their original clan ties, all the humans of the region cooperate in defense, hunting, and magic. Jalanthar rangers are proud to be in demand throughout the rest of the Silver Marches.

Mithral Hall (Large Town, 4,991): Mithral Hall was once the greatest of the northern shield dwarf holds. Around 180 years ago, it fell to a shadow dragon named Shimmergloom, let loose from the Shadow Plane into Faerûn when members of Clan Battlehammer dug too deeply in search of mithril. Shimmergloom slew most of the dwarves and took possession of the hall along with his entourage of shadow monsters and duergar. Things were not set right until 1356 DR, when Bruenor Battlehammer (NG male shield dwarf Ftr13) returned from Icewind Dale to slay Shimmergloom.

Bruenor drove out the duergar and retook the hall, proclaiming himself the Eighth King of Mithral Hall. Shield dwarves from all over the north, particularly children of the Thunder Blessing generation, have marched to Bruenor's side to mine mithril and finish cleaning out the Underdark beneath the hold. Mithral Hall's resurgence has strengthened the Silver Marches by providing Silverymoon with an energetic sister city and a staunch ally in war.

Quaervarr (Small Town, 1,212): A junior partner in the Silver Marches, Quaervarr is a woodland town of humans and half-elves. Wits in Silverymoon joke that Quaervarr is worth having in the alliance simply to preserve its fine inn, The Whistling Stag.

Silverymoon (Metropolis, 37,073): The city of Silverymoon is a beautiful place of ancient trees and soaring towers, with curving lines in its stonework and garden plantings adorning every nook and balcony. Aerial steeds carry riders on high, magic and learning is revered, music and laughter are heard often in the streets, and the city contains fascinating shops brim-full of maps, books, minor magic items, and beautiful things.

Illustration by Sam Wood

Silverymoon

Even more so than Waterdeep, Silverymoon is built on the spirit of cooperation between the races. Humans, elves, and dwarves all maintain dwellings in the same areas of the city instead of dividing into separate wards. A human home might be built around the base of a tree, with elves using the tree above as part of the walkway to their central tree home, and dwarves caverns beneath the surface.

Silverymoon is considered the foremost center of learning and culture in the North. It is noted for its musicians, its cobblers, its sculptors, and its stonemasons—as well as the mages, who are gathered here in greater numbers than in any other city of the Sword Coast lands except Waterdeep. Their might alone keeps the Arcane Brotherhood of Luskan and other evils of the North at bay—were these mages to vanish tomorrow, the civilized North might well be swept away in blood and ruin.

Silverymoon boasts a conservatory of music, a great library, parks, castlelike residences of many noble folk, and temples and shrines to such deities as Helm, Lathander, Mielikki, Milil, Mystra, Oghma, Selûne, Silvanus, Sune, Tymora, and the dwarven and elven deities. Perhaps the most famous structure is the University of Silverymoon, a school of magic composed of several formerly separate colleges. Member schools include The Lady's College (serving both sorcerers and bards), Miresk's School of Thaumaturgy, and Foclucan, a legendary bard's college that has reopened (having taken a century off after being overrun by orcs).

The city's army, the Knights in Silver, numbers over five hundred and patrols the city constantly. Harper scouts and mages assist them, and when they must turn back orc hordes, awesome magemight gathers to fight with them. Silverymoon is also protected by a number of wards that detect the presence of evil beings and the use of magic in certain areas. Even long-time Silveraen know little about the properties of the permanent magical field that augments

some magic, turns other spells wild, and negates still others, protecting the city east of its great open market. Certain areas in the palace (a place heavily guarded at all times by mages of the elite Spellguard) have an Inner Ward that requires possession of a token to allow entry at all.

The city's peace and goodwill is due to the influence of powerful local mages and the Harpers. Silverymoon's folk feel safe—and that's due to the vigilance of the mages and agents trained and established by Alustriel.

In 1369 DR, the Lady Alustriel stepped down as High Mage, yielding up the Silver Throne to Taern "Thunderspell" Hornblade (LG male human Wiz18). Alustriel is the High Lady, or Speaker, of the Silver Marches and leads the league councils.

Sundabar (Large City, 14,259): The area around Sundabar is occupied only by obsessed miners, howling orcs, and citizens of Sundabar who should know better. The double-walled city was built for war. Sundabar's ruler, Helm Dwarf-friend (NG male human Ftr10/Rgr5 of Mielikki) started his career as a member of the Bloodaxe Mercenary Company, rising to command both the mercenaries and his chosen city. He has turned out to be a wise ruler, taxing his people fairly and using the proceeds to ensure his city's defense against orc invasions, which flood in every two or three years and break on Sundabar's sturdy walls. The Everfire, a zealously guarded volcanic rift beneath Sundabar, is the source of some of the finest magic weapons of Faerûn.

REGIONAL HISTORY

Like the rest of Faerûn, the Silver Marches is built over the ruins of lands that existed long before. In this instance, the old kingdoms are the elven realm of Eaerlann formerly based in the High Forest, the dwarf realm of Delzoun underneath Ascore, and the human

empire of Netheril. None of these three occupied all the land now accounted part of the Silver Marches, but their settlements and borders overlapped in this region in various eras.

The city of Silverymoon is the heart of the Silver Marches and the bright hope of the North. Founded on a place sacred to the nature deities Mielikki and Lurue the Unicorn, Silverymoon developed around the Moonsilver Inn. The holy groves at Silverymoon Ford lay near where the River Rauvin was shallow, and could be forded in high summer and easily bridged to allow crossings year-round.

Silver Village grew slowly into Silverymoon Town, and Silverymoon became a city in 637 DR, when its first set of walls was completed. The first of twelve High Mages to rule the city thus far was elected. Ecamane Truesilver and his nine apprentices established a school and a library and set about educating the local warriors, trappers, loggers, and fisherfolk. From that day forth, successive High Mages have pursued the goal of making Silverymoon "the Myth Drannor of the North," a beacon of culture, learning, sophistication, and racial harmony.

Alustriel became the first High Mage of Silverymoon unanimously chosen by the people, and ruled long and well until 1369 DR. She stepped down, appointed Taern Hornblade as High Mage, and set about creating a new realm in the Sword Coast North with Silverymoon at its heart. Today, Silverymoon is a rich, sophisticated, and exciting place to live, truly the Gem of the North.

PLOTS AND RUMORS

Adventurers come to the Silver Marches to advance the cause of civilization by scouring the land for monster lairs, cleansing dangerous ruins, and driving orc raiders back to their mountain dens. Silverymoon's growth and prosperity have brought new enemies, though—the merchants and proud lords of cities such as Luskan and Yartar who grow jealous of the riches that flow through the Silver Marches.

Dark Deeds in Ascore: The ruined dwarven city of Ascore on the border of Anauroch was once the gateway to the realm of Delzoun, a rich seaport on the long-vanished Narrow Sea. An expedition from the city of Shade has set up a temporary camp in the ruins, driving off any adventurers who come to explore the old dwarven city. A survivor from one of these adventuring companies reports that a mighty archmage leads the shade effort, which seems to be centered around a strange pool of liquid shadow surrounded by thirteen odd, pyramidlike structures. What are the shades up to? What might they unleash in their efforts to achieve their objective?

Missing Emissary: Two tendays ago, a wizard escorted by four Everlund rangers went into the High Forest to speak with Turlang about the trees' advance upon Everlund's walls. All contact with the wizard has been lost, though divination spells indicate that the wizard, at least, is still alive. Did the wizard pay the price for delivering bad news to Turlang, or did she fall prey to one of the forest's other perils?

Illustration by Matt Wilson

KING OBOULD MANY-ARROWS

Male orc Bbn5/Ftr4: CR 9; Medium-size humanoid (orc); HD 5d12+10 plus 4d10+8; hp 87; Init +5; Spd 40 ft.; AC 17 (touch 11, flat-footed 17); Atk +15/+10 melee (2d6+9 plus 1d6 fire/17–20, *+1 flaming greatsword*) or +10/+5 ranged (1d6/×3, shortbow); SQ Darkvision, literate in Orc and Common, rage 2/day, uncanny dodge (Dex bonus to AC, can't be flanked); AL CE; SV Fort +10, Ref +3, Will +3; Str 18, Dex 12, Con 14, Int 13, Wis 12, Cha 10. Height 6 ft. 3 in.

Skills and Feats: Bluff +2, Climb +8, Diplomacy +2, Intimidate +5, Intuit Direction +3, Jump +9, Listen +3, Sense Motive +3, Spot +4, Swim +6, Wilderness Lore +4; Cleave, Daylight Adaptation, Improved Critical (greatsword), Improved Initiative, Power Attack, Weapon Focus (greatsword), Weapon Specialization (greatsword).

Special Qualities: Rage (Ex): During his rage, King Obould has the following statistics instead of those given above: hp 105; AC 15 (touch 9, flat-footed 15); Atk +17/+12 melee (2d6+12 plus 1d6 fire/17–20, *+1 flaming greatsword*); SV Fort +12, Will +5; Str 22, Con 18. Skills: Climb +10, Jump +11, Swim +8. The rage lasts 7 rounds, after which time the orc is fatigued.

Possessions: *+1 flaming greatsword*, *+1 breastplate*, *boots of the winterlands*, *crown of fireballs* (as *necklace of fireballs* with 4 3d6 fireballs).

King Obould Many-Arrows

Obould is fated for a great destiny among his people. Smarter and more intuitive than most of his kind, he completed quests for his chieftain and for his tribe's clerics before slaying the chieftain and taking control of his tribe. He faced challengers without suffering injuries amounting to more than some attractive scarring. Skilled in the arts of war and capable of fierce rages, Obould is a fearsome opponent in battle. Over the years, he subsumed other tribes into his own, and now has at his disposal a veritable army of over two thousand orc warriors, as well as their wives and children.

Obould has four wives, and eight sons who are approaching adulthood. He expects that the time will come soon enough when he must fight his upstart children to defend his throne, and he is ready for it. His only true fear is that after he is dead, they will fight each other, and everything he worked for will fade away. To avert this, he trains his warriors constantly and intends to take hold of the lowlands to the south of the Spine of the World. This dreamed-of orc empire would be large enough that he could grant a piece to each of his surviving sons, and his legacy would survive. War is on the horizon in the North, led by a sharp-eyed barbarian with a sword of fire.

The sword coast north

Capital: None
Population: 660,960 (humans 65%, dwarves 10%, orcs 8%, half-orcs 5%, elves 4%, halflings 4%, gnomes 2%, half-elves 1%)
Government: Diverse city-states
Religions: Nearly all
Imports: Books, manufactured items, magic items, miners, pottery, spices
Exports: Gems, leather goods, mercenaries, Neverwinter's crafts, precious metals, timber
Alignment: All

A region of coastal mountains, forests, and cities of smoke-wreathed ironworks, the Sword Coast North is dominated by Waterdeep at its southernmost end. (The City of Splendors is detailed separately in the Waterdeep entry, below.) The Lords' Alliance, a loose league of like-minded rulers led by Waterdeep, allies the good cities and small settlements of the Dessarin valley in this region. The Arcane Brotherhood of Luskan and the insidious Kraken Society oppose their efforts, seeking to rule this region by spell, sword, and trade.

MAJOR GEOGRAPHICAL FEATURES

Between Waterdeep and the Spine of the World lies a wedge-shaped land along the coast of the Sea of Swords, roughly six hundred miles north to south and more than three hundred miles east to west at its uppermost extent. Around the westernmost end of the Spine of the World is Icewind Dale, the northernmost settled land in this part of Faerûn, which lies between the Sea of Moving Ice and the Reghed Glacier. The Long Road stretching from Waterdeep to Mirabar defines the eastern extent of the Sword Coast North.

Ardeep Forest: A short day's ride outside the walls of Waterdeep, Ardeep was the home of moon elves who could remember when their forest had stretched all the way to the High Forest and beyond. Some echo of elven power still remains in the woods, and evil creatures do not feel comfortable among its tall blueleaf, duskwood, and weirwood trees.

Mere of Dead Men: Centuries ago, thousands of human, dwarven, and elven warriors died in this salt marsh beneath the swords of an invading orc army. Between infestations of bullywugs, sivs, lizardfolk, and the black dragon twins Voaraghamanthar and Waervaerendor, the mere has gone from bad to terrifying. Drawn by tales of treasures sunk in half-submerged castles, adventuring parties continue to trickle into the area, emerging somewhat reduced in number.

Neverwinter Wood: This charmed forest to the east of the city of Neverwinter is perpetually warmed by the Neverwinter River that flows from beneath the dormant volcano Mount Hotenow. Humans, and even orcs, fear the wood and tend to avoid it.

Unlike other forests with dangerous reputations, the Neverwinter seldom disgorges great monsters or evil forces—the unease felt by those who know they do not belong in Neverwinter Wood stems partly from a terrible anticipation that the wood *could* do them damage if it chose.

The Sea of Moving Ice: Arctic ice floes pivot around permanent rocky outcroppings in the Trackless Sea. The floes are home to orc tribes, animals, and other creatures who can or must survive in the cold.

IMPORTANT SITES

Roads and trails crisscross this corner of Faerûn. Few of them are entirely safe. Banditry and brigandage threaten travelers, especially on the wilder stretches of the road.

Goldenfields (Small City, 7,988): Tolgar Anuvien of Waterdeep (NG male human Clr16/Dis3 of Chauntea) founded this city thirteen years ago as an abbey to his deity. Under his careful administration, Goldenfields has grown into a fortified farmland covering more than thirty square miles, making it by far the North's largest city in terms of area.

Unlike the great fields of Amn and Sembia that seek only profit, Goldenfields is an ongoing act of devotion to Chauntea. Waterdeep and other cities of the North depend on Goldenfields for grain and produce. Tolgar relies on adventurers and alliances with powerful wizards for defense against frequent barbarian raids, orc attacks, and worse.

Icewind Dale (Confederation, 10,436): The northernmost human land below the great glaciers and the sea of ice, Icewind Dale is a collection of ten towns and villages populated by former nomads, tundra barbarians, rangers, hardy craftspeople, ice fishers, dwarves who live beneath the ice, and merchants willing to brave its harsh climate to purchase ivory and gems unavailable in the south. Reindeer, polar bears, elk, and yeti are more numerous than people. White dragons are thankfully not as numerous, but any number of dragons counts as a lot.

Luskan (Large City, 14,173): Also known as the City of Sails, Luskan is one of the dominant cities of the northern Sea of Swords. It is populated by Northlanders from Ruathym, most of whom sailed as pirates in the past. A council of five High Captains, all former pirate lords, rules the city, but the true power lies in the hands of the evil mage society called the Arcane Brotherhood. The Brotherhood generally avoids conflicts with Waterdeep and Amn, preferring to pick on smaller cities and merchants who cannot defend themselves.

In 1361 DR, folk of Luskan conquered the native isle of the Northlanders, Ruathym. They were forced to withdraw by the Lords' Alliance, and are so bitter about their loss of face that they now turn a blind eye when pirates who dock in their waters attempt to prey on Waterdeep's shipping.

Mirabar (Small City, 10,307): Mirabar is the mining center for the Sword Coast. The city's shield dwarves live underground to oversee their workshops. The humans above cooperate with the dwarves to handle the mining, move the ore to market, and defend the city against magical threats. The nominal ruler of Mirabar is a hereditary marchion, but the true power is an assembly called the Council of Sparkling Stones, a dwarven and human group that meets once a year to determine target production quotas and whether or not to threaten current clients with reduced output.

Neverwinter (Large City, 23,192): A walled city of humans and half-elves, Neverwinter is cultured without being arrogant, bustling without being greedy, and charming without being quaint. The city is best known for the products of its master craftsfolk: lamps of multicolored glass, precision water clocks, and exquisite jewelry. It is also famous for its gardens, heated by the supernaturally warm waters of the Neverwinter River. The gardens fill the markets with fruit in the summer and enliven winter with flowers.

The city's three architectural marvels are its bridges: the Dolphin, the Winged Wyvern, and the Sleeping Dragon. Each bridge is intricately carved into a likeness of the creature it is named after. Neverwinter and its ruler, Lord Nasher Alagondar (LG male human Ftr7/Chm4 of Tyr) nearly always side with Waterdeep against Luskan and the orcs.

Stone Bridge: This massive stone arch, a mile long and one hundred feet wide, reaches a height of one hundred fifty feet as it arches over the River Dessarin. The massive stone statues of four dwarves, two at either end, stand fifty feet tall. Dwarves built the bridge five thousand years ago to give themselves a walkway over the river no matter how high it flooded. Something in the magic of the bridge pinned the Dessarin in place: No matter how the river has snaked and changed its course, it always runs under the Stone Bridge at exactly the same point. The dwarves say the Stone Bridge has survived thousands of years of earthquakes, floods, and battles because it is sacred to Moradin.

REGIONAL HISTORY

The story of the Sword Coast North is the story of the vanishing of old, nonhuman realms and the establishment of Waterdeep and the Northlander cities. (Waterdeep's story is discussed in detail in the next entry.) The first great realm to rise in this part of the world was Illefarn, a kingdom of elves and dwarves that existed thousands of years ago. The first dungeons under Mount Waterdeep were delved by these folk.

Illefarn was a contemporary of Netheril and survived its fall, lasting until its elven rulers abandoned Faerûn for Evermeet a few hundred years before the beginning of Dalereckoning. After the fall of the great realms, humans migrated into these lands and built freeholds, towns, and keeps along the river valleys and at the harbors. The first Northlander longships arrived in the region during the last centuries of the Illefarn empire. The Northlanders colonized the island of Ruathym and spread to all the islands in the northern seas. Others migrated north, past the Spine of the World, and became the founders of Icewind Dale.

In the wake of Eaerlann's fall in the 9th century DR, elves, dwarves, Northlanders, and Netherese descendants from Ascalhorn formed Phalorm, the Realm of Three Crowns, which attempted to mirror the accomplishments of Myth Drannor to the east. It lasted only a century before orc hordes swept it away. Its successor, the Kingdom of Man, had an even briefer existence. Civilization lost its grip on these lands until Waterdeep grew strong enough to drive the orcs back to the Spine of the World. The city of Luskan was founded on the wreckage of the orc realm of Illuskan, and the towns of the Dessarin valley—Triboar, Longsaddle, Secomber, and others—were settled.

With prosperity and civilization come new threats. No orc horde can sweep away the well-established cities of this region, but powerful forces conspire to rule this land in other ways.

PLOTS AND RUMORS

Luskan's Arcane Brotherhood grows more and more aggressive each year, overtly threatening Mirabar and Neverwinter. Ten years ago the Lords' Alliance threatened war to avert Luskan's conquest of Ruathym, but few of the leaders in this area wish to embark on a bloody and expensive crusade on behalf of the pirate chiefs of Ruathym.

Fire Rescue: Something is killing the fire elementals that live beneath Mount Hotenow in Neverwinter Wood. Ordinarily, humans and elves don't care about the life and death of outsiders from the Elemental Plane of Fire, but Neverwinter relies on the supernatural warmth that flows out of the Neverwinter River as it bubbles up through the fire elementals' home beneath Mount Hotenow. If the fire elementals all leave, the river will freeze over, and winter will finally come to Neverwinter.

The Kraken's Tentacles: Semmonemily (NE doppelganger Sor12) is busily subverting the city of Yartar by uniting two disparate organizations—the Hands of Yartar, the city's fractious thieves' guild, and a powerful wererat clan lead by Nalynaul the Shriveled, a cunning illithilich. Semmonemily plots to murder the Waterbaron Belleethe Kheldorna and assume her place, making the Hands the secret rulers of the town while the Kraken Society rules the Hands.

DRIZZT DO'URDEN

Male drow Ftr10/Bbn1/Rgr5 of Mielikki: CR 18; Medium-size humanoid (elf); HD 10d10+20 plus 1d12+2 plus 5d10+10; hp 124; Init +9; Spd 40 ft.; AC 23 (touch 14, flat-footed 19); Atk +17/+12/+7/+2 melee (1d6+6 plus 1d6 cold/18–20, *+3 frost scimitar*), +16/+11 melee (1d6+4/18–20, *+2 defending scimitar*); SQ Drow traits, favored enemy (goblins +2, magical beasts +1), light blindness, rage, spell-like abilities; SR 27; AL CG; SV Fort +15, Ref +9, Will +7; Str 13, Dex 20, Con 15, Int 17, Wis 17, Cha 14. Height 5 ft. 4 in.

Skills and Feats: Climb +8, Handle Animal +9, Hide +13, Intuit Direction +5, Jump +8, Knowledge (nature) +5, Listen +20, Move Silently +15, Ride (horse) +7, Search +13, Spot +15, Use Rope +7, Wilderness Lore +8; Ambidexterity, Blind-Fight, Combat Reflexes, Dodge, Improved Initiative, Improved Two-Weapon Fighting, Mobility, Quick Draw, Track, Twin Sword Style, Two-Weapon Fighting, Weapon Focus (scimitar), Weapon Specialization (scimitar).

Special Qualities: Drow Traits (Ex): +2 racial bonus on Will saves against spells and spell-like abilities, darkvision 120 ft. *Light Blindness* (Ex): Abrupt exposure to bright light (such as sunlight or a *daylight* spell) blinds drow for 1 round. In addition, they suffer a –1 circumstance penalty to all attack rolls, saves, and checks while operating in bright light. *Rage* (Ex): During his rage, Drizzt has the following statistics instead of those given above: hp 156; AC 21 (touch 12, flat-footed 17); Atk +19/+14/+9/+4 melee (1d6+8 plus 1d6 cold/18–20, *+3 frost brand scimitar*) and +18/+13 melee (1d6+5/18–20, *+2 defender scimitar*); SV Fort +17, Will +9; Str 17, Con 19. Skills: Climb +10, Jump +10. The rage lasts 7 rounds, after which Drizzt is fatigued. He can rage once per day. *Spell-like Abilities:* 1/day—*dancing lights, darkness, faerie fire*. These abilities are as the spells cast by a 16th-level sorcerer.

Spells Prepared (1; base DC = 14): 1—*detect animals or plants*.

Possessions: +4 mithral chainmail, Icingdeath (*+3 frost scimitar*), Twinkle (*+2 defending scimitar*), *figurine of wondrous power: onyx panther* (name Guenhwyvar; see below)

Onyx Panther: This magical figurine summons the black panther Guenhwyvar, a friend and loyal companion to Drizzt. She can be summoned every other day for a period of 6 hours. If slain, she reverts to her figurine form and cannot be summoned for 48 hours. Guen understands Common and Undercommon, and has the following statistics:

Drizzt Do'Urden

Guenhwyvar: Female panther; CR 5; Medium-size animal; HD 6d8+12; hp 39; Init +4; Spd 40 ft., climb 20 ft.; AC 15 (touch 14, flat-footed 11); Atk +8 melee (1d6+3, bite), +6 melee (1d3+1, 2 claws); SA Pounce, improved grab, rake 1d3+1; SQ Low-light vision, scent; AL N; SV Fort +7, Ref +9, Will +3; Str 16, Dex 19, Con 15, Int 6, Wis 12, Cha 8.

Skills and Feats: Balance +12, Climb +11, Hide +9*, Listen +6, Move Silently +12, Spot +6; Multiattack, Weapon Finesse (bite), Weapon Finesse (claw). Includes +4 racial bonus on Hide and Move Silently checks, +8 racial bonus on Balance checks. *In areas of tall grass or heavy undergrowth, her Hide bonus improves to +8.

Despite his increasing fame (or infamy) across the Sword Coast North as a drow who dwells on the surface, is deadly in battle, fights with great agility and two magic scimitars, and can call on an *onyx panther figurine of wondrous power* to bring a battle-companion to his side, Drizzt Do'Urden remains an enigma.

He worships Mielikki and makes war on the cruel city of his birth (Menzoberranzan), his fellow drow, and all who serve Lolth. He counts as friends human warriors of the North (Wulfgar and Cattiebrie) and the dwarf Bruenor Battlehammer (whom he helped to regain the rulership of Mithral Hall). He has slain dragons and drow matron mothers. He defied fiends (Errtu) and powers (Lolth), battled perhaps the most deadly assassin currently active in Faerûn (Artemis Entreri), and sought to forge his own life on the surface.

Thoughtful and sensitive to others, Drizzt holds himself to the highest ideals but does not expect the same of others. Ever alert for treachery and danger, he speaks little but is apt to be polite (if terse) in his dealings. A perfectionist who yearns to be accepted into places and groups and to make friends widely, Drizzt is haunted by the danger he brings to those he befriends thanks to the scrutiny of Lolth and his other foes (notably Errtu and Entreri). Those he meets see his manner as grim.

Early in his surface travels, Alustriel welcomed him as warmly and personally as she does all in need, but dared not let him openly into Silverymoon at that time. His deeds have, very slowly, made Drizzt Do'Urden more welcome in the Sword Coast North.

Waterdeep

Population: 1,347,840 (humans 64%, dwarves 10%, elves 10%, halflings 5%, half-elves 5%, gnomes 3%, half-orcs 2%) (City of Waterdeep, Metropolis, 132,661)

Government: Oligarchy (the Lords of Waterdeep, anonymous meritocratic rulers)

Religions: All, especially Deneir, Mystra, and Oghma

Imports: Grain, livestock, leather, ore, timber, and exotic goods from all lands

Exports: Ale, arms, cloth, furnishings, leather goods, pottery, refined metals, and all other sorts of finished goods

Alignment: All

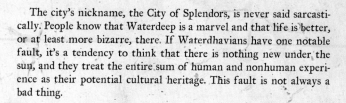

Waterdeep is the major cosmopolitan power of Faerûn. It benefits from an excellent harbor, wise rule, a tolerant spirit, and a powerful magical tradition that generally produces stronger good wizards than evil wizards. Waterdeep contains at least one of nearly everything, but it's not a melting pot—instead, it's like a gem grinder, smoothing individuals' rough edges so that their talents shine brighter.

The city's nickname, the City of Splendors, is never said sarcastically. People know that Waterdeep is a marvel and that life is better, or at least more bizarre, there. If Waterdhavians have one notable fault, it's a tendency to think that there is nothing new under the sun, and they treat the entire sum of human and nonhuman experience as their potential cultural heritage. This fault is not always a bad thing.

LIFE AND SOCIETY

The City of Splendors is undeniably a place where things happen, an important center of trade and change. Waterdhavians merely accept this as a fact and never think on why or how it became so. The astute see that Waterdeep is a city of wealth where the rich gather to trade, and in trading with others generate wealth with a swiftness unknown in backcountry Faerûn. The coins are the fire under the cauldron.

The cauldron itself, and the spoons that stir it, are the local powers locked in an endless struggle for supremacy, striving against each other in ways large and small. These are the guilds, nobles, trading costers, mercenary bands, city authorities, criminal organizations, individual citizens seeking daily sustenance, and newcomers seeking fortunes.

Some folk find life in Waterdeep to be a wine they can't stop drinking. Powers of all sorts, from cults and trade cabals to wizards' organizations and foreign rulers, find it expedient to have spies and even assassins active in Waterdeep at all times. Although the City of Splendors has plenty of room for anyone with coin to spend, it is also the place where every private moment may be seen or overheard by someone else. Many Waterdhavians rent secret rooms or establish false identities to avoid their enemies' ears.

MAJOR ORGANIZATIONS

Without some attention to the organizations that hold Waterdeep together, discussion of its various geographical features and landmarks misses the forest for all the trees.

City Watch: One of two armed bodies maintained by the city from Castle Waterdeep, the Watch functions as a police force. Watchfolk dress in green, black, and gold uniforms. They are well trained and well equipped with leather armor, clubs, and short swords. They would rather talk problems over than use force of arms, but if fighting is required, they use horns to summon reinforcements.

City Guard: Like the City Watch, the Guard is headquartered in Castle Waterdeep. Unlike the Watch, the Guard is made up of professional soldiers responsible for defending the city, protecting the gates, and guarding important citizens and locations. Guards wear scale or chain shirts and carry short swords and shortbows.

Guilds: Once upon a time, the merchants' and craftsfolks' guilds ruled the city. Waterdeep barely survived the strife. These days, the guilds focus on the commercial and professional enterprises they handle best and (usually) leave the politicking to the Lords. Waterdeep's thieves' guild, the Xanathar's Guild, has been driven into Skullport, far beneath the city.

Lords' Alliance: The Lords of Waterdeep oversee a council composed of themselves and the lords of other merchant powers of the Sword Coast, as well as those inland cities whose interests closely match Waterdeep's.

Lords of Waterdeep: A council of sixteen members who keep their identities secret rules Waterdeep. The Lords appear in public only when masked and magically protected from divinations and other forms of magic. Piergeiron the Paladinson (LG male human Pal15 of Tyr), Warden of Waterdeep and Commander of the Watch, is the only Open Lord (unmasked), and his palace in the center of Castle Ward is the seat of government. Speculation on the identity of the other lords is a sporting pastime in Waterdeep. All that is certain is that they are competent and fair rulers, which is more than most cities could hope for, much less other cities whose rulers wear masks.

Watchful Order of Magists and Protectors: All wizards and sorcerers must join this semiguild in order to practice magic in Waterdeep. Membership costs 40 gp, with no yearly dues. Members can purchase rare magical components and some magic items at the Tower of the Order, the headquarters of the guild.

MAJOR GEOGRAPHICAL FEATURES

Waterdeep commands the countryside for thirty or forty miles about, but the city itself is the chief feature. Waterdeep is divided into several major sections known as "wards," each of which contains innumerable businesses, residences, or other buildings.

Castle Ward: Castle Ward, at the center of the city, includes Mount Waterdeep, its castle, the Palace of Waterdeep (occupied by Piergeiron), and the homes of some prosperous Waterdhavians.

Dock Ward: Compared to the rest of the city, Dock Ward is dirty, smelly, clumsily built, and dangerous. In the words of Elminster himself, Dock Ward is a "riotous, nigh-perpetual brawl that covers entire acres, interrupted only by small buildings, intermittent trade businesses, an errant dog or two, and a few brave watchguards (who manage to keep the chaos from spreading beyond the docks), the whole lot wallowing in the stench of rotting fish."

North Ward: North Ward is primarily the home of the wealthy middle class, lesser nobles, and well-to-do merchants.

Sea Ward: The wealthiest ward of the city, Sea Ward is home to noble families. It features broad streets, wondrous statues, bright and expensive shops, and its own arena, the Field of Triumph.

Southern Ward: Also known as Caravan City, the Southern Ward serves as the staging, loading, and unloading zone for caravans passing through the southern gates into the city. "South," as it is known to locals, is well patrolled by the City Watch and accustomed to providing newcomers to the city with lodging, information, food, and entertainment.

Trades Ward: Waterdeep's commercial section never truly closes, and work stops only during festivals. By night, candles, lanterns, oil lamps, and *continual flames* keep Trades Ward's streets and shops glowing, with staff who sleep by day to sell to those who shop by night. The city's major guilds have their headquarters in Trades Ward, near the businesses they work for or own.

IMPORTANT SITES

Adventure awaits around every corner in Waterdeep's streets, or a short ride away in the Ardeep Forest or Sword Mountains.

Castle Waterdeep: High on Mount Waterdeep, this great fortress bristles with mighty catapults that repel invaders who attack through the harbor. The most recent victims of the castle's bombardment were the sahuagin that attacked in 1369 DR. Both the City Guard and the City Watch are headquartered in Castle Waterdeep.

City of the Dead: A huge cemetery, the City of the Dead is open to the public during the day and sealed off and patrolled at night. Citizens and strangers who want their deeds to go unobserved operate in the shadows of the tombs. The graves themselves benefit from various levels of magical protection—some tombs are actually doorways into magical planes, pocket dimensions that cannot support life but serve as burial zones for unlimited numbers of honored nobles and fondly remembered commoners.

New Olamn: One of Faerûn's few bardic colleges, New Olamn occupies the site of former mountaintop villas on Mount Water-

deep. With luck, this newly reopened incarnation of the college will rival the schools in Silverymoon.

Undermountain: Before the founding of Waterdeep, a wizard settled on the slopes of Mount Waterdeep with seven apprentices. None know the origins of Halaster Blackcloak, the Mad Wizard, but he's said to have devised many spells now widely known. Halaster summoned and bound creatures from other planes to build his tower.

Halaster's creatures—some of whom hunted humans by night—dug extensive storage tunnels beneath his abode. At length, their tunnels broke into the large, grand Underhalls, old dwarven delvings of the long-vanished Melairkyn clan. Halaster eradicated the drow infesting the halls and moved entirely into the subterranean ways, leaving behind his tower. His curious apprentices, abandoned on the surface, explored the underground lair but found only traps baited with powerful magic (and enigmatic messages hinting that "true power" awaited them below). One by one, as their courage and capabilities allowed, the seven descended in search of their master. They found a strange, dangerous labyrinth where Halaster stored his treasures, experiments, victuals and necessities, magic items, and servants—kept safe (he thought) from spying, theft, and attack.

As time passed and Waterdeep grew around the mountain's base, expeditions of armed adventurers into Halaster's stronghold grew numerous. He roamed planes to collect monsters and moved his operations deeper into the endless Underdark. Undermountain became known as a place of horrors, the lair of terrible monsters. Halaster himself grew old, mighty, and insane.

The warrior Durnan (NG male human Ftr18) and others who explored Undermountain spoke of its riches, hazards, and vast passages. Many who were desperate for wealth, bored, or escaping pursuit went down the shafts in Durnan's inn, the Yawning Portal. Some returned, now rich for life, and greed kept the adventurous coming. Some in Waterdeep whisper that the Lords still sentence defiant criminals to Undermountain, to die or find their own ways free.

Halaster, it is said, still roams the dozen levels and twice that many sublevels of Undermountain, watching from the walls. The Lords of Waterdeep turn a deaf ear to reports of entire temples below them (notably the Promenade of Eilistraee) and even an entire lawless trading community in the depths, Skullport. Sea caves are connected via great sling-hoists to the waters of Undermountain, allowing sea captains to smuggle cargoes to and from the drow and darker beings who dwell in wicked Skullport. The Lords forbid slavery in Waterdeep, but do not interfere when unsavory folk are smuggled out or down by this route.

Elminster described Undermountain best: "The most famous battlefield in which to earn a reputation as a veteran adventurer—and the largest known grave of heroes in Faerûn."

Skullport (Large Town, 2,123): The dark twin to Waterdeep's light soul, Skullport is a subterranean city connected to both Undermountain and a great sea in the Underdark. Skullport is tolerated, barely, by the Lords of Waterdeep, because the madness and chaos it houses might otherwise rise to the surface and destroy the City of Splendors. Agents of Waterdeep monitor the city's buried twin and sometimes carry out missions here, but they generally refrain from acting unless Skullport's denizens plot against the city above.

REGIONAL HISTORY

The sprawling, bustling City of Splendors, the most energetic and eclectic trading center of modern Faerûn, began as a good harbor along the storm-clawed Sword Coast, where ports for ships are sparse. An arm of Mount Waterdeep sheltered a bay where deep water came almost right up to shore.

Of the long history of this place, much has been lost. It is known that by –1088 DR, annual spring and fall trade had begun at the site. Tribes slowly settled and farmed the cleared land, and inevitably fought over it. The wizard Halaster arrived, built his tower, and abandoned it for Undermountain.

The local tribes were conquered and united by Ulbaerag Bloodhand, who was in turn defeated by Nimoar the Reaver in 882 DR. Nimoar built a permanent hold inside a wooden palisade, where the north end of present-day Waterdeep stands, and the hold withstood both pirate and tribal raids. Before his death in 936 DR, Nimoar led his warriors in the First Trollwar, scouring the lands east and north of the growing city of trolls and orcs. Later "War Lords of the Hold" fought and fell in the decade-long Second Trollwar.

In 952 DR, the wizard Ahghairon became special advisor to the War Lord of Waterdeep. His magic led to the decisive defeat of the trolls. The Free City of Waterdeep grew in size and wealth, and under the wise guidance of Ahghairon, Castle Waterdeep (then just a simple keep) was built. Over decades, the wealth and growth of Waterdeep made its rulers proud. Such a one was Raurlor, who dreamed of founding an "Empire of the North," with Waterdeep as its capital and himself on its throne.

In 1032 DR, Raurlor raised an army to conquer anyone who dared stand in his path. Ahghairon defied him in public assembly. The enraged Raurlor attacked the wizard with his sword—but Ahghairon transformed Raurlor's blade into a serpent, which bit and slew the Warlord of Waterdeep. Ahghairon then took the throne and proclaimed himself first Lord of Waterdeep. Ahghairon decreed that he would rule as an equal with masked Lords of unknown identity, gathered from Waterdhavians of all walks of life.

Ahghairon brought order to Waterdeep, founding the City Guard and City Watch. He ruled for two hundred years, during which time the city grew in size and prosperity. The city wards were established in 1035 DR, and the city's guilds in 1248 DR. The city expanded its walls several times, and the flow of wealth never ceased nor shrank, year by year.

In 1256 DR, Ahghairon's longevity magic failed, and he died. A ruling Council of Guildmasters governed until the Guildwars of 1262, in which all but two Guildmasters perished. Those two nobles proclaimed themselves the Two Lords Magister. During their rule, the Shadow Thieves established themselves in the city. Graft and corruption were rife, and public safety could only be purchased in the form of combative bodyguards.

Two long-hidden Lords, Baeron and Shilarn, emerged in 1273 DR and slew the Two Lords Magister. They established the present system of justice, with magisters who serve as judges. The Shadow Thieves were outlawed, Baeron proclaimed himself the Open Lord of Waterdeep, and Waterdeep's official permanent taxed population reached one hundred thousand.

Three years later, Baeron and Shilarn had a daughter, Lhestyn, who was to become one of the greatest Lords of Waterdeep. In that same year, the city reached its present boundaries, and the ranks of the Lords were increased to sixteen. Operating as the Masked Lady, Lhestyn later infiltrated and exposed the Shadow Thieves still operating in the city, breaking their power.

In 1302 DR, the adventurers Mirt and Durnan emerged from Undermountain as rich men. Tales of their adventures spread, luring others who followed their trail down to riches or death. Six years later, Baeron and Shilarn died. Lhestyn became Open Lord in her father's place, and the Palace of Waterdeep was built.

Upon Lhestyn's death in 1314 DR, her chosen successor, Piergeiron, became Open Lord. His rule continues to the present day, though he has been grooming his daughter Aleena Paladinstar (LG female human Ftr3/Wiz12) to succeed him. Waterdeep has survived calamities that include deities battling in the streets, the destruction of Myrkul, and the ascension of Cyric and the new Mystra. Through all these tribulations and more, the city has rolled on, ever busy and ever a source of excitement, vigor, new ventures, gossip, and adventure.

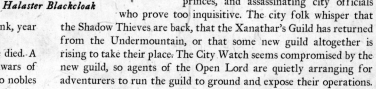

Halaster Blackcloak

Illustration by Todd Lockwood

PLOTS AND RUMORS

Waterdeep is the beginning and end of a thousand plots and schemes across the North.

Missing: The heroes are retained by an elven noble named Saeval Baelythin to find his nephew Nuvruil, an ambitious young mage. Lord Saeval has heard that his nephew was last known to be in Waterdeep, and he wants the heroes to deliver a vital message to him. On arriving in Waterdeep, though, the heroes learn that Nuvruil and his company of adventurers descended into the Undermountain a tenday past and have not been seen or heard of since. Finding Nuvruil in the Undermountain is a daunting task, to say the least, but if the young elven lord is injured or trapped, the heroes may be his only hope.

Return from Exile: For almost a century the Shadow Thieves have been banished from Waterdeep, but rumors persist of a new guild rising in the Trades Ward. Clever and resourceful rogues with potent magical assistance are pilfering the city's shops, terrifying the merchant princes, and assassinating city officials who prove too inquisitive. The city folk whisper that the Shadow Thieves are back, that the Xanathar's Guild has returned from the Undermountain, or that some new guild altogether is rising to take their place. The City Watch seems compromised by the new guild, so agents of the Open Lord are quietly arranging for adventurers to run the guild to ground and expose their operations.

HALASTER BLACKCLOAK

Male human Wiz20/Acm5/Epic5: CR 30; Medium-size humanoid; HD 20d4+60; hp 128; Init +8; Spd 30 ft.; AC 19 (touch 19, flat-footed 19); Atk +9/+4 melee (touch, spell) or +9/+4 melee (1d6–1, quarterstaff) or +14/+9 ranged touch (spell); SA Archmage abilities; SQ Enhanced ability scores, epic-level benefits, magic abilities, Undermountain entrenchments; AL CE; SV Fort +9, Ref +10, Will +18; Str 9, Dex 18, Con 16, Int 24, Wis 22, Cha 10. Height 6 ft.

Skills and Feats: Alchemy +17, Concentration +28, Craft (gemcutting) +12, Craft (trapmaking) +17, Disable Device +12, Handle Animal +3, Heal +8, Hide +6, Intuit Direction +8, Knowledge (arcana) +32, Knowledge (architecture and engineering) +27, Knowledge (the planes) +12, Knowledge (religion) +17, Knowledge (Undermountain history) +17, Knowledge (Waterdeep local) +22, Listen +9, Profession (herbalist) +11, Scry +22, Search +27, Spellcraft +34, Spot +24, Use Rope +6; Craft Magic Arms and Armor, Craft Wondrous Item, Create Portal, Delay Spell, Improved Initiative, Magical Artisan (Create Portal), Maximize Spell, Quicken Spell, Scribe Scroll, Skill Focus (Spellcraft), Spell Focus (Enchantment), Spell Focus (Transmutation), Spellcasting Prodigy.

Special Attacks: Archmage Abilities: Arcane Reach: Halaster's touch spells have a 30-ft. range. Arcane Fire (Su): Halaster may cast any spell as an energy bolt (range 600 ft., damage 5d6 + 1d6 points per spell level). Spell power +2. Mastery of Elements: Halaster can prepare any arcane spell he knows with the acid, cold, fire, electricity, or sonic designator to be cast as a different element. For example, a fireball may be prepared to deal sonic damage instead of fire damage. Mastery of Counterspelling: When Halaster successfully counterspells any spell subject to spell turning, he reflects it fully back on the original caster. A spell not subject to spell turning is merely counterspelled.

Special Qualities: Enhanced Ability Scores: Halaster has used *wish* spells to increase his Intelligence and Wisdom each by 3 points (included above). Epic-Level Benefits: Halaster has five effective levels of archmage (included above), and +1 higher-level spell ×5 (included below). Magic Abilities: Through *permanency* and *wish* spells, Halaster has the following continuous abilities: move in complete silence, *pass without trace, protection from arrows, true seeing,* walk on air as if it were firm land (as the 12th-level ability of the *phantom steed* spell). Undermountain Entrenchments (usable only when Halaster is within Undermountain): Longevity: Halaster does not age. Image Projection: Halaster may manifest up to 30 projected images of himself in different parts of Undermountain (he does not need visual contact with them, may cast spells through them, and may transfer himself to the place of any projection as a free action). Portal Control: Halaster knows if any *portal* in Undermountain is used. He may activate, deactivate, or change the destination of any *portal* within Undermountain as a standard action.

Wizard Spells per Day: 4/6/6/6/5/5/2/4/3/1/1/1/1/1. Base DC = 20 + spell level, 22 + spell level for enchantment and transmutation spells. Wizard caster level 25th.

Possessions: Ring of regeneration, horned ring (teleport 3/day when within Undermountain, negate *arcane lock* or nonprismatic magical barriers by touch, acts as a *ring of freedom of movement,* absorbs all magic missile and electricity effects), 1d20 flying daggers (animated flying objects with a +1 enhancement bonus), *robe of eyes, ring of protection +5.* In addition to these items that he always carries, Halaster has caches of magic items all over Undermountain containing powerful items of all sorts.

The creator of Undermountain, Halaster Blackcloak is widely and correctly thought of as a very old, very powerful wizard . . . who is also completely insane.

The ancient mage is expert in such diverse talents as gemcutting, engineering, and the breeding and control of monsters (living and undead) from other planes. His insanity makes him constantly

Illustration by Sam Wood

chuckle and mutter to himself, and he seems unable to follow arguments or conversations for long. However, his insanity does not prevent him from seeing danger or menace when it threatens—or defending himself with lightning speed and efficiency.

Halaster possesses literally hundreds of magic items, and when in Undermountain (where he's usually "hidden in the walls," employing his own secret network of passages), he can command constructs such as golems, helmed horrors, and crawling claws. Halaster can also call on *contingency* spells, clones of himself, and the tricks and traps of Undermountain, including a "moving portal" that can snatch up him or others and whisk them elsewhere.

Halaster's moments of sanity in Undermountain are rare, but outside it he's usually lucid. On such occasions, Halaster is fastidious, meticulous, dignified, cold, and proper. He remembers any slight or aid given him and brooks no insolence—and also tries to get his own way in everything, caring nothing for the destruction or harm he may do in the process.

The Blackcloak's chief interests include collecting new monsters and magic. After thousands of years, little of either is really "new" to him. While waiting for such delights, he amuses himself by manipulating events and politics to his whims.

MIRT

Male human Ftr8/Rog5: CR 13; Medium-size humanoid; HD 8d10+24 plus 5d6+15; hp 108; Init +8; Spd 30 ft.; AC 22 (touch 14, flat-footed 18); Atk +16/+11/+6 melee (1d8+8/17–20, *+2 construct bane longsword*), +14 melee (1d4+3/19–20, *+1 frost dagger*); SA Sneak attack +3d6; SQ Evasion, locate traps, uncanny dodge; AL CG; SV Fort +10, Ref +10, Will +9; Str 18, Dex 18, Con 16, Int 14, Wis 18, Cha 15. Height 5 ft. 10 in.

Skills and Feats: Appraise +6, Bluff +7, Climb +11, Diplomacy +11, Handle Animal +8, Intimidate +7, Jump +11, Knowledge (Waterdeep history) +7, Knowledge (Waterdeep local) +7, Listen +7, Move Silently +8, Perform (juggle) +3, Profession (fisherman) +9, Profession (gamer) +9, Profession (sailor) +9, Ride (horse) +11, Sense Motive +9, Spot +5, Swim +10; Ambidexterity, Blind-Fight, Endurance, Improved Critical (longsword), Improved Initiative, Iron Will, Leadership (15), Twin Sword Style, Two-Weapon Fighting, Weapon Focus (longsword), Weapon Specialization (longsword).

Possessions: +4 glamered mithral shirt, +2 construct bane longsword, +1 frost dagger, ring of regeneration, periapt of proof against poison +4, Lord's Amulet (acts as an *amulet of proof against detection and location,* plus allows access to magically warded areas of Waterdeep), Lord's Helm (disguises voice and acts as a *ring of mind shielding*), Lord's Robes (magically disguises wearer to appear identical to all other Lords of Waterdeep).

A fat, wheezing old rogue widely (and correctly) believed to be one of the Lords of Waterdeep, Mirt the Moneylender made his fortune in Undermountain after a colorful career as a mercenary general. As Mirt the Merciless or the Old Wolf, Mirt made many enemies, particularly in skirmishes in Amn, Tethyr, and Calimshan. He also made a few good friends, notably the adventurer Durnan.

More than one foe underestimates Mirt's agility and stealth because they see only his public act as a roaring, tipsy braggart. However, only a stranger to Waterdeep underestimates Mirt's cunning

Mirt

and his shrewd judgments of people. These qualities have made him far richer as an investor in business ventures than he ever became as a hiresword or treasure-gathering adventurer.

Mirt is a Harper as well as a Lord of Waterdeep, and has a heart of gold under his boasting and love of horseplay and tavern brawling. He wants to leave Faerûn better than he found it, and the long tales of his adventures would seem to indicate that he just might do so.

ELAITH "THE SERPENT" CRAULNOBER

Male moon elf Ftr3/Wiz9: CR 12; Medium-size humanoid; HD 3d10+6 plus 9d4+18; hp 63; Init +8; Spd 30 ft.; AC 18 (touch 16, flat-footed 14); Atk +10/+5 melee (1d8+3/ 19–20, masterwork longsword) and +11 melee (1d4+3/ 19–20, *2 dagger*) or +13/+8 ranged (1d4+5/19–20, *2 dagger*); SQ Elven traits, low-light vision; AL NE; SV Fort +8, Ref +8, Will +10; Str 17, Dex 18, Con 15, Int 16, Wis 16, Cha 17. Height 5 ft. 8 in.

Skills and Feats: Balance +7, Climb +6, Concentration +5, Hide +14, Intuit Direction +6, Jump +6, Knowledge (Waterdeep history) +6, Knowledge (Waterdeep local) +6, Listen +8, Profession (brewer) +6, Ride (horse) +7, Search +8, Sense Motive +6, Spellcraft +6, Spot +8, Swim +6, Tumble +7, Use Rope +7; Ambidexterity, Blind-Fight, Heighten Spell, Improved Initiative, Scribe Scroll, Twin Sword Style, Two-Weapon Fighting, Weapon Finesse (dagger), Weapon Focus (longsword).

Special Qualities: Elven Traits: Immune to *sleep* spells and effects, +2 on saves against enchantment effects, +2 bonus on Listen, Search, and Spot checks.

Wizard Spells per Day: 4/5/5/4/2/1. Base DC = 13 + spell level.

Spellbook: 0—all; 1st—*animate rope, burning hands, comprehend languages, feather fall, identify, magic missile, shield, sleep, true strike;* 2nd—*cat's grace, darkness, darkvision, endurance, invisibility, knock, mirror image, resist elements, web;* 3rd *dispel magic, fireball, fly, lightning bolt;* 4th—*dimension door;* 5th—*cone of cold.* Elaith prefers to use his higher-level spell slots to prepare *fireball* and *lightning bolt* spells with the Heighten Spell feat.

Possessions: bracers of armor +2, cloak of elvenkind, +2 dagger, ring of the ram (25 charges), *ring of protection +2,* masterwork longsword. Rumors have it that Elaith has stashes of other magic items and large sums of money in various places around Waterdeep, including his family's *moonblade* (a powerful elven heirloom, a magic sword with many special abilities).

Born of a noble family of Evermeet, Elaith was the last of his line when he claimed his family's *moonblade.* It rejected him, but did not slay him outright. Filled with despair, he left for Waterdeep that day and has not returned to Evermeet since.

Reaching the mainland, Elaith gave in to the cold rage and icy temper that the *moonblade* sensed within him. Solely interested in his own profit and survival, Elaith gained quite a reputation in the City of Splendors. Tavern tales circulate about various adventuring expeditions he led from which he was the only one to return.

Elaith Craulnober

Recently, Elaith was struck by a poisoned blade while recovering an elven artifact from the Knights of the Shield. As he lay dying, his thoughts turned to his infant daughter Azariah and what would happen to her after he died. This unselfish turn of thought caused his *moonblade's* power to awaken, healing him. He stores the *moonblade* in a safe place until his daughter is ready to claim it, and while he is still ruthless and evil, he avoids situations in which he might get killed, preferring to hire adventurers to do his dirty work. His contacts in all levels of Waterdeep society alert him to unusual events.

old empires

Heirs to a fallen realm that defied the very heavens, the people of the Old Empires were summoned to Faerûn millennia ago and enslaved by wizards. With the help of their foreign deities, the former slaves freed themselves and settled that lands that are now Chessenta, Mulhorand, and Unther. These countries rose to power thousands of years ago and have been in decline ever since, their vast territories since lost to younger and more vigorous realms.

Resistant to change and hostile to visitors for centuries, the Old Empires have been forced into active participation in Faerûn in recent years, and may be regaining a prominent position in Faerûnian politics and culture.

chessenta

Capital: Cimbar (theoretically)
Population: 3,386,880 (humans 82%, halflings 6%, dwarves 5%, half-orcs 4%, lizardfolk 2%)
Government: Varies by city (military dictatorship, theocracy, monarchy)
Religions: Anhur, Assuran (old name of Hoar), Azuth, Lathander, Red Knight, Tchazzar (aspect of Tiamat), Waukeen
Imports: Cheese, glass, horses, magic weapons, mercenaries, perfume, pork, slaves
Exports: Art, cattle, gold, grapes, olive oil, quality iron, silver, slaves (to Thay), statues, weapons, wine
Alignment: N, CG, LN

A group of cities considered a single nation by the rest of Faerûn, Chessenta is anything but united. The cities war against each other over old slights, philosophical differences, or economic leverage. Adventurers and mercenary companies make a good living here, hired by various governments for sneak attacks, strategic planning, or protection. The culture of Chessenta is obsessed with physical conflict, with war heroes considered very highly. The nation is friendly to dwarves and half-orcs, but uneasy with elves. The Chessentans appreciate the arts and are great fans of theater; the bardic profession is second only to that of fighters.

LIFE AND SOCIETY

The people of Chessenta are passionate, living each day to the fullest. Seen by outsiders as a drunken and riotous people, the Chessentans feast and fight often, not doing anything halfway. Their athletic competitions are popular events, particularly wrestling, and almost every citizen has some skill at fighting.

Most of the rulers of Chessenta are retired soldiers, and the title of War Hero is one of the greatest honors a person can receive, with any particular battle rarely finding more than one person worthy of such a title. This dedication to war suits the Chessentans well, for their nation has prospered through the conflicts between their rival cities.

Chessentans practice slavery, although it is less widespread than in Unther and Mulhorand. Unlike in those countries, a slave-owner can grant a slave freedom at any time, often for exceptional work. Slaves are kept illiterate, except those in Cimbar. Chessenta's sizable middle class controls the country's money. The government encourages prosperity for all, so tax revenues remain high.

MAJOR GEOGRAPHICAL FEATURES

Chessenta occupies a broad, fertile plain ringing the great Bay of Chessenta in the southeast of the Sea of Fallen Stars. Broken mountain ranges and rugged highlands mark its eastern, southern, and western frontiers.

Adder Swamp: Deadly snakes, wererats, and werecrocodiles inhabit this dangerous swamp. The werecrocodiles have a half-sunken city on the bay, and the two kinds of lycanthropes war constantly.

The Akanamere: This lake is rich in fish and inhabited by vodyanoi (aquatic umber hulks). At least one pirate vessel plagues the lake, and small tribes of lizardfolk dot the shore. The peninsula between the western and southern arms of the lake is known as the Akanal, some of the richest farmland in all Faerûn.

Akanapeaks: Containing the highest peaks in Chessenta, this range is best known for the ferocious Flaming Spike orc tribe, which numbers in the tens of thousands and inhabits a large abandoned dwarven mine. The Chessentans mine iron here in the safer areas.

Riders to the Sky: This mountain range is actually mostly hills. Inhabited by bandits on the east side, trolls and duergar on the west side, and pteranodons throughout, the hills sport ruins from an aarakocra civilization hunted to extinction by mercenaries.

Threskel: South of the dormant volcano known as Mount Thulbane and north of the Riders to the Sky lies the sparsely settled land of Threskel, claimed by both Chessenta and Unther but really part of neither. A very old vampire green dragon named Jaxanaedegor lairs somewhere in Mount Thulbane and claims the wastes of Threskel as its kingdom, although it cannot abide the touch of daylight.

IMPORTANT SITES

Chessenta is carved up between three major factions or alliances: Akanax, Cimbar, and Soorenar. Most of the other cities owe allegiance to one of these three, although some stand neutral.

Airspur (Large City, 22,282): This powerful trading port has a 30% half-orc population. For several years it took an aggressive stance against Cimbar, and the city is now rebuilding its strength and looking out for other enemies. It is ruled by a military council led by Khrulus (N male half-orc Ftr8), who is crafty, pragmatic, and greedy.

Akanax (Large City, 24,632): This town functions like a military camp. Male citizens are conscripted into the army or slain for desertion. Strangers are only barely tolerated here and viewed with suspicion. No mercenary companies are allowed within its borders. Akanax has been warring with Luthcheq for several years, and has allied with Cimbar against Soorenar. King Hippartes (LN male human Ftr19) is a tyrant but considered the finest soldier in the nation. Akanax's city population figure doesn't include the army camped outside the city, some fifty thousand soldiers.

Cimbar (Metropolis, 110,843): Hundreds of years ago, Tchazzar chose Cimbar as the center of his short-lived Chessentan Empire. Cimbar is the traditional capital of Chessenta, although it has only been so in truth for one short period of history. The city requires participation in the arts, philosophy, and music by the population, and it is known for its college of sages, and artist's college. Cimbar boasts the second largest fleet in the eastern inner sea (behind Thay). Its fleet frequently battles with cities on the north coast.

Cimbar's college of wizardry is in the process of being rebuilt after its destruction in 1370 DR during a rite of power involving an evil Shadow Weave artifact. Not long ago the ruling Sceptanar was unseated by the shadow mage Aeron Morieth (N male half-elf Wiz13/Sha3), who held the job for a few months before appointing the noble-born wizard Melisanda of Arrabar (LG female human Wiz7) to replace him. Aeron now resides in the Maerchwood, a small forest between the Smoking Mountains and the Adder Peaks along the Winding River.

Luthcheq (Metropolis, 61,580): Also known as the City of Madness, Luthcheq is led by the Karanok family, all of whom belong to the cult of Entropy (a nonsentient giant *sphere of annihilation* that they think is a deity), a group that wishes to destroy all magic. The

Tchazzar

Under the leadership of the great war leader Tchazzar, the chaotic, wealthy, always restless city-states collectively known as Chessenta were united for the first and last time. His tireless sword forged an empire.

Tchazzar ruled long and well, his mastery of the intrigues and dabblings of his people steering them into great wealth and a golden age. Chessentans are passionate, energetic, and given to doing things to extremes. Feasts and wars are frequent Chessentan pursuits—and Tchazzar was the greatest glutton and war hero of all, rising above his debaucheries to win victory after victory.

When sahuagin raided the shores of Chessenta in 1018 DR, Tchazzar rode north alone to face them, bidding his armies, "Feast and take ease, while I sharpen my sword once more." He was never seen again—save in flickering visions that appeared simultaneously in the throne and council chambers of all Chessentan cities, images of Tchazzar standing atop a heap of butchered sahuagin

with bloody blade in hand, smiling and saying, "Know that I have won my greatest victory." The Invincible Warrior was seen in Chessenta no more, and his body was never found. Without him, his empire collapsed in less than a decade.

In time, some folk came to revere "the Great Red Dragon" Tchazzar as a deity. Despite the ruin and strife that followed (and continues to this day), clergy of the Great Red Dragon in the Chessentan cities of Cimbar and Soorenar venerate him. Followers of Tchazzar believe that he will return to lead Chessenta into a new golden age. His worship is strong in Chessenta and unknown elsewhere.

Some sages say Tchazzar was not a human who used a dragon as his battle-standard, but a real red dragon. According to this line of conjecture, the dragon believed that if he took on human form, united and ruled Chessenta for a time, and then disappeared mysteriously, a cult would arise and worship him, granting him godlike powers. He was right.

Karanoks—and particularly the current head, Maelos (LE male human Ari18)—hope Chessenta's fragile alliances destroy each other so *they* can take control. No mercenary companies are allowed here.

Luthcheq dislikes users of arcane magic; known wizards and sorcerers face execution by burning. Elves (considered to be magical creatures) and dwarves (considered to be earth wizards) are similarly prosecuted, as are those who associate with the taboo folk.

Soorenar (Metropolis, 73,896): This aggressive port city is allied with Airspur and Luthcheq against Cimbar. The government consists of a representative from each of the three most powerful families in the city. They prefer to purchase victory with money and treasure, usually involving buying the services of powerful wizards (which sometimes puts them at odds with Luthcheq).

REGIONAL HISTORY

The Chessentan people spent restive centuries under the rule of Unther during the zenith of that empire. The Chessentans grew uneasy with the decadence and religious oppression of their masters, and finally rebelled under a war hero named Tchazzar. Actually a red dragon secretly polymorphed into human form, Tchazzar managed to subdue Unther itself for nearly a century.

Although the city-states of Chessenta swore fealty to a central monarch, each had a different idea of who that monarch should be, and Chessenta has since been rocked with wars between its city-states to determine supremacy. This near constant state of war has produced a nation of trained fighters and a reliance on external mercenary and adventuring groups to do dirty jobs. Chessenta engages in trade by sea with other nations and shows no signs of unifying again any time soon.

PLOTS AND RUMORS

Adventures in Chessenta generally involve aiding one city in its struggle against another.

Burning Mountain: One of the Smoking Mountains (the range that separates northern Unther from southern Chessenta) recently erupted explosively, raining down hot ash for nearly a hundred miles in every direction. The explosion displaced monsters from the rest of the range, most of which have gone north. Included in this horde are young dragons, kir-lanans, reclusive wizards, and decaying liches. Rulers of the southern cities seek to hire mercenaries and adventurers to deal with the problem before the creatures reach civilized areas.

Mulhorand

Capital: Skuld
Population: 5,339,520 (humans 95%, half-orcs 2%, planetouched 2%)
Government: Theocracy
Religions: Mulhorandi pantheon, Gond, Mask, Mystra, Red Knight
Imports: Fine timber, incense, iron, perfume, slaves (from Thay), spices
Exports: Ale, beer, blank spellbooks, gold, granite, paper, precious stones
Alignment: LN, LG, LE

One of the few ancient empires that has survived to the present day, for millennia Mulhorand existed under the rulership of physical manifestations of its deities. Now in the hands of those deities' mortal descendants, Mulhorand has begun to change and accommodate the rest of the world, opening itself to foreign trade and ideas.

With the collapse of Unther's government, Mulhorand has conquered much of its old rival's territory and may be looking to remake itself into the empire it used to be. Still unpopular in some western countries for its acceptance of slavery, Mulhorand remains an exotic land with powerful magic, old technology, and a powerful clergy.

LIFE AND SOCIETY

Mulhorand has long been a patriarchal nation, with the first son of a family inheriting two-thirds of the family's property, the second son getting the remainder, and all other children left to fend for themselves. With the removal of the deific manifestations and influence on Pharaoh Horustep III by foreign mercenaries, Mulhorand's laws have started to enforce equality between the sexes.

Clerics are still the most respected members of society, with the vast majority of them being descendants of the incarnations of the deities they serve. Wizards and sorcerers, also well respected here, spend their time researching new magic or examining old artifacts.

Religion is important to the Mulhorandi. They say prayers four times a day, clerics run the government, and the temples own all the nation's slaves (which are rented out to others). Class is also important: Bureaucrats (people of status) shave their heads and paint circles upon their foreheads. One circle indicates a freeman, two a wizard, and three a cleric. The middle class consists of artisans, craftsfolk, traders, mercenaries, and scribes.

Below the middle class are the slaves, who are treated well; harming a slave is considered vandalism of temple property. It is possible for a slave to rise to the status of a bureaucrat if given sufficient education. For the most part, adventurers are seen as little more than grave robbers. Nonhumans are uncommon aside from the dwarves and gnomes in the Sword Mountains and elves and halfelves in the Methwood.

The greatest source of dissent among the citizens is the rivalry between the churches of Anhur and Horus-Re. Anhur favors change and conflict while Horus-Re represents eternity and perpetual order. Now that Mulhorand is ruled by someone fully mortal once again, the dominance of Horus-Re is lessening, and deities from the Faerûnian pantheon are making inroads in Mulhorand while the local deities are expanding outward from their native land. Mulhorand is also unusual for its technology, primarily pumps to move water to irrigate crops. This aspect of the culture had fallen into decline for centuries but is now being revived by the clerics of Thoth and Gond.

MAJOR GEOGRAPHICAL FEATURES

Mulhorand is a vast realm, stretching from the salty lake of Azulduth through its client states of Semphar and Murghôm all the way to the Hordelands.

Alamber Sea: This sea is heavily populated by the sahuagin that hail from their undersea kingdom of Aleaxtis, thought to be in the top third of the bay. The large island is the Ship of the Gods, an active volcano and a haven for pirates.

Dragonsword Mountains: The Mulhorandi consider these high mountains impassable due to the large number of dangerous sphinxes, griffons, and yrthaks that lair here. Gestaniius the blue wyrm is the most dangerous of the mountains' denizens.

Plains of Purple Dust: This region of faintly magical sand is inhabited primarily by purple worms, with human nomads living on the plains' western border. Under the dust lie connections to the Underdark; the cities beneath are controlled by cruel lizardfolk. Most believe that the battles between the deities of Unther and Mulhorand indirectly caused this wasteland.

Raurin, the Dust Desert: This land was once the center of the Imaskar Empire. The Imaskari's battles against the Mulhorandi and Untheric deities destroyed their homeland, and the survivors moved

Illustration by Sam Wood

City of Skuld

west. Now Raurin is a wasteland of stone, sand, and dust inhabited by brown dragons, blue dragons, and a handful of rogue efreet. The desert also holds many ruins with powerful artifacts, as well as a large temple to the deity Set.

IMPORTANT SITES

The population figures below include roughly 20,000 of the Mulhorandi soldiers currently stationed in Unther.

Gheldaneth (Metropolis, 172,243): The second largest city in the nation is a sprawling port ruled by clerics of Thoth. Its most prominent buildings are the Great University and the Wizard College. The majority of the arcane magic items created in Mulhorand are made here.

Mishtan (Small City, 6,459): The temple of Osiris, Mulhorandi power of the dead, rules this town. Mishtan's claim to importance is its proximity to the Land of the Dead, the ancient burial ground for pharaohs and their families. This complex of tombs in the Dragonsword Mountains is constantly under construction, and the number of people working here increases by a factor of ten in the springtime. Animated skeletons and zombies within the tombs destroy grave robbers and defilers.

Neldorild (Metropolis, 86,121): Neldorild is a city of affluent nobles and wealthy retirees seeking escape from politics. The city is less than twenty years old, and parts of it are still being constructed to accommodate new arrivals. Ruled by the church of Nephthys, the city is intolerant of thieves, and stealing is punishable by death.

Skuld (Metropolis, 204,538): The oldest continually inhabited city in Faerûn, Skuld was founded over thirty-five hundred years ago. Its inhabitants boast (truthfully) that no invading army has ever breached its walls. The part of Skuld called the City of the Gods is the site for temples and the former residences of the incarnated Mulhorand deities, and its grandeur is all the more spectacular compared to the squalor of the rest of the city. The many laws here are strict, and taxes are both numerous and high, although those affecting nonhuman visitors have been largely dropped.

REGIONAL HISTORY

Four thousand years ago, the Imaskar Empire suffered a great plague that decimated its population. The wizard-rulers of Imaskar opened a pair of great *portals* to another world, pulling forth over one hundred thousand humans, then closed the *portals* and sealed all connections to that world forever. The Imaskari enslaved and oppressed these people (the Mulan), and the slaves offered countless prayers to their deities that went unheard because of the Imaskaran barrier.

Through the intervention of Ao, the slaves' deities were able to send powerful but mortal versions of themselves through alternate methods, bypassing the barrier. The deities battled and defeated the Imaskari, settling the lands to the west along with their followers. The nations of Mulhorand and Unther were born from these events, and after years of war, the divine manifestations agreed to abide by their common border and pursue conquest of other lands.

Nine hundred years later, another great *portal* opened to an unknown world, calling forth unnumbered hordes of orcs. The humanoids attacked the northern reaches of Mulhorand and Unther, drawing the divine manifestations into battle with the barbarous enemy. In response, the orc clerics summoned manifestations of their deities, resulting in many deaths on both sides. Eventually the orcs were defeated and fled to elsewhere in Toril.

Over the next two thousand years, Mulhorand's daughter states broke free, forming the nations of Murghôm, Semphar, and Thay. Mulhorand existed in a state of slow decline for hundreds of years until the end of the Time of Troubles, when Ao removed the Imaskari barrier. This allowed the Mulhorandi manifestations to reunite with their primary essences. Ruled by a true mortal for the first time in its history, Mulhorand went through a brief period of repression and martial law, then stabilized somewhat as the clergy, long used to ruling the country, reestablished a state of normalcy.

With the death of Gilgeam the Tyrant, Unther lost its lone manifest deity. Anhur, the Mulhorandi god of war, had long been pressing the pharaoh to take a more active role in the world, and the change in Unther was the catalyst that the young pharaoh Horustep III (LG male human Clr4/Pal6 of Horus-Re) needed. Realizing the border treaty between the deities was no longer valid without the presence of the manifestation of Gilgeam in Unther, the pharaoh allowed the clerics of Anhur to lead an army into Unther. Greatly aided by the Gold Swords, a skilled foreign mercenary company led by Kendera Steeldice (LG female human Pal11 of the Red Knight), the army of Mulhorand marched around the Alamber Sea as far north as the city of Shussel, conquering most of Unther in the process. Mulhorand's military energy is currently being used to end or divert slave revolts and train former Untheric slaves in the service of the temples of Mulhorand.

Back in Skuld, the pharaoh had become quite enamored of the mercenary Kendera, whose dedication, skill, and experience impressed him greatly. With the able-bodied men of the country camped to the west, Mulhorand faced a severe shortage of workers in all disciplines. Under Kendera's advice, Horustep III has passed a law allowing women to work in the same jobs as men and is considering plans to restructure the inheritance laws to be more equitable among all siblings.

Now Mulhorand has expanded its territory by nearly half, with the remainder of Unther barely able to organize a coherent defense. Thay, Chessenta, and other nearby nations have taken care to treat Mulhorand carefully, and diplomats from many nations visit Skuld, hoping to stay in good favor with the pharaoh. The remainder of Unther trembles at the thought of next year's campaign, but the pharaoh's military advisors caution him not to expand too quickly.

PLOTS AND RUMORS

Mulhorand's power rests on three pillars: the pharaoh and his army, the clerics and the vast possessions of their temples, and the land's wizards. The pharaoh's ascendance does not please the clerics of deities other than Anhur and Horus-Re, nor does it please the mages. Intrigues and schemes to control the young and aggressive pharaoh are becoming common in the city of Skuld.

Thieves in the Night: The church of Mask has taken advantage of the absence of the military in Mulhorand to conduct some notorious heists in Skuld. The official churches of the state have been unable to track those responsible, in part because some of the thieves have been able to melt away into thin air. Unknown to the Mulhorandi, the secret ritual discovered by the Shadowmasters of Telflamm (see Telflamm under Thesk, below) has been taught to local Maskarran clerics, and unless they are caught soon, every thief in the city will gain this ability.

unther

Capital: Messemprar (formerly Unthalass)
Population: 4,263,840 (humans 94%, dwarves 3%, halflings 2%)
Government: Magocracy (formerly direct theocracy)
Religions: Bane, the Mulhorandi pantheon, Mystra, Tempus (mainly by Chessentan mercenaries), Tiamat

Imports: Food, mercenaries, slaves, weapons
Exports: Ceramics, cloth, gold, iron, minerals, sculpture, seed oil
Alignment: CN, CE, N

Once a great empire like its sister nation Mulhorand, Unther fell far under the rule of the cruel manifestation of the deity Gilgeam. With Gilgeam's death at the claws of Tiamat, Unther was plunged into chaos. Slaves rebelled, commoners rejoiced at the death of the tyrant, and clerics of Gilgeam and nobles struggled to maintain order. The armies of Mulhorand took advantage of this unrest, invading southern Unther and placing conquered areas under martial law.

Now Unther is a country divided between those who cling to the old ways and those who hope the pharaoh of Mulhorand will treat them better than their old ruler did. Unther is a land of opportunity, where military force, diplomacy, subterfuge, and intrigue all play a part in survival and power.

LIFE AND SOCIETY

Victims of a cruel tyrant, the people of Unther had grown used to—but not complacent in—hardship and misery. While the land's exalted nobles lived a life of luxury, served by slaves and supported by the national treasury, the common people paid high taxes, and slaves were treated so poorly that the punishment for killing one was paying a fine to the owner. While the government espoused the power of law in Unther, those who enforced the laws often disregarded the rights of citizens in favor of acquiring wealth and power for themselves. Slaves worked long hours for little food and were branded on the arm as a sign of their servitude.

With the fall of Gilgeam, the lower classes glimpsed a hope that their lot would improve, but the arrival of the Mulhorandi army has confused the issue. The army is controlled by the clerics of Anhur, a warlike yet good-aligned deity—and a radical change for the people of Unther. Abuses against the conquered people are rare and rapidly punished. Untherite slaves (whether owned by temples or individuals) became property of the churches of Mulhorand, a better lot in life than they had ever known before.

The fit slaves were given rudimentary arms training and sent to root out hidden pockets of Untherite resistance, a vengeful task they performed well. Now the few free cities of Unther look to their brethren in the south and wonder if they are better served being patriots of their homeland or citizens of the new empire. Because the armies control the fertile fields in Unther and food shortages grow imminent in the free cities, leaders in the north are pressured to acquire food or surrender.

The army of Unther is ill-trained and poorly equipped with bronze swords and bronze half-plate armor. The personal retinues of the surviving nobles and temples are better armed and much more formidable in the field.

MAJOR GEOGRAPHICAL FEATURES

The River of Swords was long recognized as the border between Unther and Mulhorand, but it is no longer clear exactly what the new border will be after Mulhorand's armies cease advancing.

Black Ash Plain: This area, south of the Smoking Mountains, earns its name from the gray soot blown from the volcanic cones of that range. It is inhabited by brown dragons and black-skinned stone giants, which are locally known as ash giants. This area is not particularly fertile (it has almost no soil other than the ash itself) and was avoided by the Mulhorandi army.

The Green Lands: The soil of the Green Lands is enhanced by magic and is normally responsible for three-fourths of the food produced in Unther. The area is inhabited by androsphinxes and gynosphinxes that occasionally raid cattle farms. The Green Lands were churned into mud by the army of Mulhorand, and imports of food from the east will be needed to prevent famine in Unther this year.

Methmere: This lake is thick with fish, which are dined upon by the native plesiosaurs. Bandit settlements dot the western coast, and many refugees fled across the water when the Mulhorandi army arrived, some captured by bandits and sold into slavery, some reaching Chessenta on their own, and yet others struggling to survive on the shore.

Methwood: This thick forest once sheltered a number of druids, but they left or died out over a hundred years ago. Now home to small tribes of elves and half-elves, the Methwood is also inhabited by chimeras and an old green dragon named Skuthosiin. Legends tell of a lost city of the Turami race in the forest, possibly dating back to the time of the Imaskar Empire.

Smoking Mountains: The western end of this range has active volcanoes, while the eastern end is dormant. Guyanothaz the red dragon lairs here but hasn't been seen in centuries. The mountains are also home to pyrohydras and salamanders.

IMPORTANT SITES

The population numbers in occupied cities do not include roughly 20,000 soldiers of Mulhorand who are currently stationed in Unther.

Messemprar (Metropolis, 98,776): Once the largest city in Unther when it was a major port on the naval trade route, Messemprar shrank when merchant vessels began to avoid Unther's coast and Gilgeam's excessive trade taxes. A brief civil war within the city broke out a few years ago after a tax revolt that led to a food riot. The riot ended when the wizards of a secretly anti-Gilgeam group called the Northern Wizards took control of the city.

Now Messemprar has more than doubled in size as refugees from other cities in Unther flood into it. The Northern Wizards wished to be free of Gilgeam, but did not expect their freedom to be followed by the swords of Mulhorand. They have been working frantically to fortify their city against the army and pleading with the pharaoh for a cessation of hostilities. The Northern Wizards have a standing agreement with several adventuring groups to smuggle food into the city.

If anyone could be said to be the leader of unconquered Unther at the moment, it might be Isimud (NG male human Wiz15/Dev3 of Mystra), who is the foremost of the mages of Messemprar. His fellow mages are a fractious group whose power is not well respected by the turncoat nobles of their host city.

Shussel (Small City, 9,150): Two years ago almost the entire population of this city vanished in a single night. The war against Mulhorand had nothing to do with the disappearance of the city's population—the accounts of survivors and numerous divinations reveal that a mysterious fog descended over the city and lingered all night long, carrying away nine out of ten of the city's citizens when the morning sun broke.

Shussel-folk who were away from their home city reclaimed their empty town, now filled with entire districts of abandoned residences. Squatters and bandits followed, taking advantage of empty homes and left-behind wealth. Shussel was growing poorer anyway before the Vanishing; its iron mines are playing out, and overfarming of the fields to the north have left them little more than a desert. Now Shussel exists as a Mulhorandi garrison town, its small port under heavy guard so that ships from Skuld may dock here with supplies and fresh troops for the Mulhorandi invaders.

Unthalass (Metropolis, 164,627): In its heyday, this city was the grandest in Faerûn. Since then, it has been flooded many times, attacked by pirates, and nearly destroyed by a battle between Tia-

mat and Gilgeam during the Time of Troubles. Now the army of Mulhorand occupies the city, with about half of its former population under martial law (if free) or claimed by the church of Anhur (if slaves).

The undercity is home to monsters such as lamias and wererats, with a great lamia ruling all as a queen. The monsters are biding their time since the occupation by Mulhorand, making occasional raids on the surface as they did when the city was free. A secret temple to Tiamat also lies beneath the city. The central district, formerly inhabited by Gilgeam and his clerics, was ransacked after the deity's death.

REGIONAL HISTORY

Unther's history is strongly tied to its sister Mulhorand's, except that the people of Unther have always had a more aggressive and expansionist bent than those of their eastern neighbor. Unther's territory once included what is now Chessenta, Chondath, and cities on the southern coast of Aglarond, and its fierce and ruthless warriors were hated by those they conquered. However, the cost of this expansion bankrupted Unther's treasury, forcing the rulers to raise taxes to absurd levels.

Piece by piece, the colonies of Unther rebelled. Chessenta succeeded in conquering Unther and ruled it as a vassal state for nearly a hundred years. With the disappearance of the Chessentan hero-conqueror Tchazzar, Unther was able to free itself and turn its focus inward on its own cruel people. The country that had made great advances in sculpture, poetry, and other civilized arts became engaged in a slow decline in morale and culture, as if following Gilgeam's descent into tyranny and madness.

When Gilgeam was slain by Tiamat, Mulhorand saw an opportunity to attack and crossed the traditional border between their nations, conquering first small towns and outposts and finally the Untherite capital and cities beyond.

Left with less than a third of the territory it held a year ago, Unther is on the brink of ceasing to exist. Only the mercy of Mulhorand's pharaoh or powerful intervention by outside agents (such as the Red Wizards, the Zhentarim, or the church of Tiamat) is likely to save Unther from becoming a territory of the new empire of Mulhorand. The Red Wizards in particular are loath to see Unther fall, and are supplying both money and power to help Unther remain independent. Cautious Untherites are wary of the eventual cost of this aid, but many feel that any alternative is better than becoming subject to Mulhorand's rule.

PLOTS AND RUMORS

War, rebellion, and unrest have left vast portions of Unther in virtual anarchy.

A Man without a God: The murderous right hand of the dead god Gilgeam, the high lord Shuruppak (NE male human Ftr20/Rog3/Wiz7) was once the Chosen of Gilgeam and an agent of his lord's displeasure, usually sent to kill political or dangerous opponents. With the death of his deity, Shuruppak lost his Chosen status and went rogue, killing anyone who crosses him or whom he perceives as an enemy to Unther.

Shuruppak's long-term goals are unknown, but the church of Tiamat would like to acquire his services. He wears black robes and a red skull-mask that covers the top half of his face. This madman has been a figure of terror for so long that he truly considers himself the Reaper, a name he acquired in the service of Gilgeam.

Secret Patriot: The bandit leader Furifax (LE male moon half-elf Ftr15) is a worshiper of Tempus and former palace slave. He uses his agents to smuggle contraband and watch the army leaders, for while he wished his country to be free of Gilgeam, he didn't want it under the thumb of anyone else. He is allied with the church of Tiamat but realizes that it plans to take control once the Mulhorandi have been driven out.

NINGAL

Female air genasi Ftr4/Sor8/Brd4: CR 17; Medium-size outsider; HD 4d10+8 plus 8d4+16 plus 4d6+8; hp 92; Init +7; Spd 30 ft.; AC 25 (touch 17, flat-footed 22); Atk +14/+9/+4 melee (1d8+3 plus 1d6 cold, +2 frost heavy mace) or +16/+11/+6 ranged (1d6+2 plus 1d6 cold/×3, +2 frost shortbow); SQ Air genasi abilities, bardic music 4/day, bardic knowledge +8; AL NG; SV Fort +12, Ref +13, Will +17; Str 12, Dex 16, Con 14, Int 18, Wis 12, Cha 17. Height 6 ft.

Skills and Feats: Alchemy +9, Balance +5, Bluff +8, Climb +8, Concentration +12, Craft (armorsmithing) +11, Craft (weaponsmithing) +11, Decipher Script +7, Diplomacy +6, Gather Information +6, Intimidate +5, Jump +10, Knowledge (arcana) +9, Knowledge (religion) +7, Knowledge (Untheric history) +7, Perform +6, Ride (horse) +10, Search +8, Sense Motive +4, Spellcraft +14, Spot +6, Swim +8, Tumble +10, Use Magic Device +6; Arcane Schooling (sorcerer), Combat Casting, Craft Magic Arms and Armor, Expertise, Far Shot, Improved Initiative, Iron Will, Leadership (19), Point Blank Shot.

Special Qualities: Air Genasi Abilities: Darkvision, levitate once per day as a 5th-level sorcerer, +4 racial bonus on saves against air spells and effects. Bardic Music: Countersong, fascinate, inspire courage.

Bard Spells Known (3/3/1; base DC = 13 + spell level): 0—detect magic, light, mage hand, mending, read magic, resistance; 1st—cure light wounds, protection from evil, sleep; 2nd—cure moderate wounds, suggestion.

Sorcerer Spells Known (6/7/7/6/3; base DC = 13 + spell level): 0—arcane mark, dancing lights, detect poison, disrupt undead, flare, ghost sound, open/close, ray of frost; 1st—mage armor, magic missile, magic weapon, shield, true strike; 2nd—daylight, endurance, invisibility; 3rd—fly, lightning bolt; 4th—ice storm.

Possessions: +2 shortbow*, +2 frost shortbow, +2 frost heavy mace, ring of protection +4, ring of mind shielding, 4 +1 shields of arrow deflection*, 50 +1 frost arrows*, wand of stoneskin (25 charges), bracers of armor +8, 2 gloves of storing, helm of teleportation, cloak of resistance +3. *Ningal gives these items to her retainers, but does not use them herself.

Often referring to herself as the "daughter of the moon," Ningal is a mysterious Untherite currently organizing a rebellion against the invaders from Mulhorand. She supplies her followers with magic weapons and shields (each bearing the symbol of Selûne) to use against the Mulhorandi, warding them with abjuration magic and encouraging a hit-and-run war of sabotage.

Ningal speaks little of her origin, but her genasi nature is evident in her constantly windblown hair and skin that is cool to the touch even on the hottest day. Her followers genuinely love their leader, for she lends them strength against their enemy and heals their wounds when they have been injured.

Ningal's most faithful follower is Jeardra of Aglarond (NG moon elf female Clr9 of Selûne), who has been with her for over a year.

Jeardra believes that Ningal has been favored with a high destiny in the service of Selûne and may eventually become a Chosen of Selûne. Ningal herself makes no claim, focusing instead on the liberation of her people through her power and her faith in the Moonmaiden.

The genasi is considered a rabble-rouser and dangerous rebel by the Mulhorandi government, which has offered a bounty of ten thousand gold pieces for her capture. So far she has evaded her pursuers through careful selection of safe houses and the use of her *helm of teleportation.* The Northern Wizards of Messemprar would like to gain her as an ally, but Ningal remains wary, fearing Mulhorandi spies and assassins.

Murghôm

Once part of the great empire, this country is semi-independent from Mulhorand, giving food to its parent in times of famine and cavalry in times of war. It consists of semiautonomous farming villages each ruled by an elder known as an ataman. The atamans gather into a collective government only in times of war. The people of Murghôm are known for their skill with horses and their battles against their historic rivals in Semphar as well as the undead and monsters that infest the northern shore of Brightstar Lake.

semphar

This remote country to the east of Murghôm is another possession of Mulhorand. Although Mulhorand claims it as its easternmost province, Semphar is completely sovereign. It has grown wealthy from trade between western Faerûn and Kara-Tur, and even has a college of magic. Semphar is otherwise very much like Murghôm.

sembia

Capital: Ordulin
Population: 2,462,400 (humans 96%, halflings 3%)
Government: Plutocracy (merchants' council with elected Overmaster)
Religions: Azuth, Deneir, Lathander, Loviatar, Mystra, Shar, Sune, Tymora, Waukeen
Imports: Anything it can trade to someone else
Exports: Anything it acquires from others, books, food, livestock, pottery, spiced sausage, silk, weapons, wine
Alignment: LN, NG, LE

Sembia is a land of experienced merchants who know how to hold onto power and young traders who scheme for a share of it. Sembians relish the art of the deal, the skill of gaining advantage through negotiation instead of through outright falsehood or cheating. Although Sembia does not control as great a proportion of Faerûn's trade as Amn, trade controls Sembia much more than trade controls Amn.

Unlike the lawless thugs of the Moonsea cities and the Pirate Isles, Sembians generally observe laws of contracts, debts, and interest payments. Quite often Sembians observe these laws all too well, exploiting loopholes that others had not imagined.

Sembia conceives of itself as a young, aggressive, and expansionist nation. It has already co-opted one of the Dales, the former Moondale, and transformed it into a new capital fit for a great power: the city of Ordulin. But the Sembian elite are too interested

Ningal

Illustration by Sam Wood

in seeking advantage over each other to unite behind a single foreign policy or a single warlord.

Sembia uses its position on the northwestern shore of the Sea of Fallen Stars to serve as the broker between the north and the south of Faerûn. The Zhents of the Moonsea also trade with other countries, but the Sembians don't consider them a true competitor, because a great deal of Zhent commerce flows through Sembian ports at one point or another, mostly through Ordulin. The Sembians do think of the Zhents as a magical threat, but the foremost worry of Sembia is the magical mercantilism of the Red Wizards of Thay. The Council of Sembia has little interest in seeing Thay force its way into formerly Sembian markets by providing magical goods that the Sembians can't duplicate.

LIFE AND SOCIETY

Sembia is the land of wealth and the grasping drive to earn more. More vigorous and practical than ostentatious Amn, it's a place of costers and secret cabals, cults, and other dangerous dabblings of the bored or the desperate. As long as other folk in Faerûn still have a few coins that could be in Sembian pockets or vaults, the folk of Sembia are not content.

Most Sembians spend their lives making money, doing business, having a hearty time in ways that display wealth (chiefly fashions, fads, and revels), and gossiping about Faerûn in general and their neighbors in particular.

The cityfolk dominate Sembian life, and all citizens look down on the folk of other cities. Old money commands respect because of its extensive connections, and among the self-styled nobility of Sembia, all manner of corruption and incompetency is permitted as long as certain laws aren't breached (consorting with pirates, for instance, brings heavy fines and shunning).

All but the greediest Sembian city guards are paid well enough to be above bribery. The guards are schooled in arms, dirty tricks, politeness, and understanding the ever-shifting intrigues. As a result, they're seldom heavy-handed and widely respected.

Sembia has hot summers, rainy springs and falls, and bitter windy winters, when its harbors ice up for months. Sembian nobles own extensive farms and forested hunting estates, complete with large breeding stables and luxurious lodges, in the north and northwestern Sembian countryside.

MAJOR GEOGRAPHICAL FEATURES

Sembia is a rich agricultural land of small farms in the center and north, turning to larger farms and orchards in the south. Vineyards cover the ridges, hedgerows leading into orchards and farms occupy all the lowland. The north and far west of the country are given over to livestock. Compared to farmers of other nations, who are often at a disadvantage when selling their products at market, Sembian farmers pride themselves on running efficient businesses and selling at the best possible prices.

To the southwest, toward Cormyr, merchant families purchase huge tracts of land and practice the good life of the nobility. The self-styled nobility of Sembia maintain private armies, oversee vineyards and orchards, hunt, and pursue secret or individual passions ranging from mushroom cultivation to slave breeding. Officially, slaves are illegal in Sembia, but the nobles define legality on their own estates. The great families who maintained their wealth for generations have taken to styling themselves dukes and princes, and few choose to argue the point.

IMPORTANT SITES

Wherever ships can find good harbor, the rich cities of the southern coast cram tens of thousands of Sembians together in bustling hives of industry. When outsiders think of Sembia, they usually think of these southern ports instead of the rolling farmlands that occupy the center of the country. Each of the four great southern cities—Saerloon, Selgaunt, Urmlaspyr, and Yhaunn—is "ruled" by a merchant prince who serves at the pleasure of the true powers of the city, the merchant councils.

Daerlun (Metropolis, 52,477): Of all Sembian cities, Daerlun enjoys the closest relations with Cormyr. Centuries of intermarriage and close trading contacts with Cormyr have provided the citizens of Daerlun with a blend of Sembian business acumen and Cormyrian warmth and courtesy. Cormyrian traders who can't stomach interacting with other Sembians feel comfortable in Daerlun, a fact that the Daerlun traders are quick to exploit.

Ordulin (Metropolis, 36,330): The crossroads capital is the one area of Sembia in which politics are nearly as important as economics. Ordulin serves as the hub through which all other sections of the country interact. Ordulin is a new city, designed with care to pro-

The Dark side of sembia

Sembia is prosperous, but there is a dark side to its security and wealth. It's a haughty, ruthless, and cutthroat land, bustling with commercial intrigues. Sembians look down on the poor and all outlanders—albeit with a measure of respect when they think of wealthy and successful Amn, Thay, Waterdeep, and Westgate—and they positively sneer at elves. Sembians are outwardly tolerant of a wide variety of races, appearances, and customs . . . as long as such strange folk are here to buy.

Coins make for instant friends in Sembia, and lack of coins makes them disappear just as swiftly. The dagger, strangler's cord, and poison pose the chief dangers to life and limb, and may strike anywhere—but do so sparingly, because there are plenty of wizards-for-hire in Sembia, and local rulers pay some to use spying spells at random to check on their subjects' business dealings.

Sembians expect corruption in high places. Constant rumors speak of various city rulers conspiring with Thayans, Zhentarim, or "fell things mages can talk to from afar" to betray their citizens. Underhanded dealings are permissible and even admired—but outright theft or arson are abhorred, and justice can be harsh.

Outlanders seeking to set up shop in Sembia are warned that if they "look different" from the fair-skinned, drawling humans, business rivals seize on any excuse to start unfavorable rumors about them, because Sembians are especially quick to shun "sneaking outlanders."

Kidnappings-for-hire of business and social rivals (and of one's own undesired offspring and other relatives), "hirespell" wizards who magically spy or cast harmful spells for fees, and debtors indentured as near-slaves to work off their debts for years are all common in "Golden Sembia." The upland woods, hunting estates, and the Ghost Holds (abandoned mansions) of nearby Battledale all crawl with Sembian outlaws—folk ruined or driven off by the unwritten rules of the merchant kingdom.

claim Sembia's might and erase the memory of when this area was known as Moondale.

The city is laid out like a great sunburst, with a central core consisting of three great buildings and mighty roads radiating out from the core like the rays of the sun. At the center are the Great Hall of the Council of Sembia (the voice of the merchant class and the nation's true rulers, at least until now), the Tower of the Guards, and the Guarded Gate, Sembia's mint and chief treasury.

Rauthauvyr's Road: Sembia built its road through Cormanthor and remains determined to keep it open. Ironically, the departure of the Elven Court from Cormanthor has made Rauthauvyr's Road more dangerous rather than less. Attacks by opportunistic bandits, monsters, and drow have replaced the elven watchfulness.

Kendrick Selkirk believes he can solve these problems by establishing friendly trading relations with the new drow communities in Cormanthor. The drow should be able to keep other intruders to a minimum, and although they're not the best partners, Sembia's relations with the "good" elves were never strong enough that dealing with Vhaeraunian drow might not be an improvement.

Saerloon (Metropolis, 54,496): Saerloon's soaring gothic architecture, peppered throughout with gargoyles and other embellishments, is inherited from the Chondathan colonists who established Saerloon as their beachhead in this new land. Saerloon's citizens maintain a fever pitch of mercantile activity, seasoned by thievery and intrigue. In contrast to well-policed cities such as Daerlun, Saerloon is a happy plotting ground for thieves' guilds such as the Night Knives, slavers such as the Eyeless Mask, the Cult of the Dragon, the Red Wizards of Thay, and even the Dark Moon monks of Shar.

Selgaunt (Metropolis, 56,514): Selgaunt is the richest and haughtiest of the Sembian cities. Its nominal ruler is a hereditary merchant mayor named the Hulorn. The merchants who actually rule Selgaunt indulge in greater than normal expenditures on intrigues and power politics, as if to prove that they can afford it. Between the current Hulorn, a secretive fellow named Andeth Ilchammar (N male human Ari4/Wiz3), and the Old Chauncel (as the old nobility in town likes to call itself), Selgaunt is the Sembian city least affected by the present power struggle within the extended family of the new Overmaster of Sembia.

Urmlaspyr (Metropolis, 26,239): As Daerlun's link to the sea, Urmlaspyr maintains a steady buzz of merchant shipping. Its citizens are nearly as industrious as the people of Saerloon, without the steady diet of murderous intrigue, and nearly as friendly as the people of Daerlun, without the somewhat convoluted allegiances that plague that city's relations with its neighbors and relatives to the north. Urmlaspyr makes a point of open-mindedness, particularly where the divine powers are concerned. Hence the city is home to temples or shrines to deities such as Bane, Talos, and Umberlee—whose clerics would gladly raze the temples of Gond, Tymora, and Waukeen.

Yhaunn (Large City, 20,184): Yhaunn handles a great deal of the traffic between the Dalelands and the Sea of Fallen Stars. The city grew up on the site of an ancient quarry. The richest merchants live up high, on the slopes of the quarry. Poorer folk live farther down the slope, and so on, until the slums of the city ooze up against the well-policed section of the harbor that is reserved for commerce.

REGIONAL HISTORY

The nation of Sembia began as a colony of distant Chondath, winning its independence when the Chondathans were crushed by the elves of Cormanthor at the Battle of Singing Arrows in 884 DR. For a time, conflicts with the elves threatened to destroy the new nation, but Rauthauvyr the Raven outmaneuvered the Elven Court, cutting a trade route through the great forest up to the Moonsea.

Rauthauvyr instituted a form of government in which a merchant council elected an Overmaster to serve a seven-year term. The institution has been stable to this day—or at least until the day before yesterday. In 1371 DR, Overmaster Elduth Yarmmaster died of old age. The new Overmaster is named Kendrick the Tall (LN male human Rog4/Ftr7) of the great Selkirk trading family. Kendrick is generally regarded as a fair and honest man—but the same cannot be said of the rest of his family, whose plots and counterplots have sent the day-to-day affairs of Sembian politics lurching this way and that. Kendrick's family contains two other powerful individuals who appear to fancy themselves as future kings or queens, or at least as candidates for the next Overmaster.

Miklos Selkirk, Kendrick's eldest son, spent the previous fifteen years as an adventurer in the Sea of Fallen Stars, the Moonsea, and the Underdark. As an adventurer, Miklos called himself the Silver Raven, a name that seems to have been calculated to enhance his future in Sembian politics, since Sembia's official arms consist of the raven (representing Rauthauvyr) and a stack of silver coins. Miklos makes the twenty-two-member merchant council of Ordulin extremely nervous, because he is not only a skillful negotiator and diplomat but a deadly warrior possessed of powerful magic gained during a career as a supposedly never-defeated adventurer.

Kendrick's cousin, the Countess Mirabeta (LE female human Ari8/Rog4), appears to be Miklos's main rival for power within the family and within Sembia as a whole. Mirabeta acquired a leading interest in the Six Coffers Market trading house and established a strong relationship with the church of Waukeen. Mirabeta funded and supported the church in its early days of reestablishing itself in Sembia. These good works help conceal one widely known fact: Mirabeta is as evil as they come. Since she usually knows how to conceal her true intentions, she can safely be assumed to be sane, but that's one of the few good things that can be said about her. Her five children, and their children, are no better.

THE SILVER RAVENS

Unwilling to completely let go of his adventuring days, Miklos has formed a personal army of one hundred to two hundred skilled and loyal Sembians to improve Sembia's image abroad, gather information, retrieve magical treasures, and accomplish the types of missions he took care of himself when he was an adventurer. Some of the Silver Ravens are adventurers of good heart, but others are evil rogues who know a good deal when they can find it.

Miklos sees his Silver Ravens as a potential counter to the Harpers, who have seldom been friends of Sembia. He would prefer that his agents conduct themselves honorably, and encourages true paladins to take up his colors, but he is realistic enough to know that some missions cannot be accomplished by honorable means. For the most part, Miklos prefers agents who see things as he does—true neutrals whose loyalty is to Sembia.

Inside Sembia, Silver Ravens wear Miklos's coat of arms. Outside Sembia, Silver Ravens often go incognito, revealing their identities only when among friends.

PLOTS AND RUMORS

Sembia's merchant princes operate above the law. Competition can be fierce, and more than a few are willing to engage in whatever tactics are necessary to secure an advantage.

The Beating of Silver Wings: Outside Sembia, as the PCs are preparing to accept payment for an upcoming mission in the pursuit of a higher cause, a squad of Silver Ravens appears and offers to perform the task for free. Naturally, the Ravens intend to keep any magic treasure they find, but their stipend from the Selkirk family treasury enables them to take on dangerous adventuring missions for free. If the PCs accept the mission anyway, the Ravens race them to the goal, a rivalry that could turn friendly or lethal depending on the PCs' personalities and relations with Sembia.

Possession Equals Ownership: The PCs encounter a slave caravan or slave ship that is attempting to sneak into the northwest corner of Sembia. When the PCs defeat the slave drivers, they learn that the slaves were being taken to an estate owned by Mirabeta Selkirk's eldest son. Do the PCs attempt to turn their evidence over to Sembian authorities? Does Mirabeta's brood frame the PCs as slavers? Do Red Wizards perceive the PCs' difficulties and offer to take the whole lot of merchandise (slaves) off the PCs' hands in trade for magic?

Miklos Selkirk

Male human Ari1/Ftr6/Rog3: CR 10; Medium-size humanoid; HD 1d8+1 plus 6d10+6 plus 3d6+3; hp 61; Init +4; Spd 60 ft.; AC 22 (touch 16, flat-footed 18); Atk +8/+3 melee (1d6+2/12–20, *+2 keen rapier*) and +8 melee (1d4+2/19–20, *+2 defending dagger*) or +12 ranged (1d8/19–20, light crossbow); SA Sneak attack +2d6; SQ Evasion, locate traps, uncanny dodge (Dex bonus to AC); AL N; SV Fort +7, Ref +11, Will +6; Str 10, Dex 18, Con 12, Int 16, Wis 13, Cha 16. Height 5 ft. 10 in.

Skills and Feats: Appraise +8, Balance +11, Bluff +12, Climb +2, Diplomacy +18, Gather Information +7, Innuendo +9, Intimidate +9, Jump +4, Knowledge (arcana) +4, Knowledge (Dalelands geography) +7, Knowledge (nature) +4, Knowledge (religion) +4, Knowledge (Sembia history) +5, Knowledge (Sembia local) +4, Knowledge (Sembia nobility and royalty) +5, Listen +6, Ride (horse) +9, Search +5, Sense Motive +8, Spot +7, Swim +4, Tumble +10, Use Magic Device +4; Ambidexterity, Education, Expertise, Improved Critical (rapier), Leadership (12), Lightning Reflexes, Silver Palm, Twin Sword Style, Two-Weapon Fighting.

Possessions: *+2 keen rapier, +2 defending dagger, +2 chain shirt, boots of striding and springing, ring of mind shielding, ring of protection +1,* light crossbow.

Miklos Selkirk

A retired adventurer and the son of Overmaster Kendrick Selkirk, Miklos is best known in his homeland as the creator of the Silver Ravens, a large group of mercenary adventurers who are under his command.

A skilled negotiator and diplomat, he also is quite capable of avenging any insults with dazzling swordplay. He engages in battles of wits with other merchant nobles, but his main rival is the self-styled "Countess" Mirabeta, his father's cousin. Although he knows she is evil to the core, he cannot reveal her nature for fear of shaming his family and losing political power.

Miklos is shrewd, patient, and familiar with intrigue and bizarre

circumstances. Having spent time in the Underdark, he understands the drow and their methods of negotiation. He spends his time directing the Silver Ravens, but is called on from time to time by the Sembian Council to handle peaceful contact with the dark elves. A jack-of-all-trades, Miklos can converse on just about any subject. He keeps up-to-date on the happenings in every interesting portion of the world. This allows him better to arrange deals for his family based on excesses and shortcomings in trade, and also means he's able to respond quickly to developing situations.

the shining south

Along the southeastern coast of Faerûn stretches a vast land of magic, mystery, rumor, and legend. To the folk of the Heartlands, thousands of miles away, the South is a place of myths and tales that seem unbelievable. A land where everyone is a wizard? A kingdom of halflings? A realm ruled by drow? All of these things and more exist in the South.

The South is normally accounted to consist of the coastal lands of Halruaa, Luiren, Dambrath, Durpar, Estagund, Var the Golden, and Veldorn. It also includes the land dividing the South from the rest of Faerûn, the great grassland known as the Shaar, and the Great Rift, a mighty dwarven kingdom in the middle of the Shaar.

the Great Rift

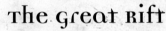

Capital: Underhome
Population: 1,308,960 (gold dwarves 90%, shield dwarves 6%, gnomes 2%, halflings 1%)
Government: Monarchy
Religions: Clangeddin Silverbeard, Dugmaren Brightmantle, Haela Brightaxe, Moradin
Imports: Fruit, grain, livestock, produce
Exports: Gems, gold, jewelry, magic items, silver
Alignment: LN, LG, N

The center of the Eastern Shaar is cut open as if by a gigantic sword in a curving, southeast-to-northwest canyon, the Great Rift. It plunges to a thousand feet below the level of the surrounding plains at its deepest point, although its floor is still well above sea level. Including the lands around it patrolled by dwarves, the Rift just outstrips the realm of Sembia in size. Quarried by dwarves for centuries, enlarged from an impressive natural canyon to its present awesome size in the process, the Rift is the most powerful kingdom held by Faerûnian dwarves today.

The Great Rift is the ancestral home of the gold dwarves. Unlike the shield dwarves of the north, the gold dwarves have flourished in one homeland for uncounted generations. The gold dwarves suffered their own ancient wars, but they turned the aftermath of the wars to their advantage. The Great Rift, a wound in the earth engineered (according to one theory) by their drow enemies thousands of years ago, is now the forbidding stronghold of the very race the drow hoped to destroy.

The gold dwarves control the Rift's floor, the tunnels and caves honeycombing its walls, the surface for a day's pony ride in all directions on the surface, and portions of the Underdark within range of dwarven patrols.

LIFE AND SOCIETY

Compared to the patriarchal shield dwarf kingdoms of the north, the gold dwarves have a long history of favoring female rulers. Males and females are equal in gold dwarven society, but females have a reputation for wise leadership. The gold dwarves' own explanation for this is that their menfolk think most of gold, power, and glory, whereas the women also remember to think of future generations. It's certain that respect for the land and for the magical ways that preserve the land are more prevalent in gold dwarven society than in the societies of the shield dwarves to the north.

Magic of all types is more common in gold dwarven society than among the dwarves of the north. Gold dwarven wizards, sorcerers, and stonesingers (their term for bards) join runecasters and clerics as valued and honored members of the Great Rift's society, working together to forge potent magic items.

MAJOR GEOGRAPHICAL FEATURES

The Great Rift is a world unto itself, an ecosystem distinct from the land above it with its own weather (wetter), animals (more plentiful, and herded or controlled by the dwarves) and plants (thriving). In some places the Rift is so wide that a person can stand on the valley floor and not even see the mighty cliffs marking the edges.

The Deepwild: The dwarves use this name to refer to the Underdark areas beneath the Shaar and south of the Shaar that they do not control. The Deepwild regions include such varied terrain as the drow city of Llurth Dreier beneath the Shaar, the Wyrmcaves (a dangerous series of dragon lairs linked by tunnels beneath the Shaar), and the Deepfall (a huge underground waterfall).

The Deep Realm: Distinct from the Deepwild, the Deep Realm is the area controlled and inhabited by the gold dwarves of the Great Rift. Some of the Realm's underground cities are detailed in the Important Sites section below.

The Riftlake: The lake at the bottom of the Great Rift is clear, cold, and fresh. The floor of the rift drains to this lake, which is also fed by great, deep springs rumored to hold *portals* to the Elemental Plane of Water. The Riftlake is the birthplace of the mighty River Shaar, which flows a short distance across the floor of the canyon only to disappear underground in a spray-filled gorge at the north end of the Great Rift. The gold dwarves pride themselves on keeping the waste products of their forges from contaminating the land and water.

IMPORTANT SITES

Most of the gold dwarves' largest settlements are in Underdark caverns surrounding the Great Rift, but the Rift gives all of them a link to the outside world that many other dwarven communities lack.

Eartheart (Metropolis, 44,008): If Underhome (see below) is the political center of the Great Rift, Eartheart is the religious center. The realm's great temples lie along Eartheart's pilgrimage roads.

Unlike surface temples, which build upward, the gold dwarves' temples to Moradin and the other dwarven deities seem to be simple shrines on the surface but build downward, spiraling through levels accessible to lay worshipers toward the Mysteries visited only by the priests in the roots of the earth. Eartheart is home to a standing army of fourteen thousand dwarves, the Steel Shields, and ruled by a Lord Scepter elected annually by the Deep Lords of the Deep Realm.

Hammer and Anvil (Small City, 7,899): The gold dwarves prefer that nondwarves come no closer to the Rift than Hammer and Anvil, a trading-moot of tents, movable huts, and watchful dwarven guards. It stands against the west wall of the soaring, spy-and-tunnel-filled dwarven fortress-city of Eartheart.

Here dwarves trade their metal goods, weaponry, and labor (especially armor-fitting and refitting, and on-the-spot gemcutting and setting) for fruit, vegetables, cheeses, fine textiles, paper, lamp oils, livestock, and other goods the dwarves need or prize. At any given time, fully half the population of this settlement is composed of nondwarves visiting for trade.

Riftedge Towers: The Stout Folk rule the Rift and the rolling plains all around for a day's pony-ride, enforcing this claim from sixty massive stone guard-towers along the canyon edges. These Riftedge Towers are entered by tunnels from beneath, and house all manner of catapults and ballistae. Over sixty dwarven warriors guard each garrison.

Dwarven sentries and lookouts patrolling the Rift floor or the lands nearby carry horns to swiftly summon "peacehammer" forces from the Riftedge Towers—a score of hippogriff-riding dwarven skyriders who throw axes with deadly skill and carry lances for close-in work. Some skyriders use magic lances that fire flame or magic missiles on command.

Underhome (Metropolis, 49,650): Underhome is the center of gold dwarven society. Its rulers are the Deep Lords, noble dwarves who lead great clans of warriors and artisans. The Deep Lords in turn owe allegiance to Queen Karrivva of the Simmerforge clan. More than any of the other cities, Underhome centers upon the Great Rift itself, maintaining responsibility for its defense and for the herds that graze around the Riftlake at the bottom.

The defense of Underhome, as well as its civic life, focuses on the community's central passage between the open air of the Rift and the city's main halls in the Underdark. Known as the Gates, the mighty seventy-foot-tall doors into Underhome's guard cavern were built to overawe visitors as much as for security. Magical wards and runes woven into the solid gold doors make them stronger and more functional than they appear. The Gates once withstood the unthinkable impact of a great wyrm hurling itself upon them with all its might, and proved stronger than the dragon.

REGIONAL HISTORY

Unlike the shield dwarves who spent themselves in fights against giants and orcs, the gold dwarves won their battles against Under-

---

who made the great rift?

Some legends say the Rift was formed when a huge cavern or series of natural caverns was torn apart by the fell sorceries of warring drow. Others claim that the collapse was caused by the divine wrath of dwarven deities, titanic hammerblows that buried drow. Still others say the collapse was caused by alhoon (illithid liches) magically summoning too-large dragons to defend them-selves in battle against beholders, or by a dragon lairing in the caverns whose entry shaft was discovered by a rival wyrm, leading to a rock-shattering struggle.

Whatever the Rift's origin, it bears no evidence of volcanic activity or raging watercourses, the common causes of such a feature.

dark foes relatively quickly. In the last dozen or so centuries, the gold dwarves have opted to remain separate from their northern cousins, who seemed to them to be laboring under a curse. The Thunder Blessing in 1306 DR and its consequences have helped to change the gold dwarves' minds.

Since the gold dwarves shared in the Thunder Blessing and were already doing well, their population has swelled to the point that some part of their people went out to settle in new lands. Some of the gold dwarves who opted against expanding the Deep Realm around the Great Rift have moved north to create colonies in the mountains of northern Faerûn. Gold dwarven outposts have been founded in the Smoking Mountains of Unther, in the Giant's Run Mountains west of Turmish, and in the North Wall of Halruaa.

PLOTS AND RUMORS

Most adventures involving the Great Rift concern it only peripherally, unless the heroes have the luck or ambition to use *portals* to travel into a place in which they're probably not wanted.

The Runaway Guardsman: While the heroes are embroiled in a battle, unexpected help comes from Matharm Derukhed, a gold dwarven warrior-wizard mounted on a hippogriff. Matharm is a long way from home, journeying to track down the murderers of his twin brother. Whether or not the PCs make an ally of Matharmm or help him in any way, the culprits turn out to be old enemies of the PCs who killed Matharm's brother for the gold and gems he wore in his hair and beard.

If the PCs ignore Matharm's quest, they may discover him dead later, apparently overcome by the murderers of his brother. Of course, the heroes are too late to retrieve any of his belongings, which are now in the hands of their enemies. To complicate matters, the dwarf is not supposed to be flying his valuable mount around northern Faerûn. He's running from his own people, intent on settling his family's vengeance before seeing to his duty.

Illustration by Todd Lockwood

Bronnia Stonesplitter

BRONNIA STONESPLITTER

Female gold dwarf Wiz7: CR 7; Medium-size humanoid; HD 7d4+21; hp 45; Init +0; Spd 20 ft.; AC 10 (touch 10, flat-footed 10); Atk +4 melee (1d6+1, quarterstaff), +3 ranged touch (by spell); SQ Gold dwarven traits, familiar benefits; AL NE; SV Fort +6, Ref +3, Will +7; Str 12, Dex 10, Con 16, Int 17, Wis 13, Cha 12. Height 4 ft.

Skills and Feats: Bluff +5, Concentration +13, Craft (blacksmithing) +8, Diplomacy +5, Intimidate +5, Knowledge (arcana) +8, Knowledge (architecture and engineering) +5, Knowledge (the planes) +8, Listen +3, Search +5, Spellcraft +8, Spot +5; Craft Wand, Improved Familiar, Scribe Scroll, Spell Focus (Enchantment), Thunder Twin.

Special Qualities: Gold Dwarven Traits: +1 racial attack bonus against aberrations, darkvision 60 ft., stonecunning, +2 on saves against poison, +2 on saves against spells, +4 dodge bonus against giants, +2 racial bonus on Appraise checks or Craft checks related to stone or metal. Familiar Benefits: Grants Bronnia Alertness when

within reach, share spells, empathic link (1 mile), familiar may deliver touch spells, speak with familiar.

Wizard Spells per Day: 4/5/4/3/1; base DC = 13 + spell level, 15 + spell level for enchantment spells.

Spellbook (* = enchantment spell): 0—*arcane mark, dancing lights, daze*, detect magic, detect poison, disrupt undead, flare, ghost sound, light, mage hand, mending, open/close, prestidigitation, ray of frost, read magic, resistance;* 1st—*animate rope, charm person*, color spray, endure elements, expeditious retreat, feather fall, identify, mage armor, magic missile, shield, sleep*, spider climb, unseen servant;* 2nd—*cat's grace, detect thoughts, fog cloud, hypnotic pattern, invisibility, knock, magic mouth, Melf's acid arrow, protection from arrows, summon monster II, Tasha's hideous laughter*;* 3rd—*dispel magic, fireball, fly, halt undead, haste, hold person*, slow, suggestion*;* 4th—*confusion*, dimension door, emotion*.*

Possessions: Cloak of resistance +1, wand of charm person (20 charges), *wand of magic missile* (3rd level, 27 charges), *wand of hold person* (18 charges), *wand of mage armor* (26 charges), arcane scrolls of *confusion, emotion,* and *feeblemind,* 2 potions of *cure light wounds* (3rd), *potion of invisibility.*

Keschk: Female quasit familiar; CR 3; Tiny outsider (chaotic, evil); HD 3d8; hp 19; Init +3; Spd 20 ft., fly 50 ft. (perfect); AC 22 (touch 15, flat-footed 19); Atk +8 melee (1d3–1 plus poison, 2 claws), +3 melee (1d4–1, bite); Face/Reach 2 1/2 ft. by 2 1/2 ft./0 ft.; SA Poison (Fort DC 13, 1d4 Dex/2d4 Dex), spell-like abilities; SQ Alternate form, damage reduction 5/silver, fire resistance 20, improved evasion, poison immunity, regeneration 2 (normal damage from acid, and from blessed and holy weapons), spell-like abilities; SR 5; AL CE; SV Fort +3, Ref +6, Will +6; Str 8, Dex 17, Con 10, Int 10, Wis 12, Cha 10. Height 2 ft.

Skills and Feats: Hide +14, Listen +6, Move Silently +6, Search +4, Spellcraft +4, Spot +6; Weapon Finesse (bite), Weapon Finesse (claw).

Special Qualities: Alternate Form (Su): Polymorph self at will into a bat or a wolf. Improved Evasion (Ex): Reflex saves for half damage are for half or none. Spell-Like Abilities (Sp): *Detect good, detect magic,* and *invisibility* (self only) at will; *cause fear* (as spell but 30-ft. radius from her) 1/day; all abilities function as if cast by a 6th-level sorcerer (DC 10 + spell level). Once per seven days, she can use *commune* as a 12th-level cleric to ask six questions.

Dissatisfied with life in the Great Rift and feeling stifled by her clansfolk, Bronnia left her home and set off across the Shaar to find money, magic, and excitement. Prone to making cutting remarks in informal situations and indifferent to the sort of person she worked for, she quickly made a number of enemies. She is on the run as often as not, especially since her twin brother Belgard constantly urges her to come home.

Bronnia hires herself out as an engineer, a blacksmith, an adventuring spellcaster, and a wandmaker. Between her greed and extensive traveling, she has worked for the Red Wizards, craftsfolk in Unther, a noble family in Sembia, and a young pasha in Calimshan;

some of these jobs ended amiably. Her familiar usually hides or takes the form of a bat when she is in public, and this demon is the only creature she treats well all the time.

Bronnia is more than willing to join other adventurers if she thinks they'll help her gain money or magic. She prefers casting spells to using her wands unless she is almost out of spells. She isn't afraid of using her magic to get her way, including casual use of *charm* spells.

Halruaa

Capital: Halarahh
Population: 1,676,160 (humans 90%, dwarves 5%, halflings 2%, elves 1%, half-elves 1%)
Government: Magocratic oligarchy (Council of Elders)
Religions: Azuth, Mystra, Shar (new cult)
Imports: Exotic magic items, precious metals
Exports: Electrum, Haerlu wine
Alignment: LG, LN, NG

Far to the south and ringed by mountains lies Halruaa, a nation of wizards. The Halruaans are descendants of refugees from mighty Netheril, a kingdom of human wizards who allowed their own power to grow unchecked, corrupt their souls, and blast all their works into splinters. Halruaa has maintained the Netherese fascination with magic, pursuing the Art with fanatical devotion and considering all other studies to be inferior pursuits. So far the Halruaans have avoided the soul-blindness that doomed Netheril.

The Halruaan wizards are a self-satisfied lot, more interested in pursuing their research in the privacy of their home laboratories than in exploring or exploiting the rest of Toril. Those who do leave their native land are merchants or agents in search of unusual spell components. Sometimes such agents are important enough to travel in one of the fabled Halruaan skyships, but the flying craft are fragile and so valuable that they are not sent outside Halruaa on anything less than major missions.

LIFE AND SOCIETY

Not all Halruaans are wizards, but they act as if they were. Halruaans observe exaggerated social courtesies, taking time for lengthy declarations of intent, ritual sharing of spell components, and other elaborate social niceties. These practices would be a waste of time in a society that didn't hinge on the worry that a fellow citizen who grows displeased with you could turn you into a toad. Halruaans often spend more time on their studies than on their families, seldom rearing large numbers of children—and populating their country more thinly than more vigorous human societies.

Halruaans receive public schooling until at least the age of thirteen. Screening for magical aptitude occurs at age five, and magic-capable students often master cantrips by the time they are fifteen.

Although practicing magic is not necessary to live well in Halruaa, it helps. Those who are capable of casting wizard spells "have the gift," even if they do not make use of their talents. Roughly one-third of all Halruaans have the gift. Of that number, approximately two-thirds have some arcane knowledge (as described in the Magical Training feat; see Chapter 1: Characters) and the rest have at least one level of wizard. To Halruaans, the true Art is wizardry—sorcery is viewed as a dangerously undisciplined and primitive approach to magic. The few Halruaans whose gifts force them to become sorcerers instead of wizards either downplay the extent of their powers or leave the country.

MAJOR GEOGRAPHICAL FEATURES

Halruaa is a warm, humid land. The higher foothills and valleys of the Walls of Halruaa are cooler and more comfortable than the lowlands.

Lake Halruaa: This central body of brackish water connects the land's river ports to the sea. Strong and unpredictable winds blowing in off the mountains make it a tricky place to sail and fish, and even trickier to fly over in a skyship.

Swamp of Akhlaur: This four-thousand-square-mile swamp is an unpleasant reminder that the disasters that destroyed Netheril could be repeated in Halruaa. Akhlaur was an ambitious conjurer who pushed his researches into interplanar connections too far, until they swallowed him whole. As Akhlaur died, the magic that he had set in motion went out of control. The Swamp of Akhlaur is fed constantly by a never-closed *portal* to the Elemental Plane of Water. The swamp grows by a hundred feet or so in all directions each year. Wizards and adventurers often enter the swamp in search of Akhlaur's fabled magical treasures or a means of turning the swamp "off." Those who survive were usually lucky enough not to encounter the magic-draining demons known as laraken that live only within the swamp.

The Walls of Halruaa: A ring of mighty mountains guards Halruaa to the west, north, and east. Three passes lead through the mountains to the often hostile kingdoms beyond. The Halruaans have largely tamed their side of the wall, but the far side is home to ogres, tall mouthers, giants, perytons, and stray outsiders that know better than to tempt the wrath of the Halruaan wizards.

IMPORTANT SITES

Halruaans prefer to live in small villages. Even the largest cities have no more than seven or eight thousand inhabitants.

Halagard (Small City, 7,500): The former capital of Halruaa is only slightly smaller than Halarahh, the present capital. King Zalathorm (LN male human Div20/Lor9) moved the capital north one hundred years ago, but residents of Halagard still think of themselves as the true bearers of the Halruaan spirit. In keeping with their stand against newfangled Halarahhan fashions, wizards of Halagard generally specialize in conjuration or evocation rather than divination.

Halarahh (Small City, 8,000): Some three thousand of the capital city's inhabitants are practicing wizards. Their towers dominate the skyline, though Zalathorm has discouraged the "tower war," a cyclic form of competition in which the wizards of Halarahh attempt to raise their towers over all rivals' towers. To gain Zalathorm's favor, lesser wizards have actually reduced the size of their towers, making the air that much safer for skyships. The seventeen members of the Council of Elders make their home in the capital.

Halarahh is a difficult place to live for those who lack the gift. Favorable treatment and promotions, in all walks of life, come to those who have the gift and somehow elude those who lack magical aptitude. The saying "as useless as a sword in Halarahh" is often on the lips of frustrated former residents of Halarahh who moved elsewhere.

Mount Talath (Small Town, 1,170): A high temple to Mystra is carved into the mountain. It consists of a grand worship space meant to inspire awe and a huge cavern complex built to store centuries of magical knowledge safely. The complex has some degree of organization—any magical fact can be located with no more than five or six years of diligent research. Halruaan wizards pride themselves on their ability to track down the information they need in Talath's caverns, devising new spells designed expressly for that purpose. Non-Halruaan wizards pay exorbitant fees just to enter the rooms reserved for Halruaan apprentices.

REGIONAL HISTORY

The first wizards of Halruaa came from Netheril in the north, fleeing the scourge of the phaerimms almost two thousand years ago. They were led by the archwizard Raumark, who foresaw the doom approaching his native land. They found a beautiful and rich country, settled sparsely by shepherds and fisherfolk.

Raumark and his retinue of loyal mages, apprentices, and their households did not set out to conquer the native Halruaans, but within a generation the two societies had grown together through intermarriage and common interest. The Netherese princes provided the simple folk of Halruaa with an organized ruling class, laws, justice, and wondrous works. Native Halruaans with a talent for magic were accepted as students with no hesitation, and the presence of so many powerful wizards in their land soon pacified the monsters and raiders who had plagued the lowlands.

The great work of Raumark and his followers in the first centuries after their flight was to prepare for the phaerimm attack that must surely follow Netheril's fall in the North. But Netheril's flying cities fell, the sands swallowed its Narrow Sea, and the fragmented realms of those who survived its fall vanished as well by the third century DR, and still the phaerimms did not attack Halruaa.

While Halruaa never fought the war that Raumark prepared for, the land was not left in peace by its neighbors. Envious of its riches and magical treasures, the barbaric Dambrathans invaded Halruaa on several instances. In 585 DR, a fleet of Dambrathan galleys attacked Halruaa's coasts and occupied all the country south of Lake Halruaa for several months, until the great wizard-king Mycontil defeated the Dambrathans and slew their leader. The last serious invasion occurred about one hundred years ago, when a charismatic satrap of Lapaliiya led a great raid through the Talath Pass. The Halruaans drove them off easily.

The present wizard-king, Zalathorm, is a diviner whose powers of foretelling have extinguished several threats before they could become serious. Zalathorm and the diviners have been so successful that the popular consensus is that Halruaa should be led by divination specialists from now on, instead of trusting evokers, conjurers, and other wizards who ruled in the days when Halruaa was actively forced to defend itself.

PLOTS AND RUMORS

Thievery, brigandage, and monstrous incursions are generally rare in Halruaa. The exciting happenings in the land (to an adventurer, anyway) revolve around the land's four hundred Elders, the most powerful wizards in the land, who scheme and intrigue in a dozen different factions. If enough Elders joined forces in a single block, even Zalathorm would be hard-pressed to gainsay them.

The Rise of Shadow: A secret peril is gathering at the edges of Halruaan society, a cloister of shadow adepts allied with the hidden faith of Shar. Proud, arrogant Elders are quietly subverted by whispering emissaries of the Goddess of Secrets, who ask the Elders whether they find Mystra's Weave to be a hindrance to their power. Several of Halruaa's powerful and ambitious wizards have already become shadow adepts. Unlike the fractious factions that form the land's Council of Elders, the shadow adepts are united in the worship of Shar and the desire to advance her cause in this most magical of lands.

Luiren

Capital: Beluir
Population: 838,080 (halflings 92%, humans 4%, elves 2%, half-elves 1%)
Government: Benevolent theocracy

Religions: Brandobaris, Tymora, Yondalla
Imports: Metalwork items, livestock
Exports: Ale, beer, fruit, grain, produce
Alignment: LG, NG, N

Luiren is the only realm of Faerûn ruled by and inhabited nearly exclusively by halflings. It is the homeland of the strongheart halflings in much the same way that the Great Rift is the homeland of the gold dwarves. Small numbers of lightfoot and ghostwise halflings live here as well, but nine-tenths of the halfling population is made up of the stronghearts—in fact, the term "Luiren halfling" is widely taken to refer to the strongheart folk, even though it's not strictly accurate.

Luiren's folk are farmers, artisans, and merchants, as are the folk of most lands. Luiren's rich fields feed the Great Rift, and its orchards produce oranges, limes, and lemons greatly in demand in northern lands. Luiren woodcarving is superb, on par with that of Tethyr, and pieces of woodworking are traded too. While few people think of halflings as possessing any real military tradition, the Luiren folk maintain well-organized militias led by the monks and clerics of the local temples and supported with powerful divine magic. Halfling archers and clerics standing their ground with strength and skill have crushed more than one invasion of humans, orcs, or gnolls from the Shaar.

Luiren boasts no real government other than local authorities, but the temples of the halfling pantheon tie together society and collectively govern the land, generally under the guidance of the Temple of Yondalla. The Devout Voice of Yondalla Faran Ferromar (LG male strongheart halfling Clr13 of Yondalla) is the preeminent leader of the faith and thus the effective leader of Luiren.

Luiren halflings don't see themselves as half of anything or anyone, and generally refer to themselves as hin.

LIFE AND SOCIETY

Most of the Luiren folk live seminomadic lives, dwelling no more than six months or a year in any one city. Luiren's cities reflect this wanderlust and mobility. Clans, families, businesses, and temples maintain permanent dwellings and hillside holes—complete with jobs and duties, normally—that are open to newly arriving individuals or families. At any given time, only three-fourths of the living quarters of Luiren's cities are occupied. Before leaving a home, halflings who want to be welcomed back clean and ready the home they've been living in for its next occupants. Unless they've been extremely bad tenants, their neighbors and friends help.

Teamwork is important to the Luiren hin. Compared to the halflings native to the north, the hin emphasize group effort and communal work over individualism. Individual halflings don't often remain in the same groups for long. The groups themselves tend to endure, but the halflings filling the roles one season are not at all guaranteed to be present, or even part of the same social group in another city, two seasons later.

Humans, elves, dwarves, and even gnomes have a difficult time understanding how Luiren society can appear so orderly and lawful when its individual members change their stripes the way other people buy new clothes. Luiren hin know that outsiders think their ways are strange, but find it disturbing that outsiders maintain the same habits all their lives.

The one habit that Luiren folk enjoy too much to leave behind them is their dedication to the Games. Luiren's Games are local, regional, and kingdomwide sporting events followed with interest by the nation's citizens. The type of sport that's played during the Games constantly changes. At the moment, the two most popular sports are ridge running and kite fighting. Ridge running is a type of competitive obstacle course in which teams from different cities compete in races. Magic cast by the competitors during the races is allowed, but participants who use magic can also be targeted by magic cast by members of the other team. Kite fighting is "Art-free," meaning it is conducted free of magic of all types.

It's rare for halflings raised in northern Faerûn to visit Luiren and have any desire to stay—most halfling immigrants find the land and its ways strange. But some northern halflings emigrate to Luiren and stay forever, and some Luiren hin can't wait to escape their home nation and live like northern folk.

Major Geographical Features

Monsters of the forests and swamps once plagued Luiren, but over many generations the hin have tamed large stretches of the land. The countryside is fertile, rich in game, and pleasant-looking. But it's also full of wildlands that resist all attempts to pacify them. These days, young hin warriors and mages keep an eye on the wildlands to keep monsters from troubling the roads and cities. Foreign adventurers are welcome to "try their luck" in Luiren's forests and swamps, and can even keep half the treasure they find—a bargain, given that the monsters obviously took the treasure from Luiren's folk in the first place.

Lluirwood: This dense forest defines Luiren's northern borders. Druids, rangers, and some rogues of Luiren feel most comfortable in the Lluirwood's southernmost parts. Other hin seldom venture into the forest, lacking the skills required to stay one step ahead of the monsters that come down into the forest from the Toadsquat Mountains. When the tall mouthers, trolls, and other beasts make the mistake of venturing out of the Lluirwood, they're usually quickly dealt with by Luiren militia, Yondalla's clerics, or hin hunters. But the Lluirwood remains dangerous to travelers.

Mortick Swamp: The Mortick Swamp, the only swamp in the region, is infested by a large number of merrow (aquatic ogres) and scrags (aquatic trolls). These hulking monsters often raid the lands nearby, carrying off livestock and plundering food stores. A powerful ogre shaman or chieftain known as the Bog King leads the merrow, and sometimes succeeds in bending the scrags to its will as well.

Southern Lluirwood: South of the Lluirwood and west of Luiren, the Southern Lluirwood is mostly untamed. The eastern flank of the forest is relatively tame, patrolled by militia units from Luiren and halfling druids and rangers. Beholders and yuan-ti roam the forest's deeper zones.

Important Sites

Luiren's cities welcome foreign travelers in peace. A small number of human merchants and craftsfolk have taken up residence in the cities.

Beluir (Metropolis, 27,210): Outsiders think of Beluir as the capital of Luiren because it's the biggest city and contains a high temple to Yondalla. None of Luiren's cities are really the center of authority, but foreign diplomats and emissaries come here first in search of the Devout Voice of Yondalla. Great Sea merchants make port in Beluir to buy Luiren's produce and handiwork.

Chethel (Large City, 14,512): This port town is one of Luiren's main trading cities. Roughly one-tenth of its inhabitants are elves and half-elves. Of all Luiren's cities, Chethel seems most like an ordinary human city. A few families who have befriended the elves choose to stay put, placing a veneer of stability over the otherwise nomadic foundation. The other long-term residents are hin who make a fine living at boat-building.

Thruldar: Lying on the easternmost verge of the Lluirwood, Thruldar is a ruined Estagundan town watched over by several nearby tribes of ghostwise halflings. About a hundred years ago, a powerful evil druid allied with dark trees and murderous plant monsters destroyed Thruldar, but the nearby ghostwise tribes slew the druid and raised magical wards to contain the druid's minions in the ruins. The druid's ghost and numerous plant monsters still lurk in ruined Thruldar, along with what is left of the town's wealth.

Regional History

Thousands of years ago, Luiren was an unsettled wilderness roamed by three great halfling tribes: the lightfoots, the stronghearts, and the ghostwise. The three races fiercely defended their woodlands against all intruders for centuries, driving off Dambrathan barbarians, packs of rabid gnolls, and sharing the Lluirwood's resources. Feuds between tribes were not uncommon, but for the most part the three tribes lived in peace.

Around −100 DR, an evil spirit entered the forest. Under the leadership of a powerful cleric named Desva, the ghostwise halflings fell into darkness, worshiping Malar and glorifying in violence and bloodshed. Feral ghostwise hunters, their faces painted like skulls, prowled the forests in search of halfling prey. They grew ever stronger as Desva led them deeper into Malar's worship, teaching the greatest hunters to take shapes as werewolves and poisoning the forest's natural predators with maddening bloodlust. For a generation the Lluirwood was a place of death.

In −68 DR, a strongheart hunter named Chand became war chief of his folk and struck an alliance with the war chief of the lightfoot tribe. The two united to root out the madness of the ghostwise halflings. Over three years each ghostwise stronghold and lair was found out and destroyed, until Chand himself slew Desva of the ghostwise in −65 DR. The fighting was merciless and awful—entire ghostwise villages were burned and their folk killed. Chand held to his purpose and saw to it that no hin warrior stayed his or her hand.

In the aftermath of the Hin Ghostwars, the ghostwise halflings were reduced to a handful of their former number. Most were exiled from the Lluirwood, although a handful who had repudiated Desva and joined with Chand's warriors were allowed to stay. Those who left settled in the Chondalwood, taking an oath never to speak until they had atoned for the animal-like savagery of their past. The atonement is long past, but to this day ghostwise halflings think long and hard before they choose to speak.

Many of the lightfoots, horrified by what Chand and the stronghearts had done, chose to leave the Lluirwood. They became a nomadic people spread across all of northern Faerûn, adopting the customs and traditions of the folk they traveled among.

The stronghearts remained in the Lluirwood. Unchecked by the lightfoot or ghostwise ways, they began to clear the forest and settled in semipermanent villages that grew larger and more permanent with each passing generation. They changed from woodland nomads to settled farmers and craftsfolk, defending their lands against numerous invasions and raids over the years. In time some lightfoots returned to the new realm of Luiren, but this is now a strongheart land.

Plots and Rumors

As with other lands far from the Heartlands, Luiren's influence may be easier to portray from a distance than to experience firsthand.

The Games: A Western Heartlands village with a substantial halfling community plans to hold its own version of the Games. Humans are encouraged to participate, and the prizes are *rich*. Humans may be cheered on lustily, but the events favor halfling competitors: rock-throwing contests, obstacle courses, chasing a greased weasel through a honeycomb of underground tunnels, and similar events.

Short and Sharp: The PCs run afoul of a gang of Luiren halflings in a busy city. These hin specialize in throwing tanglefoot bags and robbing victims who are stuck to the floor. Even arrogant adventurers may prefer handing over their valuables to being flanked and stabbed in the back.

The shaar

Capital: None (Council Hills)
Population: 587,520 (humans 60%, wemics 15%, gnolls 14%, centaurs 10%)
Government: Various nomadic chieftains
Religions: Mask, Oghma, Tempus
Imports: Armor, weapons, wine
Exports: Ivory, jewelry, slaves
Alignment: CN, N, CG

The Shaar is a vast, rolling grassland running from the Shining Sea to the distant lands of the east. Civilization has almost no hold on the area. Nomadic humans (the dozen or so tribes of the Shaaryan) and nonhumans such as centaurs, gnolls, and wemics populate the Shaar. The wemics hunt, the Shaaryan humans herd rothé and horses, and the gnolls raid. The land supports its native grasses splendidly but is ill suited for agriculture—it's not a desert, but the land bakes by day and freezes by night.

The Shaaryan humans seldom stray in large numbers from their ancestral plains, largely because their treasured horses do not do well outside the Shaar. Shaaryan horses are stronger and faster than horses from other regions of Faerûn, as long as they roam their native grasslands. The great horses grow sick and die if they do not eat the grasses that thrive only on the wide plains of the Shaar. The Shaaryan understand this, and few of them leave their native culture behind to travel Faerûn.

Illustration by Sam Wood

LIFE AND SOCIETY

The dozen or so nomad tribes known collectively as the Shaaryan have never been unified, though they share a common culture and way of life. Outsiders find it difficult to tell members of one tribe from the others, but the nomads can tell each apart instantly from clues of dress, accent, color of mount, and make of weapons.

Several of the tribes allow female warriors to ride as equals among the men, and a few have female chiefs. Chiefs are generally elected by secret votes among the elders, but two tribes have would-be dynasties of powerful charismatic families that attempt to keep a lock on power.

Traditionally, raiding parties of twenty or fewer warriors do not constitute an act of war against another Shaaryan tribe. Larger raiding parties amount to declarations of war, a risky proposition since tribes that declare war are generally not allowed to participate in the intertribal councils until they have made reparations or otherwise ceased their aggressions.

The wemics sometimes join in the Shaaryan councils. More often their chiefs pursue their own savage goals without caring for the human nomads' traditions and protocols.

MAJOR GEOGRAPHICAL FEATURES

Other types of terrain occasionally interrupt the rolling grasslands, including small sand dunes and valleys filled with tiny lakes and wildlife. The miniature oases contain ruins of earlier civilizations. Many also contain the temporary camps of present-day nomads.

Lake Lhespen: The swamps at the eastern edge of this lake are full of mangrove trees, giant eels, and water spiders. The shores are crusted with salt drawn out from the rocks beneath the waters. The nomads gather salt for their horses here when they do not wish to trade for salt at Shaarmid.

Wemics in the Shaar

The Landrise: The eastern Shaar is two hundred to four hundred feet higher than the western Shaar. The Landrise is the dividing zone, splitting the grasslands into two areas south of the Firesteap Mountains and north of the Forest of Amtar. Nomad tribes warring upon each other frequently try to occupy different sides of the cliffs, to give themselves a chance of spotting their enemies as they approach.

River Shaar: The Shaar originates in the deep, cold Riftlake, hundreds of feet below the high plains. It roars and thunders through measureless caverns for more than one hundred miles before emerging from a great cavern mouth at the foot of the Landrise. From there it pursues a course across the lower Shaar to Lake Lhespen.

The Shaarwood and the Sharawood: The nomads visit the forests to gather herbs, hunt, and occasionally hide from their enemies. The wooded land is poor terrain for horses, so the nomads have never tried to settle these lands.

IMPORTANT SITES

The nomads maintain few permanent settlements. Any cities here were established by other folk in the Shaar.

Council Hills: All the nomad tribes except those engaged in war send delegates to the Council Hills in the spring and fall to hold peace talks and drink together. The Council Hills are always considered neutral ground, off-limits to fighting between the nomads.

Lhesper: This ruined city is home to a powerful clan of yuan-ti sorcerers. Human travelers along the shores of Lake Lhespen often fall prey to bandits under yuan-ti domination and are carried back to a terrible fate in Lhesper—usually sacrifice to the yuan-ti's dark god, but sometimes transformation into monstrous servitors to the serpent race. The nomads give it a wide berth.

Shaarmid (Large City, 23,501): A free trading city populated by people who claim no kinship with the nomads, Shaarmid is accepted by the tribes as a long-time ally because the city's people have a history of brokering excellent deals for the nomads with the traders from the rest of Faerûn. Merchants flock to Shaarmid as a safe zone in a wasteland that otherwise threatens them with Shaaryan bandits and other raiders.

REGIONAL HISTORY

The history of the Shaar isn't recognizable as history to citizens of civilized Faerûn. Current events in the Shaar include small-scale conflicts with the gold dwarves, who have tired of having their trade caravans attacked by Shaaryan bandits, and an ongoing battle along the Landrise between tribes attempting to keep their rivals from reaching the Council Hills.

PLOTS AND RUMORS

The endlessly swirling politics of the nomad tribes mean that any group of adventurers can find allies or enemies aplenty in the Shaar.

Giant Cleansing: A clan of hill giants moves out of the Toadsquat Mountains into the eastern Shaar, fighting everyone they encounter. The giants eventually reach the Council Hills, occupying sacred caves that house the skulls of the nomad ancestors. The nomads have a problem: They need to remove the giants without shedding their own blood within their sacred land. Adventurers not of Shaaryan descent are under no such constraints.

Dambrath

Five hundred years ago, the barbaric human kingdom of Arkaiun became embroiled in a bitter war against a powerful drow city under the Gnollwatch Mountains. The drow proved victorious and, in alliance with a strong Loviatar cult among the barbarians, enslaved the Arkaiun people, ruling as satraps and nobles among the subjugated population. The strange and perilous realm of Dambrath is the result.

The nation of Dambrath is a human nation ruled by half-elves, most of whom are descended from drow. Elves of races loyal to the Evermeet court are not welcome in Dambrath. Loviatar is the official deity of the nation.

Durpar

Protected from the sandstorms of Raurin by the mighty Giant's Belt and Dustwall Mountains, Durpar is a prosperous merchant kingdom on the northeastern shore of the inlet known as the Golden Water. A council of merchants, made up of the leaders of the eleven wealthiest chakas (merchant houses), rules the land. The Grand Nawab Kara Jeratma (LG female human Ari4/Ill10) is the council's leader, and one of the richest people in all Faerûn.

The business of Durpar is business, and the Durpari merchant houses are the foremost traders in this portion of the world. Pious devotion to a small pantheon of Faerûnian deities worshiped together unites the Durpari in a common faith. The city of Vaelen is the capital of Durpar.

Estagund

Estagund shares a common cultural heritage with Durpar and Var the Golden. Its folk are Durpari who value trade and who honor the Adama, the pantheon and moral code common to all three kingdoms. Unlike the folk of Durpar, who are ruled by the wealthiest merchants, the folk of Estagund honor above all a class of noble warriors. The Rajah of Estagund, Ekripet Seltarir (LG male human Ari5), is not only the wealthiest merchant of the country but also the kingdom's war leader and high monarch.

The city of Chavyondat on the Bay of Kings is the capital of Estagund.

Rethild, the Great Swamp

The greatest swamp in Faerûn pools around the eastern end of Halruaa's Wall. It is a sweltering place of moss-choked cypress groves, sawgrass seas, and boggy bayous infested with giant leeches, giant toads, snakes, lizardfolk, shambling mounds, and worse. An ancient city steeped in evil lies in ruins near the center of the swamp, the retreat of some long-forgotten race.

Var the Golden

The third of the three Durpari kingdoms, Var the Golden lies on the south shore of the Golden Water. It is called "the Golden" not for the inlet to its north, but for the endless fields of grain that cover its countryside. The merchants (or nawabs), the landed nobles (called hajwas), and the priests of the Adama (the janas), compete for power over this rich land in a constant boiling intrigue that is perilously close to unseating the Sublime Potentate Anwir Dupretiskava (LE male ancient blue dragon).

Only his closest advisors known the true nature of the Sublime Potentate, although all know that he has ruled for almost two hundred years and is prone to long absences from the throne. In recent years, some of the potentate's most dangerous enemies have fallen prey to fanatical assassins, a repressive ploy that may push the nawabs or hajwas into open revolt against the potentate.

veldorn

Known as the Land of Monsters, Veldorn is bound together by the loose promise of all its monstrous inhabitants to defend one another if any of them are attacked. In times past, Durpari armies marching on one of the so-called beast-chieftains have provoked a response by a dozen more, leading to bloody, pitched battles. The beast-chieftains prey on caravans bound for Mulhorand and generally leave each other to their own devices, intervening only if some power threatens them all.

The unapproachable East

To the folks of the Heartlands, these lands are the mysterious, exotic, and deadly east, a region of terrible magic, untold wealth, and strange and capricious laws. The term "Unapproachable" generally describes the distance from the Heartlands of Faerûn, but some of these countries are considered unapproachable because of their temperament. Thay is an aggressive magocracy, Aglarond defends its borders against all intruders, and Rashemen is a cold, hard land of powerful witches and fierce warriors. The lands of the Unapproachable East trade with the Old Empires because of their proximity, and Thesk is the avenue through which exotic goods from the far eastern lands of Kara-Tur enter Faerûn.

This region is known for its powerful and strange magic. Aglarond is ruled by Faerûn's most powerful sorcerer, Thay is under the dominion of the Red Wizards, and the mysterious Witches of Rashemen guide that land's berserker defenders.

Aglarond

Capital: Velprintalar
Population: 1,270,080 (humans 64%, half-elves 30%, elves 5%)
Government: Autocratic (with representative council of advisors)
Religions: Chauntea, the Seldarine, Selûne, Umberlee (disdained), Valkur
Imports: Glass, iron, textiles
Exports: Copper, gems, grain, lumber, wine
Alignment: N, NG, GG

Aglarond is hailed as the nation that keeps the Red Wizards from attacking the rest of civilized Faerûn, and the home of the powerful sorcerer known as the Simbul. Few give the country any more thought than this, but Aglarond is a place of ancient magic that holds one of the largest half-elf settlements in the world. Its army defends its borders against Thay, and its skilled rangers scout its frontier in search of trouble. The small beaches on Aglarond's rocky coast are dotted with fishing villages, and since the Simbul has declared that all pirates are to be considered agents of Thay (and put to death if caught), the waters around Aglarond are very safe to travel. It is one of the few kingdoms that refuses to allow Red Wizard enclaves within its borders.

LIFE AND SOCIETY

The humans of Aglarond are sturdy, no-nonsense fisherfolk, farmers, and herders unconcerned with the rest of Faerûn. They are slow to warm to a person but faithful to those they trust. A serious and hard-working people, they nevertheless enjoy revelry and exuberant celebration when their chores are done. They dislike magic, pointing to the Red Wizards as proof that magic is a corrupting tool of wickedness. The exceptions are unusually good individuals, such as the rulers of their land who have always used magic to defend them. They believe in the divine powers, but have few large temples.

The half-elves of the Yuirwood are descended from wood elves. The various tribal groups that live deeper within the forest assume a nomadic and tribal culture, while those on the outskirts abide by local human customs. They have no qualms about using magic, and some of the wilder tribes know strange old elven secrets of the Yuirwood.

All people of Aglarond are respectful of the Simbul, because it is her power that has kept the Red Wizards at bay for so long. However, that same power and her impetuous nature breed suspicion of her methods and motives.

MAJOR GEOGRAPHICAL FEATURES

Aglarond is a wooded peninsula projecting westward into the center of the Sea of Fallen Stars. It divides the Easting Reach from the Alamber Sea.

Tannath Mountains: This range forms the southern edge of the Dragonjaw Mountains, south of the River Umber. The mountains are tall and rugged, flanked by wide passes. They have never been settled by humanoids, but griffons fly in the high peaks, and boulderlike creatures called galeb duhr live here. The Watchwall, a thirty-foot tall, ten-foot wide wall of smooth, seamless stone, runs for several miles from the mountains toward the fortress Glarondar in the Yuirwood.

Umber Marshes: This span of bogs, swampland, and mudflats is Aglarond's first line of defense against Thay. Inhabited by dangerous creatures such as stirges, poisonous snakes, hydras, shambling mounds, trolls, and disease-carrying insects, the swamp has foiled attacks by Thayan armies more than once.

Yuirwood: Home to the kingdom's half-elves, this forest is filled with old ruins. Detection and scrying magic cannot reach into the forest, and those who try see only a cluster of unremarkable trees rather than what they're looking for. This effect makes it difficult for enemies to discover the half-elves' settlements and fortifications. Some of the forest's stone circles act as *portals* to elsewhere in Toril (including Evermeet) and even other worlds.

IMPORTANT SITES

Aglarond proper consists of the Yuirwood and the cities on the northern coast of the peninsula. The cities on the southern coast are independent and greatly threatened by Thay.

Altumbel: This small human kingdom occupies the westernmost portion of the Aglarondan peninsula. It is loosely allied with Aglarond but has little contact with its neighbors. Its people are extremely reclusive, isolated, and outwardly hostile to nonhumans. The dreary, constantly windswept place survives by fishing.

Emmech (Small City, 7,620): This grim fortress holds over a third of Aglarond's army. A small town has sprung up around it, with the fortress looking over the town from a low hill. It holds enough supplies to feed its soldiers and everyone in the town for up to a six-month siege.

Furthinghome (Metropolis, 40,643): One of the first human settlements here, Furthinghome is a poor community, with many on the outskirts living in lean-tos and thatch huts. Its greenhouses hold the cultivated tropical flowers for which the city is known. The coastal waters are shallow, only allowing small vessels.

Relkath's Foot (Small City, 5,080): The largest permanent settlement of half-elves in the Yuirwood, this town is built around four large and very old trees. The town's militia is active in the region, frequently practicing ambushes and spying on passersby. Human rangers often seek training from the foresters of Relkath's Foot.

Velprintalar (Metropolis, 66,044): This is the only major port in Aglarond. Its narrow buildings jumbled together can be confusing to visitors, and the city has no walls. Velprintalar is the meeting-place for Aglarond's council and the location of the Simbul's palace of green stone.

REGIONAL HISTORY

Long ago, the Yuirwood was inhabited by wood elves. They mastered powerful magic, built stone menhirs and circles, and lived peacefully within their realm. Eventually monsters pushed into the elves' territory, and the elves retreated to areas deeper within the wood. Humans arrived in this region in 756 DR, settling in the south, cutting wood, and clashing with monsters and the elves. When adventurers came to slay monsters, the elves of the Yuir retreated farther into the wood.

After a time, humans penetrated the wards of the Yuir and allied with the weary elves. The humans helped the elves destroy monsters, and the two races intermarried. Their half-elven descendants began to reclaim the wood. Eventually they came into conflict with the humans on the coast, who had continued to breed, populate, and log the forest. The angry half-elves told the humans to stop but were ignored, and so they raided against the coastal dwellers, driving away or killing humans who resisted. In 1065 DR they fought the battle of Ingdal's Arm and sued for peace between the races, creating the nation of Aglarond. Some of the humans refused to share power and moved to the end of the peninsula to form the country of Altumbel.

Aglarond was ruled by a series of half-elven kings, many of whom were killed by Thayan invaders. Two heirs of the royal line, Thara and Ulae (known as the Gray Sisters) took the throne when their brother died, and they kept Aglarond safe for years. Ulae's daughter Ilione selected her apprentice, a woman known only as the Simbul, to be her heir, and the Simbul has defended her country against Thay ever since she took the throne in 1320 DR.

In 1371 DR the zulkirs approached the Simbul with an offer to cease hostilities and declare a truce, which the Simbul accepted with a healthy dose of skepticism. The Thayans seem to be holding to their end of the bargain, so the Simbul has turned her power to improving the lives of her people, as well as expanding the fortifications and wards against her longtime enemies.

PLOTS AND RUMORS

The old ruins of the Yuirwood bring adventurers to Aglarond, but the folk of the forest watch would-be plunderers and looters very carefully.

Dreams of Fire: People in the eastern portion of the Yuirwood have begun experiencing magical hallucinations of the trees burning. There is no pattern to the hallucinations, and some people have had them several times while others not at all. The only link seems to be a single carved stone half-buried in that part of the forest: A piece of the stone as long as a man's forearm has been chipped or broken from the main mass, and with it some of the elven rune-carvings.

The Sentinels: Something is causing the shambling mounds of the Umber Marshes to march toward the south. The shamblers have been forming a line just over a mile from the swamp's southern border, their bodies sometimes writhing with live snakes or buzzing with nests of insects. The plant-monsters stand in the line for days at a time; one occasionally leaves when a replacement arrives. The things attack other creatures they see, but otherwise appear to be waiting for something.

THE SIMBUL

The Simbul

Female human (Chosen of Mystra) Sor20/Acm 2/Wiz10: CR 36; Medium-size humanoid; HD 14d4+112 plus 2d4+16 plus 4d4+32; hp 210; Init +8; Spd 30 ft.; AC 26 (touch 17, flat-footed 22); Atk +16/+11 melee (1d4+6/ 19–20, *+4 dagger*), +14/+9 ranged touch (by spell); SA Chosen spell-like abilities; SQ Archmage high arcana, Chosen immunities, detect magic, enhanced Constitution, epic-level benefits, silver fire, supernatural abilities; AL CN; SV Fort +13, Ref +9, Will +18; Str 14, Dex 18, Con 26, Int 20, Wis 15, Cha 20. Height 5 ft. 10 in.

Skills and Feats: Alchemy +25, Concentration +43, Diplomacy +7, Heal +14, Intimidate +13, Knowledge (Aglarond history) +15, Knowledge (Aglarond local) +16, Knowledge (arcana) +41, Knowledge (religion) +15, Perform +10, Profession (herbalist) +12, Scry +25, Search +15, Sense Motive +7, Spellcraft +30, Spot +12, Swim +7; Craft Wand, Forge Ring, Improved Counterspell, Improved Initiative, Leadership (37), Scribe Scroll, Skill Focus (Spellcraft), Spell Focus (Evocation), Spell Focus (Transmutation), Spellcasting Prodigy (sorcerer), Twin Spell.

Special Attacks: Chosen Spell-like Abilities: 1/day—*antimagic field, delayed blast fireball, feather fall, fly, hold monster, polymorph other, prismatic wall, the Simbul's synostodweomer* (converts prepared spells into 2 hit points of healing per spell level), *web.*

Special Qualities: Archmage High Arcana: Spell power +2, mastery of elements. Chosen Immunities: The Simbul is unaffected by attacks that duplicate these effects: *charm person, circle of death, disintegrate, fear, feeblemind, finger of death, fireball, magic missile, misdirection, meteor swarm.* Detect Magic (Su): Line of sight. Enhanced Constitution: The Chosen of Mystra template adds +10 to the Simbul's Constitution. Epic-Level Benefits: Six effective levels of sorcerer and six of wizard (included in the above totals). Silver Fire (Su): See Chapter 2 for details. Supernatural Abilities: Due to *wishes* and magical experimentation upon herself, the Simbul has the following supernatural abilities: *detect magic* (always active as the 1st-round effect of the spell), *protection from evil, protection from spells, see invisibility, shapechange.* She is also protected as if wearing a *ring of protection +3* and an *amulet of proof against detection and location*. She may transform herself into a *chain lightning* effect that ends as a meteor streak traveling at speed 70 ft.; she cannot re-form for 1d4+2 hours, taking 10 minutes to do so. She has also used *wish* spells to allow her to know one more 9th-level spell than her sorcerer level would normally allow, and sometimes uses a *wish* to remove a spell she knows from her repertoire to make room for a different one.

Typical Sorcerer Spells Known (6/8/8/7/7/7/7/5/5/6; base DC = 18 + spell level): 0—*arcane mark, dancing lights*, detect magic, flare*, light, mage hand, mending, open/close, read magic;* 1st—*burning hands*, comprehend languages, enlarge*, feather fall, magic missile;* 2nd—*alter self, cat's grace, daylight, shatter*, web;* 3rd—*dispel magic, fireball*, fly, wind wall*;* 4th—*charm monster, fire shield, polymorph other*, shout*;* 5th—*feeblemind, telekinesis*, teleport, wall of force;* 6th—*chain lightning*, control weather, disintegrate*;* 7th—*limited wish, prismatic spray*, the Simbul's spell sequencer* (casting this causes the next three spells you cast of up to 4th level to be triggered simultaneously by a single verbal word); 8th—*mass charm, polymorph any object*, sunburst*;* 9th—*the Simbul's spell trigger* (as the *sequencer* but affecting up to 7th-level spells), *the Simbul's synostodweomer* (converts prepared spells into 2 hit points of healing per spell level), *time stop, wish*.

*Because of Spell Focus (Evocation) or Spell Focus (Transmutation), the base DC for saves against these spells is 20 + spell level.

Wizard Spells per Day: 4/6/5/4/4/3. Base DC = 17 + spell level, 19 + spell level for evocation and transmutation spells.

Spellbook: The Simbul knows all the wizard spells of 5th level or lower in the *Player's Handbook* and this book.

Possessions: Bracers of armor +9, ring of spell storing (identify, true seeing, wizard eye), *ring of shooting stars, wand of magic missile* (9th, 20 charges), *wand of lightning bolt* (10th, 20 charges), *+4 dagger*, 4 *potions of cure serious wounds* (10th). As a powerful spellcaster and ruler of a nation, the Simbul has access to incredible resources and can acquire almost any nonartifact item she might need, given time.

Alassra Silverhand, one of the Seven Sisters who are Chosen of Mystra, is known to Faerûnians today only as the Simbul. She is the Queen of Aglarond (called by some "the Witch-Queen," and many believe this latter term is part of her official title) and has legendary powers of sorcery and a temper to match.

She mastered metamagic long, long ago, and has singlehandedly defeated attacking Thayan armies with titanic combinations of spells. King Azoun IV of Cormyr called the Simbul "a good friend, but a deadly enemy." She is currently the lover of the famous (or if you prefer, infamous) wizard Elminster of Shadowdale. Thanks to his love, she has mitigated the worst of her dark berserker rages, which makes her even more formidable in battle—she's still fearless, but no long heedless of the damage she causes. She still seems more driven to master magic than anyone else in Faerûn . . . and seems quite likely to continue to do so.

The Simbul flits tirelessly around Toril and even other planes, never adhering to any routine, shapechanging at will (often wearing the form of a black raven). As herself, she's heedless of personal appearance, and is usually barefoot or adventurer-booted, and clad only in a tattered black robe. Her hair is always a wild, tangled mess. Even in her realm of Aglarond, people fear her, avoid her, and think her insane. Red Wizards have been known to faint at the mere thought of facing her in battle. In this, if in nothing else, their judgment is wise.

The Great Dale

Capital: none
Population: 211,680 (humans 99%)
Government: Druidic hierarchy
Religions: Chauntea, Eldath, Mielikki, Silvanus
Imports: Gold, iron tools, silver
Exports: Alchemical items, arrows, bows, carved wood, herbs, magic items
Alignment: N, NG, CG

Little more than two large forests and the strip of land between them, this land is inhabited by reclusive farmers, coolly hostile druids, and introspective rangers. The people of the Great Dale interact little with the outside world, acquiring the few iron items they cannot manufacture in exchange for herbal, alchemical, and wooden goods of exceptional quality. The soil is rich and suitable for farming, yet few other than the druids live here.

The mysterious Nentyarch, a powerful druid or sorcerer, resides in his castle of living trees and destroys all visitors. No outsiders know what he does or if he is the ruler of this place, and the people of the Great Dale answer inquiries to this effect with an uncomfortable shrug. The druids tolerate the trade route that passes between their forests only because caravaneers know that to disturb the forest is death, and accordingly they avoid it.

LIFE AND SOCIETY

The settled villagers in the small hamlets live like rural folk in other lands, although they take great pains to take only what they need from the land. They live by hunting small game, farming small spaces of open prairie, and collecting dead wood from the forest. When enemies approach, the commoners (all of whom have some skill at wilderness lore) disappear into the woods, protected by the rangers and druids who mercilessly slay anyone that causes deliberate harm to the forest.

The rangers and druids tend to the plants and animals of their land, train students in the ways of nature, make fine wooden items, acquire rare herbs, and create things of magic and alchemy for trade. Open-minded youths are trained and then sent into the larger world to speak with other druids and rangers. Some of these travelers are given a treant seedling to plant in a deserving forest, or are told to slay followers of Malar.

MAJOR GEOGRAPHICAL FEATURES

The Great Dale stretches from the Easting Reach of the Inner Sea to the great lake of Ashane on the borders of Rashemen.

Forest of Lethyr: This large forest has a thick canopy overhead, making its interior as dark as twilight even on the brightest days. Visitors report an aura of doom within its confines, and speak of sentient trees that actively resist the progressive decline of the woodlands. Large numbers of druids live in the forest; they are unfriendly to visitors, especially loggers. The southern portions enfold the small settlements of Spearsmouth Dale and Mettledale. Wandering Theskian orcs occasionally forage into the southern reach of the woodland.

Rawlinswood: This forest is a near twin to the Forest of Lethyr to the south. Its narrowest point embraces the people of Denderdale, a small settlement of woodcutters and trappers. It is also the home of the Nentyarch and his fortress Dun-Tharos, hidden near the thick center of the wood. A circle of druids camps in the northwestern-most point of the forest, preventing any encroachment by the Damaran town of Tellerth.

IMPORTANT SITES

The fallen empire of Narfell once held most of these lands, but now little remains of their cities and towers except vine-covered ruins in the forest.

Bezentil: This waymeet is marked by ten dwarf-high stones spaced along the road at intervals of ten feet, the last of which bears a carving of a tree within a circle. Caravans use it as a rest stop and barter with the locals here.

The Mucklestones: This circle of stones carved with nature-runes is a holy site for the druids of Lethyr. The stones sometimes have different arrangements and move as a whole a short distance from year to year. The stones can act as a *portal* to certain other forests in Faerûn, but some of the location-keys have been lost over time.

Nighthawk Tower: This tower is actually an elaborate platform of branches and sturdy rope, built on top of a huge oak tree. Hensoi (NG male human Drd12 of Silvanus), the druid here, has an affinity for birds of prey, and the local raptors come here if times are hard or they are injured. He is one of the more tolerant druids of the country, although hardly friendly.

Tower Threespires: This tower has a broad base with three tall spires projecting from it. Built by a forgotten human who wanted to protect the land against invasions from the east, this tower would have fallen long ago if it weren't for the incredibly thick growth of vines wrapped around it, making it look like a giant three-fingered hand reaching upward. The druids conduct a secret yearly rite in this place.

Uthmere (Small City, 8,820): Only associated with the Great Dale by proximity, this place is populated by people from Impiltur, Damara, and Thesk. It serves as a way station for traders, and the residents warn those new to this trade route of the dangers of crossing the druids. Native folk who wish to trade for foreign goods occasionally visit Uthmere.

REGIONAL HISTORY

Humans have lived in the Great Dale at least as far back as the Dalesfolk's crossing of the Dragon Reach into Cormanthor in −200 DR. In this entire time, none but humans have been known to live here. In some places of the forest, ancient elven stone markers can be found, but no other signs of elven civilization. In all likelihood, this forest suffered some sort of calamity or mass exodus of its native elven and fey population, leaving it open to the humans who arrived later.

PLOTS AND RUMORS

Adventurers come to the Great Dale to explore the forests and their strange ruins, but the land's powerful druids watch carefully over all their travels in the woods.

Ruins of Clymph Tower: Thought to be the legacy of the same person who built Tower Threespires, this ruin is cursed and avoided by the druids, rangers, and natural creatures of the forest. At times some of the outer stones of its walls glow red with heat, and crackling sounds can be heard beneath the earth. The ruin attracts fell creatures from elsewhere, making it a dangerous place.

Impiltur

Capital: Lyrabar
Population: 1,205,280 (humans 90%, dwarves 5%, halflings 4%)
Government: Monarchy
Religions: Ilmater, Selûne, Tymora, Valkur, Waukeen
Imports: Exotic goods, fruit, shipbuilders, tea, vegetables, wood products

Exports: Gems, gold, iron, silver, trade goods from the Cold Lands
Alignment: LG, LN, CG

Impiltur is a kingdom of friendly merchants, preferring peace but capable of calculated acts of war when necessary. While the Impilturans vigorously defend their own borders, the government traditionally remains neutral and leaves neighboring lands to defend themselves. Impilturans see all sorts of raw valuables come from their northern neighbors and exotic goods arrive in their ports.

Among Faerûnians elsewhere, Impiltur is often "the Forgotten Kingdom." It has the mines and pines of the northern realms, but lacks witches or tyrants who send armies to attack neighboring countries. Its shipborne trade passes through the hands of either Sembia or Telflamm, so the Impilturran origin of the copper-work, silver, and iron bars is lost to purchasers. Impiltur is also the gateway to the riches of Damara, and a land fast growing in farmers now beginning to export smoked meats, cheeses, and fireslake (strong, sour wine of poor quality but great potency).

Impiltur is at peace with its neighbors, but persistent brigands, orc and hobgoblin raids out of the Earthspur Mountains, monsters aroused by the ongoing mining and prospecting, and intrigues hatched in the cities of Impiltur by agents of Thay, the newly energetic clergies of Shar, and other dark powers keep the armies of Impiltur war-ready.

LIFE AND SOCIETY

Impiltur has grown wealthy from trade passing through it, for it is the gateway between the Cold Lands and the nations on the Sea of Fallen Stars. Its people are ready and willing to fight to defend themselves, but enjoy their peaceful lives. The strong militia is capable of fighting on the land, in the mountain lowlands, or on the water.

Typical patrols of the Warswords of Impiltur consist of twenty or more chainmail-clad, mounted warriors, armed with lances and crossbows. A meeting with formidable monsters or strong foes leads to the summoning of additional patrols, or the hiring of adventurers to serve as "swordpoints." Adventurers on swordpoint duty are allowed some measure of freedom from the usual laws of the land.

Given their country's role as a major trading state, Impilturans aren't surprised by different sorts of people, although elves and half-elves are still uncommon in this area. They are proud of the Council of Lords and the widowed Queen Sambryl (CG female human Ari5/Wiz4). The queen herself finds governing boring and prefers to let the council direct matters.

MAJOR GEOGRAPHICAL FEATURES

Impiltur stretches between the Sea of Fallen Stars and the Earthspur Mountains.

Earthspur Mountains: These tall peaks mark the western border of Impiltur, running from the Moonsea south to the Sea of Fallen Stars. A constant cold wind from the Glacier of the White Worm that rests at their center howls through the peaks. There are few trails and many monsters, but the Earthspurs are rich in gold, silver, and bloodstone. Mining communities survive here, although the dangers of the mountains contribute to a high mortality rate. Persistent rumors speak of a hidden pass leading from Impiltur west to the Vast, but no such route has ever been mapped.

The Gray Forest: Long ago this wood was inhabited by moon elves. When hobgoblins and other monsters began to encroach on their territory, the elves warred with them but lost ground steadily. Facing extinction but reluctant to abandon their homes, the elves transformed themselves into majestic trees with gray bark. Circles of these are now found within areas of normal trees. Impilturans (and other humanoids) avoid the forest entirely.

IMPORTANT SITES

Impiltur today is a land of opportunity for the hard-working and the adventurous. With each passing month the inhabitants improve the roads, clear land for farms, and push back the frontier.

Dilpur (Metropolis, 31,838): This is a moderate-sized trade city, balancing its interests against all of Impiltur. The rulers of Dilpur are aware that an increase in mining is likely to cause merchants to shift to other cities with better access to trade routes and mines, so they stockpile resources to prevent this from occurring.

Hlammach (Metropolis, 36,386): This major seaport is walled and compact, populated with merchants, tradesfolk, and sailors. Its extensive docks are filled with ships. Hlammach is the site of the kingdom's mint, and thieves constantly try to steal the coins and trade bars stored here. Its small wizard school mainly teaches magic appropriate to the sea trade and spells to protect and ward valuables.

Lyrabar (Metropolis, 52,305): The largest city in this part of Faerûn, Lyrabar is long and narrow, stretching along the waterfront for nearly a mile. Its large fleet consists of warships and merchant vessels, assuring security of its port. The city has good relations with Procampur and Tsurlagol, and it boasts a small wizard's school specializing in magic helpful to sailing.

REGIONAL HISTORY

At least two realms of Impiltur have existed along the north coast of the Sea of Fallen Stars between the Earthspur and Earthfast mountains and the Easting Reach. The present realm was founded by the war-captain Imphras, who united four independent cities to face hobgoblin hordes advancing out of the Giantspire Mountains in 1095 DR. One of the military leaders proposed uniting their strength to form a nation, and the others agreed.

Impiltur has been a monarchy since, with a council of lords (most of them paladins or of lawful or good alignment) supporting and advising the monarch. Impiltur has a history of nonintervention, letting neighboring lands handle their own affairs unless such a hands-off policy would have major consequences for Impilturans. This policy makes them good trading partners but frustrating friends in times of war, as Damara found when it was invaded by Vaasa.

Today, Queen Sambryl, the widow of Imphras IV, rules Impiltur. She prefers to travel the land inspiring her people and aiding them in individual problems, serving as a willing figurehead for the true rulers of Impiltur: the twelve Lords of Imphras II, paladins indirectly descended from Imphras. These twelve serve as the vigilant war-captains of the realm and meet in council often to adjust their defenses and devise tasks for the troublesome or formidable adventurers of the land, sending such ready blades into conflict with Impiltur's foes.

PLOTS AND RUMORS

Although the Tuigan horde never reached Impiltur, the chaos of refugees fleeing it plunged the realm into poverty, starvation, and brigandry. Order was maintained only within the walled seaport cities. Rich new mines have recently been found north of Lyrabar and near the High Pass, however, and the realm is growing in wealth, trade, and confidence.

Forest Secrets: The hobgoblins of the Gray Forest have been marshaling under a new leader. This leader is said to be either a vampire or a werewolf, commanding dire wolves that aid his tribe in their attacks. The hobgoblins may have one or more lairs in the nearby Earthfast Mountains as well as in their forest homes.

What Waits Below: One of the newest mines in the Earthspurs has broken through into an old dwarven temple. Exploration of this temple reveals it to be dedicated to Laduguer, the evil deity of the gray dwarves. Several smaller tunnels have been found leading downward. The miners are looking for a band of adventurers to explore the tunnels and determine if they connect to gray dwarven settlements in the Underdark, while at least one merchants' guild is preparing an expedition to see if the gray dwarves would be willing to engage in trade.

Rashemen

Capital: Immilmar
Population: 654,480 (humans 99%)
Government: Monarchy/magocratic gynarchy
Religions: Bhalla (Chauntea), the Hidden One (Mystra), Khelliara (Mielikki)
Imports: Cloth, food, wood products
Exports: Carvings, cheese, firewine, furs, wool
Alignment: NG, CG, N

Rashemen is a cold, rugged land, populated by hardy and fiercely independent people. Its men are berserkers, disdaining armor and fighting with axe, spear, sword, and bow. Its women wield powerful magic tied to the land, training those with magical potential to serve the land and the Rashemi race. Although Rashemen is ostensibly ruled by a powerful warrior called the Iron Lord, the true powers behind the throne are the Witches, who choose the Iron Lord.

The land is full of nature spirits, any of which can turn jealous or vindictive against those who offend them. Rashemi laws are simple and based on honor, and they disdain the trappings of civilization. The people are devoted to the warrior ideal, competing in athletic contests and other harsh physical activities such as swimming in near-freezing rivers. These challenges keep them strong, for weakness would doom them to death at the claws of the land's many monsters.

LIFE AND SOCIETY

Faerûn knows Rashemen as the Land of Berserkers, a cold, alpine-and-rock land of fierce warriors ruled by masked Witches. Colorful tales tell of the Witches' cruelty—but such stories stray far from the truth. The Witches rule with absolute authority, sternly and firmly, but they hate cruelty, having repeatedly tasted it at Thayan hands.

Rashemi warriors are fur-clad or leather-armored pony riders. Showing cowardice or incompetence at arms results in shunning. They fight in loosely disciplined warbands known as Fangs, each led by a chieftain. In time of war, Witches command the Fangs. When fighting, a Witch of Rashemen wears black robes and a mask, arming herself with magic rings and whips that dance in the air, animating to fight by themselves while their owners cast spells.

The armies of Rashemen are commanded by the Huhrong, or Iron Lord, who is expected to be the epitome of the Rashemi warrior. He is chosen by vote of the Witches, during a secret meeting at which any Witch may propose any person as Huhrong. The Iron Lord is expected to rule wisely, keeping order rather than deciding policy. It's his task to keep travel between cities safe, frontiers secure, and marauding monsters to a minimum. The Witches instruct and protect the Iron Lord, and can remove him from office at will.

Throughout the land, Witches are revered and heeded. It's certain death to harm a Witch, and usually death to disobey one (unless one is a child, another Witch, or an ignorant outlander defying the word of a Witch for the first time). Among themselves, Witches strive to

Lake Ashane in Rashemen

understand living things and their fellow Rashemi, so that open disputes are few. Their manipulation steers folk toward agreement, and the land is kept strong and united, regarding Thayans as deadly foes and Rashemen as sacred land to be protected and tended. All Witches are female; the few magic-wielding males in the country are known as Vremyonni, or Old Ones, because they are preserved by magic to great age. Kept hidden in the Running Rocks, they devote themselves to crafting new spells and the magic items the Witches use in battle.

Most Rashemi never leave the realm after the *dajemma* of their youth, a year-long journey wherein youthful Rashemi become adults and see the world. Age, experience, and accomplishment determine rank within the Witches (the age of most Vremyonni placing them high among the Wychlaran, the Witches' name for themselves), and then in the same order within all native Rashemi who cannot work magic, with outlanders ranked at the bottom.

Rashemi are a short, muscular, hardy race, given to cross-country racing in fierce winter weather, exploring the old northern ruins of fallen Raumathar, and hunting snowcats while unarmored and lightly armed. They herd sheep, goats, and surface rothé and export wool, furs, carved stone, bone, and *jhuild*, or firewine (which costs as much as 15 gp per tallglass elsewhere in Faerûn). Rashemi love *sjorl*, a heavy, smoky-flavored cheese that outlanders find horrible.

MAJOR GEOGRAPHICAL FEATURES

To visitors, Rashemen seems very wild, with few cultivated areas, roads little better than dirt tracks, and few dwellings. Rashemi farms are usually hidden in bowl valleys, forest clearings, and along stream banks, with boulder and "wild-hedge" fences. Rashemi homes are typically caves, built into hillsides or covered with earthen mounds.

Ashenwood: This ancient forest's mighty spirits live in the stones and trees. It is not settled by the Rashemi, and while they sometimes enter the wood to hunt, they do so only after paying respect to the local spirits. Owlbears, trolls, and ettercaps also live here.

The High Country: This northernmost portion of the Sunrise Mountains is a place of ancient, dark hills, old stone monoliths, and wild magic. It is home to kobolds, goblins, trolls, wolves, winter wolves, and the ghosts of Rashemi and Tuigan dead. It is sparsely inhabited by grim hunters who prefer solitude.

Immil Vale: This area north of the Ashenwood is continually warm and green even in winter. This eternal springtime temperature is due to hot springs and a small amount of volcanic activity; vents and fumaroles of steam are common, often filling the vale with mist. Like most places in Rashemen, there are many spirits here.

Lake Ashane: This glacial body of water is also known as the Lake of Tears because of the battles fought on its shores. It is protected by odd aquatic creatures—nixies, nereids, and types unknown, all ruled by a great water spirit.

The North Country: Spoken of as a different land, this region contains ruins from Narfell and Raumathar. These ruins are full of ancient magic and treasure protected by guardian spirits, spells, and monsters. Rashemi nobles explore these places to prove their bravery.

Urlingwood: This forest at the north end of the Sunrise Mountains is dense and wild. The Witches spend much time here, communing with the spirits, making offerings, performing binding rituals, and brewing the potent Rashemen firewine. Outsiders are forbidden to enter the forest, and those caught are put to death. To protect would-be visitors, representatives of the Iron Lord patrol the outer perimeter. Most Witches actually live in the nearby town of Urling.

Illustration by Sam Wood

IMPORTANT SITES

Rashemi live close to the land, preferring unspoiled wildness to gardens, fences, and elaborate buildings. Rashemi disdain cities as "the wallows of those who've gone soft," and live in the countryside, dressing lightly even in cold weather.

Immilmar (Large City, 21,210): This city is home to the Iron Lord's citadel. Crafted of iron and stone, the citadel was built with the aid of the Witches. The central portion of the city is built around the citadel, with farther-out homes more like regular Rashemi homes. The cleric of the small temple of Chauntea here makes sure that worship of "Bhalla" doesn't stray too far from official doctrine.

Mulptan (Metropolis, 39,390): This city is Rashemen's northern trading gateway to the outside world. A great field outside town is crowded with traders from many lands. The two primary noble families, the Ydrass and Vrul, sponsor contests as friendly rivals. The competition has improved both families; they are accomplished warriors, hunters, and artisans.

Mulsantir (Large Town, 4,848): This town is the primary point for Thayan attack. It has been besieged at least five times but never fallen, due to the solid stone walls created by the Witches. Its large fishing fleet nets sturgeon in the nearby lake that bears the town's name.

REGIONAL HISTORY

Rashemen is an old land, with settlements dating back to the time when it was disputed ground between Narfell and Raumathar. Years after the collapse of those two empires, the people united to form a nation, aided by the Witches, who offered their protection in exchange for the right to select the kings and war leaders, since the first one in –75 DR.

Rashemen has defended itself against Mulhorandi invasions, multiple Thayan invasions, and even the Tuigan horde, surviving it all and holding its territory. With its traditional enemies (the Red Wizards) pursuing other tasks, Rashemen is fortifying its southern border in anticipation of eventual treachery.

PLOTS AND RUMORS

Dangerous wildlands, fierce berserkers, and a suspicious population deter all but the most resourceful outlander adventurers from exploring Rashemen's mysteries.

The Hag Queen: Citadel Rashemar was besieged and destroyed by the Tuigan horde. Now a pile of shattered stone, it is used as a lair by goblins, giant spiders, and hags. These creatures have begun to harry the nearby Rashemi villages, directed by a shrewd hag with formidable sorcerous powers. Already she has slain two Witches who entered her domain, and the Wychlaran want revenge.

Walk of the Old Ones: A group of Old Ones has grown tired of living lives of isolation and wish to see more of the world. The Witches denied the Old Ones their request, fearing that their knowledge could fall into the wrong hands. The unhappy Old Ones chose to escape anyway, and they need a guide for the few tendays before they return to their duties. Meanwhile, agents of rival powers (such as the Red Wizards and the Zhents) are trying to capture the male Rashemen wizards for the information they hold. The adventurers may need to negotiate between the Old Ones and the Witches, for the latter are intolerant of those who shirk their duties.

Thay

Capital: Eltabbar
Population: 4,924,800 (humans 62%, gnolls 10%, orcs 10%, dwarves 8%, goblins 5%, halflings 4%)
Government: Magocracy
Religions: Bane, Gargauth, Kelemvor, Kossuth, Loviatar, Malar, Shar, Talona, Umberlee
Imports: Iron, magic items, monsters, slaves, spells
Exports: Artwork, fruit, grains, jewelry, magic items, sculpture, timber
Alignment: LE, NE, N

Thay is a nation ruled by cruel wizards who rely on slavery to provide them with the wealth and luxury they need to support their magical research and dreams of conquest. The land is ruled by eight zulkirs, the most powerful wizards of the land. The zulkirs in turn choose the land's tharchions, civil governors who manage the mundane affairs of the realm and serve at the pleasure of the Red Wizards.

The power of the Red Wizards extends far beyond Thay's borders. Red Wizard enclaves exist in dozens of major cities throughout the Inner Sea lands, exchanging magic items for the goods, riches, and—in some cases—slaves of a dozen lands. The Thayans are widely disliked and distrusted, but their growing stranglehold on the trade in magic devices makes them virtually indispensable to many of their clients.

The zulkirs back in the homeland grow rich beyond belief with the spread of their sinister trade. They constantly scheme and plot against their neighbors. (See Chapter 7: Organizations for more information about the individual zulkirs.) Thayan armies have marched on Aglarond and Rashemen many times, and folk think it is only a matter of time before the Thayans revert to their old habits of taking what they want through force of arms and deadly spells.

LIFE AND SOCIETY

To Faerûnians, Thay is a dark and evil empire where cruel Red Wizards endlessly crack whips over screaming, groaning slaves who are spell-transformed into weird monsters as their "reward" for backbreaking service.

The truth is only a little different.

The Red Wizards form an elite class, the nobility of the land. Through the vast, regional bureaucracy administered by their handpicked tharchions, they govern Thay's laws, commerce, and society. Free Thayans fall into one of six classes: Red Wizards, bureaucrats, priests, merchants, soldiers, and artisans or skilled workers—barely a step above slaves themselves. Neither priests nor merchants are especially common in Thay.

All Thayan children are examined for magical aptitude at an early age. Those who show signs of potential are removed from their parents and subjected to ever more rigorous schooling in the arcane arts, culminating in apprenticeships to the Red Wizards, who are notoriously careless of and abusive toward their apprentices. (Those whose talents run to sorcery channel their talents into wizardry, suppress them, or leave the country. The Red Wizards despise sorcerers, who don't follow the carefully regimented system of magical schools.) The survivors become Red Wizards upon completion of their training, but the organization is far from democratic or benevolent—to hold real power, a young Red Wizard must master as much arcane might as she possibly can, and wield it ruthlessly and without hesitation against her fellows.

Thayan policy is decided in council by the zulkirs, wizards representing schools of magical specialization. Each zulkir is elected by Red Wizards prominent in that magical school, and then serves for as long as she can hold office—alive or in undeath. Although every zulkir has rivals seeking to destroy her, zulkirs tend to be shrewd, ruthless, and good administrators (or they don't last long).

Thay is divided into "tharchs," each ruled by a tharchion responsible for local roads and bridges, sanitation, military defense, irrigation or water transport, and peacekeeping. The tharchions, or civil rulers, in turn appoint autharchs, or bureaucrats and underlings. Autharchs are generally chosen from the most competent soldiers, well-off families with a tradition of civil service, or more rarely merchants or free Thayans who simply demonstrate unusual competence. Red Wizards occasionally scheme for an appointment as a tharchion to increase their own personal power and wealth.

All of the tharchions and zulkirs can muster their own armies, and many Red Wizards have multiple bodyguards, so Thay supports a haphazard array of fighting forces. These units range from nearly naked goblins fighting in mobs to plate-armored and highly trained cavalry riding flying steeds or magically augmented mounts of various sorts. These forces often skirmish unofficially when their rulers have a disagreement, or when one catches another doing something overly illicit.

Thay used to fight Aglarond and Rashemen almost continuously, but tasted defeat far too often to continue such enthusiastic hostilities. In the increasingly uncommon "general war" situations, Thay can send at least two special units into battle: the vast Legion of Bone, a regimented unit of marching armored skeletons, and the fearsome Griffon Legion, four hundred battle-skilled Red Wizards hurling spells and dropping incendiaries from griffonback.

Thay has a small but growing "middle class" of free folk who are either servant-staff to zulkirs or tharchions, or else merchants and traveling trade-agents. Free Thayans are perhaps the closest to what the folk of Thay would be like without magical oppression. They are careful folk who show their emotions as little as possible, affect a manner of smooth politeness, and take secret glee in watching dancing, revelry, foolishness, and amusements, but never dare to participate. They tend to eat and drink prodigiously but have strong constitutions (and tolerances for poisons and bad food), and rarely show drunkenness or ill effects from what they consume.

In Thay, slaves are everywhere. Thriving slave markets hawk the living wares of slavers who bring "merchandise" from Amn, Calimshan, Chessenta, Mulhorand, Semphar, and Thesk. The majority of slaves are human, but orcs, goblins, gnolls, half-orcs, and halflings also appear for sale. Thayans still mount slaving raids on other lands, but most slaves are acquired in trade.

Although slaves may be altered in any way by their owners at a whim, they are forbidden to cut their own hair or choose their own garb (most are kept near naked). Many slaves last only a few years before dying or being put to death.

Thayans frown on those who treat slaves with wanton cruelty (crippling or weakening punishments are bad for business, wasting valuable property). Nevertheless, slaves are put to death for minor infractions, to guard against the greatest fear of all noble Thayans: a bloody and countrywide slave uprising.

The Red Wizards of Thay are infamous for their "immoral" magical experimentations—but they'd be far more of a danger to the rest of Faerûn if the internal infighting among their ranks wasn't so vicious and vigorous.

Red Wizards shave all the hair on their heads (including eyebrows and often eyelashes), and sometimes all over their bodies, and most tattoo themselves heavily. Such tattoos are often a means of magically storing spells for emergency use (the source of many "miraculous escapes" for Thayans imprisoned in other countries). In Thay, only Red Wizards are allowed to wear red robes. They learn iron self-

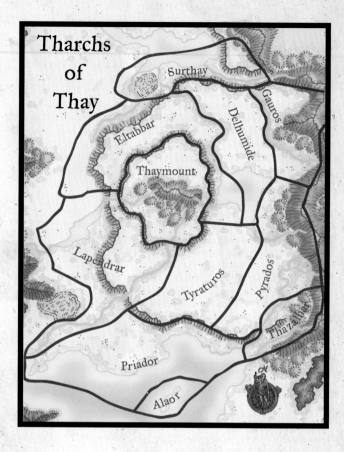

control as quiet, careful underlings to powerful senior mages, and only dare to scheme when they command a powerful roster of personal spells.

Thay is an ungainly, internally riven powerhouse of a nation—but also one that is feared, hated, and carefully watched by all its neighbors.

MAJOR GEOGRAPHICAL FEATURES

Thay is a hot, often dry, wind-scoured land where many thirst for freedom or greater power. A careful and constantly renewed webwork of spells keeps the weather good for crops with soaking rains on most nights and warm but not harsh heat during the day. The abundant slave power maintains high food production, allowing locally made beer and bread to sustain slaves along with the endlessly available boiled or pickled vegetables. Thay exports a lot of grain, but could sell a good deal more if its rulers weren't so wary of attack and didn't keep building (and filling to bursting) granary after granary.

Lake Thaylambar: This vast, deep lake provides rich fishing grounds despite its dragon turtles, which enjoy its icy depths and snack on fishing vessels. Thayan nobles occasionally go on hunting expeditions for the creatures, with about half coming home with a trophy and half never being seen again.

The Plateau of Thay: The heart of Thay is its central, heavily settled plateau. Here frequent human and gnoll patrols keep a vigilant watch for outlanders and escaped slaves, operating out of small fortresses known as tax stations.

The tax stations are surrounded by villages where free Thayans dwell, providing services and goods to the vast, fertile farms that sprawl across the plateau. Slaves labor over the crops, their lives spent swiftly and carelessly in the production of prodigious amounts of food. Every inch of the plateau is tamed. Where the land is not cleared and fenced for farms or villages, one finds the towers and demesnes of Red Wizards (who, rapt in their schemes and researches, do not welcome uninvited visitors).

Inquisitive mages of other lands who dare to scry onto the plateau discover that overlapping wards—in many places now approaching the strength of the fabled *mythals* of old—overlie the land, effectively preventing spying from afar. Those who have reason to be wary of the Red Wizards greatly regret this divination "shield" and seek other ways to learn the Thayans' schemes.

Surmarsh: Tribes of lizardfolk inhabit this dreary, fever-ridden swamp. Some of these tribes serve as occasional troops in the armies of Thay, which is considered a great honor to the scaly people. Nobles enter the swamp to hunt the monsters that flourish here.

Thaymount: At the center of the Plateau of Thay loom the rugged volcanic peaks known collectively as Thaymount. Earthquakes and ash eruptions indicate that local volcanism is increasing, but the Red Wizards haven't abandoned their fortresses on the mountain flanks. Instead, they seem to be rushing to and from them more often, called to secret councils and engaged in building new and ever larger fortifications.

Thay's military reserve (thousands of gnolls, darkenbeasts, and other fell creatures) is quartered in Thaymount, and the mountains are also known to contain both the rich gold mines that have funded the Red Wizards for years and worked-out mines that descend into the Underdark. Thaymount is home to the ancient Citadel (see Plots and Rumors, below), where it's whispered that runaway spells still rage uncontrolled.

Secret forces of magically twisted folk and monsters have emerged from the grim fortresses of Thaymount and gone out into Faerûn on sinister missions. Thay's magical workshops and armories lie in this region, too, worked by hundreds and hundreds of the younger Red Wizards at the command of their superiors.

IMPORTANT SITES

The Red Wizards have divided Thay into eleven tharchs, each ruled by a tharchion.

Alaor: This tharch consists of the pair of islands off the southern coast of Thay and houses the nation's largest naval base (large city, 20,520). Heavily damaged in the salamander war (see Regional History, below), it was rebuilt with modern facilities.

Delhumide: This tharch held the capital of the Thayan province when Mulhorand still controlled this area. The capital and other signs of civilization were destroyed in the independence war. The tharch now consists of ruins and slave farms. Its tharchion is a proponent of the magic trade, hoping to increase the prosperity of his poor territory.

Eltabbar: This tharch is of tremendous political importance. Its tharchion (Dmitra Flass, LE female human Ill7/Red8) strives to discourage feuds and intrigues among the zulkirs and advocates expanding the trade in magic items even further. She is married to the High Blade of Mulmaster, a political union that has brought Thay greater access to the Moonsea through its Mulmaster enclave.

The tharch contains the Thayan capital, also called Eltabbar (metropolis, 123,120). The city is huge, packed with slaves, and home to numerous slave auctions. The canals flowing through the city once helped to empower a spell that kept a great demon imprisoned under it, although that demon has since escaped due to weakening of the spell by an earthquake.

Gauros: This tharch on the northeastern end of Thay often skirmishes with Rashemen over its mineral-rich hills. The tharchion of Gauros hates Rashemen and constantly schemes to destroy that land, despite mandates from the zulkirs for a temporary peace.

Lapendrar: A cleric of Kossuth rules the southwestern tharch of Lapendrar. Though theoretically independent, the city of Amruthar (metropolis, 41,040) pays tribute to Thay to keep from being annexed. There is a minimal Thayan presence, and while no Red Wizards live here, some do visit. The wealthy rulers live decadently and luxuriously. Some Amrutharans want to sever all ties with Thay, making them fully independent, and some want to join Aglarond, which realistically is too far away to provide any aid. Escalant (metropolis, 28,728) has a history of alternating between independence from Thay and occupation by the Red Wizards. Currently Thay is in charge, although the locals are left to go their own way. The sprawling city is garrisoned with gnolls from the Thayan army.

Priador: The people of the Priador tharch have been terrified into submission by their tharchion, who rules with an iron fist. Currently the region prospers, but the zulkirs plan to intervene if trade falls off. Bezantur (metropolis, 136,800), Thay's largest city, is vital to the country's prosperity due to its sea trade. The city is plagued by powerful thieves' guilds. It is a major religious center, with temples to almost every deity but Azuth and Mystra.

Pyarados: The mountains of this tharch contain rich minerals. The walled city of the same name (metropolis, 54,720) is open to adventurers, even foreign ones, as long as these visitors don't threaten Thayan interests. The city's foreign quarter lies outside the city walls. The authorities turn a blind eye to crime, leaving street justice to settle matters. The city is often a launching point for adventurers delving into the Sunrise Mountains.

Surthay: This small tharch is mainly used as a staging ground for attacks against Rashemen. The locals survive through subsistence farming and trade with Theskian merchants. The city of Surthay (large city, 17,784) was originally built as a stronghold against attacks by the Rashemi, but now serves as a base for troops ready to attack that nation. Its proximity to the swamps means it often suffers strange plagues.

Thaymount: This tharch has a large military fortress and gold mines among its central mountains. Because Thaymount is used as the headquarters for the zulkirs, activities here are kept secret from all but the most privileged Red Wizards.

Thazalhar: This tharch controls trade routes to Mulhorand. Its tharchion is a retired general who extracts high tolls for caravans and travelers. The place is mostly a graveyard, since the wars with Mulhorand caused the area much damage. At night some portions are haunted by undead and the spirits of slain warriors.

Tyraturos: This well-patrolled tharch controls the two main highways through the country. The city of Tyraturos (metropolis, 68,400) is large and sprawling, with a huge slave marketplace where almost any creature can be had for a price, including exotic ones such as lamia, centaurs, and drow. Visitors must be careful to avoid being captured and sold into slavery only a few blocks from their inn.

REGIONAL HISTORY

For centuries, the region of Thay was under the rule of the powerful Mulhorandi Empire. Its native people, a Rashemi race, were subject to the rule of a noble class, the Mulan of Mulhorand. The great mage Ythazz Buvarr, a member of a Mulhorandi secret society called the Red Wizards, sought to create a separate realm where wizards would rule instead of the god-kings. Ythazz and his followers raised an army and sacked the capital of the Thayan province. The Red Wizards succeeded in destroying all opposition from their former masters and established the land of Thay in 922 DR.

In the years since then, Thay has tried many times to annex portions of Aglarond and Rashemen, sometimes with the assistance of drow, demons, assassination, or even artificially created natural disasters. Each attempt failed, mainly because the Red Wizards could never successfully cooperate with each other. The most recent attempt involved bargaining with the leaders of the efreet and salamanders from the Elemental Plane of Fire. When their allies turned on them, the clerics of Kossuth, lord of the fire elementals, were able to persuade their deity to intervene and rout the other outsiders, greatly elevating Kossuth's church in the eyes of the Thayans.

With outright conquest denied them, the zulkirs discovered that a great demand for Thayan goods—specifically magic items—exists in the cities of the Inner Sea. Given the number of Red Wizards and the traditions of years of servitude as apprentices and low-ranking members of the organization, the Red Wizards found that they could easily mobilize a large number of mages to manufacture potent magic items for sale and undercut other wizards with commercial aspirations.

Over the last several years, this trade has grown from a convenient way to fill the zulkirs' coffers and extract useful value from apprentices into an extremely rewarding enterprise. At the direction of one zulkir or another, mid-ranking Red Wizards have established enclaves—walled compounds or fortresslike footholds—in Faerûnian cities to purvey their magical goods in exchange for the wealth of a dozen lands.

Given the success of the mercantile efforts and the traditional failures of overt conquest, a new faction has arisen within the Red Wizards, supporting mercantile rather than military expansion. Grudgingly, the zulkirs (led by the lich Szass Tam, the zulkir of Necromancy and arguably the most powerful Red Wizard in Thay) have agreed to cease direct and overt hostilities against other nations for a time to see whether trade alone can accomplish their objectives. In the meantime, tenuous truces hold along the Aglarondan and Rashemi borders.

PLOTS AND RUMORS

Thay's aggressive slaving and the abominable conditions of the slaves within its borders attract good adventurers eager to strike a blow against the cruel Red Wizards.

The Buried Ones: One group of adventurers exploring the Sunrise Mountains has come back with a tale of strange pale humans they found in a newly opened cave. These humans have the same features as the ruling Mulan race in Thay, but are as pale as albinos and almost completely blind. They wield weapons of gold that are as hard as steel and cast strange magic that gives off no light. The adventurers told the story in Pyarados before they left to fight these creatures, who many in Thay believe to be a degenerate offshoot of Mulhorandi trapped centuries ago.

The Citadel: On the northern edge of the mountains in the Thaymount tharch is an old fortress simply called the Citadel. It predates the arrival of humans in this area and was built by a race of intelligent lizardfolk, possibly the progenitors of the now-primitive tribes living in the Surmarsh. Infested by troglodytes, rasts, and other subterranean species (including drow), the Citadel is said to connect to the Underdark.

Red Wizards and powerful Thayan adventurers frequently explore the fortress. Recently the number of expeditions has increased, many of them sponsored by the zulkirs themselves and often including foreigners. Whether these sponsored adventuring groups will be allowed to leave Thay with the information or treasure they find is another matter.

Szass Tam

Illustration by Sam Wood

SZASS TAM

Male lich Nec10/Red10/Acm2/Epic7: CR 31; Medium-size undead; HD 20d12+5; hp 131; Init +2; Spd 30 ft.; AC 29 (touch 14, flat-footed 27); Atk +12/+7 melee (1d6+2, *staff of power*) or +10 melee (1d8+5 [Will DC 25 half] plus paralysis, lich touch) or +12/+7 ranged touch (by spell); SA Paralyzing touch, fear aura; SQ Archmage high arcana, epic-level benefits, immunities, +4 turn resistance, damage reduction 15/+1, Red Wizard abilities, undead qualities; AL NE; SV Fort +8, Ref +10, Will +21; Str 11, Dex 14, Con —, Int 22, Wis 20, Cha 20. Height 6 ft.

Skills and Feats: Alchemy +26, Concentration +25, Craft (gem-cutting) +16, Diplomacy +7, Heal +9, Hide +10, Intimidate +11, Knowledge (arcana) +26, Knowledge (architecture and engineering) +11, Knowledge (Thayan history) +16, Knowledge (religion) +11, Listen +15, Move Silently +10, Profession (herbalist) +9, Profession (sailor) +9, Scry +26, Search +20, Sense Motive +13, Spellcraft +32, Spot +15, Swim +2, Wilderness Lore +7; Craft Staff, Craft Wand, Craft Wondrous Item, Maximize Spell, Mind Over Body, Quicken Spell, Scribe Scroll, Skill Focus (Spellcraft), Spell Focus (Evocation), Spell Focus (Necromancy), Spell Mastery (*animate dead, cone of cold, control undead, magic missile, teleport*), Tattoo Focus (Necromancy).

Special Attacks: Paralyzing Touch (Su): Creatures touched must succeed at a Fortitude save (DC 25) or be permanently paralyzed. Fear Aura (Su): Creatures of less than 5 HD in a 60-ft. radius that look at the lich must succeed at a Will save (DC 25) or be affected as though by *fear* as cast by a 29th-level sorcerer.

Special Qualities: Archmage High Arcana: Arcane reach, spell power +2. Epic-Level Benefits: Two effective levels of archmage (included in the above total), bonus spell level ×7 (included in the listing below). Immunities (Ex): Immune to cold, electricity, polymorph, and mind-affecting attacks. Red Wizard Abilities: Specialist defense (Necromancy) +4, spell power (Necromancy) +5, circle leader, Scribe Tattoo, great circle leader.

Wizard Spells per Day: 5/7/7/6/6/6/3/5/5/ 1/1/1/1/1/1/1. Base DC = 18 + spell level, 20 + spell level for evocation spells, 28 + spell level for necromancy spells. Wizard Caster Level: 22nd. Specialized School: Necromancy. Prohibited Schools: Enchantment, Illusion.

Spellbook: As a very old lich, a powerful wizard, and one of the rulers of a nation of wizards, Szass Tam has access to virtually any spell that is known and has created many unique necromancy spells known only to himself or the other Red Wizards. He normally prepares a quickened teleport and several quickened attack spells. He typically uses his 16th-level spell slot to prepare a quickened, maximized *energy drain*.

Possessions: Given his position of power and advanced magical abilities, Szass Tam can easily acquire nearly any sort of nonartifact magic item (and has access to at least two known Netherese artifacts, the *Death Moon Orb* and *Thakorsil's Seat*). He has a *staff of power*, *bracers of armor +10*, and a *ring of three wishes* in his possession at all times.

Infamous for his wise, cold cruelty and his longevity, Szass Tam is the zulkir of Necromancy in Thay, its most influential Red Wizard,

and—observers say—the true ruler of Thay. A lich for the last two hundred-odd years, Szass Tam achieved his present power through great arrogance, the skills and preparation to back up his overweening ambitions, and the brilliant schemes of one of the most cunning and intelligent beings in all Faerûn.

Like other Red Wizards, Szass Tam prefers to remain unseen, working through lackeys and servitor creatures (including vast armies of undead led by vampire generals) while he plots and schemes. His own undeath gives him patience. He's quite prepared to abandon servants and attempts that fail, and simply try again later in a better way. Tiring of the continual betrayals and slaughter within the Red Wizards, he has decided that the best future for Thay and for the Red Wizards is united under him—controlled through his magic and through fear. He's not openly exerting power yet, because he wants to preserve Thay's strength as much as possible, and in doing so control as much as he can before any open conflicts erupt.

Szass Tam possesses a truly incredible collection of magic items, ranging from rings, wands, and other trinkets up through staves and golems to artifacts. In his stronghold northwest of Tyraturos, he's almost unassailable. Those who meet him (or seemingly real magical images of himself that he creates and sends far across Faerûn) discover Szass Tam to be calm, cultured, and even pleasant. He appears as a richly robed, skeletally thin pale man. Balding, he has dark eyes, a thinning black beard, and hands that have shriveled to claws. He can, of course, use magic to change his appearance. His favorite false form is that of a tall scholar, aging but vigorous, with glittering jet-black eyes and a soft, purring voice.

Szass Tam is polite but blunt, and he can be plunged instantly into cold, controlled rage by insolence or deliberate defiance. On the other hand, he seems to admire those who cross or foil him by cleverness, as long as they treat him politely. He's always spinning more simultaneous intrigues than most Faerûnians have years in their lives, and with his domination ever growing, he seems content to view existence as a great game, with plots and schemes as the playing pieces—or, if you prefer, weapons.

Thesk

Capital: none
Population: 855,360 (humans 85%, gnomes 8%, orcs 6%)
Government: Oligarchy
Religions: Chauntea, Mask, Shaundakul, Waukeen
Imports: Gold, horses, trade goods
Exports: Food, gnome goods, iron, Kara-Turan goods
Alignment: N, NG, CG

Thesk is a land of shrewd but friendly merchants and able farmers. The trade route that leads to the far land of Kara-Tur allows the Theskians to see all kinds of people and interact with many cultures, making Thesk one of the more tolerant nations in Faerûn. After being decimated by the Tuigan horde, the people of Thesk are rebuilding their cities and towns, and they have even made a home for the orc army left behind by the Zhentarim.

The Theskians' familiarity with quality and obscure goods makes them skilled at appraising items. Arcane magic in this land is rare; that fact, along with the influence of the Shadowmasters (a thieves' guild backed by the church of Mask), makes Thesk more than just another realm of traders.

LIFE AND SOCIETY

People in the rural areas of Thesk live like common folk, tending to their soil and livestock. Unlike in other parts of Faerûn, a number of the farmers and ranchers in Thesk are full-blooded orcs. Orcs also inhabit the cities, blending in with the other merchants and workers who serve the Golden Way, the major trade route that connects Faerûn to the Utter East. Acclimatized to strange faces, languages, and goods, the people of Thesk have a long history of profiting from caravans from all parts of the world and go out of their way to welcome visitors.

MAJOR GEOGRAPHICAL FEATURES

Thesk lies between the Plateau of Thay and the Forest of Lethyr. Vast portions of the land are virtually empty—most folk live along the road from Telflamm to Two-Stars.

Ashanath: This unsettled region's good soil is covered in thick, short grass, and small herds of wild oxen and ponies roam its entire length. It would be an excellent place for farms and could easily support one or more city-states except for the tornadoes that race across the landscape in summertime, sometimes as often as once a tenday. The tornadoes are thought to be side effects of the weather-controlling magic the Red Wizards frequently use to benefit their crops. The plain is also home to bulettes and ankhegs.

Dragonjaw Mountains: The clans of gnomes in this mountain range are frequent visitors to the human city of Phent, which exists mainly to distribute the tools, inventions, weapons, jewelry, and quality iron ingots the gnomes produce. The mountain is populated by at least two copper dragons that engage in joke-contests with the gnomes on an annual basis.

Thesk Mountains: These mountains are bare and inhospitable, prone to small landslides and sudden dropoffs. Their few moderate veins of iron supply the country's needs plus a small amount for export.

IMPORTANT SITES

The Golden Way is by far the most important feature of Thesk.

Nyth (Small City, 11,501): Previously under the control of Telflamm, Nyth once again considers itself part of Thesk and trades freely with its sister cities, including Telflamm. The city received its name from the will-o'-wisplike creature that used to haunt the western edge of the Forest of Lethyr. A cabal of wizards eradicated the nyth in a battle of mutual destruction. Since that time, wizards have been respected in Nyth but are thought doomed to meet a bad end.

Phsant (Large City, 21,564): This city is famous as the site of the defeat of the Tuigan horde by the armies of the western alliance. The orc soldiers from the Zhent army settled in this area and have adapted remarkably well. Some work on farms, some have purchased small farms of their own, and others work as mercenaries, laborers, and guards. The other orcs in Thesk work as miners in the Thesk Mountains, returning here to visit with their old tribemates. Some of the orcs have married local women, but the rest are still looking for wives, drawing a steady flow of half-orc women to this area in search of strong husbands of a more civilized mindset than they might find in an orc tribe.

Tammar (Large Town, 3,594): Nearly razed to the ground by the Tuigan, this city was held for a while by a large group of bandits who extorted heavy tolls from caravans passing through their land. The oligarchy paid a squadron of one hundred orcs to root out the bandits, and now the tusked warriors are hailed as heroes in this town, which has been rebuilt and resettled by its original residents.

Telflamm (Large City, 23,361): This city sits at the end of the Golden Way, profiting greatly from the trade route by controlling access to the Sea of Fallen Stars. Independent from Thesk but closely allied with its neighbor, Telflamm is ostensibly ruled by a merchant prince. Actually, the city is firmly under the control of the Shadowmasters. This thieves' guild owns the city's inns, festhalls, and gambling halls, in addition to extorting "protection" fees from merchants and wealthy alike.

The Shadowmasters are led by the local high priest of Mask (whose temple in the city, the House of the Master's Shadow, is Faerûn's largest to that deity). He knows a ritual that allows a worshiper to exchange a portion of his or her life force for the ability to *shadow walk* once per day. This ability has served the guild greatly in the year since the ritual's discovery. The Shadowmasters maintain safe houses in every city in Thesk.

REGIONAL HISTORY

Founded in 937 DR by a coalition of friendly trading and agricultural cities, Thesk has long been a land of farmers profiting from the trade that passes through their country to and from the lands of Kara-Tur.

The Golden Way has allowed Theskians to become very wealthy, which led to their current form of government. The wealthiest person in a city becomes mayor, and joins the other mayors on a council that governs the nation. Sparsely populated and with few natural resources, Thesk has avoided the conquering gaze of the Red Wizards and is instead a reliable trade partner for food and exotic goods brought in on the Golden Way. Thesk suffered greatly from the attacks of the Tuigan horde, because the nomads used the well-trod road to attack several cities in quick succession.

Although the horde was defeated, Thesk was disrupted for years by the presence of refugees of the Tuigan attacks. The thousand orc soldiers left behind by the Zhentarim added to their paranoia, for orcs had not been seen in that region for hundreds of years, and some considered them demons. The Shadowmasters of Telflamm bribed and coerced the orcs to resettle away from their city. After being rebuffed by the druids of the Forest of Lethyr, the orcs settled peacefully in and around Phsant, where the locals eventually grew to accept them, particularly in light of their actions in helping defeat the Tuigan horde a few miles from that city.

PLOTS AND RUMORS

Unlike Rashemen or Thay, which are eastern lands that do not welcome adventurers, the folk of Thesk celebrate anyone who makes their land safer by driving out monsters. They might also welcome anyone willing to contest the power of the Shadowmasters.

Old Soldiers: Now that the Zhentarim have control of most of the Moonsea, they are looking to their remote agents in an effort to establish a firmer foothold in the rest of the world. In Thesk, these agents are the thousand orcs from their army. However, in the twelve years since arriving here, the orcs have adjusted to living in this region, and few have any interest in returning to a situation where they have to risk their lives for someone else's grand plans. The Zhents may try to woo the orcs back with money or capture them by force of arms.

The Underdark

Capital: None
Population: Unknown (aboleth, cloaker, drow, duergar, illithid, quaggoth, svirfneblin)
Government: City-states, each with different government (autocracy, magocracy, matriarchy, monarchy, theocracy, and so on)
Religions: Varies, usually racial pantheon
Imports: Armor, food, slaves, timber, weapons
Exports: Armor, exotic goods, magic, weapons
Alignment: N, LE, CE

The region called the Underdark is an entire world beneath the feet of the surface dwellers of Faerûn. Inhabited by monstrous and evil creatures that shun the daylight, the Underdark teems with entire cities and nations of derro, drow, duergar, and mind flayers (illithids). It is also home to even stranger races such as aboleths,

Travel in the Underdark

The vast, lightless Underdark is a dangerous place indeed. To non-native beings, its darkness and tight confines can be insurmountable terrors. To Underdark natives, lights mean danger—either they are lures to bring travelers to some predator, or they mark the place of creatures too powerful to fear attracting attention to themselves.

Much of the Underdark was created by volcanism, flowing or dripping water, earth tremors, and mysterious magic that left behind an intense magical radiation that the drow call *faerzress*. Any of these forces can cause sudden collapses, floods, or falling hazards.

Drinkable water is all too rare, apt to be guarded by predators or already in use by molds or fungi dangerous to other creatures. Some waters are acidic, corroding metal, flesh, or both. Bad air is another problem. Both the native cities and the ongoing volcanism can generate poisonous vapors that drift or creep for miles in the lightless depths.

The Underdark is not a static, unchanging place. Drow, deep gnomes, and other races that dwell in subterranean cities claim the prime territory. Purple worms, umber hulks, xorn, and other creatures burrow through solid rock. Fell races such as beholders and illithids wield strange spells and powers to shape the rocks around them, while the dwarves simply tunnel with skill and determina-

tion. Mysterious, unexplained appearances of chambers, caverns, and passages that pulse with strong *faerzress* are not unknown. Underdark maps thus soon go out of date. Guides can be helpful, but their loyalty is always a matter of concern.

Travel or teleport magic is usually useless over long distances in the Underdark because it is warped into deadly failure by *faerzress*, though it can still prove useful for short journeys within the same open cavern. *Portals* work in some areas but not in others, and the establishment of new *portals* is well nigh impossible, since the magic involved attracts formidable enemies very swiftly. Like the established trade routes, known *portals* are always guarded or closely watched.

Supplies are another problem. Only in Underdark cities are shops to be found, and those cities are widely seen as collections of murderers and thieves.

The very lack of supplies in the Underdark has created vigorous, ongoing trade. A merchants' caravan may provide the best protection to a visitor to the Underdark. The large amount of carried supplies and fearsome fighting capability, magical and mundane, of a caravan offers safety in unsafe territory. However, care must be taken to avoid unintentionally offering oneself as a slave while employing such a tactic.

beholders, and kuo-toas, as well as slaves of just about any intelligent humanoid found on the surface.

These evil beings battle or trade with each other for resources, magic, and power, forming alliances that collapse when plots unravel or better opportunities come along. Interspersed with the warring city-states are enclaves of gnomes, svirfneblin, dwarves, and other neutral and good folk, who remain isolated or resist encroachment by malign neighbors.

LIFE AND SOCIETY

The Underdark is a harsh realm where two overwhelming drives rule: survival and the destruction of your enemies. Perpetually dark in most regions, the Underdark is filled with creatures that long ago developed darkvision or enhanced senses to compensate, often becoming intolerant of true light as a result of their adaptation. Some places are dimly lit by glowing rocks, luminous crystals, or phosphorescent moss, lichen, and fungi. Bizarre plants are common, and visitors usually find it impossible to identify which are hostile or poisonous without magic or potentially lethal experimentation. The most precious resource is fresh water, since the Underdark has no rain and inhabitants must rely on whatever filters down from the surface. Those who discover water hoard it and protect it with their lives.

Because of the scarcity of certain resources, each city often specializes in producing a few items and trading these with neighbors in peaceful times. A typical trade caravan consists of several dozen heavily armed merchants and soldiers, with two to three patrols sent forward or behind while traveling. Although the tunnels are generally silent, echoes travel far, and a skilled Underdark scout learns to recognize subtle signs of natural animals and lurking threats by their echoes alone. Wealthier cities teleport caravans to their destinations or use existing *portals* to speed travel, and access to a convenient *portal* is often the cause of lengthy wars between nearby cities. Cities that develop a reputation for killing or enslaving caravans in peacetime (as opposed to exhibiting cool hostility and rudeness, which are expected) usually find themselves cut off from valuable resources and made easy prey for aggressors.

MAJOR GEOGRAPHICAL FEATURES

Because most of the Underdark has been only cursorily surveyed, and given that the largest caves are only a few miles long, few geographical features would be considered noteworthy to a surface dweller. Lakes tend to be the largest features, although the nearby stone may dip below the surface of the water, breaking it into quasi-separate regions that can only be identified as the same body of water by the most meticulous cartographer.

Tunnels in the Underdark extend for miles, some ballooning into caverns thousands of feet across, only to shrink to narrow spaces too small for a halfling to squeeze through. The largest cavern halls become representations of the surface in miniature, with hills, valleys, underground rivers, and lakes. In this three-dimensional environment, most races make use of the walls and ceilings of their caverns, accessing the higher levels with natural or magical flight or levitation or wall-crawling mounts such as giant spiders or certain breeds of lizards.

The Underdark is divided into three general levels. The upper Underdark is close to the surface, has considerable interaction (trade, raids, or conquest) with surface races, and is mainly inhabited by drow, beholders, dwarves, mind flayers, svirfneblin, and—under cities—wererats. Water and food are relatively abundant, and adaptation to darkness is mild.

The inhabitants of the middle Underdark tend to see surface races as slaves. These include drow, lone aboleths, cloakers, derro, mind flayers, svirfneblin, and kuo-toas. Water and food are difficult to find.

The lower Underdark is incredibly strange, filled with alien societies and bizarre cultures, hostile to any unlike them, ruled by aboleths, cloakers, derro, and mind flayers. Food and water are very rare, so the races here prey upon each other for survival. Adaptation to darkness is often extreme, with new and peculiar senses appearing in some monsters. All levels contain evil humanoids, usually as slaves in civilized cities.

Araumycos: This great fungus fills the Underdark beneath the High Forest between one and three miles below the surface. Possibly the oldest living organism in Faerûn, the fungus predates the empires of the elves. It cannot reach beyond the borders of the forest above it, and pieces of it taken away quickly die, so it may be magically or symbiotically tied to the forest. While susceptible to fire, acid, and similar attacks, it is immune to magic. No effort has eradicated much of it for long, and it sometimes unleashes psionic attacks upon its attackers. Occasionally entire portions die, revealing ruined cities or colonies of fungus folk, but the cause and origin of the growth remains unknown.

Giant's Chalice: This brackish lake in the lower Underdark curves from the northwest of Proskur, under Iriaebor, and around to Elversult. Inhabited by intelligent octopi, the Chalice is thought to have connections to the Sea of Fallen Stars. Vampiric squid introduced into the Giant's Chalice by the illithids now threaten the octopi. A glowing coral that lives only in this lake is a great prize and one of the few luxury items the octopi export.

The Labyrinth: This maze of unclaimed passageways fills the upper and middle Underdark in the region between Red Larch and Triboar on the Long Road north of Waterdeep. Used by northern Underdark merchants heading for Skullport and beyond, the Labyrinth is known to have shifting walls and dangerous inhabitants—particularly baphitaurs, sorcerous beings thought to be descended from minotaurs and demons.

IMPORTANT SITES

While great realms tend to expand to the limits of a particular cavern system, endless tunnels link the Underdark together.

Blingdenstone (currently abandoned): Founded in the Year of Fragile Beginnings (−690 DR) by svirfneblin fleeing the phaerimms, Blingdenstone became a self-sufficient city-state that only rarely made contact with other nearby civilizations. Jolted out of their isolation by Menzoberranzan's attack on Mithral Hall, the twelve thousand deep gnomes allied with the defenders of the dwarfhold and helped stem the drow onslaught.

The defeated drow had their revenge several years later: Dozens of bebiliths were summoned into Blingdenstone by *gate* and *planar ally* spells, slaughtering most of the svirfneblin. The five hundred or so survivors fled with their belongings to Silverymoon, where their small community was welcomed into the Silver Marches. The Silveraen hope to resettle and fortify the city as a defense against further drow incursions.

Cairnheim (Village, 500): Founded by stone giants fleeing a slaughter of giantkind by the dwarves of Shanatar, Cairnheim (located under the Giant's Run Mountains in the Dragon Coast) has been ruled for the last fifteen hundred years by the Dodkong, an undead stone giant chieftain. The undead monarch has corrupted the giants, and he reanimates each clan chieftain who dies, forming the Dodforer, a council of "Death Chiefs" that serves him.

Cairnheim giants use runecasting, preferring necromantic spells acquired from Velsharoon. The Dodkong is known to be a sorcerer of considerable power. At the rare times they engage in trade, the giants exchange gold, silver, and nuggets of adamantine for rothé, rare fungi, and wine. The giants of Cairnheim have darkvision and carefully watch over their access tunnels, which are protected by runes, avalanches, and deadfalls.

The fall of Blingdenstone

Illustration by Carlo Arellano

Deep Shanatar: The first and greatest shield dwarven realm, Deep Shanatar controlled the upper Underdark where Amn, Tethyr, and Calimshan are now. Originally spread across eight subkingdoms that battled in what are known as the Spawn Wars, the dwarves of Shanatar eventually convened to form a lasting peace, ruling from the *Wyrmskull Throne,* a seat of authority that could be moved from kingdom to kingdom.

Over time, the declining birthrate of the dwarves and their emigrations north caused the empire to fall apart. Wars with other Underdark races claimed the subkingdoms, leaving only Iltkazar in the modern day. Ruins from Deep Shanatar can still be found scattered over its old territory. While most ruins were looted, remote outposts turn up from time to time (often as monster lairs) with masterwork dwarven armor, weapons, and even magic items within them.

Gracklstugh (Metropolis, 36,000): Also known as the City of Blades, this duergar nation rests in the middle Underdark just south of the Evermoors. Consisting of a large grotto of hollowed-out stalagmites that borders on an Underdark sea called the Darklake, the gray dwarves use the stone pillars as smelting centers, building their homes and workshops around them. The duergar control territory for several miles around their home city, allowing only visitors intent on trade. A large standing army enforces their claim. The city is also home to derro, thousands of slaves, and a small number of stone giants from the Cairngorn clan. The city exports fish, mining equipment, and quality steel arms and armor. The derro are the true rulers, controlling King Tarngardt Steelshadow VII (LE male duergar Ftr17) and the clan leaders with bribes, magic, and threats.

Iltkazar (Small City 7,500): Surrounded by hostile neighbors, the shield dwarves of Iltkazar control little more than the city itself and its immediate surroundings under the Omlarandin Mountains in Tethyr. Iltkazar is one of the eight original dwarven kingdoms of Deep Shanatar.

Unlike other Underdark nations, Iltkazar has many tunnels to the surface, most connecting to old and carefully guarded dwarven ruins. A river and its tributary run through the city, providing fresh water and driving winches, pumps, and other mechanical devices. The city's ceiling is covered in faintly glowing silvery blue lichen. Other fungal growths are cultivated for food and as fodder for a small herd of rothé. Three-fourths of the inhabitants are shield dwarves, a little over one-tenth are humans, and the rest are rock gnomes or svirfneblin. Slavery is illegal in Iltkazar, and runecasters, warriors, and clerics guard the mithral doors that allow access to their city. The city specializes in engineering, the working of rare metals, and gemcutting.

Menzoberranzan (Metropolis, 32,000): North of the Evermoors and under the River Surbrin, Menzoberranzan is a matriarchal drow city famed as the birthplace of Drizzt Do'Urden and the launching point for the attack on Mithral Hall. The city's population is one-third drow, the rest being humanoid slaves. The city trades poisons, tasty mushrooms, riding lizards, spell scrolls, wine, and water.

The city is defended by drow troops (both full-time soldiers and armed members of the noble houses) and slave forces, with spellcasters aiding defensive efforts. Although Menzoberranzan is ruled by a council of matrons from the eight greatest houses, others in the city hold political power, such as the mercenary leader Jarlaxle (NE male drow Ftr17) and the Archmage of Menzoberranzan, Gromph Baenre (CE male drow Wiz20).

Although the drow are generally cool toward visitors, a few small businesses cater to adventurers and traders. Over one hundred tunnels link the outskirts of Menzoberranzan's territory to other parts of the Underdark, the most notable being those near Mithral Hall, in the heart of the Moonwood, and on the western edge of the High Forest. The city has recovered from its losses during the Time of Troubles and the attack on Mithral Hall, and it again plans expansion and the conquest of its neighbors and the surface realm.

Oryndoll (Metropolis, 26,000; 3,450 mind flayers): This city of illithids is in the lower Underdark, beneath the center of the Shining Plains. Hoarders of knowledge and jealous of information, the illithids are rarely visited by any but slave traders. Although it long ago fought a great war with the dwarves of Shanatar, Oryndoll is best known in the Underdark as the birthplace of the modern duergar race, bred from the dwarves of clan Duergar in the hopes of creating a loyal race of skilled dwarves with mental powers. These gray dwarves led a series of uprisings and escaped from the city, causing so much chaos that the city was saved from collapsing only by a manifestation of the illithid deity Ilsensine. The mind flayers of the city have since developed a highly religious culture and innovations in psionics. The city teems with mind-controlled slaves and an uncounted number of cranium rats.

Sschindylryn (Large City, 15,000): This drow city is on the shore of Lake Thalmiir, miles beneath the King's Forest of Cormyr. The drow of Sschindylryn are skilled in divinatory and travel magic, particularly spells and items that locate food, water, and minerals, and they trade these things with other cities through a network of *portals* in their city and in the shallow part of the lake.

The Sschindylryn drow used to be more warlike, using their portals to make surprise raids on other cities. A major defeat by Menzoberranzan curbed this practice, and they now stick to trading while they rebuild their strength. The city is built on a kuo-toan ruin, both above and below the water, and even the new architecture retains a piscine style. In addition to the magic trade, the drow fish the lake and farm local algae that thrive on faerzress.

Sshamath (Metropolis, 45,000): Rare among subterranean drow cities, Sshamath is ruled by male wizards, with the female clerics of Lolth taking lesser roles. This community under the Far Hills is the preeminent Underdark market for magic items. Considered as a strong trading partner by other cities, Sshamath is well protected by warrior-wizards.

The drow males gained ascendancy through successive generations of predominantly male births, decreasing the number of drow matrons and their power over the city. Its permanent and artistic *faerie fire*-like lights on the walls are unusual for an Underdark realm but make it convenient for surface visitors who lack darkvision. Slaves make up a fourth of the population, and visitors from other realms, undead servants, and conjured creatures bring the usual head count to sixty thousand. Anyone with skill at wizardry or sorcery is welcome to visit the city without fear of enslavement.

REGIONAL HISTORY

The history of the Underdark predates and parallels that of the surface world. Progenitor races arose in the Underdark and died out over time or were slain when their equivalents retreated underground in the face of opposition from new races such as elves and dwarves. Ancient races such as the kuo-toas disappeared from the surface before recorded human or elven history. Evidence of the illithids' origin is scarce, but sages believe that the mind flayers arose at nearly the same time as the kuo-toas or invaded from another plane during that empire's height. The aboleths are also ancient, but the history of their machinations from the lower Underdark has gone unrecorded.

The drow entered the Underdark after the Crown Wars, roughly −10000 DR, with evidence of the first drow cities built around −9600 DR. A vigorous and aggressive race, they seized a great deal of territory before falling into endless internal wars. Dwarves, always present on and below the surface, battled the drow and other Underdark races, losing the entirety of clan Duergar to the mind flayers only to see them emerge generations later as the duergar subrace, imprinted with the cruelty of their psionic masters. The derro also emerged during this time, bred from captured dwarves and humans by the illithids. In later millennia, races such as the svirfneblin, goblinoids, orcs, and grimlocks were brought or found their way into the Underdark. The most recent arrivals are the cloakers, which have been present only for the last few centuries.

War, conquest, decay, and collapse form the familiar cycle of the Underdark nations. Cities fight each other for riches, resources, or slaves, or out of age-old hatred. Stable empires grow decadent or suffer from numerous and constant skirmishes that bleed away their power. Failing empires collapse, sometimes from within and sometimes prompted by the blades of their enemies. From these broken

Araundordoom

The vast Underdark beneath Faerûn's surface is a deadly world whose inhabitants (even formidable beasts and races armed with both ruthlessness and fell magic) band together in fortified cities to survive. It's difficult to map on flat parchment because of its layers and sloping tunnels. Local control over specific locales may change with bewildering and deadly rapidity.

Many small "governed" areas of the Underdark never appear on any maps. Liches are the worst sort of this kind of minor ruler. With their dark humor and arrogance, liches to refer to their domains as "dooms." The equivalents of these undead human wizards, such as the illithid alhoon and elven baelnorn, also rule small Underdark domains.

Most lich dooms feature hiding places for magic (crevices or high ledges) and a complex tangle of passages and caverns. Liches use abandoned dwarven and gnome delves that have useful rooms and doors, if clearances are sufficient and no traps were left behind.

Araundordoom is a typical doom, ruled by the lich Araundor. Once a human wizard of Mulhorand, he long ago dwindled into a near-skeletal state and lost the last vestiges of sanity. He now exists to destroy intruders, gloat over their sufferings, and seize any magic they carry. He uses spells to read the thoughts of approaching creatures and even to steal memorized spells right out of their minds. Intruders' deeds, aims, and desires both entertain him and give him weapons against them. He can use names thus gleaned to pose as a friend or acquaintance crying for aid to lure creatures into his traps.

Like most liches, Araundor prefers to avoid crushing traps that could harm him. He employs poisons in the pools of water found in his doom, places leg-hold snares where intruders must wade, then immerses himself either underwater in the deepest pools (to avoid hostile fire magic) or in sucking mud through which intruders must struggle. His silent or stilled spells can be unleashed unimpaired from within the murk or muck.

Araundor loves to taunt foes, revealing what he knows about them and goading them into anger, fear, and recklessness—but he's smart enough to do so when only one or two opponents remain active. He animates several corpses and skeletons of past intruders to pose as himself and cause intruders to waste magic. The patient use of ruses and attacks, coupled with the labyrinth he has chosen as his doom, let him scatter bands of foes so he can deal with them one or two at a time.

cities come groups of survivors who find niches where they can scratch out an existence and eventually build new cities.

PLOTS AND RUMORS

For surface adventurers, simply entering the Underdark and returning to tell the tale is an accomplishment of note.

Dead Reckoning: A band of skeletal dwarves in full battle regalia is making its way through the tunnels, slaughtering any who attack them except for dwarves. Their dead foes shed flesh and rise as skeletons to join the march. These undead are unaffected by the turning and commanding powers of clerics, and they detour to avoid dwarven settlements. Their goal may be the reclamation of an old dwarven burial site from enemy hands or the destruction of a powerful foe, such as a deep dragon.

Hit and Run: Given the number of *portals* and undiscovered tunnels in the Underdark, it is possible for a raiding or trading party of drow, duergar, kuo-toas, or any other such race to appear in any surface area, seeking mayhem, slaves, or profit. If such a group didn't have an easy way home, it might wait out the daylight in a cave, ruin, or abandoned warehouse, or under the protection of a local wizard or evil temple.

The Vast

Capital: None
Population: 1,308,960 (humans 78%, dwarves 9%, halflings 5%, elves 3%, gnomes 2%, half-elves 1%, half-orcs 1%)
Government: City-states and feudal holdings; most cities are ruled by councils of merchants and landowners
Religions: Chauntea, Clangeddin, Eldath, Mystra, Tempus, Torm, Tymora, Waukeen
Imports: Glass, luxury goods, salt
Exports: Copper, grain, iron, livestock, nickel, parchment, silver, textiles
Alignment: LN, N, NG

The Vast is a verdant farming and hunting area on the eastern shore of the Dragon Reach, best known for its thriving ports: evil Calaunt, ever-changing Tantras, the adventurers' haven Ravens Bluff, and regimented Procampur. Orcs and dwarves vie for supremacy over the nearby mountains. Orc raids on the lowlands are rare, but troublesome enough to keep the human population concentrated along the coast. Intrigues between rival factions and a wealth of dwarven ruins beckon to adventurers.

Thanks to the Sea of Fallen Stars, the Vast enjoys a mild climate year round, with long, cool summers and short, mild winters. Most of the Vast is rolling farmland with fields divided by low walls made from rubble. Small wooded lots appear among the farms. Dozens of brooks and streams crisscross the land, but they seldom join the major rivers. Instead, they end in pools that drain into subterranean rivulets flowing toward the Inner Sea. The jigsaw water table owes its existence to broken and tilted layers of rock that lie under the deep soil of the vast. Small sinkholes, caves, and rifts are plentiful.

LIFE AND SOCIETY

Folk in the Vast have a pioneering spirit and see themselves as one with the land they inhabit. Their loyalties lie with their local communities. They always go armed (albeit usually with simple weapons such as slings, knives, and quarterstaffs), especially outside the cities. They tend to keep to themselves, but minstrels and bards are welcomed everywhere—the Vast folk delight in a well-sung ballad and news of other lands.

Boar, deer, and black-masked bears roam the forests and mountainsides of the Vast. Hunting is a way of life in the countryside, especially in the high country.

MAJOR GEOGRAPHICAL FEATURES

The Sea of Fallen Stars borders the Vast to the west and south. The Earthspur Mountains mark the area's east and north boundaries.

Earthfast Mountains: This arm of the Earthspur Mountains runs west to the Dragon Reach. Its steep slopes make mining difficult, but recent discoveries of copper, silver, and iron veins have convinced many to brave the hardships in hopes of wealth. Giant eagles and other avian creatures claim the highest peaks as their territory, while great numbers of orcs and ogres lair in the deep reaches of the mountains.

Two major passes allow land traffic to move north and south: Elvenblood Pass in the west, and Glorming Pass in the east.

Fire River: This wide and generally placid river descends from the high country and flows west to empty into the Sea of Fallen Stars at Ravens Bluff. It has one major cataract at Dragon Falls, some hundred miles upstream from Ravens Bluff.

IMPORTANT SITES

The Vast has a reputation as a place of secrets best left undisturbed, especially in the mountains and subterranean ways. Of course, the most notable places in the Vast are not secret at all.

Calaunt (Metropolis, 38,706): Currently the largest and most influential city in the Vast, Calaunt has an iron grip on legitimate traffic entering or leaving the River Vesper. Unfortunately for the rest of the Vast, the city is not as vigilant about pirates or raiders using the river, as long as they do not threaten Calaunt. Though many visit the city on business, few are fond of the place. Its major industry is tanning, and the stench of its tanneries is often noticeable for miles. (Inner Sea sailors say that Calaunt can be found by smell even in the thickest of fogs.)

Calaunt is ruled by a band of evil adventurers who call themselves the Merchant Dukes, led by one who calls himself the Supreme Scepter. These rapacious brutes think nothing of confiscating property for their own gain. Visitors to Calaunt tread softly and avoid displays of wealth or magic.

Procampur (Large City, 24,631): An old, wealthy, independent trading port at the eastern mouth of the Dragon Reach, Procampur is famous across Faerûn for its walled districts, whose buildings all have slate roofs of a particular color. Reputed to be the single richest city along the northern Inner Sea, Procampur is known for its goldsmiths, gemcutters, gem trade, paucity of thieves, and strict local government. Built on the site of Proeskampalar, a dwarven underground town built about −153 DR, the human city of Procampur dates back to 523 DR.

A hereditary overlord, the Thultyrl, rules Procampur. The current Thultyrl is Rendeth of the Royal Blood (CG male human Ari3/Ftr6), a young, level-headed warrior whose family has distinctive copper-hued hair and gray-green eyes. A loyal wizard-advisor called the Hamayarch traditionally assists the Thultyrl. Some suspect that the current advisor, Alamondh (NE male human Sor10), is less than honest and just.

Tall fortified walls protect Procampur. The walls are pierced only by pairs of coast-road gates on each side of the harbor. The bustling harbor does not operate under the city's strict rules, and its buildings are the usual chaos of different styles, sizes, and roof hues. The harbor is home to fisherfolk, shipbuilders, and foreign traders. It holds all livestock and mounts (including training facilities, equipment, and stables) not belonging to the Procampan authorities.

A single huge, guarded gate opens from the harbor onto the Great Way, an avenue that joins all city districts. The Great Way runs straight east to the Castle District, which holds the gold-roofed Palace of the Thultyrl and the High Court, and the white-roofed stables and barracks of the city guards.

Gate guards patiently explain the city's rules to all who enter. In Procampur, each activity is confined to a particular district (or the harbor), and the authorities are strict, watchful, and competent. The government has smashed countless attempts to found thieves' guilds in the city, and its forces have decisively defeated both Mulmaster and Sembia in naval battles.

Ravens Bluff (Metropolis, 28,150): Second only to Calaunt in wealth, power, and importance, Ravens Bluff's position at the mouth of the Fire River makes it the port of departure for over a third of the Vast's agricultural exports. In addition, the city has long attracted adventurers of all stripes, thanks to an indulgent local government and plenty of mysteries and intrigues to unravel (most of which arise from the city's freewheeling atmosphere or its seedier underside). Ravens Bluff is also a center for the exchange and sale of magic items.

Ravens Bluff was nearly destroyed in the summer of 1370 DR, when an adventurer called Myrkyssa Jelan descended on the city at the head of an army composed of mercenaries and fell monsters. The short war left the city without a navy and very nearly without an army or means to support itself. The tenacious and resourceful citizens of Ravens Bluff, led by their new mayor, Lady Amber Thoden, rebuilt their fortunes with outstanding speed.

Myrkyssa Jelan's reasons for attacking the city became clear when, in the early days of 1372 DR, adventurers discovered that Amber Thoden was really Jelan, and she vanished during the resultant conflict. The former mayor and adventurers' friend, Charles O'Kane (LN male human Ftr17), once again presides over the tumultuous city.

Tantras (Large City, 21,816): Famous (or infamous) as the residence of the deity Torm during the Time of Troubles, Tantras is now among the leading cities of the Vast. A major portion of Tantras was ruined in 1358 DR when the avatars of Torm and Bane destroyed each other on the outskirts of the city. (The damage has long since been repaired.) Torm, always popular in the city, is now venerated as the savior of Tantras.

Tsurlagol (Large City, 17,594): Known as the Gateway to the Unapproachable East, this busy port is the southernmost city of the Vast. It serves as a crossroads for traders from the Vast, Impiltur, the Old Empires, and the Vilhon Reach. The city also plays host to a considerable number of dwarves who pass through on errands involving their scattered kin. Tsurlagol's location has some drawbacks, and the city has the dubious distinction of having been sacked and burned more times than any other city in the region. The current city rests on a hill composed of the foundations of at least twenty previous cities.

REGIONAL HISTORY

The origin of the name "the Vast" is lost in antiquity, but sages agree the name is derived from the orc kingdom of Vastar, which once controlled the entire eastern shore of the Dragon Reach. The orcs of Vastar fought the elves of Myth Drannor, launching several invasions against the western shore of the Reach in crude wooden ships and by land across the northern end of the Reach. In time, the orcs reduced the dense forests of the Vast to the grasslands and isolated stands of timber that remain today.

Vastar eventually fell after a series of defeats at the hands of the elves, though mounting pressure from dwarves pushing in from the west contributed to the orcs' downfall. Most of the dwarven expansion took place underground, and the Vast boasts a wealth of abandoned dwarven delvings to this day.

After the fall of the orcs, the dwarves established Roldilar, the Realm of Glimmering Swords (610–649 DR), when the resurgent orcs

prevailed above and below ground. Humans were quick to exploit the power vacuum left by the collapse of the dwarven kingdom. They came from the crowded Vilhon Reach and established a foothold south of the Fire River. From there, they expanded and pushed the orcs back from the lowlands. The city of Ravens Bluff was established over the ruins of Roldilar in 1222 DR and has grown steadily ever since.

PLOTS AND RUMORS

Most adventurers passing through the Vast wind up in Ravens Bluff at one time or another. The exploration of old dwarven ruins and rumors of great vaults never uncovered draw adventurers from all corners of Faerûn.

Shadow over Scardale: The PCs hear that a powerful mercenary captain is organizing an expeditionary force of hired soldiers and adventurers to invade and seize the town of Scardale. No one knows for sure who is sponsoring the captain—merchants in Tantras or Calaunt are most likely. Scardale would be a great asset to any city on the Vast, since it would provide a toehold on the western shore of the Dragon Reach. The PCs may be hired to prevent the undertaking, or perhaps to join it.

THE VILHON REACH

Capital: None
Population: 5,505,840 (humans 95%, dwarves 2%, elves 1%, lizard-folk 1%)
Government: Various kingdoms and independent city-states
Religions: Eldath, Helm, Lliira, Malar, Nobanion, Silvanus, Talos, Tempus, Tyr
Imports: Metal
Exports: Fish, horses, slaves, stone, wine
Alignments: N, LN, LG

This region shares its name with the body of water called the Vilhon Reach, a long southern arm of the Sea of Fallen Stars. The region encompasses much of the southern shore of the Sea of Fallen Stars, from the mouth of the Reach west and north to the mouth of the Wet River, and south to the Golden Plains. It is a fertile, rich land divided up into quarreling city-states and petty nations. For all its unrest, the Vilhon remains vital to the whole of Faerûn: It forms the trade link between the Lake of Steam, the Shaar, and the rest of the world through its ports on the Sea of Fallen Stars.

With the subtropical and humid weather of the Vilhon Reach, winter temperatures rarely reach the freezing point, snowfalls are rare, and heavy winter rains are common. Spring arrives early, and summer comes hard on its heels with scorching temperatures and oppressive humidity. Autumn brings cooler weather and lower humidity, but an autumn day in the Vilhon can be as warm as high summer in more northerly regions.

The three important nations of the Reach are Chondath, Sespech, and Turmish. In addition, a large number of independent city-states and minor local authorities occupy the region.

LIFE AND SOCIETY

Most sages recognize the Vilhon Reach as the cradle from which waves of humans spread forth to conquer and inhabit Faerûn. Something of this adventuresome spirit is still present in the Reach; many of the locals leave their homeland to seek their fortunes as mercenaries. The folk of the Vilhon Reach tend to welcome visitors as bearers of news or potential trading partners.

Spellcasters are well advised to keep a low profile in the Reach, where mages have a reputation for capricious use of power. The folk of the Reach have no patience for displays of flashy magic, nor any tolerance for those who use their spells carelessly.

For such a civilized and sophisticated populace, the folk of the Vilhon Reach show a remarkable respect for nature. This is partly due to the history of the area, which is marked by plagues and volcanic eruptions, and partially due to the influence of the Emerald Enclave. This druidic organization, founded in 374 DR and headquartered on the island of Ilighôn at the mouth of the Vilhon Reach, strives to hold human civilized development to a pace that nature can endure.

The geographical features and sites noted below include only those not within the territories of Chondath, Sespech, or Turmish (see below for those entries).

MAJOR GEOGRAPHICAL FEATURES

The Vilhon Reach itself is the dominant feature in the region, along with the surrounding islands and mountains. This deep arm of the Sea of Fallen Stars extends southwest from the Eyes of Silvanus to the Deepwing and Cloven Mountains. Its two major tributaries are the Nagaflow and Nun rivers.

Cloven Mountains: These mountains rise from the southern shore of the Deepwash. They earned their name from the broad gap where the Wintercloak River flows out of the Deepwash. Several tribes of goblinoids inhabit the wild and desolate range, but they spend most of their time fighting each other. A great catlike beast stalks the Cloven's peaks and highest valleys, preying on unwary goblinoids and the occasional hunter foolish enough to come seeking it.

Deepwash: This freshwater lake is the largest in the Vilhon. Tributaries from the Cloven and Deepwing mountains fill it with clear, cold water. The Wintercloak River is its main outlet. The lake teems with fish and also harbors a massive dragon turtle that lairs near Surkh.

Eyes of Silvanus: This pair of islands guards the entry to the Vilhon Reach. The western island, Ilighôn, is home to the Emerald Enclave organization. The eastern island, Wavecrest, is an uninhabited jungle teeming with wild animals and monsters.

The islands play havoc with ship's compasses, forcing navigation by lead line and by eye. This magnetic anomaly appears to be entirely natural. Dangerous reefs surround both islands. The only safe passage between the islands is at the Strait of Silvanus, which passes between Ixinos and Wavecrest to the east and Ilighôn to the west.

Shining Plains: This vast, dry grassland gets its name from the shimmering heat waves that rise from it most of the year. It holds the human cities of Assam, Lheshayl, and Ormath. It is also home to many tribes of centaurs and wemics, of which the Tenpaw wemic tribe is the best known. The territory's total population is roughly 423,000 inhabitants.

Wetwoods: This extensive bog is often sheathed in mist and occasionally hosts bandits who harass the trade routes leading north from Assam. The mist also hides small villages of lizardfolk, halflings, and other humanoids, none of which wish to become involved in the affairs of the Vilhon.

IMPORTANT SITES

These cities are presently independent, though that status is subject to change.

Assam (Small City, 6,513): Assam is the northernmost city on the Shining Plains, yet still several leagues south of the plains' northern edge. It lies on the south bank of the Wet River, where the road from Ormath crosses over a wide ford. It is an open city in more ways than one: Assam has no walls, and it is ruled jointly by the city-states of Lheshayl and Ormath. Assam is a merchant's town, dedicated to trade. Caravans, wagons, and herds of animals encircle the city like a waiting army.

Delegates from Lheshayl and Ormath make up the ruling council. The current mayor is Honlinar Tempest (LN male human Ftr7), a master politician who keeps things running smoothly. Honlinar serves at the pleasure of Lheshayl and Ormath, and he keeps his masters happy by dealing swiftly with any business interruptions.

Hlondeth (Metropolis, 45,360; total territory population 453,600): An independent walled city-state that commands the main road (the Holondar) west out of Turmish, Hlondeth also serves as a port conveniently located directly across from Arrabar, Chondath's capital. Hlondeth is a stunning, ancient metropolis whose architecture is dominated by serpent designs and shiny green marble brought out of the Orsraun Mountains. This beautiful stone is the city's most famous product, sold both carved into statues and in uncut blocks.

Hlondeth has been known as the City of Serpents since 527 DR. The city had been all but overrun by kobolds from the Orsraun Mountains. After a tenday, the defenders of Hlondeth faltered, and all seemed lost until a noble of the city, Shevron Extaminos, emerged from his walled residence at the head of a vast mass of snakes. Shevron's counterattack broke the siege and sent the kobolds fleeing. Shevron was killed in the fighting and given a hero's burial.

The Extaminos family has ruled Hlondeth ever since. Even mixing yuan-ti blood into the line did not shake the family's power. Hlondeth is currently ruled by a yuan-ti halfblood, Dediana Extaminos (LE female halfblood yuan-ti Sor10). Dediana has a snake's tail and no legs.

Dediana apparently rules with a light hand, for the city remains profitable and has good relationships with both Chondath and Turmish, though Hlondeth jealously guards its independence.

Lheshayl (Small City, 7,165): This westernmost city of the Shining Plains produces more and finer horses than Ormath and Assam put together. Lheshayl is ruled by Chief Entawanata (CN male human Ftr5), the latest of a long line of chiefs.

Nimpeth (Large City, 12,375; total territory population 25,700): Nimpeth is best known for its wine (its vineyards are among the best in Faerûn), its mercenaries, and its slave trade. River traffic coming down the Nagaflow stops at Nimpeth before venturing out into the Sea of Fallen Stars or moving on to other cities of the Vilhon.

Ormath (Small City, 6,513): Of the three cities of the Shining Plains, Ormath is the one most likely to go to war over the slightest insult. The city keeps pace with the traffic on the Pikemen's Folly (the road leading west from Hlondeth) and controls the junction between the Pikemen's Folly and the road leading north. Ormath shares control of Assam with Lheshayl, and it would like nothing better than to have sole control. However, it is unlikely that Lheshayl would tolerate such a move.

The current ruler of Ormath is Lord Quwen (LN male human Ftr11), a mountain of a man and a true warrior at heart. He frequently leads patrols outside the city, keeping the roads clear of bandits. Lord Quwen has become concerned about reports of hostile lizardfolk in the Wetwoods.

Sapra (Large Town, 3,226): Located on the isle of Ilighôn, Sapra has become a haven for beings who seek refuge from wizards. The druids of the Emerald Enclave granted the city a fixed amount of land and will not allow it to expand even an inch, so conditions are crowded. A part-time council of six elders rules the city, meeting twice a month or as needed. The current head of the council is Mayor Thomas Flagcairn (NG male human Exp4), the town blacksmith.

Surkh (Small City, 9,770): All the citizens of this city on the north shore of the Deepwash are lizardfolk. The lizardfolk keep to themselves, though they have cordial relations with the Emerald Enclave, Nimpeth, and Lheshayl. They fish in the Deepwash and rarely venture into the nearby human territories. Nothing threatens them in their isolation, except for an ancient dragon turtle living in the depths of the lake. Many here regard death in the creature's jaws as an honor, though not one they actively seek.

In spite of Surkh's isolationism, people of the Vilhon fear it, for it is well known than any humanoid convicted of a serious crime here is put to death, then served up as food to King Griss'tok (CN male lizardfolk Bbn9), who rules the city. He seldom receives visitors, for he speaks only Draconic. Gladiatorial combat is quite popular in Surkh, and gladiators willing to risk being eaten if they lose can make even more money here than in Reth (see the entry for Chondath, below).

REGIONAL HISTORY

The earliest recorded settlement in the Vilhon was the city of Alaghôn, now the capital of Turmish. By −37 DR, Alaghôn was a thriving port. The success of Alaghôn marked the rise of trade and wealth throughout the Vilhon, which gave rise to a collection of warring city-states, each striving to command as much trade and territory as possible.

Waves of settlers from the Vilhon founded the modern nation of Sembia and reclaimed the Vast after the fall of the dwarven kingdom there. Trade rivalries and expansionism within the Vilhon also brought about numerous wars as the powerful states of Chondath and Turmish struggled against each other and against the smaller city-states that popped up around them. Shifting alliances and internecine conflicts kept the two giants locked in a stalemate. Independent cities of the Vilhon fell under the control of Turmish or Chondath, but they often managed to break free with time.

The Vilhon has suffered numerous outbreaks of plague through the centuries, thanks to its warm climate, active trade, and crowded cities. Misused magic has started plagues as well. The first great plague swept the region in 75 DR, the Year of the Clinging Death. Half the human population of the Vilhon died as the disease ravaged the cities. An even more infamous plague struck in 902 DR, when the then-powerful nation of Chondath was in its fifth year of civil war. Wizards in the cities of Arrabar and Hlath, seeking to end the war, loosed ancient necromantic magic that slew two-thirds of the population of the Nun River valley and sent a wave of panic throughout the Vilhon. The Rotting War reinforced a loathing for wizards throughout the Vilhon and gave rise to the independence of Sespech, until then part of Chondath.

The Vilhon today is a land of commerce and intrigue. The independent city-states keep a wary eye on their larger, more powerful neighbors; the large countries keep a wary eye on each other; and everyone keeps a wary eye on the elves and on the Emerald Enclave.

chondath

Capital: Arrabar
Population: 1,982,880 (humans 96%, elves 2%, dwarves 1%)
Government: Confederation of city-states
Religions: Helm, Lliira, Malar, Talos, Tempus, Waukeen
Imports: Metal
Exports: Lumber, mercenaries, salt, spices
Alignment: N, LN, NE

To look on Chondath now, a scattering of allied city-states and towns strung along the southern shore of the Sea of Fallen Stars, it's hard to believe this is the same nation that produced the merchants who settled the powerhouse country of Sembia. Most other cities in the Vilhon were once part of its empire or suffered under its cruel armies. Now, Chondath is a land darkened by its fall from glory, by the grasping ambitions of its rulers, and by foes all around it.

Trade keeps a constant flow of folk leaving and arriving in Chondath from afar, and leads to more tolerance of varying ways and outlanders than visitors expect.

LIFE AND SOCIETY

Chondathans are generally slender, tawny-skinned folk with brown hair ranging from almost blond to almost black. Chondathans have green or brown eyes. Elves and half-elves are tolerated but not loved, and nonhumans in general are a quiet minority here.

Most Chondathans spend their lives engaged in intrigue, covert manipulation, and trade with distant lands (or at least investments in trade conducted by others). Chondathans strive to perfectly control their voices, faces, and mannerisms to reflect only those emotions they desire to display.

Chondathans distrust wizards and the bold use of magic. Folk in Chondath assume that Arrabar still holds deadly plague-hurling magic for a future lunatic to unleash. Chondathans are warlike, indulging in hunting games from an early age. They dress in a wide variety of fashions drawn from all over Faerûn, though leather armor and head coverings are common, thanks to the warm, damp climate.

MAJOR GEOGRAPHICAL FEATURES

Chondath includes territory stretching from the Nunwood in the northeast to the Nagaflow River in the west, and south to the River Arran, though its political control over the whole area is in doubt.

Chondalwood: The Chondalwood is a large expanse of forest south of Chondath. It is a rarity in that its borders continue to expand, particularly to the north. Satyrs and centaurs roam this land, as well as various plant creatures such as shambling mounds and tendriculoses. Mistletoe and other parasitic plants are common, as are all sorts of mushrooms and other fungi. The druids who live within the heart of the Chondalwood are savage, angry dervishes, as willing to attack paladins as orcs in their protection of the woodlands.

A sizable nation of elves also calls the Chondalwood home. These wild elves never joined the Retreat, and they remain hidden in the depths of the wood today, ready to repel human encroachment. The secretive ghostwise halflings live here as well, a barbaric folk of nomadic clans deep within the forest.

IMPORTANT SITES

Chondath's cities are its main points of interest today.

Arrabar (Metropolis, 61,012): Arrabar is a sprawling and ancient city, the capital of a shrunken empire. Despite its age, the metropolis is clean and well maintained. Its people are fisherfolk, merchants, craftsfolk, and mercenaries. Among the latter group are members of mercenary companies who rest here between assignments, and members of private armies permanently stationed in the capital.

Arrabar marks the western end of the so-called Emerald Way, the road that runs the length of Chondath, terminating at Hlath. The Golden Road from the south also ends here. The two roads and Arrabar's location on the Vilhon Reach make it a center for trade and help keep Chondath's coffers full.

The most resplendent edifice in the city is the Generon, the ruling palace of the Lord of Arrabar and all Chondath, Eles Wianar (NE male human Wiz13/Acm1). It is a stately dome glittering in gold and silver, ringed by barracks and strong points for Wianar's personal army. Along the outer walls of the city lie various noble houses, each with its own private army. Arrabar holds enough military might to wreak havoc anywhere. Though commoners in Arrabar are as wary of wizards as anyone in the Vilhon, Eles Wianar is not, and he has granted the Red Wizards an enclave.

Hlath (Large City, 23,969): Lord Darvis Shennelm (CN male human Ftr14) rules this busy port. Its chief export is lumber cut from the nearby Nunwood, an activity the Emerald Enclave monitors carefully. Hlath is locked in a minor trade war with Iljak over the flow of goods coming up the Old Road. Mercenaries and adventurers can always find work here guarding caravans (or attacking them).

Iljak (Large City, 17,432): This centrally located port was burned to the ground thirty years ago, the victim of a vicious trade war. The city, with its newly completed walls, has no intention of being caught unprepared a second time.

Iljak's chief industries are fishing and agriculture. Its fields produce a variety of grains that eventually make their way all across Chondath. The rule of Governor Anton Yinoran (NE male human Ftr13) is fairly tolerable by Chondathan standards. Many believe him to be a puppet of Arrabar, a charge he denies.

Reth (Metropolis, 63,191): Reth is located at the far north end of Chondath's coast. It gained its independence from Chondath during the Rotting War and deals with that country as little as possible today. Once famous as a training center for gladiators, Reth still holds gladiatorial combats twice a tenday in its great arena. Most of the gladiators are freeborn adventurers seeking fame and wealth, and many of them find it.

Reth's main industries are fishing, quarrying, and logging. The latter has caused some strain between Reth and the Emerald Enclave, and the city is slowly abandoning the lumber industry. Its main source of timber, the Nunwood, lies a fair distance away, and the trade is not profitable enough to risk the wrath of the druids.

Reth is ruled by a freely elected mayor who sees to the concerns of the city's citizens. The real power lies in the hands of the Seven Senators, autocrats who each tend to a particular aspect of the government. Meanwhile, the Zhentarim have started making overtures to the city officials, trying to gain a foothold for power in the Reach both politically and through the Banite Temple of Dark Eyes here.

Shamph (Metropolis, 32,685): Known as the Crossroads City because of its location at the junction of the Emerald Way and the Old Road leading south, Shamph is a thriving city that benefits hugely from the war between Iljak and Hlath. Merchants coming from the south hurriedly sell their goods in Shamph rather than enter the war zone. Merchants in Shamph then sell those goods to the highest bidder. Mayor Tian Redown (LN male human Rog11) has no intention of letting the situation end anytime soon, and does all he can to make sure the war continues.

REGIONAL HISTORY

Along the Vilhon Reach, the population repeatedly outstrips even prodigious local crop yields. As a result, the Vilhon has been the source of many wars, and the cradle of mercenaries and merchants who seek their fortunes elsewhere. Chondath was created in 144 DR by the spreading influence of the rich city of Arrabar, whose lords built the Emerald Way trade road to Shamph and eventually to Hlath.

This road allowed Arrabar to gather lands and cities under its sway. Five hundred years ago, Chondath was one of Faerûn's mightiest trading empires, expanding into what is now Sembia. Chondath's greatness was shattered on the battlefield. First came a short war wherein Chondath was defeated with contemptuous ease by the elves of Cormanthor, then forced to abandon its northern holdings and their rich lumber. Hard on the heels of this strife came the infamous Rotting War, a struggle between the rich coastal cities of Arrabar, Hlath, and Reth. The war ended at the Battle of the Fields of Nun in 902 DR with the slaughter of Chondath's best warriors and the release of a magical plague. The country was reduced to widely separated and independent cities, wary to this day of plague-bearing outsiders and strong magic of all sorts.

Chondath is now a coastal verge of city-states that turn their backs on the wild country near the monster-haunted Chondalwood. The coast east of the River Nun is a lawless land where mercenaries skirmish endlessly, and wolves and leucrottas roam untended farms

and devour unburied dead. The Shining Lord of Arrabar nominally rules all the land between the rivers Arran and Nun, but the cities of Orbrech and Timindar and forty-odd smaller settlements lie in ruins or are held by independent adventurer-lords. These minor lords eke out a hard living by hunting, raiding, and trading, and they spit on decrees sent out from "Shining Arrabar."

Eles Wianar longs to restore Chondath to its former glory, and many of his countryfolk feel the same way, even if they have no love for Wianar. A cold and calculating man with his own personal network of spies all over the Vilhon Reach, Wianar does nothing to stop the intrigues his nobles launch against each other, and he even lets them wage war *outside* Arrabar as they please (and can afford). He knows such pursuits keep the nobles busy fighting each other and serve to cloak his own acts against the lands and independent cities around Chondath.

PLOTS AND RUMORS

In Chondath's current state of decline, strong adventurers could easily make a name for themselves by clearing territory and claiming land as their own.

External Combustion: In the Chondalwood, explorers find ancient, toppled stone towers whose cellars are packed with gold coins. The treasure is guarded by strange, ravaging magic that makes wizards go mad and causes others to burst into flame and burn like torches. Eles Wianar has called for adventurers willing to "face a little danger" to report to him in Arrabar.

Some Chondathans say the treasure rumor is false, and that the lord is recruiting formidable adventurers for another purpose. Others say the ruins hold a powerful magic-using monster of some sort, or even an adventuring band that the lord wants dealt with, but no treasure at all. Whatever the truth of the matter, adventurers are arriving in Arrabar, and Wianar is reaching quiet deals with them before they slip away.

sespech

Capital: Ormpetarr
Population: 952,560 (humans 96%, dwarves 2%, elves 1%)
Government: Feudal barony with an elected baron
Religions: Eldath, Helm, Lliira, Malar, Talos, Tempus, Waukeen
Imports: Metal
Exports: Horses, mercenaries, salt
Alignment: LG, NG, N

Sespech is a barony located at the southwest end of the Vilhon Reach. Once a part of Chondath, Sespech maintains its independence through naval power and diplomacy.

Baron Aldorn Thuragar (LN male human Ftr12), sometimes known as the Foesmasher, rules Sespech. Once a bold adventurer, Thuragar relies on several old comrades from his adventuring company, the Band of Iron, to help him govern the country.

LIFE AND SOCIETY

The people of Sespech are tall and olive-skinned like the Chondathans to the east. Some keep their beards short, but most men shave regularly. The warriors of Sespech are skilled riders, and their cavalry is second only to the riders of Lheshayl. Due to the constant danger from Chondath, all young men of Sespech enter military service for at least six years and can be recalled at any time. Sespech needs all the soldiers it can impress into service.

Magic is more deeply suspect in Sespech than it is elsewhere in the Vilhon Reach. Anyone using magic to harm another can expect a quick execution.

Illustration by Carlo Arellano

Bazaar in the Vilhon

Open rule has always been important in Sespech. Twice each month, the cities of Sespech hold communal gatherings to discuss recent political developments and other matters of public concern. A minister from the court of Baron Thuragar attends every gathering. In rare cases, Thuragar himself attends.

MAJOR GEOGRAPHICAL FEATURES

Sespech extends from the River Arran in the east to the Nagaflow in the west, and south to the Golden Plains.

Golden Plains: Named for their tall, golden grasses, these fertile lands blanket the whole area between the Nagaflow and Arran rivers.

Nagawater: A large number of water nagas live in the southern end of this deep lake. By old agreement, the nagas stick to the south half the lake, and humans remain in the north. A line of floating and submerged buoys bearing *continual flame* spells marks the boundary. Many nagas born in the lake make their way up the Nagaflow to lair in the depths of the Chondalwood.

IMPORTANT SITES

Sespech lies between two great forests—the Chondalwood and the Winterwood—and two great rivers, the Arran and the Nagaflow. Its folk live along the northern shores of the Nagawater.

Elbulder (Large City, 12,701): The Old Road leading north from Torsch provides a steady stream of travelers and trade to Elbulder. Venturesome souls who follow the road through the Chondalwood find the city a welcome place of rest, though its citizens are seldom impressed by tales of encounters with wild elves or sylvan monsters.

The current mayor of Elbulder is Gavilon Jostins (NG male human Wiz16), a retired adventurer who came to rule the city when Baron Foesmasher took over Sespech. Soon after Gavilon took control of Elbulder, Chondathan troops attacked with orders to capture the city. Gavilon drove off the soldiers with *fireball* and *lightning bolt* spells, and the citizens of Elbulder admitted that wizards could be handy to have around.

Fort Arran: This outpost guards the road south into the heart of Sespech and keeps a constant watch on Chondath. If a war is to be fought, Fort Arran may well be the site of the first battle. The garrison at the fort is charged with delaying the Chondathans until messengers can be sent to Mimph, Elbulder, and Ormpetarr. Serving at Fort Arran is considered a great honor.

General Marcius Stonehall (LG male dwarf Ftr11) leads the garrison of one thousand soldiers. Marcius served with Baron Thuragar and Lord-Mayor Gavilon of Elbulder during their adventuring days, but none of the trio discusses those adventures in public.

Mimph (Metropolis, 27,518): Mimph is only miles by sea from Arrabar, and no love is lost between the two cities. Traders normally conduct business exclusively in one city or the other. Ships from Arrabar board vessels bound for Mimph from time to time and confiscate their cargoes. This piracy led Baron Thuragar to create his navy, with Mimph as a base.

Though no road connects Mimph to the rest of Sespech, the city receives a reasonable amount of overland trade, especially from merchants who distrust Chondath. Caravans leave the Old Road at Ormpetarr and either travel cross-country or transfer their cargoes to boats that sail over the Nagawater and out into the Reach.

The current overlord of Mimph is Admiral Kalisa Tauno (NG female moon half-elf Rgr14 of Lurue), one of the few high officials in Sespech who is not one of Thuragar's old adventuring companions. The high priest of the city's newest church is Marasa Ferrentio (LN female human Clr16 of Helm), once the Band of Iron's cleric.

Ormpetarr (Metropolis, 55,037): The capital of Sespech houses Baron Thuragar Foesmasher himself, along with the bulk of the country's military. It is an ancient, walled metropolis on the east shore of the Nagawater whose major industries are trade, horse raising, fishing, and agriculture. Ormpetarr handles all the trade moving along the Golden Road from Innarlith, and it serves as a banking center as well.

The city is far from peaceful. Bandits raid the city's caravans, the baron endures assassination attempts, and the city thieves' guild forces bloody confrontation in the shops and streets. The current head of the thieves' guild, Haskar Corintis (LE male human Rog15/Asn2/Gld2), is behind the trouble. He despises the baron for bringing law and order back to the city. Chondath finances Haskar's activities, but the guildmaster would be the baron's foe even if he wasn't receiving pay from a foreign power.

REGIONAL HISTORY

The rulers of Chondath sent settlers into what was to become Sespech around 150 DR to secure a source of horses for its cavalry. Burgeoning trade from the south helped the new settlements grow rapidly, and Sespech prospered alongside Chondath for decades. Sespech declared its independence from Chondath during the Rotting War, and since that time it has been held by a number of rebels, occupying forces, and adventurers.

Baron Thuragar came to power after a mysterious series of assassinations convinced the last baron to seek safety closer to the Lord of Chondath's court in Arrabar. Thuragar has given the people stability by removing opportunists from high posts and replacing them with trusted friends. Sespech currently enjoys moderate taxes and firm, fair justice.

Thuragar has used his popularity to institute a program of conscription that insures an adequate force for self-defense. The soldiers of Sespech, conscripts and professionals alike, wear purple feathers in their helms to signify their loyalty.

The baron is engaged in a shipbuilding program. He forged a trade alliance with merchants from Hlondeth, but Thuragar's overtures to Hlondeth may be working too well. The ambassador from Hlondeth is Dmetiro Extaminos, son of the evil ruler of that city. Dmetiro is courting the baron's daughter, Glisena. Neither Thuragar nor Glisena desires the match, but Sespech cannot afford to offend Hlondeth.

PLOTS AND RUMORS

Spies from the other powers of the Vilhon, villainous merchant princes, and monsters from the dangerous forests nearby infest Sespech.

Baron for a Day: A calm, self-assured official approaches the PCs with an offer to make one of them "baron for a day." The character is offered a brief job magically impersonating the baron. The character might be asked to pay a visit to Elbulder, inspect the fleet in Mimph, or preside at a celebration in Ormpetarr.

A double might be needed for any number of reasons. Perhaps the baron is about to embark on some secret negotiations, or perhaps he needs to throw a pack of assassins off the scent. The character's companions can go along disguised as guards or members of the baronial party. The assignment is dangerous, but the pay is good (500–1,000 gp per character). If attacked, the characters are to slay their assailants if necessary, but capture them if possible. Live captives bring an additional bonus.

TURMISH

Capital: Alaghôn
Population: 1,693,440 (humans 78%, dwarves 9%, halflings 5%, elves 3%, gnomes 2%, half-elves 1%, half-orcs 1%)
Government: Republic
Religions: Chauntea, Eldath, Helm, Lliira, Loviatar, Nobanion, Silvanus, Selûne, Tempus, Tyr
Imports: Luxury goods, metal
Exports: Glass, grain, lumber, mercenaries, salt
Alignments: N, LN, LG

Gaulauntyr "Glorytongue"

The copper dragon Gaulauntyr was once a little-known but extremely effective stealer of gems and food around Waterdeep. She recently fled her former haunts after a spectacular night battle above the City of Splendors that involved two hostile dracoliches, several wizards of both the Watchful Order and the Cult of the Dragon (her true attackers), and a hastily scrambled flight of griffon-riding City Guards.

The Cult of the Dragon's agents in Waterdeep and Luskan had discovered the full extent of the activities of the Thief Dragon by piecing together reports of what they at first took to be several minor wyrms or wizards employing magical dragon disguises. When they realized that these activities were the work of the elusive dragon known to adventuring wizards as Glorytongue, they mounted a concerted attempt to destroy or magically enthrall her.

Gaulauntyr escaped the battle by luck, speed, frantic acrobatics, and the intervention of Waterdeep's defenders. Wounded and pursued, she abandoned her lair on tiny Alsapir's Rock (just off the Sword Coast near Mount Sar) and her traditional hunting grounds along the coast, from Baldur's Gate to Luskan. Gaulauntyr is a loner by nature and has often moved her domain and dwelling to avoid other dragons, preferring a life of stealth around human cities to slumbering in a lair.

This mature adult dragon now lairs in a ruined manor house in the woods southeast of Arrabar, in the wild southern verges of Chondath. She spends her days observing the doings of humans up and down the Vilhon Reach, devising new ways to steal gems or food (mainly exotic cheeses, of which she is fond).

Extremely intelligent and cautious, Gaulauntyr cloaks her true form in illusions. She sometimes hides in forest glades, ruins, or abandoned warehouses, on rooftops, or under cover of darkness. An accomplished mimic of human voices, she also has a shrewd grasp of human and draconic natures. This makes it easy for her to think several steps ahead of her opponents, so that she always has a ready escape route, a scheme to disappear, or a way to adopt a disguise, and alternative plans if the main ones fail.

Gaulauntyr's nickname comes from her habit of delivering touch spells with her elongated tongue. Many dragons and others she has robbed seek to recover their losses, but aside from the Cult of the Dragon (which seems unaware of exactly where she now lives), Glorytongue has no strong or persistent foes. Increasingly, she has taken to robbing exhausted or wounded adventurers who make camp in a stronghold they believe secure.

Turmish lies in the northwest of the Vilhon Reach. It is a rich, fertile, farming land of villages and few cities—peaceful, civilized, and well managed. Turmish features rolling fields divided by hedges or dense rows of trees, with ample room for wild creatures. The mountains to the west harbor orcs, kobolds, and other monsters, but few raid Turmish thanks to well-organized mercenary bands that serve as local militias.

Turmish's natives have an excellent reputation as fair traders, welcome throughout the Inner Sea. The area is remarkably popular with adventurers despite its lack of monsters. Buried treasure abounds (at least according to bards' tales), and the area offers plenty of ruins and wild lands to explore.

LIFE AND SOCIETY

The people of Turmish are tall, mahogany-skinned, and comely. The men of the trading class wear long beards with the ends carefully squared off. The phrase "square as a Turmian beard" signifies anything well or carefully done.

In addition to its farms, Turmish is known for its ornate and finely crafted armor. This armor is embellished with embossing, spires, and raised, fluted curves, mixing elven and human styles. It is sometimes hard to know which is more important to a Turmian fighter, his armor or his beard.

The Turmians have a variety of customs, both quaint and bizarre. Among the best known is the tradition of the guest dish. Anyone visiting a Turmian home, even on business, is expected to present a fine dish of food. Snails in an ornate bowl made from a skull are a perennial favorite.

MAJOR GEOGRAPHICAL FEATURES

The Orsraun Mountains form Turmish's western border. The Aphrunn Mountains lie to the south and the Sea of Fallen Stars to the north.

Mountains of the Alaoreum: These northernmost peaks of the Orsraun Mountains nestle against the Gulthmere Forest. Treefall Pass separates them from the rest of the Orsraun. The range includes Mount Andrus, a semiactive volcano sacred to worshipers of Talos, who are rumored to be in league with an evil being or community dwelling in the heart of the volcano. The Alaoreum also holds Ironfang Deep, a great dwarven delving that produces high-quality iron ore, gems, and gold. Ironfang Deep supplies most of Turmish's iron.

Aphrunn Mountains: These mountains have long served as a shield of stone between Turmish and the towns and city-states than have sprung up on the shores of the Reach. Travelers are familiar with Mount Kolimnis, also called Eversmoke for its volcanic activity. Over a decade ago, the mountain threatened to destroy the city of Gildenglade, but the eruption subsided before inflicting any damage.

Orsraun Mountains: The largest, tallest mountain range south of the Spine of the World is a well-known abode for all sorts of evil creatures, including kobolds, orcs, goblinoids, and red dragons. It is a wild place, untouched by the civilized lands of Turmish.

IMPORTANT SITES

Turmish is dotted with hundreds of agricultural communities too small to appear on most maps, all interconnected with winding country lanes so tangled that they would drive an invader mad. Its few large cities are the jewels of the country.

Alaghón (Metropolis, 88,704): Nearly the entire capital of Turmish is built of stone. A great fire in 352 DR razed the city, and laws have since required that all new construction must be stone or brick. Older buildings have been expanded and remodeled numerous times, and have several layers of old walls behind facades. This construction has created thousands of cubbyholes and hiding places in the city. Games of hide-and-seek are popular among Alaghón's children.

A freely elected council governs Turmish's ancient capital. Each citizen, regardless of race and social position, has a single vote. The chief speaker is chosen from the ranks of this Free Council. The duties of this chief speaker are few, the most dramatic being to maintain local and mercenary units for defense from pirates and other nations. The rest of the country is organized along similar lines.

Gildenglade (Metropolis, 48,384): This city is the second largest in Turmish, home to dwarves, elves, and half-elves. Its economy is based on woodcutting, woodworking, and mining. The elves rule the community and handle all negotiations with the Emerald Enclave. The elves are skilled enough in forestry and preservation that they probably have the best rapport with the Enclave of any city in the Reach. The dwarf population concentrates on mining the unusually pure veins of gold that honeycomb the earth below Gildenglade.

Nonthal (Large City, 12,902): The smell of manure mixed with the odor of slaughterhouses and tanneries provides an unforgettable olfactory experience for visitors to this town. Still, the lure of gold draws the curious to its streets and inns. Nonthal was named for a wizard who set up shop here over a century ago. He built a cottage behind a local inn, erected signs warning people to leave him alone, then disappeared. His house was ransacked after his presumed death, and directions were found to a place called Nonthal's Hold, a ruin said to hold a *portal* or series of *portals* to distant locales.

REGIONAL HISTORY

The origins of Turmish go back to the founding of Alaghón in −37 DR. Alaghón eventually became the capital of a powerful confederation of warlike, mercantile city-states similar to Chondath in its heyday. In 142 DR, the Lord of Alaghón, Dempster Turmish, expanded his control to include all the territory Turmish encompasses today. Dempster Turmish's efforts to expand his borders to include the city-state of Hlondeth and beyond never quite came to fruition, and by the time of his death in 150 DR, Hlondeth remained free.

After Dempster's death, Turmish had no strong leader for over a century. Political control ebbed back and forth between the various nobles and merchant houses. Turmish's commercial power remained undimmed during this period, however, because the Turmians never let their political ambitions get in the way of business. By 1242 DR, control of Turmish passed into the claws of the blue dragon Anaglathos, who insinuated himself into the capital and staged a coup. The dragon ruled as a despot for five years, nearly driving the country into ruin.

The paladin Corwin Freas slew Anaglathos and liberated Turmish in 1247 DR. Uncomfortable with ruling, Corwin abdicated the following year after creating the republic that rules Turmish today. Corwin was assassinated in a coup attempt in 1254 DR, but the coup failed and the republic stood.

Turmish remains peaceful but wary today. Its ships patrol the Vilhon Reach, keeping trade routes open, and its mercenary militia keeps the country's borders secure. Turmish worries about Chondath's rising power, but it has not offered Sespech assistance for fear of provoking Chondath.

PLOTS AND RUMORS

Like elsewhere in the Vilhon Reach, mercenary companies and adventuring bands perform jobs normally associated with a local militia. They are hired out to scout and patrol the "wild areas" of Turmish.

Vanishing Fans: Folk in Turmish are flocking to see the half-elf known as the Songbird, a singer and actor of extraordinary beauty, grace, and talent. She's performing a new cycle of ballads about the mythical Princess Arissaea, a favorite subject of songs in the Inner Sea for some centuries, who grows from sheltered innocent, to slave, to pirate, to dragon slayer. She eventually liberates her conquered homeland, ascends its throne, and finds love and happiness.

With each performance, members of the Songbird's audience disappear. No common theme (wealth, gender, trade, or place of residence) is discerned among the missing, but since the group includes several heirs to family wealth or trading companies, concern is growing. Adventurers are being hired both to locate the missing persons and to capture whoever has conducted the abductions. The Songbird herself was questioned, but she pleads ignorance of any wrongdoing. Divination spells do not seem to work on the Songbird.

western Heartlands

Capital: None
Population: 1,641,600 (humans 78%, elves 7%, half-elves 4%, halflings 4%, half-orcs 3%, gnomes 2%, dwarves 1%)
Government: City-states, each with a different government
Religions: All
Imports: Ale, fish, herbs, iron, rugs
Exports: Gold, pottery, silver, wool
Alignment: All

The Western Heartlands cover a vast area between the Storm Horns of Cormyr and the Sword Coast south of Waterdeep, from the Lizard Marsh in the northwest to the Lonely Moor on the fringes of Anauroch in the northeast, down to Beregost and Green Fields in the southwest and Easting on the border of the Dragon Coast in the southeast.

To the caravan drivers of Amn and Sembia, the Western Heartlands are known as "miles and miles of miles and miles"—windswept, grassy flats skirting impassable bogs, badlands, rolling hills, high moors, and lonely forests, all of which are filled with monsters. The farmers, frontier folk, walled-city dwellers, and other hardy souls who live here are strong and independent enough to carve successful lives out on the frontier where skill and intelligence count for more than one's bloodline. The Western Heartlands are home to dozens of separate walled cities, racial enclaves, farm towns, monasteries, fortified strongholds, and armed domains.

The Western Heartlands welcome ambitious adventurers. A dozen crumbled empires have sought to conquer or dominate the region, leaving behind fortifications built upon by waves of subsequent would-be monarchs. Others left behind treasure troves, high and perilous magic, or both. Unlike the densely packed regions in the Heartlands and the North, the Western Heartlands require long stretches of overland travel between destinations—but at least no one freezes en route.

LIFE AND SOCIETY

Inhabitants of the Western Heartlands live in scattered wilderness settlements. The people of the west tend to be stubborn, independent, and proud of their ability to thrive in a challenging environment. Their frontier spirit is complemented by a trader's willingness to greet strangers as potential friends rather than potential enemies. Unlike some civilized people of the eastern nations, the folk of the west look upon adventurers favorably, viewing them as potential customers, good allies in a fight, and possibly even as neighbors.

MAJOR GEOGRAPHICAL FEATURES

The term "Western Heartlands" is something of a catch-all. It includes a broad swath of land between Amn and the North, stretching from the Sword Coast to the Dragon Coast of the Inner Sea. Its arbitrary borders are subject to debate.

Battle of Bones: As travelers approach the region known as the Battle of Bones, the rolling grassland of the west gives way to chalky white soil dotted by stunted trees. Bones and other signs of an ancient battle begin to outnumber rocks, until the explorer stumbles through a wasteland of bleached bones that has resisted nature's cleansing elements for nearly three hundred years.

In 1090 DR, a horde of goblins and orcs out of the Stonelands met an army of humans, elves, and dwarves north of the Sunset Mountains. The warriors of Tyr, Corellon, and Moradin triumphed, killing uncounted thousands of the invading orcs in a six-day battle. Even the elves' healing magic and the clerics' powers of resurrection could not prevent thousands of the defenders from joining the orcs in death. Three hundred years later, the site of the great battle is still a cursed and haunted land, covered with bones and remnants of the battle that are nearly a foot deep and sometimes pile into great drifts.

The sixty square miles covered by the battle are horrid hunting grounds for undead: zombies, skeletons, ghouls, wights, wraiths, spectres, and even liches. Young clerics of militant faiths frequently journey to the Battle of Bones to prove themselves in battle against the undead. Their efforts are countered by clerics of Velsharoon and other deities who view the battlefield as a site for their own unholy pilgrimages.

Cloak Wood: South of Baldur's Gate and north of Candlekeep, the Cloak Wood is a thickly overgrown ancient forest that looms along the shore south of the Sword Coast. Unlike the cliffs to the north, the Cloak Wood's shoreline theoretically allows a ship to moor and send a small boat to shore for water and supplies. In practice, only desperate mariners dare the wood's nasty population of beasts, monsters, and vicious fey.

The sages of Candlekeep assert that Cloak Wood contains *portals* to several other parts of Faerûn.

Far Hills: If they were not dwarfed by the peaks of the north and south branches of the Sunset Mountains, the Far Hills might be considered mountains themselves. It's not the region's rocky ridges, hidden valleys, and thick stands of twisted trees that keep travelers away—it's the forbidding spires of Zhentil Keep's western fortress, Darkhold. Until recently, Darkhold's control on the region was absolute, but the mage Sememmon's departure has led to confusion, conflict, and laxness among Darkhold's defenders.

Fields of the Dead: Like the Battle of Bones, the Fields of the Dead is the site of an ancient battle. Unlike the orc remains that litter the Battle of Bones, the deaths on the Fields of the Dead resulted from fights between human empires, kingdoms of the Sword Coast, and Amn, who all sparred for control of the area's rich farmland. The rolling farms of the area have had five centuries to recover from the last major war, but old armor, skeletons, unused scrolls, weapons, and magical bric-a-brac resulting from the intersection of bizarre spells still turn up under the plow.

Forest of Wyrms: The great redwoods and thick pines of this wood shelter a multitude of green dragons, who think of themselves as masters of the forest. The wyrms correctly estimate their control of their territory. Dragon slayers come here to hunt, becoming heroes or dying in the attempt.

Harpers and other heroes used to journey to the forest to battle a lich who lived in a castle named Lyran's Hold, but two adventurers finally killed the lich and occupied the hold in its place. New reports indicate that the adventurers who displaced the lich have inherited its evil ways. Lyran's Hold has returned to the list of potential adventuring sites shared over firelight or mugs of ale by seasoned heroes. If new adventurers manage to kill the hold's present occu-

Illustration by Matt Wilson

The Forest of Wyrms

pants, the newcomers would be well advised to keep moving—there's no need to stay for over a tenday in the hold, unless they wish to risk suffering the same fate as the previous occupants.

Forgotten Forest: A single mighty forest once covered the center of Faerûn. The Forgotten Forest is a fragment of that ancient wood, a living cathedral of oak, walnut, and shadowtop populated by a large treant community. The treants mourn each mile that the forest has lost to the spread of the Great Desert, Anauroch. Another magical disaster to the south, the Marsh of Chelimber, has encroached upon the forest from that direction.

Druids and rangers are among the few who pass safely through the groves of treants. One of the great druids of Faerûn, Pheszeltan (N male human Drd17/Dis4 of Silvanus), lives in the thickest part of the forest. He speaks to those who have the skill to reach him, but his home is less accessible than the highest mountaintop of the Graypeaks west of the forest.

Green Fields: Over the centuries, innumerable petty warlords and ambitious merchants have established fiefdoms on the northern fringes of the grasslands north of the Snakewood and southeast of the Wood of Sharp Teeth. The current halfling-who-would-be-queen is Dharva Scatterheart (N female lightfoot halfling Exp2/Rog2/Sor6). Dharva likes the space, the running water, the lack of taxation (from anyone other than her), and the constant stream of caravans attempting the shortcut from the route through the Cloud Peaks over to Berdusk.

With the aid of a silent partner who has turned out to be a Shadow Thief of Amn, Dharva has erected a palisade town named Greenest along the trail to Berdusk. She's not entirely happy that the Shadow Thieves are her partners, but so far they've behaved themselves and confined themselves to business. That could change, of course. It wouldn't be the first time that a Green Fields enterprise failed because of incompatible partners.

Graycloak Hills: In 1335 DR, moon elves from neighboring Evereska moved into this range of high hills and small mountains. At the time, the range was known as the Tomb Hills for the elven burial sites dotting the slopes and valleys. The graves are still there, but the elven undead that formerly plagued the region were put to rest by determined moon elven clerics.

This does not mean that the hills are now open to adventurers and other travelers. On the contrary, the slopes are perpetually shrouded in gray mist. The elves move silently through the mist wearing gray *cloaks of elvenkind*, on missions that outsiders do not fully understand. Some whisper that the elves have discovered a cache of Netherese magic that they wish to keep out of the hands of outsiders. There may be Netherese magic left in the hills, but that's not what has brought the elves here. The moon elven settlements in the Graycloak Hills are forts and spyposts for watching over Anauroch and the Graypeak Mountains.

The vigilance of the moon elves has been justified, if not exactly rewarded, by the recent arrival of the Netherese city of Shade in Anauroch and the escape of the phaerimms through the shattered Sharn Wall. Evereska and its outposts in these hills face a high and dire peril far more dangerous than the occasional orc horde or flight of dragons.

The elves' focus on stealth and caution means that their control of the entire Graypeak Hills range is not absolute. Ambitious human adventurers have entered the Graycloaks without notice, quickly delving into an old tomb and escaping before the moon elves retaliate.

High Moor: Largest of the open moorlands in western Faerûn, the High Moor is infamous as the haunt of monsters who loom out of the cold mists to consume wayfarers. The High Moor is a rocky wilderness, vast and uninhabited aside from its fearsome monsters—notably trolls, though travelers who've actually crossed the moor talk more of orcs and hobgoblins.

The High Moor is bounded on the west by the Misty Forest, whose dim blue glades and deep groves have always carried a fey and deadly reputation, and on the east by the Serpent Hills, where snakes and yuan-ti lurk. These crag-studded, rolling lands are said to hide the ruins of long-fallen kingdoms—but just which kingdoms is a topic over which sages argue furiously. Minstrels sing colorful but contradictory ballads of these lost realms. ("The bones and thrones of lost lands" is a favorite phrase, all that's left of a long-forgotten song.) What is certain is that the moor holds its share of ruined castles, stone tombs, and caverns, almost all of which have yielded treasure to the bold and fortunate.

Wolves and leucrottas are scarce on the moor, since trolls, bugbears, and hobgoblins have slain the other large beasts of prey. The relative scarcity of natural predators allows hoofed grazing animals of all sorts to flourish, from small rock ponies to shaggy sheep. Large, well-armed bands of coastal farmers and down-on-their-luck merchants venture onto the moor in warm months, seeking horses to round up for training and sale elsewhere, or livestock that can be taken away. The greedy are warned that hobgoblins and worse always find and ambush large-scale intrusions, and small human bands pay for these raids with their lives.

Like the Evermoors north of the Dessarin, the High Moor is studded with moss- and lichen-festooned rocky outcrops, breakneck gullies, and rivulets of clear water that spring from rocks, wind across the moor for a time, then sink into the soil. The moor is also shrouded by frequent mists, since the prevailing winds are gentler than the chill, mist-clearing winds of the North.

Highstar Lake: High in the broken land of the northern High Moors, this eerily beautiful lake attracts human, dwarven, and elven pilgrims who come just to stare at the lake's legendary crystalline perfection. Adventurers can't believe that something so beautiful isn't loaded with strange magical powers, so they tell stories about drowned temples, sunken Netherese airships, and lost civilizations beneath the lake's waters.

Lizard Marsh: Instead of flowing freely into the Sea of Swords, the River Delimbiyr dissolves into a morass of waterways threading beneath cold-weather cypress trees festooned with hanging moss. Humans avoid the five hundred-plus square miles of the marsh, unless they intend to tangle with the lizardfolk, dinosaurs, and black dragons that lurk in its shallow waters. Few of the dinosaurs grow to great size, since they are fiercely hunted by the lizardfolk who give the marsh its name.

Under their current chief, a warrior named Redeye (CE male lizardfolk Bbn11/Chm5 of Talos), the lizardfolk have succeeded in driving all other intelligent denizens out of the marsh. They view the river waters south of Daggerford as their own hunting ground. Skirmishes with caravans and patrols from Daggerford usually go against the lizardfolk, but not so often that they avoid such fights.

Thanks in part to the proximity of the sea, the Lizard Marsh never fully freezes over, though its waters grow slushy in the deep winter. The lizardfolk hate the slush and "go to ground" during the cold spells, building lairs in the giant cypresses until the water returns to normal.

Lonely Moor: Leucrottas, perytons, and bulettes infest this high waste of dust, rock, and stunted trees. Gnolls and orcs hunt the monsters when they are not being hunted themselves. Life for the orcs is still pretty miserable, but the gnolls have recently found other employment thanks to the Zhents, who pay them to attack everyone else's caravans but leave Zhent travelers alone. The safety of the route between the Lonely Moor and the Forgotten Forest is particularly important to the Zhents now that the arrival of the city of Shade has disrupted their Anauroch routes.

Marsh of Chelimber: Some of the ruins dotting this misty lowland swamp belonged to the land's original ruler, Prince Chelimber. Chelimber feuded with a mighty wizard known as the Wizard of the Crag back in the early days of Waterdeep. The prince hired magical assassins to kill the wizard, who fought back with awful magic. The battle spiraled out of control, killing the prince and destroying his lands. A few of the old ruins are too magical or intimidating for the marsh inhabitants to tamper with, such as Dunkapple Castle.

Lizardfolk and bullywugs skulk through the thousands of square miles of the swamp that still bear Chelimber's name, occasionally striking against the Zhent caravans that pass nearby. The interior of the swamp and the oldest ruins are dominated by sivs. The sivs prefer to practice their enigmatic monastic disciplines in privacy, but adventurers are sometimes welcome as a change in diet from marsh bird and bullywug.

Misty Forest: Wood elves, hybsils, druids, and rangers move comfortably through the fogs of this evergreen forest. Others have the uncomfortable sense that they don't truly belong on its wooded slopes, particularly not the savage orcs and other barbarians that occasionally sneak through the forest from the High Moor to strike at the neighboring Trade Way. Though the Misty Forest's wood

Eldenser, the Worm who Hides in Blades

One of the strangest of all dragons currently active in Faerûn is the Lurker, a brass male wyrm more properly called Eldenser. To bards and tavern tale-tellers alike, he is the Worm Who Hides in Blades.

Eldenser uses spells to leave his withered, magically preserved body in hideaways, then transfer his sentience into the blade of any tempered, edged, metallic weapon, from where he can perceive the world and employ magic as if in his own body. He roams all Faerûn thus, inside swords, considering none of the world his territory but completely free for him to traverse. Of late, his favorite hunting ground is Amn, Tethyr, and the trading territories between Waterdeep and the Dragon Coast. He has acquired or developed magic that enables him to "jump" from one sword to another if his current carrier is engaged in activities not to his interest, or has left his chosen hunting ground.

Eldenser ignores other dragons unless they discover him. He cheerfully battles attempts to menace or control him, and he resists any dragon attempting to hoard "his" blade. A friend to ad-venturers (who as blade-carriers can bring him excitement and travel), Eldenser is wary only of spellcasters who want to magically examine the blade he's in. He actively spies on anyone working on magic that might allow a dragon to regenerate or replace an aged, crumbling body.

Eldenser is driven by the need to observe all living things and learn how they act in all stages of life. The knowledge he has acquired gives him a fine grasp of the causes and effects of deeds and events. A contented loner, Eldenser enjoys fine human-food and drink.

Currently, he devotes himself to observing the beauties of Faerûn and the entertaining strivings of its inhabitants (half-elves, humans, and elves in particular). Eldenser tries to influence political events to aid heroes, weaken authority, and promote increased opportunities for his future entertainment. He follows a mysterious process for achieving draconic immortality known as Ossavitor's Way, the details of which are unknown to humanoids.

elves are loath to admit it, they perform a valuable service for caravans and other travelers headed to Daggerford, Secomber, or Boareskyr Bridge, providing temporary respite from the constant vigilance required to survive the attention of the creatures that infest the High Moor.

River Chionthar: The River Chionthar links Baldur's Gate and the Sword Coast with the inland cities of Elturel, Scornubel, Berdusk, and Iriaebor. Barges can travel as far inland as Iriaebor, at which point they must unload and take their goods overland.

Serpent Hills: The Serpent Hills are a great expanse of rocky hills rolling and broadening to the west until they become the High Moor. The Serpent Hills see more rainfall than the moor, providing scrub cover for the region's innumerable snakes and groves of hardy trees to provide ambush shelter for the land's roving yuan-ti. Copper and red dragons fight for possession of the choicest ridgelines not already occupied by ancient silver dragons.

Skull Gorge: The orc and hobgoblin shamans who survived the six-day Battle of the Bones fled south into this narrow cut along the upper course of the River Reaching, daring their mainly human pursuers to come in and take them. The human warriors obliged them, slaying the demons and devils the orcs summoned to defend their position along with the goblinoids. Usually victors have the luxury of looting the bodies of the fallen, but the battlefield of Skull Gorge was quickly abandoned to powerful demons that outlived their summoners. Supposedly, much treasure is hidden in the river, in the white stone caverns along the gorge's walls or in the lairs of beings it would be wise not to encounter.

Sword Coast: The lands along the Sea of Swords south of Waterdeep and north of the mouth of the River Chionthar at Baldur's Gate are known as the Sword Coast. The name comes from the white cliffs that rise like a flashing blade from the shore to heights of up to half a mile, cutting off the sea and the land along hundreds of miles of coastline. It is no accident that the two greatest cities of the Sword Coast, Waterdeep and Baldur's Gate, bracket either side of the great cliffs, because these are the only sites for hundreds of miles in which ships can safely moor.

Trollbark Forest: There's scarcely a corner of Faerûn that does not have a forest, mountain range, or moor named for the trolls. Like the rest, the Trollbark Forest is thick with these monsters. The forest's dense underbrush, thick twisted stands of ash, and many bogs make it a perfect hunting ground for monsters that can crash through thorny barriers and nests of poisonous snakes without taking permanent damage.

Trollclaw Ford: The trade route known as the Coast Way does not actually run along the Sword Coast. It turns inland at Baldur's Gate to stay away from the Troll Hills and to cross the Winding Water at Trollclaw Ford at the edge of the Trollclaws. The ford is shallow and functional, but the water is black and foul, still poisoned by the death of the deity Bhaal to the north at Boareskyr Bridge. The crossing is fraught with danger, since trolls haunt the region, especially in hours of darkness.

Trollclaws: Caravans from the Coast Way that miscalculate their water rations send expeditions into the broken hills and boulder fields of the Trollclaws to find the natural springs above the tainted Winding Water. More often than not, the springs serve as watering holes and ambush spots for trolls, tall mouthers, and other murderous monsters.

Troll Hills: The Troll Hills are overrun by the same screaming, festering horde of trolls that lurks in the Trollbark Forest to the north. Some say that the trolls that live in the caverns beneath the hills have a kingdom of their own. The truth is that these trolls belong to a number of different competing realms that would be happy to eradicate each other, if not for the miracle of troll regeneration that lets them survive damage they do to each other with teeth and claws.

Winding Water: The Winding Water dips and hums across the center of the Western Heartlands, growing from a small stream flowing south out of the Marsh of Chelimber into a mid-sized river where it joins with the Serpent's Tail Stream beside the Forest of Wyrms. The Winding Water descends to the sea in a series of cataracts that can be heard from the base of the Troll Hills.

Below Boareskyr Bridge, the site of the death of Bhaal (a dark god of murder), the river's waters are foul and loathsome, flowing black until many miles west of Trollclaw Ford, when they clear slightly and turn muddy brown but are otherwise normal. The inhabitants of the Western Heartlands speak of the black water as "Bhaal water" and refuse to drink it, saying that it brings bad luck. While Bhaal water is not poisonous and can support life, intelligent beings who drink the stuff suffer unpleasant magical side effects, equivalent to enduring a *curse* spell for a day.

Wood of Sharp Teeth: This wood's reputation as a hunting ground for dire beasts, hydras, and dragons has preserved it from woodcutters and settlers from Baldur's Gate—or anywhere else, for that matter.

Yellow Snake Pass: This area was named for a winged serpent that several hundred years ago plagued this gap in the Sunset Mountains, located at the headwaters of the River Reaching. Yellow Snake Pass has lately been pressed by snakes of a different sort—the Zhents. Zhentarim patrols controlled this trade route through the pass until early in 1372 DR, when Thayan wizards and mercenaries from Hill's Edge drove the patrols into cavern shelters in the Underdark. For the moment, Yellow Snake Pass is free.

IMPORTANT SITES

Trading cities scattered along the land's great rivers and the overland routes of the Coastal Way and the Trade Way dominate the human landscape of the Western Heartlands. Centuries of conquest and scattered settlements have done nothing to tame the land—if anything, it has grown more wild.

Asbravn (Small City, 5,668): Asbravn is the central marketplace for the farmers of Sunset Vale, the rich farmlands between the Reaching Wood and the Sunset Mountains. The town resists Zhent raids from Darkhold and more subtle pressures, thanks to the services of a volunteer militia known as the Riders in Red Cloaks, whose numbers are often supplemented by friendly or retired adventurers. The town is a popular caravan stop for all but Zhent merchants, who can buy provisions but may not spend the night.

Beneath the town's well-kept farms and orderly market, catacombs left by a previous civilization of seminomadic horse riders sometimes turn up odd treasures. For a town erected upon the remnants of old tombs, Asbravn is sunny and relatively untroubled by undead.

Baldur's Gate (Metropolis, 42,103): One of the two great cities of the Sword Coast, Baldur's Gate sits on the north bank of the River Chionthar, twenty miles from where the river flows into the Sea of Swords. Situated halfway between Amn and Waterdeep, the city thrives on trade.

Trade knows no alignment, so tolerance is a virtue in Baldur's Gate, but not to the extent that visitors are allowed to conduct themselves in ways injurious to other persons or property. Guards in distinctive black helms with red stripes on either side police the city. They pay more attention to the upper half of the city, the part within the original walls, than to the newer, lower half by the river, enclosed by lower walls.

As is often the way in Faerûn, the great number of guards in Baldur's Gate is a clue to the presence of a well-run thieves' guild. Guildmaster Ravenscar (NE male human Rog10/Skr4 of Mask) maintains amiable though distant relations with Baldur's Gate's four grand dukes, including Eltan (LN male human Ftr20), the commander of the Flaming Fist mercenary company. The Flaming Fist serves as Baldur's Gate's unofficial army, providing cheap rates in return for a subsidized base of operations.

Most major cities have a few major temples, but Baldur's Gate's three major halls of worship are noteworthy. Gond's High House of Wonders houses an astonishing collection of one-of-a-kind inventions. Gnomes, inventors, and craftsfolk make the pilgrimage to Baldur's Gate for both inspiration and devotion. Tymora's temple, the Lady's Hall, is remarkable for its size and wealth. The temple to Umberlee, euphemistically known as the "Water Queen's House," is one of the few actual temples to this deity in all of Faerûn.

Berdusk (Large City, 20,242): The Jewel of the Vale occupies a fortuitous position astride both the Uldoon Trail from Amn and the River Chionthar. The city has an age-old reputation as a place for trade and for peace parleys, a status encouraged by its current administrator, the High Lady Cylyria Dragonbreast (NG female human Brd10/Ftr3/Hrp4). Cylyria is one of the leaders of the Harpers, whose most powerful base, Twilight Hall, stands beside the town's temple to Deneir. The Harpers use Berdusk as their base of operations in the West and the North.

Lady Cylyria keeps the city firmly in the Lords' Alliance and uses her influence to temper the strictly profit-minded policies of the city's rivals in Iriaebor and Scornubel. The Harpers were quick to take advantage of Darkhold's weakened grip on its territory in the Far Hills, but they are simultaneously concerned about the subtle rise in the Red Wizards' influence upon the affairs of the west.

Beregost (Large Town, 2,915): Beregost's forty or so stone and wood buildings cater to the trade between Amn and Baldur's Gate. The town has no official government, instead being run by the high priest of its major temple to Lathander. Yellow-garbed acolytes of the temple bear arms and keep the peace. Curiously, the town's founder was also a spellcaster rather than a politician—a wizard named Ulcaster established a magic school here that attracted a farming village to support it. Jealous Calishite wizards burned down Ulcaster's school three hundred years ago. The ruins still dominate the eastern side of the road, where the Morninglord's clerics graze their sheep to keep an eye on the ruins and prevent unsavory characters from going in (or coming out).

Boareskyr Bridge: This massive stone structure spans the Winding Water along the Trade Way from Scornubel to Waterdeep. The current bridge is the most recent in a long series of bridges at the site. The bridge is in fairly good shape, though the two statues of dark gods that originally guarded its ends were shattered by spells cast by worshipers of Mystra and Kelemvor.

No permanent settlement lies at Boareskyr Bridge, but the collection of merchant tents and caravan shelters that accumulate at both ends of the bridge never entirely disappears. At any given time, the tents are home to forty to nearly three hundred merchants, travelers, and hangers-on. At one time, two adventurers took the tent city under their protection and enforced a rough sort of law and order, but they moved on to retire in Waterdeep, and the estates to the north were occupied by a series of chieftains and rich merchants' entourages.

Thanks to the battle between Cyric and Bhaal that ended in Bhaal's death, the water downstream of the bridge is black, foul-smelling, and unlucky to drink. "Go drink from the west side of the bridge!" is a common curse in these parts.

Candlekeep: This citadel of learning stands on a volcanic crag overlooking the sea at the end of the Way of the Lion, a road joining it to the Coast Way trade road. Candlekeep is a many-towered fortress, once the home of the famous seer Alaundo, and it preserves the seer's predictions among its huge library of the writings of Faerûn.

The price for any traveler to enter the keep is merely a book. Those wishing to examine a work in the keep's library must gift Candlekeep with a new tome, valued by the shrewd gatekeepers of Candlekeep at no less than 1,000 gp. The monks of Candlekeep, who call themselves the Avowed, also purchase certain books brought to them and secretly commission agents to procure writings they desire.

The keep is ruled by the Keeper of the Tomes, who is assisted by the First Reader—second in authority and traditionally the most learned sage of the monastery. Up to eight Great Readers are governed by these two offices. These in turn are assisted by the Chanter, who leads the endless chant of Alaundo's prophecies, the Guide (in charge of teaching acolytes), and the Gatewarden, who deals with visitors, security, and supplies for the community. Clergy are regarded as honored guests but are not part of the monastery's hierarchy.

The citadel bears mighty, many-layered wards that prevent anything from burning except wicks and wax. No paper can ignite anywhere in the keep. These wards also block teleportation magic and destructive spells, kill all molds and insects, and have other secret properties. An additional ward prohibits entry into the Inner Rooms to all who do not bear a special token, only a handful of which exist. In the Inner Rooms are kept the most powerful magical tomes. Normally, only the Great Readers may enter, but others are admitted in the company of the Keeper or the First Reader.

The central tower of the keep is surrounded by beautiful grounds that descend to a ring of buildings along the inside of the massive outer walls: guest houses, stables, granaries, a warehouse, an infirmary, a temple to Oghma, and shrines to Deneir, Gond, and Milil. Order is kept by the Gatewarden's five underofficers: four Watchers, who take turns patrolling the monastery and watching land and sea from its tallest towers, and the Keeper of the Portal, each of whom has twelve monks (all experienced warriors) as assistants. These underofficers wield magic rods and rings to enforce their will.

No visitor can remain in Candlekeep for more than a tenday at a time, or reenter the monastery less than a month after leaving it. Visitors are forbidden to write in the library, but the monks scribe copies for visitors in good standing. Copying costs 100 gp per text, or 10,000 gp for spellbooks or any texts containing spells, magical formulae, or details of rituals, wards, command words, and the like.

The current Keeper of the Tomes is Ulraunt (LG human male Div7/Lor3), a proud and haughty wizard. It is well not to cross him. All petitioners who enter the central keep must sit at Ulraunt's left shoulder for at least one evening meal and endure his searching questions. Candlekeep has but one absolute rule: "He who destroys knowledge, with ink, fire, or sword, is himself destroyed. Here, books are more valuable than lives."

Something guards the catacombs and storage caverns beneath Candlekeep so well that few successful intrusions from below have ever reached Candlekeep proper. Few know that this sentinel wyrm was once the silver dragon Miirym. She was bound to defend Candlekeep's monks, buildings, and books by the archsorcerer Torth. Miirym is now an ancient silver dragon ghost who, if destroyed, rejuvenates in only 2d8+8 hours. Miirym defends Candlekeep diligently, but her spirit is very lonely and would rather talk than fight. She trades tales for information about current events.

Anyone who tries to trick her or launch a sneak attack can expect to have her come howling after him, hurling every spell she can in a savage, furious attack. If she meets intruders openly carrying books of any kind, the sentinel wyrm insists that they be surrendered to her for "rightful return" to Candlekeep. (As far as she's concerned, writings of any sort belong to Candlekeep.)

The scribes of Candlekeep have made at least one copy of every tome there, and an entire "mirror library" is rumored to be hidden somewhere else in Faerûn. Candlekeep-made books always bear the keep's symbol: a castle with candle flames burning atop its towers.

Corm Orp (Village, 810): The town of Corm Orp is a flea speck, slightly over a dozen permanent buildings on the Dusk Road between Hluthvar and Hill's Edge. Most of the area's inhabitants are halflings and gnomes, with a few humans who live in small homes in the hills behind the town. Corm Orp's lord, Dundast Hulteal, is a Harper sympathizer who frequently calls upon the Harpers of Berdusk for aid. Many halflings passing through the hills above Corm Orp are skilled adventurers themselves, and some of them are Harpers.

Daggerford (Village, 891): Four hundred years ago, a merchant's son armed only with a dagger stood in a shallow spot in the Delimbiyr River and fought off a lizardfolk raiding party, slaying six before his family and the rest of the caravan arrived to drive the lizardfolk off and retake the ford. Now the proud community of Daggerford, a walled settlement of nearly forty small stone buildings and a small castle, sits on the south shore of the ford, keeping it clear for caravans and travelers moving along the Trade Way or headed east to Secomber and Loudwater.

Pwyll Greatshout (LG male human Ftr5) presently styles himself as the duke of Daggerford. He is served by a small militia, supplemented by hired adventurers who patrol the local farms and hamlets. Thanks to the constant traffic along the Trade Way, Daggerford has more than its normal share of shrines, temples, and powerful priests, including full temples to Chauntea, Lathander, Shaundakul, Tempus, and Tymora.

Daggerford operates in Waterdeep's long shadow. In Waterdeep, the expression "gone to Daggerford" is taken to mean "lying low outside the city." Daggerford occasionally flirts with plans to expand its harbor and secure a portion of Waterdeep's trade for itself. This plan is popular with the town's Council of Guilds, an organization whose members go masked like the Lords of Waterdeep (but lack the magical protections that keep their identities secret from determined magicians). Privately, Pwyll Greatshout believes that the council overestimates his town's capabilities.

Darkhold: Since 1312 DR, Darkhold's black walls and towering spires have been the Zhents' western base of operations. The infighting caused by Bane's death and subsequent resurrection has weakened Darkhold's influence on the surrounding area but hasn't loosened Zhent control of Darkhold itself.

The fort itself is a high-spired keep rising from a bare rocky spur on the side of the mountain named the Gray Watcher. The black stone used to build Darkhold came from a place far from the Western Heartlands. Darkhold's massive doorways, corridors, and ceilings were constructed for giants. Legends variously ascribe the keep's construction to the days when giants ruled all of Faerûn or to elder elementals serving as slaves for the kingdom of Netheril.

Until Bane's resurrection, the wizard Sememmon was Darkhold's undisputed master. For an evil genius, Sememmon is a patient, observant, and wise man. He came into conflict with Fzoul Chembryl early in both their careers and has never sought or wished to fully repair the rift. When Bane died in 1358 DR, Sememmon held his own against Fzoul's Xvim-sponsored machinations by managing his underlings wisely, consolidating his power in Darkhold, and avoiding conflict with Fzoul. When Bane returned and Fzoul established sole control of the eastern Zhents, Sememmon assessed his situation, chose the wisest course of action, and disappeared.

Some of Fzoul's supporters have quietly claimed that Fzoul eliminated Sememmon himself, but high-ranking Zhents are not sure. Ashemmi (LE female moon elf Wiz11), Sememmon's long-time consort and lover, disappeared at the same time as Sememmon. They withdrew to fight battles they could win, rather than keep a stronghold unlikely to survive against its original headquarters to the east.

At present, the citadel houses a permanent Zhent fighting force of eight hundred warriors, slightly reduced from the days when Sememmon held the Far Hills in perfect servitude. Fzoul seems content to let the various Zhent commanders in Darkhold spar for position, including the Pereghost (CE male human Ftr7/Chm5 of Cyric). All have sworn personal oaths of loyalty to the Zhentarim cause, although the strong Cyricist influence here galls Fzoul, who wants to see all of the Zhentarim under Bane's dominion.

The intrigues and assassination attempts presently dominating Darkhold's internal politics are not openly tolerated in the eastern Zhent holdings, but for the moment Darkhold's feuds are being used to cull the weak. If a strong leader does not emerge soon, Fzoul will appoint his own commander, someone strong enough to deal with intrigues decisively.

Durlag's Tower: Durlag's Tower stands like a single massive fang atop a wall of volcanic rock that rises out of the otherwise smooth plains rolling south of the Wood of Sharp Teeth. Durlag's Tower was built by the dwarven hero Durlag Trollkiller. Durlag had an extreme case of what the dwarves call "goldeneye," an overwhelming lust for treasure.

During his adventuring career he behaved honorably, but in the last years of his life Durlag retired to his lair and devoted himself to creating a "gift" to future generations of adventurers. His tower is so full of magical treasures that it makes casters of *detect magic* spells dizzy. Magic wards, mechanical traps, and malevolent automatons ensure that adventurers who wish to depart with their lives, much less any part of Durlag's treasure, need to fight as hard as Durlag did to amass his hoard.

New rumors always surface that some new fiend has defeated the wards and taken residence in the tower. The truth is not so simple. At various times, a dragon, a squadron of will-o'-wisps, and an illithid have taken "command" of the tower, but in all cases the occupants eventually discovered that the tower had outsmarted them, turning them into a temporary part of its own defenses rather than actually yielding its secrets. At any time, multiple parties or monsters might be within the tower, fighting for a chance to take control, plunder, or escape.

Information on the current denizens of the tower is available for a small price in the tiny human and gnome settlement named Gullykin, a couple of miles from Durlag's Tower.

Elturel (Large City, 22,671): If Elturel's ruler, High Rider Lord Dhelt (LG male human Pal17 of Helm), were an evil man, his city's position atop a cliff that dominates the River Chionthar would cause no end of trouble for the other trading cities of the region. Fortunately for the peace and prosperity of the Chionthar valley, Dhelt confines his competitive instincts to running the safest, best policed, and most efficient trading and farming community in the Western Heartlands. In these harsh lands, civilization depends on military power, and Elturel proves the rule with a crack army of two hundred mounted warriors known as the Hellriders. Caravans and riverboat convoys take routes into Elturel's zone of control just so that they can relax and leave a day or two of vigilance to Lord Dhelt's soldiers.

Evereska (Large City, 21,051): In the elven tongue, Evereska means "fortress home." This great valley and the city within it, the only major settlement of moon and sun elves left on Faerûn following the Retreat, is nestled between twelve high hills that function as natural walls. Access to this refuge exists only by air or through high passes guarded by elite elven sentinels. The approach to the city leads through a crescent-shaped valley of terraced vineyards and fruit gardens. The city of Evereska itself is a masterpiece of shaped stone and crafted trees, built for architectural impact and powerful defense.

Evereska's rulers are the Hill Elders, elves of immense age, learning, and power. Thanks to the Hill Elders' care and foresight, Evereska's inhabitants are free to live deep within the elven mysteries. Some elves never leave Evereska for the outside world. Others guard the city with unceasing vigilance.

Most humans know of Evereska only through rumors or from seeing paintings or tiny sculptures given as presents to the elves' most faithful friends. Stories tell of the strength of elven magic within the city, such as its inhabitants' ability to walk straight up vertical surfaces as if they always benefited from *spider climb* spells. These effects (and more) come from a powerful *mythal*. The *mythal's* greater powers, defensive abilities of elven high magic at the peak of its power, are seldom called upon.

Hill's Edge (Small City, 9,716): Hill's Edge caters to both Zhent caravans and honest travelers. Small but prosperous, the town has a well-deserved reputation for dirty deals and odd bedfellows. Bandits, brigands, murderers, and cutthroats get to know each other in Hill's Edge's taverns, and it's hard to kill a person who bought you drinks the night before.

Officially, Hill's Edge elects a mayor every year, but suitable candidates are difficult to find. In 1371 DR, the Red Wizards brought a small enclave to Hill's Edge. It's thriving, and so is Hill's Edge, thanks to the increased spending of those who stop to purchase the Thayans' wares.

Zhent caravans still pass through Hill's Edge happily enough, but alert adventurers might play on tensions between the Thayans and Zhents. The Zhents don't appreciate the Thayans' role in the recent liberation of Yellow Snake Pass. For their part, the Harpers of Berdusk are even less happy with the Thayans, an enemy with a smiling face, than with the notoriously heavy-handed Zhents.

Hluthvar (Small City, 5,668): From the highest lookout of the fortresslike temple of Helm at the center of Hluthvar, a keen-eyed watcher can spy the black towers of Darkhold on a clear day, over sixty miles to the east. Firm vigilance, a strong ten-foot wall, and devoted worship of Helm are all that prevents Hluthvar from falling to the Zhents. Helm's high priest, Maurandyr (LN male human Clr14/Dis4 of Helm), who fights with a magical dancing sword, reinforces the town's resolve to stand strong against the Zhents.

Iriaebor (Large City, 16,193): The City of a Thousand Spires occupies a sprawling ridge above the north fork of the River Chionthar. Space to build on is at a premium atop the ridge, so Iriaebor's traders and other citizens have adjusted by building up instead of out—many-storied towers rise from all quarters of the city. Iriaebor's great merchant houses compete to build the highest, richest, and most fantastically bizarre towers, thinking to attract business the way peacocks attract their mates. Like peacocks, who fight when looks alone cannot decide engagements, the great houses of Iriaebor sometimes conspire to topple each other's towers, using magic or hired adventurers to confuse the trail.

One of those hired adventurers came to prominence in the middle of a merchants' war and took it upon himself to rule the city. Bron (LG male human Ftr5/Pal4 of Eldath) believes that his city could become a major force in the Western Heartlands if it could stop squandering its energy on internal feuds.

Laughing Hollow: A few miles north of Daggerford, a choke point in the River Delimbiyr runs through an old dwarven quarry where the dwarves used the river to flush away their mine's wastes. The miners have been gone for centuries, and the mine lies undiscovered beneath thick vegetation that covers the walls of the cliffs on either side of the river. Pixies, hybsils, and wild elves shelter in the thick brush, driving off the adventurers who come here searching for the mine and its supposed treasures.

Scornubel (Large City, 14,574): Scornubel, the Caravan City, is a sprawling buzz of mercantile activity along the north shore where the River Chionthar meets the River Reaching. It is ruled by a group of elderly or middle-aged adventurers and caravan masters, some of whom favor hiring adventurers to solve the city's problems and others who prefer that adventurers move along promptly. In all things, the ruling council chooses efficiency and profit over ideals.

Caravans of all nations, organizations, and trading costers are welcome in Scornubel. Similarly, shrines to nearly all Faerûnian deities can be found somewhere in the town's low buildings. The Red Shield merchant company runs both its military and trading caravan operations out of Scornubel. The Red Shields also serve as Scornubel's official army and police force. As an army, they're efficient. As a police force, they concentrate on relaxing, enjoying themselves, and looking after the Red Shield company's interests.

Secomber (Small Town, 1,417): Sitting along the Unicorn Run just north of the High Moor, Secomber is either the northernmost settlement of the Western Heartlands or the first village of the North, depending on who draws the map. Those who vote for the Western Heartlands point to the town's peacefulness, its thriving families of fisherfolk and farmers, its colorful gardens, and its hospitality to passing caravans. Those who think of it as part of the North point to the town's sizable community of adventurers and guides who have at least passing familiarity with the High Forest to the north.

The city welcomes travelers, particularly adventurers who use the city as a base for forays into the High Moor or the High Forest. Not coincidentally, such adventurers are called on to help out when gargoyles and worse creatures are unearthed from the ruins of long-dead Athlantar, the Kingdom of the Stag.

Well of Dragons: Throughout Faerûn, there's a legend that the great dragons have a graveyard, a place they go to die. The Well of Dragons, the hollow interior of an old volcano north of the Sunset Mountains and south of the Battle of Bones, is that graveyard. Until recently, its thousands of dragon skeletons were hidden from view by powerful spells and guarded by an undead shadow dragon called the Dire Dragon. The Cult of the Dragon learned of the Well of Dragons, made a pact of sorts with the Dire Dragon, then succeeded in unbinding the magic that kept the guardian attached to Faerûn.

Instead of enjoying easy access to the treasure trove, the Cult of the Dragon has encountered serious resistance from members of several different factions. Interested parties include dragonkin who refuse to plunder the resting place of the great dragons, yuan-ti, newly arriving lesser dragons, and various parties of adventurers and sages who are intent on looting the remains. Despite the difficulties, the Cult is secretly raising a dark and powerful fortress to watch over this place, and planning great sorceries and rites here.

REGIONAL HISTORY

The ancient history of the Western Heartlands reveals itself in the scattered tombs, broken statues, and shattered ruins of dozens of mighty kingdoms. As testified to by sites such as the Fields of the Dead and the Battle of Bones, few of those kingdoms dissolved peacefully.

Major wars in the region were rare in recent centuries, unless one counts the battle fought between the deities Bhaal and Cyric at Boareskyr Bridge during the Time of Troubles. Cyric slew Bhaal and stole his powers, the portfolio of murder.

In the centuries before the rise of Waterdeep, the greatest kingdom in the Western Heartlands was Illefarn, a kingdom of elves that rivaled Myth Drannor. Phalorm (the Realm of Three Crowns, or the Fallen Kingdom) and the Kingdom of Man ruled for a time in Illefarn's wake, but since then no single power has controlled the entire area. The trading culture of Waterdeep, Amn, and the scattered members of the Lords' Alliance comprise the longest-lived civilization to rise in the Western Heartlands since Illefarn's fall.

The mercantile cities' interests are sometimes aided and sometimes opposed by the Zhent forces operating out of the fortress of Darkhold in the Far Hills. Aside from the weather, Darkhold's changing fortunes are probably the single largest variable in the lives of inhabitants of the Western Heartlands.

PLOTS AND RUMORS

The Western Heartlands are friendly to adventurers of good heart. Uncharted mountains, wild forests, trackless hills, and haunted forests surround the small settlements of the area, and adventurers have always been the first line of defense against the evil groups—the Cult of the Dragon, the Shadow Thieves, and the Zhentarim—who seek to extend their influence into the area.

"I'd Like to Get My Things Back": The heroes might be surprised to be approached in a forthright manner by Ashemmi, the lover of Sememmon, the former ruler of Darkhold. Sememmon left some possessions behind in Darkhold when he fled, and he would like them back. These items are well hidden, but there is always the chance of accidental discovery while the keep is controlled by other commanders.

Sememmon does not want to return to Darkhold himself. Instead, he would like the heroes to break into Darkhold and retrieve his things. He even gives the PCs information to reduce their risk of being apprehended. He means to pay the PCs enormously for their services, half in advance, and informs them that the items they are gathering for him shouldn't fall into the hands of Fzoul's Zhents. If the PCs want to meet Sememmon himself instead of dealing with his lover, this can be arranged.

Sememmon is not concerned if the PCs do not accept his commission. In fact, he leaves behind a quarter of the huge fee (as many gold pieces as it takes to make the PCs gasp) as a gift, just to say that he would be willing to work with the PCs in the future. Sememmon's new plan, in the long run, is to make himself indispensable to the forces of good that he formerly opposed. The objects Sememmon wants back could be documentation of Zhentarim spies in the region, spellbooks with unique spells, or potent magic items.

Sememmon

Illustration by Todd Lockwood

SEMEMMON

Male human Wiz17: CR 17; Medium-size humanoid; HD 17d4+3; hp 49; Init +2; Spd 30 ft.; AC 20 (touch 12, flat-footed 18); Atk +8/+3 melee (1d6, *+1 quarterstaff*, or 1d4/19–20 plus *poison* spell 1/day, *dagger of venom*) or +10/+5 ranged touch (by spell); SQ Enhanced Charisma, enhanced Wisdom; AL LE; SV Fort +7, Ref +7, Will +14; Str 9, Dex 15, Con 10, Int 20, Wis 18, Cha 18. Height 5 ft. 7 in.

Skills and Feats: Alchemy +10, Bluff +9, Concentration +15, Diplomacy +13, Gather Information +6, Heal +6, Hide +17, Intimidate +8, Knowledge (arcana) +20, Knowledge (architecture and engineering) +8, Knowledge (history) +13, Knowledge (religion) +11, Listen +6, Profession (herbalist) +9, Ride (horse) +5, Scry +13, Search +8, Sense Motive +12, Spellcraft +20, Spot +9; Combat Casting, Craft Wondrous Item, Empower Spell, Great Fortitude, Heighten Spell, Leadership (21), Quicken Spell, Scribe Scroll, Spell Focus (Enchantment), Spell Focus (Evocation), Toughness.

Special Qualities: Enhanced Wisdom and Charisma: Sememmon has improved both his Wisdom and Charisma scores through the use of *wish* scrolls.

Wizard Spells per Day: 4/6/5/5/5/4/3/2/1. Base DC = 15 + spell level, 17 + spell level for enchantment and evocation spells. As the former Lord of Darkhold and former student of Manshoon, Sememmon has access to a great deal of magical lore and many spells, including many rare and unusual spells. Assume he knows all spells of 1st through 5th level, and half of the spells of 6th through 9th level, including all enchantment spells. In addition, the DM may freely assign spells to Sememmon, representing his access to rare tomes and his own brilliance in spell design.

Possessions: *+1 quarterstaff, dagger of venom, bracers of armor +8, brooch of shielding, helm of teleportation, gargoyle cloak* (wearer may polymorph self into a gargoyle for 1 hour 1/day), lavender and green *ioun stone* (24 spell levels remaining), *periapt of proof against poison, ring of regeneration, robe of blending, wand of lightning* (10th).

The able lieutenant of Manshoon for years, Sememmon long served as the Lord of Darkhold. He rose to that rank by being unfailingly polite, competent, and obedient to the letter of orders given by Manshoon, Fzoul Chembryl, and various Zhentarim beholders. Beneath his quiet politeness, he's cunning and calculating, capable of holding grudges (but not allowing himself to be driven by them) for years. He always has a ready escape from any dangerous situation and does not hesitate to use it.

Sememmon is a capable wizard, a former apprentice to Manshoon, and a survivor, swift to ruthlessly eliminate rivals and elude blame. He foiled a number of Fzoul's bids to seize command of the Zhentarim and thereby earned the priest's undying enmity—but he also protected and husbanded the power of the Zhentarim through the wildest excesses of both Manshoon and Fzoul, calmly "picking up the pieces" on many occasions. In the process, he became a master of diplomacy and foresight, a good commander of troops, and a master strategist who always has several fallback plans (and hidden magic items) at the ready.

Sememmon is mild-mannered, observant, patient, and keenly intelligent. Ruthless and tightly controlled, he's no egomaniac or lover of tyranny, and detests unnecessary violence and cruelty as wasteful. He loves and is loved by his cohort Ashemmi (LE female moon elf Wiz11). For years he remained loyal to the Black Network—indeed, in the opinion of observant Zhentarim, he *was* the Black Network, having kept everything running while his superiors raved, pursued mad schemes, and fought each other. The radical increase in Fzoul's power signaled the end of the priest's tolerance with anyone who opposes him, and Sememmon and Ashemmi fled Darkhold before Fzoul could act against them.

Sememmon is a black-haired man of handsome appearance, middling years, and excellent health, who wears conservative but well-made robes. He uses magical disguises when traveling. He seems calm even in the heat of battle and while facing great danger.

Beyond Faerûn

Even the wisest scholars of Candlekeep know only a little of what lies beyond the realms of Faerûn. While heroes, explorers, diplomats, and merchants have traveled beyond Faerûn, rare indeed is the person who has visited more than one particular region outside the commonly known lands.

Kara-Tur

The Hordelands stretch for hundreds upon hundreds of miles, east from the lands of Rashemen and Narfell. Yet east of east, beyond the sunrise, lies a vast and marvelous land of legend known as Kara-Tur. Mountains as tall as the sky, impenetrable jungles, and empty grasslands claimed by the fierce Tuigan tribes stand between Faerûn's easternmost lands and the sprawling empires of Kara-Tur.

Kara-Tur is reputed to be a land of silk, spice, and gold, a beautiful land ruled by haughty and cruel warlords. Travelers speak in awe of the Shou Empire, a kingdom thousands of miles in extent guarded by a mighty wall. In Shou Lung, it is said, the temples are roofed in gold, and the Emperor presides over a court of a thousand kings and a million swords.

From these fantastic lands a single trade route wends its way westward. The Golden Way crosses the great expanse of the Hordelands, winds through Rashemen and Thesk, and finally meets the Inner Sea at the port of Telflamm. Here Shou silk and exotic spices from the isles of Wa arrive in Faerûn after a journey covering thousands of miles and lasting many months. The Golden Way remains open only at the sufferance of the Tuigan, who sometimes exact ruinous tribute for their forbearance or shut down the road altogether.

Maztica

Ten years ago, bold mercenaries in the service of Amn dared the Trackless Sea, sailing into the sunset for week after week until they reached an unexplored land beyond the sunset—Maztica. Fighting against the strange warriors of the land, they established a foothold on the western continent. Several powerful merchant companies now struggle to wring wealth from this new land. Trade, discovery, and no small amount of fighting against hostile Mazticans and competing Faerûnians is the result.

Even less is known of Maztica than of Kara-Tur. It is a land of forbidding natural barriers and hundreds of remote, reclusive cultures, most of whom are hostile to each other. Every year more gold, gemstones, and valuable new crops such as vanilla and coffee are brought back to Faerûn in Amnian carracks, a one-sided trade that promises to enrich that nation beyond belief.

Zakhara

The best known and most frequently visited of Faerûn's neighboring subcontinents, Zakhara lies beyond the Great Sea to the south and east. Zakharan dhows are a common sight in the ports of Halruaa, Nimbral, Dambrath, and Luiren, and sea merchants of those lands report that a desert land of hidden wonders and subtle culture lies only a few hundred miles across the sea from Faerûn's southern shores.

Zakhara's shores are plagued by particularly fierce and numerous corsairs. They demand heavy tribute and sometimes close off sea travel to the exotic southern land altogether. Even when the way is open, Faerûnian travelers are not always welcomed in Zakhara's secretive cities.

Zakhara is a land of great deserts, lush oases, and powerful genies who meddle in the affairs of humankind. It is united by a powerful faith inspiring piety, zeal, and honor, yet tales tell of demon-haunted cities and godless sorcerers who wield strange magic.

The Sea of Night

The last and most fantastic of the lands beyond Faerûn is so close that every Faerûnian has seen it from afar. Above the sky lies a realm of incredible expanse, the so-called Sea of Night, where rivers of stars and worlds both strange and wonderful shimmer like silver fire in the dark.

Stories abound of wizards who seek to climb above the sky and explore its dark waters, of princes ruling castles of argent light, and crystal elf-ships that rise gleaming from the western seas into oceans vaster and more wondrous still when twilight falls over the face of Toril. In a land where wizards make castles fly and clerics bring forth godly miracles, the legendary isles and realms of the night sky are home to the wildest flights of fancy and strangest dreams of all.

Selûne

Toril's moon is known as Selûne. Through careful observations and persistent divinations, sages have determined that it circles Toril at a distance of about twenty thousand miles. While Selûne in the sky appears no larger than a human hand held at arm's length, it is a world in its own right, easily two thousand miles across.

Selûne is bright enough to cast pale shadows when full. It is accompanied in the sky by the Tears of Selûne, a number of smaller luminaries that spread across the sky in a great arc trailing the moon. Children's tales tell of pirates in flying ships who come down from the Tears to raid and plunder, but no one takes these stories seriously.

ECLIPSES

Selûne's orbit around Toril is almost in the same plane as Toril's orbit around its sun, so solar and lunar eclipses are frequent. Solar eclipses are never annular (the sun's edge cannot be seen during totality) and almost never partial, because Selûne's shadow on Toril and Toril's shadow on Selûne are quite large. Eclipses are thus spectacular but rather commonplace. Inhabitants of any particular land do not always notice such eclipses, since the rising and setting times for Selûne wander across the calendar. Solar eclipses might briefly cause nocturnal beings to awaken, but they quickly return to sleep once daylight returns.

SELÛNE'S PHASES

Selûne is full at exactly midnight, the first of Hammer, 1372 DR, and every thirty days, ten hours, and thirty minutes thereafter. The time between successive full moons is, technically speaking, one synodic month, the time from one Sun–Toril–Selûne conjunction to the next. Selûne makes exactly forty-eight synodic revolutions every four calendar years on Toril. Thus, Selûne is full at exactly midnight on the first day of every leap year, and has the same phase on any calendar day four years forward or backward in time.

One Faerûnian holiday, the Feast of the Moon, is held during a full moon that obligingly shows up on or about that day. Because Selûne's synodic period is so close to the actual length of the calendar month, Selûne is full around the first day of each month or on festival days, give or take a day or so. The annual festival days serve to correct discrepancies between the synodic and calendar months, with Shieldmeet providing a necessary correction every fourth year to keep the full moon from sliding deep into each month.

A Scholar's View of Abeir-Toril

TEARS OF SELÛNE

The Tears of Selûne are a collection of hundreds of very small but bright celestial bodies (asteroids) that orbit Toril in Selûne's wake. The Tears act like any such bodies in a Trojan point, meaning that they do not stay in place but actually orbit around a common center in whirlpool fashion. Viewed from above, the Tears appear to be a very large disk of hundreds of assorted bodies, none of any remarkable size. The Tears are visible as points of light like stars, too small for viewers to discern their actual shapes.

The individual orbits of the Tears are not exactly coplanar with the orbit of Toril and Selûne, but they are close. As a result, their appearance in the night sky of Toril is that of a flattened ellipse of bright "stars," trailing Selûne by sixty degrees across the sky, along the ecliptic. Typically, an average human can cover Selûne's image with his clenched fist at arm's length; the Tears, however, appear to span an area of the night sky almost three handspans wide and about three fingers deep at arm's length. The relative positions of individual Tears change from night to night as they orbit their common center.

The Tears are not bright enough to be seen during the day, though Selûne often is. Though the Tears are bright even when Selûne is new, they are not always visible in the night sky, since they too have rising and setting times, and thus might not be up at night. The first Tear rises or sets about four hours after Selûne does. Because it is so long, the full set of Tears takes about three hours to rise or set, from first Tear to last. The combined effect of the Tears is not enough to cast shadows at night.

Like Selûne, the Tears are believed by some sages to be inhabited, though very few people could make a reasonable guess as to who lives there. Fewer still have actually been there and reported back.

THE DAWN HERALDS

For centuries, astrologers have observed the appearance of one or two particularly bright stars close to sunrise and right after sunset. Anadia and Coliar are sometimes known as the Dawn Heralds, although they might just as easily be called the Evening Heralds too. These, too, are worlds much like Toril, only closer to Toril's sun and so never observed very far from it in the heavens. Coliar is the larger and the brighter of the two, and also the one usually found higher in the night sky.

Magical vision devices and deep divinations reveal Anadia as a small, amber-colored world with verdant green at the poles. Coliar is a streaky gray-and-white orb, rumored to hold endless oceans beneath a cloud-wracked sky.

THE FIVE WANDERERS

Deeper in the Sea of Night roam the Five Wanderers, inconstant stars that do not follow a yearly path across the sky as the other stars do. These Wanderers are markedly different from the star-rivers through which they roam; they tend to be larger, brighter, and show wondrous colors and features when scried closer.

Karpri, the nearest, is a sapphire orb with great whitecaps at top and bottom. Sages say that it roams millions of miles from Toril, if such a thing can be believed. Chandos, the next, is a brown-green smudge whose markings change oddly over a few nights' watching. Glyth is a dull gray, but surrounded by a spectacular ring and three lesser bodies, visible only with magical aid. Garden is a tiny green sparkle, rarely seen. The last, H'Catha, seems to be a very large world very far away, a gleam of diamond white.

DEITIES

The deities of Toril take an active interest in their world, channeling power through their clerics, druids, rangers, paladins, and other worshipers and sometimes intervening directly in the affairs of mortals. At the same time, they plot, war, intrigue, and ally among themselves, between themselves and powerful mortals, and with extraplanar beings such as elemental rulers and demons. In this they resemble their mortal worshipers, for to an extent deities are defined and shaped by their worshipers, their areas of interest, and their nature—for many deities are actually mortals who have gained the divine spark. Because they lose strength if their worship dwindles away and is forgotten, deities task their clerics and others to whom they grant divine spells with spreading their praise and doctrine, recruiting new worshipers, and keeping the faith alive. In exchange for this work and to facilitate it, deities grant divine spells.

worship

A weaponsmith might take Gond as his patron deity, but also pray to Tempus, Lord of Battles, before attempting to forge a fine sword. During a difficult forging or when striving to make a blade lucky for wielders, the same smith prays to Tymora. A weapon forged for guardians would involve prayers and offerings to Helm. A weapon to be wielded for justice (an executioner's blade, perhaps) would be dedicated to Tyr.

Most people of Toril worship more than one deity on a daily basis, even if they dedicate their lives to one patron deity. Some folk of Faerûn believe deities are akin to awesomely powerful mortals and are therefore prone to foibles, tempers, and the haste, mistakes, and emotions of mortals. Others see them as beyond mortal flaws or mortal comprehension. Overlaid on these extremes are beliefs as to whether deities like to intervene in mortal affairs daily, at crucial junctures, on whims, or to further mysterious or stated aims—or whether they remain aloof, influencing mortals only in subtle, hidden ways or through dream visions or cryptic auguries. With these widely varying views come a correspondingly wide range in practices of worship.

With that said, many folk make offerings both to deities they revere and appeasement offerings to deities of markedly different alignment and interests from their own to ward off holy vengefulness, spite, and divine whim. The simplest offering to a deity is to toss a few coins into a temple bowl or make another suitable offering (blood to Tempus or Malar, for example, or particular sacred or token objects to most other deities) while a plea is murmured. The formalization of this practice is the payment of a set temple fee to clergy of the deity to be appeased, who either provide the payer with a short prayer to be performed at an auspicious later time or perform a rote prayer for the payer.

patron deities

The deities of Faerûn are deeply enmeshed in the functioning of the world's magical ecology and the lives of mortals. Characters of Toril nearly always have a patron deity. Everyone in Faerûn knows that those who die without having a patron deity to send a servant to collect them from the Fugue Plane at their death spend eternity writhing in the Wall of the Faithless or disappear into the hells of the devils or the infernos of the demons.

For more information on patron deities, see the Religion section of Chapter 1: Characters.

sins and penance

Some members of the clergy believe their deities watch over every act, thought, and consequence of the deeds of every mortal worshiper. Most priests, however, see their deities as judging mortals only on deeds or on acts plus obvious intent rather than ultimate consequences.

A cleric or druid who commits a minor offense against her deity or ignores portions of the deity's dogma is guilty of a sin. He has to do some penance appropriate to the seriousness of the sin in order to remain in good standing with the church, other clerics or druids, and the deity. Paladins, rangers, and other divine spellcasters are held to this standard (to a less exacting degree) also.

Typical penance for lesser infractions includes spending an hour in prayer, making a small monetary donation to the temple (1 to 10 gp), performing minor duties in the temple (which vary by religion), and so on.

Penance for moderate infractions includes spending anywhere from a day to a tenday in prayer, making a moderate monetary donation to the temple (100 to 500 gp), or going on a small quest for the church (a short adventure).

Penance for major infractions includes a month or more of prayer, a large donation (1,000 gp or more), a quest, and possibly an *atonement* spell (which might require its own quest).

Continued abuses of the church's dogma may result in a divine spellcaster losing his class features (but not any class-related weapon and armor proficiencies) until he atones for his sins.

changing deities

It is possible for a cleric, druid, paladin, or spellcasting ranger (or any other divine spellcaster) to abandon his chosen deity and take up the faith of another deity. In doing so, the divine spellcaster loses all class features of the abandoned deity. To progress as a divine spell-caster of another faith, the character must go on a quest for his new church (often the recovery of a lost item of some importance to the deity), then receive an *atonement* spell from a representative of his new faith. Once these two conditions are met, the character becomes a divine spellcaster of the new deity, and if a cleric, he chooses two domains from the new deity's repertoire. The character then resumes the class features lost from leaving the old faith (so long as they are still applicable—turning or rebuking undead ability might change, for instance).

pantheons

A pantheon is a group of deities organized along geographic or species lines. Sometimes members of a pantheon are related to each other through familial ties. The majority of the continent of Faerûn is under the control of the Faerûnian pantheon, a group of native and immigrant deities largely unrelated to each other. The exception is the countries of Mulhorand, Unther, Semphar, and Murghôm, which are watched over by the Mulho-randi pantheon, which is mainly composed of a family group. The major humanoid races (dwarves, elves, and so on) have their own pantheons as well. Outside Faerûn, the Kara-Turan pantheon guides the peoples of Kara-Tur, and so on. Clerics of a foreign deity may travel within another pantheon's region and receive spells normally, but they are likely to be driven off or assaulted by representatives of the local deities if they attempt to convert people to their faith, establish a temple, or start a holy war. The clergy of nonhuman deities are immune to this persecution as long as they refrain from such activities while in human lands; instead, they focus their recruiting and building efforts in places owned by their own kind or frontier areas unclaimed by civilized folk.

Deity format

Each deity description follows the same format. This section discusses that format.

Deity Name (Level of power)

Each deity's listing begins with the deity's most common name. Following the name is the deity's level of power. In descending order, the levels of power are greater deity, intermediate deity, lesser deity, and demigod. These rankings do not affect the abilities of clerics, the power of the spells the clerics cast, or most anything in the mortal world. They represent relative levels of power among deities only. Incorporated into the level of power descriptor is the deity's most

commonly portrayed gender. While deities can manifest as either gender and in almost any form, most prefer one gender over the other.

common Titles

After the power level and gender are a few of the more common titles for the deity used by the faithful. Among the deity's worshipers, these names and titles are all synonymous. This is by no means a comprehensive listing.

symbol

The deity's symbol is the preferred symbol of the faithful to represent the deity. The symbol is also the form of the holy symbol used by clerics of the deity, and may be as ornate or simple as the cleric can afford or the religion requires. Note that in some cases there are limits to the decoration of a holy symbol. For example, Silvanus's clerics carry as their holy symbol a fresh oak leaf, which cannot be decorated but might be displayed in an open case of carved and lacquered wood.

Alignment

The deity's alignment is the most common alignment evidenced by the deity. Just as evil deities can act benignly to advance their cause, good deities sometimes need to be cruel to save something of importance, and so a deity's alignment is just a guideline. However, the cleric still uses the deity's alignment for determining her own alignment (using the "one step" rule from the *Player's Handbook*). A few deities permit clerics to have alignments not allowed by the one step rule. These exceptions are described in the deity's entry.

portfolio

The deity's portfolio is the topics, ideas, or emotions over which the deity has dominion, power, and control. No two beings within the same pantheon may hold the same concept in their portfolios.

Domains

The listed domains are those granted by the deity to clerics, reflecting the deity's alignment and portfolio. As with the deities listed in the *Player's Handbook*, a cleric chooses two domains from the deity's list and acquires the granted powers of those two domains.

favored weapon

The deity's favored weapon is most often a representation of an actual weapon the deity is said to carry. Sometimes, though, it is a magical manifestation or a physical object associated with the deity that is not commonly considered a weapon. (The name of a deity's weapon, when known, is given in quotation marks on Tables 5–1 through 5–8.)

Spells such as *spiritual weapon* take the form of the favored weapon (which unless otherwise specified does normal damage according to the spell, regardless of the form it takes) but use the threat range and critical multiplier of the conventional weapon given in parentheses in the deity entry (or on the appropriate table). Since the favored weapon of some deities is a particular artifact weapon of theirs (such as the Wand of Four Moons) or a force of nature (a whirlwind), the parenthetical conventional armaments also serve as the conventional favored weapons of clerics of those faiths, which most clerics use as a point of pride, though they are not required to.

TABLE 5—1: THE FAERÛNIAN PANTHEON

Name (Power)	Align.	Domains	Favored Weapon
Akadi (G)	N	Air, Illusion, Travel, Trickery	A whirlwind (heavy flail)
Auril (L)	NE	Air, Evil, Storm, Water	"Icemaiden's Caress" [ice axe] (battleaxe)
Azuth (L)	LN	Illusion, Magic, Knowledge, Law, Spell	"The Old Staff" (quarterstaff)
Bane (G)	LE	Destruction, Evil, Hatred, Law, Tyranny	The black hand of Bane [a black gauntlet] (morningstar)
Beshaba (I)	CE	Chaos, Evil, Fate, Luck, Trickery	"Ill Fortune" [barbed scourge] (scourge)
Chauntea (G)	NG	Animal, Earth, Good, Plant, Protection, Renewal	A shock of grain (scythe)
Cyric (G)	CE	Chaos, Destruction, Evil, Illusion, Trickery	"Razor's Edge" (longsword)
Deneir (L)	NG	Good, Knowledge, Protection, Rune	A whirling glyph (dagger)
Eldath (L)	NG	Family, Good, Plant, Protection, Water	Net (net or net that does damage as unarmed strike)
Finder Wyvernspur (D)	CN	Chaos, Charm, Renewal, Scalykind	"Sword of Songs" (bastard sword)
Garagos (D)	CN	Chaos, Destruction, Strength, War	"The Tentacus" [a pinwheel of five black, snaky arms each ending in a sword] (longsword)
Gargauth (D)	LE	Charm, Evil, Law, Trickery	"Corruptor" (dagger or throwing dagger)
Gond (I)*	N	Craft, Earth, Fire, Knowledge, Metal, Planning	"Craftmaster" (warhammer)
Grumbar (G)	N	Cavern, Earth, Metal, Time	A stony fist (warhammer)
Gwaeron Windstrom (D)	NG	Animal, Good, Knowledge, Plant, Travel	"Flameheart" (greatsword)
Helm (I)	LN	Law, Planning, Protection, Strength	"Ever Watchful" (bastard sword)
Hoar (D)	LN	Fate, Law, Retribution, Travel	"Retribution's Sting" [javelin of lightning] (javelin)
Ilmater (I)	LG	Good, Healing, Law, Strength, Suffering	An open hand (unarmed strike)
Istishia (G)	N	Destruction, Ocean, Storm, Travel, Water	A wave (warhammer)
Jergal (D)	LN	Death, Fate, Law, Rune, Suffering	A white glove (scythe)
Kelemvor (G)	LN	Death, Fate, Law, Protection, Travel	"Fatal Touch" (bastard sword)
Kossuth (G)*	N (LN)	Destruction, Fire, Renewal, Suffering	Tendril of flame (spiked chain)
Lathander (G)	NG	Good, Nobility, Protection, Renewal, Strength, Sun	"Dawnspeaker" (light or heavy mace)
Lliira (L)	CG	Chaos, Charm, Family, Good, Travel	"Sparkle" (shuriken)
Loviatar (L)	LE	Evil, Law, Retribution, Strength, Suffering	"Painbringer" (scourge)
Lurue (D)	CG	Animal, Chaos, Good, Healing	A unicorn horn (shortspear)
Malar (L)	CE	Animal, Chaos, Evil, Moon, Strength	A beast's claw (claw bracer)
Mask (L)	NE	Darkness, Evil, Luck, Trickery	"Stealthwhisper" (longsword)
Mielikki (I)	NG	Animal, Good, Plant, Travel	"The Hornblade" (scimitar)
Milil (L)	NG	Charm, Good, Knowledge, Nobility	"Sharptongue" (rapier)
Mystra (G)*	NG (LN)	Good, Illusion, Knowledge, Magic, Rune, Spell	Seven whirling stars (shuriken)
Nobanion (D)	LG	Animal, Good, Law, Nobility	A lion's head (heavy pick)
Oghma (G)*	N	Charm, Knowledge, Luck, Travel, Trickery	"Mortal Strike" (longsword)
Red Knight (D)	LN	Law, Nobility, Planning, War	"Checkmate" (longsword)
Savras (D)	LN	Fate, Knowledge, Law, Magic, Spell	The eye of Savras (dagger)
Selûne (I)	CG	Chaos, Good, Moon, Protection, Travel	"The Wand of Four Moons" (heavy mace)
Shar (G)	NE	Cavern, Darkness, Evil, Knowledge	"The Disk of Night" (chakram)
Sharess (D)	CG	Chaos, Charm, Good, Travel, Trickery	A great cat's paw (claw bracer)
Shaundakul (L)	CN	Air, Chaos, Portal, Protection, Trade, Travel	"Sword of Shadows" (greatsword)
Shiallia (D)	NG	Animal, Good, Plant, Renewal	"Forest's Friend" (quarterstaff)
Siamorphe (D)	LN	Knowledge, Law, Nobility, Planning	"Noble Might" [scepter] (light mace)
Silvanus (G)	N	Animal, Plant, Protection, Renewal, Water	"The Great Mallet of Silvanus" (maul)
Sune (G)	CG	Chaos, Charm, Good, Protection	A silken sash (whip)
Talona (L)	CE	Chaos, Destruction, Evil, Suffering	A scabrous hand (unarmed strike)
Talos (G)	CE	Chaos, Destruction, Evil, Fire, Storm	A lightning bolt (longspear, shortspear, or halfspear)
Tempus (G)	CN	Chaos, Protection, Strength, War	"Battle Prowess" (battleaxe)
Tiamat (L)	LE	Evil, Law, Scalykind, Tyranny	A dragon head (heavy pick)
Torm (L)	LG	Good, Healing, Law, Protection, Strength	"Duty's Bond" (greatsword)
Tymora (I)	CG	Chaos, Good, Luck, Protection, Travel	A spinning coin (shuriken)
Tyr (G)	LG	Good, Knowledge, Law, Retribution, War	"Justiciar" (longsword)
Ubtao (G)	N	Planning, Plant, Protection, Scalykind	Tyrannosaur head (heavy pick)
Ulutiu (slumbering) (D)	LN	Animal, Law, Ocean, Protection, Strength	"Harpoon of the Cold Sea" (longspear or shortspear)
Umberlee (I)	CE	Chaos, Destruction, Evil, Ocean, Storm, Water	"Drowning Death" [trident] or jellyfish (trident)
Uthgar (L)*	CN	Animal, Chaos, Retribution, Strength, War	Appropriate beast totem spirit (battleaxe)
Valkur (D)	CG	Air, Chaos, Good, Ocean, Protection	"The Captain's Cutlass" (cutlass)
Velsharoon (D)	NE	Death, Evil, Magic, Undeath	"Skull Staff of the Necromancer" (quarterstaff)
Waukeen (L)	N	Knowledge, Protection, Trade, Travel	Cloud of coins (nunchaku)

*See the deity's description for special rules regarding selection of this deity as a patron.

TABLE 5—1: THE FAERÛNIAN PANTHEON

Name	Symbol	Portfolio
Akadi	White cloud on blue background	Elemental air, movement, speed, flying creatures
Auril	White snowflake on gray diamond with white border	Cold, winter
Azuth	Human left hand pointing upward outlined in blue fire	Wizards, mages, spellcasters in general
Bane	Green rays squeezed forth from a black gauntleted fist	Hatred, tyranny, fear
Beshaba	Black antlers on a red field	Random mischief, misfortune, bad luck, accidents
Chauntea	Blooming rose on a sunburst wreath of golden grain	Agriculture, farmers, gardeners, summer
Cyric	White jawless skull on black or purple sunburst	Murder, lies, intrigue, strife, deception, illusion
Deneir	Lit candle above purple eye with triangular pupil	Glyphs, images, literature, scribes, cartography
Eldath	Waterfall plunging into a still pool	Quiet places, springs, pools, peace, waterfalls
Finder Wyvernspur	White harp on gray circle	Cycle of life, transformation of art, saurials
Garagos	A counterclockwise pinwheel of five snaky arms clutching swords	War, skill-at-arms, destruction, plunder
Gargauth	Broken animal horn	Betrayal, cruelty, political corruption, powerbrokers
Gond*	A toothed metal, bone, or wood cog with four spokes	Artifice, craft, construction, smithwork
Grumbar	Mountains on purple	Elemental earth, solidity, changelessness, oaths
Gwaeron Windstrom	White star and brown pawprint	Tracking, rangers of the North
Helm	Staring eye with blue pupil on upright left war gauntlet	Guardians, protectors, protection
Hoar	Black-gloved hand holding a coin with a two-faced head	Revenge, retribution, poetic justice
Ilmater	Pair of white hands bound at the wrist with a red cord	Endurance, suffering, martyrdom, perseverance
Istishia	Cresting wave	Elemental water, purification, wetness
Jergal	Jawless skull and writing quill on scroll	Fatalism, proper burial, guardian of tombs
Kelemvor	Upright skeletal arm holding the golden scales of justice	Death, the dead
Kossuth*	A twining red flame	Elemental fire, purification through fire
Lathander	Sunrise made of rose, red, and yellow gems	Spring, dawn, birth, youth, vitality, athletics
Lliira	A triangle of three six-pointed stars (orange, yellow, red)	Joy, happiness, dance, festivals, freedom, liberty
Loviatar	Nine-tailed barbed scourge	Pain, hurt, agony, torment, suffering, torture
Lurue	Silver-horned unicorn head before a crescent moon	Talking beasts, intelligent nonhumanoid creatures
Malar	Bestial claw with brown fur and curving bloody talons	Hunters, stalking, bloodlust, evil lycanthropes
Mask	Black velvet mask tinged with red	Thieves, thievery, shadows
Mielikki	Golden-horned, blue-eyed unicorn's head facing left	Forests, forest creatures, rangers, dryads, autumn
Milil	Five-stringed harp made of silver leaves	Poetry, song, eloquence
Mystra*	Circle of seven blue-white stars with red mist flowing from the center	Magic, spells, the Weave
Nobanion	Male lion's head on a green shield	Royalty, lions and feline beasts, good beasts
Oghma*	Blank scroll	Knowledge, invention, inspiration, bards
Red Knight	Red knight chess piece with stars for eyes	Strategy, planning, tactics
Savras	Crystal ball containing many kinds of eyes	Divination, fate, truth
Selûne	Pair of female eyes surrounded by seven silver stars	Moon, stars, navigation, prophecy, questers, good and neutral lycanthropes
Shar	Black disk with deep purple border	Dark, night, loss, forgetfulness, unrevealed secrets, caverns, dungeons, the Underdark
Sharess	Feminine lips	Hedonism, sensual fulfillment, festhalls, cats
Shaundakul	A wind-walking bearded man in traveler's cape and boots	Travel, exploration, caravans, portals
Shiallia	Golden acorn	Woodland glades, woodland fertility, the High Forest, Neverwinter Wood
Siamorphe	Silver chalice with a golden sun on the side	Nobles, rightful rule of nobility, human royalty
Silvanus	Green living oak leaf	Wild nature, druids
Sune	Face of a red-haired, ivory-skinned beautiful woman	Beauty, love, passion
Talona	Three amber teardrops on a purple triangle	Disease, poison
Talos	An explosive lightning strike	Storms, destruction, rebellion, conflagrations, earthquakes, vortices
Tempus	A flaming silver sword on a blood-red shield	War, battle, warriors
Tiamat	Five-headed dragon	Evil dragons, evil reptiles, greed, Chessenta
Torm	Right-hand gauntlet held upright with palm forward	Duty, loyalty, obedience, paladins
Tymora	Silver coin with Tymora's face surrounded by shamrocks	Good fortune, skill, victory, adventurers
Tyr	Balanced scales resting on a warhammer	Justice
Ubtao	Maze	Creation, jungles, Chult, the Chultans, dinosaurs
Ulutiu (slumbering)	Necklace of blue and white ice crystals	Glaciers, polar environments, arctic dwellers
Umberlee	Blue-green wave curling left and right	Oceans, currents, waves, sea winds
Uthgar*	That of the individual beast totem spirit	The Uthgardt barbarian tribes, physical strength
Valkur	Cloud with three lightning bolts on a shield	Sailors, ships, favorable winds, naval combat
Velsharoon	A crowned laughing lich skull on a black hexagon	Necromancy, necromancers, evil liches, undeath
Waukeen	Gold coin with Waukeen's profile facing left	Trade, money, wealth

*See the deity's description for special rules regarding selection of this deity as a patron.

God symbol illustrations by Stephanie Pui-Mun Law

TABLE 5—2: THE MULHORANDI PANTHEON

Name (Power)	Align.	Domains	Favored Weapon
Anhur (L)	CG	Chaos, Good, Strength, Storm, War	"Warhawk" (falchion)
Geb (L)	N	Cavern, Craft, Earth, Protection	"Stonemantle" (quarterstaff)
Hathor (L)	NG	Family, Fate, Good, Moon	Long cow horns (short sword)
Horus-Re (G)	LG	Good, Law, Nobility, Retribution, Sun	An ankh (khopesh)
Isis (I)	NG	Family, Good, Magic, Storm, Water	An ankh and star (punching dagger)
Nephthys (I)	CG	Chaos, Good, Protection, Trade	An ankh trailing a golden mist (whip)
Osiris (I)	LG	Death, Good, Law, Plant, Retribution	"Just Reward" (light flail or heavy flail)
Sebek (D)	NE	Animal, Evil, Scalykind, Water	"The Sorrowful Spear" (longspear, shortspear, or halfspear)
Set (I)	LE	Air, Darkness, Evil, Hatred, Law, Magic, Scalykind	"The Spear of Darkness" (longspear, shortspear, or halfspear)
Thoth (I)	N	Craft, Knowledge, Magic, Rune, Spell	"Knowledge Keeper" (quarterstaff)

TABLE 5—3: THE DROW PANTHEON

Name (Power)	Align.	Domains	Favored Weapon
Eilistraee (L)	CG	Chaos, Charm, Drow, Elf, Good, Moon, Portal	"The Moonsword" (bastard sword)
Ghaunadaur (L)	CE	Cavern, Chaos, Drow, Evil, Hatred, Slime	An amorphous tentacle (warhammer)
Kiaransalee (D)	CE	Chaos, Drow, Evil, Retribution, Undeath	"Cold Heart" (dagger)
Lolth (I)	CE	Chaos, Darkness, Destruction, Drow, Evil, Spider, Trickery	A spider (dagger)
Selvetarm (D)	CE	Chaos, Drow, Evil, Spider, War	"Venommace" (heavy mace)
Vhaeraun (L)	CE	Chaos, Drow, Evil, Travel, Trickery	"Shadowflash" (short sword)

Entries in brackets on Tables 5—1 through 5—8 give the form of a deity's weapon when it is different from the parenthetical favored weapon of the faith. They are purely descriptive.

Deity Description

The first paragraph of the deity's description includes a pronunciation of the deity's name and gives the deity's attitude, temperament, and general nature. General plans and whether the deity is usually worshiped out of respect or placated out of fear (or both) are discussed here.

The second paragraph describes the deity's church. This overview explains if the church is organized or casual, hierarchical or independent, prominent or secretive. The common duties of the clerics and members of the church are also given here. Note that buildings dedicated to a deity are casually known as temples, but that temples commonly come in three sizes: shrines (small structures), temples (structures of substantial size and at least several rooms), and cathedrals (grand structures of very large size). A household shrine or wayside shrine is not a building, but is a small space, often nothing more than a statue in an alcove or a pile of stones in a glade, dedicated to a single deity.

The third paragraph lists the time of day a deity's clerics pray for spells. If more than one time of prayer for spells is given, the cleric chooses one of those times and uses it thereafter. This section also lists well-known holy days of the faith, which the cleric is expected to observe to remain in good standing with the church and deity. Finally, the most common multiclassing options for clerics of the faith are given. (The cleric is not obligated to multiclass, is not restricted to the given classes, and is not penalized for not multiclassing or choosing classes other than those given (unless prohibited by the deity's ethos, such as a cleric of a deity of peace wishing to multiclass as a fighter). Some deities allow their clerics to multiclass freely as monks or paladins, meaning the cleric can continue to gain levels as a monk or paladin even after adding new cleric levels. (A cleric of this type could add a level of paladin, add another level of cleric, and continue to add paladin levels later, ignoring the "once you choose another class . . ." restriction in the *Player's Handbook*.)

History/Relationships: This section gives important notes on the deity's history, including his or her origin or the historic reason for current enmities. The deity's relationships indicate allies and enemies among the ranks of the divine, as well as whom the deity reports to (if anyone).

Dogma: The last paragraph gives the dogma of the deity—tenets of the religion that all clerics (and divine spellcasters) must hold dear. This paragraph is written as if it were an excerpt from a holy text of that deity. Some of the dogmatic statements are phrased in absolutes (Azuth's "Learn every new spell you discover," Chauntea's "Let no day pass in which you have not helped a living thing flourish," and so on). If a cleric is unable to perform these acts because of circumstances beyond her control (such as being locked in a dungeon cell, failing a Spellcraft roll, being involved in a lengthy religious ceremony, and the like), she is not penalized. However, if she could perform the necessary task but chose not to (for example, if a cleric of Chauntea spent the day looking for a new pair of boots instead of helping a living thing flourish), she would be guilty of a minor sin.

Azuth (Lesser God)

The High One, Patron of Mages, Lord of Spells

Symbol:	Human left hand pointing upward outlined in blue fire
Alignment:	Lawful neutral
Portfolio:	Wizards, mages, spellcasters in general
Domains:	Illusion, Magic, Knowledge, Law, Spell
Favored Weapon:	"The Old Staff" (quarterstaff)

Azuth (ah-*zooth*) is the deity of arcane spellcasters, rather than of magic itself. A somber father figure of a god, he has a dry, sardonic

TABLE 5—2: THE MULHORANDI PANTHEON

Name	Symbol	Portfolio
Anhur	Hawk-headed falchion bound with a cord	War, conflict, physical prowess, thunder, rain
Geb	Mountain	The earth, miners, mines, mineral resources
Hathor	Horned cow's head wearing a lunar disk	Motherhood, folk music, dance, the moon, fate
Horus-Rê	Hawk's head in pharaoh's crown before a solar circle	The sun, vengeance, rulership, kings, life
Isis	Ankh and star on a lunar disk	Weather, rivers, agriculture, love, marriage, good magic
Nephthys	Ankh above a golden offering bowl	Wealth, trade, protector of children and the dead
Osiris	White crown of Mulhorand over crossed crook and flail	Vegetation, death, the dead, justice, harvest
Sebek	Crocodile head wearing horned & plumed headdress	River hazards, crocodiles, werecrocodiles, wetlands
Set	Coiled cobra	The desert, destruction, drought, night, rot, snakes, hate, betrayal, evil magic, ambition, poison, murder
Thoth	Ankh above an ibis head	Neutral magic, scribes, knowledge, invention, secrets

TABLE 5—3: THE DROW PANTHEON

Name	Symbol	Portfolio
Eilistraee	Long-haired drow woman dancing before a full moon	Song, beauty, dance, swordwork, hunting, moonlight
Ghaunadaur	Purplish eye on purple, violet, and black circles	Oozes, slimes, jellies, outcasts, ropers, rebels
Kiaransalee	Female drow hand wearing silver rings	Undead, vengeance
Lolth	Black spider with female drow head hanging from a spiderweb	Spiders, evil, darkness, chaos, assassins, drow
Selvetarm	Spider on a crossed sword and mace	Drow warriors
Vhaeraun	A pair of black glass lenses that form a mask	Thievery, drow males, evil activity on the surface

wit and appreciates subtle humor. He carries the Old Staff, a divine artifact with the powers of a *staff of power* and a *staff of the magi* and the ability to reflect or absorb magic.

His church embraces the use of magic for constructive purposes and tries to acquire copies of every spell ever made (sometimes resorting to spying and temporary theft) so that the loss of a spellcaster doesn't mean the loss of a unique repertoire of spells. The Azuthan church also sponsors mage fairs, tries to curb the use of destructive or deceitful magic, and gives away spellbooks and minor magic items to people with the potential to become spellcasters.

Clerics of Azuth pray for their spells at dusk. The only official holy day of the church is the celebration of the ascension of a new Magister; however, meals within a temple are accompanied by the reading of works on the ethics of magic use and the philosophy of magic. Many clerics multiclass as sorcerers or wizards.

History/Relationships: Azuth was the first Magister, the mightiest of mortal wizards. His power was so great that he defeated the deity Savras in a protracted magical battle that lasted on and off for years. He finally imprisoned Savras's essence in a staff. Azuth later rose to divinity with the help of Mystra, and he has been her servant, friend, and advisor ever since. His subordinates are the specialized Faerûnian deities of magic: Savras, freed from the staff, and Velsharoon. He is friendly with deities of knowledge, art, and study, but opposes deities of falsehoods and wanton destruction, such as Cyric.

Dogma: Reason is the best way to approach magic, and magic can be examined and reduced to its component parts through study and meditation. Maintain calm and use caution in your spellcasting and magic use to avoid making mistakes that even magic cannot undo. Use the Art wisely, and always be mindful of when it is best not to use magic. Teach the wielding of magic and dispense learning items throughout Faerûn that the use and knowledge of magic may spread. Live and teach the idea that with magical power comes grave responsibility. Learn every new spell you discover and make a copy for the temple library. Do not hoard your knowledge, and encourage creativity in magic in all ways and at all times.

BANE (greater god)

The Black Lord, the Black Hand, the Lord of Darkness

Symbol:	Green rays squeezed forth from a black fist
Alignment:	Lawful evil
Portfolio:	Hatred, tyranny, fear
Domains:	Evil, Destruction, Hatred, Law, Tyranny
Favored Weapon:	The black hand of Bane [a black gauntlet] (morningstar)

Bane (*bain*) is the ultimate tyrant. He is thoroughly evil and malicious, and he revels in hatred and fear. A brooding power, he rarely shows himself directly, preferring to plot from within the shadows and destroy others from afar. He hopes to control all of Faerûn and dominate or subsume all other deities, although for now he is willing to work with some of them to advance his cause.

Bane's church has stabilized since the upheaval caused by his recent return, and almost all that worshiped Xvim now hold Bane as their patron, with some Cyric worshipers returning to their old deity as well. Within the church, the church hierarchy resolves internal disputes through cold and decisive thought, not rash and uncontrolled behavior. Bane's clerics and worshipers try to assume positions of power in every realm so that they can turn the world over to Bane. They work subtly and patiently to divide the forces of their enemies and elevate themselves and the church's allies over all others, although they do not fear swift and decisive violent action to help achieve their aims.

Bane's clerics pray for spells at midnight. They have no calendar-based holidays, and rituals are held whenever a senior cleric declares it time. Rites of Bane consist of drumming, chanting, doomful singing, and the sacrifice of intelligent beings, who are humiliated, tortured, and made to

Table 5-4: The Dwarven Pantheon

Name (Power)	Align.	Domains	Favored Weapon
Abbathor (I)	NE	Dwarf, Evil, Luck, Trade, Trickery	"Heart of Avarice" [diamond-bladed dagger] (dagger)
Berronar Truesilver (I)	LG	Dwarf, Family, Good, Healing, Law, Protection	"Wrath of Righteousness" (heavy mace)
Clangeddin Silverbeard (I)	LG	Dwarf, Good, Law, Strength, War	"Giantbane" (battleaxe)
Deep Duerra (duergar) (D)	LE	Dwarf, Evil, Law, Mentalism, War	"Mindshatter" (battleaxe)
Dugmaren Brightmantle (L)	CG	Chaos, Craft, Dwarf, Good, Knowledge, Rune	"Sharptack" (short sword)
Dumathoin (I)	N	Cavern, Craft, Dwarf, Earth, Knowledge, Metal, Protection	"Magmahammer" [mattock] (maul)
Gorm Gulthyn (L)	LG	Dwarf, Good, Law, Protection, War	"Axegard" (battleaxe)
Haela Brightaxe (D)	CG	Chaos, Dwarf, Good, Luck, War	"Flamebolt" (greatsword)
Laduguer (duergar) (I)	LE	Craft, Dwarf, Evil, Law, Magic, Metal, Protection	"Grimhammer" (warhammer)
Marthammor Duin (L)	NG	Dwarf, Good, Protection, Travel	"Glowhammer" (heavy mace)
Moradin (G)	LG	Craft, Dwarf, Earth, Good, Law, Protection	"Soulhammer" (warhammer)
Sharindlar (I)	CG	Chaos, Charm, Dwarf, Good, Healing, Moon	"Fleetbite" (whip)
Thard Harr (L)	CG	Animal, Chaos, Dwarf, Good, Plant	Clawed gauntlet (spiked gauntlet)
Vergadain (I)	N	Dwarf, Luck, Trade, Trickery	"Goldseeker" (longsword)

Table 5-5: The Elven Pantheon

Name (Power)	Align.	Domains	Favored Weapon
Aerdrie Faenya (I)	CG	Air, Animal, Chaos, Elf, Good, Storm	"Thunderbolt" (quarterstaff)
Angharradh (G)	CG	Chaos, Elf, Good, Knowledge, Plant, Protection, Renewal	"Duskshaft" (longspear or shortspear)
Corellon Larethian (G)	CG	Chaos, Elf, Good, Magic, Protection, War	"Sahandrian" (longsword)
Deep Sashelas (I)	CG	Chaos, Elf, Good, Knowledge, Ocean, Water	"Trifork of the Deeps" (trident)
Erevan Ilesere (I)	CN	Chaos, Elf, Luck, Trickery	"Quickstrike" (short sword)
Fenmarel Mestarine (L)	CN	Animal, Chaos, Elf, Plant, Travel	"Thornbite" (dagger)
Hanali Celanil (I)	CG	Chaos, Charm, Elf, Good, Magic, Protection	A shining heart (dagger)
Labelas Enoreth (I)	CG	Chaos, Elf, Good, Knowledge, Time	"The Timestave" (quarterstaff)
Rillifane Rallathil (I)	CG	Chaos, Elf, Good, Plant, Protection	"The Oakstaff" (quarterstaff)
Sehanine Moonbow (I)	CG	Chaos, Elf, Good, Illusion, Knowledge, Moon, Travel	"Moonshaft" (quarterstaff)
Shevarash (D)	CN	Chaos, Elf, Retribution, War	"The Black Bow" (longbow)
Solonor Thelandira (I)	CG	Chaos, Elf, Good, Plant, War	"Longshot" (longbow)

show fear before their death by flogging, slashing, or crushing. Clerics of Bane most commonly multiclass as fighters, monks, or blackguards.

History/Relationships: A mortal that gained divinity in a game of chance with the deity Jergal, Bane was a blight upon the world until slain by Torm during the Time of Troubles. However, Bane has returned, erupting from the sentient seed that was Iyachtu Xvim, his own half-demon son, and retaken his old portfolio, stealing from Cyric that which was once his. Acquiring fear as part of his portfolio, he has risen to the level of a greater deity. Bane has renewed his old alliances with Loviatar, Malar, Mask, and Talona, and hates most other deities, particularly Helm, Lathander, Mystra, Oghma, and the deities of the Triad. He has little love for Cyric either.

Dogma: Serve no one but Bane. Fear him always and make others fear him even more than you do. The Black Hand always strikes down those that stand against it in the end. Defy Bane and die—or in death find loyalty to him, for he shall compel it. Submit to the word of Bane as uttered by his ranking clergy, since true power can only be gained through service to him. Spread the dark fear of Bane. It is the doom of those who do not follow him to let power slip through their hands. Those who cross the Black Hand meet their dooms earlier and more harshly than those who worship other deities.

Chauntea (Greater Goddess)

The Great Mother, the Grain Goddess, Earthmother

Symbol:	Blooming rose on a sunburst wreath of golden grain
Alignment:	Neutral good
Portfolio:	Agriculture, plants cultivated by humans, farmers, gardeners, summer
Domains:	Animal, Earth, Good, Plant, Protection, Renewal
Favored Weapon:	A shock of grain (scythe)

Chauntea (chawn-*tee*-ah) is the humble deity of all growing things, especially those sowed by the hand of humankind. She rarely appears to mortals, nor is she fond of grand spectacles. She prefers quiet and small acts of devotion. Venerated by farmers, gardeners, and comon folk, she is beloved by all that work the soil.

TABLE 5—4: THE DWARVEN PANTHEON

Name	Symbol	Portfolio
Abbathor	Jeweled dagger	Greed
Berronar Truesilver	Two silver rings	Safety, honesty, home, healing, the dwarven family, records, marriage, faithfulness, loyalty, oaths
Clangeddin Silverbeard	Two crossed battleaxes	Battle, war, valor, bravery, honor in battle
Deep Duerra (duergar)	Broken illithid skull	Psionics, conquest, expansion
Dugmaren Brightmantle	Open book	Scholarship, invention, discovery
Dumathoin	Faceted gem inside a mountain	Buried wealth, ores, gems, mining, exploration, shield dwarves, guardian of the dead
Gorm Gulthyn	Shining bronze mask with eyeholes of flame	Guardian of all dwarves, defense, watchfulness
Haela Brightaxe	Unsheathed sword wrapped in two spirals of flame	Luck in battle, joy of battle, dwarven fighters
Laduguer (duergar)	Broken crossbow bolt on a shield	Magic weapon creation, artisans, magic, gray dwarves
Marthammor Duin	Upright mace in front of a fur-trimmed leather boot	Guides, explorers, expatriates, travelers, lightning
Moradin	Hammer and anvil	Dwarves, creation, smithing, protection, metalcraft, stonework
Sharindlar	Flame rising from a steel needle	Healing, mercy, romantic love, fertility, dancing, courtship, the moon
Thard Harr	Two crossed scaly clawed gauntlets of silvery-blue metal	Wild dwarves, jungle survival, hunting
Vergadain	Gold piece	Wealth, luck, chance, nonevil thieves, suspicion, trickery, negotiation, sly cleverness

TABLE 5—5: THE ELVEN PANTHEON

Name	Symbol	Portfolio
Aerdrie Faenya	Cloud with bird silhouette	Air, weather, avians, rain, fertility, avariels
Angharradh	Three interconnecting rings on a downward-pointing triangle	Spring, fertility, planting, birth, defense, wisdom
Corellon Larethian	Crescent moon	Magic, music, arts, crafts, war, the elven race (especially sun elves), poetry, bards, warriors
Deep Sashelas	Dolphin	Oceans, sea elves, creation, knowledge
Erevan Ilesere	Starburst with asymmetrical rays	Mischief, change, rogues
Fenmarel Mestarine	Pair of elven eyes in the darkness	Feral elves, outcasts, scapegoats, isolation
Hanali Celanil	Gold heart	Love, romance, beauty, enchantments, magic item artistry, fine art, and artists
Labelas Enoreth	Setting sun	Time, longevity, the moment of choice, history
Rillifane Rallathil	Oak tree	Woodlands, nature, wild elves, druids
Sehanine Moonbow	Misty crescent above a full moon	Mysticism, dreams, death, journeys, transcendence, the moon, the stars, the heavens, moon elves
Shevarash	Broken arrow above a teardrop	Hatred of the drow, vengeance, crusades, loss
Solonor Thelandira	Silver arrow with green fletching	Archery, hunting, wilderness survival

Her church consists of two divisions: those who work in civilized areas (clerics) and others who watch over outlying and wilderness regions (most often druids). The two branches of the church are cordial to each other, but relations are sometimes strained, as the progress of civilization continues to push the outlying branch farther afield. Both sides teach others responsibility and respect for nature, how to prevent damage and disease in plants, and how to minister to the land so that it provides year after year.

Chauntea's clerics and druids pray for spells at sundown. They have a fertility festival every Greengrass and observe solemn High Prayers of the Harvest on whatever day harvesting begins in the local community. Their few rituals are usually performed on freshly tilled land, and they say that passing one's wedding night on such a field guarantees fertility in marriage. Her clerics most often multiclass as rangers or druids.

History/Relationships: Chauntea is allied with the other nature deities of the Faerûnian pantheon, has an intermittent romance with Lathander, and opposes deities of destruction and untimely death, particularly the Gods of Fury (Auril, Malar, Talos, and Umberlee). She is a very old deity, and some consider her to be the progenitor of the natural races of the world.

Dogma: Growing and reaping are part of the eternal cycle and the most natural part of life. Destruction for its own sake and leveling without rebuilding are anathema. Let no day pass in which you have not helped a living thing flourish. Nurture, tend, and plant wherever possible. Protect trees and plants, and save their seeds so that what is destroyed can be replaced. See to the fertility of the earth but let the human womb see to its own. Eschew fire. Plant a seed or a small plant at least once a tenday.

CYRIC (greater god)

Prince of Lies, the Dark Sun, the Black Sun

Symbol:	White jawless skull on black or purple sunburst
Alignment:	Chaotic evil
Portfolio:	Murder, lies, intrigue, strife, deception, illusion
Domains:	Chaos, Destruction, Evil, Illusion, Trickery
Favored Weapon:	"Razor's Edge" (longsword)

239

Table 5—6: The Gnome Pantheon

Name (Power)	Align.	Domains	Favored Weapon
Baervan Wildwanderer (I)	NG	Animal, Gnome, Good, Plant, Travel	"Whisperleaf" (halfspear)
Baravar Cloakshadow (L)	NG	Gnome, Good, Illusion, Protection, Trickery	"Nightmare" (dagger)
Callarduran Smoothhands (I)	N	Cavern, Craft, Earth, Gnome	"Spiderbane" (battleaxe)
Flandal Steelskin (I)	NG	Craft, Gnome, Good, Metal	"Rhondang" (warhammer)
Gaerdal Ironhand (L)	LG	Gnome, Good, Law, Protection, War	"Hammersong" (warhammer)
Garl Glittergold (G)	LG	Craft, Gnome, Good, Law, Protection, Trickery	"Arumdina" (battleaxe)
Segojan Earthcaller (I)	NG	Cavern, Earth, Gnome, Good	"Earthcaller" [crystalline rod] (heavy mace)
Urdlen (I)	CE	Chaos, Earth, Evil, Gnome, Hatred	Great claw (claw bracer)

Table 5—7: The Halfling Pantheon

Name (Power)	Align.	Domains	Favored Weapon
Arvoreen (I)	LG	Good, Halfling, Law, Protection, War	"Aegisheart" (short sword)
Brandobaris (L)	N	Halfling, Luck, Travel, Trickery	"Escape" (dagger)
Cyrrollalee (I)	LG	Family, Good, Halfling, Law	"Camaradestave" [quarterstaff] (club)
Sheela Peryroyl (I)	N	Air, Charm, Halfling, Plant	"Oakthorn" (sickle)
Urogalan (D)	LN	Death, Earth, Halfling, Law, Protection	"Doomthresher" [double-headed flail] (any flail)
Yondalla (G)	LG	Family, Good, Halfling, Law, Protection	"Hornblade" (short sword)

Table 5—8: The Orc Pantheon

Name (Power)	Align.	Domains	Favored Weapon
Bahgtru (L)	CE	Chaos, Evil, Orc, Strength	"Crunch" (spiked gauntlet)
Gruumsh (G)	CE	Cavern, Chaos, Evil, Hatred, Orc, Strength, War	"The Bloodspear" [longspear] (longspear or shortspear)
Ilneval (L)	NE	Destruction, Evil, Orc, Planning, War	"Foe Smiter" (longsword)
Luthic (L)	NE	Cavern, Earth, Evil, Family, Healing, Orc	A hand with long claws (claw bracer)
Shargaas (L)	CE	Chaos, Darkness, Evil, Orc, Trickery	"Nightblade" (short sword)
Yurtrus (L)	NE	Death, Destruction, Evil, Orc, Suffering	Pale white hands (unarmed strike)

Cyric (*seer*-ick) is a megalomaniacal deity with an immense following. One of the four greater powers of evil on Faerûn, he is petty and self-centered, and enjoys misleading individuals of all inclinations so that they perform acts that ruin their lives or so that they make fatal mistakes. He drinks the tears of disillusioned dreamers and broken-hearted lovers. He is not above an alliance with another deity as long as he thinks he can betray the other divine power and come out ahead.

Cyric's church is pledged to spread strife and work murder everywhere in order to make folk worship and fear the Dark Sun. It supports cruel rulers and indulges in intrigue in such a way that the world won't be overrun by wars (and thus fall under the sway of Tempus). His church is often beset by internal feuds and backstabbing, but this conflict has decreased in recent years as Cyric has gained better control of himself and has consolidated the churches of the deities whose portfolios he took over.

Cyric's clerics pray for spells at night, after moonrise. Cyric's church has few holy days and does not even celebrate the date of his ascension to divinity. Whenever a temple acquires something (or someone) important enough to sacrifice to Cyric, its high priest declares a Day of the Dark Sun to signify the holiness of the event. Eclipses are considered holy. They are accompanied by feasts, fervent prayers, and bloody sacrifices. Cyric's clerics often multiclass as rogues or assassins.

History/Relationships: Cyric arose as a deity during the Time of Troubles. He was a mortal who assumed the portfolios of two deities slain in the Godswar and who managed to slay two other deities and then assume their portfolios. He hates most of the other deities of Toril, but he particularly loathes Mystra (whom he knew as a mortal and whose portfolio he desires), Kelemvor, and Bane (who now holds portions of the portfolio once claimed by him).

Dogma: Death to all who oppose Cyric. Bow down before his supreme power, and yield to him the blood of those that do not believe in his supremacy. Fear and obey those in authority, but slay those that are weak, of good persuasion, or false prophets. Bring death to those that oppose Cyric's church or make peace, order, and laws, for only Cyric is the true authority. Break not into open rebellion, for marching armies move the false deities to action. Fell one foe at a time and keep all folk afraid, uneasy, and in constant strife. Any method or means is justified if it brings about the desired end.

Eilistraee (Lesser Goddess)

The Dark Maiden, Lady of the Dance

Symbol:	Nude long-haired female drow dancing with a silver bastard sword in front of a full moon
Alignment:	Chaotic good
Portfolio:	Song, beauty, dance, swordwork, hunting, moonlight
Domains:	Chaos, Charm, Drow, Elf, Good, Moon, Portal
Favored Weapon:	"The Moonsword" (bastard sword)

Table 5—6: The Gnome Pantheon

Name	Symbol	Portfolio
Baravar Cloakshadow	Cloak and dagger	Illusions, deception, traps, wards
Baervan Wildwanderer	Raccoon's face	Forests, travel, nature
Callarduran Smoothhands	Gold ring with star symbol	Stone, the Underdark, mining, the svirfneblin
Flandal Steelskin	Flaming hammer	Mining, physical fitness, smithing, metalworking
Gaerdal Ironhand	Iron band	Vigilance, combat, martial defense
Garl Glittergold	Gold nugget	Protection, humor, trickery, gem cutting, gnomes
Segojan Earthcaller	Glowing gemstone	Earth, nature, the dead
Urdlen	White mole	Greed, bloodlust, evil, hatred, uncontrolled impulse, spriggans

Table 5—7: The Halfling Pantheon

Name	Symbol	Portfolio
Arvoreen	Two short swords	Defense, war, vigilance, halfling warriors, duty
Brandobaris	Halfling's footprint	Stealth, thievery, adventuring, halfling rogues
Cyrrollalee	Open door	Friendship, trust, the hearth, hospitality, crafts
Sheela Peryroyl	Daisy	Nature, agriculture, weather, song, dance, beauty, romantic love
Urogalan	Silhouette of a dog's head	Earth, death, protection of the dead
Yondalla	Cornucopia on a shield	Protection, bounty, halflings, children, security, leadership, wisdom, creation, family, tradition

Table 5—8: The Orc Pantheon

Name	Symbol	Portfolio
Bahgtru	Broken thighbone	Loyalty, stupidity, brute strength
Gruumsh	Unwinking eye	Orcs, conquest, survival, strength, territory
Ilneval	Bloodied longsword	War, combat, overwhelming numbers, strategy
Luthic	Orc rune for home	Caves, orc females, home, wisdom, fertility, healing, servitude
Shargaas	Skull on a red crescent moon	Night, thieves, stealth, darkness, Underdark
Yurtrus	White hands on dark background	Death, disease

Eilistraee (eel-iss-*tray*-yee) is the deity of good drow and those of that race who wish to be able to live on the surface in peace. A melancholy, moody deity, she is a lover of beauty and peace but is not averse to striking back against those that would harm her followers. The evil of most drow causes a great anger to burn within her.

The church of Eilistraee encourages drow to return to the surface world and work to promote harmony between the drow and surface races so that drow again become rightful nonevil inhabitants of Faerûn. Members of the church nurture beauty, craft musical instruments, sing, and assist others in need. Clerics must be able to sing adequately, dance gracefully, and play the horn, flute, or harp. Skill at swordplay is also encouraged, as is the ability to hunt.

Clerics of the Dark Maiden pray for spells at night, after moonrise. Their rituals revolve around a hunt followed by a feast and dancing (wearing as little clothing as possible). Four times a year they have a High Hunt, during which they hunt a dangerous beast while wearing nothing and carrying only a single sword. Once a year they perform a Run, when they seek out unfamiliar elven communities in order to show them kindness and bring them game and assistance, thus fostering acceptance of the drow in doing so. Eilistraee's clerics often multiclass as fighters, bards, or rangers.

History/Relationships: The daughter of Corellon Larethian and Araushnee (who became Lolth), Eilistraee was banished along with the other drow deities for her (inadvertent) part in the war against the Seldarine (the elven pantheon). She insisted upon this punishment, which was dealt reluctantly by her father, because she foresaw that the dark elves would need a beacon of good within their reach. Her allies are the Seldarine, the good deities of the Underdark races, Mystra, and Selûne; her enemies are the evil deities of the Underdark, especially the rest of the drow pantheon.

Dogma: Be always kind, save in battle with evil. Encourage happiness everywhere. Learn and teach new songs, dances, and the flowing dance of skilled swordwork. Promote harmony between the races. Befriend strangers, shelter those without homes, and feed the hungry. Repay rudeness with kindness. Repay violence with swift violence so that those that cause it are swiftly dealt with. Aid drow in distress, and give them the Lady's message: "A rightful place awaits you in the Realms Above, in the Land of the Great Light. Come in peace and live beneath the sun again where trees and flowers grow."

Gond (intermediate god)

Wonderbringer, Lord of All Smiths

Symbol:	A toothed metal, bone, or wood cog with four spokes
Alignment:	Neutral (any character can choose Gond as a patron deity)
Portfolio:	Artifice, craft, construction, smithwork
Domains:	Craft, Earth, Fire, Knowledge, Metal, Planning
Favored Weapon:	"Craftmaster" (warhammer)

Gond (*gahnd*) is a driven and energetic deity who is fascinated with making the theoretical real. He often becomes so focused on his current project that he doesn't realize the long-term consequences or implications of its use. He pushes Oghma to allow new inventions onto the face of Toril, and he often makes shady deals (paying in promises of later goods or favors) to get the strange materials he sometimes needs.

The church of Gond works to make sure the secrets of *smokepowder* and other related materials remain proprietary, eliminating rivals with sabotage, diplomacy, and financial influence. The church accepts people of any alignment as long as they are interested in crafting and craftsmanship. Clerics of any alignment may serve Gond. Clerics are discouraged from settling in one place, and they travel to discover inventions in other areas. Many support themselves by selling ammunition for *smokepowder* weapons and high-quality manufactured materials such as bells, lenses, clocks, and so on, while others work as engineers and craftsfolk. Traveling clerics establish caches of goods, invest in promising craftsfolk, and acquire or copy samples of new inventions they find. Gond's temples are said to be linked by *portals*, allowing them to easily share information and materials.

Clerics of Gond pray for their spells in the morning before the morning meal. Their one holy festival is the Ippensheir, which occurs during the twelve days after Greengrass. At this time they exhibit inventions, share innovations, feast, and drink. One of their stranger rituals occurs when they discover a new invention. The discovering cleric is charged to make two copies of it: one to be stored in a temple and the other to be smashed or burned as an offering to Gond. Some clerics multiclass as rogues, but only out of an interest in lockpicks and other small tools.

History/Relationships: Gond is an enigmatic deity. He serves Oghma but is so independent of his superior that many forget their relationship. He is friendly with Lathander, Oghma, Waukeen, and Tempus, for his inventions relate directly to creativity, knowledge, profit, and war. His only true foe is Talos, whose unhindered destruction threatens not only Gond's inventions but Gond's dominion over devices of destruction.

Dogma: Actions count. Intentions and thought are one thing, but it is the result that is most important. Talk is for others, while those who serve Gond *do*. Make new things that work. Become skilled at some craft, and practice making things until you can create devices to suit any situation. Question and challenge the unknown with new devices. New inventions should be elegant and useful. Practice experimentation and innovation, and encourage these virtues in others. Keep records of your strivings, ideas, and sample devices so that others may follow your work and improve on what you leave behind.

Helm (intermediate god)

The Watcher, the Vigilant One
Symbol: Staring eye with blue pupil on the front of upright war gauntlet
Alignment: Lawful neutral
Portfolio: Guardians, protectors, protection
Domains: Law, Planning, Protection, Strength
Favored Weapon: "Ever Watchful" (bastard sword)

Helm (*helm*) is an unflinching and dedicated deity. He is often viewed as emotionless and unconcerned with moral issues in the face of duty. However, he is merely dedicated to his work and takes pride in putting his work ahead of all other

things. He is fond of children and more tolerant of their minor infractions than of anyone else's. Many believe that Helm would give his own life to guard something entrusted to him. He is silent on the matter.

Helm's churches are often located near dangerous and evil areas, where they form a line of defense against the encroachment of powerful enemies. Major cities usually have a temple or shrine to Helm, for his clerics make excellent guards or leaders of guards. His church spreads the word that only Helm's clerics and their students are truly worthy and reliable guardians. His church and the church of Torm are coolly hostile rivals. Each church sees the other as a usurper of its chosen duties.

Clerics of Helm pray for their spells in the morning promptly after rising or just before retiring for the evening. Their one holy day is the Ceremony of Honor to Helm, which takes place on Shieldmeet. They observe important ceremonies when a cleric rises in rank or seeks to renew faith after a shortcoming. They have a strict military hierarchy, and every cleric can easily determine his rank relative to other clerics. Clerics of Helm never command undead. They most commonly multiclass as fighters or paladins.

History/Relationships: Helm saw his influence wane after the Time of Troubles and when news reached Faerûn of how his church handled the land of Maztica to the west. Helm's faith is waxing again as evil organizations and countries have strengthened and begun to expand their influence. Helm is a staunch ally of Torm (despite the difficulties between their churches). He opposes deities of destruction and deceit and has renewed efforts against his old enemy Bane.

Dogma: Never betray your trust. Be vigilant. Stand, wait, and watch carefully. Be fair and diligent in the conduct of your orders. Protect the weak, poor, injured, and young, and do not sacrifice them for others or yourself. Anticipate attacks and be ready. Know your foes. Care for your weapons so they may perform their duties when called upon. Careful planning always defeats rushed actions in the end. Always obey orders, providing those orders follow the dictates of Helm. Demonstrate excellence and purity of loyalty in your role as a guardian and protector.

Ilmater (intermediate god)

The Crying God, the Broken God
Symbol: Pair of white hands bound at the wrist with a red cord
Alignment: LG
Portfolio: Endurance, suffering, martyrdom, perseverance
Domains: Good, Healing, Law, Strength, Suffering
Favored Weapon: An open hand (unarmed strike)

Ilmater (*ill-may-ter*) is a generous and self-sacrificing deity. He is willing to shoulder any burden for another person, whether it is a heavy load or terrible pain. A gentle god, Ilmater is quiet, kind, and good-spirited. He appreciates a humorous story and is always slow to anger. While most consider him nonviolent, in the face of extreme cruelty or atrocities his anger rises and his wrath is terrible to behold. He takes great care to reassure and protect children and young creatures, and he takes exceptional offense at those that would harm them.

Unlike most other faiths, the church of Ilmater has many saints.

Clerics:

Mystra Bane Selûne Shar Torm Talos

Illustrations by Sam Wood

Perceived by most as a puzzling crowd of martyrs, the church of Ilmater spends most of its efforts on providing healing to those that have been hurt. It sends its clerics to impoverished areas, places struck by plague, and war-torn lands in order to alleviate the suffering of others..

Ilmater's clerics are the most sensitive and caring beings in the world. While some grow cynical at all the suffering they see, they still are compelled to help those in need whenever they encounter them. His clerics share whatever they have with the needy and act on behalf of those that cannot act for or defend themselves. Many learn the Brew Potion feat so that they can help those beyond their immediate reach.

Clerics of Ilmater pray for spells in the morning, although they still have to pray to Ilmater at least six times a day altogether. They have no annual holy days, but occasionally a cleric calls for a Plea of Rest. This allows him a tenday of respite from Ilmater's dictates, which prevents the cleric from suffering emotional exhaustion or allows him to perform some act that Ilmater would normally frown upon. One group of monks of Ilmater acts as the defenders of the faithful and the church's temples. These monks can multiclass freely as clerics.

History/Relationships: Ilmater is an older deity. He has long been associated with Tyr (his superior) and Torm, and together they are known as the Triad. Ilmater is also allied with Lathander, but he opposes deities that enjoy destruction and causing pain and hardship for others, particularly Loviatar, whose nature is the diametric opposite of his own.

Dogma: Help all who hurt, no matter who they are. The truly holy take on the suffering of others. If you suffer in his name, Ilmater is there to support you. Stick to your cause if it is right, whatever the

pain or peril. There is no shame in a meaningful death. Stand up to all tyrants, and allow no injustice to go unchallenged. Emphasize the spiritual nature of life over the existence of the material body.

Kelemvor (Greater God)

Lord of the Dead, Judge of the Damned

Symbol:	Upright skeletal arm holding the golden scales of justice
Alignment:	Lawful neutral
Portfolio:	Death, the dead
Domains:	Death, Fate, Law, Protection, Travel
Favored Weapon:	"Fatal Touch" (bastard sword)

Kelemvor (*kell*-em-vor) assigns the essences of the dead their proper place in the ongoing cycle of existence. Taking a different tack from his predecessor gods of the dead, he is neither malign nor secretive. He promises that the dead shall be judged in an even-handed and fair manner. He is kind, forthright, and earnest, though occasionally stern. His main flaw is that he solves problems with direct action and frequently does not anticipate the negative consequences of his haste down the road.

Kelemvor's church assists the dying, the dead, and their families. Its members see to funerals, burials, setting the affairs of the dead to right, and enacting wills. The church claims the property of those who died intestate and with no clear heirs so that its work in aiding the dying can continue. The church marks sites of disease with plague warnings, hunts down undead creatures to destroy them, recruits adventurers to fend off monsters that cause too much untimely death, and (rarely) grants swift and painless death to those for whom death would be a mercy.

Clerics of Kelemvor pray for spells at sundown. They have annual holidays on Shieldmeet and the Feast of the Moon. Both of these involve telling tales of the deeds of the dead so that they may be remembered. The remainder of the church's rituals are tied to deaths, funerals, and wakes. Kelemvor's clerics sometimes multiclass as necromancers or rangers, using their knowledge to hunt down and destroy undead. They turn undead rather than rebuking them.

History/Relationships: Once a mortal who knew Cyric, Kelemvor inherited his portfolio from Cyric after an error made by that god. Cyric hates Kelemvor and strives to regain what he lost, and Kelemvor in return fights Cyric. He also fights Talona for the many untimely deaths she causes and Velsharoon for the undead creatures he represents. Mystra, whom he knew as a mortal, and Jergal, who records the passing of the dead, are his allies.

Dogma: Recognize that death is part of life. It is not an ending but a beginning, not a punishment but a necessity. Death is an orderly process without deceit, concealment, and randomness. Help others die with dignity at their appointed time and no sooner. Speak against those that would artificially prolong their life beyond natural limits, such as the undead. Do honor to the dead, for their strivings in life brought Faerûn to where it is now. Forgetting them is to forget where we are now, and why. Let no human die a natural death in all Faerûn without one of Kelemvor's clerics at her side.

Kossuth (Greater God)

The Lord of Flames, the Firelord

Symbol:	A twining red flame
Alignment:	Neutral (you can use either N or LN when picking Kossuth as a patron)
Portfolio:	Elemental fire, purification through fire
Domains:	Destruction, Fire, Renewal, Suffering
Favored Weapon:	Tendril of flame (spiked chain)

Kossuth (koh-*sooth*), like the other elemental rulers, is an alien and enigmatic deity. He holds little affection toward his followers on Toril, but he rewards them more frequently for their attention than do his elemental counterparts. He seems to follow a private agenda, but its intended outcome or even its next steps are unknown to any but him. He actively recruits new followers, possibly because they burn out so quickly.

Kossuth's church is very hierarchical and tends toward a lawful neutral alignment and behavior, depending upon the particular temple. Kossuth appears indifferent to this regimentation, which means that clerics of Kossuth use either neutral or lawful neutral as their base alignment rather than neutral. The primary function of the church is to acquire land, wealth, influence, and power, all of which make the church appealing to potential worshipers and draw new people to the faith.

Clerics of Kossuth choose sunrise or highsun as their prayer time. They observe the birthdate of the high priest of their temple as an annual festival and undergo an Oath of Firewalking (wherein they cross a pit of hot coals) every time they gain a level or promotion within the church hierarchy. Three orders of fighting monks (the Disciples of the Phoenix, the Brothers and Sisters of the Pure Flame,

and the Disciples of the Salamander, corresponding to lawful good, lawful neutral, and lawful evil) follow Kossuth. Clerics can multiclass freely as a monk of the appropriate order. Some clerics also multiclass as wizards or sorcerers, focusing on fire magic.

History/Relationships: One of the four elemental rulers worshiped on Toril, Kossuth is prominent because of his many followers among the Red Wizards of Thay. He is less aloof to deities of fire or deities that wield it, but he is violently opposed to Istishia.

Dogma: Those fit to succeed will do so. Kossuth's faith is innately superior to all other faiths, particularly that of Istishia. Fire and purity are one and the same. Smoke is produced by air in its jealousy. The reward of successful ambition is power. Reaching a higher state is inevitably accompanied by difficulty and personal pain of some sort. Kossuth sends his pure fire to cleanse us all and temper our souls so that we can achieve a pure state. Expect to be tested, and rise to the challenge, no matter what difficulty and pain it brings. Those above you have proven their worth and deserve your service. Guide others to Kossuth's pure light so that he may reforge all life into its essential form.

Lathander (Greater God)

The Morninglord

Symbol:	Sunrise made of rose, red, and yellow gems
Alignment:	Neutral good
Portfolio:	Spring, dawn, birth, renewal, creativity, youth, vitality, self-perfection, athletics
Domains:	Good, Nobility, Protection, Renewal, Strength, Sun
Favored Weapon:	"Dawnspeaker" (light or heavy mace)

Lathander (lah-*than*-der) is a powerful, exuberant deity who is popular among commoners, nobles, merchants, and the young. Although occasionally given to excess, abundant enthusiasm, and vanity, he is an optimistic and perseverant deity who blesses new ventures and destroys undead with his mace *Dawnspeaker*. Lathander is a vibrant power that enjoys doing physical things for the sake of doing them.

The eastward-facing churches of Lathander are generally wealthy and not afraid to show it (sometimes to the point of gaudiness). There is no central religious authority in the church, and the head of each church is respected equally, regardless of the size of its flock. The church encourages its faithful to build new things, restore barren areas, foster growth in cultivated lands, drive out evil, and work to restore or lead civilizations to new heights of harmony, art, and progress. Churches sponsor athletic contests to promote unity and camaraderie, promote the arts through similar competitions, and finance the recovery of lost items.

Clerics of Lathander pray at dawn. The church holds the ceremony called the Song of Dawn on Midsummer morning and at the equinoxes. During it, the clergy and the faithful sing harmonies and counterharmonies to praise the Morninglord. Lathander's clerics are expected to keep physically fit and make regular offerings of coins, items, inventions, or food to his temples. His lawful clerics can multiclass freely as paladins.

History/Relationships: While usually shown as a young, attractive man, Lathander is an old power with a long history of driving creation, progress, and innovation. He opposes deities of evil, destruction, and death. His allies include deities of nature (particularly Chauntea), good, art, beauty, and invention. Traditionally a foe of the deity of the dead, Lathander has accepted Kelemvor's professed dislike of undead and holds no ill will toward him.

Dogma: Strive always to aid, to foster new hope, new ideas, and new prosperity for all humankind and its allies. It is a sacred duty to foster new growth, nurture growing things, and work for rebirth and renewal. Perfect yourself, and be fertile in mind and body. Wherever you go, plant seeds of hope, new ideas, and plans for a rosy future in the minds of all. Watch each sunrise. Consider the consequences of your actions so that your least effort may bring the greatest and best reward. Avoid negativity, for from death comes life, and there is always another morning to turn a setback into a success. Place more importance in activities that help others than in strict adherence to rules, rituals, and the dictates of your seniors.

Lolth (intermediate goddess)

Queen of Spiders, Queen of the Demonweb Pits

Symbol:	Black spider with female drow head hanging from a spiderweb
Alignment:	Chaotic evil
Portfolio:	Spiders, evil, darkness, chaos, assassins, drow
Domains:	Chaos, Drow, Evil, Darkness, Destruction, Spider, Trickery
Favored Weapon:	A spider (dagger)

Lolth (*loalth*) is a cruel, capricious deity who is believed to be insane by many because she pits her own worshipers against each other. Malicious in her dealings with others and coldly vicious in a fight, she covets the power given to the deities worshiped by the surface races. She can be kind and aid those that she fancies, but she thrives on the death, destruction, and torture of anyone, including those of her own worshipers that have displeased her.

Lolth's church promotes the superiority of the Queen of Spiders over all other beings. It is responsible for the perpetuation of the evil rumors and fear the surface elves hold for the drow and their deity. Even Lolth's most devout clerics hate and fear her, worshiping her only for the power she grants. In most cities, her clerics control the noble houses and thus the cities themselves. Her clerics act as the rulers, police force, judges, juries, and executioners of their society. Their cruel and capricious acts are designed to keep the citizens in fear of them and hateful of outsiders.

Clerics of Lolth pray for spells after waking from trance or before retiring to trance. Her clerics are always female. They practice monthly sacrifices of surface elves, preferring to perform them on the nights of the full moon to offend Sehanine Moonbow of the elven pantheon. Other private church ceremonies take place behind closed doors in darkened rooms with no males present, while public ceremonies allow a mix of genders. A common ritual is the summoning of a yochlol (a servitor demon with amorphous, spider, and elven shapes) for information or physical aid. Lolth's clerics sometimes multiclass as fighters or sorcerers. Drow clerics of Lolth have cleric as their preferred class.

History/Relationships: Lolth was once Araushnee, the consort of Corellon Larethian, and bore him Eilistraee and Vhaeraun. She betrayed her lover, tried to invade Arvandor with a host of evil spirits, and was banished to the Abyss in the form of a spider demon.

She is the ruler of the drow pantheon and is allied with Loviatar and Malar. Her foes include the Seldarine (the elven pantheon), Ghaunadaur, Eilistraee, nondrow Underdark deities, and Gruumsh.

Dogma: Fear is as strong as steel, while love and respect are soft and useless. Convert or destroy nonbeliever drow. Weed out the weak and the rebellious. Destroy impugners of the faith. Sacrifice males, slaves, and those of other races who ignore the commands of Lolth or her clerics. Raise children to praise and fear Lolth; each family should produce at least one cleric to serve her. Questioning Lolth's motives or wisdom is a sin, as is aiding nondrow against the drow, or ignoring Lolth's commands for the sake of a lover. Revere arachnids of all kinds; those who kill or mistreat a spider must die.

Malar (lesser god)

The Beastlord, the Black-Blooded Pard

Symbol:	Bestial claw with brown fur and curving bloody talons
Alignment:	Chaotic evil
Portfolio:	Hunters, stalking, bloodlust, evil lycanthropes, marauding beasts and monsters
Domains:	Animal, Chaos, Evil, Moon, Strength
Favored Weapon:	A beast's claw (claw bracer)

Malar (*mahl*-arr) is a savage and bestial deity who revels in the fear of the hunted. Jealous of other deities and their power, he is constantly trying to steal the portfolios and worshipers of related beings but lacks the intelligence or skill to be very successful at it. He excels at hunting, tracking, and animalistic slaughter.

Malar's church lacks a central authority and consists of small groups of worshipers scattered across uncivilized areas. His church espouses the glory of the hunt, and its members engage in ritualized hunts of wild animals, strange beasts, or even captured humanoids. They prefer to drive hunted creatures along paths dangerous to both the predators and the prey so that the final kill is more worthwhile. They try to stage the bloody finale in or near a settled area so that others can see (and fear) the power of Malar. Church members work against the expansion of farms and civilization and attack groups of nonevil druids, seeing those who promote the gentler side of nature as weak and foolish.

Clerics of Malar pray for spells at night, preferably under a full moon. Two rituals the church observes are the Feast of the Stags and the High Hunt. The Feast of the Stags consists of clerics and worshipers of Malar hunting a great deal of game before Highharvestide and then inviting all to join them at a feast, at which time they pledge to hunt in the coming winter to provide for the needy. (This is one of the few things the church does that pleases outsiders.) During the High Hunt, held each season, worshipers adorned in kill trophies hunt a humanoid, who wins his life and a boon if he escapes or survives a day and a night. Malar's clerics often multiclass as barbarians, rangers, or (if evil) druids.

History/Relationships: Malar was a deity even before the ascension of Bane and has tried over the centuries to usurp power from other deities with varying degrees of success. One of the Gods of Fury along with Talos (his superior), Auril, and Umberlee, he is also allied with Bane and Loviatar. He fights against the deities of peace, civilization, and nature.

Dogma: Survival of the fittest and the winnowing of the weak are Malar's legacy. A brutal, bloody death or kill has great meaning. The crux of life is the challenge between the hunter and the prey, the determination of who lives or dies. View every important task as a hunt. Remain ever alert and alive. Walk the wilderness without trepidation, and show no fear in the hunt. Savagery and strong emotions defeat reason and careful thought in all things. Taste the blood of those you slay, and never kill from a distance. Work against those who cut back the forest and who kill beasts solely because they are dangerous. Slay not the young, the pregnant, or deepspawn so that prey will remain plentiful.

Mask (Lesser God)

Master of All Thieves, Lord of Shadows

Symbol:	Black velvet mask tinged with red
Alignment:	Neutral evil
Portfolio:	Thieves, thievery, shadows
Domains:	Darkness, Evil, Luck, Trickery
Favored Weapon:	"Stealthwhisper" (longsword)

Mask (*mask*) is a self-possessed and confident deity fond of complex plans and intricate plots, although he has trained himself to become more direct because recently his own scheming caused him a great reduction in power and loss of the intrigue portfolio to Cyric. He is wary, but cool, never losing his temper, and he always seems to be holding back a mocking comment. His sword, *Stealthwhisper*, makes no noise and has *speed* and *wounding* properties.

Mask's church is essentially similar to a network of thieves' guilds. In large cities with several guilds, his temple is often connected to each thieves' guild by secret tunnels and is considered neutral ground for meetings by all. Mask's church promotes stealth over open confrontation, leading the more gullible to believe that Mask is dead. A wealthy religion, the church of Mask uses its resources to pay agents, sway agreements, and manipulate people. Its members spend their time nurturing plots and supporting thieves' guilds and individual thieves.

Clerics of Mask pray at night in darkness or shadows. At least once a month each major temple performs the Ritual of the Unseen Presence, involving hymns, chanted verse, and offerings of wealth, acknowledging Mask's constant scrutiny of all deeds, no matter how well hidden. Most clerics tend to multiclass as rogues or bards.

History/Relationships: Mask is a loner god who prefers to act on his own initiative, although he has occasional alliances with Bane. He hates Cyric for the theft of part of his portfolio and is opposed to Waukeen because of their rival natures. His other foes are the deities of guardians and duty, knowledge, and Selûne, from whose light his followers hide while doing their dark work.

Dogma: All that occurs within shadows is in the purview of Mask. Ownership is nine-tenths of what is right, and ownership is defined as possession. The world belongs to the quick, the smooth-tongued, and the light-fingered. Stealth and wariness are virtues, as are glibness and the skill to say one thing and mean another, twisting a situation to your advantage. Wealth rightfully belongs to those who can acquire it. Strive to end each day with more wealth than you began it, but steal what is most vital, not everything at hand. Honesty is for fools, but apparent honesty is valuable. Make every truth seem plausible, and never lie when you can tell the truth but leave a mistaken impression. Subtlety is everything. Manipulation is better than force, especially when you can make people think they

have done something on their own initiative. Never do the obvious except to conceal something else. Trust in the shadows, for the bright way makes of you an easy target.

Mielikki (Intermediate Goddess)

Our Lady of the Forest, the Forest Queen

Symbol:	Golden-horned, blue-eyed unicorn's head facing left
Alignment:	Neutral good
Portfolio:	Forests, forest creatures, rangers, dryads, autumn
Domains:	Animal, Good, Plant, Travel
Favored Weapon:	"The Hornblade" (scimitar)

Mielikki (my-*lee*-kee) is a good-humored deity who is quick to smile and confident in her actions. Fiercely loyal to and protective of those she calls friend, she considers carefully before including someone among those ranks. While she knows death is part of the cycle of life, she often intervenes to cure the injuries of an animal because she finds them hard to bear.

The members of Mielikki's church are widespread and rarely collect into large groups for any length of time. There are few temples to the Forest Queen, with most worship taking place in glades or at small shrines. The members of the church act as the voices of the trees, protectors of the forests, and warriors of the faith. They teach humans and good races to care for and respect trees and forest life, renew and extend existing forests, work against practitioners of fire magic, and assist good rangers of all faiths.

Clerics, druids, and spellcasting rangers of Mielikki pray for spells at either morning or evening. The church's most holy rituals take place on the equinoxes and solstices. They are called the Four Feasts and celebrate the sensual side of existence. The church's celebrations on Greengrass and Midsummer night are similar to the Four Feasts, but they also include planting rites and the Wild Ride, where herds of unicorns gather and allow the faithful to ride them bareback through the forest at great speed. Once a month, each cleric or druid is required to enact a ritual to call forth a dryad or treant and then to serve the creature by performing small tasks for them for a day. Almost all clerics of Mielikki multiclass as druids or rangers.

History/Relationships: Mielikki is a servitor deity of Silvanus and is allied with Toril's other nature deities. Lurue the Unicorn is said to be her mount when she rides into battle, and she is friendly with Shaundakul and Lathander. She opposes Malar, Talos, and Talona.

Dogma: Intelligent beings can live in harmony with the wild without requiring the destruction of one in the name of the other. Embrace the wild and fear it not, because the wild ways are the good ways. Keep the Balance and learn the hidden ways of life, but stress the positive and outreaching nature of the wild. Do not allow trees to be needlessly felled or the forest burned. Live in the forest and be a part of the forest, but do not dwell in endless battle against the forest. Protect forest life, defend every tree, plant anew where death falls a tree, and restore the natural harmony that fire-users and woodcutters often disrupt. Live as one with the woods, teach others to do so, and punish and curtail those that hunt for sport or practice cruelties on wild creatures.

Mystra (Greater Goddess)

The Lady of Mysteries, the Mother of All Magic

Symbol:	Circle of seven blue-white stars with red mist flowing from the center
Alignment:	Neutral good (you can use either NG or LN when picking Mystra as a patron)
Portfolio:	Magic, spells, the Weave
Domains:	Good, Illusion, Knowledge, Magic, Rune, Spell
Favored Weapon:	Seven whirling stars (shuriken)

Mystra (*miss*-trah) is a busy and devoted deity. She provides and tends to the Weave, the conduit that allows mortal spellcasters and users of magic to safely access the raw force that is magic. Essentially, Mystra *is* the Weave. As the goddess of magic, she is also the deity of the possibilities that magic can bring about, making her one of the most powerful beings involved with Toril. Although she is good and has the ability to prevent the creation of new spells and magic items that her philosophy opposes, she rarely exerts this ability unless the creation could threaten the Weave or the balance of magic in general.

Mystra's church preserves magical lore in secret and hidden places so that magic would continue and flourish in the future even if the dominant races of Faerûn were to fall. Its members also search out those skilled in magic or who have the potential to use it. Her clerics are encouraged to explore magical theory and create new spells and magic items. Sites dedicated to the goddess are enhanced by the Weave to allow any spell cast by her clerics while in one of those sites to have one metamagic effect without the requisite need to use a higher-level spell slot (the metamagic effect ends if the target of the spell leaves the site). Mystra honors the commitments that some members of her clergy made to the previous goddess of magic (who was lawful neutral). They have not been forced to leave the clergy due to alignment differences.

Clerics of Mystra pick one time of day or night to consistently pray for spells. They celebrate the 15th day of Marpenoth, the anniversary of the ascension of the current Mystra from her mortal form, but otherwise have few calendar-related rituals, focusing more on a personal style of worship. Her clerics usually multiclass as some sort of arcane spellcaster.

History/Relationships: Mystra was once a mortal wizard named Midnight. She assumed the fallen Mystra's portfolio and divinity during the Time of Troubles. Her allies are the deities of knowledge, Mystra's customary advisor (Azuth), Selûne (creator of the deity Mystryl, later called Mystra), and Kelemvor, whom she knew as a man when she was a mortal.

Dogma: Love magic for itself. Do not treat it just as a weapon to reshape the world to your will. True wisdom is knowing when not to use magic. Strive to use magic less as your powers develop, for often the threat or promise of its use outstrips its actual performance. Magic is Art, the Gift of the Lady, and those who wield it are privileged in the extreme. Conduct yourself humbly, not proudly, while being mindful of this. Use the Art deftly and efficiently, not carelessly and recklessly. Seek always to learn and create new magic.

Oghma (Greater God)

The Lord of Knowledge, Binder of What Is Known

Symbol:	Blank scroll
Alignment:	Neutral (any character can choose Oghma as a patron deity)
Portfolio:	Knowledge, invention, inspiration, bards
Domains:	Charm, Knowledge, Luck, Travel, Trickery
Favored Weapon:	"Mortal Strike" (longsword)

Oghma (*ogg*-mah) is the most powerful deity of knowledge in Faerûn. A cheerful and wise power with a gift for persuading others to his point of view, he tends to implement complex plots that he has puzzled through mentally first rather than taking direct action. He sits in judgment over every new idea, deciding if it is to remain with its creator or be allowed into the world.

The church of Oghma is responsible for the accumulation and distribution of books, scrolls, knowledge, and lore. The church accepts people of any alignment as long as they are interested in the promotion of knowledge. Clerics of any alignment can serve Oghma. The clergy consists of cloistered sages and archivists who analyze, file, and copy the temple's archives, as well as traveling clerics and bards who seek out new knowledge to bring back to the temples. Most temples support themselves by selling maps (never intentionally inaccurate), spell scrolls, and scribework.

The Chosen of Mystra

The Chosen of Mystra are powerful beings dedicated to preserving magic and holding back the onslaught of evil. The known Chosen are Alustriel, Dove Falconhand, Elminster, Laeral Silverhand, Khelben "Blackstaff" Arunsun, Qilué Veladorn (a drow elf and also Chosen of Eilistraee), the Simbul, Storm Silverhand, and Syluné (slain by a dragon, now a benign undead spirit). Each has the following Chosen abilities in common.

Bonus Spells (Sp): A Chosen gains one bonus spell of each spell level 1st through 9th per day, which can be used as a spell-like ability. Once these nine spells are selected, they can never be changed. Most Chosen select a variety of offensive, defensive, and utility spells with this ability.

Spell Immunity (Su): Chosen are immune to one spell of each spell level 1st through 9th, just as if the *spell immunity* spell were constantly in effect upon them. Once these nine spells are selected, they can never be changed.

Immunities (Ex): The Chosen are immune to aging, disease, disintegration, and poison. They have no need to sleep (although they must rest normally in order to be able to prepare spells).

Detect Magic (Su): Line of sight range.

Silver Fire (Su): All Chosen can use silver fire (see Chapter 2: Magic).

Abilities: All Chosen have a +10 enhancement bonus to Constitution.

Oghma's clerics pray for their spells in the morning. Midsummer and Shieldmeet, two days when agreements are made or renewed and contracts are signed, are holy days to Oghma. The church's two daily ceremonies are the Binding, performed in the morning and involving the writing of Oghma's symbols during silent prayer, and the Covenant, an evening service in which works of wisdom, songs, and new knowledge are shared aloud with the deity and present clergy members and worshipers. His clerics often multiclass as bards and sometimes as wizards.

History/Relationships: Oghma is an old deity with ties to many other planes. He is served by deities of knowledge, bards, and artifice and is allied with Mystra, Azuth, and Lathander. He opposes Talos, Bane, Mask, and Cyric, for they seek to corrupt knowledge, destroy it, or hoard it for themselves.

Dogma: Knowledge, particularly the raw knowledge of ideas, is supreme. An idea has no weight, but it can move mountains. The greatest gift of humankind, an idea outweighs anything made by mortal hands. Knowledge is power and must be used with care, but hiding it away from others is never a good thing. Stifle no new ideas, no matter how false and crazed they seem; rather, let them be heard and considered. Never slay a singer, nor stand by as others do so. Spread knowledge wherever it is prudent to do so. Curb and deny falsehoods, rumor, and deceitful tales whenever you encounter them. Write or copy lore of great value at least once a year and give it away. Sponsor and teach bards, scribes, and recordkeepers. Spread truth and knowledge so that all folk know more. Never deliver a message falsely or incompletely. Teach reading and writing to those who ask (if your time permits), and charge no fee for the teaching.

selûne (intermediate goddess)

Our Lady of Silver, the Moonmaiden
Symbol: Pair of female eyes surrounded by seven silver stars
Alignment: Chaotic good
Portfolio: Moon, stars, navigation, navigators, wanderers, questers, good and neutral lycanthropes
Domains: Chaos, Good, Moon, Protection, Travel
Favored Weapon: "The Wand of Four Moons" (heavy mace)

Selûne (seh-*loon*-ay) is a caring but quietly mystical deity. She is calm and placid, often seeming saddened by ancient events. In contrast to her typical demeanor are the fierce battles she has with her archnemesis, Shar, which range across the sky and onto other planes. Selûne takes many forms, reflecting the changing face of the moon itself. She is accepting of most beings.

Churches of Selûne are made up of a diverse bunch of worshipers, including sailors, nonevil lycanthropes, mystics, and female spellcasters. Despite the differences between the various worshipers and between different churches, all are friendly and accommodating toward each other. The appearance of Selûne's temples varies as much as their constituents, from small shrines in the

how the Art came to Maulaugadorn

In the days when the North was young, one ambitious man wanted to hurl back orcs and owlbears and all with his shining sword and carve himself a kingdom. This man was called Maulaugadorn. His face was handsome, his hands swift and sure, and his temper fierce. He swept all before him and came early to his dream.

As he sat upon his new and gleaming throne, the sword that had hewn many hundred heads winking naked across his knees, a restlessness came upon him, for his dream was hollow, and he wanted more. Then did his servants come to him with word that his sister, the gentle Alandalorne, was seized with a strange affliction. Fire poured from her lips and played up and down her slender curves and limbs.

Maulaugadorn the Mighty rose and strode to the chamber of his sister, who was wont to keep silent and speak but with her smiles. He found that her affliction was so, and the fires did rage, so that Alandalorne crouched bare and ashamed in a scorched corner of one room, with all smoldering around her.

He spoke to her, amazed. She swore she knew not how this malady had come upon her. At last he believed her, and straightaway commanded that his best horse and a dozen oxen be sacrificed in flames to the god Tempus, who was his god. When the flames of the roasting were a-roar, Maulaugadorn cried the name of Tempus in a great voice and prayed, demanding to know what had so afflicted his kinlady. From out of the flames came the Helm that Hovers, and the deep voice of Tempus that is all battle-steel clanging upon armor was in his mind. Tempus told him that Alandalorne suffered no malady, but was naturally able to call upon the Weave and had just now come into her power. There were many beings, human and not, who could work magic when they mastered such might, and they were called sorcerers.

Maulaugadorn asked straightaway, "So is this sorcery a weapon like my sword?"

Tempus answered him that it could be.

Then Maulaugadorn called every wise and learned person he could find to him and demanded that they tell him all the secrets of sorcery. Yet when he stood alone with all the runes they had drawn and powders they had sprinkled around him glowing, no fire came into his hands for all his straining. And he was wroth. He cried out that such trickery was ill laid upon him—and out of the glow came a quiet voice he'd not heard before. This voice told him that only a few mortals could call upon the Weave of themselves, and all others had to learn the Art by crafting spells or using the magic of others who'd gone before.

Maulaugadorn demanded to know who spoke to him, and Mystra the Lady of Mysteries made herself known.

Maulaugadorn demanded to know how this Art could be made a weapon in his hands, so that he could rule. Mystra answered that long years of study and work lay ahead of him, as it lies before all, but he could set forth, if he would, that day on the road that would take him in time to siring the Malaugrym.

Maulaugadorn frowned and set aside those words, seizing only upon the sight of the road to magic she spun with her words. He received with gratefulness a spell she placed burning in his mind. In return for it, he was never to suppress magic in others.

With this new weapon blazing in his mind, Maulaugadorn gave her great thanks and ran forth from that room. He never heard her final words: "The Art is not always a gift one should be thankful for. It is what one makes of it—a new weapon, or something much more."

Illustration by Matt Wilson

Selûne battles Shar

wilderness to open-air or skylighted buildings as large as great mansions. The temples perform fortune-telling, fight evil lycanthropes, give healing generously, and practice self-reliance and humility.

Clerics of Selûne pray at night for their spells in the direction of the moon. While most rituals of the church are performed personally and usually involve dancing and offerings of wine or milk, all clerics observe the Conjuring of the Second Moon and the Mystery of the Night. The Conjuring of the Second Moon is performed by a group during Shieldmeet. It calls the Shards, who are blue-haired female planetar servants of the goddess, to do the bidding of the clergy (usually to battle minions of Shar), after which one of the clerics joins the ranks of the Shards. The Mystery of the Night is performed annually. During it, clerics are flown high into the air to commune with the deity while in a trance. Selûne's worshipers often multiclass as bards or sorcerers.

History/Relationships: From the primordial essence of the world and heavens coalesced twin goddesses that complemented each other as light and dark. Together they created the world (bringing Chauntea into existence) and other heavenly bodies and infused them with life. The twin goddesses then battled over the fate of these things, and from their struggles were created the original deities of magic, war, disease, murder, death, and others. Eventually a balance was reached, but Selûne, the goddess of light, still tries to thwart the plans of her evil sister, Shar. The Moonmaiden's other enemies are Umberlee and Mask, but she counts among her allies many deities of fortune, light, magic, beauty, weather, and joy.

Dogma: Let all on whom Selûne's light falls be welcome if they desire. As the silver moon waxes and wanes, so too does life. Trust in Selûne's radiance, and know that all love alive under her light shall know her blessing. Turn to the moon, and she will be your true guide. Promote acceptance and tolerance. See all other beings as equals. Aid fellow Selûnites as if they were your dearest friends.

shar (greater goddess)

Mistress of the Night, Lady of Loss, Dark Goddess

Symbol:	Black disk with deep purple border
Alignment:	Neutral evil
Portfolio:	Dark, night, loss, forgetfulness, unrevealed secrets, caverns, dungeons, the Underdark
Domains:	Cavern, Darkness, Evil, Knowledge
Favored Weapon:	"The Disk of Night" (chakram)

Shar (*shahr*) is a twisted and perverse being of hatred, jealousy, and evil. She can see every being, object, and act performed within darkness and holds dominion over pains hidden but not forgotten, carefully nurtured bitterness, and quiet revenge for old slights. She spends much of her energy battling her old nemesis, Selûne, in a war that is older than recorded time. She is the creator of the Shadow Weave.

The church of Shar is made up of independent cells that have strong, authoritarian leaders. All cells in a particular region are under the purview of a superior priest. Clergy members revel in secrets, using them to tie each other together in loyalty and community. They pursue practical goals of advancing the power of the priesthood and of Shar's worshipers while avoiding direct opposition of other faiths (except that of Selûne). The clergy of Shar work to overthrow governments, promote Shar's patronage of avengers, organize secret cabals, and create false cults to further their ends.

Clerics of Shar pray for their spells at night. They have no faith-wide holy days except the Rising of the Dark, which occurs on the

Feast of the Moon and involves a blood sacrifice and the revelation by senior clerics of which plots the church will be advancing in the coming year. At least once a tenday, a cleric must attend a Nightfall, a dancing and feasting revel performed at nightfall that is followed by a small act of wickedness that the cleric reports to her superiors in the clergy. Shar's clerics often multiclass as rogues. She has an elite order of sorcerer-monks in her service that uses the power of the Shadow Weave.

History/Relationships: Shar is the dark twin of Selûne. She has battled her sister since shortly after their creation. Their primordial feud has resulted in the creation of many other deities. Rather than overtly confronting other deities, Shar seeks to gain power by subverting mortal worshipers to her faith. By her very nature, however, she is opposed to powers of light, the unsecretive Shaundakul, and her own sister. Her only frequent ally is Talona, who may eventually serve Shar to stave off the predations of Loviatar.

Dogma: Reveal secrets only to fellow members of the faithful. Never follow hope or turn to promises of success. Quench the light of the moon (agents and items of Selûne) whenever you find it, and hide from it when you cannot prevail. The dark is a time to act, not wait. It is forbidden to strive to better your lot in life or to plan ahead save when directly overseen by the faithful of the Dark Deity. Consorting with the faithful of good deities is a sin except in business dealings or to corrupt them from their beliefs. Obey ranking clergy unless it would result in your own death.

Shaundakul (Lesser God)

Rider of the Winds, the Helping Hand

Symbol:	A wind-walking bearded man in traveler's cape and boots
Alignment:	Chaotic neutral
Portfolio:	Travel, exploration, long-range traders, *portals*, miners, caravans
Domains:	Air, Chaos, Portal, Protection, Trade, Travel
Favored Weapon:	"Sword of Shadows" (greatsword)

Shaundakul (*shawn*-da-kul) is a deity of few words, letting his deeds speak for him. Kind but stern, he has a rugged sense of humor. Because he is sometimes lonely, he enjoys talking and trading jokes. He has a habit of rescuing doomed adventurers (particularly in Myth Drannor), although the price for this help is a service, usually involving the destruction of an evil being in his favorite city (which is Myth Drannor). His worship is on an upswing, and he is very aggressive in recruiting new members to the faithful.

Shaundakul's church is loosely organized, and its branches are largely independent. Because the clergy members love to wander, the temples constantly have new clerics arrive as others leave. Members of the clergy are expected to live off the land and work as guides and protectors of travelers, caravans, and mining expeditions. Ever since Shaundakul added *portals* to his portfolio, his clerics have been tasked with locating and identifying *portals* that would be useful for trade and exploration. Shaundakul has few temples. He prefers shrines, most of which are uninhabited and in remote places. He is not commonly worshiped within cities.

Clerics of Shaundakul pray for their spells in the morning right after the wind shifts from the changing temperature. Their holy day is the Windride, which is celebrated on the 15th day of Tarsakh. On this day Shaundakul causes all of his clerics to assume gaseous form at dawn so that they are carried with the wind. They return to normal (and are lowered safely to the ground) at dusk, usually in some place they have never been before. Shaundakul's clerics commonly multiclass as rangers.

History/Relationships: Shaundakul is an old deity. He predates the creation of Beshaba and Tymora from Tyche. He is allied with the deities of air, night, sky, nature, and travel, although his portfolio is similar to theirs in places. He opposes Shar because he dislikes secrets

Alorgoth, Bringer of Doom

Although many folk of other faiths think of Sharran clergy as sinister, openly cruel folk of black, cowled robes and endless plots who delight in poisonings and betrayals, the church of Shar has room to embrace less aggressive clergy. One such is the tireless wanderer Alorgoth, the Bringer of Doom, who travels about eastern Faerûn furthering the work of Shar.

Alorgoth is a tall, thin, sharp-chinned man who prefers to work alone, although he will not hesitate to recruit lesser Sharran clergy to aid him when necessary. Standing outside much of the organized faith, he is known to enjoy the personal favor of Shar and has as much authority as any archpriest of the church. Clergy who have crossed him have been as quick to taste his attacks as have the traditional foes of the faith, and when Alorgoth must engage in battle, he doesn't hesitate to summon demons to fight for him.

Disguises and misdirection are far more to his liking, however. Alorgoth spends his days conniving with rulers, nobles, or (when they are hopelessly weak, corrupt, or controlled by others) forces seeking to overthrow or supplant local authority.

He offers them the aid of Shar in persecuting their foes in return for their financial and sometimes military support, but he prefers to work not through open strife but by spreading secrets, stealing things, and kidnapping people. Alorgoth also destroys records, contracts, and documents whenever possible, and uses magic to make folk forget things.

The Bringer of Doom is forever spreading rumors and suggesting that secrets are being kept, creating an aura of mystery. In this way and by invoking the name of Shar in every act, he increases the influence and public fear of the Lady of the Night.

He delights in taking part in treasonous cabals, seductions, criminal rings, and events that spark wars and strife—but always under an assumed name and wearing a shape not his own. It is a measure of his success that he operated for decades without the Harpers discovering his name and spreading word of him.

Though he is now swiftly growing infamous, the Bringer of Doom shows no signs of slowing down. When Harpers or agents of a throne he has thrown into turmoil close in on him, Alorgoth drops out of sight by dodging through a *portal* or getting lost in a large city and lying low—working always for the greater dark glory of Shar.

and enjoys spreading the word of hidden places. He battles with Beshaba because she has been bringing suffering to the people of the Anauroch Desert under his name.

Dogma: Spread the teachings of the Helping Hand by example. Work to promote him among traders, especially those who seek out new lands and new opportunities. Unearth and resanctify ancient shrines of Shaundakul. Ride the wind, and let it take you wherever it blows. Aid those in need, and trust in the Helping Hand. Seek out the riches of the earth and sea. Journey to distant horizons. Be the first to see the rising sun, the mountain peaks, the lush valleys. Let your footsteps fall where none have tread.

silvanus (greater god)

Oak Father, the Forest Father, Treefather

Symbol:	Green living oak leaf
Alignment:	Neutral
Portfolio:	Wild nature, druids
Domains:	Animal, Plant, Protection, Renewal, Water
Favored Weapon:	"The Great Mallet of Silvanus" (maul)

Silvanus (sihl-*vann*-us) is a beneficent, paternal deity to his worshipers. He is emotionally distant when it comes to the necessity of having a balance in nature and wrathful toward those who threaten wild places. He is worshiped by those who live in or depend on the wild or remote places of the world. His great mallet fells dead trees to prevent the spread of fire and more easily let them become one with the soil.

His church favors small communities over large cities, although clusters of his clerics work in large cities to create gardenlike walled areas of wild forest within the city limits and preach the peace and purity of nature compared to the haste and corruption of the city. Most of his clergy are druids who work independently, with other druids in circles, or with rangers in the wild. His clergy work to serve the balance of forces in nature and spend most of their time stalling or reversing the encroachment of civilization. This clergy's methods sometimes involve sponsoring brigands or breeding and placing predators—activities that have to be done in secret so that outsiders continue to view the clergy as benign tree-lovers. Tending plants, nursing sick animals, and replanting trees are done publicly to promote this image.

Clerics and druids of Silvanus prepare spells at sundown or in moonlight. Holy days are Greengrass, Midsummer night, Highharvestide, and the Night the Forest Walks. This last holiday takes place when the god grows restless. He then causes trees to move, streams to change course, caves to open or close, forest creatures to stir, and forest magic to strengthen. Offerings made to Silvanus are never blood sacrifices. They are usually something made of wood that is buried in a circle of ancient trees on a hilltop. His clerics turn undead rather than commanding them. Many of his clerics multiclass as druids or rangers.

History/Relationships: Like Oghma, Silvanus is an old deity with many ties to other planes. Chauntea is his ally, and the other nonevil nature and animal deities serve him willingly. He opposes Malar, Talos, and Talona, three beings who enjoy destruction and often upset the Balance.

Dogma: Silvanus sees and balances all, meting out wild water and drought, fire and ice, life and death. Hold your distance and take in the total situation, rather than latching on to the popular idea of what is best. All is in a cycle, deftly and beautifully balanced. It is the duty of the devout to see this cycle and the sacred Balance as clearly as possible. Make others see the Balance and work against those that

would disturb it. Watch, anticipate, and quietly manipulate. Resort to open confrontation only when pressured by time or hostile action. Fight against the felling of forests, banish disease wherever you find it, defend the trees, and plant new flora wherever possible. Kill only when needful, and destroy fire and its employers.

sune (greater goddess)

Firehair, Lady Firehair

Symbol:	Face of a red-haired, ivory-skinned beautiful woman
Alignment:	Chaotic good
Portfolio:	Beauty, love, passion
Domains:	Chaos, Charm, Good, Protection
Favored Weapon:	A silken sash (whip)

Sune (*soo*-nee) is the fairest of goddesses. Benevolent and sometimes whimsical, she has been romantically tied to many of the other deities of Faerûn. She alternates between deep passions and casual flirtations, enjoys attention and sincere flattery, and avoids anyone who is horrific or boorish. She loves and protects her followers, who in turn manifest and protect the beauty of the world.

The church of Sune is a loose and informal organization. Generally, the most attractive and charismatic clerics readily rise to lead it. Sune's temples are always beautiful and are constructed with numerous picturesque paths and promenades and surprising and enchanting nooks in which to share moments of love, beauty, and passion. Sune's clerics sponsor artisans, build friendships and romances with themselves and among others, and destroy those who vandalize things of beauty. Sune has seen the benefits of Tymora's patronage of adventurers and wishes to tap into this source of worshipers, so the church supports gallant knights and explorers who are willing to search for lost jewels and priceless works of art—or who are on missions to rescue their true loves.

Sune's clerics pray in the morning after a refreshing scented bath (or after at least washing their hands). Greengrass and Midsummer Night are Sunite holy days, and the church holds a Grand Revel at least once a month. A Grand Revel is a large party with dancing, poetry recitation, and heartrendingly beautiful or soulfully rousing music to which outsiders are invited with the intent to attract converts. The influx of adventurers into Sune's clergy has reduced the huge former gender disparity in the church so that now females only outnumber males four to one. Sunite clerics tend to multiclass as bards or rogues.

History/Relationships: Sune is allied with the deities of joy, lust, poetry, youth, and the moon. She is served by Lliira and was also served by Selûne, who has now once again gone her own way. Sune's nature makes it difficult for any being to be angry with her for long, and so she has no true enemies, although she dislikes Auril, Malar, Talos, Umberlee, Talona, and Tempus, for they are often responsible for the destruction of beautiful things. (Tempus finds her dislike not worth reciprocating, since he considers her irrelevant, flighty, and not worth the conflict.)

Dogma: Beauty issues from the core of one's being and reveals one's true face to the world, fair or foul. Believe in romance, as true love will win over all. Follow your heart to your true destination. Perform a loving act each day, and seek to awaken love in others. Acquire beautiful items of all sorts, and encourage and protect those who create them. Let your appearance stir and delight those who look upon you. Love those who respond to your appearance, and let warm friendship and admiration flower where love cannot or dare not.

Talos (greater god)

The Destroyer, the Storm Lord

Symbol: An explosive lightning strike
Alignment: Chaotic evil
Portfolio: Storms, destruction, rebellion, conflagrations, earthquakes, vortices
Domains: Chaos, Destruction, Evil, Fire, Storm
Favored Weapon: A lightning bolt (longspear, shortspear, or halfspear)

Talos (*taahl*-ose) personifies the destructive aspects of nature. He is an angry, rage-filled deity that acts on his impulses and often acts just so that he doesn't appear weak or compromising to anyone. He exults in unhindered destruction and in many ways is like a twisted bully with incredible power and a short temper who proves his worth to himself by pounding upon those who cannot oppose him.

Talos's church is small and scattered, for worship of the Storm Lord is outlawed in many countries. His followers are fanatical in their love of destruction and are unafraid to call storms upon ships, towns, or cities in the name of their crazed deity. Talos's clerics often live like brigands, wandering from place to place demanding loot and threatening great destruction if they don't get it. They cow people into worshiping and placating Talos out of fear, and they occasionally recruit a new cleric into the fold. The few lands where Talos has openly established churches vacillate between cordiality and open hostility to them, which pleases Talos no end.

Clerics of Talos pray for their spells at different times of the day over the course of a year, with the time varying with Talos's whim (he rarely has them stick with the same time of day for more than a tenday). His clerics celebrate his annual festivals with great ceremonies that call down lightning and summon storms. Their most sacred ritual is Calling Down the Thunder, in which they slay an intelligent being by lightning. The most frequently seen ritual is the Fury, in which a cleric prays, then makes berserk attacks on people and items while howling Talos's name, followed by praying again (if the cleric survives). Talos's clerics tend to multiclass as barbarians, sorcerers, and wizards.

History/Relationships: Talos was formed from the first battle between Selûne and Shar. He is now the leader of the Gods of Fury, although he has rivalries with the other three, and Malar would kill him if he could. Talos has a history of elevating powerful mortals to divinity and then forcing them to deplete themselves in his service. He tried to assume dominion over wild and destructive magic but was opposed by Mystra. He has abandoned this quest due to the neutralization of most wild magic areas. He hates deities that promote building, learning, and nature, and particularly hates those that would dare to alter the weather.

Dogma: Life is a combination of random effects and chaos, so grab what you can when you can, because Talos may take you to the afterlife at any moment. Preach the might of Talos, and warn others of the forces he commands. Walk unafraid in storms, forest fires, earthquakes, and other disasters, for the power of Talos protects you. Make others fear Talos by showing the destruction he and his servants can cause. Let those who mock or do not believe know that fervent prayer is the only thing that will save them.

Tempus (greater god)

Lord of Battles, Foehammer

Symbol: A blazing silver sword on a blood-red shield
Alignment: Chaotic neutral
Portfolio: War, battle, warriors
Domains: Chaos, Protection, Strength, War
Favored Weapon: "Battle Prowess" (battleaxe)

Tempus (*tem*-pus) is random in his support, but his chaotic nature ends up favoring all equally in time. The god of war is liable to back one army one day and another one the next. Soldiers of all alignments pray to him for help in coming battles. Mighty and honorable in battle, he answers to his own warrior's code and pursues no long-lasting alliances. He has never been known to speak. He uses the spirits of fallen warriors as intermediaries.

The church of Tempus welcomes worshipers of all alignments (though its clerics abide by the normal rules), and its temples are more like walled military compounds. Tempus's clerics are charged to keep warfare a thing of rules and respected reputation, minimizing uncontrolled bloodshed and working to end pointless extended feuding. They train themselves and others in battle readiness in order to protect civilization from monsters, and they punish those who fight dishonorably or with cowardice. Collecting and venerating the weapons of famous and respected warriors is a common practice in Tempus's church. Clerics are expected to spill a few drops of blood (preferably their own or a worthy foe's) every tenday.

Tempus's clerics pray for spells just before highsun. Most of his clerics tend to be battle-minded male humans, although others are welcome. Eves and anniversaries of great battles important to a local temple are holidays. The Feast of the Moon is the annual day to honor the dead. Each temple holds a Feast of Heroes at highsun and a Song of the Fallen at sunset, and most also have a Song of the Sword ceremony after dark for layfolk. Tempus's clerics usually multiclass as fighters.

History/Relationships: Tempus arose from the first battle between Selûne and Shar. He sponsored the divinity of the Red Knight and is casually friendly with Nobanion, Gond, Valkur, and Uthgar. While he is the opposite of peaceful Eldath, he punishes those among his faithful who abuse her followers or sites, perhaps because he thinks that war has little meaning without peace to contrast it. His only foe is the upstart Garagos.

Dogma: Tempus does not win battles, he helps the deserving warrior win battles. War is fair in that it oppresses and aids all equally. It should not be feared, but seen as a natural force, a storm brought by civilization. Arm all for whom battle is needful, even foes. Retreat from hopeless fights but never avoid battle. Slay one foe decisively and halt a battle quickly rather than rely upon slow attrition. Remember the dead that fell before you. Disparage no foe and respect all, for valor blazes in all regardless of age, sex, or race. Tempus looks with favor upon those that acquit themselves honorably in battle without resorting to craven tricks. Consider the consequences of the violence of war, and do not wage war recklessly. The smooth-tongued that avoid all strife wreak more harm than the most energetic tyrant.

TORM (Lesser god)

The True, the True Deity, the Loyal Fury

Symbol:	Right-hand gauntlet held upright with palm forward
Alignment:	Lawful good
Portfolio:	Duty, loyalty, obedience, paladins
Domains:	Good, Healing, Law, Protection, Strength
Favored Weapon:	"Duty's Bond" (greatsword)

Torm (*torm*) is a stern, righteous, and unyielding deity who leads the fight against evil and injustice. His heart is filled with goodness, and he is kind and gentle when dealing with faithful friends, the weak, and the young. His greatsword "Duty's Bond" is the same holy avenger he carried when he was a mortal.

Torm's church is popular and served by several orders of warriors and paladins. The church trains, guides, provides sanctuary for, and supports guardians, loyal knights, paladins, and loyal courtiers. It sends agents to ferret out corruption in good groups, watch for impending trouble from hostile opponents, or seek out potential servitors of Torm. A few clergy of his church are assigned to explore Toril and report back so that the guardians learn more of the outside world. Each cleric must follow the three debts of the Penance of Duty, which are aiding other good religions, opposing all efforts of the followers of Bane and Cyric, and reporting and repairing areas of wild and dead magic. Torm's church has a cool rivalry with that of Helm.

Clerics of Torm pray for their spells at dawn. Torm's holy days are the Divine Death, a remembrance ceremony marking when Torm died to destroy Bane on the 13th day of Eleasias; the joyous feast called the True Resurrection, which commemorates when he returned from the dead on the 15th day of Marpenoth as a reward for his sacrifice; and the oath-making or oath-renewing event of Shieldmeet. His clerics may multiclass freely as paladins.

History/Relationships: Torm was once a mortal champion of a good king. He obeyed all commands, regardless of any danger to himself. He now serves as war leader and champion of Tyr. Torm, Tyr, and Ilmater work together often and are called the Triad. Torm's other allies are Helm (despite the conflicts between their churches), the Red Knight, and Lathander, and he opposes Bane, Cyric, and Mask. Torm is particularly combative with Bane, because it was Torm that battled Bane to the two deities' mutual destruction during the Godswar. Torm is incensed to see his return.

Dogma: Salvation may be found through service. Every failure of duty diminishes Torm and every success adds to his luster. Strive to maintain law and order. Obey your masters with alert judgment and anticipation. Stand ever alert against corruption. Strike quickly and forcefully against rot in the hearts of mortals. Bring painful, quick death to traitors. Question unjust laws by suggesting improvement or alternatives, not additional laws. Your fourfold duties are to faith, family, masters, and all good beings of Faerûn.

TYMORA (Intermediate goddess)

Lady Luck, the Lady Who Smiles, Our Smiling Lady

Symbol:	Silver coin with Tymora's face surrounded by shamrocks
Alignment:	Chaotic good
Portfolio:	Good fortune, skill, victory, adventurers
Domains:	Chaos, Good, Luck, Protection, Travel
Favored Weapon:	A spinning coin (shuriken)

Tymora (tie-*more*-ah) is a friendly, graceful, and kind deity. She is fickle but playful, never vengeful or malicious, and always able to turn something to her advantage. She enjoys jokes and has been known to play tricks on some of the more rigid deities such as Helm and Tyr, but she always finds a way to soothe hard feelings.

Shrines and temples to Tymora are spread across Faerûn. Her church is popular in cities frequented by adventurers, and such people fill its coffers in exchange for healing, making the temples wealthy. This wealth allows each temple a great deal of independence. The church encourages people to take chances and pursue their dreams rather than spending all their days planning and daring nothing. The church is duty-bound to aid those that have dared by providing them with healing and minor magic items (sometimes surreptitiously) to reinforce the good fortune that comes to those that trust in Tymora. A standard greeting among the faithful is to touch holy symbols, and worshipers often embrace to do so.

Clerics of Tymora pray for their spells in the morning. The church has only two rituals common to all temples. The festival at Midsummer is a night-long revel of daring acts, romantic trysts, and meetings between members of the Harpers (many of whom belong to the church), relatives, and allied faiths. Starfall is the church's most holy ritual. It takes place on the 23rd day of Marpenoth and is believed to commemorate the destruction of Tyche and creation of Tymora. Tymora's clerics most commonly multiclass as bards or rogues, but they have been known to try almost any class combination.

History/Relationships: Though they both sprang from the rotted husk of the former deity of luck, Tyche, Tymora is the opposite and nemesis of her twin sister, Beshaba. Friendly with most good powers and rumored to have had dalliances with several of them, she gets along particularly well with Lathander, Selûne, and Shaundakul. In addition to her dark twin, she counts Bane and Loviatar as her foes.

Dogma: One should be bold, for to be bold is to live. A brave heart and a willingness to take risks beat out a carefully wrought plan nine times out of ten. Place yourself in the hands of fate and trust to your own luck. Bear and conduct yourselves as your own masters, showing your good or bad fortune as confidence in the Lady. Chase your own unique goals, and the Lady aids the chase. Without direction or goals, you soon know the embrace of Beshaba, for those on no set course are at the mercy of misfortune, which has no mercy at all.

TYR (Greater god)

The Even-Handed, the Maimed God, the Just God

Symbol:	Balanced scales resting on a warhammer
Alignment:	Lawful good
Portfolio:	Justice
Domains:	Good, Knowledge, Law, Retribution, War
Favored Weapon:	"Justiciar" (longsword)

Tyr (*teer*) is a noble warrior who is strong in spirit and dedicated to justice. He lost his right hand to Kezef the Chaos Hound and is sometimes depicted as blind. Though he sees himself as a father figure who wants to deal with others with love, courage, and the strength of the bonds of family, he knows that such can never be in an imperfect world. He is instead viewed by outsiders as a stern arbiter of justice.

Tyr's church is strong in civilized areas. His clergy see the world in clear-cut moral terms. They want Faerûn cleansed and ordered by just laws that are applied diligently and evenly. They do not tolerate mockery, parody, or the questioning of their faith. Tyr's church is highly organized and does not deny lodging, equipment, or healing to the faithful in times of need, although later service is sometimes required for this aid. In lawless areas, Tyr's clerics serve as judge, jury, and executioner. In civilized places, they become legal experts, speaking for accused persons and dispensing advice. They never enforce a law that can be shown to be unjust.

Clerics of Tyr pray for spells at dawn. Every month they celebrate three holy days. Services on these days consist of chanted prayers, hymns, and conjured gigantic illusions. The Seeing Justice is the first holy day of every month. Its illusion is that of a gigantic hammer glowing with blinding light. The 13th of the month is the Maiming, in which the faithful see an illusion of a nimbus of burning blood around a right hand that tumbles and fades away. The 22nd of the month is the Blinding, in which two eyes turn into fountains of flaming tears (and celebrants wear ceremonial blindfolds). Tyr's clerics can multiclass freely as paladins, and most multiclass as paladins or fighters.

History/Relationships: Tyr is an interloper deity. He came to Faerûn shortly before the start of the Dalereckoning calendar. Torm and Ilmater serve him, and together the three are known as the Triad. His other close ally is Lathander. Tyr opposes Bane, Cyric, Mask, Talona, and Talos.

Dogma: Reveal the truth, punish the guilty, right the wrong, and always be true and just in your actions. Uphold the law wherever you go and punish those who do wrong under the law. Keep a record of your own rulings, deeds, and decisions, for through this your errors can be corrected, your grasp on the laws of all lands will flourish, and your ability to identify lawbreakers will expand. Be vigilant in your observations and anticipations so you may detect those who plan injustices before their actions threaten law and order. Deliver vengeance to the guilty for those who cannot do it themselves.

Umberlee
(intermediate goddess)

The Bitch Queen, Queen of the Deeps

Symbol:	Blue-green wave curling left and right
Alignment:	Chaotic evil
Portfolio:	Oceans, currents, waves, sea winds
Domains:	Chaos, Destruction, Evil, Ocean, Storm, Water
Favored Weapon:	"Drowning Death" [trident] or jellyfish (trident)

Umberlee (uhm-ber-*lee*) is a malicious, mean, and evil deity who breaks agreements on a whim and takes great pleasure in watching others die by drowning or in the jaws of sea predators. Vain and desirous of flattery, she is excessively greedy for power and revels in exercising it. Weresharks are her creations, and theirs is one of the few races that worship her out of admiration rather than fear.

Umberlant temples are mainly vehicles for sailors and merchants to make offerings of candles, flowers, candies, or coins to appease the Bitch Queen's wrath. Her clerics support themselves with these offerings and sometimes hire themselves out aboard ships as guardians, since sailors think Umberlee won't take one of her own. The church of Umberlee is disorganized and run differently in different locales. Its clerics are given to dueling each other to settle disputes of rank or ability. The church spreads respect for the goddess by preaching of the doom she has wrought on those that ignore her.

Umberlant clerics pray for spells at high tide (in the morning or evening). Their two public rituals are the First Tide and the Stormcall. The first involves a parade through town with a caged animal, which is then tied to a rock and hurled into the sea. If it reaches shore alive, it is treated as a sacred animal for the rest of its days. Stormcall is a mass prayer to summon or turn aside a storm. Its participants pray around pools upon which float candles on driftwood planks, and throw sacrifices into the pools. Umberlee's clerics tend to multiclass as rogues, fighters, or druids.

History/Relationships: Umberlee is one of the Gods of Fury. She serves Talos, along with Auril and Malar. Talos has been encroaching upon her portfolio, and since she lacks the strength to fight him, Umberlee has been trying to distract him with romantic intrigues. She fights Selûne and Valkur (to whom sailors pray to bring them home safely), Chauntea (for her dominion over land), and Sune (whose beauty she envies).

Dogma: The sea is a savage place, and those that travel it had best be willing to pay the price of challenging Umberlee's domain. Fair offerings bring fair winds to sea travelers, but those that do not pay their respects will find that the sea is as cold as Umberlee's heart. Spread the word of the might of Umberlee, and let no service be done in her name without a price. Make folk fear the wind and wave unless a cleric of Umberlee is there to protect them. Slay those who ascribe sea and shore storms to Talos.

Uthgar (lesser god)

Father of the Uthgardt, Battle Father

Symbol:	That of the individual beast totem spirit
Alignment:	Chaotic neutral (clerics and those selecting a patron deity must use the alignment guidelines of the beast totem, not Uthgar)
Portfolio:	Uthgardt barbarian tribes, physical strength
Domains:	Animal, Chaos, Retribution, Strength, War
Favored Weapon:	Appropriate beast totem spirit (battleaxe)

Uthgar (*uhth*-gar) is a proud, fierce, and independent warrior. He has few friends and has remained relatively uninvolved in divine politics. He loves a good joke, enjoys sensual pleasures of the flesh, and likes to hunt, eat, drink, and be merry with the warrior spirits that serve him. Although he is a tireless and methodical tactician, his battle strategies are not terribly inspired. He is driven to win, though, especially if the Uthgardt barbarians (his people) are threatened.

The church of Uthgar is divided among the eleven beast totem spirits that serve Uthgar as intermediaries to the Uthgardt tribes of the Savage Frontier. Uthgar is not worshiped directly, but each tribe venerates one of these servant spirits as the divine

Black Lion

Black Raven

Blue Bear

Elk

Gray Wolf

Great Worm

Griffon

Red Tiger/Snow Cat

Sky Pony

Tree Ghost

Thunderbeast

Uthgar's beast totems

Illustrations by Sam Wood

embodiment of the spirit of their tribe—the symbol of its vitality, wisdom, mystical ability, endurance, speed, and moral nature. Uthgar has neither temples nor shrines, and his clerics can perform necessary ceremonies in any location, though their tribes' ancestral mounds are their most holy sites. (Each tribe and its beast totem are tied to a particular ancestral mound.) Dogma varies from tribe to tribe depending on the nature of a tribe's beast totem, but Uthgar's clerics are responsible for spiritual guidance, performing rituals, healing, the teaching of tribal history and customs, and advising the chieftain. The spring equinox and both solstices are holy days, and all tribes converge upon their ancestral mound (or Beorunna's Well, the holiest of the ancestral mounds) during the autumn equinox to perform ceremonies, make agreements, and commune with ancestral spirits.

Clerics of Uthgar pray at dawn or sunset. They are almost exclusively male, and each worships the beast totem spirit of his tribe. Rather than follow the one step rule, clerics of Uthgar (and those who take him as a patron deity) must abide by the somewhat broader alignment guidelines of the beast totems who mediate between Uthgar and his people. Any alignment that fits the guideline for a beast totem is suitable for a cleric of Uthgar of that totem. The names and alignment guidelines of the totems are Black Lion (nonevil), Black Raven (nonchaotic), Blue Bear (nonlawful, nonevil), Elk (nonlawful), Gray Wolf (nonlawful), Great Worm (good), Griffon (nonevil), Red Tiger/Snow Cat (nonlawful, nonevil), Sky Pony (nonevil), Tree Ghost (nongood, nonevil), and Thunderbeast (nonevil). Uthgar's clerics often multiclass as barbarians, druids, or rangers.

History/Relationships: Uthgar was once a mortal Northlander who gained fame and founded a dynasty of barbarians, the Uthgardt. Sponsored by Tempus to divinity at his death, he counts the Lord of Battles as his only ally. Uthgar dislikes Helm, Ilmater, Torm, and Tyr, for they have stolen away the devotion of all but one cleric of the Black Lion tribe. He holds Malar responsible for the destruction of the Blue Bear tribe (a fragment of which survives as the new Tree Ghost tribe), and he hates Auril for turning the Elk tribe away from his worship.

Dogma: Strength is everything. Civilization is weakness. Men should fight, hunt, and raid from the weak to provide for their wives

and families. Family is sacred, and its bonds are not cast aside lightly. Arcane magic is effete, self-indulgent, and ultimately leads to weakness. Reliance upon arcane magic is an evil and false path that leads to death and ruin. Revere Uthgar, your ancestors, and your tribe's beast spirit. The beast holds wisdom and raw power that you can make your own. Make the others of your tribe fear and respect your power and knowledge so they heed the wise words your ancestors speak through you to them.

Waukeen (lesser goddess)

Merchant's Friend

Symbol:	Gold coin with Waukeen's profile facing left
Alignment:	Neutral
Portfolio:	Trade, money, wealth
Domains:	Knowledge, Protection, Travel, Trade
Favored Weapon:	Cloud of coins (nunchaku)

Waukeen (wah-*keen*) is a relatively young, vibrant, vivacious deity who is eager to get things done. She loves wealth not for itself but for what can be done and acquired with it. She enjoys bargaining and the hustle and bustle of the marketplace. She rules over deals done above and below the table—legitimate as well as black-market commerce. She is interested in innovation, but can also be stubborn and persistent, which sometimes gets her into trouble.

Waukeen's church is wealthy not because it hoards money, but because it invests wisely and uses its wealth to gain popularity, power, and renown. Waukeen's clerics travel the world aiding merchants and working with temple moneylenders, coin changers, safe storers, and covert fences. They are required to donate 25% of their income to the church, to invest in all enterprises run by the faithful that have a reasonable hope of succeeding, and to look into investing in the enterprises of businesspeople who are willing to make sizable offerings to Waukeen. The church is not above using illegal methods to influence trade, but it publicly denies such practices and makes sure that clerics who do such things act subtly.

Clerics of Waukeen pray for spells just before sundown and must initiate their prayers by throwing a coin into a ceremonial bowl or a body of water. The church celebrates a dozen high festivals spaced over the course of the year that honor accounting, textiles, wealth, generosity, benefactors, finery, deal-making, bounty, magic, guards, craft, and the dark side of wealth (a solemn remembrance of the evils of excess). Clerics often multiclass as bards or rogues to enhance their contacts and negotiating skills.

History/Relationships: Waukeen disappeared during the Time of Troubles, which caused much confusion among her faithful. She reappeared in 1371 DR after she was freed from imprisonment. She had been held in a mortal form against her will in the Abyss by the demon lord Graz'zt. She has since revitalized and reassured her worshipers of her existence and her restored divine power. She is allied with Lliira (who held her portfolio while she was imprisoned), Gond (whose inventions she appreciates), and Shaundakul (whose portfolio complements hers). Her only serious foes are Mask and Graz'zt.

Dogma: Mercantile trade is the best road to enrichment. Increasing the general prosperity buys ever greater civilization and happiness for intelligent folk worldwide, bringing people closer to the golden age that lies ahead. Destroy no trade goods, raise no restrictions to trade, and propagate no malicious rumors that could harm someone's commerce. Give money freely to beggars and businesses, for the more coin everyone has, the greater the urge to spend and trade rather that hoard. To worship Waukeen is to know wealth. To guard your funds is to venerate her, and to share them well seeds your future success. Call on her in trade, and she will guide you in wise commerce. The bold find gold, the careful keep it, and the timid yield it up.

cosmology of toril

The Material Plane that holds the world of Toril is one of many planes of existence. Beyond Toril lie the Elemental Planes, the Positive and Negative Energy planes, and the many realms of the deities, demons, and devils (collectively called the Outer Planes). The Ethereal and Shadow planes overlap the Material, with the Astral Plane connecting to all of them.

The Elemental Planes: The Elemental Planes embody the fundamental nature of Air, Earth, Fire, and Water. Inhospitable places of pure matter, they are inhabited by elementals, elemental rulers (often called "lords"), genies, and outsiders appropriate to the element in question (such as salamanders on the Plane of Fire). The Elemental Planes contain the home of Kossuth and the other elemental rulers worshiped by the people of Toril.

The Energy Planes: The Positive Energy Plane is the source of the energy of life, representing the constant force and drive of creation, and its effects bleed into and permeate the Material Plane. The Negative Energy Plane represents entropy and the inevitable decay of life into death, and it tugs at the matter of Toril on the Material Plane just like its bright twin.

The Ethereal Plane: The Ethereal Plane is a misty continuum that coexists with the Material Plane. Individuals within the Ethereal can see into the Material Plane, but not vice versa. It is accessed by spells such as *etherealness* and *ethereal jaunt*.

The Shadow Plane: The Shadow Plane is a coexistent plane that looks like a photographic negative of the Material. It is accessed through common shadows using specific spells, such as *shadow walk*. Shadow stuff may be manipulated to create objects and creatures by those skilled in its use. Sages theorize that the Shadow Plane may lead to planes currently unknown in the cosmology of Toril.

The Astral Plane: The Astral Plane is an open, weightless plane with connections to all other planes. It is an empty, mostly barren expanse of nothingness, broken only by shards of matter from other planes and *portals* leading to new dimensions. Spells such as *astral projection* and *gate* access the Astral Plane.

The Outer Planes: The other known planes are the homes of deities and outsiders. The best-known planes of this type include the Abyss, home of the countless hordes of demons (tanar'ri), and the Nine Hells, home of the hierarchies of devils (baatezu).

The planes of the deities are usually held in common between several divine powers of the same pantheon or of similar interest or temperament. Each deity associated with a plane has a private realm attached to and part of that plane, much as rooms in an inn are connected to a main hall. Within their own realms, deities rule supreme and can alter physical laws at will, but in the shared areas the physics of the plane generally conform to the rules of the Material Plane. Deities that are more powerful tend to have larger realms, although the more conservative are content with less ostentatious displays of power.

Isolationist, hostile, or paranoid deities prefer to maintain their own individual planes, the entirety of which are their realms. While this makes them each the master of an entire plane, they also become more vulnerable to a concerted attack from other deities, whereas a deity sharing a plane can rally neighbors in times of need.

Moving from One Plane to Another: All of these planes connect to Toril on the Material Plane in some way, whether through the coexistent overlap of the Astral, Ethereal, and Shadow planes or via *portals* through the Astral that connect to the deities', Elemental, or Energy planes. In a sense, the cosmology of Toril resembles a tree, with the branches (planes) growing from the center and some branches having secondary branches (realms) growing from them. It is far easier and safer to take advantage of the existing connectivity to travel between planes, using the common ground of Toril as a stopping point, rather than forcing a direct connection between two locations. To use the tree model as an analogy, it is more advantageous to climb down one branch to the trunk and then climb up another than it is to try to jump from your current branch to a distant one.

However, planar beings sometimes choose to force a direct path between two planes (at the expense of some of their available energy) rather than use the existing paths. Reasons for doing so include a hazard waiting along a more convenient path (such as a hostile power), a limited amount of time, or a desire for secrecy. In addition, deities who are friendly to each other but live in different planes sometimes create permanent connections (*portals*) to their allies for convenience. Such artificial methods are generally beyond the reach of mortals, although certain artifacts may be able to duplicate this capability.

the outer planes

The Faerûnian pantheon is unusual in that its deities have many different origins and come from many worlds. This lack of commonality prevents them from creating a common planar realm, and so they are scattered over many planes. In addition to the Faerûnian powers, the planar system of Toril houses interloper deities, humanoid pantheons, elemental beings worshiped as deities, monster pantheons, and the homes of the beings venerated in distant parts of the world.

Realms Cosmology

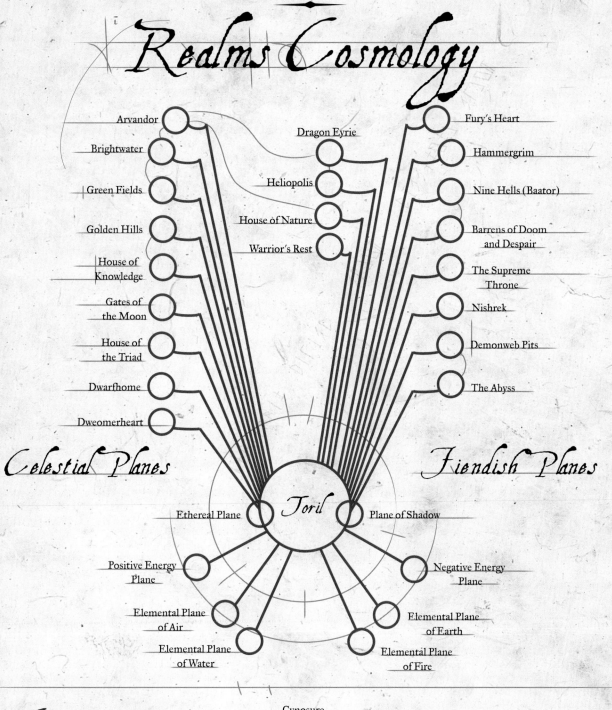

Arvandor

Brightwater

Green Fields

Golden Hills

House of Knowledge

Gates of the Moon

House of the Triad

Dwarfhome

Dweomerheart

Dragon Eyrie

Heliopolis

House of Nature

Warrior's Rest

Fury's Heart

Hammergrim

Nine Hells (Baator)

Barrens of Doom and Despair

The Supreme Throne

Nishrek

Demonweb Pits

The Abyss

Celestial Planes

Fiendish Planes

Toril

Ethereal Plane

Plane of Shadow

Positive Energy Plane

Negative Energy Plane

Elemental Plane of Air

Elemental Plane of Earth

Elemental Plane of Water

Elemental Plane of Fire

Cross Section

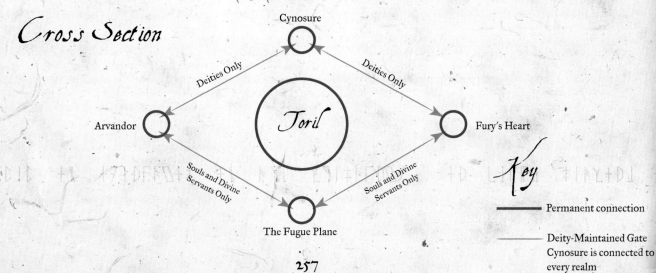

Cynosure

Deities Only

Deities Only

Arvandor

Toril

Fury's Heart

Souls and Divine Servants Only

Souls and Divine Servants Only

The Fugue Plane

Key

——— Permanent connection

——— Deity-Maintained Gate
Cynosure is connected to every realm

The following list of planes focuses primarily on the deities of Faerûn. Other Torilian pantheons (such as those of different species of humanoids, dragons, giants, other monsters, and the lands of Kara-Tur, Zakhara, and Maztica) may inhabit one plane with many domains such as the elven realm of Arvandor, or be divided among many planes as the Faerûnian pantheon is. Each plane is described below with the deities who have realms there, with mentions of known permanent connections between that plane and others. Two Faerûnian deities do not have a home in the Outer Planes: Gargauth and Ulutiu. Ulutiu is drowsing in the Astral Plane, and Gargauth, being outcast from the Nine Hells, dwells only on the Material Plane.

The Abyss: Many demon lords, demons.

Arvandor: The elven pantheon (the Seldarine) and Eilistraee. Hanali Celanil maintains a *portal* to Sune's realm in Brightwater, and the entire pantheon maintains a *portal* to the House of Nature. Erevan Ilesere maintains a *portal* to the realm of Hlal in Dragon Eyrie.

The Barrens of Doom and Despair: Bane (distant from the others), Beshaba, Hoar, Loviatar, and Talona.

Brightwater: Lliira, Sharess, Sune, Tymora, and Waukeen. Sune maintains a *portal* to Hanali Celanil's realm in Arvandor. Sharess also has a small realm on Heliopolis, the home of her native pantheon. Tymora maintains a *portal* to Green Fields.

Cynosure: No permanent residents (see below).

Demonweb Pits: Lolth and the drow pantheon. (Eilistraee has a realm here, but she rarely visits it.) The pantheon maintains *portals* to several layers of the Abyss.

Dragon Eyrie: The dragon pantheon. Tiamat maintains a *portal* to this plane. Hlal maintains a *portal* to the realm of Erevan Ilesere in Arvandor.

Dwarfhome: Moradin and the rest of the dwarven pantheon, excluding the duergar and derro deities.

Dweomerheart: Azuth, Mystra, Savras, and Velsharoon (who is unpopular but remains here to gain protection from Talos).

Elemental Planes: The elemental rulers Akadi (Plane of Air), Grumbar (Plane of Earth), Istishia (Plane of Water), and Kossuth (Plane of Fire).

The Fugue Plane: Jergal and Kelemvor.

Fury's Heart: Auril, Malar, Talos, and Umberlee.

Gates of the Moon: Finder, Selûne, and Shaundakul.

The Golden Hills: The gnome pantheon, not including Urdlen (whose realm is adjacent to the Abyss). The Golden Hills also connects to the realm of Gond.

Green Fields: The halfling pantheon. Brandobaris has a realm here, but he is rarely present, preferring to establish a small, temporary realm wherever he rests. Green Fields also connects to the realm of Tymora.

Hammergrim: The duergar powers Deep Duerra and Laduguer.

Heliopolis: The Mulhorandi pantheon and Tiamat. Tiamat maintains a *portal* to the plane of the dragon pantheon.

House of Knowledge: Deneir, Gond, Milil, and Oghma. Gond maintains a *portal* to the Golden Hills.

House of Nature: Chauntea, Eldath, Gwaeron, Lathander, Lurue, Mielikki, Nobanion, Shiallia, Silvanus, Ubtao, various animal lords, and the deities of many nature-oriented creatures (aarakocras, centaurs, and so on). The deities of this plane maintain a *portal* to Arvandor.

House of the Triad: Helm, Ilmater, Siamorphe, Torm, and Tyr.

The Nine Hells (Baator): The Lords of the Nine (archdevils), devils. A few maintain *portals* to the realms of Bane, Loviatar, and Talona.

Nishrek: The orc pantheon.

Plane of Shadow: Mask and Shar.

The Supreme Throne: Cyric.

Warrior's Rest: Garagos (hostile to all others), Red Knight, Tempus, Uthgar (distant from all but Tempus), and Valkur.

AO

Ao (*ay*-oh) stands outside of the power struggles of deities in Faerûn. A quiet and distant being, Ao is the overgod of Toril. He is responsible for the creation of the first deities of Toril and for maintaining the cosmic balance. Ao was completely unknown to mortals before the Time of Troubles. His presence was made known when he single-handedly banished all the deities to walk Faerûn in mortal forms as punishment because many of them had abdicated their responsibilities.

Ao has supreme power over all the deities of Toril, is capable of demoting, banishing, or destroying any of them, and can elevate mortals to any level of divinity if they accept the responsibilities and duties of the divine state. No being can be promoted to divinity without his approval. He is impervious to all attacks, even by a concerted effort of all the divine powers, and has no known realm among the planes. Ao is essentially the god of the deities of Faerûn. He answers no mortal's prayer, grants no spells to mortals, and has not been heard from since the end of the Godswar. It is unknown if he established the foundation of the cosmology of Toril or if that structure is something that evolved over time from the interaction of the deities.

CYNOSURE

Cynosure is a small plane located very close—cosmologically speaking—to Toril. Only deities can access it, and only from their own domains. It is considered neutral ground by all the powers of Faerûn, a place to settle disputes and decide upon punishments for those deities who upset the Balance (as defined by the guidelines Ao left). Cynosure cannot be used as a way station as Toril can, for the deities can only use the *portals* to Cynosure that lead to their own realms. Given the number of divine powers active on Toril, it is not unusual to find several meeting in Cynosure at any time, though rarely more than a dozen. At other times, the realm sits empty for several tendays. While *portals* from Cynosure lead to the realms of the elemental lords, none of them have ever been known to appear on the meeting plane.

The Afterlife

When mortals die, their souls are drawn to the Fugue Plane. Most of this place is flat, gray, bland, and nondescript, with no notable topographical features. The spirits of the dead gather here, usually unaware that they have died. From time to time (anywhere from once a day to over a tenday, depending on the deities involved), the powers send representatives—usually outsiders of the appropriate alignment—to the Fugue Plane to gather the souls of their own worshipers.

A worshiper's soul automatically recognizes an agent of its own deity, knows that it needs to go with that agent, and cannot be deceived by any means into following the agent of another divine power. The agent collects the proper souls and returns to its deity's realm, where the worshiper serves the deity in whatever capacity necessary. Agents cannot take the worshipers of deities other than those they represent.

The Baatezu

Within the Fugue Plane lurk small enclaves of baatezu. By agreement with Kelemvor, the god of the dead, they cannot harm or trick the waiting souls. However, the devils are allowed to explain to the souls that they are dead and awaiting the arrival of a divine messenger to take them back to their deity's realm. At this point, the devils attempt to bargain with souls.

The baatezu want souls that they can use to create lemures (the lowest sort of devil), which over time are transformed into more powerful devils in the service of the Nine Hells. While this probably isn't appealing to most souls, those who are pledged to evil deities or fear what punishments they may suffer in their respective deity's realm might jump at the opportunity to escape that fate. After all, in the hells you certainly know where you stand and have the opportunity for promotion, with the remote possibility of advancing to the level of a pit fiend. As a servant of an evil deity, you are always at that deity's whim and have no guarantee of being anything other than an expendable, insignificant slave.

In exchange for consigning themselves to the Nine Hells, souls may be offered early promotions from lemure to another form of devil, material riches for friends or family in Faerûn, or the execution of devilish attacks on their still-living enemies on their behalf. Especially powerful souls may bargain for automatic transformation into something other than a lemure. The success rate of the baatezu is low, but given the number of beings that die each day across Faerûn, even a small portion of that number results in enough of a gain for the hells that it's worth the fiends' time.

The city of judgment

The shared realm of Kelemvor, Lord of the Dead, and Jergal, Scribe of the Doomed, comprises a portion of the Fugue Plane. This realm, called the Crystal Spire, stands in the center of the region known as the City of Judgment. The city itself is a gray, bland, tightly packed metropolis populated by the judged dead.

While most souls wander the Fugue Plane until their deity calls them, the Faithless and the False are compelled to enter the city and be judged by Kelemvor. The Faithless firmly denied any faith or only gave lip service to the gods for most of their lives without truly believing. The False intentionally betrayed a faith they believed in and to which they had made a personal commitment.

All of the Faithless receive the same punishment: They form a living wall around the City of Judgment, held together by a supernatural greenish mold. This mold prevents them from escaping the wall and eventually breaks down their substance until the soul and its consciousness are dissolved.

The False are punished according to their crimes in life and serve their sentence in the City of Judgment for eternity. Nearly all of the beings in the city are members of the False, the rest being deceased followers of Jergal and Kelemvor who enact the will of their deities upon the doomed souls. Depending upon the severity of their crimes, some of the False may receive relatively light punishments, such as escorting visiting baatezu or patrolling the city for unauthorized guests. Others are punished in ways that would surprise the cruelest demon.

As part of his agreement with the baatezu, Kelemvor allows a few groups of devils to torment the citizens of the city. There is no respite for the False unless Kelemvor wills it, and in his tenure he has not been known to change his mind. Furthermore, once Kelemvor has made his judgment, the soul cannot be raised or resurrected without the intervention of a deity (represented by at least the use of a *miracle* or *wish* spell), who will almost certainly have to negotiate with Kelemvor.

The tanar'ri

While the lawful baatezu have a contract with Kelemvor that allows them to acquire souls, the chaotic tanar'ri employ another method: They steal them. From time to time, a demon ruler creates a *portal* between the Abyss and the Fugue Plane. Dozens of servitor demons spill through the opening to claw a hole in the wall of the Faithless, tearing some of the doomed free to be brought back to the Abyss. The demons then raid the city, gathering as many souls as they can before retreating. The minions of Kelemvor and Jergal act as guards and soldiers against these attacks, as do the devils, who are always willing to take on their ancient enemies. Kelemvor tolerates these attacks if they are not too frequent and don't cause much collateral damage.

However, when the demons become greedy, some of Kelemvor or Jergal's divine servants are taken, or Kelemvor feels he needs to teach the demons a lesson, he steps up his realm's defenses or makes raids into the Abyss to harass as many demons as possible. He prefers sorties and campaigns that make the demon rulers look weak and ineffectual. These reprisals are rarely needed and primarily serve to keep the number of tanar'ri attacks low.

Creatures of the outer planes

In addition to deities and the souls of their followers, outsiders of many shapes, sizes, and temperaments inhabit the planes. These native creatures include planar animals, guardinals, tieflings, and elemental creatures. Within the realm of a divine power, the natives are loyal to that deity. Creatures native to a plane shared by several deities have an affinity for all of them.

On their home planes, these creatures are the natives and therefore not subject to outsider-based warding magic (such as the bodily contact prevention aspect of *protection from evil* spells, if evil) or attacks that would send them back to their home plane. Note that in the planes and realms it is still possible to use summoning spells, although quite often a summoned creature of like alignment to the current plane is actually summoned from the plane the caster is on, much as with a *summon nature's ally* spell.

Spells such as *summon monster* and other effects that bring outsiders to Toril follow rules based on the nature and resonance of Toril and its associated planes. All summoned outsiders come from a realm or plane appropriate or similar to their alignment and type. The deity living in a realm determines a realm's alignment, and a plane created and shared by several deities reflects all of the alignments of the powers living there. If a priest summons a creature that is appropriate to his deity's plane or realm, the creature actually comes from there.

For example, an outsider dog brought by *summon monster I* (see Chapter 11 of the *Player's Handbook*) has a lawful good alignment and comes from any plane or realm that has a lawful good alignment, such as the realm of Torm (a lawful good deity) or the Golden Hills (a plane inhabited by lawful good, neutral good, and neutral deities). An outsider eagle brought by *summon monster II* has a chaotic good alignment and comes from the realm of Sune (a chaotic good deity) or from Arvandor (a plane inhabited by neutral good, chaotic good, and chaotic neutral deities). A neutral evil salamander might be a native of the Elemental Plane of Fire (because it is a fire creature), the realm of Shar (neutral evil), or the plane of Fury's Heart (chaotic evil, neutral evil).

There are some exceptions to these rules. For example, the gnome deities have an affinity for burrowing creatures such as badgers. There *are* badgers in the Golden Hills, even though the summoned badger listed in *summon monster I* is chaotic good and no chaotic good deities live in the Golden Hills.

HISTORY

F aerûn is an old land, full of long-lost empires and wonders. One after another, the great ancient races rose and fell, finally giving rise to the Time of Humans—the last three to four thousand years of Faerûn's history. Even within this epoch, great empires and shining kingdoms have risen and fallen, passing into the dust of centuries past, leaving only their cryptic ruins and fell lore behind.

The current date is Midsummer, 1372 DR, the Year of Wild Magic. Flamerule is past, and Eleasias—Highsun—is yet to come. If the DM chooses, the Shieldmeet festival to occur the day after Midsummer night provides a good starting point for a FORGOTTEN REALMS campaign.

Creation of the world

While mythology and religion rarely hold much sway for historians, certain legends are echoed in so many Faerûnian religions that they have become accepted as fact. Thus, the history of Faerûn began when Lord Ao created the universe that now holds the world of Toril. After this creation came a period of timeless nothingness, a misty realm of shadows that existed before light and darkness were separate things. Eventually this shadowy essence coalesced to form beautiful twin goddesses, polar opposites of each other, one dark and one light. The twin goddesses created the bodies of the heavens, giving life to Chauntea, the embodiment of the world Toril. Toril was lit by the cool radiance of the goddess Selûne and darkened by the welcoming embrace of the goddess Shar, but no heat yet existed in this place.

The war of light and darkness

Chauntea begged for warmth so that she might nurture life and living creatures upon her form, and the twin goddesses disagreed over whether this should be done. The two fought, and from their divine conflict the deities of war, disease, murder, death, and other fell forces were created.

Selûne reached beyond the universe to a plane of fire, using pure flame to ignite one of the heavenly bodies so that Chauntea would be warmed. Shar became enraged and began to snuff out all light and warmth in the universe. Desperate and greatly weakened, Selûne tore the divine essence of magic from her body and hurled it at her sister, tearing through Shar's form and pulling with it similar energy from the dark twin. This energy formed Mystryl, the goddess of magic. Composed of light and dark magic but favoring her first mother, Mystryl balanced the battle and established an uneasy truce between the two sisters.

Shar, who remained powerful, nursed a bitter loneliness in the darkness and plotted her revenge. Selûne waxed and waned with the light, but drew strength from her allied daughters and sons, and even interloper deities from other planes. Their battle continues to this day.

Advancing the years

The first FORGOTTEN REALMS game product, the FORGOTTEN REALMS Campaign Set (known fondly as the Old Gray Box), was released in 1987 and set the campaign date at 1356 DR. Over the course of nearly one hundred game products in the original and 2nd Edition ADVANCED DUNGEONS & DRAGONS® games, the timeline of the setting was advanced to 1371 DR. This new edition of the FORGOTTEN REALMS Campaign Setting, in addition to updating the setting for the new DUNGEONS & DRAGONS game, moves the timeline ahead to the middle of 1372 DR.

From this point forward, we expect to advance the timeline of the world about two years per five years of game products and novels. In other words, for every five months that pass in the real world, we'll advance Faerûn by two months.

The Creator Races

While the deities battled, many intelligent beings arose on Toril. Modern scholars call the five greatest the *creator races*. The first of these was a saurian race that built an extensive if short-lived civilization. Its survivors eventually became the nagas, lizardfolk, troglodytes, and similar creatures.

Supreme among the creator races were the dragons, powerful enough to raid large cities of the other races with impunity. Dragons dominated the surface world, claiming vast areas of territory and battling each other for land, mates, and status. The great drakes suffered setbacks only when lesser races mastered magic, and they remain influential today despite the advances of such rabble.

An aquatic race of shapechangers that became amphibious developed late during the saurian civilization and crept onto the land, building proud cities. These creatures contributed to the downfall of the saurians, but they themselves eventually fell into barbarism under pressure from sahuagin, merfolk, and tritons. The survivors of this race are the locathah in the sea and doppelgangers on land.

Least known of the creator races are the sylvan people that populated the forests and other wooded areas, living in harmony with nature and leaving few traces. It is believed that their civilization fragmented after a great plague created by a draconic or demonic power. Their descendants are the sprites and other small woodfolk that populate secret parts of Toril today.

The last creator race, and the one that spent the longest time in a primitive state, is the humans. Always adaptable and ingenious, humans made advances with incredible speed and efficiency when circumstances allowed for their rise to prominence. Of the five creator races, only the humans truly survive as a cohesive civilization today. The individual dragons war with each other, and the others have vanished from the world or splintered among their subraces.

The First Flowering

With the discovery of magic by the creator races, talented individuals began experimenting with planar travel, contacting and visiting other worlds. Through these early *portals* came natives of these other worlds—dwarves, treants, elves, and mind flayers, in that order. Other races appeared, either through crossbreeding, planar immigration, or transformation by magic. Sharns and phaerimms are believed to have appeared during this time, and may have been birthed by the primal energies of the Weave.

The Newcomers

Halflings, gnomes, and giants arose on Toril. The mighty giants built great kingdoms and battled the dragons, although the giant civilization was never great enough to merit inclusion as one of the creator races. Goblinoids migrated to Toril in small waves when they discovered *portals,* and humans from other worlds migrated to places such as Kara-Tur, Maztica, and Zakhara. Nonhumanoid creatures such as beholders, wemics, and centaurs established territories, while pegasi and winged creatures such as aarakocras filled the skies while the dragons slept.

Of these arrivals, elves and dwarves proved the most resourceful. Each race began to acquire cultural, technological, and commercial power, establishing strong kingdoms across the face of Faerûn and other continents. This event, known as the First Flowering, heralds the ascension to civilization by races that still exist in great numbers today.

The friendly gnomes worked as go-betweens for the dwarven and elven nations, trading rare goods and exotic weaponry for magic and lore. During this time, the kingdoms of the benevolent humanoids developed a social structure of clans, houses, or families, each focusing on certain arts and ideals. These factions would eventually develop rivalries that would result in the downfall of their great kingdoms.

The Crown Wars

The elves colonized the islands of Evermeet and parts of the future Moonshaes, taking the first steps toward what would someday be known as elven high magic. This powerful arcane knowledge allowed the elves to contest with and finally drive back the dragons for the first time in history. With strong magic and many allies, the elves built great cities and mighty kingdoms. Little did they know their greatest threat was to come from within their own race.

The actual spark that set elven tempers ablaze is unknown. The conflict known today as the Crown Wars involved all the existing elven nations and lasted three thousand years. Entire kingdoms fell, and countless elven lives were wasted in battle. Punished for their loyalty to the corrupt elven goddess Araushnee (now Lolth), the dark elven nation of Ilythiir fell with her, banished to the Underdark to become known as the drow.

At the end of the Crown Wars, only two elven realms emerged with their civilizations intact. The Keltormir elves, inhabiting their namesake forest (which used to cover what is now Amn, Tethyr, and Calimshan), wearily settled into a much-needed peace. Unfortunately, they would soon come into conflict with a new human nation to the south. Illefarn, an elven nation near the Sea of Swords, made peaceful contact with nomadic tribes of elves and human settlements. The elves traded the knowledge of magic to the humans for food and trade goods. This event signaled the beginning of the age of humans, for these simple folk would found the magical empire of Netheril.

Netheril

Originating as seven fishing villages that came together for mutual protection, Netheril was destined to become incredibly powerful and doomed to overwhelming arrogance. Taught the basics of magic by their elven neighbors, the Netherese made moderate progress in the Art, bolstered by frequent contact with the elves of Illefarn and the much younger elven settlement of Eaerlann. The four peoples engaged in trade and fought against the orcs that swarmed from the Spine of the World every few years. Netheril weathered the war that erupted between its elven neighbors, and through one fortuitous discovery was launched onto a path of greatness and ruin.

The Nether Scrolls

An unknown adventurer discovered a set of magical writings that held vast secrets of the Art. These Nether Scrolls gave insight to spellcasting, the creation of magic items and constructs, the relations and structure of the planes, and even the making of artifacts. Although all of the Nether Scrolls were lost or stolen over the next two thousand years, the information changed the entirety of Netherese society.

The fledgling spellcasters of Netheril studied the scrolls and invented types of magic never before seen in Toril. The Netherese wizard Ioulaum created the *mythallar* that gave power to nearby items, negating the need for expenditure of a spellcaster's energy to create magic items. The *mythallar* also allowed the creation of flying cities, formed by slicing off and inverting the top of a mountain. Netheril's people took to the skies in these flying enclaves of magic, safe from human barbarians and hordes of evil humanoids. Every citizen wielded minor magic, and the Netherese traded with nearby elven and dwarven nations, expanding the reach of their empire greatly.

The fall of Netheril

The phaerimm onslaught

The first check to the power of Netheril was the phaerimms, a race of magical creatures living under the surface of the earth. This evil race suffered from the extensive use of magic by the Netherese. In retaliation, the phaerimms began to cast magic- and life-draining spells upon the lands of Netheril, turning lush fields and forest into barren desert. The humans eventually realized the intelligence behind the strange attrition, and a protracted magical war resulted. Eventually the drain on magic began to affect the functioning spells in the cities. Slowly at first, the archmages left in search of places where magic did not go awry, and the common folk whose fields had been turned to desert began to flee the land.

Karsus, an incredibly talented archmage responsible for bizarre advances in magic, felt it was his duty to hold the nation together in its time of need. Casting a spell he had been researching for a decade, Karsus created a link to Mystryl so that he could steal her power and become a deity. Upon completing the spell, his body swelled with divine power and his mind expanded with unimaginable knowledge—including the knowledge of the horrible mistake he had just made. Having stolen the divinity from the one being capable of constantly repairing the damage to the Weave the magic-gluttonous Netherese and phaerimms caused, Karsus threatened the existence of magic on Faerûn, since he was not prepared for such a task.

Mystryl sacrificed herself to save the Weave before the damage was irreparable. This severed her link to Karsus, petrifying him and temporarily negating all magic in the world. The Netherese flying cities plummeted, and Karsus's stony form, still containing a fading omniscience, watched as all he knew and cared about was destroyed because of his folly. Despite this catastrophe, sages know Karsus as the one being who attained godhood with a single spell.

The goddess of magic was reincarnated as Mystra, and in recreating the Weave was able to safely bring to earth three of the flying cities—Anauria, Asram, and Hlondath—that were high above the ground at the time of Karsus' act. This new Weave had stricter requirements for spellcasting, preventing the heights of power and potential for destruction the Netherese had attained. Clerics of Mystra were told the truth of the fall of Netheril as a warning so that such a thing might never happen again.

Meanwhile, the survivors of the now-grounded cities fled the phaerimms, humanoid hordes, and encroachment of the desert, founding the daughter states of Netheril to the south. The greatest empire of humans was dead, leaving a legacy of broken artifacts and a magically created wasteland now called Anauroch.

Fallen Empires

Meanwhile, far to the east, other kingdoms had formed beyond the immediate reach of Netheril. The greatest and oldest of these was Imaskar, a nation ruled by sorcerers known as the Imaskari or the Artificers, founded where the Raurin Desert now stands. Heady with power and hubris, the Imaskari refused to bow down before any divine entity. They worked mighty magic and researched strange technologies, fending off the predation of humanoids, dragons, and strange creatures native to their homeland. When their population was decimated in a terrible plague, the Imaskari created a pair of *portals* to another plane and raided that place to acquire countless slaves. When the raids were finished, they closed the *portals* and worked a great spell to forever close the physical connections between the two planes. The slaves eventually contacted their deities, who found a way to send physical manifestations to Toril through the Astral Plane, bypassing the Artificers' barrier and eventually destroying the empire of Raurin. The fallout from their battle became the Raurin Desert. The freed slaves traveled westward to found Mulhorand and Unther.

Six centuries before the fall of Netheril, two empires of magic rose east of the Sea of Fallen Stars. Narfell, great and cruel, was greatly feared, for its leaders made pacts with demons that marched into battle with the Nar soldiers. Raumathar, its neighbor, was similarly

Illustration by Sam Wood

mighty, and famous for its battle-wizards. The two clashed often, and Narfell even attempted an invasion of Mulhorand and Unther but was repelled. Eventually Narfell and Raumathar destroyed each other in a great battle involving demons, dragons, and magic that burned entire cities, creating the Endless Waste. To this day, the former lands claimed by Narfell remain known to some as the Demonlands.

The surviving cities of Netheril—Anauria, Asram, and Hlondath—formed settlements on the borders of Anauroch, poor shadows of their parent's glory. Asram, known for its City of Magicians, preserved the spirit of Netheril if not its wisdom, and was devastated by plague a mere three hundred years after its founding. Anauria, known for its magic and swordmaking ability, was destroyed less than five hundred years after Netheril's fall. Hlondath, which survived the longest, largely abandoned magic and became a nation of loggers and shepherds. The advance of Anauroch eventually swallowed all three. Other refugees from Netheril fled farther south and founded Halruaa, which still exists today.

Other ill-remembered and little-known empires included the dwarven nation of Delzoun that traded with Netheril, and the elves of Illefarn. Many communities of elves have vanished over time as they retreated to the sanctuary-home of Evermeet, but these are not true fallen empires in the same sense as the others mentioned here, because the elves left voluntarily rather than being beset by war and catastrophes.

The old Empires

The freed slaves of the Imaskari moved west after the destruction of their oppressors, led by their manifested deities. They settled on the southeastern portion of the Sea of Fallen Stars, forming two nations separated by the River of Swords. These kingdoms, Mulhorand and Unther, grew at a prolific pace and conquered or colonized the nearby lands. Unther's expansion stopped when the elves of the Yuirwood and the gold dwarves of the Great Rift held the empire at bay. A mages' rebellion halted Mulhorand's growth and caused the realm to look inward for centuries.

The orcgate wars

One *portal* opened by Mulhorand's rebellious wizards led to a world populated by savage orcs. These orcs used the *portal* to invade Faerûn, overrunning settlements and slaying thousands. The manifestations of the god-kings of both Mulhorand and Unther battled the orcs, and the orcs retaliated by summoning divine avatars of their own deities. During these conflicts, known as the Orcgate Wars, the orc god Gruumsh slew the Mulhorandi sun god Re, the first known deicide in the Realms. Many of the Untheric deities were slain as well. The human deities eventually prevailed and the orcs were slain or driven northward or westward.

The deities Set and Osiris battled to succeed Re, and Set murdered his rival. Horus absorbed the divine power of Re and became Horus-Re, defeated Set, and cast the evil god into the desert. Isis resurrected Osiris. All of the Mulhorandi pantheon but Set united in support of Horus-Re. The two old nations paused to rebuild their power and lick their wounds. In Unther, the chief god Enlil abdicated in favor of his son Gilgeam and vanished. Ishtar, the only other surviving Untheric deity, gave the power of her manifestation to Isis and vanished as well. Gilgeam began his two-thousand-year deterioration into despotic tyranny as the ruler of Unther.

The Long Decline

Settled in their ways and careless toward their distant conquests, Mulhorand and Unther were ripe for internal conflict and resentment from their daughter states. Over the next thousand years, Unther's northern cities seceded, and the country shrunk by half when its western cities declared themselves the free nation of Chessenta. Mulhorand suffered another mages' revolt that resulted in the loss of the province of Thay, and, despite a later invasion attempt to reclaim it, Mulhorand was eventually forced to accept Thay as an independent nation. Semphar and Murghôm won their relative independence, and Mulhorand and Unther became known to many as the two "living" fallen empires.

calimshan

Calimshan has a long history that predates even mighty Netheril. While never achieving the heights of magical power as Netheril did, Calimshan was a driving force in the history of the south of Faerûn because of its great population and military power.

Calim, a noble djinni, founded his empire when he, his retinue of djinn nobles and servants, and thousands of human slaves arrived from another plane. They repelled attacks from dragons and established border agreements with the nearby nations of elves and dwarves. A thousand years after Calim's arrival, an efreet mercenary named Memnon created a *portal* to Toril and founded his own realm to the north of the Calim empire.

After three centuries of coexistence, the two nations went to war and begin the Era of Skyfire, battling over the next four hundred years. Their war was brought to an end by the actions of their elven neighbors, who used elven high magic to fuse the two genie lords and most of their genie servitors into a large gem thereafter known as the *Calimemnon Crystal*. Eventually, the humans of the twin empires managed to drive out or bind the remaining djinn and efreet with the help of their dwarven neighbors. The humans called their united nation Coramshan.

Over the next four thousand years, under many different names and governments, Coramshan expanded to cover modern-day Amn and Tethyr, the entire Lake of Steam region, and as far south as the Chultan peninsula and the Landrise in the Shaar. Their expansions kept them busy battling Jhaamdath (now known as Chondath), the dwarven nation of Shanatar, and small elven kingdoms. Although intrigue, rebellions, monsters, and conquest caused the borders of Calimshan to collapse and expand several times (eventually resulting in the territory it holds today), Calimshan always maintained its status as a mercantile power, moving goods from the Chultan peninsula to the North and back again.

Rise of chondath

Founded shortly after the liberation of Coramshan by humans, the nation of Jhaamdath began as a collection of fishing and logging villages north of what is now called the Chondalwood. Jhaamdath and its central Twelve Cities of Swords grew quickly along the land and sea, and soon came into conflict with Coramshan when its borders approached the Lake of Steam. The two nations finally reached a peaceful settlement when they both agreed to abandon the contested lake. With Coramshan to the west and Unther to the east, Jhaamdath had nowhere to go but across the Sea of Fallen Stars, and so it focused its attention on trade, fortification of its borders, and northern expansion across the Inner Sea. Jhaamdath settled what is now Impiltur, Thesk, Sespech, Turmish, and the Vast, establishing colonies that enriched Jhaamdath with trade goods and prestige gained from large land holdings.

In time, the logging of the Chondalwood greatly angered the elves of that forest, and war between the races began. Within twenty years, all the elven cities in the forest except one had been destroyed, and nine out of ten elves in the wood had been slain. In retaliation, the surviving elven wizards used elven high magic to summon a great wave that scoured all of Jhaamdath from the face of the world and reshaped that area into the current coastline of the Vilhon Reach.

The few survivors fled to the colonies along the northern coast of the Sea of Fallen Stars. In time, other scattered survivors and folk from its old colonies returned and formed the country of Chondath, which rose to become a mercantile power but was broken again by wars and plague. The Chondath of today is only the palest shadow of its former greatness, but its legacy lives on in its colonial descendants, who eventually expanded west and founded the powerful nations of Sembia and Cormyr.

Ages of Unity and Dissolution

Dalereckoning began with compacts between the human settlers of what became the Dalelands and the elves of Cormanthor, who raised the Standing Stone as a symbol of the vows to respect each other's ways of life. That stone still stands, despite the chaos and pain of more than thirteen centuries. Below are discussed only a few of the more relevant events from the time of the early empires to the modern day.

Faerûnian history records numerous attempts by all the races to live together peaceably. Two of the most prominent were at the elven capital of Myth Drannor in the Cormanthor forest and on the Sword Coast in the country known as Phalorm, the realm of Three Crowns (for its elven, human, and dwarven co-rulers). While both grand realms had their internal pressures, their demises came from without—invasion by orcs and humanoids (and, in Myth Drannor's case, extradimensional creatures). Despite their falls, these kingdoms stand as a testimony to the ideal that the varying races *can* live and thrive together.

A divine event now known as the Dawn Cataclysm resulted in numerous transformations among the deities, though the only known impacts on Toril came from a schism in Tyche's church that led to her demise and the rise of the goddesses Beshaba and Tymora. The schisms took place during the 8th century DR.

Some centuries before the Dawn Cataclysm (mortals have difficulty dating events involving the deities), the first Magister, Azuth the High One, battled his rival Savras the All-Seeing for supremacy in service to Mystra. The battle lasted years, ending when Azuth finally imprisoned Savras in a magic staff.

Other events in this time period may be tied to the Dawn Cataclysm, such as the ending of the second empire of Unther, the formation of the Harpers, the arrival of demon-king Iyachtu Xvim the Baneson in Westgate, and the imprisonment of Moander.

The Time of Troubles

Seeking power over other deities, Bane (in his previous incarnation) and Myrkul (the former god of the dead) stole from Lord Ao the *Tablets of Fate*, divine records that state the responsibilities of all the deities of Faerûn. This act convinced Ao that the gods were unconcerned with their worshipers and more concerned with their battles against each other. To punish them and force them to attend their followers, Ao forced the deities out of their extraplanar realms and into mortal bodies called avatars.

The Avatars

The divine avatars walked the earth, interacted with mortals (some more ruthlessly than others), and scrambled to find a way to return to their extraplanar homes, for the normal paths were barred. Known variously as the Time of Troubles, the Godswar, and the Avatar Crisis, this period in the history of Faerûn is the most chaotic in recent memory.

Sudden mortality wreaked havoc on the deities. Helm alone retained his divine power and was commanded by Ao to guard the path to the Outer Planes. Because Helm was successful, much of the destruction caused by the Avatar Crisis is laid at his feet. Mystra was destroyed and her essence merged with the land, causing magic to function erratically and creating many wild magic and dead magic areas.

Gond the Wonderbringer fell to earth as a gnome on the shores of Lantan. In gratitude for the sanctuary, he taught the Lantanese the secrets of *smokepowder*. Tymora appeared at her temple in Arabel, and it is thought that her presence there spared the city much destruction. Ibrandul, god of caverns, was slain by Shar in secret and his portfolio stolen.

Malar battled Nobanion and was hunted by Gwaeron Windstrom. Shaundakul battled and destroyed the avatar of a minor orc deity. Sharess took the form of the favorite concubine of the pasha of Calimport and was liberated from the growing influence of Shar by Sune. The Red Knight appeared in Tethyr, helping that nation defeat monsters raiding from the Wealdath. Hoar slew Ramman, Untheric god of war, but lost his foe's portfolio to Anhur. Clangeddin Silverbeard battled Labelas Enoreth on the isle of Ruathym over a misunderstanding. Shar and Selûne fought another round of their age-old battle as mortals in Waterdeep. Waukeen vanished, and her ally Lliira claimed custody of her portfolio for safekeeping. The avatar of the godling Iyachtu Xvim, half-demon offspring of Bane, was imprisoned under Zhentil Keep. Gilgeam, the god-king of Unther, was slain by his rival Tiamat, ending his two-millennia rule of that nation.

Bhaal, the god of murder, was greatly weakened during the Godswar and existed only as a murderous force that could possess living beings. When Bane challenged Torm, the Black Lord slew all of the Bhaal-worshiping assassins in Faerûn and absorbed their essence, further weakening Bhaal.

The Mortals

Forging an alliance with Myrkul, Bhaal kidnapped the mortal wizard Midnight and discovered one of the *Tablets of Fate*. But at the Boareskyr Bridge the mortal Cyric killed Bhaal with the sword *Godsbane* (the avatar of Mask). Cyric absorbed some of Bhaal's power, while the rest went into the Winding Water, poisoning the river.

Cyric then slew Leira, goddess of deception and illusions, with *Godsbane* and absorbed her portfolio. He later broke *Godsbane*, greatly weakening Mask.

Torm destroyed Bane during a battle in Tantras, and Ao later gave the Black Lord's portfolio to Cyric. Torm himself was slain in the conflict with Bane, but since his realm at the time was actually Toril and because he died in service to his ethos (obedience and duty), Lord Ao restored him to life and reinstated him as a deity.

Myrkul's avatar battled Midnight, who destroyed him. Midnight became the new incarnation of Mystra, absorbing the essence of the previous goddess from the land. Cyric became the new deity of strife, tyranny, murder, and death, holding the portfolios of the slain Bane, Bhaal, and Myrkul. (Years later, Cyric lost the portfolio of death to the mortal Kelemvor when he was temporarily driven mad by an artifact he created.)

The close of the Avatar Crisis brought a change to the way the deities of Faerûn relate to their followers. By Ao's decree, a deity's power is in part derived from the number and fervor of his worshipers, and so deities can no longer afford to ignore their faithful. While the Time of Troubles reshaped the land and altered the Faerûnian pantheon dramatically, the new accountability of divinity remains its most powerful legacy.

The Tuigan Horde

For centuries the Endless Waste was believed an empty land lightly populated by skilled horsemen, until a great leader arose who would change the perception of that isolated land forever. The son of his tribe's khan (leader), Yamun was a charismatic young man with drive and ambition. After slaying his father to attain control of his tribe, Yamun made alliances with other tribes and eventually united almost all the Tuigan natives into a powerful military force, earning the title of khahan, or "great khan." With over three hundred thousand horsemen under his command, Yamun's army rode east, easily defeated the armies of the Shou, then broached the Dragonwall. Soon turning his eyes westward, Yamun Khahan swept toward Thay. Surprised by the aggression of their normally undisciplined eastern neighbors, the Thayans suffered tremendous losses. Eventually Szass Tam, Thay's zulkir of necromancy, bargained with the Tuigan, arranging to teleport the khahan's forces to Rashemen in exchange for no further attacks against Thay. The horde battled the berserkers of Rashemen and was eventually pushed back by the Witches, but avoided a devastating defeat with the aid of more magic from the Thayan wizards.

Only temporarily halted by the Rashemaar, the horde progressed toward Thesk. News of the horde eventually reached western ears. Given its size, it seemed likely to easily overrun Thesk and Impiltur and move through the Vast and into the Dales, Sembia, and Cormyr. This great threat temporarily unified the people of the Heartlands, and they formed an army to combat the Tuigan. King Azoun IV of Cormyr led a force composed of the Purple Dragons and War Wizards of Cormyr, skilled mercenaries from Sembia and the Sword Coast, Dales militiafolk, dwarves of Earthfast, and even a division of Zhentarim orcs. This patchwork army reached Thesk while the horde was besieging its northern cities. The two armies met, and the allied army carried the day in the greatest battle of the last hundred years. Under Azoun's leadership, the allied force broke the Tuigan horsemen, and the king slew Yamun Khahan in the conflict.

Demoralized at the loss of their leader and reduced to less than a fourth of their original numbers, the Tuigan retreated from the battlefield and began the long retreat back to their homeland. The people of Cormyr, Sembia, and the Dalelands returned to their homes. The orcs, however, had orders from their Zhentarim masters to remain in Thesk, and did so despite protests from Azoun. Not wishing to overextend his resources any further, the king left the small contingent of orcs in place, although he never forgot this tarnished spot on the Heartlands' otherwise bright victory.

Illustration by Todd Lockwood

LOCKWOOD

The return of Bane

Recent Years

The last few years have seen numerous upheavals. The followers of dead gods had to contend with worshipers of the new holders of those portfolios. The greatest among these battles were between Cyric and the "heretic" followers of Bane, Bhaal, and Myrkul. These internal conflicts slowed the expansion of the church of Cyric for some time and resulted in secret purges and crusades. When Iyachtu Xvim was released during the destruction of Zhentil Keep, another holy war began between his followers and those of the "usurper" Cyric. The return of Waukeen caused some confusion among her following, although Lliira gratefully returned her portfolio and the two faiths sorted things out quickly.

The peaceful kingdom of Cormyr suffered a series of tragedies, destabilizing a healthy, benevolent nation and affecting its ties to other countries. The Red Wizards of Thay greatly expanded their mercantile efforts into other lands, extending their reach into the Heartlands. Mulhorand, sensing weakness in its old neighbor and rival, invaded Unther and took the first step toward becoming a great empire again. The elves ended their Retreat just in time to combat the arrival of drow in their abandoned forests.

These events pale in comparison to the return of Bane. For many years, Iyachtu Xvim was known as the Baneson, said to be the offspring of Bane and a greater demon. Xvim acquired Bane's portfolio of tyranny and hatred and touted his church as the true church for those who once worshiped the Black Hand. Led by Fzoul Chembryl, Chosen of Xvim, the church of the Baneson gained many converts from the temple of Cyric, and the two faiths battled mercilessly.

On Midwinter night of 1372 DR, the priests of Xvim dreamt of their god, his demonic form glowing with hellish green light. The flame burned and split Xvim's skin, and from this shell burst forth a black armored figure—the traditional image of Bane—with an upraised right hand. The green flames collected in that hand, which clenched suddenly, forcing the light outward from between the fingers. "Serve no one but Bane," the figure intoned, at which point the clerics woke, their right hands surrounded by cold green flames that persisted for nearly an hour.

The highest members of the church speculate that the creation of Xvim had always been part of Bane's plan to thwart his own death. Xvim thought himself an independent being but was actually nothing more than a seed of Bane's power, which finally ripened so that the Black Hand could return. Conversion of Xvimlar faithful to the worship of Bane was complete within a matter of days. The reborn god acquired the unclaimed portfolio of fear and returned to his status as a greater god. With the church of Bane full of zeal and guided by an experienced and intelligent deity, the forces of good fear a shift in the balance of power in the world.

What the Future Holds

Faerûn is a land of constant change. Wars are fought, bright kingdoms fall, and dead gods are reborn to work their evil. Individuals of skill, power, and determination will write the next page of history—if they dare to take up the challenge.

An Abbreviated Timeline

Date (DR) Events

-20000 By this time, the elven realms of Eiellûr, Orishaar, Syòrpi-ir, and Thearnytaar are established in the forests around the Lake of Steam. To the south lies long-established Illythiir and to the north and west are Aryvandaar and Illefarn.

-17800 Elven realm of Keltormir is established in the great forest that stretches from present-day Amn (Bowl of the Gods) down to the shores of the Shining Sea.

-14000 Tribal barbarian clans of humans roam Keltormir.

-12000 The Crown Wars of the elves begin.

-11700 Tethir, the first elven dragonslayer, slays Xaxathart the Retributer. Human clans settle in the clearings and meadows created by the dragon fires around Keltormir.

-11200 The elven realms of Eiellûr, Orishaar, Syòrpiir, and Thearnytaar fall to the Ilythiir. The Ilythiiri skirmish with the elves of Keltormir.

-11000 Dwarves establish the first holds of Deep Shanatar in the southern Underdark, beneath the Almraiven Mountains and the Lake of Steam.

-10500 The Dark Disaster engulfs the elven kingdom of Miyeritar in killing storms.

-10450 The Fourth Crown War: Ilythiir's elves make open use of corrupting powers granted by evil gods.

-10270 The Stone and Claw Campaigns: The withdrawal of Keltormir's forces to defend its own borders pits the forces of Aryvandaar and Ilythiir against each other.

-10000 Corellon's magic, directed through his priests and High Mages, transforms the corrupt Ilythiiri and others into the drow, who retreat into the Underdark. Elven Court forms in the eastern woods, later named Cormanthor.

-9600 Rise of the first drow civilizations in the Underdark beneath southern Faerûn.

Lost Empires

The city-states and kingdoms of Faerûn stand on the wreckage of older lands. Ruined cities, ancient plagues, and slumbering evils still wait for those foolish enough to disturb them. Some of the most famous of these realms include the following.

Anauria: One of the few cities of Netheril to survive the failure of magic caused by Karsus in his mad bid for godhood, Anauria was swallowed by the desert Anauroch more than twelve hundred years ago. Its towers and citadels still lie under the sands of the Sword in southern Anauroch.

Askavar: An elven community in what is now the Wood of Sharp Teeth, Askavar was abandoned in the Retreat about eight hundred years ago.

Asram: Another survivor of Netheril. Its capital, Orolin, was known as the City of Magicians. Like Anauria, it fell to the relentless encroachment of Anauroch.

Athalantar: Athalantar, also known as the Kingdom of the Stag, was the long-ago birthplace of Elminster, the Old Mage, the last true prince of the realm. It stood in the Western Heartlands in the lands south of the High Forest. It fell under the cruel dominion of usurping Mage Kings but had a brief restoration after their fall. The realm fell to orc hordes a few scant generations later.

Cormanthyr: The great elven kingdom of the forest of Cormanthor, Cormanthyr grew from the ashes of the Crown Wars and later survived the loss of its capital city, Myth Drannor, for hundreds of years. The Elven Court was abandoned in the Retreat, but some of Cormanthyr's elves stayed on in the settlements of Semberholme and Tangled Trees. In recent months numerous drow from several clans have invaded the ruins of Cormanthyr, seeking to reestablish their surface realms.

Delzoun: A powerful dwarven kingdom in the North, Delzoun lay beneath the Ice Mountains and the Rauvin Mountains. Ascore, its most important trading city, is a sand-swept ruin at the western border of Anauroch. Some of Delzoun's other cities, including Mithral Hall, Citadel Adbar, and Citadel Felbarr, are in dwarven hands again, or never fell. Other strongholds of Delzoun have been held by orc tribes for centuries.

Eaerlann: A powerful elven kingdom that sprawled across the eastern High Forest and the Delimbiyr Vale, Eaerlann survived for many thousands of years. Many of its folk left for Evermeet or helped form various elven and allied realms along the Sword Coast. The weakened kingdom was swept away by the orc hordes and demons of Hellgate Keep when the city of Ascalhorn fell to the fiends in 882 DR.

Hlondath: Third and longest-lasting of Netheril's surviving cities, Hlondath was a realm of loggers and shepherds that lay on the northwest verge of Anauroch, in the vicinity of the Fallen Lands. Like Asram and Anauria, it fell to the desert's growth.

Illefarn: A very old kingdom of elves that welcomed human tribes and dwarven miners in its territory, Illefarn stretched along the northern Sword Coast, including the territory that would become Waterdeep. It fell under repeated orc attacks from the North as well as the pressures of increasing encroachment by human settlements.

Imaskar: One of the earliest human empires, Imaskar rose in the region that is now Raurin, the Dust Desert, and the Plains of Purple Dust. The Imaskari, also known as the Artificers, were extremely powerful and haughty wizards who worked great wonders with magic and created *portals* to many worlds. Slaves they abducted from other worlds eventually rose up and overthrew them, becoming the folk of Mulhorand and Unther.

Jhaamdath: Later known as Chondath, this kingdom gave rise to the human settlers who migrated into much of the northern Inner Sea and the Dragon Coast in the centuries before Dalereckoning. Most of Jhaamdath was swept away by elven high magic worked to defend the Chondalwood from its aggressive incursions.

Kingdom of Man: After the fall of Phalorm, the Kingdom of Man arose in its wake, unifying the humans and few surviving elves and dwarves of the Sword Coast North under human rule. The realm lasted only two human generations. Like its predecessor, the Kingdom of Man was swept away by goblinoid hordes—but in dying, it dealt such a blow to the nonhuman populations that humanity gained the opportunity to expand without serious challenge and came to dominate the Sword Coast as it does to this day.

Miyeritar: An elven realm that stood where the High Moor now exists, Miyeritar was destroyed during the Crown Wars by terrible elven high magic that blanketed the entire realm for months in a *killing storm* (only a remnant of that magic survives today as

−9000	Crown Wars end. High Forest is abandoned so the gods might restore its peace. The Wandering Years of elven colonization begin. Many elves migrate to the Elven Court in its eastern forest. Illefarn and Keltormir are the sole realms to emerge intact from the Crown Wars.	−6800	Memnon the efreeti arrives north of the River Agis. He begins building the country of Memnonnar.
−8600	Evereska founded in secret by surviving clans of Eiellûr, Miyeritar, and Orishaar as an elven haven in the woods east of Aryvandaar.	−6500	A group of elves, mainly survivors from Syòrpiir, settle the great forest now known as the Chondalwood.
−8500	Fire-sundered and otherwise ravaged, the forest of Keltormir fragments into three separate forests.	−6500	Era of Skyfire. Memnon and Calim bring their forces to bear one against the other in twenty-two cataclysmic battles over the next four centuries.
−8100	Eight dwarven realms unite and form the empire of Shanatar, which is ruled from the *Wyrmskull Throne*.	−6100	Era of Skyfire ends with elven high magic binding the noble genies Memnon and Calim in eternal struggle. Creation of the Calim Desert.
−7800	The djinn arrive in the area of present-day Calimport and build the Calim Empire.	−6060	Humans oust the last genies of Calim's realm. These lands become the human nation of Coramshan. Calimport and Keltar are rebuilt.
−7790	Calimport falls before a flight of dragons. Calim begins a campaign against the dragons of the Marching Mountains and drives them north from the peaks.	−5960	High Shanatar is founded by the dwarves along the River Agis.
−7690	The djinni noble Calim reaches an accord with the elves and dwarves and the borders of his empire halt at the southern banks of the River Agis.	−5800	Jhaamdath is founded north of the great forest now known as the Chondalwood. Jhaamdath eventually meets Coramshan near the Lake of Steam, and the two empires struggle for centuries over control of this area.

Lost Empires (cont.)

the spell *storm of vengeance*). When at last the curse ended, nothing was left of the elven kingdom but a few subterranean ruins.

Mulhorand: Mulhorand, of course, is not a dead empire. But it is lost in the sense that it once was a mighty realm that spanned thousands of miles in the lands east of the Sea of Fallen Stars. Thay, Semphar, Murghôm, and the Plains of Purple Dust were under Mulhorandi dominion a thousand years ago, and are independent (or independent in all but name) now.

Narfell: The barbarians who roam this cold, hard land remember the days of their forefathers' glory only in tales and songs. Narfell was a warlike, cruel nation whose leaders were evil priests allied with demons. The Nars fought in the Orcgate Wars as mercenaries and contended with Mulhorand and Unther for rule over these lands for centuries, but their great enemy was the realm of Raumathar. Narfell and Raumathar destroyed each other in a great magical battle roughly one hundred fifty years before the raising of the Standing Stone. Nar ruins litter the northern lands.

Netheril: The most renowned of human empires, Netheril was a nation of great archwizards that arose along the Narrow Sea in the fair and verdant plains between the Icewall Mountains and the Desertsmouth Mountains, where Anauroch now lies. Netheril's mages crafted works of magic whose like has not been seen since, but they fell to the power of the phaerimms and the act of a single archmage whose pride and power doomed his people.

Oghrann: A dwarven nation that once surrounded the vale of the River Tun, Oghrann lay beneath the Sunset Mountains and the Storm Horns of Cormyr. Like many dwarven realms, Oghrann fell to an onslaught of orcs, ogres, and other such creatures.

Phalorm: This kingdom is most often referred to as the Fallen Kingdom and is also known as the Realm of Three Crowns. Its formation in the early 6th century DR united native humans, elves from abandoned Illefarn, fallen dwarven realms, and scattered communities of gnomes and halflings for the first time along the Sword Coast. At its height Phalorm echoed what had already been achieved in Myth Drannor to the east, but the kingdom lasted a bare century before it was torn apart by concerted humanoid invasions. The realm's survivors became the founders of the Kingdom of Man.

Raumathar: The rival and enemy of ancient Narfell, Raumathar lay between the lands of the Nars and the Old Empires. At first mercenaries in the armies of Mulhorand and Unther, the Raumathari gained a reputation as skilled sorcerers and battle-wizards. They destroyed (and were destroyed by) Narfell more than a thousand years ago.

Shanatar: A mighty realm of shield dwarves that lay in the Underdark below Calimshan, Tethyr, and the Deepwash, Shanatar consisted of eight smaller kingdoms united by the *Wyrmskull Throne*. Only one of the kingdoms (Iltkazar, under Tethyr) still stands; evil Underdark races have destroyed or plundered the rest. Most of the dwarven realms of the Sword Coast sprang up as colonies from this realm, which outlived nearly all of them.

Shandaular: A strange mystery envelops this long-lost city. Reputed as a site of great magic and fantastic wealth, it is said to lie somewhere in the Shaar . . . or perhaps in Narfell. No one knows if there was one Shandaular or two, or if both are somehow the same city.

Shoon: The Shoon Empire arose in Calimshan and carried that ancient land to the zenith of its power under human rule. It dates back to the first four centuries DR and at its height subdued a vast portion of southwestern Faerûn.

Tethyamar: The Mines of Tethyamar were a rich dwarven realm beneath the Desertsmouth Mountains. They fell to an assault of bloodthirsty demons at the end of a great horde of goblins, ogres, and giants. The fall of Tethyamar is relatively recent, having happened only a few hundred years ago (two or three dwarven lifetimes). Many of Tethyamar's folk still wander rootless, dreaming of the day when they reclaim their home.

Unther: Like Mulhorand, Unther is not strictly a lost empire—but it seems to be undergoing its final disintegration at the hands of its ages-old rival. At its height, Unther ruled most of the lands south of the Sea of Fallen Stars and the city-states on the south side of the Aglarondan peninsula. Its conquests included Chessenta, the Shaar, and portions of Dambrath and Estagund. None of these lands remain under Untheric rule, although the zigguratlike Untheric temples still can be seen in some of the cities of these regions. The death of the god-emperor Gilgeam in the Time of Troubles heralded the final collapse of a realm that had been in decline for a dozen centuries.

−5005   A truce between Coramshan (soon renamed Calimshan) and Jhaamdath ends the war and limits their expansion over the Lake of Steam.

−4700   Elves settle Eaerlann.

−4400   Drow and duergar destroy the Elven Court and the dwarven nation of Sarphil.

−3983   Birth of the elven kingdom of Cormanthyr.

−3900   Establishment of Delzoun, the Shield Kingdom of the dwarves.

−3859   Villages on the shores of the Narrow Sea combine for mutual protection. The new realm is named Netheril.

−3830   Elves of Eaerlann open dialogues with Netheril. Humans begin to learn magic from the Eaerlanni elves during the following decade.

−3605   Orcs pour from the Spine of the World but elves turn them back in a great slaughter with help from fledgling Netheril. This orc incursion lasts nineteen years.

−3533   The Nether Scrolls are uncovered in the ruins of Aryvandaar, and the humans soon abandon the magic taught by the elves for greater power.

−3520   Elves of the North begin aiding the escapes of gnome slaves from Netherese captors, helping them move south and east across Faerûn.

−3419   The Netherese approach the dwarves of Delzoun at Ascore to conduct trade. After three years of deliberation, they set up a trade route through the safest and most heavily patrolled sections of the Underdark.

−3095   One set of the Nether Scrolls is stolen by elves of Cormanthyr and secreted away by the High Mages.

−3000   Hunting clans and fishing villages on the Sword Coast North unite under a single leader. The humans call their new community Illusk.

−2954   The first floating city rises above Netheril.

−2637   In Chult, the deity Ubtao founds Mezro.

−2600   The last of the known dwarves of High Shanatar fall in battle against the Tavihr Dynasty of Calimshan. The dwarves seal the last known entrance to Deep Shanatar.

−2550   Ulutiu, a minor sea deity, exiles himself to the Astral Plane. His ice necklace sinks, creating the Great Glacier.

−2488   Empire of the Imaskari in Raurin is destroyed.

−2381   Beholders plague the Alimir Mountains. The bakkal of Calimshan is assassinated and the Tavihr dynasty ends.

−2135   Mulhorand founded.

−2103   A horde of orcs, led by giants and their ogre generals, razes the human civilization of Illusk.

−2087   Unther founded.

−1967   First Mulhorand–Unther War.

−1961   Mulhorand and Unther agree on a common border, the River of Swords.

−1900   The Caltazar Hills come under regular attack from the beholder nations around and beneath the Lake of Steam.

−1838   The great red wyrm, Ylveraasahlisar the Rose Dragon, conquers and rules Calimshan.

−1726   Ylveraasahlisar is slain by the Cajaan noble family.

−1700   Calishite nobles begin hunting elves in the northern forests as a pastime.

−1570   Zazesspur, a simple fishing town, becomes a fortified city and center of the Emir of Tethyr's rule.

−1428   The beholders of the Alimirs swarm out of the mountains and conquer every city in Calimshan and Iltkazar.

−1402   The Drakhon priest-princes lead the nation of Calimshan to freedom from the beholders.

−1400   The attacks on the Caltazar Hills by the beholder nations of the Lake of Steam end.

−1088   First record of trading at the future site of Waterdeep.

−1087   The wizard Thayd leads a rebellion of wizards against Unther and Mulhorand.

−1081   Thayd and his conspirators are defeated. He is executed, but prophesies that Mulhorand and Unther will decline.

−1075   Orcgate Wars in Thay.

−1071   Orc god Gruumsh kills Mulhorand deity Re in the first known deicide.

−1069   Orcs in Thay defeated; many flee north and west.

−900   Rise of Narfell and Raumathar.

−790   The Night Wars begin: Drow attack outlying reaches of the Calimshan Empire.

−680   *Year of Creeping Thieves:* Calimshan begins to colonize the Lake of Steam.

−553   *Year of Plentiful Wine:* The Shadow Plane discovered by Netherese wizards.

−530   *Year of Meager Means:* The Night Wars between the drow and Calimshan end.

−461   *Year of Bold Pioneers:* The phaerimms begin to cast the spells that create Anauroch.

−425   *Year of Ancestral Voices:* Netherese settlers refound Illusk as a magocracy.

−387   *Year of Shattered Walls:* Calishite-controlled Zazesspur is sacked in a surprise attack by Tethyrian barbarians.

−354   *Year of Many Maws:* The first recorded clash between sharns and phaerimms occurs.

−351   *Year of Glassharks:* As the phaerimms' magic drain depletes more of their available power, several of Netheril's archwizards abandon their cities and relocate to parts unknown. Civil unrest rises in some cities.

−349   *Year of Bold Poachers:* Netherese wizard Saldrinar destroys Kisonraathiisar, the dragon ruler of Westgate, and becomes the city's first human king.

−339   *Year of the Sundered Webs:* Karsus causes the fall of Netheril, and most of its cities fall to earth and are destroyed. Mystryl is destroyed but is reborn as Mystra, who alters the function of magic to prevent such an event in the future. Anauria, Asram, and Hlondath (the survivor states of Netheril) established.

−288   *Year of Eight Lightnings:* Calimshan accedes independence to Tethyr and its people.

−286   *Year of Foul Awakenings:* Westgate falls during the course of a single night to a small army of elite mercenaries led by the vampire Orlak.

−255   *Year of Furious Waves:* Jhaamdath falls to elven high magic as a great wave is summoned to scour the southern shores of the Inner Sea. The coastline of the present-day Vilhon Reach is formed. The survivors head north and settle the lands of present-day Cormyr, Sembia, the Dalelands, and a portion of the Vast.

−212   *Year of High Thrones:* Battle of the Purple Marches forces the second Calishite surrender of Tethyr. Darrom Ithal is crowned the King of Tethyr.

−200   *Year of Stonerising:* Candlekeep founded; Calendar of Hartos begun. The humans who are to become the first of the Dalesfolk cross the Dragon Reach to the southern region of Cormanthor.

−160   *Year of the Stone Giant:* Narfell and Raumathar destroyed.

−153   *Year of the Starry Shroud:* Proeskampalar, later renamed Procampur, is founded by dwarves and quickly becomes an important trading partner of Westgate.

−133   *Year of Silent Screams:* Great sea storms erupt along the Sword Coast. A tidal wave envelops the city of Velen in Tethyr, decimating its population.

−111   *Year of Terrible Anger:* Illusk falls again to orc hordes.

−100   *Year of the Black Unicorn:* Delzoun falls to encroaching phaerimms and other dangers; surface citadels survive.

−75   *Year of Leather Shields:* Witches of Rashemen choose the first Iron Lord of that nation.

−68 to −65   *Hin Ghostwars:* Many lightfoot and ghostwise halflings depart Luiren.

−52   *Year of the Choking Spores:* First permanent farms in Waterdeep area.

−33   *Year of Slowing Sands:* Asram falls victim to a plague, from which there are no survivors.

1   *Year of Sunrise:* The Standing Stone is raised by the elves of Cormanthyr and the Dalesfolk. Start of the Dalereckoning calendar.

10   *Year of Dreams:* Netheril region renamed Anauroch.

20   *Year of the Fallen Fury:* The human Calendar of Harptos adopts the elven holiday of Cinnaelos`Cor (The Day of Corellon's Peace) and renames it Shieldmeet, celebrating it every four years since.

25   *Year of Many Runes:* Church of Deneir founded.

26   *Year of Opening Doors:* Cormyr founded by Obarskyr family.

27   *Year of Shadowed Blades:* Start of the Age of Shoon in Calimshan.

37   *Year of Dark Venom:* Five tidal waves strike Calimshan, destroying between a third and two-thirds of each of the five port cities of the nation.

75   *Year of Clinging Death:* Plague racks the civilized lands (Calimshan, Lake of Steam, Vilhon Reach). Alaundo the Seer arrives in Candlekeep.

111   *Year of Fallen Guards:* Anauria is destroyed by an orc horde, though it also destroys the horde. Orc numbers are reduced for centuries in this area.

112   *Year of the Tusk:* Cormyrian cartographers create the first map of Cormyr, Cormanthor, and the Dalelands.

168   *Year of Scattered Stars:* Halaster's Hold is built near Waterdeep's farms. Halaster Blackcloak begins creation of the great dungeon of Undermountain.

171   *Year of Unkind Weapons:* The elves of Cormanthyr destroy the sole surviving temple of Moander in the northern forest at the site of modern Yûlash. From this time forward, Moander remains a lurking evil trapped beneath the ruins of his final temple.

241   *Year of the Hippogriff's Folly:* Elminster Aumar enters the city of Cormanthor to serve Mystra's will.

244   *Year of the Elfsands:* Evereska's existence is discovered by nonelves, though the secret is kept for centuries by the human tribes of the Graycloak Hills.

261   *Year of Soaring Stars:* The elven city at the heart of Cormanthor becomes the unified city of Myth Drannor with the raising of a *mythal.*

273   *Year of the Delighted Dwarves:* The first migration of dwarves arrives at Myth Drannor in three small clans from Ammarindar and Citadel Felbarr.

284   *Year of Fallen Flagons:* A halfling migration hundreds strong arrives at Myth Drannor from Tethyr via the first open *portals* set up to bring folk to the city.

324   *Year of Freedom's Friends:* The Harpers at Twilight are formed in secret deep in Elven Court woods by Dathlue Mistwinter, the Lady Steel.

329   *Year of the Closed Scroll:* Hlondath's grain fields are consumed by the expansion of Anauroch, and the city-state is abandoned, its folk migrating east to the Moonsea or south into the Dales and beyond.

376   *Year of the Leaping Hare:* Ashar Tornamn of Valashar extends the borders of the Shoon Imperium to the High Moor. The army of Crown Prince Azoun I of Cormyr drives Shoon forces back through Amn, Tethyr, and Valashar before sacking Ithmong and returning home.

379   *Year of Seven Stars:* Seven mages build the first school of wizardry open to all the races of Myth Drannor.

384   *Year of Dreaming Dragons:* Silverymoon Ford, a lowly wood and rope bridge, is built across the River Rauvin.

449   *Year of Killing Ice:* Silvyr Ithal marches to Ithmong and takes the crown as the rightful King of Tethyr, sparking rebellion in Tethyr and Amn. Silvyr is killed in combat by Amahl Shoon VII.

450   *Year of the Corrie Fist:* Prince Strohm of Tethyr avenges his father by slaying Amahl Shoon VII and ending the Age of Shoon.

480   *Year of the Winter Sphinx:* Lyonarth, a white-furred androsphinx, claims the crown of Westgate.

482   *Year of the Blighted Vine:* Northern cities begin to become independent of Unther.

523   *Year of Trials Arcane:* Rise of Phalorm, the Realm of Three Crowns in the North.

574   *Year of the Gored Griffon:* Silverymoon rises to become a small trading post town.

615   *Year of the Lamia's Kiss:* The Winter Sphinx of Westgate falls prey to the charms of the lamia Nessmara, who has assumed the guise of a gynosphinx, and they rule in tandem. Phalorm falls to humanoid hordes.

616   *Year of the Ensorceled Kings:* A visiting wizard shatters the illusions guarding Westgate's lamia queen, and she and the androsphinx battle to the death.

627   *Year of the Bloodcrystals:* Ecamane Truesilver and his nine apprentices arrive in Silverymoon. The mages create a school of magic patterned on elven teachings.

640   *Year of the Fanged Beast:* First mining and trading encampments at Zhentil Keep.

659   *Year of the Hunting Ghosts:* Many wizards migrate to Silverymoon and begin establishing its role as a sister city to Myth Drannor.

668   *Year of the Telling Tome:* Halaster Blackcloak of Undermountain begins magically abducting wizards from Myth Drannor.

679   *Year of the Scarlet Sash:* Hillsfar is nearly destroyed by an army of deepspawn-bred monsters emerging from the Beast Marches to the west. Unther is forced to recognize the independence of the cities on the southern fringes of the Yuirwood.

694   *Year of the Ominous Oracle:* The first divinations and portents of the approaching doom of Myth Drannor arrive via the diviner Darcassan. This knowledge is kept from the public to prevent a panic.

708   *Year of Bound Evils:* Three battalions of elven mages battle a resurgence of evil beasts and cultists of the fallen god Moander near the site of his fallen temple. Three fiends are freed from their extradimensional prison and build an army of orcs, goblins, and other evil creatures.

710   *Year of the Toppled Throne:* Drow attacks in Cormyr claim the lives of three noble families of the realm; while believed dead, most of the nobles survive as slaves in the Underdark. A gate to the Abyss opens above the palace of Westgate, and a large host of tiefling warriors invades. The leader of the tieflings, Iyachtu Xvim the Baneson, seizes the throne of Westgate.

711 *Year of Despairing Elves:* Late in the autumn, the Army of Darkness (led by the three fiends) overruns the mining encampments on the western Moonsea. The Weeping War begins on the Feast of the Moon as the Army of Darkness engages elven patrols and destroys many villages and clan enclaves in Cormanthor.

712 *Year of the Lost Lance:* The Weeping War continues through the year, resulting in the deaths of many heroes and most of the Harpers at Twilight.

713 *Year of the Firedrake:* The war at Myth Drannor rages on, though the allies manage to eliminate two of the three fiends leading the Army of Darkness.

714 *Year of Doom:* Myth Drannor falls under siege by the Army of Darkness. Only two hundred elves and allies out of three thousand escaped to tell of its passing.

720 *Year of the Dawn Rose:* The Gathering of the Gods at the Dancing Place inspires the refounding of the Harpers. In attendance are all fifteen of the Harpers at Twilight who survived the previous decade, including Elminster and Khelben Arunsun.

734 *Year of the Splendid Stag:* The reign of Iyachtu Xvim comes to an abrupt end in Westgate as he is forced by a host of mercenaries to flee the city.

756 *Year of the Leaning Post:* Fisherfolk settle in Aglarond.

796 *Year of the Gray Mists:* Merrydale becomes Daggerdale following vampiric infestation.

863 *Year of the Wondrous Sea:* The Chultan city of Mezro disappears.

864 *Year of the Broken Branch:* Beneath Calimport, the lich Rysellan the Dark founds the Twisted Rune, a group of undead spellcasters with plans to control the world through subtlety and intrigue.

882 *Year of the Curse:* Demons take control of the elven citadel Ascalhorn, later known as Hellgate Keep. Fall of the realm of Earlann.

900 *Year of the Thirsty Sword:* Civil war erupts in Chondath. The Vault of the Sages is built in Silverymoon.

902 *Year of the Queen's Tears:* The Rotting War in Chondath decimates the country. Chondath renounces claims on Sembian city-states. The Cult of the Dragon creates the first dracoliches.

906 *Year of the Plough:* Shadowdale founded.

913 *Year of the Watching Raven:* Sembia founded under the Raven banner.

922 *Year of the Spouting Fish:* Battle of Thazalhar in Thay. Red Wizards declare Thay independent of Mulhorand. End of the Second Mulhorand Empire.

929 *Year of Flashing Eyes:* Chessenta rebels against Unther.

934 *Year of Fell Wizardry:* First Thayan invasion of Rashemen.

937 *Year of the Turning Wheel:* Thesk founded along the Golden Way.

974 *Year of the Haunting Harpy:* Castle Waterdeep built.

975 *Year of the Bent Coin:* Telflamm established as a royal city-state.

976 *Year of the Slaying Spells:* Mulhorandi invasion of Thay repelled.

1018 *Year of the Dracorage:* Death of Tchazzar, unifier of Chessenta. Sapphiraktar the Blue comes from the Calim Desert and destroys Calimport and Keltar.

1021 *Year of the Howling Axe:* Thay strikes against the Harpers. Harpers go underground.

1022 *Year of the Wandering Wyvern:* Refounding of the Harpers.

1030 *Year of Warlords:* Zulkirs established as rulers of Thay.

1032 *Year of the Nightmaidens:* Ahghairon, premier mage of the North, saves Waterdeep and creates the Lords of Waterdeep. The city grows into the largest in the North.

1038 *Year of Spreading Spring:* Glaciers retreat. Lands of Narfell, Vaasa, and Damara are fully free of ice. Large-scale immigration begins to these lands. Aencar declares himself king of the Dales.

1065 *Year of the Watching Wood:* Humans and elves in Aglarond agree to peace, electing a half-elf, Brindor, as the first king of the new kingdom of Aglarond.

1074 *Year of the Tightening Fist:* Zulkirs quell rebellions and rule in Thay.

1090 *Year of Slaughter:* The Battle of the Bones. Followers of Malar mount the Great Hunt.

1095 *Year of the Dawndance:* Imphras unites Impiltur.

1097 *Year of the Gleaming Crown:* Imphras crowned king of Impiltur.

1099 *Year of the Restless:* New trade routes forged. First modern contact with Kara-Tur and Zakhara.

1117 *Year of the Twelverule:* Chessenta breaks up into city-states through 1154 DR.

1150 *Year of the Scourge:* Plague throughout the Sword Coast. Worship of Talona and Loviatar soars. Khelben Arunsun arrives in Waterdeep.

1164 *Year of Long Shadows:* The pirate Immurk the Invincible raids a merchant-ship of Procampur, capturing the coronation crown of Cormyr's new king, Palaghard I. This marks the rise of piracy in the Inner Sea. The nations of the Inner Sea begin building their own warships, seeking to defend their merchant fleets and hunt the pirates in their own lairs.

1179 *Year of the Stalking Satyr:* Malaugryms attack Arunsun Tower but are turned back by Khelben, Elminster, and an assortment of Waterdeep mages.

1180 *Year of Sinking Sails:* Sembia loses fleet in Pirate Isles.

1182 *Year of the Tomb:* The malaugryms are discovered in Faerûn. Start of the Harpstar Wars.

1194 *Year of the Bloody Wave:* Battle of the Singing Sands. Aglarond defeats Thay.

1197 *Year of the Sundered Shields:* Battle of Brokenheads. Aglarond bests Thay.

1209 *Year of the Blazing Banners:* The plundering of the pirates is curtailed after a massive confrontation outside the Dragonisle by the combined forces of Sembia, Impiltur, and Cormyr.

1222 *Year of the Horn:* The Harpstar Wars end with the destruction of the Harper King.

1232 *Year of the Weeping Wives:* Destruction of Sessrendale by Archendale.

1235 *Year of the Black Horde:* Largest orc horde in history masses out of the North and engulfs the Sword Coast in war. Waterdeep besieged. Many Calishite nobles slain.

1237 *Year of the Grotto:* Thesk and Aglarond ally.

1241 *Year of the Lost Lady:* A well-respected Tethyrian noblewoman is captured and slain by orcs. In her memory, orcs are wiped out throughout the South.

1242 *Year of the Yellow Rose:* Monastery of the Yellow Rose founded in Damara. The venerable wyrm Anaglathos arrives in Turmish and stages a coup.

1245 *Year of Pain:* Loviatar worship gains great popularity—most of the modern temples in the North are founded.

1247 *Year of the Purple Basilisk:* Anaglathos overthrown in Turmish by popular rebellion and slain by adventurers.

1260 *Year of the Broken Blade:* Many peace treaties signed this year. Halacar of Aglarond is poisoned and his sister Ilione, tutor to the Simbul, takes the throne.

1261   *Year of Bright Dreams:* Manshoon claims his seat on the Zhent council. Manshoon founds the secret organization of the Zhentarim.

1280   *Year of the Manticore:* Thay nearly conquers Mulhorand before being repulsed.

1298   *Year of Pointed Bone:* Lhestyn, the Masked Lady, infiltrates the Shadow Thieves guild and exposes it. Within the span of one bloody week, the Shadow Thieves of Waterdeep are either dead or fleeing.

1306   *Year of Thunder:* Moonsea War. Mulmaster vanquished by alliance of other cities. Vangerdahast of Cormyr founds War Wizards. Moradin's Thunder Blessing begins, causing dwarven populations to multiply.

1307   *Year of the Mace:* Azoun IV of Cormyr born.

1312   *Year of the Griffon:* Darkhold seized by the Black Network as Manshoon slays its lich-queen. Teziir founded on the Dragonmere.

1316   *Year of the Gulagoar:* Teshendale becomes part of the Zhent lands.

1317   *Year of the Wandering Wyrm:* Great Plague of the Inner Sea, also called the Dragon Plague.

1320   *Year of the Watching Cold:* The Simbul becomes queen of Aglarond.

1321   *Year of Chains:* The Harpers are reorganized. Twilight Hall founded in Berdusk.

1323   *Year of Dreamwebs:* Thayan wizards attempt to control others through dreams, but the plan is thwarted.

1333   *Year of the Striking Falcon:* Amnian Trade War. Founding of the Council of Six, unification of Amn.

1336   *Year of the Highmantle:* Azoun IV takes the throne of Cormyr. The Zhentarim conquer Daggerdale.

1340   *Year of the Lion:* Battle of the River Rising in Featherdale between the forces of Sembia and the Cult of the Dragon.

1344   *Year of Moonfall:* Retreat of the elves from Cormanthor begins.

1345   *Year of the Saddle:* Plagues claim many among the Sword Coast port cities south of Baldur's Gate.

1347   *Year of the Bright Blade:* Zhengyi the Witch-King rises in Vaasa. Alemander IV dies in Tethyr. Tethyrian civil war begins.

1350   *Year of the Morningstar:* Elminster retires to Shadowdale.

1351   *Year of the Crown:* Warlock's Crypt discovered. Plague in Baldur's Gate.

1352   *Year of the Dragon:* Barbarians of the Ride destroy Zhentarim force en route to Glister.

1353   *Year of the Arch:* Night Masks become secret rulers of Westgate.

1355   *Year of the Harp:* Zhentil Keep takes Citadel of the Raven as its own. Retreat of elves from Cormanthor reaches its peak. Yûlash falls in civil war. Zhentil Keep and Hillsfar move troops to Yûlash.

1356   *Year of the Worm:* Lashan of Scardale attempts to take over the Dalelands and fails. Cormyr seizes Tilverton. Flight of dragons over the Dales and Moonsea. Death of Syluné of Shadowdale. Mithral Hall reclaimed.

1357   *Year of the Prince:* King Virdin of Damara killed in battle with Zhengyi the Witch-King. Horustep III (age 11) takes the throne of Mulhorand. Moander, god of corruption, is accidentally woken from a magical slumber and causes much devastation before being banished.

1358   *Year of Shadows:* The Time of Troubles: Gods walk Toril. Destruction of Bane, Bhaal, Gilgeam, Ibrandul, Myrkul, and other deities. Ascendancy of Cyric and Mystra. Dead magic and wild magic areas appear.

1359   *Year of the Serpent:* Zhengyi the Witch-King is destroyed. Damara united by Gareth Dragonsbane, who is soon crowned as its king. Tuigan horde united beneath Yamun Khahan. Tuigan horde battles Thay. Szass Tam negotiates with the horde and allows it to pass through Thay to attack Rashemen, where it is defeated by the Witches.

1360   *Year of the Turret:* Tuigan horde invades Faerûn. Crusade against the Tuigan. King Azoun IV kills Yamun Khahan.

1361   *Year of Maidens:* The First Banedeath begins as a holy war in Zhentil Keep. Orthodox Banite worship driven underground in that city by clerics of Cyric. Explorers from Amn discover Maztica.

1363   *Year of the Wyvern:* Mezro reappears.

1367   *Year of the Shield:* Tethyr's Reclamation Wars begin.

1368   *Year of the Banner:* Cyricists begin the Second Banedeath. Zhentil Keep is destroyed. Hellgate Keep is destroyed.

1369   *Year of the Gauntlet:* The Reclamation Wars of Tethyr end with the coronation of Tethyr's Queen-Monarch Zaranda and King Haedrak III. Randal Morn reclaims the throne of Daggerdale. Xvim is freed from his prison under the ruins of Zhentil Keep and becomes a lesser god. Trade with Maztica hampered by attacks from sea creatures. Fzoul becomes leader of the cult of Xvim and converts many holdouts of Bane to worshiping Xvim.

1370   *Year of the Tankard:* Trade between the sea folk of the Sea of Fallen Stars and ports along the Inner Sea increases sharply in the aftermath of a great undersea war. The Shaking Plague decimates Scardale. War in southern Amn as ogre mages and their minions ally with the temple of Cyric. Fzoul Chembryl forges the *Scepter of the Tyrant's Eye.* Manshoon is slain by Fzoul and the Zhentarim purged of Manshoon's supporters, giving Fzoul control over most of the organization. Several clones of Manshoon awake at once and create havoc as each tries to claim the Zhent wizard's possessions and place.

1371   *Year of the Unstrung Harp:* The Harpers divide into factions because of the departure of Khelben the Blackstaff, and these conflicts are only grudgingly held at bay by greater issues. A red dragon leads an army of orcs and goblins and despoils much of Cormyr. The dragon and King Azoun IV slay each other in battle, leaving an infant heir on Cormyr's throne. Evermeet is nearly destroyed by a sneak attack of rebel elves and drow. Mulhorand invades Unther. The Silver Marches is declared a new country.

1372   *Year of Wild Magic:* By the midpoint of the year, several events have signaled a shift in the balance of power for all of Faerûn.

Hammer: City of Shade appears.

Midwinter: The return of Bane.

Mirtul: Tilverton obliterated.

Midsummer: Campaign begins (Shieldmeet 1372).

Organizations

Hideous trolls and fire-breathing dragons may account for the doom of many noble heroes, but even more meet their end from the knife in the dark or a smiling face that conceals black-hearted treachery. Faerûn is home to fell powers that choose to work through stealth, intimidation, intrigue, and terror. Bold knights and battle-wise wizards alike have fallen to foes they never even suspected in cities or courts they deemed safe.

Hundreds of guilds, cabals, societies, and orders exist in Faerûn's wide lands. Some assemble to wage war against evil, swearing solemn oaths of goodwill and protection as binding as any paladin's. But most are alliances of ambitious, wealthy, and frequently ruthless people interested only in advancing their hidden agendas, regardless of who or what gets in their way.

The Cult of the Dragon

The Cult of the Dragon is a secret society dedicated to bringing about the "inevitable" rule of Faerûn by undead dragons. Founded by the mad archmage (and later lich) Sammaster, the Cult's information-gathering, illegal acts, magical research, and alliances with evil dragons all help it acquire power and wealth. With these tools the Cult fortifies its holdings and proceeds toward its goal: converting dragons to the most terrible form of undead, the dracolich.

The Cult reveres dragons to an extent resembling divine worship (and in fact some dragons are wor-shiped as gods, although they are not deities and cannot grant spells). Cult members serve the dragons by giving them treasure, offering healing, exchanging spells, modifying lairs by adding mechanical traps, and tending eggs and hatchlings. In exchange, the Cult members are allowed to hide in the dragons' lairs in times of crisis and receive promises of aid from the dragons. Above all, the Cultists handle the preparations for transforming a dragon into a dracolich.

The Cult is organized into independent cells that work together toward their greater goals. Some rely upon legitimate business to bring in wealth, including trade, selling information, and hiring adventurers to investigate ancient sites (Myth Drannor in particular) in exchange for a share of the profits. Other cells rely upon smuggling, kidnapping, blackmail, protection rackets, selling illicit or dangerous goods, usury, gambling, or brigandry to support themselves.

Each cell has a hierarchy of individuals, with the lowest being those serving the Cult without knowing it and the highest being the Wearers of Purple, so known for their ceremonial purple robes. Most of the important members of the Cult are wizards, particularly necromancers, who manufacture magic items, prepare the dracolich-transformation potions, and create undead. A typical servant of the Cult is a 6th-level wizard specializing in the school of Necromancy.

The group's symbol is a flame with eyes burning above a dragon's claw, displayed only in the few places where the Cult gathers openly—many groups such as the Harpers and the churches of Mystra, Lathander, Torm, and Tyr attack Cultists on sight.

While they are devout in their appreciation of dragons, few actual clerics serve within the ranks of the Cult. Those who do are typically clerics of Bane, Shar, Talos, Talona, or Velsharoon. A smaller number worship Cyric, Gargauth, Malar, or Tiamat. Because of their conflicts with the church of Mystra, many of the Cult wizards choose to worship Velsharoon to avoid paying even lip service to the Lady of Mysteries.

The Cult is rumored to have a secret headquarters or hidden fortress somewhere in the Western Heartlands, not far from the Battle of Bones.

Typical Cult Wizard: Human Nec6; CR 6; Medium-size humanoid; HD 6d4+12; hp 30; Init +2; Spd 30 ft.; AC 14 (touch 14, flat-footed 12); Atk +2 melee (1d4–1/19–20, claw bracer) or +6 ranged (1d8/19–20, masterwork light crossbow); SQ Familiar; AL CE; SV Fort +6, Ref +4, Will +6; Str 8, Dex 14, Con 15, Int 16, Wis 12, Cha 10.

Skills and Feats: Alchemy +12, Concentration +11, Knowledge (arcane) +10, Listen +4, Speak Language (Draconic), Spellcraft +12, Spot +4; Brew Potion, Exotic Weapon Proficiency (claw bracer), Great Fortitude, Scribe Scroll, Spell Focus (Necromancy), Greater Spell Focus (Necromancy).

Special Qualities: Toad familiar, hp 15; see Chapter 2 of the *Player's Handbook.*

Spells Prepared (5/5/5/4; base DC = 13 + spell level): 0—*detect magic, disrupt undead*†, ghost sound, ray of frost, read magic;* 1st—*burning hands, chill touch*†, mage armor, ray of enfeeblement*†, spider climb;* 2nd—*Aganazzar's scorcher, ghoul touch*†, invisibility, resist elements, summon swarm;* 3rd—*fly, haste, lightning bolt, vampiric touch*†.*

*These spells belong to the school of Necromancy, which is this character's specialty. Prohibited school: Divination.

†Because of Greater Spell Focus (Necromancy), the base DC for saves against these spells is 17 + spell level.

Possessions: amulet of natural armor +1, wand of magic missile (3rd), *ring of protection +1,* arcane scroll of *darkvision, potion of hiding,* 2 *potions of cure light wounds* (1st), masterwork light crossbow, 20 bolts, silvered claw bracer.

Emerald Enclave

Based on the island of Ilighôn off the Vilhon Reach, the Emerald Enclave is an organization of druids and other people who protect the natural resources of the Vilhon Reach and nearby lands. The members of the Enclave, known as the Caretakers, eschew good and evil to focus on the needs of the natural world and resist the encroachment of mankind. Founded in the Year of the Thoughtful Man (374 DR), the actions of the Enclave have influenced the lives of the high and the low.

The Enclave is organized into a hierarchy of circles, each with a different responsibility. The three members of the Elder Circle are the Chosen of Eldath, Mielikki, and Silvanus. The group accepts new members as long as they do not serve good or evil, are not members of another organization (except the churches of the aforementioned deities), are innocent of any crimes against nature, and have performed a significant act that benefits nature in the Vilhon Reach.

The tenets of the Caretakers are sixfold: preserve nature in all its forms, control human expansion, recognize that nature encompasses more than just forests, agree that magic should not be used for mass destruction, warn against the use of magic on a grand scale for fear of unexpected side effects, and present a united front to the outside world. Most members worship Eldath, Mielikki, or Silvanus, and all wear some sort of green symbol. They travel often, searching for threats to the natural resources in the Reach and potential allies in other lands.

While the Emerald Enclave's primary goal is to preserve nature, its members are not direct opponents of progress. They prefer to work with civilized folk to promote the health of the natural world rather than using acts of violence to deter it. The druids have been known to allow woodcutters to work in areas of forests that need culling, although they still oppose indiscriminate logging.

Recently the Enclave has started splinter cells in other areas that they believe may become threatened, such as the High Forest, Cormanthor, the Wealdath, and the forests of the Great Dale. These cells are small, often consisting of only one or two people, but they keep a close eye on organizations dangerous to their aims, such as the church of Talos or the People of the Black Blood.

Fire Knives

Originally a band of assassins based in Cormyr, the Fire Knives were driven from that land in 1341 DR after their ties to the assassination of a local lord were revealed. The current group consists mostly of exiled nobles of Cormyr's house Bleth and Cormaeril, who rebuilt the organization after adventurers broke its power in 1357 DR. Now they scheme to assassinate those Cormyrians who oppose their return, reserving their special hatred for House Obarskyr.

The Fire Knives are based in Westgate, existing there with the permission of the Night Masks (the thieves' guild that runs the city). The guild's new headquarters is under Castle Cormaeril in Westgate. Bitter about their exile, the former nobles of the Fire Knives have a strict hierarchy under the Grandfather of Assassins. Lord Tagreth Cormaeril (LE male human Ftr3/Rog7/Asn7) tolerates no dissent among the ranks of his followers. Agents of the guild exist in all of the major cities in Cormyr and many of the smaller towns, with a few scattered among Sembia, the Dales, and Chessenta. Since Cormyr is unaware of the rebirth of the guild and has its own problems, the Fire Knives have been able to act unopposed, placing assassins close to targets who only await a command from the Grandfather.

Because most of the Fire Knives were born to the nobility, they are schooled in diplomacy, subtle language, and high society. Most have acquired some skill at disguise. Forced to flee Cormyr with what they could carry, many have heirloom magic items and jewelry, some of which they were forced to pawn in the months before the guild was formed. Fire Knives tend to use giant wasp poison on their weapons when performing an assassination, but don't shy from poisoning their target's food and drink when possible.

Recently Lord Tagreth has been urging his followers to dissociate themselves from the Night Masks, sensing trouble on the horizon as the vampire leader of the Masks exerts his influence more forcefully upon the Knives. Tagreth has purchased a large mansion and a scroll with *teleportation circle,* which he plans to use to evacuate his followers should the Masks turn against them.

The Fire Knives are dangerous due to their ability to blend in with elite society and their fixation on the destruction of Cormyr's house Obarskyr. They are willing to accept other assassinations at very low rates just for the opportunity to hone their skills. This eagerness makes them popular with those who would otherwise be unable to afford such services.

Typical Fire Knife: Human Rog4/Ftr1/Asn2; CR 7; Medium-size humanoid; HD 4d6 plus 1d10 plus 2d6; hp 29; Init +9; Spd 30 ft; AC 20 (touch 13, flat-footed 12); Atk +8 melee (1d8+2/19–20, *+1 longsword*) or +9 ranged (1d8+2/19–20, masterwork light crossbow); SA Sneak attack +3d6, poison use, death attack (DC 14); SQ Evasion, uncanny dodge (Dex bonus to AC), +1 save vs. poison; AL NE; SV Fort +3, Ref +10, Will +0; Str 12, Dex 16, Con 10, Int 14, Wis 8, Cha 13.

Skills and Feats: Balance +7, Bluff +10, Climb +1, Diplomacy +8, Disguise +10, Hide +22, Innuendo +10, Intimidate +10, Listen +6, Move Silently +12, Pick Pocket +9, Spot +6, Tumble +8; Dodge, Improved Initiative, Mobility, Thug, Weapon Focus (longsword).

Assassin Spells per Day: 1. Base DC = 12 + spell level.

Possessions: +1 chain shirt, +1 buckler, +1 longsword, cloak of elvenkind, masterwork light crossbow, 20 bolts, 6 doses greenblood oil (DC 14, initial damage 1 Con, secondary 1d2 Con).

Harpers

Those Who Harp believe in the power of individuals, the balance between the wilderness and civilization, and the good of humankind and its allied creatures. They preserve the tales of the past so that others may remember its lessons when dealing with the present. Powerful individuals such as Elminster, Alustriel Silverhand, Dove Falconhand, and Storm Silverhand support the Harpers.

The Harpers usually operate in secret, alone or in small groups, traveling throughout the North and the Western Heartlands. Many members are elves, rangers, or bards. While they lack a main base of operations, Harpers are common in Berdusk (in Twilight Hall, a building complex associated with the temple of Deneir) and Shadowdale (often sheltered by Elminster or other powerful allies).

The Harpers are opposed by evil organizations such as the Cult of the Dragon, the Iron Throne, the Red Wizards, the Zhentarim, and in particular the resurgent church of Bane. Harpers identified by their enemies risk torture and death, making it essential that the Harpers protect their identities from all who might reveal their allegiance. Despite these dangers, Harpers are brave folk, facing dire perils with little more than their hearts and their hands.

Harpers have no standard equipment, although most are familiar with the use of magic items, and powerful members tend to have a large number of such items. A Harper agent might be an elf warrior in mithral full plate or a penniless human ranger in leather. Harpers spread knowledge, aid common folk in small ways, thwart the schemes of villains, and manipulate the affairs of civilized races in order to preserve their idea of balance. In addition to these active Harpers, many folk serve as their spies, give them shelter when in trouble, watch for enemies, or report unusual occurrences.

Harpers often secretly aid adventurers and other groups that promote good causes, whether this aid consists of a pointer to a friendly innkeeper in a hostile town, a traveling cleric appearing just when the group is hurt, or a surprise attack against a common foe.

The highest-ranked Harpers are called the High Harpers, and they are responsible for most of the long-term planning for the organization. The High Harpers are voted into their position by a secret ballot among the other High Harpers, with the criteria being experience, exceptional service, and discretion in implementing the Harpers' plans. Some of the High Harpers gain the favor of deities that support the Harpers, achieving special powers and status much like the Chosen of a deity. (Chosen are characters specially selected by deities to serve them at particularly dangerous tasks and who are therefore given special powers.)

KHELBEN "BLACKSTAFF" ARUNSUN

Male human (Chosen of Mystra) Wiz20/Acm3/Epic4: CR 31; Medium-size humanoid; HD 20d4+160; hp 210; Init +3; Spd 30 ft.; AC 26 (touch 18, flat-footed 23); Atk +15/+10 melee (1d6+5, the *black staff*) or +13/+8 ranged touch (by spell); SQ Archmage high arcana, Chosen immunities, Chosen spell-like abilities, detect magic, enhanced Constitution, enhanced Wisdom, epic-level benefits, silver fire; AL LN; SV Fort +16, Ref +11, Will +21; Str 14, Dex 16, Con 26, Int 22, Wis 20, Cha 15. Height 6 ft.

The Meaning of the pin

Some members of Those Who Harp can be identified by the magical silver crescent moon-and-harp pins they bear; but a Harper can otherwise be just about anyone from any walk of life. They're disorganized, secretive, and tend to have many lone wolves in their ranks. Most work informally as solo agents who never band together. Elminster (a founder of the Harpers) once differentiated the Harpers from other secret societies as the only such group that "habitually worries about the effects of their actions on others." Senior Harpers tend to be cautious and careful, whereas younger Harpers tend to want to change the world personally, immediately if not sooner.

Others have called them "the meddlers of Faerûn," and the comment is largely correct. All work for what they see as good (though individual Harpers often sharply disagree on just what "good" is), and most do so in a style that involves deception, misdirection, and covert action rather than open conflict.

The Harper Code is simply stated but hard to follow: to work against villainy and wickedness, to keep folk free of fear and tyranny, to support law and order to gain peace wherever laws are just and fairly enforced, and to prevent extremes of power and influence and imbalances of wealth and opportunity.

In following these aims, Harpers do whatever must be done without thought of personal pride or comfort. They police themselves (traitor Harpers must die), are free to rebuke and disagree with other Harpers, aid other Harpers without hesitation or thought of cost (or expectation of payment), and try to record and preserve the past, accumulating written lore for all.

Some Harpers prefer to work actively in cooperation with other Harpers, following a hierarchy and long-range plans. That faction is based in Twilight Hall in Berdusk and led by the half-elf bard Lady Cylyria. Others prefer to subtly manipulate events behind the scenes, practicing politics amid great secrecy. Khelben "Blackstaff" Arunsun is the most powerful of these, and he and his followers are often abrasively at odds with the other Harper branches. (In fact, Khelben's "Moonstars" have fallen out with Cylyria's followers altogether and no longer consider themselves part of the same organization.) The third sort of Harper prizes independent adventurers acting more or less as secret agents. These agents are led by Storm Silverhand in Shadowdale, aided by her sister Dove Falconhand and Elminster.

In the Sword Coast North, Cormyr, and the Dales, most common folk see Harpers as heroes; in Amn, Tethyr, and Calimshan, they're considered no better than the Zhentarim and other sinister cabals.

Illustration by Sam Wood

Skills and Feats: Alchemy +26, Bluff +4, Concentration +32, Craft (painting) +11, Diplomacy +4, Gather Information +4, Intimidate +7, Knowledge (arcana) +30, Knowledge (the planes) +16, Knowledge (religion) +11, Knowledge (Waterdeep history) +11, Knowledge (Waterdeep local) +16, Perform (drama) +4, Ride (horse) +4, Scry +25, Search +10, Sense Motive +9, Spellcraft +34, Spot +7, Wilderness Lore +8; Artist (painter), Craft Staff, Craft Wondrous Item, Forge Ring, Iron Will, Quicken Spell, Scribe Scroll, Skill Focus (Spellcraft), Spell Focus (Evocation), Spell Focus (Transmutation), Spell Mastery (*blackstaff, chain lightning, fly, magic missile, teleport without error*), Still Spell, Weapon Focus (quarterstaff).

Special Qualities: Archmage High Arcana: Arcane reach, mastery of counterspelling, mastery of elements. Chosen Immunities: Khelben is unaffected by attacks that duplicate these effects: *blindness, circle of death, disintegrate, energy drain, forcecage, ice storm, lightning bolt, magic jar, magic missile, Otto's irresistible dance.* Chosen Spell-Like Abilities (all 1/day): *Alustriel's fang* (causes the next weapon the recipient throws to return as if it were a returning weapon), *antimagic field, brain spider* (allows the caster to read the thoughts of up to eight people and even pry for more information), *gaseous form, gauntlet* (sheathes one hand in a gauntlet of force that gives damage reduction 30/— to that hand and prevents all contact with it but also prevents the use of that hand to cast spells), *minor spell turning* (as spell turning but affects only 1d4 spell levels and cannot partially turn spells), *Muirara's map* (provides a mental map consisting of the recipient's location, another's location, and two landmarks known to the recipient), *the Simbul's skeletal deliquescence* (convert's target's bones to jelly, turning it into an ooze-like creature), *the Simbul's synostodweomer* (converts prepared spells into 2 hit points of healing per spell level), *sphere of wonder* (a variant of globe of invulnerability that allows the caster to choose which spell effects may enter the sphere). Detect Magic (Su): Line of sight. Enhanced Constitution: The Chosen of Mystra template adds +10 to Khelben's Constitution. Enhanced Wisdom: Khelben used *wish* spells to increase his Wisdom. His Wisdom score has a +4 inherent bonus included in its value. Epic-Level Benefits: Bonus spell level ×4 (included in the listing below), three effective levels of archmage (included in the above total), Silver Fire (Su): See Chapter 2 for details.

Wizard Spells per Day: 4/6/6/5/5/5/5/2/3/4/1/1/1/1. Base DC = 16 + spell level, 18 + spell level for evocation and transmutation spells. Caster level 23rd.

Spellbook: Khelben makes it his business to know hundreds of worthwhile spells and a few odd spells that lesser wizards find of little interest. He knows most of the wizard/sorcerer spells in the *Player's Handbook* and in this book.

Possessions: The *black staff* (a *staff of power* with a permanent *blackstaff* spell upon it that allows it to *dispel magic* as an 8th-level caster by touch, channel various mind-affecting spells, or cause a touched spellcaster to lose a prepared spell or expend an unused spell slot), *bracers of armor +8, ring of protection +3.* As a very powerful wizard, Khelben has access to incredible resources and can acquire or make almost any nonartifact item he might need, given time.

A Chosen of Mystra and a grim, inflexible proponent of law and order, Khelben Arunsun (called "the Blackstaff" for his magic staff and several spells that create stafflike effects) is the Lord Mage of Waterdeep and the husband of Laeral Silverhand of the Seven Sisters. Few know of Khelben's youth in lost Myth Drannor, or even his true age—but many have learned to fear him.

Khelben dresses in nondescript black robes and never appears in public without his black staff. He has a dignified, imposing manner. He prefers to intimidate or frighten people rather than revealing his dry sense of humor or his keen, playful intelligence and quick wits. More than one shrewd observer of humankind say they see an old, underlying guilt in the Blackstaff, one that eats away at him—but no one knows (or will say) what this may be.

In Khelben's pursuit of law and order, he has founded or supported organizations (such as the Lords' Alliance) and then abandoned them (the Harpers) when they no longer suited his purposes. He recently resigned from the Lords of Waterdeep and later broke with the Harpers over a disagreement about his methods. He formed his own group of likeminded ex-Harpers, known only as the Moonstars.

Khelben acts as the gravely wise, stern tutor who manipulates agents and adventurers he meets by reluctantly dispensing information on a firm "only what you need to know" basis, never volunteering even paltry tidbits. In his words, "A secret isn't a secret if you tell anyone."

His beloved Laeral is probably the only person who is privy to all of Khelben's plans. She is a match for him in both intellect and personal power, and their deep bond of true love has created one of the most formidable magical alliances in contemporary Faerûn.

Khelben "Blackstaff" Arunsun

Lords' Alliance

Also known as the Council of Lords, this group was formed to oppose the Zhentarim and the other sinister factions that seek to dominate the North through trade or treachery. Primarily a lawful good organization, it represents the interests of rulers of cities in the North and the Western Heartlands. The rulers of Waterdeep, Silverymoon, Neverwinter, and other free cities and towns in the region make up most of the Alliance.

The various Lords differ on issues of trade,

magic, relations with foreign nations such as Thay, and even the treatment of humanoids such as orcs and goblins. The members of the Alliance are all equal in discussing Alliance matters, regardless of station outside the group. Given the increase in Zhentarim holdings in the North, the Lords have been trying to encourage other cities to join their cause, but so far such efforts have been met with little success. Luskan is notoriously independent and feels threatened by the new nation of the Silver Marches, one of the major members of the Alliance. The Shadow Thieves of Amn are the antithesis of the Alliance, and Calimshan does not consider the Zhentarim (or the Shadow Thieves, for that matter) to be serious threats to its trade.

The agents of the Alliance include sophisticated bards, zealous paladins, talented sorcerers, and grizzled warriors. They are chosen primarily for their loyalty and then trained in observation, stealth, innuendo, and combat. Backed by the wealthy and the privileged, they carry quality equipment (often disguised to appear common), and spellcasters tend to have a large number of scrolls with communication spells.

The Alliance has a history of hiring adventurers, both to raid Zhentarim strongholds and to scout out sources of Zhentarim activity. Local adventuring groups with an interest in combating evil have quickly gained status and valuable contacts by their association with the Lords' Alliance, and just as quickly made enemies of the Black Network because of it. The Alliance pays these groups in information, travel arrangements, and masterwork items, as well as in cold, hard gold.

ALUSTRIEL

Female human (Chosen of Mystra) Wiz20/Sor2/Acm2: CR 28; Medium-size humanoid; HD 20d4+120; hp 162; Init +7; Spd 30 ft.; AC 23 (touch 15, flatfooted 20); Atk +10/+5 melee (1d8/ 19–20, longsword-arm from *sword pendant*) or +13/+8 ranged touch (by spell); SQ Archmage high arcana, Chosen immunities, Chosen spell-like abilities, detect magic, enhanced Constitution, epic-level benefits, immune to nonmagical metal (*ring of lesser ironguard*), name and song attunement, silver fire; AL CG; SV Fort +11, Ref +8, Will +19; Str 11, Dex 16, Con 23, Int 20, Wis 17, Cha 17. Height 5 ft. 11 in.

Alustriel

Skills and Feats: Appraise +8, Bluff +11, Concentration +33, Craft (gemcutting) +10, Diplomacy +13, Gather Information +11, Heal +5, Hide +13, Intimidate +8, Intuit Direction +5, Knowledge (arcana) +28, Knowledge (religion) +10, Perform (dance) +8, Profession (herbalist) +9, Scry +20, Search +21, Sense Motive +8, Spellcraft +32; Combat Casting, Craft Rod, Craft Wand, Craft Wondrous Item, Forge Ring, Improved Counterspell, Improved Initiative, Quicken Spell, Scribe Scroll, Skill Focus (Spellcraft), Spell Focus (Enchantment), Spell Focus (Transmutation).

Special Qualities: Archmage High Arcana: Mastery of shaping, spell power +2. Chosen Immunities: Alustriel is unaffected by attacks that duplicate these effects: *chill touch, disintegrate, feeblemind, flesh to stone, forcecage, lightning bolt, maze, poly-*

morph other, time stop, web. Chosen Spell-like Abilities (all 1/day): *antimagic field, clairaudience/clairvoyance, comprehend languages, detect thoughts, hold monster, minor creation, polymorph any object, shapechange, teleport without error.* Detect Magic (Su): Line of sight. Enhanced Constitution: The Chosen of Mystra template adds +10 to Alustriel's Constitution. Epic-Level Benefits: Four effective levels of wizard (included in the above total). Name and Song Attunement (Su): Whenever Alustriel's name or the Rune of the Chosen is spoken, she hears it along with the next nine words that person speaks. Silver Fire (Su): See Chapter 2 for details.

Wizard Spells per Day: 4/6/6/5/5/5/4/3/4/4. Base DC = 17 + spell level, 19 + spell level for enchantment and transmutation spells. Caster level 22nd.

Sorcerer Spells per Day: 6/5. Sorcerer Spells Known: 0—*detect magic, detect poison, light, mage hand, read magic;* 1st— *comprehend languages, feather fall.* Base DC = 15 + spell level, 17 + spell level for enchantment and transmutation spells. Caster level 2nd.

Possessions: Alustriel's sword pendant (transforms the wearer's arm into a nondisarmable longsword blade for 40 minutes once per day; grants the user Martial Weapon Proficiency (longsword) as a bonus feat; dismissible), *bracers of armor +8, boots of elvenkind, cloak of elvenkind, amulet of proof against detection and location, ring of lesser ironguard, ring of protection +2, wand of light,* 3 *potions of cure serious wounds* (10th). As a 24th-level character and the ruler of a small country, Alustriel has many other items not listed here at her disposal.

The longtime High Lady of Silverymoon and new ruler of the Silver Marches is both a powerful mage and one of the Seven Sisters. Folk in the North revere Alustriel for her gentle, kindly thoughtfulness and caring stewardship of her people. Her serene manner is legendary, and she tends and cherishes the places and people she rules, turning to battle-magic only as a last resort.

Alustriel spent her rebellious youth adventuring and learned very early in life that happiness is something that must be shared, not won alone. She tirelessly pursues dreams of peace, races dwelling together in harmony, and a place where arts would be prized and nurtured: Silverymoon.

It's seemingly impossible to make Alustriel confused or angry (though she'll weep at the personal misfortunes of her people), or to overload her concentration on multiple matters at once. This, coupled with her natural talent for perfectly remembering faces, names, voices, and mannerisms, makes her nearly the perfect ruler. Her wits and experience enable her to better anticipate future events in the North than almost anyone else in Faerûn.

Folk of Silverymoon love her as their "Lady Hope" or "Shining Lady." Alustriel has the knack of befriending most people she meets, helping them (even in small ways) with their concerns and needs of the moment. Only injustice and intolerance anger her, but she seldom shows rage in anything more than cold, pointed speech. She is a builder and an administrator whose success is rooted in her understanding of others.

malaugryms

The malaugryms—sometimes known as the shadowmasters—are immortal shapeshifters from the Plane of Shadow. Despite the similarity in name, the shadowmasters have nothing to do with the Shadowmasters of Telflamm, a thieves' guild strongly tied to the church of Mask. The malaugryms are described in *Monster Compendium: Monsters of Faerûn*.

Intent on invading Faerûn, the malaugryms are hindered by their inability to master interplanar magic, trapping them in the Castle of Shadows on their home plane. Only the most powerful spellcasters of the race can master spells that send the malaugryms to the Material Plane to wreak havoc.

Malaugryms can perfectly duplicate the form of any creature they have seen or assume horrifying nonhumanoid forms. The only nonmagical way to recognize their nature is by the hard-to-spot golden light shining in their eyes (Spot check DC 20). Theoretically immortal, they can be slain by weapons (and are vulnerable to silver) and seem to suffer a slow debilitation due to aging, since the leader of the race—the Shadowmaster—is periodically unseated by a younger, stronger malaugrym. Their numbers seldom exceed one hundred, and since they cannot breed with each other, they must mate with humans and steal their own offspring.

The malaugryms are obsessed with magic and spend much of their time in Faerûn searching for powerful items and magical lore. In the past they fought a secret war against the Harpers, sought to acquire the secret of spellfire from Shandril Shessair, sent a large force into Faerûn during the Time of Troubles, and tried to eliminate Khelben Arunsun and Laeral Silverhand of Waterdeep. It is unknown if any of them have learned how to use the Shadow Weave or if they are associated with the Netherese of the city of Shade.

Malaugryms are very independent and only work together when directly supervised by the Shadowmaster. If left to their own devices, they wander off to "play with" humans, acquire magic items and spells, or delve into excessive hedonism. Cruel and evil, they think nothing of befriending someone for any purpose and then turning against or killing their ally if the mood strikes them or if doing so advances their plans. Although true mortal allies of the malaugryms are rare, those who do exist are likely to have powerful spells and items at their disposal.

people of the Black Blood

The People of the Black Blood collectively include several large groups of lycanthrope worshipers of Malar. Because they can travel incognito and form new bands in other places, it is not known how widespread they are, but groups are known to be active in the Chondalwood, Cormanthor, and the High Forest. They exist for the hunt, following the will of the Beast Lord and their own animal instincts. They hunt normal animals but prefer intelligent prey, often kidnapping victims in humanoid form and releasing them in a wilderness area to be pursued by the entire pack. Such hunts usually end in the consumption of the victim.

The group's membership consists of true and infected lycanthropes, primarily evil with a scattering of feral neutral members. They disdain people who live in cities, particularly wererats, and often commit acts of great violence against would-be interlopers on their territory. The churches of Gwaeron, Mielikki, and Silvanus often mount searches into the forest to discover and destroy the People's lairs.

To join the People, an individual need only worship Malar and be infected with lycanthropy. Many rangers, barbarians, and druids are counted among the packs. When the ranks grow thin, they infect others with their kind of lycanthropy to gain more followers. A pack's leader, called a Bloodmaster, is decided by physical prowess. Werewolves and wereboars are the most common Bloodmasters due to their physical strength.

As an organization, the People of the Black Blood do not have a political agenda. Like wild animals, they wish to protect their territory and thrive, which means they attack creatures that approach them. Occasionally they ally themselves with the church of Malar or are hired by evil groups such as the Zhentarim, but their independent natures mean that such alliances tend to be short-lived. Because they disdain civilization, what minor equipment they have is usually ill kept, but most packs have an amazing variety of potions devised by their spellcasting members (since potions can be used by creatures that cannot speak and lack hands). Most packs consist of only one or two types of lycanthropes and normal or dire animals of the same type.

Notable members of the People include Heskret of the High Forest (N male werebat Ftr5), Narona of the High Forest (CE female werewolf Rgr6), Totoruan of the Chondalwood (N male wereboar Bbn4), and Vakennis of Cormanthor (NE female werewolverine Drd8). Each has been a Bloodmaster for at least five years and has defeated many challengers.

SENGAL

Male lightfoot halfling werewolf Drd5 of Malar: CR 7; Small shapechanger; HD 5d8+5; hp 36; Init +2; Spd 15 ft.; AC 18 (touch 13, flat-footed 16); Atk +3 melee (1d6–1/×3, halfspear), +7 ranged (1d6–1/×3, halfspear); SQ Animal companions, halfling (lightfoot) traits, language (Druidic), lycanthropic empathy (wolf), nature sense, resist nature's lure, trackless step, wild shape 1/day, woodland stride; AL NE; SV Fort +8, Ref +6, Will +9; Str 8, Dex 14, Con 12, Int 10, Wis 14, Cha 12. Height 3 ft. 1 in.

Skills and Feats: Animal Empathy +3, Climb –2, Concentration +5, Handle Animal +3, Heal +5, Hide +4, Intuit Direction +4, Jump +0, Knowledge (nature) +4, Listen +8, Move Silently +3, Search +4, Spot +11, Swim +0, Wilderness Lore +6; Improved Control Shape, Run, Simple Weapon Proficiency.

Hybrid/Animal Form: Medium-size shapechanger; Spd 50 ft.; AC 18 (touch 14, flat-footed 14); Atk +7 melee (1d6, bite) or +3 melee (1d6/×3, halfspear, hybrid only) or +8 ranged (1d6/×3, halfspear, hybrid only); SA Curse of lycanthropy, trip; SQ animal companions, halfling (lightfoot) traits, language (druidic), lycanthropic empathy (wolf), nature sense, resist nature's lure, trackless step, wild shape 1/day, woodland stride; AL NE; SV Fort +10, Ref +8, Will +9; Str 10, Dex 18, Con 16, Int 10, Wis 14, Cha 12.

Skills and Feats: Animal Empathy +3, Climb +2, Concentration +7, Handle Animal +3, Heal +5, Hide +5, Intuit Direction +4, Jump +4, Knowledge (nature) +4, Listen +12, Move Silently +8, Search +8, Spot +15*, Swim +1, Wilderness Lore +6**; Blind-Fight, Improved Control Shape, Improved Initiative, Run, Simple Weapon Proficiency, Weapon Finesse (bite). *+14 in animal form. **+10 if tracking by scent.

Special Qualities: Animal Companions: Vaes (tiny viper), Skaeoss (raven), Baraen (3 HD wolf). Halfling (Lightfoot) Traits: +4 size bonus on Hide checks, +2 racial bonus on Climb, Jump, Listen, and Move Silently checks, +2 morale bonus on saves against fear, +1 racial attack bonus with thrown weapons. Lycanthropic Empathy (Wolf): Can communicate simple comcepts to wolves or dire wolves and gains a +4 racial bonus to checks when influencing those animals' attitudes.

Druid Spells per Day: 5/4/3/1. Base DC = 12 + spell level.

Possessions: Amulet of natural armor +1 (holy symbol of Malar), *wolf skull helm* (acts as *eyes of the eagle*), *wand of entangle* (25 charges, looks like a lock of hair bound in a leather thong), *Quaal's feather token* (whip), *dust of illusion*, halfspear (Sengal may use this weapon without violating his druidic oaths because Malar's favored weapon is a spear), hide armor (worn only in humanoid form).

Sengal is a feral halfling who surrendered to his primitive instincts. A druid of Malar and a member of the People of the Black Blood, he is well respected among other werewolves despite his youth and size. Sengal acts as a scout and message-carrier for the bands of the People and the other druids of his faith within the High Forest.

In combat, he prefers to observe opponents to learn their strengths and weaknesses, then strikes from ambush, with his wolf companion attacking unarmored spellcasters. If he anticipates a battle, he rounds up another wolf or two or other members of the People, for he is too cunning to engage multiple opponents without any hope of winning.

Sengal emulates wolves even in normal activities. When he gets angry, he leans forward and growls. When in the presence of a powerful ally, he lies on his back with his belly exposed. He has never been outside the High Forest and considers those who live in cities to be weak.

Red Wizards

The Red Wizards are the magocratic leaders of the country of Thay. The most powerful Red Wizards are the zulkirs, each specialized in one of the schools of magic. These eight choose the tharchions (regional governors) who handle the day-to-day leadership of Thay while the zulkirs scheme and plot to rule the entire world.

Long-standing factions split the power of the zulkirs. Some push for isolating their land in order to safeguard their vast magical knowledge, while others advocate wars of conquest. Currently a faction favoring trade and mercantilism rules the day, rising from a class of ambitious, entrepreneurial mages with their eyes on the rich commerce of the Inner Sea and the kingdoms of the west. The Red Wizards' ability to forge and trade magic items in great quantities has given them control of a lucrative and influential trade. Thayan enclaves exist in dozens of cities around the Sea of Fallen Stars, walled compounds in which the Thayans enjoy immunity from local laws and tariffs while providing access to their many and varied magical wares.

Sengal

Given their different magical specializations and conflicting philosophies, the Red Wizards may be involved in almost any sort of venture, from smuggling to adventuring to slaving. (Active slaving is currently discouraged by the zulkirs in places where such activity is illegal, since such efforts generate ill will toward the mercantile efforts.) A typical group includes a Red Wizard leader of 7th level or higher, one or two wizard subordinates, a cleric of Kossuth, and at least five bodyguards of moderate skill. All in the group are likely to be armed with magic items, with the spellcasters having many useful charged items.

The zulkirs each have their own plots, intrigues, and interests.

Aznar Thrul (CE male human Evo10/Red10/Acm3) is the cruel and savage zulkir of Evocation and the tharchion of the Priador. Although Thrul loathes Szass Tam, the lich holds him in check through some secret information or advantage.

Druxus Rhym (NE male human Tra10/Red10/Acm4) is the steadfast zulkir of Transmutation. He is the greatest spokesperson of ruthless trade over isolation or military aggression, using his power and his alliance with Szass Tam to encourage the others to cooperate.

Lallara (CE female human Abj10/Red10/Acm1) is the zulkir of Abjuration, a chaotic and unreliable ally of Szass Tam and a woman with a taste for decadent pleasures. She collects unusual magic items and enjoys torturing slaves.

Lauzoril (NE male human Enc10/Red10/Acm2) is the handsome zulkir of Enchantment, a scheming and dangerous opponent. He opposes Szass Tam and only grudgingly refrains from marching his armies on Thay's neighbors.

Mythrellaa (CE female human Ill10/Red7/Sha3) is the zulkir of Illusion. She prefers isolation and rarely fraternizes with her peers, devoting her time to studies of the Shadow Weave.

Nevron (NE male human Cjr10/Red10/Acm2/Epic2) is the hateful, aggressive, fiend-touched zulkir of Conjuration. The other zulkirs suspect he plans a surprise attack on Aglarond, which they would be forced to oppose in order to avoid the loss of valuable trade that would result. Aglarond doesn't trade with Thay, but other lands sympathetic to Aglarond do.

Szass Tam (NE male human lich Nec10/Red10/Acm2/Epic7) is the shrewd zulkir of Necromancy. Over two hundred years old, he has tried to unite the zulkirs under his banner but lost prestige recently after a failed attempt to harness the power of a long-imprisoned demon.

Yaphyll (LE female human Div10/Red5/Lor4) is the youthful zulkir of Divination. A strong supporter of Druxus and Szass Tam, she uses her magic to monitor the other zulkirs and events in Thayan enclaves throughout Faerûn.

Illustration by Todd Lockwood

Thayan Enclaves

Thayan enclaves are independent mercantile and political entities within an urban area in a non-Thayan country. Here people interact with Thayans in a peaceful manner, buy magic items, and make deals with the Red Wizards who control the enclave.

An enclave is established after a Thayan diplomat negotiates with the local authorities. These negotiations usually entail lists of benefits for the local rulers, such as an increased amount of magic for their guards and protectors, as well as for the authorities themselves. Depending on the nature of the local authorities, the diplomat presents gifts or offers bribes in order to sweeten the deal. For peaceful or good nations, the gifts are benign or useful items such as *potions of cure* spells, *wands of fly*, magic shields, and so on. For more aggressive countries, the bribes are often items that can be used for illicit deeds, such as *potions of invisibility*, or combat items such as a *wand of fireball* or magic weapons. Once both parties agree that an enclave can be built, they discuss the exact terms.

The Thayans always require the local government to agree to three demands (known as the Three Laws of the Enclave) and refuse to establish an enclave unless the other party agrees to all of them. The Three Laws prevent abuse at the hands of those who oppose the presence of the Red Wizards on moral, cultural, or religious grounds. If such abuse occurs, the Thayans can claim that the local authorities have failed to provide protection for diplomatic envoys acting within the confines of the law, which would make the local government accountable to Thay itself.

The Law of Sovereignty: The enclave is treated as Thayan soil. Thayan law applies within, the Red Wizards are responsible for patrolling the enclave themselves, and the law of the rest of the country does not apply. The enclave's inhabitants are not immune to prosecution; for example, local authorities can demand that a man who murders someone elsewhere in town and then retreats to the enclave be turned over to the local law, whereupon the Thayans must comply. Slavery is permissible within the enclave, although if the local laws forbid slavery, few Thayans force this point by keeping slaves in the enclaves.

The Law of Trade: The Thayans price their goods and services at 10% below the normal cost. Their merchandise is primarily magic items, and some enclaves also sell mundane equipment such as tapestries and weapons. Technically the sale of slaves is permitted, but since local laws apply outside the enclave, this is futile in lands where slavery is outlawed. An enclave normally sells scrolls of 0-level spells for the cost of creating them if the customer buys an equal number of other magic items (including potions and scrolls of 1st level or higher). The Law of Trade also states that the Thayans can accept slaves as payment for items, and these slaves can be legally transported within the borders of the sovereign nation on the way to Thay. Most antislavery countries require that a potential slave in this situation must either be willing (such as a man selling himself into slavery to provide for his family) or a criminal convicted of a serious offense (such as murder or treason). The local government sometimes even trades criminals in exchange for Thayan goods.

The Law of Crafting: This law dictates what the Thayans will and will not create for sale to the general public. Normally an enclave only produces potions, scrolls (of up to 4th-level spells), wands, *+1 armor*, *+1 weapons*, and minor wondrous items. None of these may have abilities easily used for crime (such as *potions of invisibility* or a *wand of charm person*) or overtly destructive (such as a *wand of fireball*). They may also cast spells for hire. In general, the Thayans never create an item worth more than 2,000 gp, because such items dominate limited resources that could be used to produce cheaper and more desirable products. All items produced in an enclave are required to bear the mark of the Red Wizards and the insignia of the city where the enclave is located. They also refuse to create dangerous items (as described above) because should someone be harmed with an item created in an enclave, the Thayans could be held responsible. This policy also prevents such items from being used against them.

In exchange for these demands, the Thayans agree to donate 1% of the enclave's profits to the local government. The actual amount is rather soft, since an accurate count is not provided for the local government, and some enclaves allocate a portion of these funds to bribe local guardsmen and officials. Most enclave contracts include brief but regular periods of military service by the wizards in the enclave's employ, which allows the local government access to more spellcasters.

Since the inception of the Thayan enclave, their numbers have increased quickly. Within the lands bordering on the Inner Sea, nearly every (90%) metropolis-level location has an enclave of one sort. Most (75%) large cities have one, many (50%) small cities do, some (30%) large towns do, and a few (10%) small towns have an enclave, while smaller settlements might have a single Thayan representative or none at all. A typical enclave holds a number of Thayans equal to 1% of the settlement's population. Guards and other support staff for the wizards, including servants, assistants, and mundane artisans, make up at least half of the enclave population. The remainder are wizards of various levels (some with levels in the Red Wizard prestige class). The highest-level wizard is the leader of the enclave, and always has at least one level in the Red Wizard prestige class.

Khalia

Khalia

Female human Tra6/Red4: CR 10; Medium-size humanoid; HD 10d4+10; hp 35; Init −1; Spd 30 ft.; AC 9 (touch 9, flat-footed 9); Atk +4 melee touch (by spell) or +4 ranged touch (by spell); SQ Red Wizard abilities; AL LN; SV Fort +6, Ref +6, Will +15; Str 8, Dex 8, Con 12, Int 17, Wis 15, Cha 14. Height 5 ft. 10 in.

Skills and Feats: Alchemy +9, Concentration +11, Craft (woodcarving) +8, Diplomacy +8, Innuendo +7, Knowledge (arcana) +9, Knowledge (Thayan history) +8, Knowledge (Thayan nobility and royalty) +12, Ride (horse) +3, Spellcraft +15; Brew Potion, Craft Wand, Craft Wondrous Item, Iron Will, Lightning Reflexes, Scribe Scroll, Tattoo Focus (Transmutation).

Special Qualities: Red Wizard Abilities: Specialist defense (Transmutation) +2, Spell power (Transmutation) +2.

Wizard Spells per Day: 5/6/6/5/4/3. Base DC = 13 + spell level, 16 + spell level for transmutation spells. Caster level 10th.

Spellbook: 0—*arcane mark, detect magic, detect poison, disrupt undead, mage hand*, mending*, open/close*, prestidigitation, ray of frost, read magic, resistance*; 1st—*animate rope*, burning hands*,* *comprehend languages, endure elements, enlarge*, expeditious retreat*, feather fall*, identify, mage armor, magic weapon*, protection from evil, scatterspray*, spider climb*;* 2nd—*alter self*, blindness/deafness*, bull's strength*, cat's grace*, continual flame, create enchanted tattoo, darkvision*, eagle's splendor*, endurance*, glitterdust, knock*, levitate*, Melf's acid arrow, protection from arrows, scare, see invisibility, summon swarm, whispering wind*;* 3rd—*analyze portal, clairaudience/clairvoyance, dispel magic, flame arrow, fly*, halt undead, haste*, hold person, keen edge*, phantom steed, slow*, tongues, water breathing*;* 4th—*dimension door*, fear, fire stride*, Leomund's secure shelter, minor globe of invulnerability, polymorph other*, polymorph self*, scrying, stoneskin;* 5th—*animal growth*, fabricate*, prying eyes, stone shape*, teleport*, wall of stone.*

*These spells belong to the school of Transmutation, which is this character's specialty. Prohibited schools: Enchantment, Evocation, Illusion.

Possessions: Khalia's robe (acts as *cloak of resistance +2* and grants 3rd-level *cat's grace* 1/day), *Khalia's flaming mask* (grants 5th-level *burning hands* 1/day and *endure elements (fire)*; user may ignite or quench at will), *wand of darkvision* (3rd level)**, *bag of holding III, wand of fly* (5th level)**, *potions** (spider climb, protection from arrows, levitate, cat's grace, haste).*

**These items are used as gifts in Khalia's negotiations.

Khalia is a cautious and skilled diplomat in the service of the Red Wizards of Thay. She visits the rulers or ministers of cities and kingdoms and convinces them to allow the Red Wizards to lease a space within their territory to create an enclave. In addition to passionate arguments and negotiations about profits, trade, and friendly relations, she offers gifts to the nobles and leaders she visits—typically magic items useful in supporting an army or guard force. As her people are still held in low regard, she has been forced to flee negotiations that turned sour (her owl familiar was slain during a recent incident).

She prefers to travel in the company of Thayan bodyguards, normally hired from an enclave in a nearby city. Khalia chooses to memorize spells that cause a minimum of damage, to avoid tainting the reputation of the Red Wizards any further should a conflict arise. She replenishes her stores of items from enclaves she visits, using their resources to construct whatever she needs. For her fellows in the enclaves, she brings news of home, letters from other enclaves, and the opportunity to travel.

Khalia has a gentle manner and prefers to avoid arguments and conflict, despite insults directed at her. Given time and access to an enclave, she can have a large amount of money or magic items at her disposal. She is not averse to using them to acquire the services of others to forward her goals, such as hiring local adventurers to supplement her guards or to petition a local noble on her behalf. Extremely intelligent, she knows that she has a lot of work ahead of her and tries to be the most restrained and reasonable Red Wizard that anyone might ever meet.

The seven sisters

For centuries, seven women of great beauty, power, and heart have battled injustice and tyranny across Faerûn. The Seven Sisters are legendary figures whose deeds are sung by bards in every land. They are not an organization, they are not particularly secret, and they do not even share many common goals—but their actions, their very existence, have changed Faerûn more than any mighty cabal of wizards or mad cult.

Few in Faerûn know the beginning of their story. The Seven Sisters were born to a ranger named Dornal Silverhand and his wife Elué, the Lady of the Gate, a powerful sorcerer, in the years 761 through 767 DR. Unknown to Dornal, during this time Elué harbored Mystra, the goddess of magic, in her body, so that the couple's children were in fact Mystra's daughters as much as her own. Elué perished in 767, consumed by the divine power she held, and Dornal abandoned his family in grief. The young sisters were fostered to various folk throughout Faerûn.

Syluné (NG female human spectral harpist Wiz20/Sor2/Ftr2), the eldest, is dead now, slain defending Shadowdale from the attack of a red dragon. She was known as the Witch of Shadowdale, and she survives as a powerful but good-hearted ghost who still watches over the lands and people she loved in life.

Alustriel, the second sister, is the Lady of Silverymoon. She has devoted her life to building a realm of peace, learning, and strength in the Silver Marches of the North. (See Alustriel's description earlier in this chapter.)

Dove Falconhand (CG female human Rgr14/Sor9/Rog4/Hrp1) is unusual among her siblings in that her magical abilities are secondary to her skill at arms. She won renown as a Knight of Myth Drannor and is married to Florin Falconhand of the same band.

Storm Silverhand, the famed Harper knight and the Bard of Shadowdale, has been a leader among the Harpers for many years. (See her description in Chapter 4: Geography.)

Laeral Silverhand (CG female human Wiz19/Sor4/Rgr7) is known as the Lady Mage of Waterdeep. Along with her husband Khelben "Blackstaff" Arunsun she leads the Moonstars, a Harper splinter group that seeks to order the destiny of cities and nations in the North.

The Simbul (whose birth name, Alassra, is known only to her few closest allies) rules Aglarond as its Witch-Queen. She is the most powerful wielder of arcane magic in Faerûn, a sorcerer of such unfettered strength that she has single-handedly preserved her realm against the Red Wizards of Thay for generations. (See her description in Chapter 4: Geography.)

The youngest sister enters into few tales. Qilué Veladorn (CG female drow Clr16/Dis3) is a powerful cleric of the drow goddess Eilistraee and a drow herself (the circumstances of her birth were exceptional, to say the least).

All of the Seven are Chosen of Mystra, unaging mortals who hold some portion of the power of the Weave at Mystra's request. They serve as Mystra's agents in the world and aid all good folk against those who would harm or enslave them.

THE RUNE OF THE CHOSEN

Seven bright stars in the sky I see.
Seven for those who watch over me.
Seven be the smiles down they send.
Seven be the troubles swift they mend.

shades

Long ago, during the collapse of ancient Netheril, one of the empire's flying cities survived the realm's destruction by shifting completely into the Plane of Shadow. Safe from outside predators and the disasters that befell their kin, the city-dwellers were free to practice their magic and experiment with the stuff of shadow. After generations of living within the Plane of Shadow, the rulers of the city became suffused with the dark energy of that place, achieving strange and remarkable abilities.

Returning to Faerûn in 1372 DR, the people of the renamed city of Shade began magically exploring the world and fortifying their defenses against old and new foes, such as the phaerimms. The shades consider all of Anauroch their territory, and once they have established their borders it is likely they will try to expand their realm. Backed by the arcane might of ancient Netheril and the alien power of shadow, the shades are a serious threat to the safety and security of people all over Faerûn.

The true goals of the shades are unknown. They may turn up in almost any part of the world looking for information, sowing dissent, defying authority, or looting old caches of Netherese items. The shades may try to ally themselves with magocracies (such as Thay or Halruaa), groups with ties to shadows (such as the Shadowmasters of Telflamm or the church of Shar), or far-reaching political organizations such as the Zhentarim, if only for the purpose of acquiring information about the world their ancestors fled almost two thousand years ago.

Having lived in a magical society for generations, the shades are completely comfortable with magic, and most have at least some magical ability. Because of their isolation and aloofness, their mannerisms and equipment are exotic and old-fashioned. Ruled by powerful wizards and sorcerers, the shades have access to an almost unlimited number of potions, scrolls, and minor magic items. (For two representative shades, see Hadrhune in Chapter 4 and Leevoth in Chapter 9.)

Illustration by Sam Wood

The Xanathar's Guild

The Xanathar's Guild is a group of thieves and cutthroats operating out of the bowels of Waterdeep. From its main offices in Skullport, the Xanathar's Guild has access to several *portals*, with prominent ones leading to an alley in Waterdeep, a rock outcropping near Calimport, and a small Guild-owned warehouse in Westgate.

The Guild is led by an elder beholder called The Xanathar. It is at least the second such creature to claim the title, since it destroyed its predecessor. Few outside the inner circle of Masters know of The Xanathar's nature, because it is reclusive and guarded by undead beholders. Eleven Masters each control one of the Guild's businesses: assassination, blackmail, bookkeeping, enforcement, extortion, information gathering, magical defenses, mercenaries, slavery, smuggling, and thievery. Most of the Guild's work involves slavery or thievery.

Members of the Guild are well trained and skilled in stealth, tactics, and discretion. They have excellent arms and armor, and those who need to use *portals* as part of their work are usually multiclass spellcasters or at least trained in rudimentary spell-

casting. The elite troops that work for the slavers (known as the Hands of the Eye) are all at least 4th level.

Avaereene (LE female human Wiz11) is the First of the Hand and Master of Magic, a beautiful and cruel woman who has worked with the Xanathar for years and speaks for the beholder in most affairs. Colstan Rhuul (LE male human Clr10 of Bane) is the Second of the Hand and Master of Assassins, a patient and calculating man who personally leads an elite team of assassins as well as running the Guild's entire assassination business. Ahmaergo (LE male dwarf Ftr9) is the Third of the Hand and Master of Slavers. Known as "the horned dwarf" for his magic spell-turning platemail, he's thinking about splitting his followers from the Guild to form another slaving group.

The Xanathar

Typical Xanathar Slaver: Human Rog3/Ftr2; CR 5; Medium-size humanoid; HD 3d6+3 plus 2d10+2; hp 27; Init +7; Spd 30 ft.; AC 17 (touch 13, flat-footed 14); Atk +6 melee (1d6+3/ 19–20, *+1 short sword*) and +6 melee (1d6+1/19-20, masterwork short sword) or +7 ranged (1d8/ 19–20, light crossbow); SA Sneak attack +2d6; SQ Evasion, uncanny dodge (Dex bonus to AC); AL CE; SV Fort +5, Ref +6, Will +1; Str 14, Dex 16, Con 13, Int 12, Wis 10, Cha 8.

Skills and Feats: Appraise +3, Balance +5, Bluff +3, Climb +10, Escape Artist +5, Hide +9, Intimidate +5, Jump +8, Listen +6, Move Silently +9, Search +5, Spot +6, Tumble +7, Use Rope +7, Swim +4; Ambidexterity, Improved Initiative, Twin Sword Style, Two Weapon Fighting, Weapon Focus (short sword).

Possessions: +1 studded leather, +1 short sword, potion of invisibility, potion of cure moderate wounds (3rd), masterwork short sword, light crossbow, 20 bolts.

Zhentarim

The Zhentarim, also known as the Black Network, is an evil organization intent on dominating the land from the Moonsea to the Sword Coast North. Originally a secret society, for years the Zhents have operated openly in the Moonsea area, particularly around their greatest base of operations, Zhentil Keep. People who live near Zhentarim strongholds grow used to caravans with its symbol but live in fear that someday they will see armies marching under that banner.

While many of the Zhentarim are nothing more than opportunistic merchants, some resort to illegal acts such as attacking rival caravans, extorting villages for food, or more serious crimes such as arson and murder. The Zhentarim hire bandits to attack other caravans and towns, or have wizards conjure up or enrage monsters. Recently they have begun sending older members to frontier nations such as the Silver Marches, where they buy land and become peaceable homesteaders with families, biding their time until they are needed.

The agents of the Zhentarim are well equipped with both mundane and minor magic items. Masterwork items are common, and nonspellcasters usually have at least a potion of some sort. Spellcasters in good standing with the Black Network gain a scroll of two spells of any spell level they can cast every time they gain a spellcaster level (most wizards immediately add these spells to their spellbook).

Fear of this cabal has spread from the Moonsea lands across the Heartlands to the Sword Coast, where everybody "knows" the Black Network is a sinister, murderous organization of spies, informants, armies, and flying-monster-riding wizards engaged in all sorts of secret and terrible activities.

Folk who live in the Dragon Reach lands know rather more about the Zhentarim. They can tell you that it rose to open rule and power in Zhentil Keep, seized control of the Citadel of the Raven from the other Moonsea cities that shared it, conquered Teshendale, Voonlar, and Yûlash, and plotted the conquest of Shadowdale, Daggerdale, and Mistledale. The Zhents have entire armies hidden away in the Citadel and a sinister fortress, Darkhold, somewhere in the Western Heartlands. Zhent gold and sorcery govern affairs west across Anauroch (until the arrival of the shades, anyway) to the vales of the Gray Peaks, east to the walls of Mulmaster, north through the Ride and the Cold Lands to the Great Glacier, and south through the weaker Dales.

The Zhents are soldiers (from black-plate-armored veteran warriors to marauding orc mercenaries) commanded by aggressively cruel minor wizards of more ambition than power, who report to truly powerful mages headed by the sly-tongued Lord Manshoon. The Zhentarim seem bent on enriching themselves and controlling towns, villages, and entire realms along a trade route linking the Moonsea with the Sword Coast (specifically the Waterdeep area) via Darkhold. They smuggle slaves, poisons, and contraband.

They have spies everywhere. In their ranks are an evil unholy knight known as the Pereghost and Zhentil Keep's charismatic champion, the lady Scyllua Darkhope. (Scyllua administers the defenses and day-to-day affairs of the keep itself.) Anyone could be a Zhentarim, and some of them seem to want to seize all the magic they find, while others want to rule every town and steading between Shou Lung and Evermeet.

How much of any of this is truth, and how much exaggerated speculation, is the topic of endless conjecture in whispered conversations across half the Heartlands.

Zhentarim Spy: Human Rog2/Sor7; CR 9; Medium-size humanoid; HD 2d6+4 plus 7d4+14; hp 45; Init +6; Spd 60 ft.; AC 18 (touch 13, flat-footed 16); Atk +4 melee (1d6–1/18–20, masterwork rapier) or +7 ranged (1d8/19–20, masterwork light crossbow); SA Sneak attack +1d6; SQ Evasion, familiar; AL LE; SV Fort +7, Ref +8, Will +8; Str 8, Dex 14, Con 14, Int 12, Wis 10, Cha 16.

Skills and Feats: Alchemy +8, Bluff +6, Concentration +9, Diplomacy +8, Disguise +8, Escape Artist +7, Forgery +6, Gather Information +8, Hide +7, Innuendo +5, Intimidate +6, Jump +9, Listen +2, Move Silently +7, Read Lips +5, Scry +8, Spellcraft +8, Spot +4; Brew Potion, Heighten Spell, Improved Initiative, Iron Will, Spell Focus (Illusion).

Special Qualities: Familiar (rat)—Int 9, natural armor +4, improved evasion, share spells, empathic link, touch spells, speak with master, speak with animals of its type, Alertness feat to master (figured in).

Spells Prepared (6/7/7/5; Base DC = 13 + spell level; arcane spell failure 10%): 0—*detect magic, ghost sound*, light, mage hand, ray of frost, read magic, resistance;* 1st—*change self*, charm person, color spray*, shield, silent image*;* 2nd—*invisibility*, misdirection*, Snilloc's snowball swarm;* 3rd—*lightning bolt, major image*.*

*Because of Spell Focus (Illusion), the base DC for saves against these spells is 15 + spell level.

Possessions: +1 mithral chain shirt, ring of protection +1, cloak of resistance +1, boots of striding and springing, brooch of shielding, arcane scrolls of *blur, dispel magic, expeditious retreat, fireball,* and *levitate, wand of magic missile* (3rd level, 25 charges), masterwork rapier, masterwork light crossbow, 20 bolts.

manshoon and fzoul

The Black Network was founded almost one hundred years ago by a dark and powerful lord of Zhentil Keep, the wizard Manshoon. Through guile, murder, intrigue, and his ever-increasing magical might, Manshoon created a cabal of like-minded wizards (the so-called Black Cloaks), beholders, wealthy Moonsea merchants, and servants of evil temples whose purposes did not cross his—most notably, the temple of Bane.

While Zhentil Keep was nominally under the rule of a council of lords, the real power in the city was Manshoon, absolute master of the Zhentarim. Through a small number of handpicked lieutenants (chief among them Sememmon, his second) he ran a secret empire of thousands of merchants, mercenaries, spies, and agents. In the years preceding the Time of Troubles, Manshoon cemented an alliance with Fzoul Chembryl, an ambitious cleric of Bane, to strengthen the Zhentarim even further.

In the last twenty years, the reach of the Zhentarim has extended to every corner of Faerûn, forging what amounts to a not-so-secret empire over much of the Moonsea and the North. But the Zhents have also suffered many setbacks, most notably the fall of Bane, internecine strife between Banite faithful and those who turned to Cyric, the destruction of Zhentil Keep in a holy purge, and vicious feuds between Manshoon's Black Cloaks and Fzoul's clerics. The winner in all this turned out to be Fzoul Chembryl, who assumed control over the organization and nearly destroyed Manshoon, driving the archmage into hiding for a time.

At the time of this writing, Fzoul Chembryl is the master of the Black Network, Lord of Zhentil Keep, and the Chosen Tyrant of Bane. Sememmon, Fzoul's longtime rival, has abandoned the fortress of Darkhold and is in hiding, conceding control of the western Zhentarim. Manshoon has recovered from Fzoul's attack and, ironically, returned to the Zhentarim in some kind of secret accommodation with Fzoul. The founder of the organization serves as a member-at-large, a free agent with the power and the authority to direct Zhentarim assets as he sees fit in the pursuit of power and influence across Faerûn.

With the Zhentarim fully under the thumb of Fzoul and the church of Bane, the Black Network is finally starting to see some of its major plans come to fruition. Over time, Fzoul plans to make the Zhentarim an arm of Bane's church in all but name.

MANSHOON

Male human Wiz20/Acm2/Epic3: CR 25; Medium-size humanoid; HD 20d4+80; hp 133; Init +3; Spd 30 ft.; AC 24 (touch 15, flat-footed 21); Atk +12/+7 melee (1d6+2, *staff of power*), +13/+8 ranged touch (by spell); SQ Archmage high arcana, enhanced Intelligence, epic-level benefits, permanent spells; SR 17; AL LE; SV Fort +12, Ref +12, Will +19; Str 10, Dex 16, Con 18, Int 23, Wis 16, Cha 19. Height 5 ft. 9 in.

Skills and Feats: Alchemy +17, Concentration +25, Craft (gemcutting) +12, Diplomacy +9, Disguise +7, Handle Animal +7, Intimidate +7, Knowledge (arcana) +26, Knowledge (architecture and engineering) +10, Knowledge (Moonsea geography) +10, Knowledge (Moonsea history) +16, Knowledge (Moonsea local) +11, Listen +7, Profession (herbalist) +8, Ride (dragon) +9, Ride (horse) +7, Scry +20, Spellcraft +30, Spot +9, Wilderness Lore +7; Combat Casting, Craft Staff, Craft Wand, Craft Wondrous Item, Create Portal, Forge Ring, Maximize Spell, Quicken Spell, Scribe Scroll, Skill Focus (Spellcraft), Spellcasting Prodigy, Spell Penetration, Spell Focus (Conjuration), Spell Focus (Enchantment).

Special Qualities: Archmage High Arcana: Arcane fire, spell-like ability (*teleport* 4/day). Enhanced Intelligence: Manshoon read a *tome of clear thought +3*. His Intelligence score has a +3 inherent bonus included in its value. Epic-Level Benefits: Two effective levels of archmage (included in the above total), bonus spell level ×2 (included in the listing below), +1 Constitution (included in the listing above). Permanent Spells: Through the use of *permanency*, Manshoon has the following permanent continuous magical abilities: *comprehend languages, darkvision, protection from arrows*, and *see invisibility*.

Wizard Spells per Day: 4/6/6/6/9/4/5/ 5/3/3/1/1. Base DC = 17 + spell level, 19 + spell level for enchantment and conjuration spells. Caster level 22nd.

Spellbook: Manshoon knows more than one hundred spells, including most wizard/sorcerer spells in the *Player's Handbook* and this book.

Possessions: Staff of power, brooch of shielding, Manshoon's battle gorget (protects against neck-targeted attacks, +4 natural armor, quickened *lesser ironguard* 1/day, *feather fall* 2/day, *repulsion* 1/day, *lightning bolt* 1/day, all at 17th caster level), *ring of spell storing, ring of wizardry IV, black robe of the archmagi*.

Manshoon

For years a lord of Zhentil Keep and leader of the Zhentarim, Manshoon fit the archetype of the sly-tongued, sinister, and decadent evil master spellcaster. He ruthlessly quelled revolts in the ranks of the Black Network, slaughtered his rivals, and weeded the ranks of the young and ambitious by sending such upstart mages on impossible missions to slay Elminster or seize the spellfire-wielder Shandril Shessair. Hated and mistrusted by his ally Fzoul, Manshoon calmly manipulated the priest as he did all others—remaining arrogant, untouchable in his power, and faintly amused by everything.

That all came forcibly to an end in 1370 DR, when Fzoul and Lord Orgauth managed to slay Manshoon—and found themselves facing not the sole clone they expected but a dozen or more stasis clones Manshoon created. No one knows who activated all the clones or why, but the chaos caused Faerûn to come alive with ruthless evil archmages, each convinced that he was, in fact, the "real" Manshoon and inexplicably compelled to slay his rival clones.

Most of the clones perished in battle, and the caches of magic items formerly hidden across Faerûn by Manshoon are now scattered into other hands. Only three Manshoons remain. One reclaimed his place among the Zhentarim, conceding leadership of the organization to Fzoul Chembryl but arriving at an understanding with the Chosen of Bane that allows him to make use of the resources and manpower of the Zhentarim. One is rumored to have assumed a position of power among the thieves of Westgate, calling himself Orbakh. A third has taken refuge with Halaster of Undermountain. Those who survive have mastered the slaying-compulsion by means of various spells and devices.

For all intents and purposes, the Manshoon with the Zhentarim appears to be "the" Manshoon. A master tyrant and diplomat, he's accustomed to ruling and manipulating from behind the scenes, and is likely to employ adventurers to work his will wherever he can't dupe local authorities to do so. Relieved of the responsibility of administering the Black Network, he is free to concoct far-ranging designs for the advancement of the Zhentarim, and seems to have learned a lesson in caution and patience from the travails of the last two years. He has redoubled his arcane researches, seeking ways to transfer his consciousness from one clone to another at will.

THE COLOR OF AMBITION

In this adventure, the player characters discover the illegal activities of an ambitious Red Wizard operating out of an enclave in a small town. The enclave serves as an example of how a small enclave is structured and can be used for that purpose independent of the adventure.

ENCOUNTER LEVELS

"The Color of Ambition" is a short adventure for four characters of 1st or 2nd level. It would be helpful if the party had characters with tracking ability, arcane magic, and some skill at diplomacy. A careful group can handle this adventure with just one good fight at the end, but a careless one is likely to become overwhelmed by enemy reinforcements.

ADVENTURE BACKGROUND

Three months ago the Red Wizards of Thay established a small compound outside a small- or moderate-sized town. Led by a fledgling Red Wizard, the wizards and their bodyguards have a small operation in which they produce potions, scrolls, and occasionally minor magic weapons and armor. The lesser members of the group divide their time between making items and going on short adventures. The leader, Hinnar, runs a tight operation. She does not tolerate activities that bring public disfavor upon the group, and she works with local leaders to smooth relations. She even lends her minions, armed with potions and scrolls, to the local military to aid in rousting out small groups of monsters (which gives the wizards a way to gain experience so they can craft more magic items).

However, one of the mid-level wizards in Hinnar's group, Kizzaf, has ambitions of her own. Armed with a few *charm person* spells (renewed every few days), several *potions of love*, and an *animate dead* scroll, she has acquired some faithful friends and servants, and

she plans to sell the charmed ones into slavery through a Thayan merchant she knows. The disappearance of these "friends" triggers the investigation by the heroes.

ADVENTURE SYNOPSIS

When in town, the adventurers hear rumors of the disappearance of two young men who never returned to their homes the night before. The men were strong, healthy, and fit, working in jobs appropriate to the area (such as logging or blacksmithing). Investigating the disappearance, they discover that the men were last seen at one of the local taverns, speaking with a tall woman with long, dark hair. The men left with her, and the three were spotted walking out of town as a group.

Characters who pick up the trail find that the tracks meet up with those of a wagon and horses. But while the wagon tracks continue along their path, the steps of the woman proceed alone and slowly circle around the town to approach the Thayan enclave. A confrontation there results in an attack by the woman responsible (Kizzaf), supplemented by her zombie servants. Whether the other Thayans join in to defend her or aid the PCs in capturing her depends on the heroes' actions up to this point.

character hooks

- The woman (coincidentally) resembles someone the adventurers are looking for, whether an enemy or an information contact.
- One of the missing men is a friend, relative, or employee of one of the heroes.
- A merchant friend of the heroes is owed money by one of the missing men, and the heroes are asked to find him to make sure he's not trying to dodge his obligations.

encounters

Each of the first four items in the following series can be treated as an encounter with one or more people, depending upon the effectiveness of the adventurers' questions.

- The two young laborers are named Talf and Elonn. They left the tavern last night with a tall woman with long, dark hair. This woman does not live in town and has only been spotted here a handful of times, starting about a month ago.
- Those present at the tavern the night before remember that the men seemed to recognize the woman and were friendly toward her, leaving in good spirits.
- A drunk man dozing in the street was awakened by the trio's

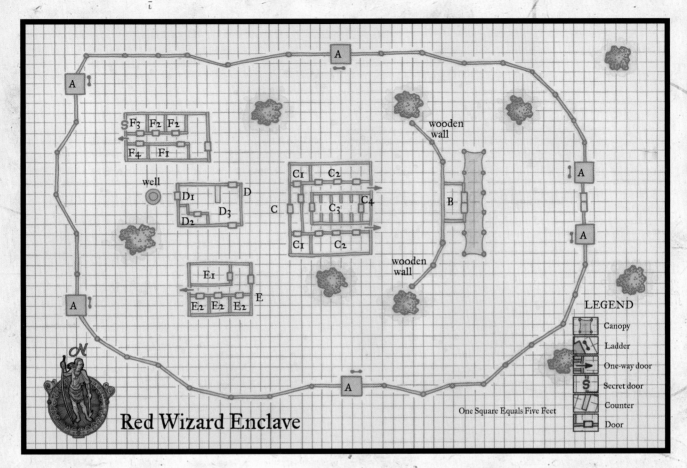

Red Wizard Enclave

One Square Equals Five Feet

LEGEND

Canopy
Ladder
One-way door
Secret door
Counter
Door

laughter as they passed and saw them head out of town together. In exchange for 1 sp, he tells the direction they went.

- Following the drunk's directions, the characters can find and follow the trail with a Wilderness Lore (Track) or Search check (DC 9). About a mile outside town, the trail intersects with the tracks of a wagon drawn by two horses, and the tracks of several people move all around the wagon at this point. The wagon and horse tracks continue on as before (DC 8 Search or Track check to follow the wagon), but the other trail thereafter consists of only the woman's footsteps.

- The wagon has a good head start and travels more quickly than characters on foot, so unless the heroes are mounted they can only catch up if they continue moving after the wagon stops for the night. With the wagon is a Thayan merchant named Mahzed (Exp2, 8 hp, hand crossbow and dagger) and his two guards (War1, 6 hp each, studded leather, scimitar, light crossbow).

- The wagon holds the missing Talf and Elonn, both drugged into unconsciousness, as well as two other men (criminals) sold to the merchant to pay for their debts. The merchant acquired these "slaves" legally and is hesitant to give them up for nothing. If pressed, the merchant informs them that the person he bought the slaves from is a Thayan, and he suggests the PCs travel to the nearby enclave for more information.

- The solo trail is only slightly more difficult to follow (DC 10). It curves around the town at a roughly fixed radius and eventually leads to the entrance of the small fenced enclave owned and inhabited by the potion-selling wizards of Thay.

The Enclave

The Red Wizard enclave is a large fenced compound, over 250 feet long and more than 150 feet wide. The fence is 4 feet high and made

of pairs of cut logs affixed to vertical posts set 10 to 20 feet apart. Each of the posts has a *continual flame* spell cast upon it, so the entire formation is lit up at night. Six wooden platforms (marked A on the map) are built into the fence, each accessed by a ladder. The platforms have 3-foot-high walls, providing one-quarter cover to anyone standing behind them.

The enclave itself is mostly open, with five buildings, a few trees, and a well. It is home to ten guards (Ftr1), ten wizards (five Wiz1, three Wiz2, and two Wiz3), and one Red Wizard leader (Wiz5/Red1). The two day shifts of guards consist of one at a watch platform, another patrolling the enclave, and a third standing watch at the sales booth (area B). At night the gate is closed, and two guards patrol the interior of the enclave (keeping just beyond the illumination of the fence lights and completing a circuit in less than 2 minutes), while a third alternates between platforms approximately every hour. Under normal circumstances, if the compound is attacked, the remaining guards and novice wizards move out to counterattack while the other wizards hang back to evaluate the threat and determine strategy.

A. WATCH PLATFORM

The floor of this walled platform is 5 feet above the ground, supported by four thick wooden posts. It has a cloth canopy suspended by a wooden frame. Any guard using one of the platforms carries a longspear to be able to attack foes on the ground in melee.

B. SALES BOOTH

This small building is little more than a wooden countertop mounted in front of a set of shelves. The great wide doors have no lock, because they are designed only to keep the weather out when the shop is closed at night (the merchandise is locked up in the main barracks at that time). In front of the booth is a canopied area so that potential customers can be shielded from the rain or sunshine. The back wall of the booth joins an 8-foot-high wooden wall that shields the view of the rest of the compound from the customers, allowing those living here some privacy. When the shop is open, it holds two of each of the following potions: *cat's grace*, *change self*, *comprehend languages*, *darkvision*, *endurance*, *endure elements (cold)*, *endure elements (fire)*, *fly*, *levitate*, *love*, *protection from arrows*, and *spider climb*. Also posted is a list of other potions or scrolls the wizards can make (as appropriate from the spell lists of the resident wizards, although they obey the guidelines for creating magic items as described in the *Player's Handbook* and the *Dungeon Master's Guide*).

Like all Thayan enclaves, they sell their potions at a 10% discount from the prices in the *Dungeon Master's Guide*. The wizards can take an arcane scroll and make a potion from it (if its spell can be made into a potion) for the normal potion cost. Any items specially ordered (whether from the list or an offered scroll) take from two to five days to complete; next-day results add an extra 50% to the normal cost. They also sell scrolls of *detect magic*, *detect poison*, *light*, *mending*, *read magic*, and *resistance* at cost if the buyer is purchasing an equal number of 1st-level or higher items.

The booth is run by three of the 1st-level wizards (exactly which ones varies daily) and guarded by one guard. On slow days, two of the wizards assist those making the items or visit the town for supplies and to promote their items. When the town has a festival, the enclave normally donates one or more potions (usually *endure elements [fire]* and *levitate*) to the cause to promote good will and provide entertainment.

C. Main Barracks

This large building serves as the housing for four guards (two in each room marked C1) and the 1st-level wizards (divided between the C2 rooms), as well as the place where the creation of potions and scrolls occurs (the alcoves in C3). Room C4 is a storage area for supplies necessary to make items (it currently holds 500 gp worth of the proper materials) and any prepared potions. The door to the storage area has a good lock (Open Lock DC 30), and Hinnar has the key. During the day, the 2nd- and 3rd-level wizards and any 1st-level wizards not working elsewhere spend most of their time here, with occasional item creation done by Hinnar.

D. Kitchen

This building houses the kitchen (D1), pantry (D2), and a walkway where the residents can pick up food (D3)—this last doubles as a cramped cafeteria in bad weather. The food is normally prepared by one of the guards.

E. Second Barracks

This barracks is the home of three guards (E1) and the three 2nd-level wizards (E2).

F. Leader's Barracks

This building is the home of three guards (F1), the two 3rd-level wizards (F2), and Hinnar (F3). The last room (F4) is a storage room, holding building tools, extra cookware, a cask of fine wine, and other minor luxuries.

Approaching the Enclave

If the characters follow the solo trail, it takes them to the entrance of the Thayan enclave, between the two watch platforms on the east side of the fence. The gate is open during the day, and a guard is stationed in one of the watch platforms adjacent to it. The guard accosts all who approach, asking their names and their reasons for visiting the enclave, and is not averse to answering questions. If the characters try to enter the enclave without speaking with a guard, by jumping the fence instead of going through the gate, or by any other means, the occupants of the enclave consider such action an attack and react accordingly (see Tactics, below).

At night the gate is closed, and the watch platforms next to it are likely to be vacant. However, any characters who come within 20 feet of the gate (or any other part of the fence) will be visible in the light of the *continual flame* spells on the fenceposts; all they need to do is stay in the light for a minute or two, and a patrolling guard will notice them.

Talking with the Guard (EL 4)

Other than Kizzaf herself, none of the Thayans know of the kidnapping of Talf and Elonn. If the characters question a guard about this event, the guard calls one of the wizards to talk. The one who answers his call is Kizzaf. Note that Kizzaf is bald when in Red Wizard garb (she shaves her head) and wears a wig in her slave-recruiting trips, making it unlikely that she can be recognized as the "long-haired woman" the heroes are looking for. She denies any knowledge of the missing men, and if pressured she tries to antagonize the heroes into attacking. If the heroes don't attack, eventually the guard calls for Hinnar (proceed to Concluding the Adventure). The guard defends Kizzaf against attacks but does not initiate attacks against the heroes unless attacked himself.

Tactics (EL4+)

The guard calls an alarm on the round the heroes attack. The other guards on duty and one novice wizard from building C respond, running to defend their fellows (making a double move each round). This group is EL4.

On the next round everyone from building F pours out of that location to investigate. When she sees the battle, Hinnar is outraged. She loudly exclaims that her people have worked hard to keep the peace with the local authorities and she will make complaints once these rabble-rousers are defeated. Should the heroes confront her with accusations of kidnapping, she orders a temporary cessation of hostilities so they may discuss the matter (proceed to Concluding the Adventure). The wizards use spells to disable opponents so they can be turned over to the local authorities for justice.

concluding the Adventure

If the heroes decide to speak with Hinnar, the woman questions them about the kidnapping accusations. At this point, Kizzaf realizes she's about to be caught and decides to try escaping, yelling for her "minions" to attack the adventurers. These minions are the two humanoid zombies she created (using a prized scroll she acquired while aiding a local military patrol), which lie buried 40 feet inside the gate. The zombies dig themselves free and shamble forward to attack the heroes. When this treachery is revealed, Hinnar tries to use her spells to disable Kizzaf before the woman escapes out of range.

If Kizzaf is caught, Hinnar agrees to have her brought to the town constable for questioning. Once the truth comes out, Hinnar apologizes for her underling's actions and leaves her in the hands of local justice. She also gives four potions to the town as compensation for their trouble and offers another as a reward for the successful return of Talf and Elonn.

⬧ **Medium-Size Zombies (2):** hp 16, 15; see *Monster Manual*.

TREASURE

Kizzaf's equipment is claimed by the Thayans, but Hinnar gives the adventurers 300 gp worth of potions from her enclave's stock (based on the undiscounted prices given in the *DUNGEON MASTER's Guide*) to thank them for discovering this potential threat to their economic and social security.

CREATURES

In all, the enclave is home to ten guards (Ftr1), five novice wizards (Wiz 1), three minor wizards (Wiz2), two lesser wizards (Wiz3—one is Kizzaf), and one Red Wizard (Wiz5/Rwz1).

➤**Chamon, Gaera, Barlos, Hena, Daedus, Wuxor, Lanaus, Xera, Nikka, and Kyros:** Male and female human Ftr1: CR 1; Medium-size humanoid; HD 1d10+2; hp 12; Init +1; Spd 20 ft.; AC 18 (touch 10, flat-footed 18); Atk +5 melee (1d10+2/19–20, masterwork bastard sword) or +3 melee (1d8+2/×3, longspear) or +2 ranged (1d8/×3, composite longbow); SV Fort +4, Ref +1, Will +1; AL LN; Str 15, Dex 13, Con 14, Int 10, Wis 12, Cha 8.

Skills and Feats: Craft (any one) +4, Listen +3, Spot +3; Exotic Weapon Proficiency (bastard sword), Point Blank Shot, Weapon Focus (bastard sword).

Possessions (each): Splint mail, large steel shield, masterwork bastard sword, longspear, composite longbow, quiver with 1d20 arrows, 3–4 gp.

➤**Arrit, Dymia, Ekass, Ibron, and Tolmen:** Male and female human Wiz1 (see below); CR 1; Medium-size humanoid; HD 1d4+1; hp 5; Init +2; Spd 30 ft.; AC 12 (touch 12, flat-footed 10); Atk –1 melee (1d4–1/19–20, dagger) or +2 ranged (1d8/19–20, light crossbow); AL LN; SV Fort +1, Ref +2, Will +3; Str 8, Dex 14, Con 13, Int 15, Wis 12, Cha 10.

Skills and Feats: Alchemy +6, Concentration +5, Knowledge (arcana) +6, Scry +6, Spellcraft +6; Extend Spell, Scribe Scroll, Tattoo Focus (each with a different school: Abjuration, Divination, Enchantment, Illusion, and Transmutation, respectively).

Spells Prepared (4/3; base DC = 12 + spell level, 13 + spell level in specialized school): varies with what scrolls are needed that day, but typically 1 attack spell, 1 defensive spell, and 1 spell for a scroll. Each of these wizards is specialized in the school of magic indicated by his or her Tattoo Focus feat. Prohibited school: Evocation.

Spellbook: 0—arcane mark, daze, detect magic, detect poison, disrupt undead, ghost sound, mage hand, mending, open/close, prestidigitation, ray of frost, read magic, resistance; 1st—burning hands, change self, comprehend languages, endure elements, sleep, spider climb.

Possessions (each): Dagger, light crossbow, 20 bolts, 10 gp.

➤**Alasitra, Devanto, and Tatyl:** Male and female human Wiz2 (see below); CR 2; Medium-size humanoid; HD 2d4+2; hp 8; Init +2; Spd 30 ft.; AC 12 (touch 12, flat-footed 10); Atk +0 melee (1d4–1/19–20, dagger) or +4 ranged (1d8/19–20, masterwork light crossbow); AL LN; SV Fort +1, Ref +2, Will +4; Str 8, Dex 14, Con 13, Int 15, Wis 12, Cha 10.

Skills and Feats: Alchemy +7, Concentration +6, Knowledge (arcana) +7, Scry +7, Spellcraft +7; Extend Spell, Scribe Scroll, Tattoo Focus (each with a different school: Abjuration, Divination, and Transmutation, respectively).

Spells Prepared (5/4; base DC = 12 + spell level, 13 + spell level in specialized school): varies with what scrolls are needed that day, but typically 1 attack spell, 2 defensive spells, and 1 spell for a scroll. Each of these wizards is specialized in the school of magic indicated by his or her Tattoo Focus feat. Prohibited school: Evocation.

Spellbook: 0—arcane mark, daze, detect magic, detect poison, disrupt undead, ghost sound, mage hand, mending, open/close, prestidigitation, ray of frost, read magic, resistance; 1st—burning hands, change self, charm person, comprehend languages, endure elements, expeditious retreat, shield, sleep, spider climb, true strike.

Possessions (each): Dagger, masterwork light crossbow, 20 bolts, 25 gp.

➤**Kizzaf and Muxos:** Female human Div3 (Kizzaf), male human Tra3 (Muxos); CR 3; Medium-size humanoid; HD 3d4+3; hp 12; Init +2; Spd 30 ft.; AC 12 (touch 12, flat-footed 10); Atk +1 melee (1d4–1/19–20, masterwork dagger), +4 ranged (1d8/19–20, masterwork light crossbow); AL LE (Kizzaf), LN (Muxos); SV Fort +2, Ref +3, Will +4; Str 8, Dex 14, Con 13, Int 15, Wis 12, Cha 10.

Skills and Feats: Alchemy +8, Concentration +7, Knowledge (arcana) +8, Scry +8, Spellcraft +8; Brew Potion, Extend Spell, Scribe Scroll, Tattoo Focus (each with a different school: Divination for Kizzaf, Transmutation for Muxos).

Spells Prepared (5/4/3; base DC = 12 + spell level, 13 + spell level in specialized school): varies with what potions are needed that day, but typically 1 attack spell, 1 or 2 defensive spells, and 1 spell for a potion for each spell level. Each of these wizards is specialized in the school of magic indicated by his or her Tattoo Focus feat. Prohibited school: Evocation.

Spellbook: 0—arcane mark, daze, detect magic, detect poison, disrupt undead, ghost sound, mage hand, mending, open/close, prestidigitation, ray of frost, read magic, resistance; 1st—burning hands, change self, charm person, comprehend languages, endure elements, identify, mage armor, shield, sleep, spider climb, true strike; 2nd—alter self, blur, cat's grace, darkvision, endurance, levitate, protection from arrows.

Possessions (each): Masterwork dagger, masterwork light crossbow, 20 bolts, potion of cure light wounds, 60 gp. Kizzaf also has a cloak of resistance +1 (not included above).

➤**Hinnar:** Female human Tra5/Red1; CR 6; Medium-size humanoid; HD 6d4+6; hp 23; Init +2; Spd 30 ft.; AC 12 (touch 12, flat-footed 10); Atk +3 melee (1d4+1/19–20, +1 dagger) or +5 ranged (1d8/19–20, masterwork light crossbow); SQ Specialist defense; AL LN; SV Fort +5, Ref +4, Will +8; Str 10, Dex 14, Con 13, Int 16, Wis 12, Cha 14.

Skills and Feats: Alchemy +11, Concentration +7, Diplomacy +6, Intimidate +4, Knowledge (arcana) +9, Knowledge (Thay local) +7, Scry +9, Spellcraft +11; Brew Potion, Craft Magic Arms and Armor, Extend Spell, Great Fortitude, Scribe Scroll, Tattoo Focus (Transmutation).

Special Qualities: Specialist Defense: +1 bonus on all saving throws against transmutation spells.

Possessions: +1 dagger, masterwork light crossbow, 20 bolts, potion of cure moderate wounds, potion of invisibility, wand of ray of enfeeblement (10 charges), scrolls (dispel magic, invisibility), cloak of resistance +1, 300 gp.

Spells Prepared (5/5/5/4; base DC = 13 + spell level, 14 + spell level for transmutation spells): varies with what magic items are needed that day, but typically 1 or 2 attack spells, 2 defensive spells, and 1 spell for a magic item for each spell level. Hinnar is specialized in the school of Transmutation. Prohibited schools: Evocation, Conjuration.

Spellbook: 0—arcane mark, daze, detect magic, detect poison, disrupt undead, ghost sound, mage hand, mending, open/close, prestidigitation, read magic, resistance; 1st—burning hands, change self, charm person, comprehend languages, endure elements, identify, shield, sleep, spider climb, true strike; 2nd—alter self, blur, cat's grace, darkvision, endurance, invisibility, levitate, protection from arrows; 3rd—dispel magic, displacement, fly, gaseous form, gentle repose, protection from elements, tongues, water breathing.

Running The Realms

At its heart, the FORGOTTEN REALMS is neither an imaginary world of shining heroes and terrible monsters nor a real world whose mystic echoes are lost in our past. It's a setting for your DUNGEONS & DRAGONS campaign. This book provides an entire world (well, a continent, anyway) in which you can create all kinds of adventures for your players and link them together in the ongoing story of Faerûn.

This chapter is aimed at the Dungeon Master, providing tips and rules for creating your own FORGOTTEN REALMS campaign and running DUNGEONS & DRAGONS adventures in the world of Toril. The subjects covered here appear in the same order in which they're covered in the *DUNGEON MASTER's Guide*. Each topic expands on the information in that book. If you're not sure where to find a piece of information about how to run a DUNGEONS & DRAGONS game, refer to the *DUNGEON MASTER's Guide* if you don't see it in this chapter.

characters

The FORGOTTEN REALMS campaign takes advantage of several options and variants for characters described in the *DUNGEON MASTER's Guide*. The players are encouraged to create any kind of character they can imagine within the rules of the game, but as the Dungeon Master it falls to you to ground these characters in the setting and help the players bring them to life. Chapter 1: Characters contains everything players need to create characters suitable for a campaign set in Faerûn. This chapter offers additional options and information on character creation to help you anchor the player characters in your FORGOTTEN REALMS campaign.

additional pc races

Humans, dwarves, elves, halflings, and the other races described in Chapter 1: Characters comprise the vast majority of the adventurers found in Faerûn. However, there are many intelligent races on Toril, and most of those give rise to the occasional individual of exceptional ability or drive who is willing to take up the career of the adventurer.

The most common of these monstrous races include the drow, duergar, svirfneblin, and planetouched—all described in some detail in Chapter 1. Some of the other races that could reasonably become adventurers are summed up on Table 8–1: Common Monstrous Adventurers.

TABLE 8–1: COMMON MONSTROUS ADVENTURERS

Race	Level Adjustment	Source
Aarakocra	+2	*Monster Compendium*
Alaghi	+11*	*Monster Compendium*
Bugbear	+4*	*Monster Manual*
Centaur	+7*	*Monster Manual*
Fey'ri	+2	*Monster Compendium*
Gnoll	+2*	*Monster Manual*
Goblin	+0	*Monster Manual*
Hobgoblin	+1	*Monster Manual*
Hybsil	+2	*Monster Compendium*
Kobold	+0	*Monster Manual*
Kir-lanan	+8*	*FR Campaign Setting*
Lizardfolk	+4*	*Monster Manual*
Ogre	+8*	*Monster Manual*
Orc	+0	*Monster Manual*
Shade‡	+5	*FR Campaign Setting*
Siv	+1*	*Monster Compendium*
Troll	+11*	*Monster Manual*
Wemic	+8*	*Monster Compendium*
Werewolf**†	+3	*Monster Manual*

*These races have more than 1 Hit Die.
**Choose a standard race for the creature's base race.
†Character must be at least 2nd level.
‡Character must be at least 5th level.

Level Adjustment: Add this figure to the character's character level to determine his effective character level. For example, a 3rd-level alaghi cleric is effectively a 14th-level character.

Source: The sourcebook in which the creature's monster description appears: the *Monster Manual*, *Monster Compendium: Monsters of Faerûn*, or Chapter 9 of this book.

monster levels

Creatures with more than 1 Hit Die function as multiclass characters with levels in a favored "racial" class equal to the creature's base Hit Dice. For example, an alaghi has 9 Hit Dice, so an alaghi PC begins play with nine levels of "alaghi." As player characters, their first racial Hit Die has its maximum value. A creature's HD is not always the same as the creature's level adjustment, since creatures with many special abilities have a level adjustment higher than their actual Hit Dice.

A race's level adjustment measures just how powerful the race is compared to a standard character race such as human or dwarf. When creating a character of this race, add the level adjustment to the character level of the creature to determine the effective character level, or ECL.

Because characters of these powerful races possess a higher level than just their character level alone, they do not gain levels as fast as a normal character. The character uses his ECL to determine how many experience points he needs to reach a new level. See Table 1–2: ECL Experience Requirements for a summary of how a character's ECL affects the XP needed to advance a level. The table covers characters with a level adjustment of +1 (planetouched), +2 (drow and duergar), and +3 (svirfneblin). For level adjustments greater than +3, extrapolate from the given information to determine the character's XP requirements.

For example, a centaur has a level adjustment of +7, so a 1st-level centaur paladin has an ECL of 8 (1 character level plus the level adjustment of +7). A normal 1st-level character needs 1,000 XP to get to 2nd level, but this centaur paladin is an 8th-level character beginning play with 28,000 XP who needs to reach 9th level before he can add another character level. In this case, he needs a total of 36,000 XP to become a 2nd-level paladin, a total of 45,000 to become a 3rd-level paladin, a total of 55,000 to reach 4th level, and so on. Essentially, instead of needing your character level × 1,000 to reach the next class level, your character needs your ECL × 1,000 to reach the next class level.

ABILITY SCORES FOR MONSTROUS PCs

Ability scores for these races are generated according to the procedure described in Chapter 2 of the *Dungeon Master's Guide*. The unusual races covered in Chapter 1 of this book (the drow, duergar, svirfneblin, and planetouched) do not follow this procedure; their racial ability score modifiers can be found in the race descriptions.

ALLOWING POWERFUL RACES IN PLAY

Since these are not standard character races, you should decide if you are willing to allow a player to generate a character from any of these races.

If the character's ECL is higher than the average character level of the other player characters in the group, the character is probably too powerful for the current group. You should not allow this character into the group unless you are willing to deal with the difficulties associated with a group composed of characters of varying power levels. An inequality of one level for high-level characters is probably not a problem, but it can make a significant difference in a low-level group.

Even if the character falls within the power range of the rest of the group, you can disallow it if you don't think the character suits your campaign—you have the final say on what sorts of characters the players can create for your game.

creating characters above 1st level

You may choose to begin your campaign with relatively experienced heroes instead of 1st-level novices. If you do so, use Table 2–24 in the *Dungeon Master's Guide* to determine the value of the character's equipment. If the character chooses a class encouraged by his native region (see Chapter 1: Characters), add 300 gp to the value

characters above 20th level

Some of the characters described in this book go beyond 20th level. They use terms that are fully detailed in the upcoming D&D *Epic Level Handbook.* When present in the character statistic block in the class/level area, the word "Epic" refers to a character's epic-level benefits. At each level beyond 20th, a character selects a single epic-level benefit. Characters do not gain level-based ability score increases and feats beyond 20th level as they did before. Those epic-level benefits that a character has are described in the Special Qualities section of the character's statistic block.

+1 Effective Level: The character gains a level in a class, acquiring the class features and skill points for that class level, and increasing his maximum skill rank by 1. He does not increase his base attack bonus, Hit Dice, hit points, or base saving throws. You cannot use effective levels to increase a character's class level above 20. You cannot use effective levels to increase a character's level in a class that he abandoned (such as becoming an ex-cleric, ex-monk, or ex-paladin).

When a character chooses an effective level as an epic-level benefit, the class/level portion of the character's statistic block shows the modified level of that class (actual levels plus effective levels) rather than being listed as "Epic" and a number. So Elminster is listed as a Ftr1/Rog2/Clr3/Wiz20/Acm5/Epic4, even though he actually has fifteen levels above 20th character level. Six of those

levels are effective levels of wizard (included in the "Wiz20"), and five are effective levels of archmage (included in the "Acm5"). The remaining four are other epic-level benefits.

+1 Ability: Add 1 to one ability score. This epic-level benefit replaces the ability score increase that characters normally get every four levels.

+1 Attack: Add +1 to base attack bonus. (Monks also add this to their unarmed attack bonus.) This bonus does not increase the number of additional attacks you get due to a high base attack bonus (so a 20th-level fighter's base attack bonus increases to +21/+16/+11/+6 without getting a fifth attack at +1).

+1 Bonus Spell Level: The character gains 1 spell slot per day whose level is one higher than the highest level spell he can already cast in a particular class. This benefit is only available if a character already has 20 levels in a spellcasting class. For example, if Elminster chose this benefit, he would gain one 10th-level wizard spell slot. If he chose it again, he would gain one 11th-level spell slot. If the character has a high enough ability modifier to gain a bonus spell for this spell level, he also gets that bonus spell of this new level. No spells exist of a spell level above 9th for wizards, sorcerers, clerics, and druids; 4th for paladins and rangers; or 6th for bards. However, these spell slots can be used for lower-level spells or metamagical spells.

shown on the table to allow for the bonus equipment the character received at 1st level. The character does not have to begin with this bonus equipment—after all, he's had some time to use it up, wear it out, or trade it in. (This rule applies to NPCs as well as PCs.)

If the character is a member of a powerful race, use the character's effective level to determine the character's equipment.

patron Deities

As noted in Chapter 5, Faerûn has many gods, and most intelligent people worship more than one god, or at least pay homage to different gods when the circumstances are appropriate. Still, most residents of Faerûn feel a special attachment to one particular deity.

A character's choice of a patron deity never restricts which deities that character may honor. All the gods of Faerûn recognize that their fellow gods have their own portfolios and spheres of control, and none prevent their followers from recognizing the same thing.

A character's choice of a patron deity does not create any special obligations for that character. Choosing a patron merely indicates which deity happens to be the character's personal favorite. A character's choice of a patron reflects the character's ambitions and self-image (most people want to be as much like their patron deity as possible for a mortal), and reflects the character's values.

Unless she is a divine spellcaster, a character is under no obligation to proselytize on her patron deity's behalf, make special sacrifices, or even tell other mortals which patron deity she honors. Even clerics and druids aren't expected to constantly seek converts. An adventuring cleric represents her faith through her actions and the causes she fights for, not by haranguing her comrades at every opportunity.

Half-orc giant-killer

PATRON DEITIES AND THE DEAD

A character who has chosen a patron deity can be brought back from the dead by all the normal methods, provided the character is willing to return. The process is somewhat more difficult for a character who did not choose a patron deity in life.

Kelemvor, the god of the dead, eventually disposes of unclaimed souls, trapping them and making it impossible for them to return to life. This process of disposal takes 1d10 days. During this time, characters who died without a patron deity can be raised, resurrected, or reincarnated if the spell that brings them back is cast before Kelemvor deals with the soul. After this time, only a *miracle* or *wish* can restore the character to life.

Even if a player has not chosen a patron deity for his character before the character meets her death, the player can choose one at the time of the character's death. If the player decides not to choose

a patron once his character has died, the character is truly faithless and must take his chances with the rest of the unclaimed souls of the Fugue Plane. If the player decides to declare a patron, he should choose a deity the character has shown at least some interest in. Even if the character has never actively shown interest in any particular god, the way the character has been played usually will suggest a god. For example, a character of good alignment who has devoted himself to magic would naturally gravitate toward Mystra, whereas an adventurer of almost any class or alignment might naturally gravitate to Shaundakul if he had a zest for travel or exploration.

In short, there is one cardinal rule regarding characters and patron deities: Never punish a player for not writing down a patron deity on his character sheet.

optional Rules

Most FORGOTTEN REALMS game products will assume that the only rulebooks you are using are the three core rulebooks, this book, and *Monstrous Compendium: Monsters of Faerûn*. The campaign setting assumes that you have access to the monsters described therein.

In general, any optional rule you care to add will work as well for a campaign set in Faerûn as it will in any other D&D campaign. The various optional prestige classes and other material from the Builder's Guidebook series easily fit into a Faerûnian campaign with little or no adjustments.

The upcoming *Epic Level Handbook* is fully supported in the FORGOTTEN REALMS campaign. In fact, many of the characters described in this book make use of advancement rules from the *Epic Level Handbook*. Refer to the Characters Above 20th Level sidebar on the previous page.

PSIONICS

This book presents Faerûn, and indeed all of Toril, as a nonpsionic world. That does not mean, however, that you cannot use the *Psionics Handbook* rules for your Faerûnian campaign. Psionic powers are rare, and most people find little difference between psionics and magic. Do not use the Nonmagical Psionics variant described in Chapter 3 of the *DUNGEON MASTER's Guide* in your Faerûnian campaign.

Reactions to Psionic Characters

Psionics are rare on Faerûn and largely unknown except in areas where psionic monsters live. Such areas include the South, where the yuan-ti have influence (particularly the city of Hlondeth on the Vilhon Reach) and the Underdark (thanks to the influence of the mind flayers). Waterdeep undoubtedly holds a few characters with psionic abilities, as do large urban areas such as Amn and Calimshan.

Illustration by Carlo Arellano

In general, psionic characters can expect the same reactions and attitudes that arcane spellcasters encounter. Areas that welcome or at least accept wizards will welcome psionic characters with equal enthusiasm (or lack thereof). In areas where wizards are feared or shunned, such as Amn, psionic characters will have to tread carefully.

Many spellcasters are likely to view psionic characters as potential magical rivals, so psionic characters might consider concealing their talents anywhere they are likely to meet a jealous wizard or cleric (in Thay, for example).

Psionics and Regional Feats

The psion and psionic warrior classes are not favored in any region of Faerûn. Regional feats (and regional bonus equipment) are not available to such characters.

If you decide that you want psionics to play a greater role in your campaign, you can relax these restrictions somewhat. Tashalar, Chult, the Vilhon Reach, and the Gray Dwarf "regions" are more likely than other parts of Faerûn to give rise to psionic characters and might be considered preferred regions for psions and psionic warriors.

Running the Game

All the rules, situations, and guidelines described in the *Player's Handbook* and *Dungeon Master's Guide* apply to campaigns set in Faerûn. Combat runs in the same order, saving throws are calculated in the same way, hazards and special attacks operate as usual.

The only additions to the rules for running the game are time-keeping and extra information on using maps for terrain and overland movement.

Timekeeping

The calendar of Faerûn is described in Chapter 3: Life in Faerûn. Many Dungeon Masters find it useful to keep a close eye on the passage of time in their campaigns. At the most basic level, keeping track of time helps you to administer the use of special abilities that can only be used once a week, or once a year, or in other increments. For example, a paladin is limited in how often she can use *remove disease*, and from time to time a game situation may crop up in which several characters are suffering from disease and it's important to know when the paladin's ability becomes available again.

TRACKING TIME

The most accurate and thorough way to keep track of the passage of time in your game is to create a campaign journal. A blank grid like a monthly appointment book works good—you can number the days as they appear on the Calendar of Harptos, and use the space provided for each day to note major occurrences or the use of time-controlled special abilities.

From time to time you should give the player characters some significant "down time," a window of several weeks or months in which no adventures take place. This is important because it gives characters an opportunity to undertake tasks such as item creation, which is an important game ability for many characters. If every adventure in your campaign follows hard on the heels of the last one, wizards and clerics will never get a chance to engage in spell research or craft items.

You don't need to roleplay session after session of nothing happening, of course—you can simply skip ahead by several weeks or months and ask the players if they have any long-term projects they want their characters to work on. This also helps to suspend the disbelief engendered when a character shoots from 1st level to 10th level in a few months of play. The player characters simply enjoyed some respites from their continuous adventures and used up more calendar time than the sum of their adventures would indicate.

TENDAYS VS. WEEKS

Faerûn's Calendar of Harptos divides its 30-day months into three tendays each, which are the closest equivalent to a week on Faerûn. While it would make some sense to tie time-controlled abilities to tendays instead of weeks, you might not want to do that. First of all, an ability usable once per ten days is weaker than an ability usable once per seven days. Second, Faerûn's calendar includes festival days that don't fall into any tenday of the year. If you want to use tendays instead of weeks, you should consider each of the five festival days to "belong" to the tenday that immediately precedes them—which means that five weeks of Faerûn's year are actually eleven days in length, not ten, weakening time-controlled abilities even more.

If you track time-controlled abilities by the passage of days instead of tendays, simply make a note seven days from the time the ability is used. If an ability can only be used once per week, the character can't do it again until seven days pass. If it's usable multiple times per week, each "use" must wait seven days before it becomes available again.

Terrain and Movement

In the FORGOTTEN REALMS campaign, there are great adventures to be found in strange and distant lands. You have an entire world to describe to your players, filled with hundreds of unique locations and cities for their characters to explore. Your characters may trek across Anauroch to explore the dwarven ruins of Ascore, sail the Sea of Fallen Stars to reach the undercity of Westgate, or strike out into the ogre-infested hills of Thar in search of a ruined castle to plunder.

TERRAIN TYPES

The poster map of Faerûn shows most of the continent at a scale of 120 miles to the inch. Only the largest features can be included at that scale—you can assume that thousands of tiny hamlets and villages, myriad ponds and lakes and streams, and countless copses, groves, and woodlands exist on the map but simply aren't shown. The following types of terrain can be found on the map.

Barren/Badlands: Rugged areas with very sparse vegetation. Badlands are crisscrossed with labyrinthine valleys separated by weirdly shaped hills and rock formations.

Cleared/Mix: Open areas that have been cleared for agriculture. Cleared area may contain small stands of trees, low hills, and other geographical features. Mixed areas are naturally open and rolling, and include a variety of minor landforms such as low hills, prairies, scattered trees, and small brooks.

Forest: Any area thickly covered with tall trees. The trees may be coniferous or deciduous.

Glacier: A large mass of ice in high mountains or in high latitudes. The ice is in motion (albeit very slowly), creating crevices, pressure ridges, and other hazards.

Grasslands: Open and fairly flat areas covered mostly with grass. Some trees and shrubs may grow near open water.

High Mountains: Areas covered with steep, rocky peaks. Areas of high mountains have at least some peaks tall enough to remain snowcapped throughout the year, even in temperate or warm climates. Tall mountains also have distinct tree lines. Mountainous areas contain passes and valleys that are lower than the surrounding peaks.

Hills: Rugged areas that are lower and less steep than mountains. Like mountainous areas, hilly areas can also contain valleys that are lower than the surrounding hills.

Jungle: Exceptionally thick and damp forest.

Lake: An inland body of fresh water. The Lake of Steam is an exception—it's really a saltwater inlet of the Shining Sea. Azulduth, the Lake of Salt, is saltwater instead of freshwater.

Low Mountains: Areas taller, steeper, and more rugged than hills, but less so than high mountains. Low mountains are not tall enough to have tree lines or to retain permanent snowcaps in temperate or warm areas. Mountainous areas contain passes and valleys that are lower than the surrounding peaks.

Marsh: Low, waterlogged areas that support stands of reeds and other low vegetation, but few trees. Marshes may contain islands of fairly dry land separated by stagnant water or sluggish streams.

Moor: Open areas, often fairly high but poorly drained. Moors tend to be grassy, with patches of low shrubs and bogs.

River: Flowing water too deep and wide to cross without swimming or using a bridge, boat, or ford.

Road: A route with a smooth and firm surface, covered with packed earth or gravel and graded to shed rainwater.

Rocky Desert: An arid region covered with sunbaked rocks and scrub.

Sandy Desert: An arid region covered in shifting sand and sand dunes.

Swamp: A low, waterlogged area, similar to a marsh but covered with trees.

Trail: An unimproved track that marks a reasonably efficient route through an area.

OVERLAND MOVEMENT

Powerful wizards may teleport themselves from one point to another, but most of the rest of Faerûn's inhabitants walk, ride, fly, or sail from place to place. Use the rules in Chapter 9 of the *Player's Handbook* for overland movement in Faerûn. The poster map of Faerûn includes terrain not shown on Table 9–5: Terrain and Overland Movement in the *Player's Handbook*. Use Table 8–2 here instead.

TABLE 8—2:
TERRAIN AND OVERLAND MOVEMENT IN FAERÛN

Terrain	Road	Trail	Trackless
Barren/Badlands	×1	×1	×3/4
Cleared/Mix	×1	×1	×1
Forest	×1	×1	×1/2
Glacier	—	—	×1/2
Grassland	×1	×1	×1
High Mountains	×3/4	×1/2	×1/8
Hills	×1	×3/4	×1/2
Jungle	×1	×3/4	×1/4
Low Mountains	×3/4	×1/2	×1/4
Marsh	×1	×3/4	×1/2
Moor	×1	×1	×3/4
Rocky Desert	×1	×1	×3/4
Sandy Desert	×1	—	×1/2
Swamp	×1	×3/4	×1/2

In local areas, many more roads and trails exist than are shown on the poster map—only the major cross-country routes are noted. Flying creatures ignore movement penalties in all terrain types except low mountains and high mountains, which they treat as hills and low mountains respectively.

OTHER RESOURCES

The Dungeon Master has a number of available resources to enhance a FORGOTTEN REALMS campaign. Aside from future game products, both *DRAGON®* and *DUNGEON®* magazines support the game setting. *DUNGEON* in particular is an excellent source for a DM looking for adventure material, since most adventures can be easily adapted to fit the FORGOTTEN REALMS setting.

Also, the Wizards of the Coast website (www.wizards.com/dnd) is frequently updated with game information, adventures, characters, and locations for both the DUNGEONS & DRAGONS game and specifically for the FORGOTTEN REALMS campaign.

ADVENTURES

Adventures in Faerûn are much like adventures in the core DUNGEONS & DRAGONS game, except that many will feature Toril-specific monsters, villains, and background. In this section we'll discuss dungeons of Faerûn and specific local encounters.

DUNGEON ARCHITECTS

What makes Faerûnian dungeons different from dungeons in other worlds? History, mostly. No matter what its original or current function (see Chapter 4 of the *DUNGEON MASTER's Guide* for a discussion of dungeon types), a dungeon in Faerûn will bear the stamp of its original builders and of the various groups that have occupied it over the centuries. Few dungeons in Faerûn stay empty for long.

No matter who built a dungeon, *portals* may connect it to other dungeons the same species or group has built, forming a network that past residents once used and that now provides player characters with a quick way to hop from dungeon to dungeon. Likewise, many dungeons contain connections to the Underdark.

Adventurers: This category of dungeon builders includes mad wizards such as Halaster, the architect of the vast dungeon of Undermountain, successful adventurers looking for safe places to stash their wealth, and enterprising folk who build safe places to hide from their enemies when things get rough. Adventurers' dungeon features vary widely. Areas protected against scrying and astral travel are common, as are *portals* leading almost anywhere.

More bizarre features might include zoological or botanical collections (sometimes contained, sometimes running amok), extradimensional prisons holding fiends or elementals, labyrinths and traps built to guard special treasures, complexes of miniature chambers accessible only to visitors who are magically reduced in size, and vast laboratories containing deadly experiments still in progress after centuries.

Beholders: Beholders frequently carve out underground lairs using slave labor (courtesy of their *charm* abilities) and their *disintegrate* powers. Beholder lairs usually feature vertical architecture that can be hard to negotiate without flying or levitating. They are often stuffed with magical oddities and other treasures.

Dwarves: The premier dungeon builders of Faerûn, dwarves build everything from simple mines to underground cities carved out of bedrock. Dwarf-built dungeons usually have fortified surface entrances in mountainous or hilly areas. Later residents who have the means to keep the defenses in good repair usually take advantage of them.

Even small dwarf-built dungeons feature living areas with safe water supplies and storage areas for food, trade goods, and weapons. Permanent settlements usually feature temples and catacombs, heavily protected by stonework traps, magical runes, and guardian constructs such as golems.

Dragons: Dragons sometimes excavate their own subterranean lairs, but more often they move into natural caverns or force weaker residents out of dungeons they have built. A dragon-occupied dungeon will have at least one big, lofty chamber or cavern that allows the dragon to fight on the wing. Unless the dragon can teleport, its lair also will feature an entrance that the dragon can fly or swim through.

If the dragon has allies or servants, they will be housed nearby in some area where the dragon can access, such as a side cavern or surface village.

Drow: Unlike dwarves, who tend to construct dungeons from the surface down, drow build up toward the surface from the Underdark. Drow dungeons serve as jumping-off points for raiding, trade, or colonization. They usually contain only spartan living quarters. Supplies (including water) are usually stolen from the surface or carried in from the Underdark. Drow dungeons often contain holding cells for prisoners and slaves.

Halflings and Gnomes: Halflings and gnomes burrow into hillsides to create private homes, mines, or small protected communities. Both favor forest settings over hills and mountains.

Humans and Other Surface Races: Many dungeons in Faerûn are simply the lower reaches of structures built on the surface. The subterranean levels of these buildings often remain long after the main structures have been destroyed. These dungeons can be exceedingly dangerous to explore. They may prove structurally weak and prone to collapse, especially when adventurers toss around *fireball* and *lightning bolt* spells. Many of these dungeons include old catacombs, which tend to be heavily protected with traps and magical wards but contain very little treasure.

Power Groups: The various organizations and secret cabals of Faerûn construct all manner of dungeons to serve as safe houses, training centers, fortresses, and way stations for members on the move. The more active dungeon builders include the Cult of the Dragon, who are constantly seeking out sites to house new dracoliches, and the Zhentarim, who favor secret fortresses and out-of-the-way spots that contain existing *portals*.

Known Dungeons of Faerûn

Adventurers across Faerûn have taken to calling every cellar and underground passage a dungeon, even places clearly never intended or used for incarceration. Some time ago, the word came to mean any place of old stone where monsters may lurk, treasure may lie hidden or has been found, and adventurers go exploring.

By that definition, Faerûn holds thousands of dungeons, from landmarks to truly lost places remembered only in old tales and records. A very few of the most famous are listed here because of their fabled wealth, sheer size, location near cities or trade routes, notorious history, or potential importance.

Ardeep Forest: This small forest, the remnant of an elven kingdom, lies close to the bustling city of Waterdeep. Ardeep Forest's pleasant verge conceals thickly grown woods whose interior is all ridges and breakneck gullies cloaked in thick vines and shrubbery where mists are constant, wild boars roam, and ruins lie hidden. Outlaws and a few lonely elves dwell in Ardeep. The occasional owlbear, wolf, or stirge lurks here as well, but nothing worse—except the mad undead elven hero Reluraun.

Reluraun's tomb at the very heart of Ardeep is guarded by at least three baelnorns (good liches; see *Monstrous Compendium: Monsters of Faerûn*), who keep the living away. Twisted by evil magic in his final battle, Reluraun is now a mad, aggressive flying pair of skeletal hands and eyeballs. Shrieking, he hacks with a magic sword at anyone who ventures too near.

Ardeep also holds the famous Green Glade, the Dancing Dell, and some ancient tunnels and storage cellars from the days of the lost kingdom of Phalorm, some of which may still hold treasure or link with the Underdark.

The Green Glade is named because within its protective ring of elms, no matter what the season outside, conditions are always springlike. Good-aligned creatures are welcome, and healing magic used in the glade has unusually strong effects. No trail to the Glade survives for more than one night.

The Dancing Dell is a small, smooth bowl valley of soft moss, short grasses, and ferns. The Ladystone, a needle of rock sacred to Eilistraee, stands at its center. Drow who worship Eilistraee often dance in the Dell on moonlit nights, sometimes led by Qilué Veladorn of the Seven Sisters. The Ladystone's powers guard the Dell, and the goddess has been known to manifest here.

Castle Grimstead: This small, ruined keep lies in the woods of western Shadowdale, west of the River Ashaba and north of the Northride. Reduced to foundations overgrown with moss and creepers, its cellars are pierced with drow undertunnels that connect to the cellars of the Twisted Tower and descend through miles of passages to a huge subterranean lake, beyond which lies unmapped Underdark territory. The residents of Shadowdale wisely cede the castle and its associated caverns to the attention of traveling adventurers. None have deemed Grimstead's teetering walls, rotted timbers, and monster-haunted basements worth reclaiming for surface society.

Castle Krag: Jyordhan, Shadowdale's false ruler, claimed this ancient drow tower as his seat. He aimed to build the fort into a keep to rival Darkhold in the west. Fortunately for Shadowdale, Jyordhan's architectural skills were as flawed as his morals, and Castle Krag fell easily after the Zhentarim agent's death. No one has openly claimed the ruins, but occasionally a rock slams into town from the north, apparently launched by one of the old catapults within Castle Krag. Someone unknown keeps repairing the old siege engines and firing missiles into Shadowdale's outlying farms below. Few of Shadowdale's farmers are interested in rushing into Castle Krag to catch the sniper in the act.

Castle Spulzeer: Spulzeer Vale lies in eastern Amn, not far from the town of Trailstone. Elves and wild animals alike avoid the overgrown valley, even though all traces of its haunted keep, Castle Spulzeer, are now gone. There are wild legends about magical explosions, battles with liches, and a *mythal*-cloaked city visible only in moonlight. Whatever the truth of the matter, the activities (and vanishings) of local adventuring bands suggest that there's still something dangerous to be found where Castle Spulzeer once stood.

It should be noted that many other *mythal*-guarded ruins not listed here are hidden in Toril (some underground, and some underwater), and most have a better than fair chance of holding both danger and treasure.

Cavern of Death: A small "natural" network of caves in the southern Stonelands, cut by the streams that still trickle through them. The former wizard Asbaron, now a lich, guards his home against intruders with a collection of monsters brought from all over Faerûn. He's reputed to have driven off several determined Zhentarim attacks, and on several occasions unleashed monsters to roam the Stonelands and imperil Zhent patrols and caravans.

Caverns of the Claws: A notorious troll-hold in the Stonecliff (the cliff-face that adjoins the High Road, east of Eveningstar) in Cormyr. Despite repeated scourings by Purple Dragon patrols, trolls from the Stonelands lair in this simple cavern complex over and over again.

Crumbling Stair: This broken marble spiral staircase rises out of overgrown foundations on a ridge in the Sword Hills east of Waterdeep, between Ardeep Forest and Uluvin. It was once the mansion of Taeros, home to the sorcerer Ybrithe, who founded a wizards' school for young women here. Their fading spells hold aloft the fragmentary stair (which apparently leads up to nothing), where a will-o'-wisp lurks. The staircase is also haunted by a murderous ghost: a floating, glowing sword, helm, or human form.

Its other end descends into extensive underways, haunted by such apparitions as a disembodied human hand cupping a glowing selection of (sometimes whirling) gems; a dark, shadowy, and swift-gliding cowled human figure that points, beckons, or waves a sword; and a wild-eyed, finely gowned lady elf in chains, who screams soundlessly and gestures imploringly to be rescued. Their origins and purposes are unknown, but some of them lure intruders into deadly traps. The cellars are prone to ceiling collapses, and may harbor beholders.

Crypt of the Wondermakers: Located in a tavern cellar in Scornubel, this crypt is said to hold liches, along with the many magic items they collected, crafted, and now wield in undeath. Guardians under their control include helmed horrors, strange golems and other automatons, and an eater of magic (nishruu) in a stasis sphere.

Dragonspear Castle: This famous ruined fortress dominates the long, lonely run of the Trade Way south from Daggerford (past the High Moor). The once-mighty castle of the adventurer Daeros Dragonspear has become home, over the centuries, to a succession of fell beasts and monsters, from orc armies to dragons and dark fiends. Scoured out repeatedly by intrepid adventuring bands, its crumbling, plundered halls are taken as a lair by brigands or monsters, only to be cleansed again.

A decade ago, armies from Waterdeep and the other trading towns of the west mustered to purge Dragonspear of fiends who had slipped into Faerûn via a *portal* in the castle's lower levels. Priests of Tempus erected a shrine within the castle walls to keep a lid on Dragonspear's monstrous emigrants, but the shrine exists in a state of perpetual siege against bugbears, chitines, devils, drow, orcs, quaggoths, and other beings that find a way into Dragonspear through the Underdark. Adventurers who visit Dragonspear to assist the Tempuran defenders will be gratefully received and allowed any plunder they can wrest from the castle's unwelcome denizens.

Dread Lair of Alokkair: In northeastern Shadowdale, not far south of the farm of the famous Harper and adventurer Storm Silverhand, is a forest-cloaked and cave-riddled limestone cliff-face known as Fox Ridge. One of the caves in its northern face has long been reputed to be haunted, and leads to an ancient tomb. The tomb in turn connects to an underground chasm known in legend as the Grinding Gulf, beyond which is said to lie great magic. This is the abode of the lich Alokkair, Wizard-King of lost Hlontar, and although adventurers are known to have penetrated its chambers, there's great debate about the fate of Alokkair himself—even if all or most of his treasures yet lie undisturbed.

Dungeon of the Crypt: This fabled dungeon complex lies under Waterdeep's City of the Dead burial district, reached by a secret stair descending from one of the crypts. The Company of Crazed Venturers, famous adventurers of Waterdeep, spoke of battling vampires, nagas, and nasty traps, notably around a fireplace. The Dungeon of the Crypt connects underground with the uppermost level of fabled Undermountain—but since the Crazed Venturers retired from adventuring, no one else has (yet) been able to find a way into it.

Dungeon of Death: A onetime gem mine of the Deepdelve dwarven clan, this subterranean complex gained its present fell name from its use by the troll king Glarauuth as a prison for human slaves destined to become troll meals. It lies under a grassy hill just within the southern edge of the Lurkwood in the Sword Coast North, near the headwaters of Shining Creek. Glarauuth perished centuries ago, and the latest news about this locale is that "imps and fiends" have been seen atop the hill.

Dungeon of the Hark: Somewhere in the rocky ridges on the northern edge of the High Moor is a set of ruins and a subterranean stronghold used by brigands. The most recent are wererats and a mysterious bandit leader known as the Hark.

Dungeon of the Ruins: Due north of the confluence of the Rivers Rauvin and Surbrin, near Settlestone in the Sword Coast North, is a small, monster-infested subterranean complex beneath ruins that were once a school of wizardry. In ancient times, before the school was built from the shell of a dwarven keep, the dungeon was an ancient dwarf hold. Barbarians avoid the area because great froglike forms (bullywugs? slaad?) have been seen there dancing around pyres. The dungeon remains unscoured and presumably contains the bones of the Company of the Riven Orb adventuring band, who disappeared here.

Dungeon of Swords: Somewhere in the Serpent Hills due east of the High Moor lies an abandoned gnome silver mine: several underground rooms connected to a worked-out shaft. It served several adventuring parties as a home before the Cult of the Dragon found it—infested with monsters and guarded by deadly animated, flying magic swords. Still unscoured after the deaths of several Cultists, it's said to hold in its depths a one-way *portal* to the northern Evermoors.

Endless Caverns: In the High Forest, due south of the Star Mounts, a spring that joins the Unicorn Run river flows out of this large network of limestone caverns (and a few deliberately hewn linking passages) that stretches for many miles underground, ultimately connecting to the Underdark. Older than the fallen elven realm of Eaerlann, it has been home to several now-slain dragons (some of whose hidden treasure hoards may still lie in it), and more recently illithid-led drow slaver bands who mount raids into the surface realms.

Fell Pass: In the Sword Coast North, this pass between Mount Arinratha and Mount Thalangabold was the grave of an entire orc horde, slaughtered in desperate battle long years ago by the dwarves of Delzoun. It is haunted by the ghosts of that battle—and still holds the means by which the dwarves won the battle: an underground stronghold that let dwarven warriors burst forth to charge the orcs from all sides. It's said beholders and gargoyles infest these treasure-rich chambers.

Gauntlgrym: Located somewhere under the Crags south of Mirabar in the Sword Coast North, this large, ancient subterranean city was built by the dwarves of Delzoun. Its peaktop ventilation shaft was taken over by a recently vanished red dragon for its lair, and the shaft descends to at least three levels of chambers said to now be infested by many monsters, including mind flayers and ghosts. The lowest cellars of the city lead down ultimately into the Underdark—and the uppermost reaches are now home to The Hargrath, a strange, mismatched band of adventuring monsters (alaghi, a leucrotta, and the like) led by a cambion. They defend their territory against the illithids with endless monsters disgorged by deepspawn they captured and placed in strategic underground chambers.

Halls of Four Ghosts: On the western edge of the High Forest in the Sword Coast North stands the crumbling great hall of a ruined, long-abandoned dwarf hold, now haunted by the ghosts of four dwarves who beckon urgently to any dwarves approaching the ruins. Diligently exploring adventurers found an underground stronghold opening out of one side of a now-dry well shaft that descends from the hall. Home to many trolls (including giants of that race), these chambers connect via many miles of mine tunnels (used by drow and illithid slavers) to the Underdark.

Halls of the Hammer: In the northeastern High Moor, due east of Highstar Lake, is a pit quarry connected to a long-abandoned dwarf hold. Nearby stands Hammer Hall, a palisaded, long-abandoned lodge constructed by adventurers exploring the hold. Many bands have come to grief exploring the hold, which is named for a glowing, flying, animated warhammer (according to dwarven lore, it guards the hold and won't leave). Adventurers tell tales of helmed horror guardians; a huge central chamber that's sometimes full of a hundred human corpses dangling from a forest of ceiling chains and is sometimes empty; and at least five roaming watchghosts (see *Monstrous Compendium: Monsters of Faerûn*).

Haunted Halls of Eveningstar: Dug out of the rock of the western wall of Starwater Gorge just north of the farming village of Eveningstar in northern Cormyr is a former bandit hold. Dwarven stonemasons built this subterranean stronghold of orderly walls and chambers for the human bandit Rivior. After his death, various monsters used the halls as their lair. Mages settled in it and used magic to compel some monsters to be their door guards—only to be slain by other monsters or other wizards. The hauntings caused by many violent deaths over the years have given the halls their current appellation.

Recently used for caravan cargo and contraband storage by local Zhentarim agents and infested with kobolds, the Haunted Halls still lure hopeful adventurers and thrill-seekers, primarily from Cormyr and Sembia. The local temple to Lathander, the House of the Morning, provides accommodation and guides for hopeful treasure-seekers.

Heroes' Tomb: A simple network of subterranean burial chambers built by dwarves for adventurers fallen long ago, this monster-infested crypt underlies the forest-overgrown ruins of the lost village of Thruldar at the eastern end of the Lluirwood (north of Luiren). Adventurers have scoured these rooms many times in search of a legendary Crypt of the Magicians that's said to be somewhere under Thruldar, holding the bones—and all the magic—of several dead archwizards.

Hidden House: A state secret of Cormyr, this maze of ever-changing walls and passages was once the abode of the Netherese sorcerer Phaeryl. It's reached via a *portal* in the uppermost room of Tessaril's Tower in Eveningstar and has served as both a refuge and a hunting ground for foes playing deadly games of hide-and-seek. There are no maps of the Hidden House—and in the words of Elminster, "Its doors do not always open into the same rooms they did the last time ye opened them—even if that last time was but a few breaths ago."

Holdfast: This elf-constructed safehold (one of many similar lost, hidden, or forgotten hideaways scattered across Faerûn) is reached by stepping in just the right direction off the top of the Standing Stone, in Cormanthor. According to some old elves now in Ever-

meet, it's a series of *portal*-linked rooms full of stored magic and magic traps, plus a few animated guardian constructs. Adventurers who've fled it in disarray say it's now home to an undead human mage who is somehow trapped there.

House of Stone: On the east edge of the Ardeep Forest sits an immense square tower built at least a thousand years ago by dwarves and elves of Illefarn. The moon elves used to keep all outsiders away from the House of Stone, but when they left the tower became fair game.

The House of Stone contains hundreds of rooms, atriums, halls, temples, and towers locked together like the pieces of a maze. Some chambers have been shattered by long-ago battles or roof collapses, others rise and fall in shafts, and a few sport silent, hurrying armed phantoms of elves, dwarves, and humans. Not surprisingly, many rooms are now home to ghouls and shadows.

Legends speak of dwarven gold, gems, and an armory of weapons hidden here. Originally called Stoneturn, it was built to defend Stoneturn Well, still at its heart. The Stoneturn waters well up from a deep lake of the Underdark known as Asmaeringlol ("Giantgout"), and many monsters come up into the House of Stone from the Underdark to feed on adventurers.

Ironguard: This is a typical "stonedelve," one of many similar small, simple tombs, dwellings, and guard shelters cut into the rocks all over Faerûn. This particular delve in the Stonelands is guarded by magically animated flying daggers of the same sort encountered in the upper levels of Undermountain.

Lonely Tower: A tall, white tower due west of the Cold Wood in the northernmost Sword Coast North is now said to be home to a mighty wizard who has orc and elemental guardians and firmly desires no visitors. The Company of Crazed Venturers drove an earlier owner out of the tower: the evil mage Arbane and his apprentices and consorts Tantra and Werendae. The company reported that the tower has many cellars, one of which contained an eerie glowing healing pool that seemed sentient.

Lyrar's Hold: Due east of Boareskyr Bridge, on the western edge of the Forest of Wyrms, this former bandit lord's hold has lost its keep to the ravages of time (and dragons battling over a good lair-site). All that is left is an extensive underground complex of storage caverns and passages—now inevitably monster-infested.

Martek's Tomb: Somewhere in the Desert of Desolation in Raurin lies the lost tomb of Martek, Grand Vizier of Raurin, "the

the haunted halls of eveningstar

Famous this underground fortress may be, but it's more than a kobold stronghold, bandit hideaway, and longtime lair for many monsters. Through the years it's been used as a testing ground for adventurers, justice-by-peril for criminals, and even as a way fortress of the Mages-Regal.

Heard of them? Thought not. They were wizards who sought to control realms without ruling, by a judicious slaying here, the proper word there, a deft deed yonder, the casting of the right illusion in one place, and the spreading of a particular rumor in another.

Arrogant, aye, and dangerous—but that's the way of mages. There were never many Mages-Regal, and they had their feuds and battles with the malaugryms and others. Some say they created a Torilwide network of forgotten and hidden *portals*, but I suspect they simply added traps and controls to *portals* they found, the work of even older and more mysterious hands. In the Haunted Halls they left at least two operating *portals*, a deepspawn (one of those fell monsters that spew forth living beasts), and spell scrolls.

What spells? Ways to open *portals*, close *portals*, hide *portals*, and govern *portals*. Magic enough to rule all Toril, behind the thrones—just as the Mages-Regal tried to do. Some say Regals watch all who venture into the Halls, seeking the right ones to become their successors—or mind-magic-controlled pawns. Others say they're but fading dust, leaving behind a monster-roamed, kobold-infested death trap of dark passages and moldering bones that the War Wizards should have scoured out long ago.

I've walked the Halls, and I fought vicious beasts to the death and had to run from both Zhentarim using the place as a contraband shelter and Red Wizards exploring it for a lark. I say there's more than that—and not just chambers still sealed and treasure not yet found. I think something lurks in the Halls, watching—and waiting for something.

—*Brimbelve Gabror, veteran adventurer*

Greatest of Mages." Local legends speak of a pyramid, a curse that dried up a river and with it a verdant land, an oasis, temples, a city, and much magic all lying beneath the shifting sands.

Mussum: In 472 DR, this "cursed" coastal city of Chondath was abandoned to the plague so swiftly that most of its goods and belongings still lie in houses now roamed by monsters and littered with the gnawed bones of its plague-slain citizens. Few venture into the ruins today. Those who do still find the bodies of previous explorers who have died in the streets. Whatever strikes down the victims turns their skin pale green and leaves welts and abscesses all over their bodies.

Myth Drannor: See Chapter 4: Geography.

Myth Rhynn: A truly ancient *mythal*-cloaked city now abandoned to the forest, Myth Rhynn lies at the heart of the Wealdath. It was once an elven tomb city, where the dead were laid to rest with all honor (and much treasure). The magic of its *mythal* prevented animation or raising of the dead and warded off dragons, but over the passing centuries the *mythal* has decayed and now corrupts the forest around it. Moreover, some sort of flying skeletal undead being that seeks to slay all elves (and can teleport about) now dwells in Myth Rhynn, as do will-o'-wisps and possibly a lich. Adventurers report being attacked by powerful spells as they clambered through the vine-choked, tree-riven stone city. They also say many tombs have been broken open by the unhealthy-looking trees and creepers.

Nameless Dungeon: In the northeastern High Forest (near Tall Trees) stands a ruin of fallen Eaerlann, a crypt beneath a shattered and overgrown mansion. There's also a small subterranean storage complex near the mansion (not guarded by the elves, and not connected to the mansion crypt). It's said by some to be a long-abandoned dwarven or gnome dwelling.

Purple Halls: Located under a hill somewhere in Tethyr, this small subterranean stronghold has an identical twin in the Spiderhaunt Peaks north of Brightstar Lake in eastern Faerûn, linked by *portals*. The Tethyrian one gains its modern name from its use by a mercenary band known as the Purple Claw, and since their deaths in battle has become a monster-infested dungeon.

Sarbreen: The flooded, silt-choked, fallen City of the Hammer, once a jewel of the dwarven kingdom of Roldilar, lies beneath present-day Ravens Bluff (and forms much of its sewers). Secret passages descend to unknown depths beneath the old city.

Shoonach: The former seat of the evil Shoon Empire, the ruined metropolis called Shoonach is to Tethyr what Undermountain is to Waterdeep. Filled with residual magical effects from old battles, Shoonach is guarded by something like a *mythal* that prevents undead from escaping, maximizes fire magic, minimizes cold magic, slows projectiles to a crawl, and negates divine necromantic spells.

Miles upon miles of crumbling buildings and toppled walls cloak the land, studded here and there with still-active magic. Adventurers who enter Shoonach and survive to escape report seeing lamias, thousands of undead, beasts that seemed like hard-shelled lizardfolk, gnolls, goblins—and even drow, in the extensive undercity that underlies the Imperial Mount at the center of the ruins. Temples, palaces, and mighty state buildings stand more or less intact atop the high hill of the mount. Undead rule the mount now, and some of them wield wands and other magic that was formidable enough long ago, in the hands of the living.

Southkrypt: Tunneled into the southern flanks of the Sword Mountains, north of the Kryptgarden Forest in the Sword Coast North, is an abandoned dwarf hold and former silver mine. Sometimes called Southkrypt Garden because the dwarves started a farm around it of astonishing verdancy and yield (it has since grown wild and tangled), this hold is universally described as a maze of chambers and passages roamed by many, many monsters.

Spellgard (Saharelgard): On the western edge of Anauroch, due east of the Graypeak Mountains, is a labyrinthine castle-city, a vast, mold-encrusted fortress. Until recently the home of the lich Saharel, this remnant of Netheril is now the lair of various roaming monsters. A few elven adventurers who fled it recently report that its southern end holds a temple to a hawk-headed god (perhaps a self-styled "god wizard" of Netheril)—and that it's prowled by a skulking human adventurer who pounces on intruders or leads them to waiting monsters and traps.

Temple of the Splendor of Splendors: Though minstrels' tales have confusingly applied this name to several places in Faerûn, the real temple lies underground, somewhere in the Chessentan countryside. Its clergy were slain centuries ago by monsters, who then fell to fighting among themselves and were easily driven out or killed by other intruders. Later used by a thieves' guild as a headquarters and then claimed by monsters again, it has become a monster-infested dungeon once more—and the doom of many adventuring parties. The Splendor of Splendors was a magic gem (sentient due to storing the intellects of several mages) that served the deity Savras, but quite different tales of its nature have been told, and it may no longer be in the subterranean temple.

Tomb of the Archmage: At the back of a wyvern-lair cavern in the northeastern flanks of the Mountains of Tethyamar (near the headwaters of the River Tesh) lies a small labyrinth of rooms bristling with magic traps and guardians deadly enough to turn back the Knights of Myth Drannor. They found the magic-rich tomb of a long-ago archmage, but were forced to retreat before a Zhentarim onslaught—which released some formidable undead that tore apart more than three dozen battle-ready Zhentarim wizards. The tomb itself is thought to still lie undisturbed.

Undermountain: See Chapter 4: Geography.

Warlock's Crypt: Located at the mouth of the Winding Water, this is "Larloch's Crypt," its name corrupted over the centuries. Larloch the Shadow King is a lich of awesome power who rules a horrid city of wraiths, wights, liches, vampires, and lesser undead. Larloch desires nothing so much as to be left alone by the rest of the world. If anyone ventures too close to the crypt, Larloch sends lich after spell-hurling lich out to destroy them or drive them into flight. Beyond these assailants wait *spellwebs* (fields of magical force holding many waiting spells that affect intruders blundering into them), and more battle-mighty liches. Rumors say that Larloch is a survivor from the ancient kingdom of Netheril.

Warriors' Crypt: Dug into a bare rock ridge in the Stonelands north of central Cormyr is this small subterranean tomb complex. Its burials were plundered long ago, and the Zhentarim now use it as a storage cache/refuge/food resupply encampment, guarding it with several gargoyles and magically animated constructs.

Whisper's Crypt: Attached to the Haunted Halls in the Stonelands north of Eveningstar in Cormyr by a long tunnel, this underground storage area was a Zhentarim caravan way station administered by the Eveningstar Zhent agent and minor mage Whisper, who dwelt here until his death. Beyond its collapsed entry tunnel, the Crypt is said to consist of a dozen or so rooms, one of them containing Whisper's spellbooks and large collection of potions.

Local Creatures

Some locales host greater than normal concentrations of certain creatures. A few of the most notable such areas are described below.

Anauroch: Bedine humans, Netherese shades. The Bedine usually are encountered in scouting groups or patrols, both mounted on horses or camels. Bedine scouts include 1d3+1 1st-level warriors and 1d2 rangers of level 1d3+2. A Bedine patrol has 1d4+4 1st-level warriors, 1 3rd-level cleric, and 1 leader of level 1d3+3. To determine the leader's class, roll d%: 01–75, fighter; 76–85, ranger; 86–90, cleric; 91–95, sorcerer; 96–100, wizard. The Bedine can be of any good alignment.

Battle of Bones: Undead of all varieties.

Bay of Chult: Dragon turtles.

Border Forest: Dryads, pixies, satyrs, sprites.

Chondalwood: Dryads, ghostwise halflings, pixies, satyrs, sprites, wild elves.

Chult: Chuuls, dinosaurs, dwarves, goblins, human tribesfolk, wild pterafolk, yuan-ti. Less common are aarakocras, hydras, nagas, troglodytes, trolls, and wyverns. Use the information on the Bedine (in the Anauroch entry, above) for the humans and dwarves.

Cloven Mountains: Bugbears, goblins, hobgoblins, orcs.

Cold Wood: Uthgardt barbarians; use the information on the Bedine (in the Anauroch entry, above).

Cormanthor: Drow, elves.

The Deepwash: Dragon turtles, lizardfolk.

Deepwing Mountains: Griffons, hippogriffs, manticores, red dragons, wyverns.

Dragon's Run Mountains: Hill giants, stone giants, undead giants (patrols from Cairnheim in the Underdark). Use the statistics for huge zombies from the *Monster Manual*.

Dragonspine Mountains: Bugbears, goblins, hobgoblins, orcs, red dragons, and white dragons among the peaks. Stone giants, frost giants, and hill giants in lower peaks and most of the valleys.

Earthspur/Earthfast Mountains: Bugbears, drow, goblins, hobgoblins, orcs.

Evermoors: Trolls.

Flooded Forest: Assassin vines, black dragons, dark trees, lizardfolk, shambling mounds, shriekers, tendriculoses, violet fungi.

Forgotten Forest: Treants.

Forest of Wyrms: Green dragons.

Galena Mountains: Dwarves, giants, goblins. (Underdark is nearby with drow, derro, and duergar.)

Giantspires: Bugbears, hill giants, hobgoblins, ogres, stone giants.

Graycloak Hills: Elves.

Graypeak Mountains: Stone giants.

Hazuk Mountains: Stone giants.

High Forest: Centaurs, treants, wood elves.

Icelace Lake: Dire bears (on shore).

Lizard Marsh: Dinosaurs, black dragons, lizardfolk.

Long Forest: Tall mouthers, trolls.

Lonely Moor: Gnolls, leucrottas, orcs, perytons, bulettes.

Lurkwood: Orcs.

Marsh of Chelimber: Bullywugs, lizardfolk, sivs.

Mere of Dead Men: Lizardfolk, bullywugs, sivs.

Mhair Jungles: Wild dwarves.

Misty Forest: Hybsils, wood elves.

Moander's Road area: Fungi, oozes.

Moonwood: Lycanthropes (all types except werecrocodiles).

Naga flow/Naga water: Water nagas.

Peaks of Flame: Salamanders, other fire creatures.

Rauvin Mountains: Goblins, orcs.

Reaching Woods: Centaur, hybsils, satyr druids.

Serpent Hills: Copper, red, and silver dragons, snakes, yuan-ti.

Southern Lluirwood: Beholders, yuan-ti.

Spiderhaunt Woods: Chitines, ettercaps, monstrous spiders of all types.

Tashalar (Black Jungles): Yuan-ti.

Trollbark Forest: Trolls.

Trollclaws: Trolls, tall mouthers.

Troll Hills: Trolls.

Troll Mountains: Bugbears, goblins, hobgoblins, orcs, trolls.

Valley of Lost Honor: Batiri (human tribe); use the information on the Bedine (in the Anauroch entry, above). Also natural predators (lions, tigers, bears, and so on).

Wood of Sharp Teeth: Dire beasts, dragons, hydras.

Wyvernfang: Wyverns.

NPCs IN THE COMMUNITY

Wizards and sorcerers are somewhat more prevalent in Faerûn than they are assumed to be in the *DUNGEON MASTER's Guide*. On Table 4–43, Highest-Level Locals (PC Classes), treat the sorcerer entry as 1d6 + community modifier (instead of 1d4) and the wizard entry as 1d8 + community modifier (again, instead of 1d4). Just about every thorp or hamlet boasts at least one wielder of the Art, even if that person is a humble hedge wizard.

campaigns

Since its debut in 1987, the FORGOTTEN REALMS campaign setting has generated literally hundreds of FORGOTTEN REALMS novels, adventures, and supplements. The only portions of this body of material that matter are the parts you choose to incorporate into your campaign.

In preparing to run a FORGOTTEN REALMS campaign, you have several choices. First, you should consider which optional rules to allow in your game. Second, you should decide where your campaign is set. Faerûn is a big place, and your campaign can fit quite comfortably into one small corner of the continent with room to spare. Designing the particular locations, characters, and plots of your version of the FORGOTTEN REALMS campaign is covered in more detail in the next section, World-Building.

RULE 1: IT'S YOUR WORLD

This campaign setting is packed with details about Faerûn and the world of Toril, but the book provides only a broad sampling of the people, places, and things the world contains. The real details are left up to you. Make additions as you see fit. For example, if you need a village, a small town, or a dungeon in some locale to make an adventure work out right, go right ahead and add it.

Likewise, the details in this book reflect what the people of Faerûn know about their world—but only you know the truth. So if your players read this book and try to dictate details of the world for you ("No, the river runs through Silverymoon!"), stand firm. It's *your* world. Don't be a slave to the map or this book, and don't be afraid to alter anything you want to.

RULE 2: MAKE THE PCs THE STARS

Faerûn is home to numerous established characters: Drizzt Do'Urden, Elminster, Scyllua Darkhope, and Artemis Entreri, just to name a few. But Faerûn is a big place—big enough for many heroes and many stories. Your campaign should focus on your PCs, with the rest of the world and the other characters as a backdrop.

It's okay to allow your PCs to cross paths with an important NPC once in awhile (after all, these NPCs are part of what makes Faerûn a unique and colorful place), but your PCs should confront and explore the world on their own terms. When you create an adventure, create it for your PCs. Don't assume that some powerful or famous NPC is going to drop in and make things right if the heroes falter. Let your PCs handle the consequences of their own failures and reap the rewards for their own successes.

campaign locations

Faerûn is large enough to hold several campaigns at once. You can run anything from a game of courtly intrigue and politics around the throne of Calimshan to a game of barbaric riders and nomads hunting monsters on the plains of Narfell.

So where should you set your campaign? Two areas presented in this book suggest themselves: the Dalelands and the Silver Marches. These areas are thematically close to the central vision of the FORGOTTEN REALMS setting, feature many of Faerûn's signature villains and monsters, and also receive a lot of support in the form of sourcebooks, novels, and magazine articles. You can rapidly exhaust the game materials available for Narfell (not a bad thing, if you really enjoy world-building), but you'll find a wealth of adventure ideas, suggestions, and source material on the Dales and the North.

THE DALES

This area offers a fairly civilized locale where adventurers can rest safely between adventures and buy common supplies. Drow incursions into neighboring Cormanthor and pressure from the Zhentarim to the north provide a source of conflict and numerous starting points for adventures of many kinds. Entrances to the Underdark and numerous old ruins also beckon to adventurers.

The Dales are a great place to run a simple explore-the-dungeon game in which the PCs venture underground (or into the forest), then return to a nearby town to rest and reequip.

The Dales are an equally good place to set a campaign that takes advantage of many of Faerûn's ongoing stories. As mentioned earlier, the Dalesfolk are under pressure from the drow of Cormanthor and the schemes of the Zhentarim. The Dales are affected by the end of the Elven Retreat, turmoil in Cormyr, and the economic vigor of Sembia. The Moonsea and the Vast, both simmering with longstanding intrigues and rivalries, are also near.

THE SILVER MARCHES

This fairly isolated northern area has connections to the rest of Faerûn, both literally and figuratively. The great city of Waterdeep lies just down the road to the southwest. Anauroch, with its resurgent Empire of Shadows, lies to the east. Several power groups are interested in the area, including the ever-present Zhentarim, the Red Wizards, and the People of the Black Blood.

The Silver Marches is a perfect setting for a campaign with a frontier atmosphere where the PCs must be self-sufficient. Players interested in carving out personal domains for their characters will find Lady Alustriel a useful ally (and potential sovereign). Enterprising adventurers might also try their luck in the nearby Spine of the World Mountains, which are well supplied with abandoned dwarven keeps, dragon lairs, and hordes of orcs and barbarians.

OTHER AREAS

Of course, the Dales and the Silver Marches are not the only great places to set campaigns. If you crave an urban setting, it's hard to beat cosmopolitan Waterdeep. The Moonshae Isles offer a locale with a Celtic or Viking flavor. Chult in the far south could be home to a campaign featuring primitive technology (not to mention marauding dinosaurs). Calimshan and the Vilhon Reach offer settings similar to that of *The Arabian Nights*. The eastern end of the Sea of Fallen Stars has a Mediterranean or North African flavor. If you have something special in mind, you probably can find a corner of Faerûn where your campaign would fit.

WORLD-BUILDING

The country of Impiltur is shadowed by monster-infested mountains and plagued by pirate raids along the coast. Wealthy merchants scheme for influence and power over the land's throne, and mysterious ruins from sacked dwarven cities and long-vanished elven realms lie hidden in the kingdom's woodlands. A dozen great ports and trading cities offer intrigue, deception, and plots to seize power. But all these possibilities for adventure and resources for the DM take up less than two pages in this manuscript.

You can draw two conclusions from this: One, you aren't meant to play in Impiltur (the wrong conclusion). Two, if you choose to set your game in Impiltur, you have a free hand to add to the details by spinning your own intrigues and mapping out your own cities and dungeons (the right answer). Of course, doing this is a fair amount of work, but it is the single best way for you as a Dungeon Master to make the FORGOTTEN REALMS setting your campaign, not ours.

In this section, we'll examine the demographics and settlement patterns of Faerûn to help you flesh out the areas you want your players to explore at greater length.

DEMOGRAPHICS

The human states of the Heartlands range from sleepy, independent counties or cantons such as Battledale to vast empires spanning thousands of miles, such as the mighty realm of Mulhorand in the south. In Faerûn, a single powerful individual—an archmage, for instance—can wield more power than an entire army. Tiny states that might be absorbed by larger and more aggressive neighbors frequently remain free because a single individual, a dangerous guild, or an interested deity does not wish to see the smaller realm swallowed up. This leads to a patchwork of cities, realms, and frontiers impossible to explain in a few sweeping generalizations.

Nonhuman realms can generally be described in similar terms. The lands of dwarves, elves, orcs, or goblins are best described as small and reclusive kingdoms or city-states. With some exceptions (the Great Rift of the gold dwarves, Evermeet of the elves), few nonhuman states grow to the size and power of a human land such as Cormyr or Damara.

The community size guidelines in Chapter 6 of the *DUNGEON MASTER's Guide* apply to most areas of Faerûn.

FRONTIERS

Vast portions of the North, the Western Heartlands, the lands about the Moonsea, the Cold Lands, and the Unapproachable East are frontier—territory unclaimed by any state capable of enforcing its laws or desires there. Human settlements are thorps and villages isolated by vast tracts of virgin forest or impassable mountains, with the occasional small town rising in a place where rivers and roads meet or where a particular resource attracts those who would exploit it. Companies or governments of more civilized regions sponsor some of these settlements. For example, the town of White Horn beyond the Tortured Land is really nothing more than a Zhent mining camp.

In areas that humans regard as untamed frontier, nonhumans frequently outnumber humans. The orc and goblin hordes of the Spine of the World, the Galena Mountains, or the Earthspurs terrorize the thinly settled lands surrounding these humanoid strongholds. The wood elf realm of the High Forest is a far stronger and more well organized state than any human land for hundreds of miles about.

- Frontiers average one town for every 2,000 square miles or so (a region 40 miles by 50 miles in extent).
- The next town is 2d20+20 miles away, through uncharted wilderness.
- In frontier regions, apply a −20% modifier to the roll on Table 4-40: Random Town Generation in the *DUNGEON MASTER's Guide*.

CANTONS OR FREE CITIES

Isolated independent cities, counties, or regions are fairly common in Faerûn. A canton is a small, independent rural region, usually centered on a handful of large villages or small towns. A free city is the same thing, consisting of a small city and its immediate area. Unlike a true city-state, a free city has little ability to exert power abroad, but cantons and free cities have been known to resist the aggression of larger states with tenacity and determination.

The best examples of cantons in Faerûn are the Dalelands. They're not really frontier lands, and most aren't city-states—they're somewhere in between. Many nonhuman realms might be considered cantons or free cities, too. A gnome village with a few miles of wilderness around it, a dwarven fortress, or the dismal caverns, rifts, and high clefts of a small mountain orc tribe all fall under this category.

- Cantons average one town for every 500 square miles or so (a region 20 miles by 25 miles in extent).
- The next town is 2d10+10 miles away, through sparsely settled farmlands, light woods, and rangeland.
- A free city has at least one large town or small city. Apply a –15% modifier to the roll on Table 4–40: Random Town Generation in the *Dungeon Master's Guide* for all other towns in the free city's borders, and all towns in cantons.

CITY-STATES

Dozens of strong, independent city-states exist throughout the Heartlands. Most are trading powers that grew up around cities at the great crossroads of Faerûn—along the navigable rivers or beside the best harbors with access to the interior. Unlike a smaller free city, a city-state is in a lot of ways a one-city kingdom, often controlling the land for dozens, if not hundreds, of miles around. The city is large and strong enough to support armies far from home or dictate trade terms, treaties, and other concessions to other states.

On the Sword Coast, the city of Waterdeep is an outstanding example of an exceptionally powerful city-state. Most of the land within a hundred miles of the city is subject to the will of the Lords of Waterdeep. On the Inner Sea, Westgate is a more sinister city whose power shapes the Dragon Coast.

- City-states average one town for every 150 square miles or so (a region 15 miles by 10 miles in extent).
- The next town is 2d6+6 miles away, through densely settled farmlands.
- A city-state has at least one large city. Apply a –10% modifier to the roll on Table 4–40: Random Town Generation the *Dungeon Master's Guide* for all other towns within the city-state's borders.

KINGDOMS AND EMPIRES

A kingdom is a single political entity generally incorporating a number of cities and towns and claiming an area at least a hundred square miles or more in extent. Anything smaller is better described as a canton, although much larger kingdoms are not uncommon. A kingdom stops being a kingdom and starts being an empire when it includes lesser, subject realms that are ruled by the central power.

The terms kingdom and empire are somewhat misleading, because not all states of this size are monarchies. Sembia is a very powerful land ruled by an oligarchy of merchant princes, but for purposes of this discussion it's a kingdom because it includes a dozen or so major cities and shares a common culture, language, and government.

The best example of a kingdom in the Heartlands of Faerûn is Cormyr, a powerful and civilized land now fallen on hard times. More empires now lie in the past than exist today, each undone by magical folly or the simple tide of change. Mulhorand is the best example of a surviving empire, since it holds (however tentatively) the states of Murghôm, Semphar, and most of Unther as subject territories.

- Kingdoms and empires average one town for every 150 square miles or so (a region 15 miles by 10 miles in extent).
- The next town is 2d6+6 miles away, through moderately settled farmlands.

faerûnian creatures

The following creatures referenced in this book can be found in the *Monster Compendium: Monsters of Faerûn* product: aarakocra, air genasi (planetouched), alaghi, alhoon (illithilich), asabi, baelnorn (lich, good), brown dragon, bullywug, chitine, crawling claw, dark tree, darkenbeast, deep bat, deep dragon, deepspawn, dragonkin, duergar (gray dwarf), earth genasi (planetouched), eyeball behold-erkin, fang dragon, fey'ri, fire genasi (planetouched), gold dwarf, green warder, helmed horror, hybsil, ibrandlin, leucrotta, lythari, malaugrym, nishruu, nyth, peryton, phaerimm, pterafolk, quag-goth, shadow dragon, sharn, shield dwarf, siv, song dragon, spectral harpist, tall mouther, tiefling (planetouched), tomb tapper, watchghost, water genasi (planetouched), wemic, werecrocodile, wereshark, wild dwarf, yuan-ti.

rewards

Most of the rules in Chapter 7 of the *Dungeon Master's Guide* apply to campaigns set in Faerûn. Some adjustments and changes are required, as noted below. In addition to the "hard" rewards of experience and treasure, the FORGOTTEN REALMS setting is a great place for softer rewards such as the patronage of a powerful NPC, the gifting of lands and titles, or the chance to join elite organizations such as the Harpers. Many players enjoy having their characters earn a title or a favor even more than discovering wealth that could more directly contribute to their characters' power.

awarding experience

When making a standard XP award, use the procedure outlined below. This differs from the *Dungeon Master's Guide* in that it tends not to reward powerful characters adventuring with weak parties, since the party level is not averaged before determining experience awards.

1. Determine each character's level. Don't forget to account for effective character level if any of the characters are of a powerful race.
2. For each monster defeated, determine that single monster's Challenge Rating.
3. Use Table 7–1: Experience Point Awards (Single Monster) in the *Dungeon Master's Guide* to cross-reference one character's level with the Challenge Rating for each defeated monster to find the base XP award.
4. Divide the base XP award by the number of characters in the party. This is the amount of XP that character receives for helping defeat that monster.
5. Add up the XP awards for all the monsters the character helped defeat.
6. Repeat the process for each character.

Example: A party of five PCs defeats two ogres and their pet hell hound. The characters include a 4th-level human ranger, a 3rd-level drow paladin, a 3rd-level air genasi wizard, a 4th-level strongheart halfling rogue, and a half-elf fighter/ranger of level 2/1.

The human ranger is 4th level. The ogres have Challenge Ratings of 2 and the hell hound has a Challenge Rating of 3.

According to the table, a party of 4th-level characters should earn 600 XP for defeating an ogre and 800 XP for defeating the hell hound. Because there were five characters, the ranger gets 120 XP (600 ÷ 5 = 120) for each ogre and 160 XP (800 ÷ 5 = 160) for a total of 400 XP (120 + 120 + 160 = 400).

The drow paladin has an effective level of 5th (because drow add +2 to their character level to determine their effective character level). According to the table, 5th-level characters receive 500 XP for each CL 2 ogre and 750 XP for the CL 3 hell hound. The paladin gets 100 XP (500 ÷ 5 = 100) for each ogre and 150 XP (750 ÷ 5 = 150) for the hell hound, for a total of 350 XP (100 + 100 + 150 = 350).

The genasi is effectively 4th level (because genasi add +1 to their character level to determine their effective character level), so the genasi gets the same XP award as the ranger.

The rogue also is 4th level, and receives the same XP award as the ranger.

The fighter/ranger is only 3rd level. Each ogre is still worth 600 XP to a party of 3rd-level characters, but the hell hound is worth 900 XP instead of 800 XP. The half-elf earns 120 XP for each ogre, and 180 XP (one-fifth of 900) for the hell hound, for a total of 420 XP.

Gems of Faerûn

Table 8–3: Gems, below, replaces Table 7–5 in the *Dungeon Master's Guide*. It includes a wider variety of stones, some unique to Faerûn. Some stones are described after the table.

TABLE 8–3: GEMS

d%	Value	Average Value
01–25	4d4 gp	10 gp

Examples: azurite, agate (banded, eye, fire, moss, or tiger eye), blue quartz, crown of silver, fluorspar, freshwater pearl, greenstone, hematite, hyaline, ivory, lapis lazuli, malachite, nelvine, obsidian, rhodochrosite, sanidine, turquoise, violine

d%	Value	Average Value
26–50	2d4×10 gp	50 gp

Examples: andar, aventurine, bloodstone, carnelian, chalcedony, chrysoprase, citrine, hydrophane, iol, iolite, irtios, jasper, moonstone, onyx, orprase, peridot, phenalope, quartz (rock crystal, rose, smoky, or star rose), sard, sardonyx, spodumene, tchazar, zircon

d%	Value	Average Value
51–70	4d4×10 gp	100 gp

Examples: amber, amethyst, angelar's skin, chrysoberyl, coral, garnet (red or brown-green), jade, jet, Laeral's tears, spinel (red, red-brown, or deep green), pearl (golden, pink, silver, or white), tourmaline (white, golden, pink, or silver pearl), waterstar

d%	Value	Average Value
71–90	2d4×100 gp	500 gp

Examples: alexandrite, aquamarine, black pearl, deep blue spinel, golden yellow topaz, violet garnet

d%	Value	Average Value
91–99	4d4×100 gp	1,000 gp

Examples: corundum (fiery yellow, rich purple, black, or blue), emerald, opal (black, fire, water, or white), orl, ravenar, red tears, sapphire, star ruby, star sapphire (black or blue), tomb jade

d%	Value	Average Value
100	2d4×1,000 gp	5,000 gp

Examples: beljuril, clearest bright green emerald, diamond (blue, blue-white, brown, canary, or pink), jacinth, king's tears, ruby

Alexandrite: Favored for focal use in items of magic that confer good luck, favor, or protection.

Amber: Often used as a good luck charm to ward off diseases and plague.

Amethyst: Rumored to ward off drunkenness and convert poisons to harmless substances (folk belief).

Andar: Green-red or brown-red, translucent, durable.

Angelar's Skin: Fine pink coral, opaque, delicate.

Aventurine: Golden, medium to light green, or dark to pale blue, spangled with mica crystals, sometimes called love stone.

Banded Agate: Used as as "soothe stones" that merchants handle to relieve tension during negotiations.

Beljuril: Seawater green, periodically blazing with a sparkling, winking, flashing light, also known as fireflashils, durable and very hard.

Bloodstone: Dark green-gray quartz flecked with red crystal impurities that resemble drops of blood.

Blue Quartz: Favored jewels for *gems of seeing*.

Chalcedony: Used to make magical items that ward against undead.

Crown of Silver: Silver chalcedony with brilliant metallic black bands.

Emerald: Used in spell ink formulae, as a spell component, and in items concerned with fertility, health, and growth.

Fire Agate: Translucent, iridescent red, brown, gold, and green chalcedony.

Fire Opal: Favored in *helms of brilliance*.

Fluorspar: Pale blue, green, yellow, purple, pink, red (gemstones), purple-and-white banded (carving).

Garnet: In folktales, garnets are the hardened blood of divine avatars.

Greenstone: Gray-green, soft, used in *greenstone amulets*.

Hematite: Prized by fighters, often used in magical periapts.

Hyaline: Milky (or white) quartz, often flecked with gold.

Hydrophane: Frosty-white or ivory opal, opaque, used in water-oriented items.

Iol: Color-changing straw-yellow, blue, and dark blue, sometimes with an internal star effect, strong associations with magic in Faerûnian legend.

Irtios: Colorless or very pale yellow, hard, translucent crystals, often found on sword scabbards and wizards' staves.

Ivory: White substance that comprises mammal teeth or tusks, carved and polished. Unicorn horns are technically not ivory, since they are not teeth. It should also be noted that unicorn horns are not used for ornamental carving and that they command prices of thousands of gold pieces from alchemists. On a cautionary note, certain Faerûnian religions—especially followers of Mielikki and Lurue the Unicorn—take great exception to people hunting unicorns for their horns. They have even been known to put to death people convicted of the evil act of killing unicorns.

Jacinth: Fiery orange jewel also called hyacinth or flamegem, the true corundum jacinth is found only in Faerûn.

Jade: Said to enhance musical ability and worn as a lucky stone by musicians.

Jet: The stone of mourning and sorrow in wealthy cities.

Kings' Tears: Clear, teardrop-shaped, smooth-surfaced, and awesomely hard, sometimes called frozen tears or lich weepings, very rare.

Laeral's Tears: Large colorless, crystalline, soft, brittle stones named for the famous sorcerer Laeral.

Lapis Lazuli: Dark to sky-blue with gold flecks, opaque.

Malachite: Used as jewelry among poorer folk.

Moonstone: Used in magic items that control lycanthropy, affect lycanthropes, or protect against lycanthropy, considered sacred to Selûne.

Moss Agate: Said to promote serenity and stability.

Nelvine: White, cream, fawn, or brown-pink feldspar with celestial blue iridescence, soft and fragile.

Obsidian: Can be chipped into arrowheads or weapons.

Opal: Used in a number of magic items and spells.

Orl: Red (most valued), tawny, or orange crystals.

Orprase: Colorless or faintly straw-yellow, brittle, medium hardness, popular with followers of Tymora.

Peridot: Used in items that provide protection against spells and enchantments.

Phenalope: Rose-red or pink, said to protect against magical flame.

Ravenar: Glossy black tourmaline, mainly valued in the North.

Red Tears: Vivid cherry-red, blood-crimson, or fiery orange crystals also called *Tempus's weeping*, legends say they are the tears of lovers shed for their beloveds who were slain in battle.

Rock Crystal: Used for optics and prisms.

Ruby: Held as lucky objects in folklore.

Sanidine: Pale tan to straw yellow feldspar, favorite of the Bedine.

Sapphire: Widely used in the making of magic swords and other magic items, especially those related to magical prowess, the mind, and the element of air.

Sardonyx: Used in spells and in creating magic items that affect wisdom.

Smoky Quartz: Black variety called morion and used by necromancers.

Spodumene: Pink-to-purple gem also known as ghost stone because its color fades with the time.

Star Sapphire: Used in devices that offer protection against hostile magic.

Tchazar: Fragile, soft, straw-yellow gemstone.

Tiger Eye Agate: Golden agate with dark brown striping, legends state that nonmagical tiger eyes are useful in repelling spirits and undead creatures.

Tomb Jade: Rare, highly prized jade that has turned red or brown through being buried for great lengths of time.

Topaz: Often mounted on protective magic items, the preferred jewel in the making of a *gem of brightness*.

Turquoise: Prized by elves for use in sky-related spells, mages use turquoises in the creation of items concerned with flight.

Violine: Purple volcanic gemstone.

Water Opal: Clear, translucent variety of opal used as ornaments around mirrors and windows or in the crafting of magical scrying devices (such as *crystal balls*).

Waterstar: Colorless, rare tourmaline.

Zircon: Occasionally passed off as more valuable gemstones (Appraise check DC 10).

scrolls

The following two tables are provided for DMs who want to randomly generate scrolls of spells described in this book (see Chapter 2: Magic). To include these scrolls in any random generation of magic items, refer to Table 8–2 in the *DUNGEON MASTER's Guide* and divide the "Scrolls" line into two parts:

Minor	Medium	Major	
47–64	51–58	46–50	Scrolls
65–81	59–66	51–55	Faerûnian scrolls

The numbers above give an equal chance of generating a regular scroll (of spells found in the *DUNGEON MASTER's Guide*) or a Faerûnian scroll. If you want the chance for a Faerûnian scroll to be higher or lower, adjust both sets of numbers accordingly.

Follow the process outlined in Chapter 8 of the *DUNGEON MASTER's Guide* to see whether the Faerûnian scroll is arcane or divine and what levels of spells it contains. Then use one of the following tables to determine the spells a scroll contains.

TABLE 8–4: ARCANE SPELL SCROLLS

Minor	Medium	Major	Spell (Level)	Market Price
01–15	—	—	*Scatterspray* (1st)	25 gp
16–30	01–02	—	*Aganazzar's scorcher* (2nd)	150 gp
31–35	03–04	—	*Claws of darkness* (2nd)	150 gp
36–38	05–06	—	*Create magic tattoo* (2nd)	150 gp
39–48	07–08	—	*Eagle's splendor* (2nd)	150 gp
49–63	09–10	—	*Shadow mask* (2nd)	150 gp
64–70	11–12	—	*Shadow spray* (2nd)	150 gp
71–85	13–14	—	*Snilloc's snowball swarm* (2nd)	150 gp
86–90	15–30	01	*Analyze portal* (3rd)	375 gp
91–95	31–40	02	*Blacklight* (3rd)	375 gp
96–100	41–50	03	*Flashburst* (3rd)	375 gp
—	51–70	04–24	*Fire stride* (4th)	700 gp
—	71–90	25–44	*Thunderlance* (4th)	700 gp
—	91–95	45–60	*Grimwald's graymantle* (5th)	1,125 gp
—	96–100	61–75	*Lesser ironguard* (5th)	1,125 gp
—	—	76–89	*Gateseal* (6th)	1,700 gp
—	—	90–94	*Flensing* (8th)	3,000 gp
—	—	95–99	*Great shout* (8th)	3,000 gp
—	—	100	*Elminster's evasion* (9th)	28,825 gp

TABLE 8–5: DIVINE SPELL SCROLLS

Minor	Medium	Major	Spell (Level)	Market Price
01–25	—	—	*Cloak of dark power* (1st)	25 gp
26–34	01–02	—	*Analyze portal* (2nd)	150 gp
35–56	03–04	—	*Gembomb* (2nd)	150 gp
57–85	05–06	—	*Moonbeam* (2nd)	150 gp
86–90	07–25	—	*Anyspell* (3rd)	375 gp
91–95	26–45	—	*Eagle's splendor* (3rd)	375 gp
96–100	46–65	—	*Moon blade* (2nd)	375 gp
—	66–70	01–05	*Armor of darkness* (4th)	700 gp
—	71–80	06–20	*Darkbolt* (5th)	1,125 gp
—	81–90	21–35	*Moon path* (5th)	1,125 gp
—	91–100	36–45	*Spiderform* (5th)	1,125 gp
—	—	46–50	*Fantastic machine* (6th)	1,650 gp
—	—	51–60	*Gateseal* (6th)	1,700 gp
—	—	61–70	*Greater anyspell* (6th)	1,650 gp
—	—	71–75	*Spider curse* (6th)	1,650 gp
—	—	76–80	*Maw of stone* (7th)	2,275 gp
—	—	81–85	*Stone spiders* (7th)	2,275 gp
—	—	86–90	*Waterspout* (7th)	2,275 gp
—	—	91–94	*Maelstrom* (8th)	3,000 gp
—	—	95–96	*Greater fantastic machine* (9th)	3,825 gp
—	—	97–98	*Moonfire* (9th)	3,825 gp
—	—	99–100	*Spider shapes* (9th)	3,825 gp

*Found only as a domain spell and not usable by divine spellcasters who do not have access to that domain.

Green Bones

Character Hooks

- Having been tricked by the dragon or her minions into acquiring treasure only to have it stolen, the adventurers seeking their lost loot have at last found her lair.
- The adventurers have been directed by one of the dragon's minions to the lair under the assumption that the dragon is weak, young, or otherwise not much of a threat compared to the potential rewards.
- The heroes have encountered the dragon while she was patrolling or consorting with one of her minions and have followed her back to her lair.

Encounters

The main event in this adventure is the assault on the dracolich's lair, which is depicted in the map on page 305. The following descriptions are keyed to locations on the map.

A. Observation Posts

Signs of habitation mark this small cave, with many footprints and a small pile of thick furs that might be used as a chair. The altitude of the opening is higher than the tree line, which gives a good view of the nearby land.

These two caves are occasionally used by the medusas or werewolves as observation posts.

1. Entrance

The natural earthen ramp that leads to this cave opening continues for another 30 feet before apparently merging with the hillside. The cave itself is over 10 feet wide and slopes downward after a few paces.

The cavern entrance is about 30 feet above the level of the ground and smells faintly of predatory animals. There are enough tracks on the earth and soft ground that anyone can spot multiple wolf tracks if they look hard enough (Search DC 10). A character with the Track feat can detect (Search DC 17) a few faint human bootprints in this area, no more than three days old.

Encounter Levels

Green Bones is an adventure site for four characters of about 16th level. The number of minions in the lair can be increased or decreased to accommodate a weaker or stronger adventuring party.

Adventure Background

Eight years ago, the green dragon Azurphax was attacked in her lair by a group of powerful dragonslayers. They drove her off and stole a large portion of her loot. When they returned for more, she was better prepared and succeeded in slaying them, although greatly wounded. The Cult of the Dragon heard of the attacks and offered her immortality and treasure. In her weakened state, she accepted and was transformed into a dracolich.

Since her transformation, she has been a reluctant ally of the Cult, preferring to go her own way and work on rebuilding her hoard and strengthening her defenses. She has subdued or enslaved several local creatures and has a few servants who act as her agents beyond the forest. The dragon's agents plant rumors about a dragon's hoard among the foolish and investigate tales about caches of treasures within her forest that she might plunder. The heroes can become involved through these agents, dealing with traps and monsters only to be attacked and robbed (possibly by the dragon herself) when they emerge from a dungeon. Eventually the heroes can learn where the dragon actually lairs and plan an attack upon her home.

In this adventure, the heroes explore the lair of an adult green dragon named Azurphax, who has been transformed into a dracolich. She is served by living and undead minions and slaves. Azurphax has several contacts in far parts of the world and is always looking for ways to expand her wealth and control over the forest that surrounds her well-defended lair.

2. FIERY HALLWAY

> This part of the tunnel is scorched on the ground and the lower part of the walls.

Any character who closely examines the floor (Search DC 20) detects a very faint residue, left from alchemist's fire (Intelligence or Alchemy DC 15 to recognize the residue).

Trap: A tripwire just above the floor in this area leads to a false ceiling that supports eight flasks of alchemist's fire. When the trap is triggered, the ceiling pops open, spilling the flasks into a 5-foot-by-10-foot area. Each creature within the target area is attacked by up to two flasks. Any flasks that don't hit targets crash to the floor for splash damage. All creatures within 5 feet of a targeted square (including those in the other targeted squares) take splash damage. Any direct hits burn the next round for the same damage.

↗**Alchemist's Fire:** CR 4; +10 ranged touch (1d6 fire per flask, splash 1 fire); Search (DC 20); Disable Device (DC 20).

Development: If this trap is triggered, the noise from it and the reactions of the target creatures is sufficient to alert creatures in areas 3 and 4, if any (Listen DC −5 and 3, respectively). Light in this area alerts any creature in area 3.

3. WOLF DEN

> This area smells of dog and spilled blood. The earth has been dug up in a few places to make simple bed for animals. A small pile of bones stands in the western end of the room.

This room is used as a lair by the werewolves when in wolf form and also as a place where prey animals are skinned and cleaned. There is a 25% chance that one of the werewolves is resting here. Otherwise, the room is empty. The bones are all those of animals.

4. COMPLEX ACID TRAP

> The ceiling of the narrow cave lowers to little more than 5 feet above the stony floor, but the tunnel continues to slope downward, leveling off about 20 feet ahead and turning to the right.

The ceiling above this area is actually an *illusory wall*, which conceals a small cubbyhole containing a number of acid flasks and thunderstones supported by a slender framework of thin wooden poles. This part of the trap is activated by the *glyph of warding* (see below) on the floor.

Trap: The floor is guarded by a *glyph* triggered by any nonevil creature that enters the area. The blast ignites the wooden poles above the illusory ceiling, causing them to burn through on the round after the *glyph* is triggered, releasing the thunderstones and flasks of acid. Eight flasks of acid and four thunderstones are distributed evenly over a 5-foot-by-10-foot area across the corridor. All creatures within 5 feet of a targeted square (including creatures in the other targeted square) take splash damage from the acid, and all creatures within 10 feet of the targeted squares must save against the thunderstones. The noise of the thunderstones is loud enough to alert everyone within the lair and anything within 1,000 feet of it.

↗**Glyph of Warding:** CR 4; 5-ft. fire blast (5d8); Reflex half (DC 16); Search (DC 28); Disable Device (DC 28).

↗**Acid Flask and Thunderstone Trap:** CR 8; +5 ranged touch (1d6 acid per flask, 1 acid splash); sonic attack (Fortitude save DC

15 for each thunderstone); Search (DC 20, possible only if searcher first succeeds at a DC 17 Will save against illusory wall in ceiling); Disable Device (DC 28)

5. DRIED DEPRESSION

> The floor of this area is smooth and slightly sunken, with many stains from varying water levels within this now-dry pool.

The trap in area 4 formerly released a great deal more acid, which tended to rush downhill and pool here, making it too difficult for the other denizens of the lair to get in and out. Someone with knowledge of alchemy or stoneworking can recognize (Alchemy or Craft DC 15) that the floor has been smoothed by acid, with the effect lessening uphill toward the entrance.

6. WEREWOLF LAIR

> Glowing coals in a firepit provide dim illumination for this room. Five piles of straw and furs mark this as a sleeping area. A bow and several hunting spears are near each bed, watched over by wolf-women.

The women are the werewolf guardians of Azurphax's lair, who also acquire food for those living here and interact with rural settlements and other isolated creatures on behalf of the dracolich. They verbally threaten anyone who tries to enter their room, warning visitors away. If the unwelcome guests don't leave, two of them fire bows while the others enter melee. On the second round, the remaining werewolves enter melee. The lycanthropes are all siblings and are loyal to each other. They have fought together often and take advantage of flanking and their trip ability if possible. Noise from combat in this area alerts the cleric in area 7 and the inhabitants of areas 9 and 10. The tunnel in the northwest is covered by an *illusory wall*.

Creatures (EL 11): Werewolf Rgr4 (5).

➤**Female Werewolves Rgr4 (hybrid or animal form):** CR 6; Medium-size shapechanger; HD 4d10+8; hp 34, 29, 31, 38, 43; Init +6; Spd 50 ft.; AC 14 (touch 12, flat-footed 12) as wolf or hybrid; Atk +6 melee (1d6+3, bite) or +7 melee (1d6+3/×3, masterwork half-spear) or +7 ranged (1d6+2/×3, masterwork halfspear); SA Curse of lycanthropy, fight with two weapons, trip; SQ Alternate form, damage reduction 15/silver, favored enemy +1 (humans), scent, wolf empathy; AL CE; SV Fort +11, Ref +4, Will +4; Str 14, Dex 15, Con 15, Int 10, Wis 10, Cha 10 (in wolf or hybrid forms).

Skills and Feats: Hide +9, Listen +17, Move Silently +9, Search +8, Spot +17, Wilderness Lore +7*; Alertness, Blind-Fight, Great Fortitude, Improved Control Shape, Improved Initiative, Track, Weapon Finesse (bite). *+4 racial bonus on Wilderness Lore checks when tracking by scent.

Special Attacks: Curse of Lycanthropy (Su): Any humanoid hit by a lycanthrope's bite attack in animal form must succeed at a Fortitude save (DC 15) or contract lycanthropy. Trip (Ex): A werewolf that hits with a bite attack can attempt to trip the opponent as a free action (see Chapter 8 of the *Player's Handbook*) without making a touch attack or provoking an attack of opportunity, or leaving herself open to a trip if the attempt fails.

Possessions (each): Hide armor (not worn), masterwork halfspear, *potion of healing, cloak of resistance +1*, gem (100 gp amethyst), 70 gp.

7. CLERIC'S CHAMBER

> This sparsely decorated chamber has only a simple bed, desk, and three-legged stool. A hooded lantern burns on the desk.

The lantern burns with a *continual flame*. This is the residence of Varlae, the Cult of the Dragon ally of Azurphax. A cleric of Bane, she serves as the Cult's liaison to the dracolich and as an agent of the creature in the more civilized areas. In her spare time she checks on the *glyphs of warding* she creates, works with Azurphax to think up more traps, and writes poems glorifying Bane.

Creatures (EL 11): Varlae (Clr11 of Bane).

Tactics: Since she probably has been alerted by the thunderstones in area 4 or fighting in area 6, Varlae has prepared herself for an upcoming battle, passing through the *illusory wall* in the hallway near her door. Her preparations include donning her armor, drinking her *potion of fly*, using her scroll of *protection from elements: acid*, and casting *deathwatch* and *spell immunity* (*fireball*, *lightning bolt*). She waits with her face and hands showing through the *illusory wall* (so she stands in the 5-foot-wide space between the *illusory wall* and the glyph trap in area 8), casting spells or using her wand until discovered. Detecting her is possible with a Spot check (DC 20), although range may limit the heroes' ability to see her (she is at least 50 feet away from area 6, putting her out of range of torchlight or even low-light vision with torchlight).

Once spotted by her opponents, she flies toward area 9, first attacking from darkness anyone who succumbs to the trap in area 8. Then she lurks in the upper portions of area 9, using her wand and spells to attack targets from the darkness while they fight the dragon. If forced to flee, she passes through the *illusory walls* (areas 11) in that chamber, healing herself and either returning via the other end of the loop or through the secret tunnel to her bedchamber.

Treasure: Paper, writing supplies, treasure chest (in secret tunnel) trapped by fire blast glyph (contains 500 gp).

⚡ **Glyph of Warding** (on chest): CR 4; 5-ft. fire blast (5d8); Reflex half (DC 16); Search (DC 28); Disable Device (DC 28).

🗡 **Varlae:** Female human Clr11 of Bane; CR 11; Medium-size humanoid (human); HD 11d8+33; hp 82; Init +4; Spd 20 ft.; AC 19 (touch 10, flat-footed 19); Atk +11/+6 melee (1d4+3, *+2 spiked gauntlet*) or +10 ranged (1d8/19–20, masterwork crossbow and masterwork bolt); SA Rebuke undead 4/day, convert spells to *inflict* spells; AL LE; SV Fort +10, Ref +5, Will +10; Str 13, Dex 10, Con 14, Int 10, Wis 17, Cha 12. Height 5 ft. 6 in.

Skills and Feats: Alchemy +4, Concentration +16, Heal +8, Knowledge (arcana) +5, Knowledge (religion) +5, Spellcraft +6; Brew Potion, Craft Wand, Improved Initiative, Lightning Reflexes, Scribe Scroll.

Spells Prepared (6/7/6/6/4/3/2; base DC = 13 + spell level): 0—*create water, cure minor wounds, detect magic, light, purify food and drink, read magic*; 1st—*bane, deathwatch, doom*, entropic shield, obscuring mist, sanctuary, shield of faith*; 2nd—*darkness, desecrate, endurance, scare*, silence, spiritual weapon*; 3rd—*animate dead, bestow curse*, dispel magic, invisibility purge, meld into stone, prayer*; 4th—*dismissal, emotion* (hate)*, *spell immunity, summon monster IV*; 5th—*circle of doom, greater command*, insect plague*; 6th—*blade barrier, geas/quest**.

*Domain spell. Domains: Hatred (+2 profane bonus on attack rolls, saving throws, and armor class against one opponent of her choice for 1 minute, 1/day), Tyranny (compulsion spells add +2 DC to targets' saving throws).

Possessions: *+1 full plate, +2 spiked gauntlet*, masterwork light crossbow, 10 masterwork bolts, *amulet of health +2, wand of cure serious wounds* (10 charges), *wand of hold person* (10 charges),

scrolls (*heal, harm, neutralize poison, protection from elements, raise dead*), *potion of fly*, holy symbol.

8. COMPLEX TANGLEFOOT TRAP

> The walls of the hallway grow rough, with many ridges for easy climbing and odd globular protuberances, as if the stone has run like hot wax in its history. The hallway broadens and continues roughly to the west, the ceiling rising quickly.

The descriptive text assumes the characters are coming from the east toward area 9. The ridges are actually thin wooden dowels. The globules are tanglefoot bags or clay hemispheres containing alchemist's fire. All have been bound together with string and painted to look like stone. Recognizing the deception requires a Spot check (DC 15). All these are part of a trap activated by the *glyph of warding* in this area.

Trap: The floor is guarded by a *glyph* triggered by any nonevil creature that enters the area. The blast ignites the wooden poles and the string, causing the alchemist's fire and tanglefoot bags to be hurled about on that same round. When the trap is sprung, six flasks of alchemist's fire and six tanglefoot bags are divided evenly among the three squares warded by the *glyph*. All creatures within 5 feet of the alchemist's fire take splash damage, including those directly affected by a different flask. Anyone glued to the floor by a tanglefoot bag is unable to roll on the ground to extinguish any fires. The noise of this trap is sufficient to alert creatures in areas 3, 6, 9, and 10.

⚡ **Glyph of Warding:** CR 4; 5-ft. fire blast (5d8); Reflex half (DC 16); Search (DC 28); Disable Device (DC 28).

⚡ **Alchemist's Fire and Tanglefoot Bag Trap:** CR 6; +5 ranged touch (1d6 fire per flask, 1 fire splash); entangle (Reflex save DC 15 if tanglefoot bag hits); Search (DC 20); Disable Device (DC 28).

9. LARGE CHAMBER (EL 16)

> The ceiling of this large chamber is 20 feet high at the entrances and slopes sharply upward into the darkness overhead. In the distance can be seen two large stone pillars, one of which has a large reptilian skeleton curled in front of it. The room reeks of acrid chemicals, and the floor and walls nearby have been artificially smoothed as if scoured by heat or acid.

The ceiling quickly reaches 50 feet in height, and near the middle of the pool of water (area 10) it approaches 70 feet. Six skeletons of large lizards are in the room, all animated and under the control of the dracolich. However, she prefers to leave them where they are, to distract foes who would use *detect undead* or try to turn them. Only the skeleton by the pillar has wings (it is the dead body of a minor rival), all others being merely giant lizards.

The entire room (as well as area 10, the pool) is warded by an *unhallow* spell, giving a –4 profane penalty on all turning checks and filling the entire area with a *magic circle against good* effect, which gives all evil creatures within it a +2 deflection bonus to AC and a +2 resistance bonus on saves. The *magic circle* effect also prevents good outsiders from entering or being conjured into the warded area.

In the northeast portion of the room are two *illusory walls* 35 feet above the floor, concealing an illuminated tunnel. The dracolich hides here, poking her head and staff out just enough to fire upon her foes. The secret tunnel here connects to Varlae's chambers, and

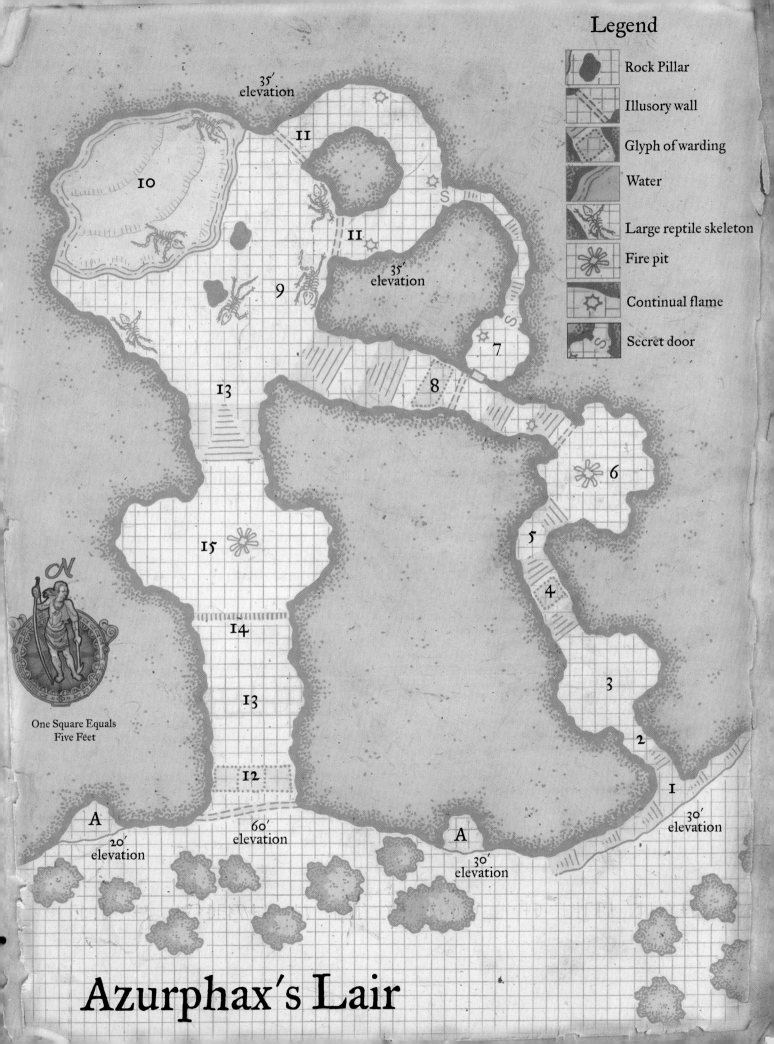

Azurphax's Lair

Legend

- Rock Pillar
- Illusory wall
- Glyph of warding
- Water
- Large reptile skeleton
- Fire pit
- Continual flame
- Secret door

One Square Equals
Five Feet

35′ elevation

35′ elevation

30′ elevation

30′ elevation

20′ elevation

60′ elevation

the evil cleric is generally ready to channel prepared spells into *inflict* spells to heal the dragon, either from this place or from her flying position.

Creatures (EL 16): Six lizard skeletons (two initially hidden in the pool) and one dracolich.

➤**Huge Winged Skeleton:** hp 30; see *Monster Manual*.
➤**Large Lizard Skeletons (5):** hp 16 each; see *Monster Manual*.
➤**Azurphax the Dracolich:** hp 130; see page 307.

Tactics: Azurphax uses her darkvision, blindsight, and knowledge of her lair to best advantage. She prefers to hide in the upper reaches of her lair, clinging to the ceiling with *spider climb*, swooping upon her opponents to make a round of melee attacks and use her snatch ability, dropping foes into the acid pool (area 10) or diving under with them and holding them there. She uses her frightful presence, paralyzing gaze, and paralyzing touch to panic and disable foes. She enjoys using her spells, breath weapon, and staff to strike at opponents from the darkness and is not above retreating to the acid pool for defense, since she can use all her spells and abilities normally within it (including her breath weapon). She is used to working with Varlae and the medusas, planning attacks accordingly. Once battle starts here, the medusas from area 15 hasten to her aid. If desperate, Azurphax uses her *control undead* ability to direct the skeletons at her attackers and then flees through the tunnel to the south.

Azurphax's phylactery is not here. The Cult keeps it in a safe place for her. Should the dracolich be slain, Varlae tries to flee to notify the other Cultists of the need to reunite Azurphax's spirit with a body.

10. ACID POOL

> This broad pool has a bitter smell to it, and it is almost certain that nothing normal lives within its waters.

Through the dracolich's breath weapon and her alchemical skill, the lake is somewhat acidic. Since she is immune to acid, she bathes in the pool regularly and retires to it when she wishes solitude. Almost 30 feet deep at its deepest point, it holds several chests of treasure, kept in specially greased wooden boxes that resist acid. The area around the chests has been warded with a *forbiddance* spell, affecting creatures not of lawful evil alignment. The entire pool is under the effects of the *unhallow* spell as described in area 9.

Trap: Touching the acid pool is harmful, immersion in it even more so. Note that characters dropped into the acid need to swim to get out, taking damage each round.

⚔**Acid Pool:** CR 1; 1d6 acid (immersion) or 1 acid splash (contact); Search (DC 5).

Treasure: 3,000 gp, gems (10 gp ×2, 50 gp ×6, 100 gp ×11, 500 gp ×2, 1,000 gp ×2), 25 alchemist's fire, 8 thunderstones, 9 acid vials, 9 tanglefoot bags, 12 tindertwigs, 12 smokesticks.

11. SECRET LOOP

> This long, curving hallway has an oversized alchemist's lab built into one of the walls. The large working surface, flasks, beakers, and a stove are all sized for a creature much larger than a human.

Two entrances to this area are 35 feet above the ground in area 9; the other is through a secret door in area 7. The dracolich is too large to fly within here, so she normally flies toward the opening, furls her wings, and lands.

The alchemist's lab is just like any other, although it has more materials and everything is sized for a dragon's hands.

Treasure: 500 gp worth of alchemical supplies can be salvaged from the lab, weighing 60 pounds.

12. GLYPH TRAPS

> The broad hallway has a set of steep stairs leading down to the north and a stone wall to the south. The ceiling is 20 feet or more high.

The entrance to this area is 60 feet above the ground. The ceiling is high enough to allow the dragon to fly from this secret entrance all the way to her central lair in area 9. Ten feet past the *illusory wall* that guards the entrance to this tunnel is a series of three *glyphs of warding* that cover the entire floor. Each *glyph* is activated by nonevil creatures and triggered independently. The noise of a *glyph* activating alerts the medusas in area 15.

⚔**Glyph of Warding (4):** CR 4; 5-ft. electricity blast (5d8); Reflex half (DC 16); Search (DC 28); Disable Device (DC 28).

13. STEEP STAIRS

> These steep stairs stretch across the entire width of the tunnel. The ceiling lowers only slightly toward the north.

The stairs are steep enough to reduce speed by half for Medium-size characters, although no Climb check is needed. If the medusas in area 15 are attacked, they take advantage of their flight ability to avoid this obstacle, using the stairs against the heroes if possible, hitting them with ranged attacks while melee combatants attempt to close.

14. SMOKESTICK TRAP

If the trap has not been activated, read the following text:

> This part of the tunnel is not unusual except for a series of ropes, pitons, and pulleys that connect to a long wooden frame near the ceiling.

If the trap has been activated, read this text:

> A 10-foot-high wall of smoke fills the entire width of the corridor. Ropes, pitons, and pulleys can be seen attached to the walls nearby, with some lines reaching into the smoke and others toward the ceiling.

Less a trap than a means of delaying pursuit, this device is a wooden frame hanging near the ceiling. Ropes affixed to the frame reach into the southern parts of area 15. Pulling these ropes (whether from the ground or while in the air, such as with the dragon's wingtip) causes the frame to swing downward in an arc toward the north. The bottom of the frame comes close enough to the ground to scrape several tindertwigs, igniting them and the smokesticks to which they are bound. The result is a 10-foot-tall, 10-foot-thick region of smoke filling the hall. Creatures within or beyond the smoke have total concealment (if the attackers can locate the target square at all).

Anyone within 10 feet of the frame when it reaches its lowest point (where it crashes to a stop) must make a Reflex save (DC 15) or take 1d8 hit points of damage. Crossing the smoky area safely (without falling) is a move-equivalent action; otherwise, a DC 15 Reflex save is necessary to move faster than half speed without falling down. Other ropes allow the frame to be hoisted into place, which takes 2 full rounds.

If the dragon is pursued by ground creatures, it activates the trap with its wing as it flies by, providing a temporary obstacle for anyone following it. The medusas are likely to use it for a similar purpose or to detain anyone who considers using this tunnel as an exit.

15. SNAKY SISTERS (EL 11)

> This large cavern has two sleeping pallets and a coal-filled fire pit. Some sort of meat is slow-roasting on the coals. The ceiling is about 30 feet high, and large exits lead north and south.

If alerted to intruders, the medusas drink their *potions of fly* before the party arrives and wait in the upper parts of the cavern. They prefer to attack with their bows, revealing their faces when foes come within 30 feet. They lead adversaries toward area 9, where they can be backed up by the dragon. Since the dragon is immune to their gaze attack, they reveal themselves fully when supported by their patron, although they are more careful when Varlae is present.

Creatures: 2 medusas.

➤**Corinye and Kathala:** Female medusas Ftr2; CR 9; Medium-size monstrous humanoid; HD 6d8+6 plus 2d10+2; hp 47, 49; Init +6; Spd 30 ft.; AC 20 (touch 12, flat-footed 18); Atk +13/+8 ranged (1d6/×3, masterwork shortbow [Corinye] or 1d6+1/×3, *+1 shortbow* [Kathala] and masterwork arrow) or +8/+3 melee (1d6/×3, halfspear) and +5 melee (1d4 plus poison, snakes); SA Petrifying gaze, poison; AL LE; SV Fort +6, Ref +7, Will +6; Str 11, Dex 15, Con 12, Int 12, Wis 13, Cha 15.

Skills and Feats: Bluff +11, Diplomacy +4, Disguise +11, Intimidate +4, Move Silently +9, Spot +12; Improved Initiative, Point Blank Shot, Precise Shot, Weapon Finesse (snakes), Weapon Focus (shortbow).

Special Attacks: Petrifying Gaze (Su): Turn to stone permanently, 30 ft., Fortitude save (DC 16). Poison (Ex): Snakes, Fortitude save (DC 15); initial damage 1d6 temporary Strength, secondary damage 2d6 temporary Strength.

Possessions (Corinye): +1 chain shirt, masterwork shortbow, 40 masterwork arrows, halfspear, cowled cloak, grappling hook, 50 ft. hemp rope, 2 *potions of fly*, potion of cure moderate wounds, 650 gp, 10 gems (50 gp each).

Possessions (Kathala): +1 chain shirt, +1 shortbow, 40 masterwork arrows, halfspear, cowled cloak, grappling hook, 50 ft. hemp rope, 2 *potions of fly*, potion of cure moderate wounds, Quiver of Ehlonna, 400 gp, 9 gems (50 gp each).

concluding the Adventure

If the dragon is slain, the Cult goes into action to find her another body that she may use as a host. In a new body, Azurphax proceeds to acquire contacts and agents in order to find her slayers and reclaim her treasure. It is likely she retaliates against any nearby settlements, both to bolster her ego and to draw out those who attacked her. Should her minions be slain, she contacts the Cult to have them provide her with assistance until her defenses are back to normal. Finding where the Cult has her phylactery hidden is quite a task, making it difficult for her to be permanently slain.

➤**Azurphax:** Adult female green dracolich; CR 15; Huge undead; HD 20d12; hp 130; Init +0; Spd 40 ft., fly 150 ft. (poor), swim 40 ft.; AC 29 (touch 8, flat-footed 29); Atk +26 melee (2d8+8 plus 1d6 cold plus paralysis, bite), +21 melee (2d6+4 plus 1d6 cold plus paralysis, 2 claws), +21 melee (1d8+4 plus 1d6 cold plus paralysis, wings), +21 melee (2d6+12 plus 1d6 cold plus paralysis, tail slap); Face/Reach 10 ft. by 20 ft./10 ft.; SA Breath weapon, frightful presence, paralyzing gaze, paralyzing touch, *suggestion*; SQ Blindsight, control undead, damage reduction 5/+1, half damage from piercing or slashing weapons, invulnerability, immunities (acid, cold, electricity, polymorph, standard undead immunities), keen senses, water breathing; SR 24; AL LE; SV Fort +12, Ref +12, Will +15; Str 27, Dex 10, Con –, Int 16, Wis 17, Cha 18. Length 20 ft.

Skills and Feats: Alchemy +13, Appraise +8, Bluff +12, Concentration +24, Diplomacy +19, Escape Artist +10, Hide –8, Intimidate +8, Knowledge (arcana) +10, Knowledge (geography) +10, Knowledge (local) +10, Listen +25, Search +23, Sense Motive +9, Speak Language (Auran, Common, Dwarven, Elven, Sylvan), Spellcraft +23, Spot +25; Alertness, Flyby Attack, Hover, Power Attack, Snatch, Wingover.

Special Attacks: Breath Weapon (Su): Corrosive (acid) gas, usable every 1d4 rounds, 50-ft. cone, 12d6, DC 24.

Frightful Presence (Ex): The dracolich can unsettle foes with her mere presence. The ability takes effect automatically whenever she attacks, charges, or flies overhead. Creatures within a radius of 180 feet are subject to the effect if they have fewer than 20 HD. A potentially affected creature that succeeds at a Will save (DC 24) remains immune to her frightful presence for one day. On a failure, creatures with 4 or fewer HD become panicked for 4d6 rounds and those with 5 or more HD become shaken for 4d6 rounds. Dragons ignore the frightful presence of other dragons.

Paralyzing Gaze (Su): The gaze of a dracolich's glowing eyes can paralyze victims within 40 feet if they fail a Fortitude save (DC 24). If the saving throw is successful, the character is forever immune to the gaze of that particular dracolich. If it fails, the victim is paralyzed for 2d6 rounds.

Paralyzing Touch (Su): A creature struck by a dracolich's physical attacks must make a Fortitude save (DC 24) or be paralyzed for 2d6 rounds. A successful saving throw against this effect does not confer any immunity to further attacks.

Suggestion (Sp): As the spell, 3/day as a 5th-level sorcerer.

Special Qualities: Blindsight (Ex): A dracolich can ascertain creatures by nonvisual means (mostly hearing and scent, but also by noticing vibration and other environmental clues) with a range of 180 feet.

Control Undead (Sp): Once every three days, a dracolich can use *control undead* as a 15th-level sorcerer. The dracolich cannot cast other spells while this ability is in effect.

Immunities: Immune to acid, cold, disease, electricity, mind-influencing effects, paralysis, poison, polymorph, sleep, stunning. Not subject to ability damage, critical hits, death from massive damage, energy drain, or subdual damage (see *Monster Manual*).

Invulnerability: If a dracolich is slain, its spirit immediately returns to its host (phylactery), from where it may attempt to possess a suitable corpse.

Keen Senses (Ex): A dracolich sees four times as well a human in low-light conditions and twice as well in normal light. It also has darkvision with a range of 600 feet.

Water Breathing (Ex): The dracolich can freely use its breath weapon, spells, and other abilities while underwater.

Spells Known (6/7/5; base DC = 14 + spell level): 0—*daze, detect magic, disrupt undead, flare, mage hand, read magic*; 1st—*shield, spider climb, true strike, ventriloquism*; 2nd—*hypnotic pattern, invisibility.*

Possessions: Clay scrolls (*confusion, wall of ice*), *staff of fire* (40 charges).